Composers of the **Twentieth** Century

The Music of

YALE UNIVERSITY PRESS   New Haven and London

Alban Berg

DAVE HEADLAM

For Sylvie

Set in Postscript Monotype Garamond type by
The Marathon Group, Durham, North Carolina.
Printed in the United States of America by BookCrafters, Inc.,
Chelsea, Michigan.

Library of Congress Cataloging-in-Publication Data
Headlam, David John.
   The music of Alban Berg / Dave Headlam.
      p.   cm. — (Composers of the twentieth century)
   Includes bibliographical references (p.   ) and index.
   ISBN 0-300-06400-4 (cloth : alk. paper)
      1. Berg, Alban, 1885–1935—Criticism and interpretation.
I. Title. II. Series.
ML410.B47H43   1996   95–46936
780'.92—dc20   CIP
                         MN

A catalogue record for this book is available from the
British Library.

The paper in this book meets the guidelines for
permanence and durability of the Committee on
Production Guidelines for Book Longevity of the
Council on Library Resources.

10 9 8 7 6 5 4 3 2 1

Contents

Acknowledgments

This book is the culmination of many years of work on the music of Alban Berg. I still distinctly remember the time in the listening room of the School of Music at the University of Michigan when I, as a first-year master's student feeling distinctly inferior in repertoire to my colleagues, flipped open the card catalogue to "B," then to "Berg" and *Wozzeck*. As I sat listening I was transfixed; it was a singular moment, to be followed by a master's thesis, doctoral dissertation, papers, articles, and finally this book. Happily, despite the untold hours, weeks, months, and years I have devoted to this music, I recently taught Act III, scene iii of Berg's first opera and was still moved by the experience.

Through my work on Berg's music I became a part of a small but growing community of musicians whose insights I have pondered many times; these writers become familiar characters in the little superscript numbers that adorn the following pages. I wish to thank Douglass M. Green, Mark DeVoto, Douglas Jarman, and Glenn E. Watkins, who read and commented on parts of this book. One debt I particularly want to acknowledge is to George Perle, whose exemplary scholarship and devotion to Berg and advice on many musical matters have long guided my efforts. As I note below, I view this book as a further tilling of soil already broken by Perle. The personal and professional contact I have had with this remarkable musician is one of the most rewarding outcomes of my studies.

I would also like to thank Allen Forte, editor of the series Composers of the Twentieth Century, for the opportunity to contribute this volume and for his kind advice through the process. My editors, first Jeanne Ferris, then Harry Haskell and Susan Laity at Yale University Press have been extremely helpful as well. I acknowledge Robert Freeman, director of the Eastman School of Music, for granting me a semester's leave and for furnishing assistance toward the production costs of this book. I was greatly assisted at the Austrian National Library by Günter Brosche and Rosemary Hilmar and at the Vienna City Library by Ernst Hilmar. For allowing me to examine the Berg manuscripts in their collection I am grateful to Dr. Marie Rolf and Robert Owen Lehman. I also acknowledge European American Music Distributors Corporation and Musikverlag Robert Lienau for permission to reproduce examples from Berg's music.

For their help during my days at the University of Michigan, I want to thank the graduate students and professors I was fortunate enough to work with—in particular Howard Cinnamon, John Covach, my thesis advisor Edward Chudacoff, and my dissertation advisor Andrew Mead. I was also given free rein at the Michigan Music Theory Conference IV to indulge in Berg's music, an opportunity provided by the Music Theory Department and the chair Ralph Lewis. At the Eastman School of Music I have been fortunate to find myself among the finest scholars and students in music theory. I especially wish to mention countless hours of discussion with Matthew Brown, encouraging comments from Robert Wason, and the students participating in my two seminars on Berg's music for their indulgence and many insights: Michael Buchler, Ed Jurkowski, Paul Laprade, David Lefkowitz, Mary Linklater, David Palmer, Adam Ricci, Yayoi Uno, and Keith Waters. To Ed Jurkowski, Pat Long, and David Palmer I also owe thanks for many of the musical examples, to Aleck Brinkman and Martha Mesiti my regards for the contour graph of Berg's op. 4, no. 2, and to Kimberly Fox and Robert Fink gratitude for their 600 dpi special. Finally, for their years of faithful service, with only a few hard drive crashes to keep life interesting, I salute my old Pronto computer (retired), my slightly newer IBM AT (soon to be retired), and my deluxe new Power Macintosh (still active); I have spent more time with these contraptions in the past years than with anything or anyone else.

In closing, I wish to thank my wife, Sylvie Beaudette, for her love and support and continual best wishes as I labored. It is to Sylvie that this book is dedicated, for I should surely be incurably insane without her.

A Note on Terminology

employ several terms and symbols in common use in theory parlance, given below. Two terms are somewhat unusual: (1) *Tn-class sets* are sometimes distinguished from *TnI-class sets*; and (2) *Pn* is used to indicate pitch-class levels of Tn-class sets, as well as to indicate (as usual) pitch-class levels from prime forms of serial motives or twelve-tone rows; *Tn* is reserved for relative transpositional levels between two sets.

$< ->$	an ordered series of elements, e.g., $<C-D-E>$
$\{ , \}$	an unordered group of elements, e.g., $\{C,D,E\}$
Contour	the contour of a group of pitches is given in relative terms, with 0 as the lowest position; $<C_4-B_3-E_4>$ have contour $<102>$. Contours are given within angle brackets with no punctuation
Cycle	an ordered series resulting from successive equal gradations, e.g., a 1-cycle of pitch-classes is $<C-C\sharp-D-D\sharp-E-F-F\sharp-G-G\sharp-A-A\sharp-B>$
In	a label given to a serial motive or twelve-tone row, where n is a variable indicating the initial pitch-class; e.g., I_5 is the inversional form beginning on F

Interval; pitch-class interval; interval-class	the span in semitones between two pitches; the same span equivalent to within an octave; and the same span equivalent to within an interval-6 boundary
$M7$, $M5$	the multiplicative operators that multiply intervals or pitch-classes by 7 or 5; e.g., {C,E,G} by $M7$ yields {C,E,C♯}; {C,E,G} by $M5$ yields {C,A♭,B}; $M7$ and $M5$ yield inversionally related sets or series
Number notation	the numbers 0–B, where A = 10 and B = 11, used to represent the twelve pitch-classes, intervals, and order positions. Occasionally 10 or 11 is used instead of A and B to avoid confusion
Order position	the ordered place of an element in a series or row. Order-position numbers (ops) are underlined or labelled *ops*
Partition	an ordered series of notes extracted non-segmentally from a serial motive or twelve-tone row, e.g., <C–E–G> from <C–F–E–G♯–G>
Pitch, pitch-class	pitches are numbered as C_4 = middle C, etc. Pitch-classes are equivalence-classes of pitches related by octaves; there are twelve pitch-classes
Pn	(1) a label given to a Tn-class to indicate its pitch-class content, with *n* the lowest note in normal order; e.g., P4 [047] represents the notes {E, G♯,B}. (2) a label given to a serial motive or twelve-tone row, where *n* is a variable indicating the pitch-class of the initial note; e.g., P5 is the prime row beginning of F
R (In) or R (Pn)	labels given to retrograde-form serial motives or twelve-tone rows; e.g., R(P5) is the retrograde of the prime form beginning of F; R(I5) is the retrograde of the inversional form beginning on F
Row	an ordered series of the twelve distinct pitch-classes, appearing in four forms: prime (P), inversion (I), retrograde of prime (R(P)), and retrograde of inversion (R(I))
Segment	an ordered series of a serial motive or twelve-tone row, e.g., <C–E–G> within <C–E–G–A>
Series	an ordered group of elements, e.g., <C–E–G>
Set	an unordered group of elements, usually pitch-classes, eg., {C,E,G}
Set-class	an alternate name for TnI-class

Time Point	a point in time coinciding with the attack of a duration; e.g., the series of durations eighth, sixteenth, quarter, half has the time-point series $<0-2-3-7>$, with 0 as the initial attack and units of sixteenths
Tn	a transpositional level relative to some fixed pitch or pitch-class level, where n is a variable indicating pitch or pitch-class interval; e.g., {C} is at T_5 from {G} and {G} is at $T-5$ from {C}
Tn-class	an equivalence class from groups of pitch-classes related by transposition, e.g., Tn [047] from {C,E,G}, {C♯,E♯,G♯}, etc.
TnI-class	An equivalence class from groups of pitch-classes related by transposition and inversion; e.g., TnI [037] from {C,E,G}, {C,E♭,G}, {C♯,E♯,G♯}, etc. Often abbreviated as [037]
Z-relation	a relationship between two set-classes of the same size, wherein they share the same interval-class content

"...but I would first like to ask a favor of you—that you forget everything that I've tried to explain about musical theory and aesthetics when you come ... to see a performance of *Wozzeck.*"

"We are all the more justified, even compelled (if we wish to form a judgement about music), to give an account of this [piece] from a musico-theoretical point of view as well, and further to make it as precise and foolproof as possible."

Introduction

These two quotes from Alban Berg (1885–1935), the first from his lecture on *Wozzeck* (1929) and the second from a reply article to the composer Hans Pfitzner (1920), aptly reflect two reactions to his music.[1] On the one hand, Berg's music transports us to realms of profound emotion and human understanding that defy the power of words; think of the delicate beauty of the *Altenberg Lieder*, the majesty of the Three Pieces for Orchestra Op. 6, the poignant Act III interlude in *Wozzeck*, the tragic song in the finale of the *Lyric Suite*, the despairing "Liebestod" of the Countess Geschwitz in *Lulu*, and the resigned peace of the chorale "Es ist genug" concluding the Violin Concerto. On the other hand, the symmetry of form, intricacy and variety of motivic transformation, the complexity of rhythmic treatment, and the coherence in the pitch language compel a rational, considered response to Berg's music which, over time, yields a deep intellectual satisfaction. Of course, these two apparently opposite responses intertwine and feed back into one another in the circle that acts as a metaphor for many aspects of Berg's music. As Berg's pupil Theodor W. Adorno commented, "Few things are as noticeable in Berg as the combination of near imponderable subtlety with planning so manic that it reaches the point of number games."[2]

Another factor in considering Berg's music is, of course, the man himself.

Research has revealed that the composer is as fascinating and enigmatic as is his contemporary fin-de-siècle Viennese society, with its intellectual, cultural, and artistic ferment, and that the two reflect each other in myriad ways. Berg lived and wrote in the midst of the events that shaped the twentieth century, politically, socially, and artistically, and a complete account of his life and work must both focus in on his day-to-day existence and radiate out from it to the larger forces that governed his society. As Douglas Jarman has noted, a definitive biography is a pressing need and a priority in Berg research, but for me, at least, the time has not yet arrived for such a monumental task.[3]

In the interim, in spite of many excellent studies, Berg's legacy in the music still beckons with unlocked secrets and unexplored depths. This volume, building on the work of others, particularly George Perle, is a contribution—in the spirit of the second quotation given above—to the continuing study of Berg's music. A purely musical discussion is, of course, incomplete, but I regard my efforts as part of a larger body of writings from a community of scholars who are devoted to a more complete understanding of this remarkable musician.

Berg Scholarship: An Overview

Scholarly research into Berg's music falls into three eras, dividing approximately at the late 1950s, with the 1957 publication of Hans Redlich's book on Berg's life and music and George Perle's 1959 article on the music of *Lulu*, and the late 1970s, with the revelation of the secret program of the *Lyric Suite* in articles by George Perle (1977b) and Douglass M. Green (1977b), Douglas Jarman's 1979 book on Berg's music, and the publication of Rosemary's Hilmar's catalogue of Berg manuscripts and writings in the first volume of *Alban Berg Studien* (1980). The third and most recent era commenced with the premiere of the completed three-act *Lulu* on February 24, 1979, and the first conference on the music of Alban Berg, held in Vienna in 1980.

The principal sources on Berg's music and life of the first period stem from Berg himself—his extensive writings, notes, sketches, articles, and letters on his own and others' music—and from writers who knew Berg personally and who frequently cite his authority: Theodor W. Adorno, Ernst Krenek, René Leibowitz, Willi Reich, and Erwin Stein. Although the purely musical aspects of the secondary sources have largely been superseded, Berg's analytical writings—particularly concerning *Wozzeck*, the *Chamber Concerto*, and the *Lyric Suite*—continue to be a valuable resource. The biographical information offered, however, particularly by Reich, has proved to be not only incomplete and unreliable but misleading, as had been demonstrated by Mark DeVoto, Green, Jarman, and Perle.

The end of the first and the beginning of the second era of Berg scholarship is marked by Redlich's book, in which a critical viewpoint and an acknowledgment of the limitations of existing knowledge are evinced for the first time. The second era features the emergence of the most significant writer on Berg's music, George Perle, beginning with his seminal trio of articles first on *Lulu* (1959, 1964b, 1965a), then on *Wozzeck* (1967c, 1967e, 1971), and the study "Berg's Master Array of the Interval Cycles" (1977a), which collectively brought analytical writing on Berg's music into the modern age of music theory. Other important contributions include Bruce Archibald's dissertation on harmony in Berg's early works (1965), DeVoto's study of the *Altenberg Lieder* (1967)—pieces that, remarkably, were virtually unknown until DeVoto's pioneering efforts—Klaus Schweizer's exhaustive account of Berg's use of sonata forms (1970), and Jarman's seminal book (1979) on Berg's complete oeuvre, in which attention is focused on Berg's systematic approach to rhythm and form as well as to pitch. Important studies on Berg documents and reception history appeared from Volker Scherliess and Ernst Hilmar, and Berg's biography was forever changed by the unveiling of the autobiographical program of the *Lyric Suite* by Green (1977b) and Perle (1977b). The second era also featured the formation of the International Alban Berg Society in 1966 and the inaugural issue of the society's *Newsletter* in 1968. The import of this endeavor is reflected in the founding members: Igor Stravinsky, president; Hans Redlich, vice-president; and a board including Benjamin Britten, Luigi Dallapiccola, Mark DeVoto, Harald Goertz, Donald Harris, Ernst Krenek, Gian Francesco Malipiero, Darius Milhaud, George Perle, Roger Sessions, and Claudio Spies.

The third era of Berg scholarship received its formal articulation with the completion of Berg's second opera *Lulu* by the Austrian composer Friedrich Cerha and its somewhat infamous world premiere in Paris in February 1979. This era, which has also witnessed two conferences devoted to Berg, in Vienna in 1980 and Chicago in 1985, has two aspects. The first is the continuation of analytical studies from the second era, now supplemented by sketch materials and access to all of Berg's writings, notes, manuscripts, and unfinished compositions; notable authors include Mark DeVoto, Allen Forte, Douglass M. Green, Patricia Hall, Douglas Jarman, Robert Morgan, George Perle, Janet Schmalfeldt, and Joan Smith. In addition, the availability of source material has begun to allow for complete compilations of letters and other documents, as in the translation of the Berg-Schoenberg correspondence by Juliane Brand, Christopher Hailey, and Donald Harris (1987), and the establishment of a critical edition of Berg's compositions under the stewardship of Rudolf Stephan.

The second aspect of the third era is the steady unearthing of letters, documents, and other biographical information. The discovery of the annotated score and hidden song revealing the secret program in the *Lyric Suite* has led to similar disclosures in the *Violin Concerto* by Jarman (1982a) and the *Chamber Concerto* by Brenda Dalen (1989), and to related musical details in the second version of "Schließe mir die Augen beide" and in *Lulu* by Perle (1985) and *Der Wein* by Andrew MacDonald (1988), Perle (1985), and the present author (1990). Studies of Berg's life in relation to his social, cultural, and historical heritage and the *Rezeptionsgeschichte* of his music are also appearing in greater numbers. As Jarman (1991b) has noted in his contribution to the collection of published papers from the second Berg conference, recent developments allow for at least a glimpse of the scope required for a definitive Berg biography.

Autobiographical, Symbolic, and Historicist Aspects

Among the works of the three composers of the Second Viennese School, autobiographical, symbolic, and what might be termed "historicist" aspects play the most integral role in the composition and reception of Berg's music. Autobiographical elements, both obvious and hidden, are found in musical quotation and in references both obvious and hidden in numbers and notation. Many musical features—including tonality itself—are given symbolic associations by Berg, particularly in the operas, through both their inherent expressive characteristics and their musical and dramatic contexts. Historicist features are reminiscences and quotation of previous music used as commentary in a wider musical and cultural context. All reflect the intensely personal, self-conscious nature of many arts and artists in the late nineteenth and early twentieth centuries.[4] A particular musical model in this aspect is Gustav Mahler, a composer whom Berg met and admired. Limits of space in the present volume do not allow for an adequate exploration of these important aspects of Berg's music, but they have been discussed widely by many other writers. Here I want only to acknowledge these elements and to add a few thoughts of my own.

Berg's music has been widely recognized for its autobiographical features. The composer commented on personal reflections in the third movement "Marsch" of his Orchestra Pieces op. 6—referred to in a letter to Schoenberg as "the march of an asthmatic"—with the character Wozzeck from his first opera and in relation to the community of musicians surrounding Schoenberg in the *Chamber Concerto*.[5] In this last piece and in the remainder of his compositions, Berg followed a pattern of including both overt programmatic references and clues to highly personal "secret" aspects which often lend new meaning to his public acknowledgements. Brenda Dalen discovered what may be the first secret program, in the *Chamber Concerto*, which concerns Schoenberg's first wife as well as the painter Richard Gerstl.[6] In later pieces, the private references are based primarily on Berg's relationship with Hanna Fuchs-Robettin, as Perle discovered from a score of the *Lyric Suite* annotated by Berg himself.[7] Slightly prior to this discovery, Green deciphered a text in a sketch of the final movement of the *Lyric Suite* that reveals a song, a lament over the tragic love story told throughout the quartet.[8] Jarman has uncovered several private aspects to the Violin Concerto, including references to Berg's illegitimate daughter, Albine, as well as to Fuchs-Robettin; the reference to Berg's daughter also points back to the association of himself with Wozzeck.[9] These autobiographical references take many forms: numbers, such as 3 and 7 in *Wozzeck*, 3 and 5 in the *Chamber Concerto*, and 23 and 10—reflecting Berg and Fuchs-Robettin—in the later music in numbers of notes and bars, formal proportions, and tempo markings;[10] the note group {A,B♭,B,F} from the initials of Alban Berg and Hanna Fuchs-Robettin (B for B♭ and H for B♮ in German), particularly in the *Lyric Suite* and the second "Schließe mir die Augen beide" setting;[11] and quotations, from Zemlinsky's *Lyric Symphony* and Wagner's *Tristan und Isolde* in the *Lyric Suite*, from Beethoven's Ninth Symphony and Wagner's *Ring* in *Der Wein*, and even from *Wozzeck* and the *Lyric Suite* in *Lulu*.[12]

A second important feature of Berg's music is the symbolism imparted to musical events. It has often been noted that with various composers certain keys seem to have a symbolic value. In Berg's music, keys or notes of focus analogous to key centers invariably include the note D, as a center in its own right or set in relation to G in an analogous fashion to a dominant. These notes emerge in many contexts; for instance, in *Wozzeck*, a D center is symmetrically placed between the tones of the referential dyad {F,B}, and emphasized notes {B♭,B} are symmetrical between focal notes G and D in later works. These notes D and G seem to have a symbolic significance, for one or both are prominent in almost every piece, creating a continuous thread throughout Berg's life. In explanation, many writers have referred to the influence of Beethoven's Ninth Symphony and Mahler's Sixth Symphony, and, in a literary connection, David Schroeder has written about Berg's use of D minor in relation to the writings of August Strindberg, an author well known to Berg and his circle, who also used D-minor musical pieces in his plays.[13]

A more immediate symbol in Berg's music is the representation of fate by rhythmic motives, often labeled *Hauptrhythmus* (RH), in a type of gesture clearly derived from Mahler's music. In *Wozzeck*, both Marie and Wozzeck seem helpless before a merciless fate that controls their destinies; a symbol of that fate is the RH that appears immediately following Marie's death in Act III, scene ii, then pervades Act III/scene iii, where Wozzeck attempts to escape but is accused by the crowd at the inn, leading to his return to Marie's body and eventual drowning. In the pieces following *Wozzeck*, except for the second "Schließe mir" song, at least one formal section is controlled to some extent by a rhythmic motive. In *Lulu*, the fateful RH appears as the basis of "monoritmicas" of varying lengths at the death of each character. In the Violin Concerto, the RH in the first part of the second movement is associated with the illness and death struggle of the young girl.

Berg also lent purely musical processes an extra-musical significance, particularly in his later music where twelve-tone techniques are used symbolically. For instance, he described the successive intervalic changes in the row of the *Lyric Suite* as "submitting to fate," in a reflection of the ill-fated love depicted in the quartet.[14] Many authors have noted that palindromes appeared to have a symbolic meaning for Berg, related to completed cycles and circular time. The effect of Berg's palindromes is twofold: on the one hand, time is arrested and seems to retreat, suspending chronological time and forward motion; on the other hand, new aspects of the music emerge in retrograde, creating a forward impetus.[15] The dichotomy between prime and inversional forms of material, basic to the twelve-tone system, is given a symbolic aspect by Berg in his setting of the dialectical text to the "Lied der Lulu" and in representations of the duality in the character of Dr. Schön in *Lulu*, particularly in the latter's "five-strophe aria."[16]

Another symbolic effect in Berg's music comes from the varying treatments of the ends of pieces. The *Chamber Concerto* ends, as does the first of the *Altenberg Lieder*, with repeated figuration of successively decreasing duration and number of notes, over a held chord. As a result, the ending is prolonged seemingly indefinitely, so that no one point is marked as the definitive close. The *Lyric Suite* concludes similarly, with a diminuendo oscillation between the notes {Db,F} (stipulated not to end on Db, which would lend an impression of resolution) for an indeterminate amount of time, as a symbol of the dying out of the tragic love in the program. At the other extreme, *Wozzeck* ends with an abrupt cut-off of the oscillating chords and foreshadows a similar abrupt ending of canonic statements of the *Hauptrhythmus* at the end of *Lulu*. The effect is an unresolved state, broken off rather than ended.

Aside from the autobiographical and symbolic aspects, the most common comment on Berg's music concerns his use of tonal materials, ranging from allusion to outright progression.[17] Berg's generation is unique in that once tonality had ceased to be the only language available, it gained associations that composers could exploit, such as the invocation of a nostalgic, simpler era, or, in neoclassical music, as an active engagement with the past employing parody or distortion. The tonal elements in Berg's music are part of a larger, conscious invocation of his musical culture in many forms, ranging from quotations to reminiscences of styles, often in the nature of commentary, and his influence on the music of the past by this invocation. In this sense, Berg took an actively historicist position in relation to his heritage.

Like Mahler, Berg invoked popular elements of Viennese nineteenth-century music, placing them in contexts that comment on their traditional associations. The allusions to a more controlled and innocent world of folk-like meter and tonality often clash poignantly or brusquely with atonal surroundings. In the Orchestral Pieces op. 6, Berg takes reminiscence through commentary to distortion and perhaps even to "deconstruction" of his past. The first movement, which emerges from and returns to a primordial state of raw, unpitched sound, reflects the dying gasps of romanticism and its organic ideal. The second movement, *Reigen* ("Round Dance"), has waltz passages in two places (mm. 20–35, 94–100) bearing the indication *Walzertempo*, with an emphatic triple meter supported by a regular harmonic rhythm and traditional "oom-pah-pah" accompaniment figure and even a hint of a tonicized key of B♭. Although the waltz infuses the entire movement, it faces constant opposition in which the characteristic rhythm and gestures struggle pathetically to survive, attempting to invoke the gaiety of the past in an uncertain present.[18]

In the "Marsch" op. 6, no. 3, Adorno has noted that "four shattered old-fashioned march formulae are stitched together and reconstituted into form by the same force that had disintegrated them."[19] Perle has described the "Marsch" in terms invoking the relationship between Ravel's *La Valse* and the Viennese waltz; rather than a march, it is a commentary on the demise of the march and the world it represented. In its military connotations, the "Marsch" foreshadows the horrors of the First World War, in which nineteenth-century cavalry marches, charges, and military etiquette were obliterated and grimly rendered obsolete by the more effective, deadly, and chaotic weapons of the twentieth century.[20]

Like other composers of his time, Berg also invoked popular contemporary jazz-related music as a symbol of decadence and decay.[21] The texts of *Der Wein* and *Lulu* both concern Parisian demimonde. *Der Wein* uses three poems from a set of five, "Le Vin," from Baudelaire's *Les fleurs du mal*, in a translation by Stefan George. *Lulu* is based on Frank Wedekind's plays *Erdgeist* and *Die Büchse der Pandora*, written in Paris between 1890 and 1895. Both *Lulu* and *Der Wein* contain tangos and English waltzes, and in both a jazz band is extracted from the orchestra.[22] In *Lulu*, Berg integrated the popular elements into his language and imbued them with a larger meaning in the context of Lulu's fate. The jazz world is part of Lulu's character, associated with her dancing (Act I, scene iii), and it is played out dramatically and musically in the course of the opera. The Wedekind song added in Act III of *Lulu* is originally a cabaret song, sung by Wedekind himself; the text, ruminating on different aspects of love, sex, and power from a woman's first-person view, reflects the different aspects of Lulu's character.[23]

Aside from questions of musical quotation or reminiscence, Berg's very composition of *Wozzeck* has been regarded as a historicist act. Adorno has suggested that in setting Büchner's play *Woyzeck* in his opera *Wozzeck*, Berg altered the perception of the earlier work, in effect influencing the past: "*Wozzeck* aims to revise history: it is a process in which history, too, is included; the modernity of the music underlines the modernity of the book precisely because the latter is old and was not recognized in his own day."[24] Although written before 1837, Büchner's play *Woyzeck* was pieced together only in the 1870s but soon came to influence many writers. The extent to which Büchner's play foreshadowed later expressionist literature is remarkable; Berg's role in its history was to highlight these features through his expressionist musical setting.[25]

Finally, Berg's use of quotation, musical names, references to his predecessors, contemporary cultural signposts, and musical symbols reflects an attitude toward his own musical heritage.[26] Redlich noted that Berg seemed to establish, through allusions and quotation, a "spiritual link" to his past.[27] Green has commented on the "return to" tendencies of early twentieth-century composers: Stravinsky turned to neoclassicism, Webern to pretonal polyphony, Schoenberg to eighteenth-century dance types, and Berg to cantus firmus and choral writing in *Wozzeck*, *Lulu*, and the *Violin Concerto*.[28] Green quotes a statement by T. S. Eliot (1919) that anticipates the postmodernist view that no work of art can be understood in and of itself: "No poet, no artist of any art, has his complete meaning alone. His significance, his appreciation is the appreciation of his relation to the dead poets and artists . . . the existing monuments form an ideal order among themselves which is modified by the introduction of the new (the really new) work of art among them. Whoever has approved this idea of order in the form of European literature will not find it preposterous that the past should be altered by the present as much as the present is directed by the past. And the poet who is aware of this will be aware of great difficulties and responsibilities."[29]

Joseph Straus has elaborated similar views, pointing out that much early twentieth-century music is "permeated by the music of the past" as composers "grapple with their musical heritage."[30] The dominance of the past emerged with Beethoven's influence in the nineteenth century, and by the early twentieth century the past was a weight that composers, particularly Stravinsky and Schoenberg, had to bear. Stravinsky resorted to neoclassicism whereas Schoenberg felt compelled to push his German heritage to its progression toward the twelve-tone system and analyzed the music of his predecessors to show the inevitability of his own musical developments. Straus discusses three models of artistic influence on composers, derived from the writings of the literary critic Harold Bloom: (1) influence as immaturity, where young composers emulate past styles and masters; (2) influence as generosity, where mature composers write "within a tradition, and their work—including the most individual works of their maturity—reflect [*sic*] the shaping impact of that tradition," often as an act of self-denial and subordination to the past; and (3) influence as anxiety, where composers feel a need to replace the past. Schoenberg is a quintessential example of the latter; he was obsessed with the past and felt compelled to improve on his predecessors while continually paying them homage.[31]

Straus discusses the influence of the past in many works, including Berg's *Lyric Suite* and the Violin Concerto.[32] In my view the quotations from Zemlinksy and Wagner in the *Lyric Suite* and from the Bach chorale in the Violin Concerto have a dual nature. On the one hand, Berg integrated this material into his musical language: the quotations are related musically to prevailing rows and to Berg's cyclic harmonic and melodic shapes. Thus, they do not disturb the purely musical coherence, as Berg pointed out, noting that the *Tristan* quote emerges naturally from a "strict observance of the 12-tone rows."[33] On the other hand, despite their integration, the quotations stand apart by their symbolic associations, outside the bounds of the immediate piece, to invoke a spiritual and historical world within a larger cultural context.

Berg's employment of the symbolic associations of the quoted material has, however, another effect: it affects not only our perception of the Violin Concerto and the *Lyric Suite* but also of the pieces quoted, in a retroactive change of perspective. Thus, in addition to being influenced by the past, Berg also influenced the past. The new contexts in which these quotes occur alter our perception of the source pieces. Bach's chorale "Es ist genug" and the opening of Wagner's *Tristan* are never again quite the same after we have heard Berg's Violin Concerto and *Lyric Suite*.

Berg's commentary on and reworking of the past stem not from an influence of anxiety, however, but from a comfortable incorporation of a tradition.[34] Whereas Schoenberg struggled with the past, Berg freely took from his heritage, in a manner closer to Straus's definition of the "influence of generosity." He self-consciously borrowed from the past, invoking symbols outside the bounds of the immediate pieces, to create new meaning not only in his own music but in the works from which he borrowed. Berg was, however, sufficiently concerned with the integrity of individual pieces to create cogent musical relationships between his borrowed material and the language of each piece. Berg's music is, therefore, susceptible to both a modernist approach, treating each piece as a self-contained musical entity, and to a postmodernist approach, searching for meaning in the works' symbols and references, history and context, both past and present, and the effect on the listener.

Theories and Analyses of Berg's Music

Studies of the purely musical elements in Berg's compositions radiate from two related sources: Berg himself, and George Perle.[35] Berg's writings have formed the basis for commentary and discussion of his music since his inclusion of a formal chart for *Wozzeck* in the published piano-vocal score. Particularly in his lecture on *Wozzeck* and his "Open Letter" on the *Chamber Concerto*, Berg touched on virtually every aspect of his music, providing detailed formal charts and discussions of rhythmic motives and referential harmonies, as well as hints of symbols and programmatic meanings. The recent cataloguing and availability of Berg's notes, sketches, and documents have supplemented the published writings and reveal the uncanny depth to which Berg carefully considered and placed every musical element.

By a strange but perhaps inevitable path, the score of Berg's *Lyric Suite* ended up in the hands of George Perle in 1937. The music catalyzed a compositional and analytical technique nascent in Perle's musical endeavors of the time, and from the early 1940s to the present Perle has developed a theory of "twelve-tone tonality" that encompasses his own music as well as the music of Berg and Béla Bartók principally, but many other composers of the late nineteenth and early twentieth centuries to varying degrees. Perle's theories center on symmetry manifested in interval cycles and inversional complementation as "normative" structures in certain types of post-tonal music. In his book, *The Listening Composer*, Perle summarizes and extends his previous analyses into a true theoretical system that defines a class of compositions across many different composers according to their exploitation of symmetry. Elliot Antokoletz (1984) has further documented the systematic use of symmetry in the music of Bartók in a comprehensive study, extending and refining Perle's work, and the present volume seeks to accomplish a similarly exhaustive account of Berg's music.

My approach, then, begins from the premise of a normative structure based on symmetry and cycles. Compositional units are interpreted as cycle-based, with built-in dissonance providing the impetus for compositional unfolding that takes full advantage of both the redundant intervalic and combinatorial properties of interval cycles and cyclic collections as well as the intervalic variety and multiplicity of interpretation provided by the ubiquitous dissonant elements. In considering Berg's tonal music I have attempted to detail the composer's own cyclic reinterpretation of tonality as an explanation of the ease with which he seamlessly invoked tonal features throughout his music. In the "atonal" music—a term I use with reservation, but which has common currency and which can be understood here as specifically connoting Berg's music—I supplement my approach with some aspects of pitch-class set theory, following writings by Allen Forte (1973) and Janet Schmalfeldt (1983), rhythmic approaches from the generalized intervals of David Lewin (1987), and contour studies from Robert Morris (1987). For the "twelve-tone" music—also a term used advisedly, but again one that gains a specific meaning as applied to Berg's music—I include explanations of order position transformations derived from work by Andrew Mead (1988–89) and Michael Stanfield (1984–85), as well as strategies for combining pitch-class sets in combinatorial contexts established from the basis of Milton Babbitt's writings by Lewin, Mead, Morris, and others.

Ultimately, the underlying cyclic basis of Berg's music transcends surface distinctions of "tonal," "atonal," and "twelve-tone" periods, terms which, although used as chronological guidelines, should be regarded as signifying differences in degree rather than kind. The cyclic aspects of Berg's pitch language have also been extended here to include his rhythmic techniques and twelve-tone order-position manipulations, tempo relationships, and even orchestration. Thus, this book seeks to demonstrate that Berg achieved a synthesis in his treatment of all musical elements, one that foreshadows later developments in the music of many composers. Chapter 1 introduces Berg's tonal music, includes a discussion of cycles in tonal music through examples from the early songs, and concludes with detailed analyses of the Piano Sonata Op. 1 and three of the Four Songs op. 2. The second and third chapters concern the atonal music: chapter 2 serves as an introduction and chapter 3 presents a detailed examination of pitch, rhythmic, formal, and orchestrational techniques, with examples drawn from all the atonal works, followed by detailed analyses of the song op. 2, no. 4, the *Altenberg Lied* op. 4, no. 4, the clarinet piece op. 5, no. 1, and the Orchestral Piece op. 6, no. 1. The forth and fifth chapters discuss the twelve-tone music: chapter 4 introduces the topic and chapter 5 presents separate analyses of each of the twelve-tone pieces, beginning with the transitional *Chamber Concerto* and ending with Violin Concerto. The opera *Lulu* is described first in general terms, then through the music associated with each of the main characters.

My intention in organizing the book into more general introductions and accompanying detailed chapters and sections is to make the discussions accessible to a wide range of readers. Those interested in Berg's music in more general terms may read the introductory sections and follow footnotes to other sources; readers who wish to pursue Berg's compositional techniques in individual pieces may proceed to relevant sections in the analytical chapters. The beginning of chapter 3 offers a detailed demonstration of the cyclic basis that forms the core of my approach. As always in an analytical study, familiarity with the sound of the music and access to scores are prerequisites to the reader's full participation. My closing wish is that those drawn to Berg's music will gain some insights from this volume to enhance their experience when engaging this extraordinary musician.

1 Tonality, Cycles, and Berg's Opus 1 and Opus 2

Berg's tonal music consists of about eighty-two songs (1901–8)—including those later collected and orchestrated as the *Seven Early Songs*—numerous study pieces for Schoenberg including the Piano Variations (1907), and unfinished works such as the five piano-sonata fragments written from about 1908 to 1910.[1] The two tonal works from his complete mature output, although still written under Schoenberg's tutelage, are the Piano Sonata op. 1 and the first three of the Four Songs op. 2.

Berg's songs and other early compositions exhibit styles characteristic of nineteenth-century music in varying degrees of sophistication.[2] Many of the songs contain unusual harmonic progressions and even begin and end in different keys, but in these earlier efforts well-defined motives are relatively rare. The later songs, under the influence of Schoenberg, show increasing motivic content and manipulation and a more coherent use of keys and harmonies, culminating in the Piano Sonata, which features a high degree of motivic economy and complex motivic transformations. The harmonic language of the Sonata, although tonal, features extensive use of whole-tone collections and "quartal" (interval 5 – based) chords. Used sparingly in Berg's early songs, these elements are common in the music of his immediate predecessors and contemporaries, as described by Schoenberg in his *Theory of Harmony* (1983; first published 1911). The op. 2 songs are also characterized by increased tonal resources, including different alignments of two or more horizontal voices, each consisting of successive interval 1s or 5s, which yield harmonies commensurate not only with the tonality of the first three songs but also with the "atonal" context of the last song. As described below, the multiple harmonic and voice-leading possibilities available from "cyclic" collections such as whole-tone scales and quartal chords and alignments of interval cycles are singular events in the evolution of Berg's musical language.

Tonality and Cycles

From the time of equal temperament, when the octave was divided into twelve equal semitones as a practical compromise to allow the full spectrum of tonal keys, the commonly available pitch space has been a cyclic space of equal, repeating gradations.[3] Pitch space can be traversed by increments of one semitone in a "1-cycle," of two semitones in a 2-cycle, three semitones in a 3-cycle, and so on through 4-, 5-, and 6-cycles. Such cycles can proceed ad infinitum, but it is useful to generalize pitch space to modular pitch-class space. Here cycles are defined by intervals 1–6 (ex. 1.1); cycles of intervals 7,8,9,A,B yield the same pitch-class collections as cycles 5,4,3,2,1 and can be read from these corresponding cycles in reverse order. When examining Berg's music, it is relevant to consider cycles both as pitch interval cycles and more generally as pitch-class interval cycles with their resulting pitch-class collections. In terms of pitch-class collections, cycles 2, 3, 4, and 6 each result in different numbers of distinct

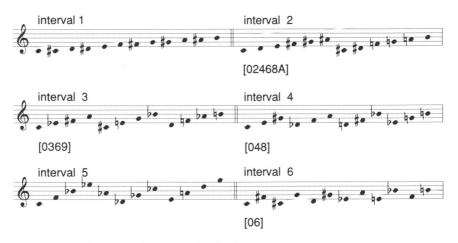

Example 1.1. Collections from interval cycles 1–6

forms and notes per form: a 2-cycle yields two six-note whole-tone collections [02468A], a 3-cycle yields three four-note [0369]s, a 4-cycle yields four three-note [048]s, and a 6-cycle yields six two-note [06]s. The 5-cycle is akin to the 1-cycle in that both yield all twelve notes, since 12 is not divided by 1,5,7,B.

Although the cyclic equal-tempered pitch space was created partly in response to the harmonic operation of tonal modulation, tonality itself is based on asymmetrical divisions of musical space, most notably the division of the octave into a perfect fourth and a perfect fifth. In the course of tonal composition, however, composers discovered that tonality can accomodate cyclic motions and collections. The most common tonal cycle is an extension of the perfect fifth-relationship between tonic and dominant chords, in a "circle of fifths" or 5-cycle that traverses the twelve distinct pitch classes. In a typical circle of dominant-seventh chords, a bass interval 5-cycle aligns with two voices in parallel descending interval 1-cycles—which in pitch-class set terms yields a succession of [026]s—and, if a third voice with a staggered descending interval 2-cycle is included, a series of [0258]s (ex. 1.2). Such alignments of 1-, 5-, and 2-cycles are common in tonal music, particularly in sequential passages of dominant-type chords, and are important features of Berg's music.

Example 1.2. Alignment of descending 1-, 2-, and ascending 5-cycles in a tonal "circle of fifths" progression

In addition to intervals and more generally interval-classes 1, 2, and 5, tonal chord and key relationships occur by interval-classes 3 and 4. In his *Structural Functions of Harmony*, Schoenberg generalized key relationships in a two-dimensional cyclic space, using a "Chart of the Regions" to demonstrate secondary keys around a tonic (fig. 1.1, with tonic C), in which the vertical axis is 5-cycles and the horizontal axis (lower left to upper right) is 3-cycles.[4] The latter reflects Schoenberg's nomenclature for more distantly related keys, described in terms of mediants and submediants. Another such cyclic map comes from David Lewin, originally to demonstrate just intonation but also generalized for use in an equal-tempered system.[5] Lewin's chart has horizontal 5-cycles and vertical 4-cycles, and he defines harmonic relationships in terms of the two intervals, such

Figure 1.1. Cyclic key relationships

Schoenberg: 3- and 5-cycles

G♯/g♯				D♭/d♭
	E/e	G/g	B♭/b♭	
C♯/c♯				G♭/g♭
	A/a	C/c	E♭/e♭	
F♯/f♯				C♭/c♭
	D/d	F/f	A♭/a♭	
B/b				F♭/f♭

Lewin: 4- and 5-cycles

C♯	G♯	D♯	A♯
A	E	B	F♯
F	C	G	D
D♭	A♭	E♭	B♭

as the intervals <7−7−4> transformational path <C−G−D−F♯> from C to F♯. Charts such as Schoenberg's and Lewin's, which have their roots in nineteenth-century and even eighteenth-century music theory, indicate possibilities for cyclic progressions within the tonal system.

In nineteenth-century music, cycles in vertical chords or horizontal voices tend to occur either in transitional, modulatory sections or within extended dominant functions. The cyclic chords are 3-cycle diminished-seventh chords, 4-cycle augmented chords, 2-cycle- or whole-tone−based French sixths, and 5-cycle or "quartal" chords. In Schoenberg's *Theory of Harmony*, the chapters "The Whole-Tone Scale and Related Chords" and "Chords Constructed in Fourths" outline the use of whole-tone and quartal collections as altered dominant chords and in motivic contexts in his own pieces, such as *Pelleas und Melisande* (1902), as well as in pieces by Debussy, Strauss, Wagner, Liszt, Dukas, and Mahler.[6] Schoenberg also discusses properties of interrelated cyclic chords. For instance, he demonstrates how whole-tone and 5-cycle chords can succeed one another (*Theory of Harmony*, ex. 337), and several examples (*Theory of Harmony*, ex. 339) aggregate combinations of cycles and cyclic collections transposed by other cycles, such as [036]s transposed by a successive descending 2-cycle (of four notes), to yield a collection of ten distinct pitch-classes: <{C,E♭,G♭}−{B♭,D♭,E}−{A♭,C♭,D}−{F♯,A,C}>. After discussing the role of diminished-seventh chords as dominants (p. 366), he combines these chords with added roots from the notes of another diminished-seventh chord to yield four T_3-related ninth chords (ex. 1.3a, b, f, g), sets a diminished-seventh chord against a scale of two interlocking diminished sevenths (to produce what is now commonly referred to as an "octatonic collection," ex. 1.3c) and to complete the aggregate (ex. 1.3d), and shows several instances of "pedal-point" settings (ex. 1.3e).

Cycles of all six interval-classes either within voices, between voices in vertical alignments, and/or in successive transpositions of harmonies or melodic units

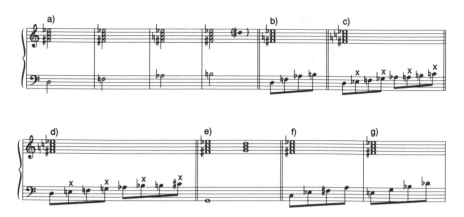

Example 1.3. Alignments of 3-cycle [0369]s (Schoenberg *Theory of Harmony*, ex. 304)

have been uncovered in music by Liszt, Wagner, Beethoven, Tchaikovsky, Chopin, Schubert, and other composers, by Schoenberg and other writers.[7] Although cyclic collections are easily accommodated within tonality, as in octave prolongations by major thirds or 3-cycle–based octatonic scales from diminished-seventh chords embellished with chromatic neighbors, the most interesting cases occur where the cyclic collections or procedures operate independently of tonal processes. For instance, Howard Cinnamon has distinguished equal interval cycles that are subordinate to a I–V progression from those that are not, citing the first movement of Lizst's *Faust* Symphony, which features major third or 4-cycles, as an example of the former and the introduction to the movement as the latter.[8] Among other pieces of the latter persuasion, hovering around the divide between tonal and "atonal" music, are the first version of Lizst's *La lugubre gondola*, based on [048]s; Debussy's *Voiles*, based on outer whole-tone sections and an inner 5-cycle or "pentatonic" section; and Bartók's "Diminished Fifth" from *Mikrokosmos* and Scriabin's Prelude op. 74, no. 3, both based on 3-cycles within the octatonic collection. These pieces, without a triadic basis or a defined dominant and tonic relationship, yet with referential or prioritized groups of pitch-classes, are part of a relatively small group of pieces based on purely cyclic collections. Many more pieces, including those by Berg, feature pitch organization based on cyclic collections but with complex relationships between cyclic and non-cyclic elements as an important element of the language.

Berg's Early Songs

Berg's songs up to 1908, including the *Seven Early Songs* as well as the first setting of "Schließe mir die Augen beide," feature varied musical and textual characteristics; here I will concentrate only on the aspects that have a direct bearing on the following analyses of the Piano Sonata op. 1 and the Songs op. 2.

Berg's later reliance on cycles and cyclic collections is not particularly evident in his early songs, which seems to indicate a later development of around 1907–8 for the cyclic interpretation of tonality described below in regard to his op. 1 and 2. Nonetheless, the few examples that appear are interesting in hindsight. The song "Am Strande," in A major, divides into two repeating halves, mm. 1–18 and mm. 18–35, which both proceed from a prolonged V to I. Some typical uses of cyclic collections occur—a succession of voice-leading through 3-cycle diminished-seventh harmonies over the prolonged V (mm. 1–6, 18–20), and an internal motion from VI to V/V effected by a descending bass 3-cycle arpeggiation <A–F♯–D♯–C–(B)> (mm. 12–13)—but in the second half of the song a progression from VI to I proceeds by aligned ascending and descending 1-cycles in "wedge" voice-leading, with vertical whole-tone chords. By the odd interval voice-leading, the chords alternate source whole-tone collections between the "C" collection {C,D,E,F♯,G♯,A♯} and the "C♯" collection {C♯,D♯,F,G,A,B} (ex. 1.4, mm. 23–26).[9] This combination of horizontal 1

Example 1.4. Wedge interval 1 voice-leading and vertical whole-tone harmonies, "Am Strande" mm. 23–26

cycles in wedge voice-leading and vertical whole-tone chords is characteristic of Berg's music throughout his life. Another such wedge appears in "Schilflied" from the *Seven Early Songs* (mm. 10–12), where outer-voice A♭s converge onto a central D (harmonically III–V/II in F minor), with largely 1-cycle horizontal voices yielding vertical whole-tone and 3-cycle chords interspersed with triads.[10]

The two most interesting instances of cyclic materials occur in "Traurigkeit" and "Nacht," the latter from the *Seven Early Songs*. The former is in three sections (mm. 1–7, 8–12, 13–16) with outer sections in A minor and a middle section based largely on successive whole-tone chords from alternating C♯ and C source collections, ending on a whole-tone dominant over E (ex. 1.5; the notes F, G, and C♯ in m. 10 are an appoggiatura and passing tones in this context.)[11] "Nacht," in A major, is a ternary form with an opposite organization: whole-

tone aspects in the outer sections (mm. 1–8, 25–38) contrast with an inner triadic section (mm. 9–25, which divides into mm. 9–15 and their varied repeat in
mm. 16–25, with mm. 11–12 transposed at T5 in mm. 19–20).[12] The song
ends open with a whole-tone half cadence in A on {E,G#,B#}. The opening five
measures of "Nacht" prolong a whole-tone dominant of A, with the C whole-
tone collection over a functional bass E, {E,F#,G#,A#,C,D}, set in oscillating
chords that shift to the neighboring C# whole-tone collection and back (ex. 1.6).
The main melodic motives (mm. 2–3, voice) are also whole-tone. In m. 6, the
harmony becomes triadic, with diatonic versions of the opening vocal motive—
originally comprised of two [048]s <E–B#–G#> and <Bb–F#–D>—in the
tonicization of E leading to the tonic A by m. 9. In the middle triadic-based section of the song, this motive returns as an interval 5–based line with [0167]
<F#–C#–C–G> extended by the 5-cycle–based collection <C–G–D–
F–Bb> (mm. 9–10). Later (m. 24) it leads to the restatement as an almost continuous 5-cycle segment <F–C–Bb–F–C–G–(F–E–Eb)–D>. The transformation of motives from whole-tone to 5-cycle–based collections, found
here in a tonal context, is characteristic of Berg's atonal music and assumes a
more structural role in the absence of tonality.

Berg's mature compositions are characterized by rhythmic motives that exist
independent of pitch realizations, and the origins of these motives are evident
in the songs. Of the earlier songs, "Grenzen der Menschheit" is characterized
throughout by a periodic rhythm in an upbeat grouping relative to the notated
meter (ex. 1.7a), and "Über den Bergen" also has a metric rhythmic figure in
each bar of the accompaniment. From the *Seven Early Songs*, "Schilflied" has a
syncopated rhythmic motive in mm. 1–8 of successive eighth–quarter dura-

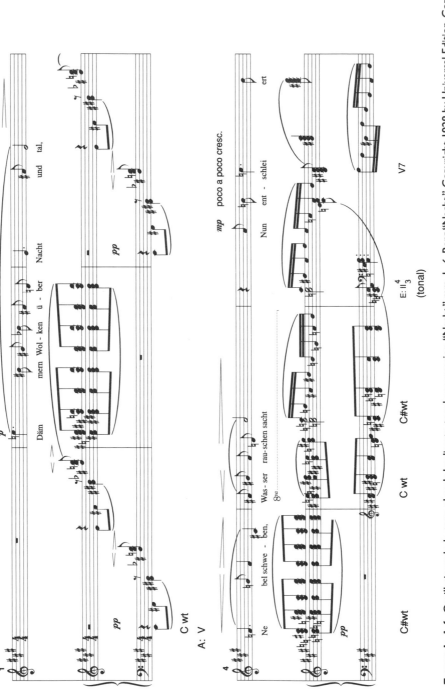

Example 1.6. Oscillating whole-tone chords leading to tonal progression, "Nacht," mm. 1–6. Berg "Nacht." Copyright 1928 by Universal Edition. Copyright renewed. All Rights Reserved. Used by permission of European American Music Distributors Corporation, sole U.S. and Canadian agent for Universal Edition A.G., Wien.

Example 1.7a. Opening rhythmic motive in "Grenzen der Menschheit." Berg "Grenzen der Menschheit." © Copyright 1985 by Universal Edition A.G., Wien. All Rights Reserved. Used by permission of European American Music Distributors Corporation, sole U.S. and Canadian agent for Universal Edition A.G., Wien.

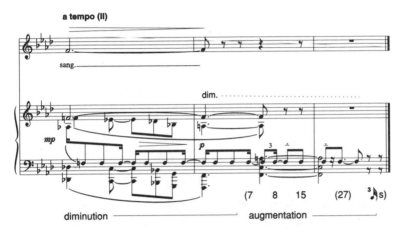

Example 1.7b. Diminution then augmentation of opening rhythm at the end of "Schilflied." Berg "Schilflied." Copyright 1928 by Universal Edition. Copyright renewed. All Rights Reserved. Used by permission of European American Music Distributors Corporation, sole U.S. and Canadian agent for Universal Edition.

tions that is transformed and diminuted at the return of the opening material (m. 19). This diminuted form, now as successive off-beat attacks, returns at the end of the song (ex. 1.7b) and is prolonged with each of the last four attack points spaced successively further apart from one another (in triplet thirty-second proportions, $<7-8-15-(27)>$), in a written-out deccelerando characteristic of Berg's later rhythmic techniques.

The song "Schließe mir die Augen beide" in Berg's first setting (he set the text again in 1925 as his first twelve-tone work) is written in $\frac{5}{4}$, but each vocal gesture spans four beats (ex. 1.8). In the first part (mm. 1–4), where the harmonies support the notated bar lines, each vocal phrase has a preceding quarter rest, so that the voice begins on beat 2 for mm. 1–3; the rest is omitted in the fourth vocal phrase, which begins on beat 1 in m. 4. In the second part (mm. 5–9), the vocal four-beat gestures, supported now by four-beat harmonic groups, are con-

Tonality, Cycles, and Opus 1 and Opus 2   21

Example 1.8. "Schließe mir die Augen beide," first setting, mm. 1–2, 5–6. Berg "Schließe mir die Augen beide" (1900). Copyright 1955 by Universal Edition A.G., Wien. Copyright renewed. All Rights Reserved. Used by permission of European American Music Distributors Corporation, sole U.S. and Canadian agent for Universal Edition A.G., Wien.

tinuous, overlapping the notated five-beat bars so that the initial note of each vocal phrase falls cyclically on beats 1, 5, 4, and 3, respectively. The penultimate vocal gesture comes to rest on the downbeat of m. 8 ("Herz"), with the following repeat of the final text phrase ("mein ganzes Herz") ending on the downbeat of m. 9. The continuous setting of the four-beat vocal phrases within a five-beat bar in the latter part of the song, with the result that the initial notes of the vocal phrases change beats in a cyclic succession, foreshadows rhythmic and metric arrangements in Berg's later music.

Piano Sonata Op. 1

Berg's Piano Sonata op. 1 was written in 1907–8 and first performed on April 24, 1911.[13] The sonata is tonal, in B minor, with unusual but by no means unprecedented harmonic relationships—extended passages of whole-tone based harmonies and lesser amounts of "quartal" or 5-cycle–based chords.[14]

The intervalic qualities of the main motives reflect these cyclic collections, but ultimately the cyclic harmonies and motives serve triadic tonality, with the tension between the tonal functions and cyclic materials an integral aspect of the piece. To illustrate the tonal course of the exposition, a Schenkerian voice-leading graph is given in example 1.9; for the most part, clear harmonic areas are connected by cyclic passages in largely interval 1 voice-leading.[15] Motivically, the sonata is highly unified, with all the motivic material stemming from the opening phrase, which acts as a *Grundgestalt*.

The sonata has the conventional three sections, a repeated exposition (55 × 2 = 110 bars, mm. 1–55), a development section of the same size (55 bars, mm. 56–110), and a slightly expanded recapitulation (69 bars, mm. 111–79), yielding the roughly equal proportion 1:1.1 for the repeated exposition to the combined development and recapitulation (fig. 1.2).[16] The internal sections fall into roughly equal divisions of twenty-six to twenty-eight measures; the climax in m. 83 divides the development into twenty-eight (mm. 56–83) and twenty-seven bars (mm. 84–110), the second theme area in the recapitulation is extended by four bars to a total of thirty (mm. 137–66), and the coda is about half that length at thirteen bars. Smaller passages of corresponding measures between the exposition and recapitulation also show integral relationships, such as the proportions 1:2 between mm. 1–10 and 110–30; 38–48 and 144–66; and 49–55 and 167–79. The tempo and dynamic groupings also define and support the sonata-form divisions, with *Tempo I* in the first area and *langsamer als Tempo I* in the second. The use of tempo in the definition of form becomes an increasingly important component of Berg's later music.

The first theme area is ternary, ABA' (fig. 1.2), with A' (mm. 16–28) doubling as the transition. The first A divides internally into three parts, a, development, a', and the contrasting B section is in two parts. In the recapitulation, the developmental passage in mm. 4–7 is greatly expanded (mm. 114–28), and the B section doubles as the transition (mm. 131–36), with the A' section omitted. The second area is in two parts (themes 1 and 2), with a sequential expansion (mm. 155–62) in the recapitulation. The closing theme (mm. 49–55) expands from seven to thirteen bars in the recapitulation with the addition of the five-bar codetta (mm. 175–79).

The initial phrase in Berg's sonata is an open-ended auxiliary cadence II–V–I (ex. 1.10; cf. ex. 1.9), with formal consequences, particularly large-scale formal overlaps.[17] The closing theme of the exposition leads toward I with a motion through V and ♭II, that is, F♯ and C (mm. 49–55); the arrival on I is delayed, however, until the cadence ending the first phrase, overlapping the formal division between the end of the exposition and the beginning of the repeat.[18] In a similar overlap at the divide between the development and reca-

Example 1.9. Graph of the exposition, Piano Sonata op. 1

Example 1.9. Graph of the exposition, Piano Sonata op. 1 (*Continued*)

Figure 1.2. Form of Sonata opus 1

Exposition				keys (M/m)		Recapitulation		
			bars			bars		
1st theme	A mm.	1–10	28			26	111–130	1st theme A
	a	1–3		b	b		111–113	a
	dev.	4–7					114–128	dev. expansion
	a'	8–10		D: ii–V			128–130	a T4
	B mm.	11–16					131–136	B/transition
	b	11–13		D: I			131–132	b
	b'	14–16		D: V	to E:V/V		133–136	b'
Transition	A'mm.	16–28		b				
	a	16–18						
	a'	18–23						
	y	23–28		D: vi–V/V				
2nd theme	mm.	29–48	27			30	137–166	2nd theme
	theme 1	29–32		D: V–ii	E: V–ii		137–140	theme 1
		33–38			to D		141–144	
	theme 2	38–39		Bb: V–I	D		144–145	theme 2
		F#					146–149	
		40–42		Bb: V	Bb: V		150–152	
		43–44		to b: ii	to b: ii		153–154	
							155–162	seq. expansion
		45–48		b: IV–V	b: IV–V		163–166	
closing theme/ retransition		mm. 49–55	7	b: V/bII–I		13	167–179	closing theme/ Coda

Development: motive 1: mm. 56–70
  bridge theme/motive 2 mm. 70–99, bass \<F#-G-C-F-B>
    mm. 82–86/86–88 T5
  2nd theme 100–107 (T −5)
  2nd theme/theme 2/retransition: mm. 108–110, B: IV–V

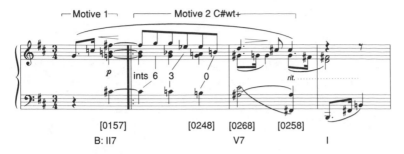

Example 1.10. Opening phrase of Piano Sonata op. 1

pitulation sections (mm. 100–110), a prolonged E (IV) moves up through G (VI), leading into the II–V–I return of the opening phrase (mm. 111–13). The cadential I chord is elided here, however, and waits until the final cadence to make its second definitive statement.

TONALITY AND FORM

The sonata is in B minor, with the tonic asserted locally in the opening phrase (ex. 1.10) and over a larger span by an arpeggiation of I–III–V (mm. 1, 29, 49) in the exposition (ex. 1.9). In the recapitulation, the opening cadential tonic is elided, but the overall progression is I–IV–V (mm. 111, 137, 167) with a definitive V–I at the end (ex. 1.11c, mm. 174–75). The elision of I in the recapitulation (mm. 111–13) is foreshadowed in mm. 16–20 of the exposition, where the opening phrase returns in a two-part sequence with a deceptive II–V–VI motion straddling the sequential pair (ex. 1.12, mm. 16–18, 18–20). The move to the dominant as a function rather than a key area for the closing theme in the exposition (ex. 1.11c, mm. 49ff.) obviates the need for transposition in the recapitulation and reduces considerably the traditional formal opposition between the main key and the keys of the second area.

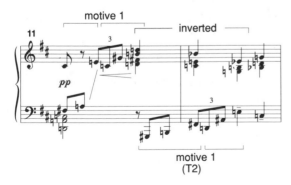

Example 1.11a. Bridge, from doubled motive 1, mm. 11–12, Piano Sonata op. 1

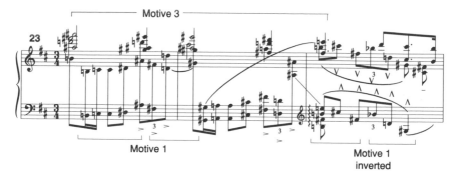

Example 1.11b. Motive 3 and varied motive 1 in transition, mm. 23–26, Piano Sonata op. 1

Example 1.11c. Motive 1 varied in m. 38; as the closing theme, mm. 49–50; and inverted in the final cadence, mm. 171–76, Piano Sonata op. 1

Example 1.11d. Motive 1 varied in second theme, mm. 28–29, Piano Sonata op. 1

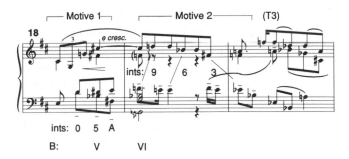

Example 1.12. Transposed restatement of opening, mm. 18–20, Piano Sonata op. 1

The secondary key area in the exposition, III (the relative major), appears first in a bridge within the first theme area (ex. 1.11a, mm. 11–16) led to by the fifth-motions E–A–D. The harmony progresses from D (I) to A (V) in m. 14, but the latter leads back to II^7 in B for the restatement of the opening phrase (m. 16). The key of D returns as the second key area, again led to by a fifth-motion, now VI–II–V, B–E–A, but the second theme appears over a V of D (ex. 1.11d, mm. 28ff.); the expected resolution to the tonic D is elided by a move to E (m. 31), and a cadence to D never appears. In the recapitulation, the bridge material returns in D (mm. 131–36), but over an F♯ that becomes V of V in E, to lead to the transposed second area (mm. 137ff.).

One of the defining features of a tonal sonata is the transposition of second theme material from the exposition when it recurs in the recapitulation. The second theme group in Berg's sonata begins in D (Ex. 1.9, m. 29) and proceeds through tonicizations of E (mm. 32–37) and B♭ (mm. 37–43), leading to II of B (mm. 44–48), which proceeds to V for the closing theme (mm. 49–55). In the recapitulation, the second theme begins not in the expected key of B (I) but in E (IV), transposed up a major second from its initial statement in D in the exposition (mm. 137–39), but again without a definitive cadence to I. The ensuing material is varied and proceeds through tonicizations of F♯ (mm.

140–41), D (mm. 142–45), F♯ (mm. 146–49), and B♭, which leads to II of B (mm. 150–54 are the same as mm. 40–44), with a sequential extension to V (mm. 155–66). The closing theme again features V and ♭II, leading finally to I with a codetta (mm. 167–79). The second theme also appears in the development (mm. 100–110) in A, also without a confirming cadence to I.

The three second-theme keys of D, A, and E form a 7-cycle, but in each case the key is strongly implied by the dominant notes only: A, E, and B. In the exposition and recapitulation, motions to tonics D and E are elided by tonicizations of II—E and F♯, respectively. The tonicization of E in the exposition foreshadows the key of the recapitulated second theme, but in the latter the key of E is implied by its dominant, B, which is, of course, also the tonic note in a larger sense. Thus, the emphasis on B as a dominant in the second key area is a fresh and somewhat novel treatment of the sonata requirement that second theme material be recapitulated closer to the tonic key. In a similar situation with the second theme statement in the development, the dominant E of the implied key of A becomes the subdominant of B.

A striking harmonic event is the combined T6-related V and ♭II chords at the ends of the exposition and recapitulation (ex. 1.11c, mm. 49–53, 167–79). The penultimate chord {C,E,G,F♯,A♯} at the structural cadence (mm. 174–75) merges the perfect fifth and semitone motions of a dominant and augmented-sixth-to-tonic progression. The chord is whole-tone based [02368], and it foreshadows the [013679]s from T6 related [037]s that occur in Berg's later music.[19]

TONAL CYCLES

The cycles evident in the sonata are, as might be expected, mostly of intervals 1 and 5, with the former tending toward the melodic, the latter the harmonic dimensions. Keys are established mostly by 5 or 7 cycles. The 5-cycle pattern is set in the chord roots of the initial phrase, <C♯–F♯–B>, as II–V–I in B minor (ex. 1.10), a progression that recurs throughout (mm. 44–55, 107–13, and 163–79, varied as IV–V–I). Corresponding 5-cycle motions occur in the bridge within the first area, in D as II–V–I <E–A–D> (mm. 8–12) and V/V–V <E–A> (mm. 13–16), and in the second theme areas: (1) in D in the preceding bars as VI–V/V–V–(I) <B–E–A–(D)> (mm. 25ff.); (2) in E as II–V–I <F♯–B–E> (mm. 31–36, 136–42); and (3) in A, as II–V–(I) <B–E–(A)> (mm. 99–102). In the development, the climax on a bass G is followed by a 5-cycle motion to C and F (mm. 84–90), which initiates an interval 1 descent to B (m. 97). Overall, the emphasis on the key of E along with the recurring dominant F♯ frames the tonic B in its surrounding 5-cycle neighbors E and F♯ throughout.

In addition to 5- and 1-cycles, 4-cycles appear within key areas. The recapitulation features a 4-cycle of tonicized keys <D–B♭–F♯> (mm. 142ff.) after the initial key of E. In the corresponding bars of the exposition, the 4-cycle <D–B♭–F♯> is interrupted by the key of E between D and B♭; E, however, is from the same whole-tone collection as the other notes, in the larger context for 4-cycles that is common in Berg's later music. These motions may be interpreted as expansions of the traditional minor-key tonal interval 4 motion from III to V (here D to F♯).

Between structural tonal functions, harmonies are often whole-tone, with interval 1 voice-leading (ex. 1.9) in both parallel motion and "wedges" from inversionally-related 1-cycles (mm. 3–10, 16–24, 49–50, 56–70, 91–99, 113–29, 167–68). Lesser areas of quartal or 5-cycle harmonies voice-lead similarly between tonal functions (mm. 25–28, 43–44, 94–96, 153–55). A recurring cyclic alignment pairs descending horizontal 1- and 4-cycles. The alignment yields vertical intervals in a 3-cycle, in permutations of intervals <6–3–0–9>; for instance, in the opening measures (ex. 1.10) descending 4-cycle <G–E♭–B> over descending 1-cycle <C♯–C–B> yields vertical intervals <6–3–0> (also mm. 17, 111), and in m. 19 <D–B♭–F♯> over <F–E–E♭> yields intervals <9–6–3> (ex. 1.12, also mm. 109–10, 111–12). A slightly different alignment of an ascending interval 1 cycle combined with a descending interval 4 cycle in m. 18 yields vertical intervals <0–5–A> in a 5-cycle: <D–D♯–E> over <D–B♭–F♯> (ex. 1.12). Such cyclic alignments become prominent in Berg's atonal music.[20]

GRUNDGESTALT, MOTIVES, AND CYCLES

Berg's early songs show an increasing use of motives, undoubtedly in response to Schoenberg's teaching, culminating in the songs "Traumgekrönt" and "Sommertage." The Piano Sonata, however, takes a distinct leap forward in its motivic integration. The first phrase acts as a *Grundgestalt* that establishes the motivic and harmonic basis of the entire piece (ex. 1.10).[21] Virtually all the motivic and harmonic material is derivable from the two motives presented at the outset: motive 1 comprises ascending intervals 5 then 6 spanning interval B in a dotted rhythm, forming set-class [016], and motive 2 descends in a 4-cycle in repeated notes followed by an ascent to an appoggiatura resolving by interval 1 to a note in the whole-tone collection of the preceding 4-cycle, forming whole-tone–based [01248]—a type of whole-tone collection with an added note that becomes a defining characteristic of Berg's later harmonic language. Other influential features of the opening phrase are the interval 1 voice-leading in the accompanying voices, the 5-cycle, II–V–I <C♯–F♯–B> harmonic motion, the <G–F♯> 6̂–5̂ motivic motion, and the Tristanesque sequences of harmonies ranging from whole-tone [0248] and [0268] to half-diminished and dominant-seventh

[0258] chords. The only motivic material not appearing in the opening is the descending tetrachordal motive 3, which evolves through the exposition in various intervalic guises (ex. 1.11b). The three motives, in whole or in part, are sequenced—often by cyclic transpositional levels—liquidated, rhythmically transformed, and combined throughout. In several cases, as in the song "Nacht," motives change cyclic content, in a variation technique increasingly common in Berg's later music.

Motive 1, initially [016], takes on whole-tone characteristics in its "doubled" form as <F♯–A–E/C–G♯–D> (from the C whole-tone collection with an added note A) associated with the bridge (ex. 1.11a, m. 11), where it is immediately imitated at T2, maintaining the same whole-tone collection, then sequenced at T7 changing to the C♯ whole-tone collection (m. 14). This doubled form appears in a few variants, with added notes and changed rhythms: with a repeated note as a figure in the transition (mm. 23–24, ex. 1.11b, lower voice), inverted (mm. 25–28, middle voices <E–C♯–F♯–B♭–D–G♯>, ex. 1.11b), and as a 3-cycle–based form <F–C–F♯–A–E–E♭> (containing 3-cycle {F♯,A, C,E♭}) in the second theme area, which is restated in varied intervalic settings but returns with its original intervals in rhythmic augmentation as the closing theme (ex. 1.11c). In the final bars of the movement, the closing theme beginning on E is sequenced to begin at T6 on A♯ (mm. 169–70, in the whole-tone–based form <A♯–B–F♯–C–E–B–A♯>), then inverted in sequence to lead to the final cadence (ex. 1.11c). In the course of the sequence, the initial notes <G–C–E> outline ♭II under an upper-voice oscillation of <C–B> ♭2̂–1̂. In the opening of the development, motive 1 is presented in a large-scale 3-cycle sequence, with upper notes F♯ (m. 57), C (m. 59), A (m. 62), and D♯ (m. 64) (the sequence is continued by a 4-cycle <F♯–A♯–D>, mm. 66–68). Finally, the contour of motive 1 is altered, with the dotted rhythm maintained, in the second theme, where the [016] is extended to [0167] (m. 29, ex. 1.11d).

Motive 2 is initially whole-tone based, but it appears with the intervals of motive 1 as [0167] in the second phrase (mm. 4–5, <(F)–E–E♭–B♭–A>). Motive 2 is also transposed down by T5 (mm. 3–4), and TB (mm. 8–9) in the first area, reflecting the interval-classes of motive 1 [016]. At the return of the opening (mm. 16ff.), motive 2 is sequenced from G through 3-cycle <D–D–F–A♭>, then in a 7-cycle <A♭–E♭–A♯> as part of the transition (mm. 21–23). In the recapitulation, the restated mm. 7–8 are transposed at T4 in mm. 127–28, maintaining [048] {C,E,G♯} within the motive; other transpositions of motive 2 change the internal [048] <G–E♭–B> (mm. 1, 16, 22, 111) to <D–B♭–F♯> (mm. 3, 19, 113–14), <G♯–E–C> (mm. 8, 128–30), and, completing the aggregate, <F–D♭–A> (m. 20, mm. 73–76). Motive 2 also appears in a varied but still whole-tone form following motive 1 in the second theme (ex.

1.11d), and is set in counterpoint with motive 1 in the development (mm. 74–77).

Motive 3 is a descending tetrachord, either as [0135], [0235], or the whole-tone [0246]. It appears first in the transition (mm. 23–25, ex. 1.11b) and recurs at climactic points throughout: in the exposition harmonized by 5-cycle chords (mm. 43–44), in the development juxtaposed with motive 1 (mm. 81–84) and in a transformation to a form of motive 2 (mm. 90–99), and at the climax of the recapitulation extended and sequenced in a tripartite sentence structure (mm. 153–54, 155–56, 157–60).

Overall, the sonata features a characteristic formal balance and clarity based on repetition, but a still-tonal style of developing variation of motivic material, where all motives derive organically from the opening phrase. In Berg's later music, motives are varied contrapuntally to a much greater extent, and varied less intervallically, retaining their identity. The cyclic structures—which will be defined primarily by identification with motives—are still in embryonic form in the sonata, submissive to the tonality, but some of the progressions and alignments that typify Berg's style are already in evidence. Once the basis of tonality is weakened and finally removed, as in op. 2, these elements take on a life of their own.

Four Songs Op. 2

The four songs in Berg's op. 2 (1908–10) group internally in several ways: (1) the first three are tonal, the fourth is "atonal"; (2) the first is in the Romantic lied tradition, the following three are successively further removed from that tradition; and (3) the second and third songs group together by the V–I motion E♭ to A♭ bridging the end of the second to the beginning of the third, creating proportional blocks of thirty bars for song 1, thirty bars for songs 2 and 3, and twenty-five bars for song 4.[22] Opus 2 is unified by recurring images in the texts, shared pitch motives, pitch-class sets, rhythms, and a D-minor passage in the third song recalling the first, but most notably by relationships based around intervals 1 and 5, in scale-degree and key relationships, and particularly by alignments of horizontal 5- and 1-cycles in each of the songs. Different alignments of these cycles create both tonal progressions and, in op. 2 no. 4, "atonal" chord successions (see the discussion of op. 2, no. 4 in chap. 3). A pivotal chord resulting from these cyclic alignments, <D–A–F♯–C–F> beginning opus 2, no. 1 and T–3 <B–F♯–E♭–A–B> ending op. 2, no. 4, rounds off the work in a return of opening material characteristic of Berg's later music. The cyclic aspects of op. 2 demonstrate clearly how Berg moved from tonal to atonal spheres by first interpreting tonality cyclically, then by maintaining similar compositional procedures while changing harmonic contexts away from tonal functional relationships.

The text of op. 2, no. 1 is the fourth of eleven poems collected together as *Dem Schmerz sein Recht* (1836) by Friedrich Hebbel (1813–63). The texts of the remaining three songs are from the collection *Die Glühende* (1896), subtitled *Glühende in einem neuen Heimat-Urgefühl*, by Alfred Mombert (1872–1942).[23] Despite the sixty years that separate these texts, they present similar images of sleep and repose—or death—after a difficult journey through adversity (dark seas, mountains, giants) to one's homeland, representing heaven, away from life's tumult. The images in the first three songs are quite similar to one another; the fourth is somewhat different, although it retains references to death. As Redlich notes, however, the rhymes and stanzas of Hebbel's poem and Berg's more romantic setting in the first song are markedly different from Mombert's "mystical visions in free meter" and Berg's successively more progressive forays away from the traditional lied in the second, third, and fourth songs.[24]

The first three songs in op. 2 are tonal, in characteristic late nineteenth-century style, with rhythmic displacements of consonances, resolution of dissonance into changes of chords, and extended dominants by cyclic voice-leading and collections. In all three songs, tonic chords are expressed with dominant characteristics and thus have an ambiguous status as I or V of IV: D as I or V of G in op. 2, no. 1; the final E♭ chord in op. 2, no. 2 as V of A♭ of the following op. 2, no. 3; and, in op. 2, no. 3, A♭ as I or IV of E♭ and, in the area of ♭II, A (B♭♭) as I or V of IV in D (E♭♭). The keys of the three songs are related internally and externally by interval-classes 1 and 5. The first song is in D, with a secondary area of G, and both D and G are embellished by interval 1 neighbors D–E♭ and G–A♭); op. 2, no. 2 is in E♭, and op. 2, no. 3 is in A♭, with a secondary key area of B♭♭ (A), and, within B♭♭ (A), IV or E♭♭ (D).[25] In op. 2, no. 3, the principal harmonic and scale-degree relationships are around notes {A♭,B♭♭,F♭,E♭}, or the conventional nineteenth-century emphasis on scale degrees $\hat{1},♭\hat{2},♭\hat{6},\hat{5}$; these scale-degree relationships are reflected harmonically in motives that can be described in pitch-class set terms as [01]s, [016]s, and [0156]s.

The principal horizontal cycles are aligned ascending 5- and descending 1-cycles, with the basic three-voice model an ascending 5-cycle voice aligned with two descending 1-cycle voices in parallel interval 6s, yielding consecutive [026]s (ex. 1.13a, open noteheads).[26] In op. 2, no. 3, the model is elaborated by an additional 5-cycle voice in parallel interval 7s with the bass, yielding successive [0258]s; in context, the chords are applied dominants in a "circle of fifths" progression ending with a triad (♭II: V–I = V/IV–IV; cf. ex. 1.13a and 1.17, mm. 4–6). In op. 2, no. 2 the model is elaborated by two additional descending interval 1 voices, yielding successive [0268]s (ex. 1.13b); in context, the [0268]s are part of a prolonged dominant of the main key E♭. In op. 2, no. 1, the model is elaborated by two voices creating successive whole-tone chords (ex. 1.13c;

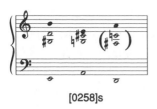

[0258]s

Example 1.13a. Aligned 1- and 5-cycles yielding [0258]s, op. 2, no. 3, mm. 4–6

[0268]s   Eb: V --- V

Example 1.13b. Aligned 1- and 5-cycles yielding [0268]s, model and musical prolongation of V of Eb, op. 2, no. 2, mm. 1–4

wt   D: V -------------------------------- V [V] IV   A sub

Example 1.13c. Aligned 1- and 5-cycles yielding whole-tone chords, model and musical prolongation of V of D, with bass note A substitute, op. 2, no. 1, mm. 11–14

filled-in noteheads to the right are dissonant within the whole-tone context of each chord); in context, the progression prolongs V of D, with some variation in the voice-leading (noted by parentheses in ex. 1.13c), dissonant appoggiatures in the vocal part (flagged grace notes), and an interval 1 inserted in the bass interval 5 cycle, E to Eb (at T6 from the expected A), which, while maintaining the whole-tone content of the chords, allows the succession to begin and end on the same pitch-class C♯. Finally (as discussed at the end of chap. 3), in the atonal op. 2, no. 4, the alignment is supplemented by an additional descending interval 1 voice creating parallel descending [016]s, yielding alternating all-interval-class tetrachords Tn [0256] and [0137]. These chords are transposed versions of the chord pairs over Eb, A, and D in mm. 1–10 of the first song (ex. 3.37b), and their use in both tonal and atonal settings demonstrates the links across Berg's change in language.[27]

The op. 2 songs are also unified by recurring rhythmic figures—foreshadowings of Berg's later *Hauptrhythmus* motives—characterized by changing duple- and triple-beat divisions with beat articulations suppressed by ties (ex. 1.14).[28] In op. 2, no. 1, a repeated triplet figure with tied beats occurs in the opening (mm. 1–10) and closing bars (mm. 20–30); characteristically, the rhythm repeats as an echo or afterthought following the closing chord. The second song features a similar rhythm following the cadential chord (mm. 17–18); this same rhythm then returns in op. 2, no. 3, mm. 3–4 and 10–12, and a variant recurs in op. 2, no. 4, mm. 5–6 (piano). Aside from these unifying rhythmic figures, the three tonal songs are metric and relatively straightforward rhythmically.

OPUS 2, NO. 1

The poem "Dem Schmerz sein Recht" has eight lines, alternating eight and seven syllables in length, grouped into two four-line stanzas with rhyme scheme *abab cdcd* (fig. 1.3).[29] Berg's setting is almost completely syllabic, with only a few

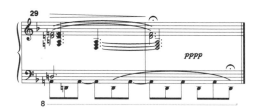

Example 1.14. Similar rhythmic motives in op. 2, no. 1, mm. 29–30; op. 2, no. 2, mm. 17–18; and op. 2, no. 3, mm. 10–12

Figure 1.3. Form of op. 2, no. 1

				rhyme
mm.	1–10	I established	1. Schlafen, Schlafen, nichts als Schlafen!	a
			2. Kein Erwachen, keinen Traum!	b
	11–16	V to V/IV to IV	3. Jener Wehen, die mich trafen,	a
			4. Leisestes Erinnern kaum,	b
			5. daß ich, wenn des Lebens Fülle	c
	16–21	IV	6. Niederklingt in meine Ruh',	d
			7. Nur noch tiefer mich verhülle	c
	21–24	IV-V-I	8. Fester zu die Augen tu!	d
	24–30	I Coda		

corresponding bars in palindromic return

mm. 1	2	3	4	5	6	7	8	9	10
mm. 30	29	28	27	26			24	25	

two-note slurs (*keinen*, m. 8; *Traum*, m. 9; *Leisestes*, m. 13; *Fülle*, m. 16; and *Augen*, m. 23). Musically, the song divides into five sections: the establishments of I (mm. 1–10); V–V/IV–IV (mm. 11–16); IV (mm. 16–21); IV–V–I (mm. 21–24); and coda confirming I (mm. 24–30) (cf. fig. 1.3 and ex. 1.15, middle level). The first two sections coincide with the text lines, but the third overlaps lines 5 and 6 in mm. 16–17, and the fourth overlaps lines 7 and 8 in mm. 21–22; the overlaps are set to *Fülle* and its rhyme *verhülle*.

The climax of the song—registrally, texturally, and dynamically—is in mm. 16–17, spanning the end of line 5 and the beginning of line 6; at this point of highest tension in the poem the two worlds of the narrator—the painful outside world and the inner escape world of sleep—are directly juxtaposed. From this extreme condition, the narrator returns to the initial state of detachment and repose, signaled by the restated opening gestures, first in IV, then in I (mm. 21–24). The circular nature of this return is also reflected by the palindromic formal and tonal restatement of mm. 1–10 in reverse order with respect to measures in mm. 24–30 (fig. 1.3). The correspondences suggest an arch form around the climax in mm. 16–17 which is supported by texture, the progressive thickening from one to seven voices and back (mm. 1, 16–17, 30), and dynamics, which increase from *ppp* to *f* and back to *pppp* (mm. 1, 16, 30); the song ends as it began, extremely soft in the low register.[30]

The insistent quality in the first line of text, "Schlafen, Schlafen, nichts als Schlafen," is reflected in the increasing dissonance over mm. 1–5: the initial triadic D-minor chord is transformed to a chord with dominant characteristics: scale degrees $\hat{1},\sharp\hat{3},\hat{5},\hat{7},\hat{9}$ <D–A–F#–C–F> ([01469]), with the upper dissonant

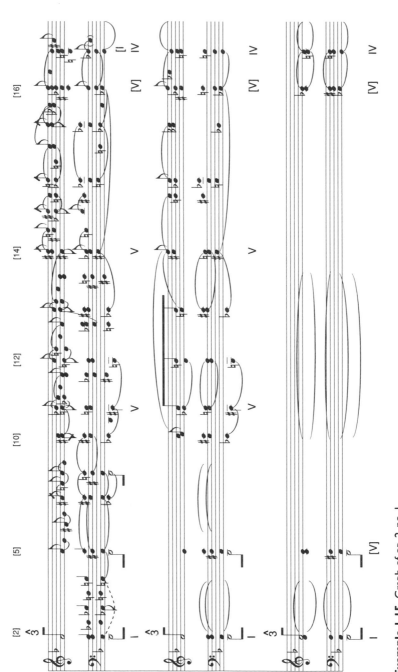

Example 1.15. Graph of op. 2, no. 1

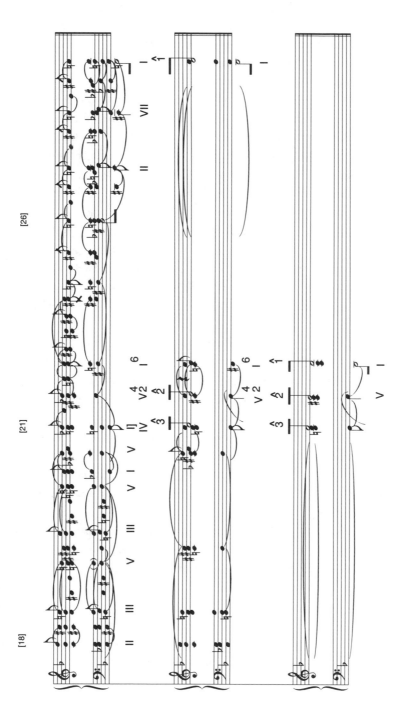

Example 1.15. Graph of op. 2, no. 1 (*Continued*)

voice F resolving to E to yield a whole-tone–based dominant-ninth chord
<D–A–F♯–C–E> ([02469]) (ex. 1.15). This chord is prolonged throughout
mm. 5–10 by an upper-neighbor chord built on E♭ and A, <E♭–A–G–
C♯–F♯>, with each note related by T1 except for the held A, under an upper-
neighbor motion F♯–F. The coda's closing measures (mm. 24–29), which
reverse the opening, take the D dominant-ninth chord and resolve the inner
voices back to a D-minor tonic triad, using various forms of neighboring chords
along the way, as the narrator returns to a quiet sleep.[31]

The D/E♭ chords in mm. 5–10 have a corresponding chord pair at T5, the
level of IV or G, in mm. 16–17. This key is associated with the intrusion of the
outside world into the narrator's sleep. The A♭ chord is a whole-tone–based
neighbor chord with "dissonant" (not in the C whole-tone collection) notes A
and F, the latter from the vocal motive <F5–E♭5–D5> (ex. 1.15). These two
dissonances resolve over a change of chord, however, whereupon they are again
dissonant. This second chord, over G, is also a whole-tone–based chord, in
which the A♭ resolution of the A is dissonant, as is the D resolution of the
melodic <F–E♭–D>.[32] The G (IV) chord is subsequently established by its
own progression (mm. 17–21), but in m. 21 it is transformed to a T5 transposition of the chord of m. 5, complete with a preceding neighbor chord on D
(analogous to the neighbor chord on A in mm. 5–10). The G chord as IV then
leads back to I via V $\frac{4}{2}$ (mm. 22–23).

The bass motion and chord progressions of the song are almost entirely by
interval-classes 5 or 1 (ex. 1.15). After the opening D–E♭ alternation, embellished by a bass fifth A–D, the cyclic sections of mm. 11–14 combine ascending
5- and descending 1-cycles with vertical whole-tone–based chords (cf. exx.
1.13c and 1.15). The vocal line consists of appoggiaturas, mostly resolving by
falling half-step into the whole-tone collection of the accompaniment. The
entire progression, a prolonged whole-tone dominant of D, is divided into two
sequential pairs, mm. 11–12 and 13–14, signaled by the descending interval 1 of
E–E♭ in the bass, causing a large double neighbor around the bass C♯ of
<C♯–B/E♭–C♯>.

At the arrival on the C♯ chord in m. 14, the bass descends by interval 1 to A♭
underlying a transformed D chord as a whole-tone dominant of G. After the
oscillating A♭- and G-based chords in mm. 16–17, the key of G is established by
an ascending progression, <G–A–A♯–B–C–C♯–D>, mostly interval 1
except for the interval 2 <G–A>. This unique bass interval signals the diatonic
tonicization of G (IV). The tonicizing progression is also marked by a 5-cycle
chord on B (which recurs in op. 2, no. 3). At mm. 20–21, G arrives as local tonic,
but in the dominant-ninth–chord guise of the opening (at T5); then leads, as IV,
through V $\frac{4}{2}$ to I6 over descending interval 1 G–F♯. The remainder of the song

transforms the tonic chord back into a triad, with the bass succession <Ab–
D♯–E–C–C♯–G♯–A–D> circling around the notes D and A with largely
interval 1 motions.

The three levels in ex. 1.15 are arranged as in a conventional Schenkerian
graph, with the foreground upper level a "normalization" of the surface with
harmonic areas clarified. Dissonances are shown as flagged notes, with slurs to
notes of resolution, some of which are themselves dissonant in the changed
harmonic context. The middle and bottom levels are successively higher
abstractions, modeling the previous level. As often occurs in eighteenth- and
nineteenth-century tonal music, the overall third progression <F–E–D> in
the bottom level—a deep middleground—is replicated at different levels
throughout, as on the surface at the climax of the vocal part (mm. 16–17) and
over a larger span at the outset (mm. 1–10).

OPUS 2, NO. 2

The poem of op. 2, no. 2 (fig. 1.4) has six lines in an irregular syllabic and rhyme
scheme, but a repeated phrase *in mein Heimatland* which Berg sets with the same
music (mm. 1–4, 15–18), creating a rounded form.[33] The poem is linked to that
of the first song by the images of sleep and of the places sleep allows access
to, specifically the native country (*Heimatland*).[34] The song, in Eb minor, is in a
ternary song form in three sections marked by dynamics and tempo, with the
outer sections pianissimo in *Tempo I* and the middle section forte and in *Tempo
II*. The middle two lines of the poem, which recount the narrator's journey
from the foreign place to a homeland, begin with the loudest, highest point in
the vocal line (m. 9) and are set by the only clearly triadic bars in the song (mm.
9–12, ex. 1.16b), perhaps reflecting Berg's journey from his tonal beginnings to
a new harmonic world in the course op. 2.

The introduction in mm. 1–9 and the coda in mm. 13–18, with mm. 1–4
restated in mm. 15–18, consists almost entirely of combinations of ascending
5- and descending 1-cycle voices creating vertical [0268]s that begin and end
functionally on a whole-tone dominant of Eb (compare ex. 1.13b and 1.16a).[35]
The bass 5-cycle in mm. 1–4 extends from Bb to T6-related E—scale degrees

Figure 1.4. Form of op. 2, no. 2			
A	introduction:	mm. 1–9	Schlafend trägt man mich
			in mein Heimatland.
B	tonal progression:	mm. 9–12	Ferne komm' ich her,
			über Gipfel, über Schlünde,
A'/coda:		mm. 13–18	über ein dunkles Meer
			in mein Heimatland

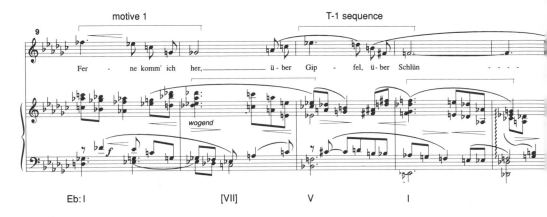

Example 1.16a. op. 2, no. 2, mm. 1–4

Example 1.16b. op. 2, no. 2, mm. 9–12

$\hat{5}$ to ♭$\hat{2}$ of E♭—to pass through the six distinct forms of [0268], ending at T6 with the notes of the first chord. Characteristically, the first [0268] is set with a dissonant note, C♭, in the voice, which "resolves" to a consonant B♭ in the third chord. In mm. 13–15, [0268]s occur in parallel descending interval 1s, and in the closing bars the restated opening progression returns, with the end bass E resolving to E♭. The final E♭ [0268] chord has the tonic note in the bass but the structure of a dominant chord which resolves into the A♭ beginning of op. 2, no. 3.

The tonal progression in mm. 9–12 is I–VII/V–V–I; the bass descending interval 7 B♭–E♭ recalls the opening ascending interval 5 B♭–E♭. The end I chord functions as a tonic, but as a whole-tone–based sonority {E♭,F,G,D♭} it is simultaneously a pivot back to the [0268]s in the coda. The bass interval 2 descent from E♭ to D♭ in m. 12–13 is unique (recalling the unique G–A bass motion in song 1, mm. 17–18) and sets off the end of the tonal section from the return to the whole-tone–based 1- and 5-cycles of the opening.

The two principal motives are stated at the outset in counterpoint, motive 1 in the piano (upper line) and motive 2 in the voice (ex. 1.16a). The two are closely related at T6—<F♭– E♭–C–G–G♭–F–E> and < C♭–G–B♭–A♭–G♭–F–D♭–C–B–B♭>—although clearly differentiated by contour. Motive 2 is spun out sequentially and liquidated on the surface in mm. 4–8, in a whole-tone–based sequence at successive T2. In the middle, tonal section, motive 1 appears with a new rhythm in mm. 9–12 in a T−1 sequence (mm. 9–10, 11–12) in the voice (ex. 1.16b); the counterpointing piano part alternates between motive 2 and a partial variant of 1, also in sequence. The closing section begins with a vocal motive 2, beginning on E; then its final portion <B3 – G4– G♭4> is sequenced by T6 to the original level, <F4–D♭5 – C5>, and imitated in the piano at T−1 <B♭3– G♭4– F4>. The final vocal motive 2 is extended to A over the cadential E♭ chord while the piano restates motive 1 (mm. 15–18).

OPUS 2, NO. 3

The images in the poem of op. 2, no. 3 are similar to those of op. 2, no. 2: in a dream the narrator finds the way home after a journey filled with obstacles to arrive in the throes of sleep (fig. 1.5).[36] The matching images are home attained (*heimfand*) and sleep (*schlafbefangen*), with an added magical touch, the guiding hand from a mysterious fairy tale. Tonally, the guide leads the narrator back to the home tonic (A♭) from the point of furthest remove—the tritone or the "darkest land" (D as IV of ♭II). The ending in sleep is inconclusive, however, signified by the closing E♭ sonority, V of A♭.

The song is a ternary form, with each section taking two lines of the poem, but grouping across the two three-line stanzas. The key is A♭ minor, but the song ends tonally open on a V chord, with an arpeggiated <E♭– A♭– E♭> in the bass (m. 11, ex. 1.17) including A♭ rather than a B♭, emphasizing the dominant nature of the chord. The secondary key area is ♭II, B♭♭ respelled enharmonically as A, achieved by reinterpreting F♭ (♭VI of A♭) as V of ♭II (B♭♭). The restated opening in m. 8 is condensed and disguised, allowing for two possible tonal interpretations: (1) the return is only voice-leading, bridging from ♭II to ♭VI (ex. 1.17, upper system); (2) the return is structural, as part of a large-scale I–♭II

Figure 1.5. Form of op. 2, no. 3

A	mm.	1–5	I-V-♭II	Nun ich der Riesen Stärksten überwand
				Mich aus dem dunkelsten Land heimfand.
B	mm.	5–8	♭II	an einer weissen Märchenland —
				Hallen schwer die Glocken
A'	mm.	8–12	I to V	und ich wanke durch die Gassen
				Schlafbefangen.

Example 1.17. Graphs of op. 2, no. 3

−I−♭VI−V progression, with the second I restoring scale degree $\hat{3}$ in the upper line (ex. 1.17, lower system). In the latter case, the first note of the returning A♭ is given a [0268] setting, {A♭,F♯,C,D}, recalling this sonority in op. 2, no. 2. The overall chord progression, as in the previous songs, is almost entirely by fifth or by semitone, both within sections and overall, using chords I, ♭VI, ♭II, and V.

The most interesting passage occurs in the alternating D-triadic and B−5-cycle neighboring chords in mm. 6−8 (enharmonically E♭♭ and B♭♭), which in harmony and gesture recall op. 2, no. 1. The apparent key of D presents a T6 challenge to the tonic of A♭. The circle-of-fifths progression from aligned ascending 5- and descending 1-cycles in mm. 4−6 may be interpreted as [V]−V−I in D minor, but given the tonal context a preferable alternate reading is V−I arriving as V/IV−IV (in ♭II). Thus the true key opposition comes from B♭♭ as ♭II of the main key of A♭, rather than E♭♭ or D as ♯IV of A♭, a tonal situation which is untenable.[37] In this latter reading, the unusual feature of the form is the ending of the middle section on a back-relating IV of ♭II (the D or E♭♭ chord), followed by a return of the opening, with no harmonic connection across the formal boundary in m. 8.

Although the E♭♭/D minor section has a subordinate harmonic role (to B♭♭) in op. 2, no. 3, it has an extremely important formal and dramatic function in its reference to op. 2, no. 1. The neighboring B/C♭−based quartal or 5-cycle chord recalls a similar chord in op. 2, no. 1 (mm. 18, 19), and the primary motives in op.

2, no. 1—the falling fifth and the neighbor motive—also occur in the D/E♭♭-minor section in op. 2, no. 3.

The primary motive in op. 2, no. 3, an aggressive gesture that reflects the narrator's struggles with "the strongest of giants," appears only in the piano (ex. 1.18). The motive, an [0156], reflects the interval 1- and 5–based elements of op. 2. In each case, it is an arpeggiation that locally connects one harmony to another, and overall the motive begins on the notes $<A♭-C♭-(D♯)/E♭>$, outlining the tonic triad: $<A♭4-C6-G4-D♭4>$ I–IV (mm. 1–4, 8), $<C♭2-E♭3-B♭2-F♭2>$ ♭VI–V (mm. 3–4, mm. 9–10), and $<D♯4-G4-D4-G♯3>$ V/♭II–♭II (mm. 4–5). A varied statement of the motive, as $<B♭4-B4-C5-G4-D4>$, with a 5-cycle segment in the last three notes, occurs in mm. 8–9 of the return within the E (F♭) ♭VI chord with an upper neighbor note C (ex. 1.17). This E/F♭–based chord, which arrives via the accelerando in the bass motion of mm. 8–9, appears before the V chord, unlike in the initial section where it enters only after the initial V$_4^6$ (mm. 3–4). Although the voice part does not include the primary motive, it also embellishes the tonic triad by two cycles: a 4-cycle $<C♭3-E♭4-G4>$ resolving to A♭4, where G4 in a lower neighbor (upbeat to m. 1, ex. 1.18); and a 3-cycle $<A♭4-C♭4-D5>$ resolving to E♭, where D is a lower neighbor (mm. 3–4).

The first three songs of op. 2 described above feature tonality in a cyclic guise—with horizontal interval 1 and 5 cycles and vertical whole-tone or 5-cycle–based sonorities in sequence. These set the stage for the remarkable song op. 2, no. 4, which displays the cyclic features of the preceding songs but with non-triadic harmonies and without a tonal context. Thus, these songs truly map out Berg's path to atonality. To understand this path, however, requires a fuller explication of the cyclic basis of Berg's atonal music. This is given in the next chapter; a complete analysis of op. 2, no. 4 follows.

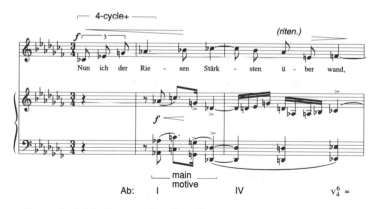

Example 1.18. Opening of op. 2, no. 3

"Beyond the bounds of the universe you glanced musingly."[1]

"When I decided some fifteen years ago to compose 'Wozzeck' a peculiar situation in music existed. We of the Vienna school (under its leader Arnold Schoenberg) had just outgrown the infancy of that movement which was—quite erroneously—classified as the movement of Atonality. Composition in that style was primarily confined to the creation of musical miniatures—such as songs, pieces for solo piano and for orchestra—or (in the case of more extensively planned works like Schoenberg's 'Pierrot' melodramas or his two one-act operas) concentrating on a formal species which received its shape exclusively from its text and dramatic action. Until then works of bold dimensions—such as four-movement symphonies, oratorios and large-scale operas—were missing from the sphere of atonal composition. The reason for this deficiency? That style renounced Tonality and thereby gave up one of the most effective means of building either small or large musical structures."[2]

2 The Atonal Music: Introduction

n this statement from his *Wozzeck* lecture of 1929, Berg reflected back on the musical problems he and his colleagues faced when they abandoned tonality. Berg's assessment is somewhat modest with respect to his own compositions; although he composed small-scale atonal pieces—the song op. 2, no. 4 (1910), the *Altenberg Lieder* op. 4 (1912), and the Clarinet Pieces op. 5 (1913)—he developed a language that also produced the substantial String Quartet op. 3 (1910) and Orchestral Pieces op. 6 (1913–15).[3] In *Wozzeck* (1914–22), text and instrumental forms combine in a remarkable synthesis to create an extended atonal music drama.

Berg's response to the challenge presented by Schoenberg's turn from tonality was to create an internally consistent language in which arrangements of musical elements characteristic of tonality were incorporated into a larger system. Pitch relationships in Berg's atonal music are based to a large extent on collections derived from interval cycles; these collections are used as self-defining bases of the language but retain their original tonal associations. Within the system, allusion to these associations is one option among many. Rhythmic patterns are analogously freed from metric constraints to allow their periodic (or cyclic) durational aspects to develop independently, yet also to invoke their metric origins if desired. The dual nature of these cyclic collections of pitches and durations is responsible in large part for the particular affect of Berg's music.

The remainder of this chapter discusses formal, motivic, pitch, and rhythmic aspects of Berg's atonal music in general terms. The following chapter contains a more detailed exposition of the purely musical aspects of Berg's atonal music—pitch, rhythm, motive and form, and orchestration—ending with analyses of op. 2, no. 4; op. 5, no. 2; op. 4, no. 4; and op. 6, no. 1.

Form, Treatment of Motives, and Text

Berg's atonal pieces vary in form and motivic treatment from the brief song op. 2, no. 4 and the Clarinet Pieces op. 5, which lack traditional motivic features and defined forms, to the *Altenberg Lieder* op. 4—songs with prominent, repeating motives but brief, concise forms—and the larger String Quartet op. 3, the Orchestral Pieces op. 6, and several scenes in the opera *Wozzeck*, all characterized by motivic and even thematic development within the repetition forms of tonal instrumental music. Other scenes in *Wozzeck* are variation forms on traditional features such as themes and chord progressions, but some vary more unusual elements—rhythms, a single chord, and a note.

In the midst of Berg's diverse formal practice, three formal and motivic features stand out. The first is the tendency for motives to be systematically unfolded by slowly introducing one or a few notes at a time, and to be similarly dissolved or liquidated by the successive truncation of a few notes at a time or by a gradual disintegration.[4] The continual emergence and dissolution of motivic materials also shapes formal areas based on similar principles, as in op. 6, no. 1, which begins with non-pitched percussion and slowly develops from small pitch cells into the longer themes of the middle section, then, in symmetrical retrograde, dissolves from themes into cells and eventually back to unpitched percussion. Adorno claims a similar form for the op. 4 songs as the formal principle most characteristic of Berg's music: "gradually, with concurrent dynamic build-up, compositions are led from the amorphous to the articulate and then, occasionally with acts of destruction, back into the indeterminate."[5] Circular or retrograde constructions, hinted at in op. 2, no. 1 (fig. 1.3), occur in op. 4, no. 2 and in *Wozzeck* Act I, scene i.[6] In the last, the circular return of the opening material extends to the music and text of the entire opera—the hopeless cycle in which Wozzeck and his progeny are trapped—as reflected in Berg's comment in his lecture that "the initial bars of the opera could easily link up with these final bars and thereby close the circle."[7]

A second feature of Berg's formal and motivic practice is the appearance of the same motives in different movements of a work, even when motivic recurrence within movements is minimal.[8] Such recurring motives unify the songs of op. 2, particularly the atonal op. 2, no. 4 with its tonal predecessors, and the String Quartet op. 3, where the second movement features varied and explicit returns of motives from the first movement. Both the *Altenberg Lieder* op. 4 and Orchestral Pieces op. 6 feature extensive intermovement motivic appearances, and in *Wozzeck* thematic recurrences take the form of leitmotivs associated with characters, objects, and dramatic subjects throughout the opera.[9] The exception is the largely athematic Clarinet Pieces op. 5, in which only a few traditional motivic recurrences take place.

Finally, forms in Berg's atonal music tend to be rounded off by the return of opening material. Such returns take the form of sonatas in op. 3, nos. 1 and 2, and in *Wozzeck*, Act II, scene i; traditional ABA structures in op. 4, nos. 2 and 3, and in *Wozzeck*, Act II, scene iv; brief restatements or motivic occurrences from earlier points in the movement or the work at the end of op. 2, no. 4, op. 3, nos. 1 and 2, op. 4, nos. 4 and 5, and op. 6, nos. 2 and 3; and retrograde returns in op. 4, no. 2, op. 6, no. 1, and *Wozzeck*, Act I, scene i.

SCHOENBERG, NON-REPEATING FORMS, AND TEXTS

Berg's most radical atonal expressions, in op. 2, no. 4, op, 4, no. 4, op. 5, op. 6, no. 3, and *Wozzeck*, Act II, scene iii and Act III, scene ii, are those in which formal and motivic repetition is largely eschewed. As many writers have noted, the movements of op. 5 in particular were influenced by trends exemplified in Schoenberg's Piano Pieces op. 19 (1911). With regard to the developments in his music of the time, Schoenberg noted that, from a large number of motives and themes in his late tonal music, he came to "formulate ideas in an aphoristic manner, which did not require continuations out of formal reasons; secondly, to link ideas together without the use of formal connectives, merely by juxtaposition;[10] and, in the most extreme position, to abandon repetition altogether: "to find further liberty of expression . . . I and my pupils believed that now music could renounce motivic features and remain coherent and comprehensible nevertheless."[11] In a letter to Webern, Berg described *Wozzeck*: "For example, normal operatic scenes with thematic development, then others *without* any thematic material, in the manner of [Schoenberg's monodrama] *Erwartung.*"[12]

Berg's op. 5 pieces fall most closely into the categories outlined by Schoenberg. There are relatively few internal repetitions of motivic material, either within or across different movements, compared to the highly motivic op. 4 and op. 6. Formally, the first, second, and fourth movements in op. 5 have only the briefest of returns. The unusual motivic and formal features have a corresponding anomaly in the harmonic language: op. 5 is the least characteristic of Berg's atonal pieces in terms of harmony.

Of Berg's other pieces that lack internal repetition, op. 2, no. 4, op. 4, and *Wozzeck*, Act II, scene iii and Act III, scene ii are texted. As Berg was quoted at the beginning of this chapter, he and his colleagues were dependent on text in their initial atonal efforts. Rather than traditional text and music relationships, however, where either the text setting is subordinate to melodic motives or the music depicts elements in the text, Schoenberg asserted a new relationship between the two elements.[13] Text was freed from music, in part by *Sprechstimme*, a recitative-like declamation in which the singer follows the rhythms and inflections of the text unimpeded by the demands of musical motives. But at the same time music was freed from text, as Schoenberg rejected all external correspondences, such as traditional word painting and text depiction.[14]

Berg's text setting is somewhat more traditional than the position outlined by Schoenberg. In his songs the vocal line is generally independent of the accompaniment but follows the phrasing of the text in settings that are almost completely syllabic, with only a few melismas. Vocal effects foreshadowing *Sprechstimme* appear in op. 2, no. 4 and op. 4, nos. 1 and 4, and *Sprechstimme* as well as the more songlike *Sprechgesang* appears throughout *Wozzeck*. In op. 4, no. 5, a passacaglia, the vocal treatment is significantly different, however; the vocal line is motivic and doubled throughout in the orchestra as part of the symphonic texture.[15] This texture appears in places in *Wozzeck* (Act I, scene i, mm. 115–32; Act I, scene iii, mm. 346–50; and parts of Act II, scenes i, ii and iv and Act III, scene i), but is more characteristic of Berg's later concert aria *Der Wein* and his opera *Lulu*. The form of op. 4, no. 5 also foreshadows Act I, scene 4 in *Wozzeck*, a passacaglia with three themes.

STRING QUARTET OP. 3 AND THREE ORCHESTRAL PIECES OP. 6

The Quartet op. 3 and the Orchestral Pieces op. 6, both large-scale works with repeating forms and motivic development, were strongly influenced by Schoenberg. The Quartet was the last piece written under Schoenberg's tutelage, and, particularly in the strictly balanced formal areas of the sonata-form first movement, it bears the traces of an assigned task. The following op. 4 songs and the Clarinet Pieces op. 5 were Berg's first independent forays, and Schoenberg complained about the experimental nature of the first and the insubstantial dimensions of the second.[16] Following Schoenberg's subsequent suggestion to write an orchestral suite, Berg composed his op. 6 pieces and wrote in a letter to Schoenberg that "the three Orchestral Pieces really did grow out of the most strenuous and sacred endeavour to compose character pieces in the manner you desired, of normal length, rich in thematic complexity, without striving for something 'new' at all costs, and in this work to give of my best."[17]

As quoted in the epigram heading this chapter, Berg alluded to the difficulty of creating large forms without the unifying force of tonality. In his larger works, op. 3 and 6 and some scenes in *Wozzeck*, Berg was undoubtedly influenced by Schoenberg's assertion that form in tonal music stems from tonality and motivic and thematic organization, but that in the absence of tonality, the latter is sufficient to create a coherent form.[18] In many tonal forms, particularly sonata forms, however, repetition is motivated by tonal reasons, to reassert the tonic key and reconcile wayward material by transposition. Such tonal motivations are absent in atonal works. Where Berg used tonal repeating forms in op. 3, op. 6, and *Wozzeck*, the redundacy of large-scale formal restatement is balanced by continuing development of material and even the introduction of new motives.[19] Such development rarely includes transposition, however, since motives in Berg's music generally recur at the same transpositional levels.

WOZZECK

The text of Berg's opera *Wozzeck* (1914–22) was adapted from the play *Woyzeck* by Georg Büchner, written before 1837.[20] The vocal treatment falls into two main categories. The first is described by Berg in his lecture, where he stated that, although *Wozzeck* was not a "bel canto opera," it is "bel cantare" in that almost no recitative is present. Instead, influenced by Schoenberg's *Pierrot Lunaire*, Berg used *Sprechstimme*, a rhythmic declamation that has, according to Berg, three virtues: (1) it allows for "all formal potentialities of absolute music which play no part in Recitative"; (2) it insures that words are understood; and (3) *Sprechstimme*, as well as *Sprechgesang*, has shadings from "the pitchless whispered word to the true bel parlare of broad speech melodies" as a "welcome addition and attractive contrast to the sung word."[21] *Sprechstimme* is prominent throughout, but in Act I, scene ii, where Wozzeck and Andres are distinguished by *Sprechstimme* and singing, respectively, and in Act III, scene i, where a contrast between Marie's reading of the bible story to her child and her cries for mercy is created by a similar alternation, *Sprechstimme* becomes part of the formal structure.

The other principal vocal treatment in *Wozzeck* is the use of folk elements, corresponding to numerous folksongs in Büchner's play.[22] Melodies in folksong style appear in Andre's song in Act I, scene ii; Marie's "Soldaten" song in Act I, scene iii; Marie's three songs to her child in Act I, scene iii, Act II, scene i, and Act III, scene i; the inn scenes Act II, scene iv and Act III, scene iv; and the children's song in Act III, scene v. These passages, with their restricted vocal ranges and relatively simple metric and harmonic structures, represent the external, everyday world, in contrast to the irregular, dissonant, and more complex language associated with Wozzeck's inner torments.

The feature of *Wozzeck* that has elicited the most commentary is Berg's declared use of self-contained forms associated with instrumental music in each scene.[23] Berg insured this focus for his critics by including the formal plan of the opera along with the vocal score[24] and by emphasizing the formal aspects in his writings about the opera, and apparently influencing his students to do the same. For instance, Berg's student Fritz Heinrich Klein wrote: "For Berg has written not an internationally conventional 'music drama' but an opera with a completely new kind of structure in which the themes, springing from the dramatic situation, undergo a formal musical development and in which the opera itself is divided into sections which include almost all the forms of absolute music."[25]

The opera is in three acts with five scenes per act; Berg's chart of the forms is given in figure 3.24. The three acts were, according to Berg's lecture, built on "the venerable tripartite formal pattern a-b-a," corresponding to an "exposition, dramatic development, and catastrophe and epilog." The first and third acts are both in five separate scenes, whereas the scenes of the second act are grouped together as a five-movement symphony. The scenes throughout are connected by interludes, which have different functions: a traditional development of the material in the previous scene (Act I, scene i–ii); an epilogue of reminiscenes from the previous scene (Act I, scenes ii–iii); a continuation or completion of the previous scene (Act I, scenes iii–iv; Act II, scenes i–ii, ii–iii, and iv–v; Act III, scenes i–ii and iii–iv); a prelude to the following scene (Act I, scenes iv–v; Act II, scenes iii–iv; Act III, scenes ii–iii); and the Act III interlude, a "development section" of themes associated with Wozzeck, with one new theme that acts as a "commentary" on the tragedy of the opera (Act III, scenes iv–v).[26]

In his article "A Word about *Wozzeck*," Berg commented on the central issue in opera—the relationship of text and music—asserting that, although music ultimately serves the text, it must do so only in accordance with certain inviolate musical laws: "The music was to be so formed that at each moment it would fulfil its duty of serving the action. Even more, the music should be prepared to furnish whatever the action needed for transformation into reality on the stage. The function of a composer is to solve the problems of an ideal stage director. On the other hand this objective should not prejudice the development of the music as an entity, absolute, and purely musical. No externals should interfere with its individual existence."[27]

Berg outlined the close correspondence between the musical forms and the text in several scenes from *Wozzeck* in his lecture.[28] But although acknowledging Berg's masterful combining of music and text in the opera, many writers have commented on the strictness of the given musical forms, their audibility, and their relevance to an understanding of the opera.[29] They are, for the most part, imperceptible to audiences, unlike the traditional operatic forms like recitative-aria or cabaletta-cavatina pairings. Adorno wrote, "Although these [the much-discussed forms of absolute music in *Wozzeck*] are used to organize the score over a relatively broad time span, they neither need nor ought to be perceived as absolute forms; rather they are invisible, like the row of a good serial composition in later music."[30] Berg felt his particular accomplishment in the opera was that "no one in the audience . . . pays any attention to the various fugues, inventions, suites, sonata movements, variations and passacaglias . . . No one gives heed to anything but the vast social implications of the work which by far transcend the personal destiny of Wozzeck."[31]

Despite the many references to strict forms, with the exception of the sonata form in Act II, scene i and the scherzo with two trios in Act II, scene iv, the forms are rather loosely constructed. A few scenes, Act I, scenes i, iii, and v, Act II, scene iii, and Act II, scene v, are sectional, with some recurring elements. Two scenes, Act II, scene ii and Act III, scene i, divide into sections based on variation treatments of themes and imitative, fugal passages. The remainder are essentially variation forms, on a chord progression in Act I, scene ii, a passacaglia on a twelve-note theme treated like a serial motive in Act I, scene iv, and several themes in the first section of Act III, scene i. The variation forms Berg described as "inventions," "new forms, based on novel principles," appear in Act III, with variations on the register, instrumentation, and dynamics of realizations of pitch-class B in Act III, scene ii, on a rhythmic motive in Act III, scene iii and on a fluctuating pulse in Act III, scene v, and on a referential chord in Act III, scene iv. The latter "invention on a chord" is undoubtedly influenced by Schoenberg's "Farben" op. 16, no. 3 (1909), although Berg's chord is treated more like a pitch-class set (arranged in different contours and rhythms) than the relatively fixed registral relationships of the pitch set in Schoenberg's movement. The invention on a rhythm in Act III, scene iii was novel, however, as Fritz Heinrich Klein stated: "This idea of invention is surely unique in music: I at least have not yet found anything similar in music literature."[32]

The other "invention" mentioned by Berg in Act III of *Wozzeck* refers to the interlude between scenes iv and v. As Perle has noted, the term "invention on a tonality" is problematic and he does not include it as one of the variations of the act. The interlude marks, however, an interesting addition in Berg's adaptation of the play. Berg's "objective" formal stance in relation to the character Wozzeck, reflected in the absolute music forms, is only broken, as noted in the lecture (1957, p. 284), in the interlude of Act III where a subjective commentary acts as an "epilogue" to the tragedy: "[the interlude] should also be appreciated as the composer's confession, breaking through the framework of the dramatic plot and, likewise, even as an appeal to the audience, which is meant to represent Humanity itself."

The change in musical language in the early years of the twentieth century from tonal to so-called "atonal" organization and relationships has fascinated and frustrated musicians from that time up to our own day. As Berg pointed out in his talk "Was ist atonal?" (1930), the term "atonal" was originally used as a criticism, a synonym for "unmusical." Following similar arguments by Schoenberg, Berg replied that, although the harmonic basis might be different, the music he and his colleagues were writing contained all the elements "formerly" associated with music, new perhaps only in expression, but not unprecedented when compared with developments in the music of Mozart to Mahler. Schoenberg speculated that the new harmonic language undoubtedly had a systematic basis, but one that awaited discovery.[33]

Theories and analyses of atonal music have ranged from traditionalist views stressing continuity with the past to modernist beliefs in a historical break to a fundamentally different and self-contained language. Many musicians have attempted to find an explanatory theory for atonal music comparable to that for tonality, in which every note has its functional place within a hierarchical network of pitch and intervalic relationships. Others have rejected the assumption that the negative appellation "atonal" describes a unified language, instead allotting each piece its unique space and relationships between events and invoking generalizations for analysis only where explicitly warranted. Most, however—including the present author—inhabit a middle ground between the twin poles of an entirely theoretical or analytical basis. In the following discussion, I begin with theories relevant to Berg's music, from Berg himself, Schoenberg, George Perle, David Lewin, Robert Morris, and Allen Forte, then proceed to an explanation of my own theory.

ALBAN BERG AS THEORIST

On July 27, 1920, Berg sent a letter to Schoenberg describing a "theoretical trifle" he had discovered while writing *Wozzeck*.[34] The letter contains a sheet of twelve-stave manuscript paper on which is written a two-dimensional array of twelve pitch interval cycles from intervals 1 to 12 (12 = octave) aligned vertically and horizontally; each cycle begins on the note C2. A pitch-class representation of Berg's matrix is given in figure 2.1. Berg labels every horizontal cycle by the traditional interval name (interval cycle designations are added at the left) and notes the resulting vertical collections in the same terms: a unison, the chromatic scale, the whole-tone scale, a diminished-seventh chord, an augmented triad, a chord of fourths, and the tritone, then the inversional forms of these collections in reverse order. He drew arrows between the inversionally comple-

Figure 2.1. Berg's array of the interval cycles (uns. = unison; chr. = chromatic chord; w.t. = whole-tone chord; dim7 = diminished-seventh chord; aug. = augmented triad; 4ths = quartal chord; tri. = tritone; 5ths = quintal chord; 8ve = octaves)

cycles

0	octave:		C	C	C	C	C	C	C	C	C	C	C	C	C
B	major	7th:	C	B	Bb	A	Ab	G	Gb	F	E	Eb	D	Db	C
A	minor	7th:	C	Bb	Ab	F#	E	D	C	Bb	Ab	F#	E	D	C
9	major	6th:	C	A	F#	Eb	C	A	Gb	Eb	C	A	F#	Eb	C
8	minor	6th:	C	G#	E	C	Ab	E	C	Ab	E	C	Ab	E	C
7	perf.	5th:	C	G	D	A	E	B	Gb	Db	Ab	Eb	Bb	F	C
6	dim.	5th:	C	Gb	C	F#	C	F#	C	Gb	C	F#	C	F#	C
5	perf.	4th:	C	F	Bb	Eb	Ab	C#	Gb	Cb/B	E	A	D	G	C
4	major	3rd:	C	E	Ab	C	E	G#	C	E	Ab	C	E	Ab	C
3	minor	3rd:	C	D#	F#	A	C	D#	Gb	A	C	Eb	F#	A	C
2	major	2nd:	C	D	E	F#	Ab	Bb/A#	C	D	E	F#	Ab	Bb	C
1	minor	2nd:	C	C#	D	Eb	E	E#	F#/Gb	G	Ab	A	Bb	B	C

uns. chr. w.t. dim7 aug. 4ths tri. 5ths aug. dim7 w.t. chr. 8ve

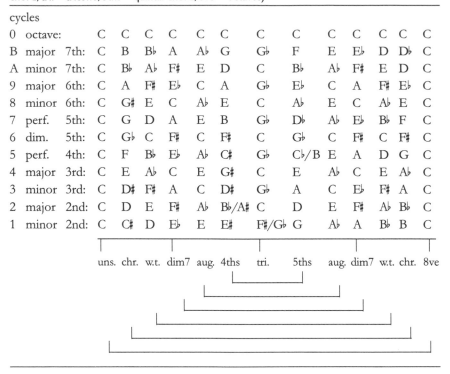

mentary cyclic collections symmetrical around the middle tritone, and another arrow joins the unison and octave, diminished-seventh chords, and tritone. This remarkable document demonstrates Berg's awareness of the interval cycle alignments and collections that, as has been pointed out by Perle, are characteristic of his music from the songs op. 2.[35]

Berg also makes a number of remarks about aspects of his language in the *Wozzeck* lecture. He clearly emphasizes the tonal aspects of many of his materials, particularly the cadential chords of each act, ending on a "tonic" G; the polytonality and tonal chaos of the military march in Act I, scene iii and the inn scene Act II, scene iv; the hierarchical relationship of the three chords of Act I, scene ii, analogous to those of tonic, subdominant, and dominant chords; and the dominant chord consisting of twelve notes from the three distinct diminished-seventh chords leading into the reprise of the Act III interlude. In his discussion of folk style in the opera, he notes that the harmonic language is characterized by whole-tone scales and chords constructed in perfect fourths; as discussed below, these formations are simplified versions of the harmonies used throughout his music. This harmonic parallel in the "folk" sections, like the tonal aspects of his cyclic materials in general, allows Berg to move seamlessly between "atonal" and "tonal" relationships.

SCHOENBERG

Schoenberg's *Harmonielehre* of 1911, for which Berg compiled the index, contains discussions of cyclic collections and their combinations (as described in chap. 1). In the final chapter, "Aesthetic Evaluation of Chords with Six or More Tones," Schoenberg outlines several features of the harmonies emerging in his and other's music around 1911 that are relevant to Berg's music. He particularly emphasizes spacing and number of notes as paramount to the logic, coherence, and identity of chords. Registral spacing can, according to Schoenberg, imply resolutions to more familiar chords. He shows an example from *Erwartung* (mm. 382–83) in which the implied resolution is to diminished-seventh (or 3-cycle) based harmonies. Schoenberg adds, however, that dissonant chords are in no way dependent on "possibilities of or tendencies toward resolution."[36] It is in Berg's music that Schoenberg's comments are most relevant, in the consistent "tonal" spacing and tendencies toward "resolution" in the voice-leading. Berg's musical materials are not dependent on tonal interpretations for their coherence, but they nonetheless retain tonal implications within a broader cyclic context.

GEORGE PERLE

Perle has described a duality in atonal music between "reflexive" elements characteristic of individual pieces and "normative" elements that underlie the surface in similar ways across a number of pieces. Although these normative elements may or may not constitute an all-encompassing theoretical system analogous to tonality, they exist to varying degrees in the music of many different composers, including Berg, Bartók, Schoenberg, Scriabin, Stravinsky, Varèse, and Webern. The normative procedures stem from the symmetry of the twelve-tone equal-tempered collection, manifested as interval cycles and collections based on interval cycles, and from transpositional and inversional complementation.[37] Perle points out, as did Schoenberg, that cyclic collections (whole-tone, diminished sevenths, augmented triads, quartal chords, etc.) emerged in the tonal music of nineteenth-century composers such as Mahler, Lizst, Wagner, Debussy, and Richard Strauss as "windows of disorder," then gained an independent status in non-tonal contexts as "windows of order."[38] He distinguishes pieces and composers by the extent to which symmetrical elements are operative in their music—with Bartók and Berg at the high end—in a weighing of the proportion of normative versus reflexive elements.[39]

In Perle's terms, symmetry results not only from the division of pitch space into equal parts, related by either transposition or inversion, but in a more general sense from relationships derived from defining symmetry in pitch-class terms. Here the emphasis shifts to the maintenance of structural intervalic relationships between elements in a modular space, exemplified by the difference between fixed axes of symmetry and abstract sums or index number relationships. Different symmetries may also combine, vying for allegiance among pitches and pitch-classes, and some pitches or pitch-classes may lie outside the symmetrical system or be transitional to some new system. Thus, it is possible to establish a hierarchy of symmetrical and non-symmetrical notes and to suggest that, where it occurs, symmetry is in a constant state of interruption and regeneration, of tension and release, somewhat analogous to tonal stability and instability by motion away from and back to the tonic key.

Pitch interval cycles are formed by successive gradations of the same pitch interval. In pitch space, interval cycles define voice-leading by the successive equal intervals of the cycle: successive semitones are "1-cycles," successive whole steps are "2-cycles," successive minor thirds are "3-cycles," and so on. The cyclic interval and the particular notes of the cycle are privileged and define the hierarchical status of "cyclic notes" and "cyclic intervals" versus "non-cyclic notes" and "non-cyclic intervals," which coexist in relative "consonant" and "dissonant" states. Composition can be motivated on small and large levels to fill gaps within cycles, to span cyclic intervals across registers, to transpose or invert cycles, or to change to different cycles. Intervalic spans can be defined and redefined cyclically, such as an interval 6 partitioned into a four-element 2-cycle, (e.g., <C–F♯> into <C–D–E–F♯>), then a three-element 3-cycle (e.g., <C–F♯> into <C–E♭–F♯>).[40] Cycles can align with themselves in parallel or with other cycles, to create vertical intervals; the resulting vertical intervals occur in predictable patterns stemming from the difference between the two cycles. In one familiar phenomenon, cycles aligned with their inversionally complementary cycles create "wedges."

When interval cycles are treated in pitch-class space, "cyclic collections" based on the pitch-class content of interval cycles arise in which not all adjacent elements are related by the cyclic interval. In the case of 2-, 3-, 4-, and 6-cycle collections, the relatively small size and the redundant interval content render the relationship between the cycle and the cyclic collections immediately recognizable and functionally equivalent. With 1- and 5-cycle collections, which both yield all twelve tones if completed, the cyclic identity of the collection depends to an ever-greater extent on the presence of the cyclic interval in proportion to the increase in size of the collection. Because of the redundant intervalic content of cyclic collections, the latter exist in small numbers of distinct forms and have correspondingly high degrees of invariance. Compositional strategies can thus include the transposition or inversion of cyclic collections to yield gradations in numbers of common tones defining relationships of "remoteness" or "closeness" to the original, the former often associated with the completion of the aggregate.[41]

Many collections have multiple possibilities for cyclic interpretation. The three interval-6 based tetrachords are the most notable examples. For instance, {C,C♯,F♯,G} [0167] may be regarded as a combination of segments of a 1-cycle <C−C♯> and <F♯−G>, 5-cycle <C−F> and <C♯−F♯>, or 6-cycle <C−F♯> and <C♯−G>; {C,D,F♯,G♯} [0268] as a combination of segments of a 2-cycle <C−D> and <F♯−G♯>, 4-cycle <G♯−C> and <D−F♯>, or 6-cycle <C−F♯> and <C♯−G>; and {C,E♭,F♯,A} [0369] as the combination of a 3-cycle <C−E♭−F♯−A> or segments of 6-cycles <C−F♯> and <E♭−A>. Such collections are highly susceptible to reinterpretation in different cyclic contexts and are extremely significant in Berg's later music, particularly in *Lulu*.

Cyclic and *non*-cyclic collections may be transformed cyclically. One common transformation is a "wedge" in which collections are subjected to diverging or converging voice-leading based on one or more axes of symmetry or sums of complementation. Another transformation is by cyclic transposition levels, such as successive T_4s to cycle through three forms and return to the original (in modular space). Cyclic collections are often embedded in larger non-cyclic collections as subsets, but the cyclic properties of the subsets affect transformations of the larger collections, especially in transpositional or inversional levels that either retain or alter the pitch-class content of the cycle subset, in some strategy involving invariance or aggregate completion of different forms of the cycle.[42] In different contexts, alternate cyclic subsets may be highlighted, changing the hierarchical status of notes in the larger set.

Inversional complementation may also be defined in both pitch and pitch-class space. Pitch space is divided by inversion into two or more equal and complementary sections by a central axis of symmetry. From the vantage point of the central "mirror" axis (either a pitch or the joining of two pitches), complementary pitches are in the same but opposite relationships to the axis, and pitch formations on either side of the axis are in the same but opposite relationships to each other. In pitch space, inversional complementation creates a static field, with the axis exerting its control over melodic or harmonic formations. Superimposed different axes create expanded possibilities for combined relationships and allow for the possibility of "modulation" between axes.

In pitch-class space, a fixed axis is no longer defined; instead, pitch-classes are associated by constant sums—sums of complementation.[43] Each pitch axis has an analogous pitch-class sum. Even sums group the twelve distinct pitch-classes into five fixed dyads and two single pitch-classes that map into themselves, creating all even intervals; odd sums group the twelve distinct pitch-classes into six fixed dyads, creating all odd intervals. A passage may include relationships between materials at different sums, which creates competing pitch-class pairs, or single pitch-classes that have multiple sum partners. Perle defines different sums as "keys" and relates pieces, as with the sum-9 relationship (pairing E/F, Eb/F#, D/G, Db/G#, C/A, and B/Bb) between Berg's *Lyric Suite* and Bartók's Fourth Quartet, on this basis.[44] As with interval cycles, inversional complementation does not require an all-or-nothing approach: pitches or pitch-classes may be outside the prevailing sums or axes as "non-chord" tones.

The multicyclic collections have built-in multiple axis or sum possibilities. For instance, {C,D,F#,G#} [0268] may be defined by sum-2 pairs {C/D} and {F#/G#} or sum-8 pairs {C/G#} and {D/F#}; for each sum, two potential pitch axes related by interval 6 are possible, equivalent to pitch-classes found at one half of the sum (mod 12): from sum 2, the axes are 1 (C#) or 7 (G); from sum 8, axes 4 (E) or 10 (Bb). These multiple axes provide for reinterpretations or "modulation" between axes. In addition, as noted above, the three tetrachords [0167], [0268], and [0369] contain multiple potentials for "difference" or intervallic combinations: [0167] as transpositionally related [01]s, [05]s, or [06]s, for instance. Both of these types of internal relationships, by transposition and inversion, are central aspects in Perle's analytical and compositional uses of symmetry.

Perle's approach privileges symmetrical and cyclic voice-leading and intervalic formations within the pitch and pitch-class universes for their influence and referential quality, but it does not require that these elements account for every note. "Non-chord tones" may be defined simply by their exclusion from the prevailing symmetrical system, or they may be part of some other motivic, cellular, pitch-class set, or other set of relationships. Perle's views on this music are thus similar in some ways to those of David Lewin but differ from those of Allen Forte and classical pitch-class set theory.

DAVID LEWIN

Lewin's focus throughout his writings has been on the spans between musical objects, such as pitches or pitch-classes, attack points, articulations, and so forth, rather than on the objects themselves. These spans, called *intervals* in a generalized sense (and italicized here when used in this more inclusive sense), are regarded as active rather than passive, transformational rather than simply measurable or classifiable, ordered in time and space, and interpretable in a multitude of ways according to relative rather than absolute criteria. By combining defined musical spaces ("S"), divisions of those spaces into *intervals* (IVLS), and defined operations mapping objects onto one another by specific *intervals* (function "int" mapping s onto t), Lewin's analytical apparatus, the "Generalized *Interval* System" (GIS), encompasses aspects of many existing music theories—of both tonal and atonal music. The successive *intervals* transforming one object through a succession of other objects are displayed in transformational networks, which are themselves internally ordered and logical and independent of the objects being transformed.

Like Perle, Lewin defines spans between pitches or pitch-classes both as differences and, although he does not use the term, sums; instead, inversional complementation is defined as inversional "balance," as pitch or pitch-class axes that associate surrounding notes. The pitch registral or pitch-class dyadic completion of an inversional dyad, either at one axis or at competing axes, is often a compositional premise and may occur embedded within other, non-symmetrical, notes. Although Lewin allows for the equivalences of pitch-class set theory, he often stresses pitch relationships with registral extremes or boundary tones as important elements.

In Lewin's analyses, pitch or pitch-class are storehouses of potential energy in the form of projections of sum or difference relationships constantly transforming musical objects. The internal intervals and notes have a tendency to propagate as other intervals or notes or as transpositional or inversional levels. Relationships between pitch-class sets include all possible shared intervals, abstract subsets, and numbers of common tones, and not only transposition and inversion but combinations of transposition and inversion, described as "Klumpenhouwer networks," analogous to Perle's combinations of sum and difference relationships generalized with his compositional "cyclic sets."[45]

Lewin's approach has many similarities to Perle's and has advantages for analyzing Berg's music. Both approaches combine transposition and inversion in a search for symmetries of different kinds, not only of pitch or pitch-class inversion but, for instance, the symmetry of a set of transformations. In Lewin's transformational view, however, symmetry is not a prerequisite, and non-symmetrical passages in Berg's music may be analyzed by projections of intervalic and pitch relationships as generalized *intervals*.

A related generalized approach to musical *intervals* or spaces is Robert Morris's definitions of generalized relative "contour" spaces, in which "*intervals*" of contour, pitch, rhythm, tempo changes, and so on can be defined in relative or absolute terms, quantified, and measured by comparison matrices ("COM matrices") that tabulate relative changes in successive intervals between objects, then allow for a classification of objects based on percentages of these changes as measures of similarity.[46] Elizabeth West Marvin has expanded on Morris's contour theory applied to rhythm, positing equivalence classes based on analogs to the twelve-tone operations.[47] The premises of Lewin's and Morris's approaches, when applied to Berg's music, reveal the remarkable degree to which he treated relationships involving pitch and pitch-class, rhythm and meter, and even tempo in structurally similar ways.

Another approach to Berg's music, taken by several writers but most notably by Allen Forte in articles on Act III, scene i and the Act III interlude of *Wozzeck*, and by Janet Schmalfeldt on the entire opera and the Sonata op. 1, is Forte's pitch-class set theory.[48] In this view, all notes on the surface are members of pitch-class sets, codified as set-classes equivalent under transposition and inversion, and related through a hierarchical network to a central nexus set or sets by interval-class relationships defined between sets and their literal and abstract complements. The intervalic relationships that result from the twelve-tone equal-tempered system, such as the similar invariance and intervalic structures of complementary sets, the tendency of hexachords to be nexus sets, and the presence of Z-related pairs of sets, form the "normative" structure against which the "reflexive" elements of individual pieces unfold. The structural units are generally tetrachords, pentachords, and hexachords and their complements, occurring both segmentally on the surface and over larger spans, linked by register or instrumentation, and more recently displayed in graphs somewhat similar to Schenkerian graphs. Smaller and larger sets are defined in terms of their supersets or subsets. Like basic cell analyses, pitch-class set theory is not dependent on the presence of traditional motives or surface motivic groupings: the intervalic network is independent, to varying degrees, of the surface features of the piece. Unlike in Lewin's and Perle's approaches, there are no "non-chord tones" in pitch-class set theory, which adopts the democracy of tones as well as the principle of complementation from twelve-tone music.

Because of the intervalic redundancy of the cyclic collections characteristic of Berg's music, pitch-class set theory yields useful results in analysis. The types of cyclic collections in Berg's atonal pieces may be conveniently catalogued and related in pitch-class set terms. My focus in this book is not on pitch-class set relationships per se, but many of my observations could be couched in those terms.

In my own interpretation of Berg's music, I have tried to account directly for my experience of the surface: hierarchical pitch and pitch-class relationships analogous to tonal "chord tones" and "non-chord tones," with voice-leading between the two states, as well as reinterpretations in which chord tones become non-chord tones and vice versa. The harmonic language has a consistency, and although harmonic progressions to inevitable goals are rare, strongly directed successions occur, motivated by cyclically defined consonance/dissonance resolutions of chord and non-chord tones and by voice-leading in pitch space by interval cycles and sequences. Pitch and rhythm are treated in similar ways, and the latter is raised to an equal status in an alliance rare in previous music.

My approach begins from Perle's assertions about the "normative" structures based on symmetry, interval cycles, and inversional complementation that span Berg's tonal, atonal, and twelve-tone music. The typical late nineteenth- and early twentieth-century use of symmetrical collections and procedures within the context of tonality appears in Berg's Piano Sonata op. 1 (as described in chap. 1). In his next piece, the op. 2 songs, Berg extracted the symmetrical aspects of tonality from the first three songs for use in the fourth song, freeing them from any tonal obligations with regard to harmony. He still found it useful, however, to exploit the tonal appearance of cyclic combinations, such as alignments of ascending interval 5s and descending interval 1s (ex. 1.13). The song op 2, no. 4 sets a familiar pattern in Berg's music of tonal allusions within cyclic procedures.

The occasional "tonal" moments in Berg's atonal music are, however, largely illusions, double entendres that open a window onto a familiar world only to find a mirror that returns the music to its atonal setting. The programmatic invocation of tonality in Berg's music has expressive and historicist aspects that are extremely important to its spiritual world and to *Rezeptionsgeschichte*, but in purely musical terms the procedures are based largely on interval cycle alignments and cyclic collections; the influence of the supposed "tonal" passages does not exceed the boundaries of their cyclic origins. For example, in the opening of op. 6, no. 1 (ex. 3.43), an apparent I–[VII]–V (tonic, applied VII of V, then dominant) progression in G stems from the combination of 5-cycle and whole-tone–based chords. The implication of G as tonic, however, extends no further than the fourth chord; the basis of the passage is the interaction of the whole-tone and 5-cycle systems. The illusory nature of the tonal implication is demonstrated at the end of the movement, when the opening chords return in retrograde, tonally as V–[VII]–I, a nonsensical progression; retrograde is not a viable transformation in tonality. In another instance, at the end of op. 3, no. 2 (mm. 228–32), a 3-cycle–based collection, {C♯,E,G,B♭,D}, apparently "resolves" briefly to a D-minor triad, then all voices leap to an {F,F♯,G,A♭} interval 3 bounded 1-cycle cluster.[49] The articulation of the "tonal" arrival on D, despite earlier registral and durational emphases on D, is an illusion here, with a purely local effect. The consonant state of D results from its inclusion in the 3-cycle collection {D,F,A♭,B} [0369].

Despite the evidence for symmetrical procedures in Berg's music, problems arise in explaining Berg's diverse harmonic language exclusively in terms of the reduced intervalic and pitch or pitch-class relationships and pitch-class sets privileged by symmetry and interval cycles. Purely symmetrical or cyclic passages are infrequent and of relatively brief duration, and their static nature conflicts with the diversity found in Berg's music. Although procedures and transformations are based on symmetrical models, clearly the compositional units are not purely symmetrical in construction. Instead, in order to maintain variety of intervalic content, a hierarchical distinction between "chord tones" and "non-chord tones," the possibility and voice-leading implications of real, implied, or deceptive "resolutions" of "dissonant" non-chord tones, and the rich possibilities of reinterpreting chord tones in new harmonic contexts, Berg's principal harmonic elements are cyclic collections with, usually, one added note. The strategies for unfolding these cyclic collections with added notes occur on two levels: (1) to create a local forward impetus by accounting in some way for the consequences of the built-in dissonant notes, searching for resolution that never arrives; and (2) to contrast, locally and over larger spans, cyclic collections of different cyclic bases. The cyclic bases generally group into (1) interval 2 and 4 cycles, which combine under the rubric of "whole-tone" based collections (a more accurate label would be "even-interval collections," but I will use the more familiar term "whole tone" even though the label is misleading because the cyclic basis is not always "whole-tone" or 2-cycle in structure); (2) collections based on interval 3 cycles; and (3) collections based on interval 5 cycles. These three cycles form the harmonic basis of a large amount of Berg's music, usually with two primary cyclic bases per piece and the third in a secondary position. Interval 1 and 6 cycles are generally used horizontally and in combination with other cycles.

The large-scale conflicts between the three cyclic bases for collections and procedures do not constitute, however, a "normative" basis for a hierarchical distinction analogous to tonics and dominants. Instead, the designations of primary and secondary are purely reflexive. For instance, in *Wozzeck*, whole-tone and 5-cycle based collections are primary; Wozzeck is associated with whole-tone based collections, and Marie with 5 cycle based collections. In the op. 4 songs, however, 3- and 5-cycle based collections are primary, with whole-tone based collections secondary.

An example of Berg's use of a cyclic collection with different possible interpretations occurs in *Wozzeck*. In the opera, the character Wozzeck is associated throughout with whole-tone – based collections with one added note (see ex. 3.1). The added notes are dissonant in their whole-tone contexts — not included in the source whole-tone collection — creating odd intervals dissonant with the other notes and providing for forward impetus toward resolution and motivic connections to other materials, such as the [014] motive associated with Marie (see ex. 3.2). When a collection of the same type appears as one of the final cadence chords, however, the changed spacing and context cause a new interpretation, of a 7-cycle chord with a "gap" in the cycle <G–D–A–()–B> (see ex. 3.1f). The note D, originally dissonant in the whole-tone-plus-added-note context, is reinterpreted as consonant in its new supporting role in the interval 7 cycle. Furthermore, the relative spacing and register (recalling Schoenberg's comments above) strongly suggest a tonal interpretation of a focal G as a local "tonic," with D in a supporting "dominant" role. The 7-cycle and "tonal" interpretations depend heavily on spacing and the presence of the cycle interval—in a pattern found throughout Berg's music—whereas the whole-tone-plus-added-note definition depends only on interval-class content.

One important question in evaluating the role of registral cyclic unfoldings in Berg's music is whether the cycle is being "prolonged" in a tonal sense or is merely associative or referential. The pitch analyses in the following chapters are often presented with reductive graphs, with cyclic "chord tones" differentiated from "non-chord tones" (the former indicated largely by open noteheads, the latter by filled-in noteheads), the latter often moving between statements of the former. If the "consonant" cyclic notes are grouped together and considered to constitute "prolonged" events, then unfolded cyclic collections resemble the "tonic sonorities" posited by Felix Salzer and Roy Travis and commented on by Joseph N. Straus.[50] A prolonged event is, in the simplest terms, an active, hierarchically superior force even when not physically present. Straus outlines four criteria for prolonged musical events: (1) a consistent consonance-dissonance relationship; (2) a hierarchy of consonant harmonies; (3) a consistent basis for determining embellishment from structural tones; and (4) a distinction between harmony and voice-leading. The questions of consonance, dissonance, and embellishing tones in Berg's music hinge on the dichotomy between the underlying cyclic collections and transformations and the surface collections, which contain cyclic and non-cyclic elements. The problem is similar to that in late tonal music, where the functional basis of the system is often difficult to separate out or decipher from the surface. For the most part, it is possible to distinguish cyclic-based chord and non-chord tones and their dissonance-consonance relationships in Berg's music. The cyclic-based collections present no hierarchy or distinction between harmony and voice-leading, however, except where established contextually; for instance, voice-leading by interval 1 through whole-tone–based vertical chords is a common feature in Berg's atonal music. In my view, the cyclic collections in Berg's atonal music are referential and the basis of the pitch language, but they are not prolonged in a tonal sense. Cyclic collections are quickly superseded, are not "in force" in their absence, and require constant reiteration for their continuing referential status. Thus, I do not posit large-scale cyclic collections comprised of largely non-adjacent notes spanning a piece or large sections.[51]

In Berg's atonal music, passages of an expository nature are characterized by distinctive cyclic materials in clear presentations; however, long "dissonant" passages also occur in which distinctions between materials are not as clear. This dichotomy is reminiscent of late nineteenth-century music, which, although tonal, contains long passages of extended dissonance and harmonic ambiguity. Opus 6, no. 3, for instance, has few cyclic signposts, and the density of the texture allows for so many pitch-class – set relationships that any consistent intervalic definition is short-lived at best. The "basic cell" approach similarly yields a rich harvest of relationships but also suffers from an overload of information. In high-density and highly motivic pieces such as op. 6, no. 3, an approach that invokes purely relative relationships between motivic contours, such as Morris's contour theory, yields useful distinctions, and motivic families can be defined on this basis. Relationships based on contour are especially relevant for Berg's music, since he generally maintains consistent motivic contours; for instance, in op. 4, no. 1, transformed motives (an instance is shown in ex. 3.8) may be related by equivalences among contours; with pitch collections varied cyclically.

Finally, it proved particularly useful in the analyses of op. 2, no. 4, op. 4, no. 4, and op. 5, no. 1 to consider the harmonic language in terms of projections of intervals, along the lines of David Lewin's analysis of the opening of Webern's op. 5, no. 2.[52] One obvious projection of intervals is onto interval cycles or onto symmetrical registral grids, but these may be regarded as parts of a larger class of transformations that include non-cyclic projections of intervals in combinations, in both ascending and descending directions and between both adjacent and non-adjacent notes. In op. 5, for instance, the opening clarinet figure acts as a *Grundgestalt* for the entire work, as a repository combining pitch-class – set properties, a symmetrical wedge-type function, and multiple cyclic intepretations of combinations of interval class 1s in sets [0123] and [0156].

RHYTHM

In his "Open Letter" to Schoenberg on the *Chamber Concerto* (February 9, 1925), Berg noted that his use of rhythm in a "constructive" role began in *Wozzeck*, Act III, scene iii. The "thematic importance" of the rhythmic motive of this scene is described in the *Wozzeck* lecture: the rhythm appears continuously throughout, underlying melodies and accompaniment, in augmented and diminished forms, shifted relative to the barline, superimposed on itself, varied in subdivision, and combined in canon (see ex. 3.22 – 24). This scene is a culmination of the development in Berg's unprecedented raising of rhythm to an equal status with pitch in his atonal music. Two characteristic uses of rhythm particularly stand out: (1) rhythms are freed from the obligations of meter, and structured in cycles and cyclic transformations analogous to pitch cycles; and (2) rhythmic motives play a thematic role, with an identity apart from their association with pitch motives. Beginning with the op. 2 songs, Berg's music invariably contains rhythmic motives, often introduced by a percussion instrument or as a repeated note to establish their identity; these motives are treated analogously to pitch motives and are an integral part of the formal and motivic structure.[53]

Just as Berg interpreted tonality in its cyclic aspects, so that he could maintain tonal characteristics in his cyclic-based atonal language, meter is similarly defined as a particular cyclic alignment, as one option among many in the cyclic treatment of rhythm. The most common rhythmic cycles are "graduated" cycles, which lengthen or shorten durations successively by absolute or relative amounts—for instance, in durational or time-point patterns such as $<1-2-3-4-5>$. Lewin has investigated the metric potential of a cyclic rhythm of successively larger units, $<2-3-4-5>$, a type that Berg regularly employs.[54] A time-point series, here $<0-2-5-9-14>$, is constructed to define the rhythm, then all possible relationships between these time points are explored using a time interval vector. The $+5$ combinations of time points $0-5$ and $9-14$ and the $+9$ combinations of time points $0-9$ and $5-14$ support impulses (or accents) at time points 5 and 9, creating larger periodicities influencing any perceived meter that may arise. The analyses in the following chapters of Berg's op. 5, no. 2 and of *Wozzeck* Act III, scene iii based on Lewin's method demonstrate the extent to which Berg's systematic cyclic procedures characterize all aspects of his musical language.

The proof of any theoretical approach is, of course, in the analyses that result. The following chapter presents aspects of the pitch, rhythmic, formal, and orchestrational language with analytical examples drawn from all of Berg's atonal works. The chapter ends with detailed analyses, combining the approaches and elements described previously, of op. 2, no. 4, op. 4, no. 4, op. 5, no. 1, and op. 6, no. 1. The musical examples include reductive graphs in which cyclic notes are highlighted, with non-cyclic notes—where indicated—identified in intermediary roles. The criteria for note choice in these hierarchical interpretations include traditional emphases created by dynamics and duration and boundary status conferred by register and formal placement, as well as consistency, context, and cyclic content. As with Schenkerian graphs of tonal music, however, criteria of harmonic or linear content—here cyclic—are primary and may override other factors; for example, a relatively brief unaccented tone may be hierarchically superior, with regard to cyclic content, to a longer stressed tone close by. As with other theories of music, my methods may be accused of circularity—the cyclic collections are the means and the ends—but, equally as with other theories, the relevance or applicability of my cyclic interpretations is testable both aurally and intellectually. Ultimately, no single analytical method can reveal all the intricacies of a composer's music, but a method worthy of attention should lead to a greater understanding and appreciation and an enriched experience for both the heart and mind.

3 The Atonal Music: Detail and Analysis

Pitch Language

As outlined in the preceding chapter, Berg's atonal pitch language draws on what George Perle has termed "normative" elements: symmetry manifested in interval cycles and inversional complementation. The principal compositional units in Berg's music are cyclic-based pitch collections with added "dissonant" elements. The cyclic basis of these collections allows for the symmetrical and invariance properties of the cycle, whereas the dissonant element(s) allow for intervalic variety, distinctions between consonance and dissonance, and the potential for reinterpretation of collections. Voice-leading is often by intervals excluded from the collection or by those created by the dissonant elements (an odd interval in a whole-tone–based collection, for instance), to yield variety of pitch-class content. The intervalic redundancy of the cyclic-based collections also yields the superset/subset relationship described in pitch-class set theory, and the tendency for interval cycles to continue completing themselves registrally or modularly, often creating symmetries by pitch or pitch-class inversional complementation, yields transformational networks.

Collections stemming from interval cycles are distinguished primarily by interval-class content. Of these collections, those based on even intervals, known as whole-tone collections, are the most distinctive intervalically. The eleven pitch-class intervals can be grouped into the even intervals {0,2,4,6,8,A} and the odd intervals {1,3,5,7,9,B}. Even intervals in combination yield only other even intervals; thus, they constitute a closed system of two groups of six notes: {C,D,E,F♯,G♯,A♯} and {C♯,D♯,F,G,A,B}, the two complete whole-tone collections. Subsets of the whole-tone collection form exclusive groups of nine Tn-classes and eight TnI-classes excluding Tn[046] (fig. 3.1).[1] With the exception of the whole-tone hexachords, complements of whole-tone collections are not purely whole-tone.

Figure 3.1. Whole-tone–based collections

pure whole-tone					
prime form	distinct forms		whole-tone+		
[024]	12	[0124]	[01246]	[012468]	[012468A]
[026]	12	[0126]	[01248]	[013579]	
[046]	12	[0135]	[01268]	[023468]	
[048]	4	[0137]	[01357]		
[0246]	12	[0146]	[01468]		
[0248]	12	[0148]	[02346]		
[0268]	6	[0157]	[02368]		
[02468]	12	[0236]	[02458]		
[02468A]	2	[0247]	[02469]		
		[0258]			

With their exclusive interval content, whole-tone collections transposed by any even interval maintain the same overall collection. Odd intervals are thereby dissonant in whole-tone contexts and function as agents of "modulation" from one whole-tone collection to the other. In *Wozzeck*, for instance, the "fanfare" leitmotiv associated with the Drum Major, comprised of notes from a C♯ whole-tone collection, is verticalized as two chords that alternate between the C and C♯ whole-tone collections by odd interval 1 voice-leading (ex. 3.1d, m. 332). Such arrangements, vertical even intervals and horizontal odd intervals, with clearly distinguished harmonic and voice-leading functions, occur frequently in Berg's music.

Purely whole-tone–based collections like the fanfare motive are rare in Berg's music; however, most whole-tone–based motives and harmonies contain added notes, referred to here as "whole-tone+" collections. Such collections are similar to one another in their predominantly even intervals but differ by the specific

Example 3.1a. "Anguish" leitmotiv, *Wozzeck*, Act II, mm. 313–14

Example 3.1b. "Wir arme Leut" leitmotiv, *Wozzeck*, Act I, mm. 136–37

Example 3.1c. "Entrance and exit" leitmotiv, *Wozzeck*, Act I, m. 427

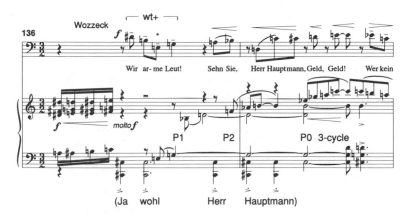

Example 3.1d. "Fanfare" leitmotiv, *Wozzeck*, Act I, mm. 330–32

Example 3.1e. Interlude theme, *Wozzeck*, Act III, mm. 320–23

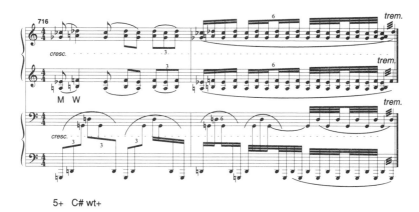

Example 3.1f. Two cadence chords, *Wozzeck*, Act I, mm. 716–17 ("M" = Marie, "W" = Wozzeck). Berg WOZZECK, OP. 7. Full Score copyright 1926 by Universal Edition A.G., Vienna. English Translation copyright 1952 by Alfred A. Kalmus, London. Full Score copyright renewed. Pocket Score copyright 1955. Pocket Score copyright renewed. All Rights Reserved. Used by permission of European American Music Distributors Corporation, sole U.S. and Canadian agent for Universal Edition, A.G., Wien.

odd-interval relationships between the purely whole-tone subset and the added dissonant note. The possible whole-tone+ collections as TnI-classes are given in figure 3.1.[2] With the exception of those with purely whole-tone intervals, trichords are uninterpreted in whole-tone+ contexts. Complements of whole-tone+ tetrachords and pentachords contain more than one added element and thus require a clear context to register as whole-tone+ collections.

Whole-tone+ collections appear throughout *Wozzeck* as leitmotivs associated with the main character, drawn largely from the C♯ whole-tone collection: the "anguish" motive (ex. 3.1a, C♯wt + A♭, where "wt" means "whole-tone collection"); the four-note "Wir arme Leut" motive (ex. 3.1b, <D♯–B–E–G> [0148], C♯wt +E); the "entrance and exit" motive (ex. 3.1c, Cwt +E♭), the "earrings"

(Act II, mm. 7–10) and "guilt" motives (Act II, mm. 105–6—both of which represent Marie's betrayal of Wozzeck; Andres's folksong motive (Act I, mm. 213–14), which reflects his friendship with Wozzeck; the purely whole-tone closing theme of the sonata form in Act II, scene i (mm. 93–96), which anticipates the anguish motive; the purely whole-tone fanfare motive that relates Wozzeck and the Drum Major as soldiers (ex. 3.1d); the theme of the Act III interlude, a commentary on Wozzeck's death (ex. 3.1e, lower voice, Cwt +A); and one of the two cadence chords that end each act (ex. 3.1f, marked "W," C♯wt +D).[3] The added note and odd intervals lend each of the whole-tone+ motives a distinctive profile and create internal motivic relationships. For instance, in the "Wir arme Leut" motive <D♯–B–E–G> [0148] (ex. 3.1b)— which may also be regarded as a more distinctive 4-cycle+ collection—the added note E creates an interval-class 5 with the adjacent preceding note B, the interval-class associated with Marie in the opera. In the "anguish" motive (ex. 3.1a) the added note A♭ creates a closing turn figure <A–F–A♭> [014], the same TnI-class as the Marie "mother" motive (ex. 3.2a). A♭ is dissonant: in the whole-tone+ context it is the added note from the other whole-tone collection, and in Marie's 5-cycle–based harmonic context (described below) the A♭ is the added element in a vertical 5-cycle chord <D–G–C–A♭>. The anguish motive is similar in intervalic content and gesture to the opening motive of op. 3, also a whole-tone+ collection with an internal [014] created by a closing turn, <F–E♭–D♭–A–C–B> (ex. 3.6a below).

The whole-tone+ leitmotiv in *Wozzeck* are summarized in one of the cadence chords ending each act: a whole-tone+ chord <G–D–B–F–A–C♯> from the referential C♯ whole-tone collection (ex. 3.1f).[4] The dual nature of the chord reflects the possibilities for reinterpretation of whole-tone+ collections. In its whole-tone+ guise, related to the whole-tone+ motives associated with Wozzeck in the opera, the chord contains an added note D. Arranged in an open spacing with D over the bass note G, however, the chord presents a strong tonal implication of a G tonic in which the D is consonant. Similar reinterpretations, also strongly dependent on context, spacing, and register, occur elsewhere in the opera. For instance, the theme beginning the interlude in Act III (ex. 3.1e) is a whole-tone+ collection with A as an added note, associated with Wozzeck, but in the immediate tonal focus on D the A is consonant, and the whole-tone notes A♭ and B♭ are local dissonant neighbors.

Whole-tone+ collections often occur as the harmonic regions in expository sections of Berg's atonal pieces, with alternation from one whole-tone collection to the other by horizontal odd-interval voice leading. In op. 3, no. 1, mm. 1–10 (ex. 3.5 below), for instance, the opening C♯ whole-tone collection establishes the context for the alternating C and C♯ whole-tone+ areas that complete the first phrase (to m. 9). Characteristically, a G focus in the bass is created in mm. 6–9 in which D is a pivotal note: it is dissonant in the C♯ whole-tone+ context but consonant as an interval 7 support over G.

Although whole-tone collections may be expressed as even-interval cycles, the latter are infrequent in Berg's music. More common are even intervals created by aligned, inversionally complementary notes, either symmetrically disposed around a pitch or related by an even sum. In *Wozzeck*, Act I, scene iv, variation 12, inversionally-related C whole-tone pitch collections symmetrical around A4 (celeste and harp), C♯2 (cellos 1 and 2), and G5 (violins 1 and 2) yield vertical as well as horizontal even intervals. The circular formations reflect the text —"Lines and circles, strange figures, would that one could read them!" (Act I, scene iv, m.561: *Linienkreise, Figuren / Wer das lesen könnte!*)—as Wozzeck recounts his hallucinations from Act I, scene ii to the Doctor. The three canonic statements of the twelve-note passacaglia theme <E♭–G–B–C♯–C–F♯–E–B♭–A–F–A♭–D> in the surrounding voices (trumpet, oboe, bassoon), which each begin with a four-note segment <E♭–G–B–C♯> from the C♯ whole-tone collection, create whole-tone+ collections with the C whole-tone symmetrical figures.

Odd intervals, unlike their even counterparts, do not constitute a closed system: odd intervals in communication yield even intervals; only combinations of odd and even intervals create odd intervals. Thus, there are no exclusively odd-interval collections other than the six odd-interval dyads {1,3,5,7,9,B}. Odd-interval collections may be defined as those with only odd intervals between adjacent notes, although these collections are much less distinctive as TnI-classes, excluding only the whole-tone and whole-tone+ collections. Odd-interval successions that highlight one interval, or odd-interval cycles, are distinctive, however, and occur frequently in Berg's atonal music. Cycles of intervals 1/B and 5/7 yield all twelve notes (1, 5, 7, and B are prime to 12), and cycles by intervals 3/9 yield the three forms of tetrachordal [0369]s (ex. 1.1).

Odd-interval cycles—unlike the infrequent even cycles—occur throughout Berg's atonal music. For instance, in *Wozzeck*, Act I, scene i, as the Captain discusses concepts of time passing with Wozzeck, his mention of eternity is reflected in a nine-note descending interval 5 cycle (mm. 33–34, F4 down to C♯1). Descending or ascending interval 1 cycles in the lower voices are common and lend a directed motion by virtue of their similarity to chromatic voice-leading in late nineteenth-century music. In op. 6, no. 2, for instance, an ascending interval 1 cycle in the bass from C♯1 to D2 (mm. 4–15) helps to organize the opening measures and to create an orientation to D in the larger context of the G focus in the movement. In *Wozzeck*, the climactic statement of the passacaglia theme in Act I, scene 4 (variation 21, mm. 638–42) is harmonized with massive block chords over a descending interval 1 cycle in the bass, lending a goal-directed focus to the final bass note D♯/E♭—accompanying the Doctor's triumphant cry of "immortal!" (*Unsterblich!*). In Act II, scene ii, as the Doctor mercilessly spins out his paralyzing prognosis to a petrified Captain, an upper-voice descending 1-cycle from G5 to C4, harmonized in varied tetrachords, leads to an articulating cadence apparently asserting F minor (mm. 227–31); although the bass F is actually part of an overall bass C♯ whole-tone collection in this waltz, which concludes with the focal point of G, in this and many other instances in Berg's atonal music the interval 1 cycles coerce listeners into hearing goal-directed contexts reminiscent of tonality.[5]

Collections from odd-interval cycles appear in three forms: (1) as cyclic segments (fig. 3.2); (2) as cyclic segments plus an added note (fig. 3.2); and (3) as "gapped" collections, cyclic segments with one or possibly two gaps in the cycle. Because of their mix of even and odd intervals, odd-interval–based collections lack the harmonic distinctiveness of whole-tone collections. Although 3-cycle collections are sufficiently restricted in content to be recognizable even when the cyclic interval does not appear between all adjacent elements, collections from 1/B and 5/7 cycles rely on the presence of the cyclic interval for definition in their gapped and larger forms. For instance, tetrachords [0158] and [0358] appear frequently but may be identified only in interval 5 contexts as gapped 5-cycle chords; larger sets similarly require a context for a cyclic interpretation. As with whole-tone+ collections, trichords are neutral as odd-interval cycle collections except for the purely cyclic [012], [036], and [027]. An important aspect of several of the cyclic+ collections listed in figure 3.2—tetrachords [0124], [0127], [0157], [0236], and [0247]—is their potential for multiple interpretations: for instance, [0124] as a 1-cycle+ or whole-tone+ collection. These collections may thereby act as pivots between cyclic systems.

Figure 3.2. Odd-interval cycle collections

pure odd interval			odd interval+			
1/B	3/9	5/7				
[012]	[036]	[027]	[0124] (1+, wt+)	[01235] (1+)	[012346]	(1+)
[0123]	[0369]	[0257]	[0125] (1+)	[01236] (1+)	[012347]	(1+)
[01234]		[02479]	[0126] (1+)	[01237] (1+)	[012479]	(5+)
[012345]		[024579]	[0127] (1+, 5+)	[01257] (5+)	[023579]	(5+)
[0123456]		[013568A]	[0136] (3+)	[01368] (5+)	[012579]	(5+)
[01234567]		[0123578A]	[0236] (3+, wt+)	[01369] (3+)		
[012345678]		[01235678A]	[0157] (5+, wt+)	[02357] (5+)		
[0123456789]		[012345789A]	[0237] (5+)		[0124579]	(5+)
[0123456789A]	[0123456789A]		[0247] (5+, wt+)		[0234579]	(5+)
[0123456789AB]	[0123456789AB]					

In *Wozzeck*, 5-cycle collections are associated with the character Marie and the related surrounding characters the Drum Major and the child (ex. 3.2). Marie's "mother" leitmotiv first appears as a melodic [014] <A♭ – F – E> and its sequential repetition <E – D♭ – C>, with the first note of each motive, A♭ or E, dissonant in their vertical 5-cycle+ harmonic contexts (ex. 3.2a). The sequential repetition of the [014]s may be interpreted in two ways: (1) in terms of even intervals, associating Marie and the child with Wozzeck, as a transposition of <A♭ – F – E> by T−4 to <E – D♭ – C>, outlining 4-cycle <A♭ – E – C>; or (2) in terms of a 5-cycle context matching the harmonies, as an interval-class 5 mapping of A♭ to D♭ and F to C, with the pivotal E held invariant. The supporting chords are purely 5-cycle ("5"), 5-cycle segments with added notes, or 5-cycle+ ("5+"), and combined non-adjacent 5-cycle or a "gapped" 5-cycle ("5g") segments (ex. 3.2a); the latter are dependent on an established 5-cycle context for their identity. In the two "5+" chords, the dissonant upper notes A♭ and E "resolve" down by interval 3 to the consonant notes F and D♭, creating pure 5-cycle chords <D – G – C – F> and <B♭ – E♭ – A♭ – D♭>. The "cradle" motive (ex. 3.2b) presents a similar juxtaposition of 5-cycle – based chords and melodic [014], with the upper note D of the [014] {B,D,B♭} dissonant in its local harmonic 5+ context (as are the upper [014] notes A♭ and E in ex. 3.2a). The interval 1 wedge voice-leading transforms the gapped 5-cycle segments <A – D/F – B♭> into 5-cycle <G♯ – C♯ – F♯ – B>.

Marie's "waiting" motive (ex. 3.2c) initially combines interval-class 5s {C,F} and {A,E} into a gapped 5-cycle [0158]. The bass motion of C to B (Act I, scene iii, mm. 412 – 25), however, creates [0157] {B,F,A,E}, interpretable as both a 5-cycle+ collection related to Marie and a whole-tone+ tetrachord related to Wozzeck. The musical alteration reflects Marie's fate: as she waits for Wozzeck

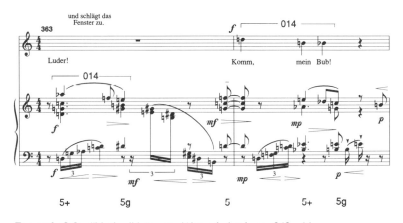

Example 3.2a. "Mother" leitmotiv, *Wozzeck*, Act I, mm. 363 – 64

Example 3.2b. "Cradle Song" leitmotiv, *Wozzeck*, Act I, mm. 372–73

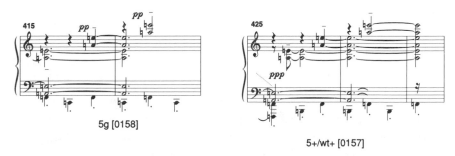

Example 3.2c. "Waiting" leitmotiv, *Wozzeck*, Act I, mm. 415–16, 425–26

Example 3.2d. "Drum Major" leitmotiv, *Wozzeck*, Act I, m. 667. Berg WOZZECK, OP. 7. Full Score copyright 1926 by Universal Edition A.G., Vienna. English Translation copyright 1952 by Alfred A. Kalmus, London. Full Score copyright renewed. Pocket Score copyright 1955. Pocket Score copyright renewed. All Rights Reserved. Used by permission of European American Music Distributors Corporation, sole U.S. and Canadian agent for Universal Edition A.G., Wien.

to arrive, her "waiting" motive changes, via leitmotivs of the Drum Major ("fanfare," ex. 3.1d, and "military march" from Act I, scene iii, mm. 334ff.), to reflect her entrapment with Wozzeck. The {F,B} dyad connotes "fate" in the opera, foreshadowing death: F associated with Wozzeck (from his C♯ whole-tone collection) and B with Marie.[6]

The role of the Drum Major's motives in the transformation of Marie's "waiting" motive reflects his influence on her downfall. When the "fanfare" motive first appears in Act I, scene iii, the Drum Major marches outside Marie's window (ex. 3.1d). Whereas the C# whole-tone collection with dyad {F,B} relates the Drum Major to Wozzeck as a soldier, the accompanying 5-cycle+ chord {A,D,E,G+B♭}, held from the preceding interlude, reflects his future ties to Marie. In the seduction scene, Act I, scene v, the Drum Major is associated with another motive (ex. 3.2d), melodically an interval 5 {C#,F#} but accompanied by even vertical interval 4s {A,C#} and {A♭,C}, the latter creating the whole-tone trichord {A♭,C,F#} [026] associating the Drum Major with both Wozzeck's whole-tone and Marie's 5-cycle collections. The combined collection, [01457], is a superset of an important collection that links Marie and Wozzeck, the 3-cycle+ [0147], associated with the child, used particularly in Act II, scene i.

Marie's association with 5-cycle collections may account for the chord in the "invention on a chord" scene, Act III, scene iv—the scene of Wozzeck's death (ex. 3.3). Since the scene features only Wozzeck, a whole-tone+ collection might be expected; however, the principal chord of the scene is a gapped 5 cycle+ hexachord, [012479], related to the 5-cycle collections associated with Marie. The chord, approached from "white-note" gapped 5-cycle chord [013568] {B,C, F,A,D,E} with voice-leading by interval 1, has an internal 5−cycle arranged as two contiguous interval 7 segments {<C#–G#–E♭>, <B♭–F>}, with added note E. The harmony of the chord reflects the dramatic situation in which Wozzeck has killed Marie and has been irrevocably changed by her death, symbolized by his association with the 5-cycle+ chord. The upper note of the chord, F, is Wozzeck's half of the fateful {B,F} dyad; the lack of an accompanying B reflects Marie's death. A prominent transposition of the chord at T7 {F,A♭,B,E♭,B♭,C} (which yields the maximum invariance of four notes) restores

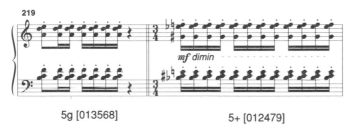

5g [013568]   5+ [012479]

Example 3.3. 5-cycle+−based [013568] to [012479], *Wozzeck*, Act III, mm. 219–20. Berg WOZZECK, OP. 7. Full Score copyright 1926 by Universal Edition A.G., Vienna. English Translation copyright 1952 by Alfred A. Kalmus, London. Full Score copyright renewed. Pocket Score copyright 1955. Pocket Score copyright renewed. All Rights Reserved. Used by permission of European American Music Distributors Corporation, sole U.S. and Canadian agent for Universal Edition A.G., Wien.

the {F,B} dyad, with F as the bottom note of the chord, representing Wozzeck's memory of Marie. The scene, however, ends with the chord at the original level, without the note B.

Of the two cadential chords that end each act of the opera (ex. 3.1f), the whole-tone+ chord [013579] reflects Wozzeck and the other, [013589], is associated with Marie and may be regarded in this context as a gapped 5-cycle+ chord <G–D–A–( )–B–F♯> with an added note {E♭}.[7] The two chords symbolize the opposition of the two characters but also their relationship, by the shared [0247] tetrachord {G,D,A,B} (the maximum number of common tones possible between the two chords), which is interpretable both as a whole-tone+ and 5-cycle+ collection.

ALIGNED CYCLES

In Berg's letter to Schoenberg mentioned in the previous chapter, Berg wrote out an array of the twelve interval cycles aligned horizontally (fig. 2.1). Although the latter was written while he was composing *Wozzeck*, aligned cycles appear as early as the op. 2 songs (ex. 1.13). The aligned 1- and 5-cycles found in each of the op. 2 songs also appear in a motivic figure in the first movement of Berg's String Quartet op. 3 (ex. 3.4a). The alignment, of a descending interval 1 cycle and a descending interval 5 cycle, yields vertical odd intervals <3–7–B>.[8] Elsewhere in the first movement of op. 3 (mm. 108ff., ex. 3.4b), the two cycles align differently, yielding vertical even intervals <0–4–8> and <2–6–A>, in a varying of vertical intervalic content characteristic of Berg's music. At the end of the movement, a descending interval 2 cycle is added to the original cyclic alignment as a middle third voice <F–E♭–D♭> ex. 3.4c). The addition of the first-violin B transforms the final trichord into the whole-tone+ or 5-cycle+ collection {G,D♭,F♯,B} [0157], reconciling four important elements in the movement: aligned odd-interval cycles, whole-tone+ motives, 5-cycle–based collections, and the focus on G.

In the second movement of op. 3 an accompanimental figure to the recapitulated opening theme features aligned cycles of intervals 5 (cello), 4 (violin 2), and 1 (viola), with a held E♭ (violin 1) (mm. 153–54, ex. 3.4d). The interval 1 cycle (viola) is, however, altered by an interval 2 to become a gapped 1-cycle <D–E♭–E–F♯–G>. A possible reason for the change, other than a "dissonant" break in the symmetry characteristic of Berg's cycle+ collections, is the effect it has on the final chord, which is purely whole-tone in the altered version, whereas it would be a whole-tone+ chord if the 1-cycle were maintained (and the final note in the viola cycle an F♯). In *Wozzeck*, Act II, scene iii (m. 380), a similar alignment occurs, but as four cycles in four different instruments: interval 1 (cello), 2 (oboe), 3 (solo viola), and 4 (A clarinet) all beginning on C4,

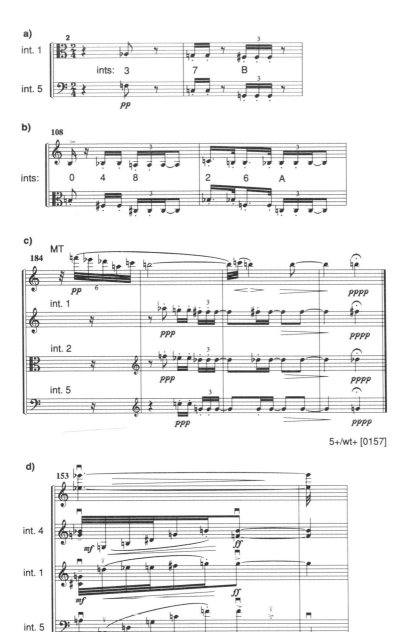

Example 3.4. Aligned cycles in String Quartet, op. 3: (a) first movement, mm. 2–3; (b) first movement, mm. 108–9; (c) first movement, mm. 184–87; (d) second movement, mm. 153–54. Berg STRING QUARTET, OP. 3. Copyright 1925 by Universal Edition. Copyright renewed. All Rights Reserved. Used by permission of European American Music Distributors Corporation, sole U.S. and Canadian agent for Universal Edition A.G., Wien.

as a partial statement (consisting of only eight notes) of the complete cycle alignment shown in figure 2.1. In accordance with Berg's use of cycle+ collections, however, an added violin part, which ends with a four-note 3-cycle <G–E–C#–Bb>, "spoils" the purely cyclic verticals and creates cyclic+ chords.[9]

OPUS 3, FIRST MOVEMENT

The first movement of Berg's String Quartet op. 3 opens with many features characteristic of his atonal pitch language (ex. 3.5): the unfolding and definition of registral space by interval cycles and cyclic collections, whole-tone+ harmonic areas, wedge voice-leading formations, horizontally unfolding 3-cycle collections, aligned 1- and 5-cycles, motivic basic cell [014]s, and a focus on pitches G and D determined by registral placement, spacing, and collectional content.[10] As is common in Berg's music, two cyclic collections are primary, here whole-tone+ and 3-cycle+–based, with the other, 5-cycle+–based, secondary.

Several registral spans are defined and redefined in the opening nine bars of the first movement of op. 3, with four at the outset: (1) F4–G5, (2) B3–F4, (3) F3–B3, and (4) G2–F3. Each span is characterized by one or more cyclic divisions. Register 2 is defined initially by the C# whole-tone+ <F–Eb–Db–A–C–B> main theme (ex. 3.6a). The dissonant note C (not in the C# wt collection) resolves to the consonant B—this C–B resolution (which foreshadows the C–B in Marie's waiting motive in *Wozzeck*, ex. 3.2c) occurs throughout the movement in all registers—but then is reactivated as the center of a sum-o wedge expanding out from C4 to A3/Eb4 (to m. 6), delineating the 3-cycle collection <A–C–Eb> (anticipated by the A3–C4> dyad in the main theme).[11] The Eb4 expected in m. 6 is delayed and arrives up an octave in m. 7, opening up register 1, as the initial note of a secondary whole-tone+ motive. This whole-tone+–based secondary main theme in mm. 7–9 (SMT, ex. 3.6a) defines register 1, but it returns to register 2 for the cadence in m. 9, with F#4/E4 as neighbors to the initial F4. The voice under the secondary main theme in register 2 alternates A3–B3 but ends on C4, the midpoint of the A3–C4–Eb4 wedge and the initial "dissonant" note.

Register 3 is defined initially by a 3-cycle <F3–Ab3–B3> division of the interval 6 <F–B> (m. 2), contrasting the whole-tone division of <F4–B3> in the opening main theme. The Ab3 then descends by interval 1 cycle to D3 by m. 5, where the registral space <D3–Ab3> is reinterpreted by the return of the initial whole-tone+ main theme at T–9, <Ab–Gb–E–C–Eb–D>, now based on the C whole-tone collection (by virtue of the odd transpositional level). The boundary notes D3 and Ab3 link with D4 in m. 5, the latter two as the 3-cycle midpoints of the opening <F3–B3–F4> spans, and together defining a large-scale P2 3-cycle <D3–F3–Ab3–D4–F4>. The dissonant note Eb3 of the

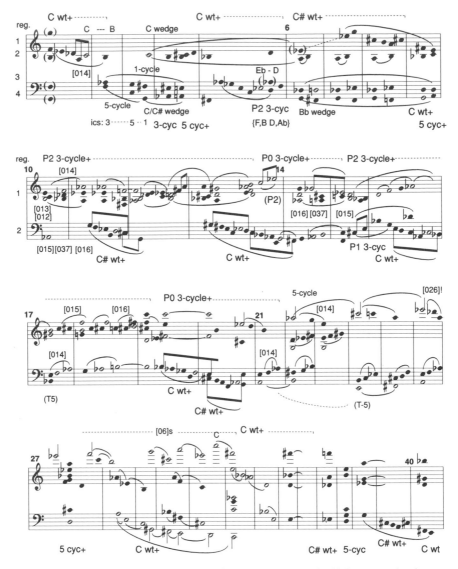

Example 3.5. Cyclic pitch structure, op. 3, first movement, mm. 1–40 (open noteheads marked for emphasis)

main theme in m. 5 resolves repeatedly to D3 in mm. 5–9. Like the dissonant C in the initial whole-tone+ motive, E♭ is a significant pitch-class in the movement; as shown in m. 6, for instance, the shift of the expected E♭4 to E♭5 opens up register 1 and initiates the secondary main theme.

Register 4 combines with register 3 throughout the passage. The span <G2– F3> is defined by a 5-cycle descent <F3–C3–G2>, which aligns with the 1-cycle descent from <A♭3–(G3)–F3> (mm. 2–3) in a cyclic motive (CYC, ex.

Example 3.6a. Opening of op. 3, first movement: main theme (MT), cyclic motive (CYC), wedge motive (WGE), and secondary main theme (SMT)

Example 3.6b. Bridge motive, op. 3, first movement, mm 10–11, 14–15

3.6a; cf. ex. 3.4a). The aligned cycles yield vertical odd interval-classes $<3-5-1>$ contrasting with the predominantly even interval-classes of the opening whole-tone+ motive. The G_2 in m. 3 (which completes the C♯ whole-tone collection of the opening main theme) emerges as a focal pitch in register 4. The lowest voice combines with the register 3 voice in a sum-1 wedge pairing around C/C♯ then a sum-8 wedge around B♭ (mm. 3–4, 6–9). In the cadence chord of m. 9, G is reunited with its sum-1 pair F♯, now an octave higher as F♯$_4$, but the passage ends with outer voice sum-1 neighbors A2, E4.

Example 3.6c. Second-area themes 2ndth1 and 2ndth2, op. 3, first movement, mm. 45–49

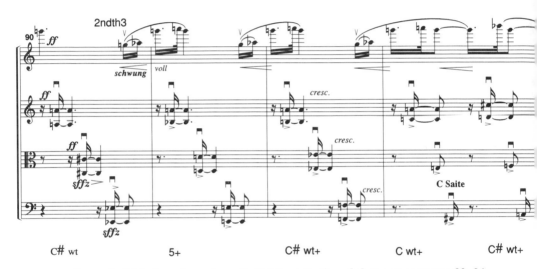

Example 3.6d. Second-area theme 2ndth3 (in violin 1), op. 3, first movement, mm. 90–94

Example 3.6e. Second area theme 2ndth4, op. 3, first movement, mm. 58–60

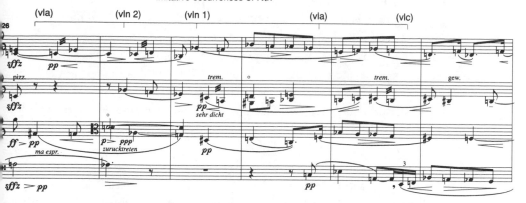

Example 3.6f. New theme (Nth) in the recapitulation, op. 3, first movement, mm. 126–31. Berg STRING QUARTET, OP. 3. Copyright 1925 by Universal Edition. Copyright renewed. All Rights Reserved. Used by permission of European American Music Distributors Corporation, sole U.S. and Canadian agent for Universal Edition A.G., Wien.

Harmonically, the opening C♯ whole-tone+ collection sets the stage for the alternating C and C♯ whole-tone+ areas in mm. 5–9. The intervening mm. 2–4 introduce contrasting odd interval-classes (mm. 2–3), the 3-cycle chord {B3, E♯3, A♭2} (from the referential {D,F,A♭,B} 3-cycle collection), and the wedge-voice-leading–related 5-cycle+ chord {A2,E3,B3,C♯4} (m. 4). The phrase ends with an "open" cadence (m. 9): a C♯ whole-tone+ chord {G,B♭,D,F♯} leading to a less structural neighboring 5-cycle+ chord {A,D,C,E}. The principal registral span combining registers 2 and 3 outlines 3-cycle <F3–G♯3–B3–D4>, but a competing 3-cycle <A3–C4–E♭4> (completed by F♯4 in m. 9) anticipates the contrast of these two collections in the following bars. As in many Berg pieces, the focus on the bass G2 in mm. 3–9 sounds vaguely tonal; characteristically, the upper D3 in mm. 6–9 has a dual role as a dissonance in the C♯ whole-tone+ context and a consonant upper interval 7 support for G2.

The exposition of the main theme (MT) is followed by a bridge motive (cf. Ex. 3.6b), initiating an antecedent–expanded consequent phrase-pair (mm. 10–13, 14–20). Here the registers are simplified to two areas, divided between the upper three instruments and the cello, and the registral collectional content is roughly reversed: the lower register is defined by whole-tone+ collections, as the MT takes an accompanying role, and the upper register by 3-cycle collections and basic cell [014]s.

The lower register continues the focus on G2 with surrounding notes, descending from <A♭2–G2–F2> to end again on G2 (m. 20). This register is defined by the MT in paired statements, spanning <G3–C♯3/C♯3–G2>in mm.

11-12, then expanding out in a sum-2 wedge to a span of <G#3–D3/C3–F#2> (mm. 13–14) and eventually to a span of <Bb3–E3/C#3–G2> to end the section (mm. 18–19), with the latter boundary tones part of the remaining 3-cycle collection {C#,E,G,Bb}. The interval between the two whole-tone+ MTs at each occurrence expands successively from a unison (<G–C#/C#–G>) through interval 2 (<G#–D/C–F#>) to interval 3 (<Bb–E/C#–G>).

The upper and middle registers in mm. 14–19 are saturated with motivic [014]s. The initial bridge motive in the antecedent phrase (mm. 10–11) and its consequent pair (mm. 14–15) (ex. 3.6b) are both melodic [014]s accompanied by horizontal [013] and [012] trichords (<C4–Db4–Eb4> and <B3–Bb3–A3> in the antecedent, and <D4–C#4–B3> and <Ab3–A3–A#3> in the consequent, stemming from the trichordal collections caused by the intrusion of the dissonant C in the opening MT, {Db,A,C} [014], {A,C,B} [013], and {Db,C,B} [012]). The cyclic succession of trichords continues in the first violin part (mm. 17–19) as [015] <C5–C#5–F5> and [016] <C5–C#5–F#5>. The voices accompanying the first bridge motive (m. 10) begin with the <B3/C4> dyad prominent in the opening bars, and similarly expand to a 3-cycle wedge <C4–A3/Eb4> (mm. 10–11) and result from a transposed reverse wedge <D4/Ab3–B3> (mm. 14–15). The intervals between vertically adjacent notes of the initial bridge motive (mm. 10–11) follow an ascending series similar to the cyclic succession of vertical harmonies: intervals 1 <B3–C4>, (4 <C4–E4>), 3 <Bb3–Db4>, 4 <Db4–F4>, 5 <Eb4–Ab4>, 6 <A3–Eb4>, and 7 <Bb3–F4>. The outer intervals similarly expand, but in a "gapped" 2-cyclic pattern: intervals 5 <B3–E4>, 7 <Bb3–F4>, and 11 <A3–Ab4> and <F#3–F4>.

The intervening mm. 11–13 and 15–20 develop the [014] cell by imbricated sequences, guided by primary 3-cycle collection P2 {F,Ab,B,D}, with contrasting 3-cycle P0 {F#,A,C,Eb} in the outer voices of the cadence at m. 13 overlapping into the upper voice of the bridge motive consequent <G4–Gb4–Eb4> in m. 14 and returning in the upper voice to end the section (m. 20). The boundary notes of the final MT in the lower voice, C#3 and G2, are supported at this cadence by E3 as part of a P1 3-cycle {C#,E,G,Bb}. The upper C5, momentarily dissonant, revolves to B only later as a part of a restated MT in m. 28. In the 3-cycle context, the [014]s are generally consonant [03]s with a dissonant added note, as in the initial bridge motive <E4–F4–Ab4> (m. 10), where the E is dissonant in the P2 3-cycle context, {D,F,Ab,B}.

One other cyclic relationship, introduced in mm. 2–4 (CYC motive), is by interval-class 5, emerging in the low register in mm. 14–19. The [014] motives in this register begin on notes <G2–C3–E3–G3–D4>, with an underpinning of T5 from F2 to Bb2 (mm. 15, 17).

The remainder of the first area, mm. 21–38, divides into further [014] developing variation (mm. 20–27), a transition with the combined main theme and bridge motive (mm. 28–31), and a varied return of the opening bars (mm. 32–40). The first violin begins with [014]s in a 5-cycle+ of transpositional levels, <E♭4 – A♭4 – C♯5 – E♭5>, changing to [026] at m. 26, then continuing as the MT in a transpositional whole-tone+ cycle spanning interval 7, <F5 – G5 – A5 – C5>. The cello complements the violin's 5-cycle transpositions with two 5-cycle+ collections of transpositional levels of [014] figures related by T–5 (<A2–B2>, mm. 21–23 to <E2–F♯2>, mm. 24–27), then as part of two sequential statements of the bridge motive at whole-tone+ [0148] transpositional levels <A3–E3–C3–G♯2> (mm. 28–29) and <B♭3–F♯3–C♯3–D2> (mm. 30–31), as part of a bass whole-tone descent <G♯2–F♯2–E2–D2–C2>.

The first violin main theme beginning on C5 in mm. 31–32, at T7 from the opening, initiates a descending sequence of the motive at C whole-tone related transpositional levels <C6–E5–A♭4–B♭3>. This sequence combines with the previous statements of the MT (mm. 28–31), each spanning an interval 6, to exhaust the possibilities of interval 6 boundary notes (F/B, G/C♯, A/E♭, C/F♯ to E/B♭ and A♭/D). In its initial appearance, the end of the main theme evolves into a wedge (mm. 3–6); in the closing mm. 33–37, each voice features the oscillating end notes of the main theme leading to a return of the secondary main theme from mm. 7–8, with its C♯ whole-tone context, but now in the lower register (mm. 38–40). The first area concludes with a rare purely consonant C whole-tone chord in m. 40, acting as a cadence.

The second-area motives of the movement (mm. 41ff.) maintain the whole-tone+ context from the first area, but with a 5-cycle internal organization replacing the 3-cycle elements of the first area. The second-area motives are presented in whole-tone+ harmonic contexts: 2ndth1 (mm. 45–47, cello, ex. 3.6c), 2ndth2 (mm. 48–52, violin 1, ex. 3.6c), 2ndth3 (mm. 90–94, violin 1, ex. 3.6d), and 2ndth4 (mm. 58–62, viola, ex. 3.6e). 2ndth1 is characterized by an expanding opening <–5,–1> to <–6,–1> interval pattern (recalling the expanding trichords in the harmonization of the bridge motive in mm. 10–11); the interval-class 5 content is reflected in the interval 7 created by the added note G in the whole-tone+ harmony with the bass note C (characteristically, the interval 7s over the bass allude to a local "tonal" stability). The closely related 2ndth2 is bounded by notes E♭ and F♭; it and the 2ndth4 combine interval 5 elements in an overall harmonic whole-tone+ context. The 2ndth3 in the development section (mm. 90ff.) has primarily whole-tone+ harmonies, with a contrasting 5 cycle+ chord, and the notes of the motive typically change their relative consonance and dissonance status with each new harmony.

Overall, the T3-related notes C and E♭ are prominent throughout the movement. The note C begins as a dissonance in the first main theme, resolving to B, then becomes the center of a wedge (ex. 3.5). The note pair C/B reappears in the harmony to the bridge motive (m. 10), a long-range C5-to-B5 resolution occurs in mm. 19–29, and C returns at the restatement of the MT as the highest note (C7) in the first area, in m. 31. The resolution of C to B reappears prominently in mm. 165–71 and 182–87 at the end of the movement (violin 1, ex. 3.4c). E♭ is the dissonant note in the second main theme statement (m. 5), and it resolves to D repeatedly in mm. 6–9 as <E♭3–D3>, while in the upper register E♭5 begins the whole-tone SMT (m. 7). In the continuation of the first area, E♭5 is the final upper note of the antecedent bridge motive (mm. 10–13) and begins the violin 1 [014]s in m. 20. In the second area, E♭2 is the first note (m. 41) and the first note of motives 2ndth1 (m. 45, E♭4 over a bass C), 2ndth2 (E♭4, m. 47), and 2ndth4 (m. 58, E♭4, viola). The most dramatic appearance of the two notes, in tandem, occurs at the end of the development section (mm. 100–106), where E♭6 repeatedly moves to C6 by an interval 1 cycle in violin 1, then C finally resolves to B at the start of the recapitulation, in m. 105.

The final chord of the first movement, <G4–D♭5–F♯5–B5> (ex. 3.4c), acts as a traditional cadence chord in the sense of a summary and reconciliation opposing tendencies in the movement: it is both a whole-tone+ and 5-cycle+ collection, the outer voice {G,F♯} is carried over from the preceding embellished version of the CYC motive, B5 is the resolution of a dissonant C5 (from a motion beginning in m. 164 and continuing in the first violin through elaboration from F4–C4 in mm. 174–75, <F4–C4–B3> in mm. 182–83, <F5–E♭5–C5–B4> in mm. 183–84, and finally the full motive <F6–E♭6–D♭6–A5–C6–B5> in mm. 184–187), and the bass note is the focal G. The vertical harmonies of the embellished CYC motive, [03], [037], and [016], stem from the vertical [015], [037], [016] harmonies of the bridge motive in m. 10 (ex. 3.6b). The final note D♭5 comes from an upper E♭5 in the added voice of the CYC motive, which has "resolved" to D throughout the movement, but here the motion to D is delayed until the second movement, where D is emphasized throughout.[12]

ALTENBERG LIEDER, OP. 4

In the op. 4 songs, 3- and 5-cycle collections are primary, whereas whole-tone+ based collections are secondary.[13] The songs also include an emphasis on G, by registral placement and inclusion in the principal P1 3-cycle+ collection <G–A♭–B♭–C♯–E>, and by emphasis on D as an interval 7 support, analogous to a "dominant" of G.

The opening mm. 1–15 of op. 4, no. 1 establish the cyclic context by the use of cycles as successive transpositional levels. Five superimposed motives, motives 4/1, 4/2, 4/3, 4/4, and 4/5 (ex. 3.7) are transposed by different cycles at dif-

Example 3.7. Motives in op. 4

ferent rates (fig. 3.3): the T = <0−1−3−6−9> of motive 4/1 is a horizontal projection of the [01369] motive 4/b, and the T = <0−1−3−6−A−3−9−4> of motive 4/2 yields an almost complete 3-cycle−based "octatonic" collection. Toward m. 15, all motives are liquidated and transformed to map onto the notes of the principal 3-cycle+ <G−A♭−B♭−C♯−E> collection (motive 4/b).

Figure 3.3. Cyclic transposition of motives in op. 4, no. 1, mm. 1–14

(1) motive 4/1, 3+ T = 01369 (piccolo, clarinet 1, glockenspiel, violin 1)
(2) motive 4/1, diminuted, 2-cycle (clarinet 2, viola)
(3) motive 4/3, 1 cycle (trumpets)
     motive 4/4, 1 cycle (celeste)
     motive 4/5, 1 cycle (piano)
(4) motive 4/2, gradated cycle T = 0136A394 (flute, violin 2)

Motive 4/4 undergoes a remarkable cyclic transformation in mm. 1−15 (ex. 3.8), with its contour retained in the traditional manner of a varied motive. From its initial 5-cycle basis—it contains the notes of 5-cycle <A−D−G−C> on every other note[14]—it is transposed by 1-cycle and simultaneously altered through a whole-tone+ form into 5-cycle−based motive 4/a, which consists of two 5-cycle segments joined by descending interval 4 (A♭−E). The motive continues its transformation, becoming first two 5-cycle segments joined by an interval 1, and finally the "tonic" 3-cycle+ collection of motive 4/b, {G, A♭, B♭, C♯, E}. The [0167] in the middle four notes of the penultimate motive form is used as a motive in op. 4, no. 2, and undergoes a somewhat similar cyclic transformation to appear in op. 4, no. 4 as whole-tone+ motive <A♭5−E5−D5−B♭5−F♯4−C♯4−G♯3−D3> (solo viola, mm. 19−21).

contour 1 2 3 0 4 7 6 5   0 2 3 1 4 7 6 5   0 1 3 2 4 5 7 6

contour 0 1 3 2 4 5 7 6   0 1 2 3 4 5   0 1 3 2 4 5

Example 3.8. Cyclic transformation of motive 4/4, op. 4, no. 1, mm. 1–15

The succession of contours closely relates the stages in the cyclic transformation of motive 4/4. From the first to the second contours, only the two lowest notes exchange positions (contour numbers 1 and 0). In the second to third contours, positions <0231> change to <0132> and <4765> to <4576>, maintaining the overall upward motion in the consecutive three-note groups beginning each motive form. The third, fourth, and sixth contours are identical, the latter being a shortened version. The fifth contour is unique in its unidirectional thrust, derived from the unidirectional segments of the other motive forms.

Motives 4/2, 4/b, and 4/c are 3-cycle based materials in the opening bars of op. 4, no. 1 (ex. 3.7). Motive 4/2, originally an interval 3 {D♯, F♯}, is transposed successively by an increasing "+1 cycle," traversing the notes of an octatonic collection and ending on {G,B♭}, part of the principal 3-cycle+ <G–A♭–B♭–C♯–E>. The final four upper notes, [0167] <E–A–E♭–B♭>, reflect the 5-cycle motives mentioned above. At two formally significant places in the work, in the first and last songs, motive 4/b <G–A♭–B♭–C♯–E> moves by interval 1 wedge motion to motive 4/c <F♯–A–B–D–F> (song 1, mm. 14–15), then returns to <G–A♭–B♭–C♯–E> (song 5, mm. 50–55). The motive 4/c harmony [01469] sounds, in context, like a 3-cycle–based chord, {<F♯–A>, <B–D–F>}. This motion from motive 4/b to 4/c and back is part of a large-scale formal symmetry in the five songs of op. 4 and foreshadows the large-scale progression of the chord in *Wozzeck*, Act III, scene iv, <B♭–C♯–E–G♯–E♭–F>, to the D-minor–based chord <A–D–F–A–E> of the interlude in Act III (cf. ex. 3.1e and 3.3).

The 3-cycle motive 4/b is reflected in op. 4, no. 2 by an elaborate harmonic and voice-leading structure based on interval 3 cycles (ex. 3.9). The lower-voice accompaniment begins with P2 3-cycle collection <F–()–B–D–F–A♭>, interrupted by a partial P0 3-cycle <F♯–A–C>, leading to P1 3-cycle <G–B♭–D♭–E–G> and finally to a completed vertical P0 3-cycle+ collection <F–C–E♭–A–F♯> in the chord at m. 7. The horizontal 3-cycles are doubled throughout at parallel interval 4s, creating "octatonic" collections from the parallel 3-cycles. The combination of interval 3s and 4s is reflected in the ascent <B–E♭–F♯> to the chord in m. 7, and in the [014] basic cell in the song, which marks the entrance of the accompaniment (m. 3), where [014] <F–E–G♯> is doubled in interval 3s <D–C♯–E> in the vocal part.[15]

The second section of the song, mm. 8–11, partially restates the previous ascending accompanying 3-cycles but in a descending retrograde, ending on the referential F2 in the bass. The registral shape of the piece is clear from the contour graph included in ex. 3.9, which plots register on the vertical axis and duration on the horizontal axis.[16] After the initial solo vocal line, the register from F1 or G♯5 is established by boundary notes (the low F1s are not shown on the pitch

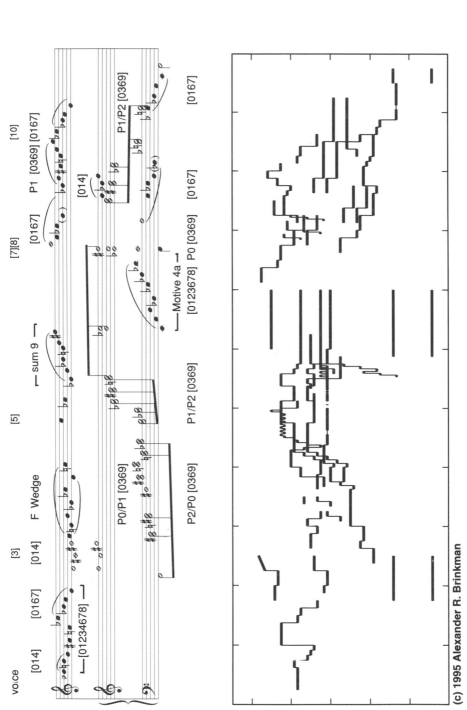

(c) 1995 Alexander R. Brinkman

Example 3.9. Cyclic pitch structure in op. 4, no. 2, with contour graph

graph in ex. 3.9), then gradually filled in, ascending from low to high. The rapid ascent of motive 4a immediately preceding the climactic chord of m. 7 retraces the ascent. Following the climax, all parts descend back to the lower register, in a roughly symmetrical motion, but highly condensed. The status of the bass F2 (actually an F1/F2 dyad, clearly visible in its three occurrences in the contour graph), consonant in the initial P2 3-cycle collection, dissonant in the P0 3-cycle collection of the chord in m. 7, and consonant again at the end in the adumbrated restatement of the opening in retrograde, reflects the arch-shape of the song. The note F as F4 is also the center of a wedge in the vocal part that includes [0167] <E♭–A♭–D–A>, a set-class important throughout (mm. 3–5, stemming from motive 4/d).

The opening vocal phrase in op. 4, no. 2, <B♭–B–G–F♯–F–E♭–B♭–A–E>, symmetrical around A4/B♭4, is inversionally related at sum 7 to the lower-voice motive 4/a <E–A–D–B♭–E♭–A♭–D♭–C> preceding the chord in m. 7 (cello). This sum is one of the two sums 1,7 of [0167] <E♭–B♭–A–E> in the vocal part (m. 2), the four notes that the opening vocal phrase and motive 4/a hold in common. When this vocal motive returns in mm. 8–9 at T6 as <A–E–E♭– (B)–B♭>, a B is interpolated; the sum-7 pair for B, G♯/A♭, appears as the upper voice in the accompanying descending interval 4s. The interpolated B delays the B♭ and connects the two vocal phrases: B♭ both completes the <A–E–E♭–B♭> gesture and initiates a rising 3-cycle <B♭–C♯–E–G>. Sums 1 and 7 return in the principal [0369] {D,F,A♭,B} in the accompaniment, and the secondary [0369]s {C,E♭,F♯,A} and {G,E,C♯,B♭} may be related to each other at sum 7: {C/G, E♭/E, F♯/C♯, A/B♭}.

The [0369] of the m. 7 chord, {F♯,A,C,E♭}, has internal sums of 3,9, foreshadowed by the immediately preceding symmetrical sum-9 vocal notes <E♭–G–B♭–B–D–F♯>. The sum-9 pair for F, the additional note in the m. 7 chord, is E, which occurs as the second vocal note, E4, following the chord. The other sum relationships involving F are the sum-10 wedge around F and the sum-7 pairing of F with D; the two appear in a dyad in m. 2, beat 4 ({D4,F5}), and in the [014] <D5–D♭5–F5> in the celeste in mm. 8–9. The latter figure is embellished by 5-cycle–based grace notes in a cyclic increase of two, three, and four notes (<A4–D5>, <E♭4–A♭4–D♭5>, and <D4–G4–C5–F5>, not shown in ex. 3.9).

The wedge around F stems from the wedge motive 4/d, which originates in motive 4/3 from the opening measures of op. 4, no. 1 (ex. 3.7). Motive 4/d is a twelve-note wedge motive containing all six interval-classes twice, along with internal [014] and [0167] to relate motivically to surrounding material. Motive 4/d focuses around C in op. 4, no. 1 (mm. 9–14, viola), F in op. 4, no. 2, and around C and F (sums 0 and 10) in op. 4, no. 5.

The wedge motive 4/d is also reflected in a large sum-4 wedge with whole-tone harmonies in op. 4, no. 1 (mm. 17–24, ex. 3.10). The wedge expands from two to five voices, with a four-voiced whole-tone tetrachord ascending by interval 1 in the upper voices against a bass descending interval 1 cycle. The alignment produces whole-tone chords at each vertical from alternating whole-tone collections, and the succession of vertical whole-tone chords ends in a characteristic motion reminiscent of an "augmented 6th–V⁷" in G. The voice

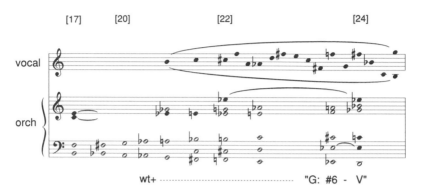

Example 3.10. Whole-tone–based wedge with wedge-like vocal part, op. 4, no. 1, mm. 17–24

part and the wedge are systematically unfolded in mm. 20–22; the voice moves through <B4–C4–C#4>, sung cyclically in a textural progression of closed mouth, half-open mouth, and open mouth, and the wedge unfolds in successively larger waves as <A2–Ab2–G2>, <A2–Ab2–G2–F#2>, and <Ab2–G2–F#2–F2–E2>, in a threefold expansion characteristic of Berg's motivic treatments. The voice part, roughly wedge-like in its expansion out from B4 to G5/B3 (mm. 20–26), aligns consonantly with the whole-tone collections of the chords, but the held Eb in the violin (mm. 22–24) is alternately consonant and dissonant, creating whole-tone+ collections in the latter case. In the form of the song, mm. 20–26 are completely controlled by the wedge, with no other motives appearing, in contrast to the highly motivic surrounding sections.

A wedge similarly controls the middle section of op. 4, no. 3 (mm. 12–16), where principal 3-cycle notes <G2–E3–Bb3–Db4> diverge to whole-tone+ or 5-cycle+ [0157] <Eb2–G#3–A3–Db4>. The outer sections of op. 4, no. 3 are controlled by an aggregate chord (ex. 3.11) containing [0167] and [0369] segments: the bottom four notes are [0167] <C#2–Ab2–D3–G3>, sums 3/9, and an internal segment forms Po [0369] <D#4–F#4–A4–C5>, also sums 3/9. The upper [016] <E5–F5–B5> groups into either sum-9 {E,F} or sum-3 {B,E} dyads. In fact, adjacent dyads in the chord are almost all sum 9: {C#/Ab, D/G, Bb, Eb/F#, A/C, E/F, B}, with the exception of Bb and B, the remaining sum-9 pair.[17]

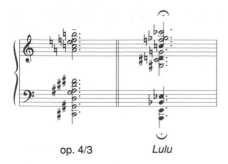

op. 4/3   *Lulu*

Example 3.11. Aggregate chord from opening of op. 4, no. 3, with Lulu's death-cry chord from *Lulu*, Act III, m. 1294

Opus 4, no. 5 features dual emphasized notes G and E, both in the primary 3-cycle+ {G,Ab,Bb,C#,E}, with G as the first bass note and E initializing motive 4/a as <E−A−D−Bb−Eb−Ab−Db−C> (m. 7). The association of these two notes extends back to the initial statement of motive 4/1 (ex. 3.7), where the second note E is the added note in the whole-tone+ context. In op. 4, no. 5, these two pitch-classes are the focus of mm. 31−46 (ex. 3.12). The upper line arpeggiates <G5−Ab5−Bb5−C#6−E6>, accompanied by an inner-voice sum-o wedge <F4−E4−D4−(Bb3)−Ab3> and the E-based motive 4/a, and harmonized with whole-tone+ chords that characteristically alternate source collections C and C#. From m. 36 the bass repeatedly descends from G to E. The clearest statement of the tonal and cyclic emphasis on G occurs in mm. 35−36,

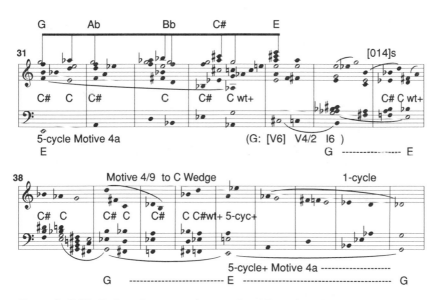

Example 3.12. Cyclic reduction, emphasis on G and E, op. 4, no. 5, mm. 31−46

where a "V of V" A-major chord in "first inversion" descends through a "V $\frac{4}{2}$" over C to a B underpinning the <G–Ab–Bb–C#–E> "tonic" cyclic chord. The B is, of course, dissonant in the 3-cycle context as the momentary tonal implication dissolves. In m. 39 the wedge motive 4/d around C (sum o) begins, soon joined by motive 4/a to end on G in m. 46. A bass pedal G dominates the following variation 8 (mm. 45–51), and in the final bars the 3-cycle+ collection {G, Ab, Bb, C#,E} is stated in its closest spacing over G (<G3–Ab3–Bb3–C#4–E4>, flute, clarinet, harp, piano), simultaneously with its most open spacing (<E2–Db3–Bb3–Ab4–G5> strings), with E in the bass.[18]

OPUS 5

The op. 5 pieces are the least characteristic of Berg's atonal works in their brevity, lack of repeating motives, and few distinctly cyclic collections or transformations. The exception is op. 5, no. 2, in which the overall progression of the bass voice is controlled by 4-cycles, with secondary upper-voice 3-cycle–based materials (ex. 3.13); in this aspect it is a counterpart to op. 4, no. 2, where 3-cycles are primary and interval 4-based material secondary (ex. 3.9).[19] The structural bass in op. 5, no. 2 consists of P2 [048] {D,F#,Bb} connecting the initial section and the return (mm. 1–4, 8–9), with P1 [048] {F,A,Db} defining the middle section (mm. 5–7). In the symmetrical setting, consecutive [04]s are related by interval 3: {D,F#}/{F,A} and {Db,F}/{Bb,D}. Although there are hints of Po and P3 [048]s in the clarinet part, the upper voices are more clearly organized in 3-cycles: Po {C,Eb,F#,A} in the opening bars, P1 {C#,E,G,Bb} aligned with a bass interval 1 cycle from G# to Db in mm. 5–6 (piano), and P2 {D,F,Ab,B} in m. 7 (clarinet). The clarinet descends repeatedly to P1 3-cycle note G4 in mm. 5–6

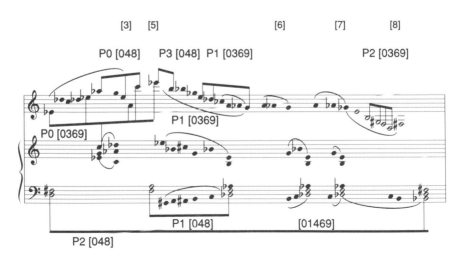

Example 3.13. Cyclic pitch structure in op. 5, no. 2

before breaking through to E4 in m. 7 by way of the notable interval 2 <A♭4–G♭4>. The momentum carries the clarinet through an arpeggiation of notes <E4–B3–G♯3–F3> of the D♭-based [01469] chord of m. 6, but the end note is changed to D to complete the P2 3-cycle <B–G♯–F–D> and to act as a pivot to 4-cycle <D–F♯–B♭>. This pivot on D provides an alternate 3-cycle interpretation of the bass line throughout: P2 [0369] from D to F (mm. 1–4), then G♯ through B to a repeated "dissonant" D♭, then a resolution of D♭ to D in the clarinet, while in the piano a retreat back through B, with a subsequent "resolution" of the {D,F,G♯,B,(D♭)} 3-cycle+ collection to the bass B♭ and 4-cycle {B♭,D,F♯}.

Aside from the cyclic relationship in op. 5, no. 2, most of the pitch relationships in the op. 5 pieces are derived from the opening clarinet figure (ex. 3.14) in the manner of a *Grundgestalt*.[20] As described below in the analysis of op. 5, no. 1, features of this figure are: (1) the interval-classes and pitch-class–set identity of the first six notes <A♭–E♭–G–A–C–E> Tn [012589], TnI-class [012569], which acts as the "nexus" set for harmonic and melodic groups throughout op. 5; (2) the registral wedges associating <A♭5–A5>, <E♭5–D5>, <E♭5–E5>, and <G4–F♯4>; (3) the cyclic unfolding of intervals, <−5, −8 (= −1), +2, +3, +4, +5, (), −7, −8> between successive notes; and (4) the tonal implication of the final "D-major triad" in the emphasis on D in the first three pieces. A secondary emphasis on whole-tone+ harmonies derives from the segmental [0126] <A♭–E♭–G–A> and [02469] <C–E–A–D–F♯> collections and 5-cycles from the segmental gapped collection <G–A–C–E–A–D–F♯> (<C–G–D–A–E–()–F♯>) in the context of surface interval-class 5s.

In op. 5, no. 2 (ex. 3.13), the notes in the opening clarinet line and the right-hand piano chords to the downbeat of m. 5, <E♭3–D♭4–C4–A♭4–G4–E4–A3>, contain not only {E♭,C,A♭,G,E,A} [012569], the same notes as the

ints: (-1) 2 3 4   5 () -7   -8

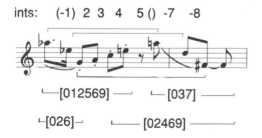

⌞—[012569] —⌟   ⌞—[037] ——⌟

⌞[026]⌟   ⌞—— [02469] ——⌟

Example 3.14. Opening clarinet motto, op. 5, no. 1, m. 1. Berg 4 PIECES, OP. 5. Copyright 1924 by Universal Edition. Copyright renewed. All Rights Reserved. Used by permission of European American Music Distributors Corporation, sole U.S. and Canadian agent for Universal Edition A.G., Wien.

opening hexachordal figure (the entire figure is completed by adding the piano dyad {D,F#}, but also {Db,C,Ab,G,E,A} [012569] and {Eb,Db,C,Ab,G,E} [013478]—the Z-related pair to [012569]—when the added note Db is included. This Db, which appears twice in the clarinet part as well as in the piano chords {Eb,G,C,Db,Ab} ([01568], a subset of [013478]), is prominent in the combined bass interval 4s, {D,F#/F,A/Db,F}, forming a collection which, with the passing tone C (mm. 5−7), yields [012569]. The note Db also underlies the [01469] chord of m. 6, {Db,F,Ab,B,E}, which with the surrounding C also yields [012569]. The role of C in the completion of these sets which include Db is foreshadowed in the reiterated upper line C4−Db4 of the opening piano chords and in the clarinet's insistent articulation of C5 in m.4.

The clarinet descent from Eb6 to G4 in m. 5 (with the preceding note C6) may be segmented into <C6−Eb6−B5−Bb5−Gb5>, an [012569] completed by the G4 that arrives at the end of the descent, and into <E5−Db5−(Cb5)−A4−Ab4−G4>, in what would be an [012569] with C5 instead of Cb5. The Cb5 in the clarinet descent is a curious note: if it were C5, the [012569] would be complete; if it were Bb4, P1 [0369] {E,Db,Bb,G} would be clearly established. If the clarinet descent is regarded cyclically in segmented pairs, however, as <Eb6−B5, Bb5−Gb5, E5−Db5, Cb4−A4, Ab4−G4>, the intervals are a cyclical <4−4−3−2−1>; the process reverses itself through the remaining clarinet notes: intervals <1−2−3−4> in <A4−Ab4, G4−E4, B3−G#3, (F3), D3−F#3>. Ultimately, despite the appearances of [012569], op. 5, no. 2 is ordered by cycles: the ending on P2 4-cycle {Bb, D, F#} is ambiguous from the point of view of [012569], but it resolves the controlling 4-cycle aspects of the harmony.[21]

In Opus 5, no. 3, the opening piano figure, <C4−G#4−E4−G4−B4−C5−C#5> is at T4 from the original [012569], maintaining notes {C,G#,E,G} but substituting {B,C#} for {A,Eb} (ex. 3.15a); two of the remaining notes of the original at T4, {Bb,F#}, are in the first two notes of the clarinet. The substitute notes {B,C#} are reiterated in the clarinet figure in m. 15 as <C#5−B4>, which then initiates a cyclic descent (interval 2 and 1 cycles) to D3. The piano part in this final section (mm. 14−18) returns to the original [012569] with {C,E} reiterated in mm. 14−15 and {Ab,Eb,G,A} as the final piano chord. The "D" emphasis from the original is reflected in the symmetry around D4 in the right hand piano in mm. 14−17, in the neighboring D−Eb−D motion within the piano chord <Ab−A−D−G>, moving to <Ab−A−Eb−G>, and the final clarinet D3 (mm. 16−18). Immediately preceding the final section, the end of the trio (mm. 9−13) is marked by [012569] {F#,B,F,Bb,G,D} with an added Eb. The D6 in the upper-voice clarinet resolves a long-range Eb6 from op. 5, no. 2 (m. 5), reflecting the emphasis on these pitch-classes throughout, stemming from the interval 1 motion of Eb5−D5 in the original clarinet figure (ex. 3.14).

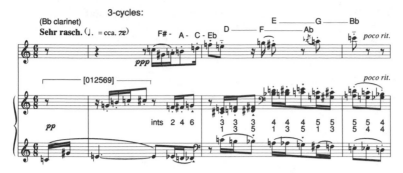

Example 3.15a. Opening of op. 5, no. 3, mm. 1–3 (clarinet in B♭)

Example 3.15b. Recurring motive in op. 5, no. 1, m. 2 (piano), op. 5, no. 3, mm. 5–6 (clarinet). Berg 4 PIECES, OP. 5. Copyright 1924 by Universal Edition. Copyright renewed. All Rights Reserved. Used by permission of European American Music Distributors Corporation, sole U.S. and Canadian agent for Universal Edition A.G., Wien.

Like op. 5, no. 2, this third piece has important cyclic aspects as well. The setting of the opening piano figure (ex. 3.15a), with the doubled note C, asserts 4-cycle [048] <C4–G♯4–E4> and 1-cycle <B4–C5–C♯5>. The piano continues with a series of wedged [012]s over a descending interval 1 line from E4 to D3. The voice pairs create wedges, first with intervals <2–4–6>, then with repeated <1–3–5>s, with a third voice added in parallel to the upper voice at increasing intervals of 3,4,5. In the concurrent clarinet part, a series of 3-cycle collections unfolds. The final piano chord, P2 [048] <D–G♭–B♭>, recalls the opening [048] in the piano and reflects the symmetrical registral extreme of the clarinet part, <F♯4–D5–B♭5>; the same pitch-classes return at the extremes of the chord in m. 13: <F♯2–B♭3–D6>. The note D is then extracted and emphasized as an axis of symmetry in a series of whole-tone chords (piano, mm. 14–16).[22]

In op. 5, no. 4 the opening piano chord <C–G–E–G♯–D♯> combines with the clarinet note A, part of parallel interval 1 descents <B3–B♭3–A3> (m. 2) and <C♯4–C4–B3–B♭3> (m. 3), to complete the notes of the original [012569] (ex. 3.16a). The emphasis on A is reflected in the prominent bass As in the final

Example 3.16a. Opening chords and rhythmically transformed restatement, op. 5, no. 4, mm. 1–2 and 11–12

bars of the movement (ex. 3.16b). When the opening piano chord returns in mm. 11–12 (ex. 3.16a) the clarinet reiterates a B–C♯ sum-o dyad, which served as an axis of symmetry for the whole-tone chords of the middle section; the <B–C♯> stems from the first notes of the clarinet descents in mm. 2 and 3. The combination of piano chord {C,G,E,G♯,D♯} and {B,C♯} yields [012569] with an added E♭, recalling the same collection from the opening of op. 5, no. 3 and the emphasis on {B,C♯} and added E♭ in the [012569] (m. 13) of that movement.

In the closing section, the sum-o dyad <B3–C♯4> expands to <B♭3–D4> and adds F♯4 to complete a P2 4-cycle (ex. 3.16b). The piano figure continues expanding to include <E♭–A♭–C–A–B>, then chord <A–B–C–E–G>, all of which yields the original [012569] with an added B. The clarinet reiterates the interval 1 span from the notes <E–G> of this collection, recalling its interval

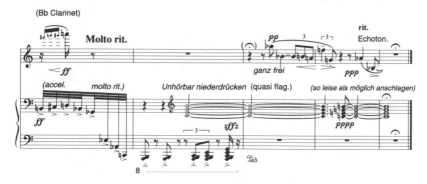

Example 3.16b. Closing mm. 17–20, op. 5, no. 4. Berg 4 PIECES, OP. 5. Copyright 1924 by Universal Edition. Copyright renewed. All Rights Reserved. Used by permission of European American Music Distributors Corporation, sole U.S. and Canadian agent for Universal Edition A.G., Wien.

1 cycle figures in the opening bars of the fourth piece. The closing may be interpreted as the original [012569] <A♭–E♭–G–A–C–E> plus the note B, with the piano tetrachord {C,E,G,B} and notes {A♭,A,G,E♭} from the final clarinet line <G♭–A♭–A–G–E♭–F–G♭–A♭>. Whereas the original figure, <A♭–E♭–G–A–C–E> would be [014568] with a B instead of a C, here {B,C,E,G} forms [014568] with the closing clarinet notes <G♭–A♭> or with the penultimate pair <E♭–F>. Tetrachord {B,C,E,G} would form [012569] with notes {A♭, D♭} or {B♭,E♭}, but B♭ and D♭ are omitted and instead the tetrachord forms [01358] with A. Although the stage would seem to be set to end with the actual "Schoenberg" form of [012569], with B and B♭ in {B♭,B,C,E♭,E,G}—a form prominent in op. 5, no. 1—no B♭ appears.[23]

In the absence of a convincing [012569]-related conclusion, we may turn, as elsewhere in op. 5, to a cyclic interpretation. Registrally, the final bars group from the bottom up into [048] <A♭3–C4–E4>, [012] <F4–G♭4–G4>, and 4-cycle <G4–B4–E♭5>, or two 4-cycle collections with a linking 1-cycle. The closing clarinet notes <E♭5–F4–G♭4–A♭3> are thus arranged symmetrically around the piano's symmetrical <C4–E4–G4–B4>, in sum-11 pairs <A♭–C–E–F–G♭–G–B–E♭>. The arrangement strongly recalls the [048]- and [012]-based opening of op. 5, no. 3 (ex. 3.15a) but also reflects the opening of op. 5, no. 4. Here the opening chord <C2–G2–E3–G♯3–D♯4> is symmetrical (sum 3) but lacks B2 to balance E3; instead, the clarinet enters with B3, which creates a symmetry of <E3–G♯3–B3–D♯4> (sum 7) and completes [014589] {C,E,G♯,G,B,D♯} (the same pair of 4-cycle trichords that occur symmetrically at the close of the movement. The emphasis on 4-cycles recalls op. 5 no. 2, whereas the symmetry recalls op. 5, no. 3; thus op. 5, no. 4, and op. 5 as a whole, ends convincingly in terms of cycles and symmetry rather than pitch-class sets.

Berg's systematic treatment of rhythm and tempo, analogous in many ways to his use of pitch, is one of the most distinctive traits of his music. In tonal music, rhythmic patterns are generally constrained by the requirements of meter and often tied to particular pitch motives. Although these traditional rhythmic roles occur in Berg's music, in connection with waltz or march patterns, for instance, rhythm is also used independently, freed from the organizing forces of meter or pitch. Two characteristic uses of rhythm particularly stand out: (1) rhythms structured in cycles or transformed cyclically; and (2) the independent, "constructive" role of rhythmic motives, to the extent of forms based principally on rhythm.[24]

With the freeing of rhythm from meter, questions naturally arise about the status of notated meter and barlines. In Berg's music, the measure span is often supported by the durations of at least one musical event, but on one periodic level rather than on the multiple synchronized levels usually associated with meter, and conflicting rhythmic patterns invariably exist. Thus, the notated meter exerts a weak force perceptibly, and notated "syncopations" do not have the effect they appear to have on the page. Barlines often mark significant formal divisions, however. For instance, in op. 4, no. 1, the first unison attack, an important motivic transformation, and the climax of the introduction occur on the downbeat of m. 15, at what might be termed a "structural downbeat."[25] In op. 6, no. 1, the downbeat of the notated meter is supported by unison attacks on a prominent pitch-class D-based chord in the A sections (mm. 9, 42), the beginning and middle of the B section (mm. 15, 28), and the climax (m. 36). In *Wozzeck*, Act I, scene i, after the Prelude each dance form begins on a notated downbeat (m. 30, Pavanne; m. 51, Cadenza; m. 65, Gigue; m. 109, Cadenza; m. 115, Gigue; m. 127, Double I; m. 133, Double II) until the climactic Air. Here the motivic "Jawohl, Herr Hauptmann" rhythm, which occurs throughout the scene, is freed from metric constraints in an augmented form, beginning on the second quarter of a $\frac{3}{2}$ bar as it accompanies the "Wir arme Leut" motive (ex. 3.1b, m. 136). The momentary freedom from meter of this rhythmic motive is ironic, as it underlies Wozzeck's cry of the yoke borne by his lot, "Poor folk like us."

METER AND CYCLES

A pulse may also be regarded as a rhythmic cycle; for instance, in a pulse of sixty events per minute the duration between events is a second, forming a "second-cycle." Meter arises when at least two rhythmic cycles, of different durations but related by integral proportions, are synchronized to coincide at cyclic durational intervals.[26] In a meter of $\frac{4}{4}$, for instance, with the duration of an eighth note as the basic unit, the eighth-beat level is a 1-cycle, the quarter-beat level a 2-cycle, the half-beat level a 4-cycle, and the whole-beat level an 8-cycle. The barline establishes the 8-cycle modular limit, although metric groups of measures, or hypermeasures, may also be grouped.[27] Alterations such as hemiola may be regarded as a division of a durational span into a different cycle, such as a quarter-note duration of two eight notes redefined as three triplet eighths. A hemiola is thus analogous to the redefining of an intervalic span: for instance, the division of the interval 6 span <B−F> first by a 2-cycle <B−C#−D#−F>, then by a 3-cycle <B−A♭−F>, at the beginning of the first movement of op. 3 (ex. 3.5).

Another type of rhythmic cycle is a gradated cycle that increases or decreases additively, in either absolute or relative terms, such as <1−2−3−4−5> or <10−8−5−4−1>. These gradated cycles occur often in Berg's music as successive numbers of notes, bars, durations of notes, or note groups. Gradated cycles also occur on different rhythmic levels; in *Wozzeck* Act II, scene ii (mm. 249−58), for instance, the indications *viertaktig, dreitaktig, zweitaktig,* and *eintaktig* indicate a cycle decrease in the number of bars in successive hypermeasures, from four bars down to one. The accelerando of decreasing hypermeasures is part of the overall comic contrast in tempo between the Captain (*langsam*) and the Doctor (*pressiert!*) in this scene.

Berg's rhythmic motives tend to have well-defined rhythmic profiles, ranging from the strongly periodic or metric to the highly irregular, supporting or conflicting with the notated meter. David Lewin has developed a "weighting" system for durations in rhythmic patterns that is useful for determining internal periodicities; these periodicities provide a durational profile that can be used to describe the relationships between rhythmic motives and their rhythmic and metric surroundings.[28] Lewin calculates durational weights on a time-point scale, beginning from time point 0, then lists the durations between all attack points and their frequencies, somewhat analogously to the determination of an interval-class vector from a pitch-class set. For instance, the cyclic series of four durations <2−3−4−5> may be placed on a time point series, of <0 (+2) 2 (+3) 5 (+4) 9 (+5) 14>. The list of all durations within this time point series, given in figure 3.4, includes two durations of 5 and 9 (5−0 = 5, 14−9 = 5, and the corollary 14−5 = 9 and 9−0 = 9). The multiple occurrences of durations 5 and 9 mark the internal periodicities of the rhythm and tend to impart a weight to the boundary tones of these durations: the durations of 5 lend a weight to time points 0,5 and 9,14; the durations of 9 lend weight to time points 0,9 and 5,14. Lewin notes that typical listeners' metric responses to the durational series <2−3−4−5> place a "downbeat" on the first and third durations, which may be accounted for by the double weight given these notes by the internal double

Figure 3.4. Durations between time points <0-2-5-9-14>, from Lewin 1981

durations:	0	2	3	4	5	7	9	12	14
occurrences per	2	1							
time point	5		1		1				
	9			1		1	1		
	14				2		2	1	1

periodicities of 5 and 9 (the relative weight and definition of the fourth duration depend on the presence of a following attack). In the following discussions I use Lewin's "durational vector" in a somewhat restricted sense, mostly to identify internal periodicities and to contrast and compare the inherent metric weights within rhythmic patterns to Berg's settings.

METER

Meter has such a close affiliation with tonal music that its mere presence in atonal contexts coerces listeners into attempting to hear tonal progressions. In op. 6, no. 2, for instance, waltz gestures, meter, and tempo (mm. 20–34, 94–100) combine with a somewhat tonal bass line to create a local implied focus on B♭ in places. Many sections of *Wozzeck* similarly combine meter with pitch combinations reminiscent of tonality and add balanced phrases and sections in mutually reinforcing relationships: in Act I, scene ii in Andres's folksong settings (mm. 212–22, 249–69); in Act I, scene iii in a military march (mm. 326–63) and a lullaby (mm. 372–416); in Act I, scene iv (mm. 565–601) and Act II, scene ii (mm. 202–47) in a waltz; in Act II, scene iv in a ländler and waltz (mm. 412–47, 481–569, 592–99, 671–736); in Act III, scene i in folksong (mm. 34–42); in Act III, scene iii with popular music at the inn (mm. 122–44, 154–57, 169–79); and in the Act III interlude outer sections (mm. 320–38, 365–71). The metered, tonal sections have dramatic as well as musical functions; for instance, in Act II, scene iv, the regularity of the ländler and waltz (first in the orchestra, then in the stage band) reflects the outer world of dancing and revelry, including Marie and the Drum Major and the other people in the inn, whereas the ametric atonal sections (mostly orchestral) reflect Wozzeck's inner anguish.

CONFLICTING METERS AND GROUPINGS

Berg often juxtaposed two or more conflicting meters, leaving the notated barline relatively unsupported, at times rendering it imperceptible. In such cases it is not always clear why the notated meter was chosen. The opening mm. 1–9 in op. 4, no. 1, for instance, feature five pitch motives in seven total durations; each motivic setting has different internal note values, some including rests (fig. 3.5;

the durations and motives begin to change in m. 10; for motives, see ex. 3.7). Of the motives, only 4/3 and 4/5 support the notated meter of $\frac{4}{8}$ (an added motive 4/d entering in m. 10, viola, also supports the meter) by their durations of sixteen and four sixteenths, respectively. The durational arrangement is such that the motives would align again only after 1680 sixteenths, or 210 bars of the notated $\frac{4}{8}$.[29]

If we establish a time-point line for mm. 1–9 with a scale in sixteenth-note durations, yielding a total expanse of seventy-two points, we may then weigh each time point by the number of pairs of motivic durations that coincide at that time point and observe a rhythm of patterns emerging (fig. 3.5). The time-point chart indicates that the notated downbeats of $\frac{4}{8}$ measures, or units of eight sixteenth-notes, are all supported by at least one occurrence of a paired periodicity, except for m. 2 (at time point 8, marked as [8] in the lower part of fig. 3.5), but that time points in units of twelve sixteenths, implying a meter of $\frac{6}{8}$ or $\frac{6}{16}$, have the greatest weights. Within the implied $\frac{6}{8}$, time points 48 and 60 have the greatest number of coinciding pairs, six. Thus, Berg's notated meter of $\frac{4}{8}$ conflicts with the natural metric weights that emerge from the combination of the five motives and seven durations in this section; the conflict avoids any impression of a meter until the entrance of the viola theme (entering in m. 10, from motive 4/d). A somewhat similar combination of conflicting motives occurs in the final section of the song, mm. 29–38, and, in changing groupings, in op. 6, no. 2, mm. 83–93.

Opus 4, nos. 2 and 3 both contain conflicts between meters of $\frac{3}{4}$ and $\frac{4}{4}$ in formal statements and returns. Opus 4, no. 2 is notated in $\frac{4}{4}$, but mm. 1–3 group in $\frac{3}{4}$, $\frac{3}{4}$, $\frac{3}{4}$, and $\frac{2}{4}$ (beginning on the notated second beat) by the vocal phrasing and the attacks of the low octave Fs (fig. 3.6). By the alignment of the notated and sounding meters, however, the notated meter is supported in m. 2 and again in m. 4 (underscored in fig. 3.6). In the corresponding mm. 8–11 in the second part of the song, the opening vocal line returns, set in canon at two beats with the cellos. (The canon can be seen clearly in the contour graph of the song included in ex. 3.9). Because of this canonic interval, one of the two canonic voices, each in $\frac{3}{4}$, coincides with the downbeats of the notated $\frac{4}{4}$ meter at m. 9 and 10 (again underscored in fig. 3.6). The rhythmic groupings in surrounding parts, however, conflict with this relatively weak assertion of the notated meter.

In op. 4, no. 3, the vocal part supports the notated $\frac{3}{4}$, but the orchestral accompaniment attacks group in conflicting units of four quarter notes (fig. 3.7). The two parts would coincide at the notated downbeat of m. 5 except that the voice has a hemiola with extension in mm. 4–6, which delays their coincidence until m. 6, beat 2, the point at which the regularity in both parts and the notated meter begins to break down. The hemiola from the voice part returns as

Figure 3.5. Motivic durations and metric weights in the opening of op. 4, no. I

motive	instruments	internal durations	total durations (in 16ths)
4/1:	picc, clar 1, glock, xyl	8ths	10
4/1:	clar 2,3, vla	16ths	7
4/1:	vln1	triplet 32nds	10
4/3:	flute, vln2	32nds	16
4/2:	trpt	triplet 32nd, 16ths	3
4/4:	celeste, harp	32nds, 16ths	6
4/5:	piano	16ths, 8ths	4

time points of
periodicities of
duration pairs
from units of
3, 4, 6, 7, 10,
16 (sixteenths):

3:4	=	12, 24, 36, 48, 60, 72
3:6	=	6, 12, 18, 24, 30, 36, 42, 48, 54, 60, 66, 72, 78
3:7	=	21, 42, 63
3:10	=	30, 60
3:16	=	48
4:6	=	12, 24, 36, 48, 60, 72
4:7	=	28, 56
4:10	=	20, 40, 60
4:16	=	16, 32, 48, 64
6:7	=	42
6:10	=	30, 60
6:16	=	48
7:10	=	70
7:16	=	-
10:16	=	-

Figure 3.5. Motivic durations and metric weights in the opening of op. 4, no. I (Continued)

time points (in sixteenths) (tp)	0	6	12	16	18	20	21	24	28	30	32	36	40	42	48	54	56	60	63	64	66	70	72
and weights by numbers of pairs of coinciding durations: (no. of pairs)	1	3	1	1	1	1	1	3	1	3	1	3	1	3	6	1	1	6	1	1	1	1	3
resulting $\frac{4}{8}$	0	[8]		16				24			32		40		48		56			64			72
implied meters: $\frac{6}{8}$	0	(6)	12		(18)			24		(30)		36		(42)	48	(54)		60			(66)		72

Figure 3.6. Conflicts between groupings and notated meter in op. 4, no. 2

```
                    m.   1           2           3           4
mm. 1–4  notated meter:  1  2  3  4  1  2  3  4  1  2  3  4  1          4/4
         vocal surface groups:  1  2  3  1  2  3  1  2  3  1  2  1      3,3,3,2
                                                                        4,4,4,4

                    m.   8           9           10          11
mm. 8–11 notated meter:  1  2  3  4  1  2  3  4  1  2  3  4  1  2  3  4   4/4

              voice:  (2 3)  1  2  3  1  2  3  1  2  3                    3/4
              cello:        (2 3)  1  2  3  1  2  3  1  2  3              3/4
```

Figure 3.7. Metric conflict in opening of op. 4, no. 3

```
                    m.       1     2     3     4     5     6     7
mm. 1–7  notated meter:  1  2  3  1  2  3  1  2  3  1  2  3  1  2  3  1  2  3  1   3/4

    4/4  orchestra:  1  2  3  4  1  2  3  4  1  2  3  4  1  2  3  4  1  2         4/4
    3/4  voice:         1  2  3  1  2  3  1  2  1  2  1  2  3  1  2               3,2
                                                                                 4,4
                              (hemiola)
```

the rhythmic feature of the restatement (mm. 18ff.), where the $\frac{3}{8}$ voice part is set against a $\frac{6}{16}$ orchestral accompaniment.

A conflict of three against four in a more pronounced metric setting occurs in op. 6, no. 2 (ex. 3.30 below). Here the waltz section (mm. 20ff.) begins with a typical waltz accompaniment pattern (low strings, harp) and tune (bassoons, trumpet), with a countermelody (violin, E♭ clarinet). Despite the clear $\frac{3}{4}$ organization of the countermelody, the violin and E♭ clarinet are instructed to phrase in a conflicting $\frac{4}{4}$ ("Geige u. Es-Klar. noch im 4/4 Takt zu phrasieren") in a parody of waltz phrasing, part of the programmatic implication of a musical and societal breakdown that pervades op. 6. Berg even added a stave above the violin part with the countermelody notated in the conflicting $\frac{4}{4}$; due to its internal organization in three, the melody shifts in relation to the $\frac{4}{4}$ barlines, coinciding only at m. 24. When this section returns (mm. 94ff.), the countermelody is relegated to an accompanying figure that conforms to the meter (flute, xylophone, harp, celeste, mm. 96–97).

In op. 6, no. 3, the strong duple meter of the opening and of the two returns of the opening (ex. 3.31 below, mm. 15ff. and 155-60) represents the "March" of the title. Part of the "deconstruction" of the march is the dissolution of this meter by conflicting metric and ametric parts throughout. For instance, pronounced structural downbeats occur on the notated third beats in mm. 66 and 142 and on the notated second beat in m. 91. Passages such as mm. 91–98, where the horns parts struggle to assert a duple grouping supporting the notated meter with fanfare-like motives against irregular groupings in surrounding parts, exemplify the conflict that pervades the movement.

CYCLIC RHYTHMIC TRANSFORMATIONS IN METRIC SETTINGS

Characteristic of metric settings in Berg's music is the use of "gradated cycles," series such as <1 2 3 4 5> or <5 4 3 2 1>, in successive subdivisions of beats into smaller durations (two eighths to triplet eighths) or groupings within beats into larger durations (triplet eighths to duple eighths) with corresponding greater or lesser numbers of notes to maintain the integrity of the beat. The aural result is an accelerando or ritardando without changing temp. In the CYC motive of op. 3 (ex. 3.4a), for instance, three successive dyads occur in a series of 1, 2, and 3 attacks, each time occupying an eighth-note duration with a following eighth rest, the eighth-note durations being divided into an eighth, two sixteenths, and three triplet sixteenths, respectively. The CYC motive also appears in variants without the intervening eighth rests but with the final duration extended (ex. 3.4b, mm. 105ff., mm. 109ff., and mm. 185ff.).

One of the two rhythmic motives in op. 4, which I have labeled RH1 (following Berg's later use of the RH marking [*Hauptrhythmus*] to notate rhythmic motives), similarly consists of consecutive beats subdivided into successively smaller subdivisions but with correspondingly greater numbers of attacks. RH1 appears on repeated notes ending the first and second entries in a canon in op. 4, no. 1 (mm. 26–29, ex. 3.26b below) and in three-part metric canons in op. 4, no. 2 (mm. 5–6, cello, violin, harp) and op. 4, no. 5 (mm. 30–31: clarinet, horn and cello, viola; and mm. 31–33: clarinet, trombone and cello; horn and viola, oboe).[30] Similar figures occur in op. 5, no. 1 (mm. 8ff.), and irregular versions, where successive but not necessarily consecutive beats are systematically further subdivided, appear in op. 2, no. 4 (mm. 1–6), op. 4, no. 2 (mm. 8–9, celeste grace notes), and op. 5, no. 1 (mm. 4–6, clarinet).

The reverse process, successive beats internally grouped into larger subdivisions, characterizes the drowning music of *Wozzeck*, Act III, scene iv (mm. 284–302). The 5-cycle+ chord of the scene (ex. 3.3) ascends in interval 1 cycles, subdividing quarter beats in a cyclic succession of five sixteenths (m. 284), four sixteenths (m. 287), three triplet eighths (m. 289), two eighths (m. 291), three triplet quarters across two beats (m. 293), and finally one quarter (m. 295). The successively longer durations create a ritardando with no change in indicated tempo, reflecting the slowing of Wozzeck's movements until he drowns. A similar successively larger grouping of internal beats occurs at the end of op. 5, no. 1 (mm. 10–12, piano and clarinet), which, combined with a ritardando, slows the piece to its conclusion.

Subdivisions of beats into smaller units often occur in tandem with the establishment or liquidation of pitch motives. In op. 5, no. 4 mm. 17ff., the piano coda figure <B–C♯–D–B♭–F♯–E♭–A♭–C–A> (ex. 3.16b) is gradually unfolded through a successively greater number of notes and correspondingly smaller subdivisions of the beat (from five notes in eighths, six, then seven, notes in triplet eighths, eight notes in triplet sixteenths, and nine notes in thirty-seconds). In op. 4, no. 1, the opening mm. 1–14 are characterized by the dissolution of the motivic identity of each voice with successive subdivisions into smaller note values (to sixty-fourths and triplet thirty-seconds) and liquidation of pitch content to one- or two-note subsets of <G–A♭–B♭–C♯–E>. Similar subdivisions occur at the end of op. 6, no. 2, where all parts reduce to trills and thirty-second notes, culminating in a statement of a *Hauptrhythmus* of the work (m. 119; RH from op. 6, no. I, shown in ex. 3.42 below).

CYCLIC TRANSFORMATIONS IN IRREGULAR, AMETRIC SETTINGS

In cyclic subdivisions or groupings of beats in a metric setting, the beat is maintained by a corresponding increase or decrease in the number of notes. When, however, a single durational unit is successively truncated or increased by equal durations, a non-metric setting may result. The aural result is an ametric accelerando or ritardando as the decreasing or increasing durations between attacks are perceived as a change in tempo. For instance, in op. 4, no. 1 (mm. 22–25, ex. 3.17), the second violin note E♭5 steadily decreases in duration: (in sixteenths) <12–10–8–6–6–4–3–2–1> (ending in a variant of the rhythmic motive RH2).[31] The four accompanying wedge chords in the strings and brass have their own time-point rhythm of 6, 12, 14, and 12 sixteenths (mm. 22–24),

Example 3.17. Ametric rhythmic relationships in op. 4, no. 1, mm. 22–25. Berg 5 ORCHESTERLIEDER, OP. 4. Copyright 1953 by Universal Edition A.G., Wien. Copyright renewed. All Rights Reserved. Used by permission of European American Music Distributors Corporation, sole U.S. and Canadian agent for Universal Edition A.G., Wien.

Atonal Music: Detail and Analysis

with a counterpointing timbral rhythm, alternating winds and strings, of mostly prime units of 5 and 7 sixteenths. The lack of coordination between the violin and orchestra parts, and between these and the notated meter, renders the passage highly ametric and polyphonic in many dimensions.

In the closing section of op. 4, no. 1 (mm. 29ff., voice, celeste, and violin 1, ex. 3.18), the unfolding <G – A♭ – B♭ – C♯ – E – A – E♭> vocal motive divides into alternating Gs and upper notes, both in successively longer durations, but at differing rates.[32] The proportions in durations of the upper notes to the preceding repeated Gs increase through <1 – 1.6 – 1.7 – 3 – 3.9 – 5.3>. The effect is a systematic ritard, with the upper part leading. In a somewhat similar gesture in the harmonium in the same bars (mm. 28–33, ex. 3.19), the harmonium chord increases in duration in a series of <6 – 7 – 10 – 12 – 13> (sixteenths) while the intervening rests decrease in a series of <13 – 6 – 4 – 3 – 1> (sixteenths). The effect is an accelerando of successively longer durations. The differing cyclic

Example 3.18. Vocal decelerando in op. 4, no. 1, mm. 29–36. Berg 5 ORCHESTERLIEDER, OP. 4. Copyright 1953 by Universal Edition A.G., Wien. Copyright renewed. All Rights Reserved. Used by permission of European American Music Distributors Corporation, sole U.S. and Canadian agent for Universal Edition A.G., Wien.

Example 3.19. Harmonium chord decelerando in op. 4, no. 1, mm. 28–33. Berg 5 ORCHESTERLIEDER, OP. 4. Copyright 1953 by Universal Edition A.G., Wien. Copyright renewed. All Rights Reserved. Used by permission of European American Music Distributors Corporation, sole U.S. and Canadian agent for Universal Edition A.G., Wien.

patterns of the voice and harmonium parts, along with the varying lengths of the accompanying motives in other instruments, create the complex series of rhythmic relationships ending this song.

OP. 5, NO. 2: A RHYTHMIC ANALYSIS

In terms of pitch material, op. 5, no. 2 divides into a three-part ABA form: mm. 1−4, 5−7, and 8−9 (ex. 3.13). Tempo defines a two-part division of mm. 1−4 and 5−9, both beginning *a tempo*, then slowing, with the return of opening material in mm. 8−9 marked *Noch langsamer*, markedly slower than in the original appearance. The climax, marked by the loudest dynamics, occurs in the second half of m. 6. The piece is notated in $\frac{4}{4}$, and the notated meter is supported by the clarinet in mm. 2−5 and 7−8 and by the piano in mm. 5−6. However, the piano part, particularly the left hand in mm. 1−4 and 8−9, and the clarinet part in mm. 5−6 also present strongly conflicting groupings.[33]

The left hand of the piano part in the opening four bars (ex. 3.20) presents dyad {D/F♯} in the pattern of durations shown in figure 3.8. The pattern is in two sections, with the second a variant of the first, beginning on the second eighth note in m. 3 at the direction *Etwas langsamer*. The first half has a total of 108 basic durations (measured as triplet thirty-seconds), the second 99 durations, for a difference of nine and a proportion of 12:11. The patterns of durations vary systematically in each half: in the first half they decrease in duration from units of 10 down to 3, then increase to 27; in the second half the process accelerates as durations decrease twice, from 10 down to 3 and from 11 to 3, then increase to 18. The rhythms group into either 9, 18, or 27 larger durations, or durations of a dotted eighth, dotted quarter, or half tied to a sixteenth, suggesting a natural metric weight in units of a dotted eighth or its multiples. The resulting implied meters of $\frac{3}{16}, \frac{6}{16},$ and $\frac{9}{16}$ are shown in the rewritten version of the opening bars included in example 3.20. The implied meter strongly conflicts with the $\frac{4}{4}$ of the clarinet part, with a basic conflict between the dotted eighth unit of the left hand of the piano part and the eighth note unit of the right-hand and clarinet parts.

By the groupings into 9, 18, or 27 units (fig. 3.8), the internal relative proportions of the rhythmic pattern in the piano left hand are 3:1:3:2:3 in the first section and 3:3:3:2 in the second. The middle of the "hairpin" dynamic markings in mm. 1 and 3 emphasizes the beginning of the second "3" proportion in each section. The successive differences between durations are also dominated by 3 and its multiples (three triplet thirty-second = one sixteenth), particularly in the first half, supporting the implied $\frac{3}{16}$-based meters noted above.

In both sections, the number of attacks in the successive proportional areas decreases cyclically, <4−3−2−1−1> in the first, <6−4−3−1> in the second.

Figure 3.8. Patterns of durations in op. 5, no. 2, piano, left hand, mm. 1–4, 8–9 (units are triplet thirty-seconds)

	section 1: 108 units	varied repeat: 99 units
	m. 1 m. 3	m. 3
diff. btn durs	6 3 1 3 0 0 9 3 3 9	6 0 1 0 0 8 4 1 2 15 12 12
durations:	10 4 7 6 3 3 12 15 18 27	10 4 4 3 3 3 11 7 6 3 18 6 18
durational groups	27 9 18 27	9 18 9 18 27
implied meter	$\frac{3}{16}$ $\frac{9}{16}$ $\frac{6}{16}$ $\frac{9}{16}$	$\frac{3}{16}$ $\frac{6}{16}$ $\frac{(2)}{16}$ $\frac{3}{16}$ $\frac{6}{16}$ $\frac{6}{16}$
proportions	3 : 1 : 2 : 3	3 : 3 : 2
no. of attacks	4 3 2 1 1 6	4 3 3 1

formal return of opening

	mm. 8 9
durations:	10 4 7 6 3 3 3 3
durational groups	27 9
implied meter	$\frac{3}{16}$ $\frac{9}{16}$
proportions	3 : 1

Example 3.20. Opus 5, no. 2, mm. 1–4, with rewritten version. Berg 4 PIECES, OP. 5. Copyright 1924 by Universal Edition. Copyright renewed. All Rights Reserved. Used by permission of European American Music Distributors Corporation, sole U.S. and Canadian agent for Universal Edition A.G., Wien.

Closure is thus indicated by the smallest number of attacks per durational sub-section. The number of attacks within proportions is, however, extremely varied: groups of 27 are articulated by 6,4,3,2,1 attacks, groups of 18 by 3,2,1 attacks, and groups of 9 by 3,2 attacks. In the second section, the second and third groups of 27 overlap on a basic duration of "3" (underlined in fig. 3.8); the overlap is marked locally by the change in the dyad from D/F♯ to F/A (m. 4) and indicates the formal change about to take place over mm. 4–5.

In the final section of the movement, mm. 8–9, the opening pattern returns in almost the same proportions as the opening, with an added fermata. Whereas at the outset, however, the piano part establishes its own metric context, in m. 8 the octave B♭s in the lower piano create a "downbeat" on beat 2 of m. 8, providing a fixed point against which the rhythm takes on a strongly syncopated quality.

The right hand of the piano in mm. 1–4 (ex. 3.20) reiterates two chords in an alternating pattern of mostly *increasing* and decreasing durations <*1*– 4– 4–2– *5*–1–*3*> (unit = eighth). The first chord {E♭,G,C} (italicized) increases in duration <*1–4–5–3*> until it is cut off by the beginning of the middle section in m. 5, whereas the second chord {C,A♭,D♭} decreases in duration <4–2–1> successively by a factor of 2. The pattern of the two chords is independent of the left-hand rhythms but fits with the clarinet duple rhythms. Marking the close of the section in m. 4, the three parts attack together for the first time (beat 3, second eighth), with the right- and left-hand piano parts synchronized for two attacks, foreshadowing the simultaneous attacks in the middle section.

In mm. 5–7, the piano chords largely support the notated meter, although they also feature a successive decrease in duration and number of elements. The piano chords group into three larger units, each consisting of a chord series ending with reiterated <D♭–F–A♭–B–E> chords. The three groups successively decrease in total duration (from 58 to 26 to 14 triplet thirty-second units), ending in dissolution (m. 7). Within the groups, the chords within the series decrease in number (from 5 to 2 to 1), in individual durations (from eighths to triplet eighths to sixteenths), and in total duration (from 30 to 8 to 3 units). Within the reiterated pairs of <D♭–F–A♭–B–E> chords, the first is relatively stable (at <12–12–11> units) whereas the second decreases in duration (from 16 to 6 units) to dissolution. The grouping of durational units strongly supports the notated meter in mm. 5–7.

The clarinet line in mm. 5–7 begins metrically in an accelerando (quarters to triplet eighths to sixteenths) descent, then a repeating group of <A4–A♭4–G4> gradually increases in individual durations by a factor of two (sixteenths to eighths to quarters in the continuation) in a rising total durational pattern of 6,8 (sixteenth units) against the notated meter and the decreasing pattern of group-

ings in the piano. The third repetition of the clarinet figure is altered to <A3–
A♭4–G♭4> to begin an accelerando into m. 7 (quarter to eighth to triplet eighth).
The *ritardando* marking over mm. 6–7 emphasizes the clarinet increase in duration, but mediates the piano decrease in duration and the following clarinet
accelerando. Much as in mm. 1–4, the clarinet and piano parts do not share
attacks after the fourth beat of m. 5 until the penultimate sixteenth in m. 6,
when the pattern changes.

Overall, the piano and clarinet in op. 5, no. 2 move within different rhythmic
spheres. In mm. 1–4 and 7–9, the clarinet is relatively consonant with the
notated meter, while first the left hand (mm. 1–4) then the right hand (mm.
7–9) of the piano are dissonant in conflicting groupings. In mm. 5–6, however,
the piano changes to a consonant metric position while the clarinet conflicts.
The only places where the two coincide are at formal junctures: the end of m.
4 and beginning of m. 5, at the formal divide between the first two sections, and
in the corresponding divide to the final section, where the piano echoes the clarinet's closing <D–F♯>, in mm. 7–8.

WOZZECK, ACT III, SCENE III: A RHYTHMIC ANALYSIS

The most notable rhythmic motive in Berg's atonal music is the *Hauptrhythmus* in
Wozzeck, Act III, scene iii.[34] The rhythm is associated with Marie's death by its
appearance at the end of Act III, scene ii. Here it occurs as a timbral rhythm in
the attack points of the canonic instrumental entries between the strings and the
woodwinds and brass (ex. 3.21) within a crescendo on the unison B3, a note
associated with Marie (mm. 109–13). The macrorhythm of the canonic RHs
yields an accelerando in groups of <2224/224/24/11118> (in eighths), to
emphasize the crescendo. The following dramatic solo bass drum statement

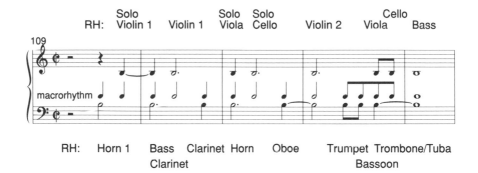

Example 3.21. *Hauptrhythmus* canon, *Wozzeck* Act III, mm. 109–12

Atonal Music: Detail and Analysis

then makes the RH explicit (mm. 114–15).[35] A second tutti crescendo ensues, to lead into the beginning of Act III, scene iii. The RH is the basis of the musical organization of this scene, acting as a constant reminder of Marie's death in what Berg described in his lecture as an "invention on a rhythm."

The RH consists of eight attacks, with relative durational proportions <4–6–2–6–6–1–1–()> (ex. 3.22); the final duration, marked "()," is variable and depends on both the prevailing meter and following attacks for its definition. Three situations arise in the scene with regard to the final duration. First, where the last attack is followed immediately by another event in the same voice, the

Example 3.22. *Hauptrhythmus* proportions in *Wozzeck*, Act III, scene iii

final duration is proportionally 2; the pattern then takes seven beats, with a beat defined as the first duration of the rhythm, and is labeled "a" in example 3.22. Second, when, in a duple meter, the final duration is followed by a rest, the rest if perceived as completing the metric unit; the final duration is proportionally 6 for a total of eight beats, labeled "b." Third, in a similar situation with a triple meter, the rest following the final attack fills out the triple metric unit; the final duration is proportionally 10 for a total of nine beats labeled "c." The RH patterns are also labeled by the note value of the first duration, with numbers from 1 to 8; patterns are thereby identified as, for instance, "RH 3b" for the form that begins with a quarter beat and has a final duration of a dotted quarter, for a total of eight beats. A few variants on the RH are shown to the right in example 3.22.

If the durations of the rhythm are placed on a time-point line, with the first attack at time point 0, the RH yields the pattern <0−4−10−12−18−24−25−26>. This pattern yields a number of differing durations and durational patterns between all elements: for instance, the durations of 6 between time-points 4−10, 12−18, and 18−24. The number of occurrences of each duration within this pattern is shown in figure 3.9. The internal periodicities of the RH lend a maximal metric weight to durations of 6, 8, 12, and 14, with time points 12 and 18 coinciding with the greatest number of beginning and end points of these durations. These periodicities are maximized in the metric settings shown in example 3.23. The setting maximizing units of 12 (ex. 3.23a), notated in $\frac{3}{4}$, then $\frac{6}{8}$, reveals the conflict between duple and triple groupings inherent in the rhythm itself; this conflict is reflected in the scene by the presentation of the RH in, first, duple settings (mm. 122−54), then in triple settings (mm. 155−79). The setting maximizing units of 6 is notated in $\frac{3}{8}$ (ex. 3.23b). The first $\frac{4}{8}$ setting maximizing units of 8 (ex. 3.23c) appears in the scene in mm. 142−45 (RH 3b), 149−52 (RH 6b), and 154−60 (RH 6b) (ex. 3.24). The second $\frac{4}{8}$ setting (ex. 3.23d), with only two coincidences with the RH attacks, is used in mm. 131−33 (RH 1a) (ex. 3.24). The internal durations of 14 in the RH (fig. 3.9) are reflected in the scene by the use of the seven-beat "a" form of the rhythm, in mm. 131−33, 145−47, and 152−53, and in the implied $\frac{7}{2}$ meter beginning in m. 187 (ex. 3.24)—where every point in the successive RHs is thus related by 7 or 14 units.

Example 3.23. Maximally metric settings of the *Hauptrhythmus* in *Wozzeck*, Act III, scene iii

Figure 3.9. RH time points and chart of internal metric weights in *Wozzeck*, Act III, scene iii

RH time points: 0 4 10 12 18 24 25 26

metric weights

durations:	1	2	4	6	7	8	10	12	13	14	15	16	18	20	21	22	23	24	25	26
number of occurrences:	2	2	1	3	1	3	1	2	1	3	1	1	1	1	1	1	1	1	1	1

durations of 6:   time points
                       4–10, 12–18, 18–24
8:                   4–12, 10–18, 18–26
12:                0–12, 12–24
14:                4–18, 10–24, 12–26

maximal periodicity metric settings

time points =	0	4	10	12	18	24	25	26	
units of 12:									
0:	0			12		24			(ex. 3.23a)
6:		4	10	12	18	24			(ex. 3.23b)
8:		2	10		18			26	(ex. 3.23c)
8:		4		12		20	(28)		(ex. 3.23d)
14:		4			18				
14:			10			24			
14:				12				26	

Example 3.24. Chart of *Hauptrhythmus* occurrences, *Wozzeck*, Act III, scene iii

In the course of the scene, the rhythm is subject to different metric settings, including those that maximize the internal periodicities of the rhythm; these can be compared and differentiated by placing the metric beats on the time-point line of the rhythm (fig. 3.10). The three duple meter settings used begin on time points 0, 2, and 4 of the RH, exploiting the inner periodicities of eight in the rhythm. In the first metric setting (m. 122, RH 3b, ex. 3.24), beginning at time point 0, the rhythm is syncopated against the barline, coinciding only at time points 0 and 24. In the second setting (m. 131, RH 1a, ex. 3.24; cf. ex. 3.23d), the downbeat coincides with the second attack of the RH, rendering the initial attack an upbeat; this setting of the RH begins metric, coinciding at time points 4 and 12, but ends syncopated. The third setting (m. 142, RH 3b, ex. 3.24; cf. ex. 3.23c) is the most straightforwardly metric; after an upbeat beginning and syncopated first attack, downbeats coincide with the rhythm at time points 10, 18, and 26; a particularly striking feature of this setting is the coincidence of the eighth attack with a barline, creating an end accent which overlaps into the beginning of the next section.

The RH is also set in triple meter; each of the RH 4cs in mm. 161–69 has its sixth and seventh attacks doubled in duration to yield a varied rhythm of <4–6–2–6–6–2–2>, time points <0–4–10–12–18–24–26–28>. The first triple setting (m. 161, RH 4c, ex. 3.24; fig. 3.10) is the most straightforwardly metric, coinciding at time points 0, 12, and 24. The other three (mm. 163–66, RH 4c, ex. 3.24) are mostly syncopated, but the change in the sixth and seventh durations causes the RH 4c's beginning in mm. 163 and 166 (with a half-note upbeat) to end on metric downbeats.

The setting of greatest metric conflict occurs beginning in m. 180, where a

Figure 3.10. Time points of metric settings of the RH in *Wozzeck*, Act III, scene iii

	0	2	4	8	10	12	16	18	20	24	25	26	28	
rhythm:	0		4		10	12		18		24	25	26		
duple meter:	0			8			16			24				m. 122, RH 3b
			4			12			20				28	m. 131, RH 1a
		2			10			18				26		m. 142, RH 3b

	0	2	4	10	12	14	16	18	22	24	26	28	
rhythm:	0		4	10	12			18		24	26	28	
triple meter:	0				12					24			m. 161, RH 4c
			4				16					28	m. 163, 166, RH 4c
		2				14					26		m. 163, RH 4c
				10					22				m. 164, RH 4c

	0	6	15	16	18	27	32	38	38.7	39.4	
rhythm:	0	6	15		18	27		38	38.7	39.4	
conflicting meter:	0			16			32				m. 180, RH 5b

variant of RH 5b is stated five times in canon at the duration of a $\frac{4}{4}$ bar (ex. 3.24). The variant has an extended fifth duration and shortened sixth and seventh durations, yielding a pattern of $<36-54-18-54-65-4-4-(52)>$ and time points of approximately $<0-6-15-18-27-38-38.7-39.4>$ (ex. 3.22 right side, and fig. 3.10). The notated $\frac{4}{4}$ meter coincides only at time point o with the entrances of the canonic statements of the rhythm.

Formally, the scene divides into three parts: an opening section (mm. 122–54), its varied repeat with triplet settings of the RH (mm. 155–86), and a closing canonic section that overlaps into the following interlude (mm. 187–211, 212–19). The music shifts between the duple meters of the piano-based music of the inn (mm. 122–44, 155-57, 169–79) and more complex orchestral passages with multiple RH statements that reflect Wozzeck's inner turmoil over the death of Marie (mm. 145–54, 158–68, 180–86, 187–218).

The opening section (mm. 122–45, ex. 3.24) is in a strongly metric $\frac{2}{4}$, reflecting the popular music of the inn, with correspondingly strongly syncopated statements of the RH 3b. The RH patterns 3b and 6b establish four- and eight-bar hypermeasures in mm. 122–41. In the initial four-bar $\frac{2}{4}$ setting of RH 3b (mm. 122–26) the RH coincides with a downbeat metric accent on the first and fourth bars, and in the intervening bars agogic accents on beats (in eighths) 3 then 2 cyclically work their way back to the downbeat. In the RH 6b, attacks coincide with downbeats at mm. 130, 131, 133, and 136, in a cyclic pattern of increases of one-, two-, and three-bar units between these coincidences.[36] A four-bar codetta (mm. 142–45) completes the twenty-four–bar unit, but the upbeat setting of the RH 3b—which maximizes the internal periodicities of the rhythm (cf. ex. 3.23c)—causes it to overlap into the first half of the $\frac{2}{2}$ bar in m. 145, ending on the downbeat. This RH 3b setting appears in the timpani, the first instrumental part added to the voice and piano, on interval-class 6 {B♭,E}. The metric shift in RH 3b and the upbeat RH 1a embedded in mm. 131–33 represent the agitation lurking beneath Wozzeck's attempts at merriment.

After exhorting his fellows to dance in the first section of the scene, Wozzeck sings a song (mm. 145–52), his non-RH voice part in triple divisions of the $\frac{2}{2}$ meter (anticipating the following triple meter section, mm. 160ff.); his thoughts of Marie are betrayed, however, by his use of the cradle song motive (ex. 3.2b). The orchestral accompaniment features RH 6b (mm. 145–48), with RH 1a in a conflicting implied meter of $\frac{7}{8}$ (on the small drum, continuing the association of percussion sounds with conflict in the scene); the underlying conflict reflects the shadow of Marie's murder that hangs over Wozzeck.

In the second phrase of Wozzeck's song (mm. 149–52), the meter breaks down with the appearance of conflicting RHs: first, a canonic RH 6b at a quarter beat to the main RH 6b (piano versus strings); then, as Wozzeck suddenly breaks off his song with a cry of "Verdammt" and a *meno allegro* in the middle of m. 152 (marked by a tempo change to quarter = 60), conflicting RHs 1a and 3b. The RH 1a appears in the timpani, on the bass notes {B,F} of an allusion to Marie's waiting motive, and in a parallel to the timpani statement of RH 3b on {B♭,E} in mm. 141–45. (Although the RH 1a in m. 152–53 has no immediately following event, and thus could be identified as 1b, it is labeled 1a to parallel the previous RH 1a's of this section.)

The second section of the scene begins, like the first, with the piano four-bar RH 3b (mm. 154½–157) notated with its own 2/4 beginning in m. 154½, but accompanied by an RH 6b overlapping the sectional division. In view of the upcoming 2/2 meter signature (m. 158), the setting can be interpreted as beginning with a quarter-note upbeat to an implied 2/2 bar in the middle of m. 154, and grouping across the 2/4 mm. 154½–155 and 156–57, strongly anticipating the following 2/2 meter. Wozzeck then exhorts Margaret to sing, set to triplet division RH 2cs in varied forms (mm. 158–60, ex. 3.22, right side), followed by one RH 4c, then three RH 4c's in three-part canon (mm. 161–69) and a final RH 4c (m. 166) overlapping onto the downbeat of m. 169. The RH 4c's in this section are all similarly altered (ex. 3.22, right); the time points of the three-voice canon of RH 4c's, given in fig. 3.11, yield the maximal number of internal coincidences, and, thus, the canon is relatively consonant in a rhythmic sense. (The initial timbral canon of the RH, ex. 3.21, is arranged as are entries 1 and 2 in fig. 3.11.)

Figure 3.11. Three-part canon mm. 163ff. of *Wozzeck*, Act III, scene iii (time point 0 at attack of first entry, time points = ³♪)

entries	m.	164			165			166		
1.	0	4	10 12		18	24	26 28			
2.	2	6	12 14		20		26 28 30			
3.		6 10		16 18		24		30 32 34		

Margaret's folksong (mm. 168–79), which reestablishes duple divisions, divides into two groups of six bars (mm. 168–73, 174–79). The RH 6a and 3a (in a varied form; cf. ex. 3.22) are each preceded by a rest to complete an even eight beats, in four and two bars. The initial RH 6a, overlapping with previous rhythms, is set with its first attack in a triplet context. Since the RH is subordinate to the meter of the piano accompaniment in Margret's song, the variation to RH 3a—changing the fifth duration from a proportion of 6 to 4—may have been to emphasize the text parallels *nit* (m. 171) and *nit* (m. 173), and *Schuh* (m. 177) and *zu* (m. 179), by their occurrences on beat 4 of the respective bars.

Margaret's song does not, however, cause Wozzeck to forget Marie; he takes her reference to "shoes" and declares that "one can go to hell barefoot" (mm. 180–82, *man kann auch blossfüssig in die Höll' geh'n*). This foreshadowing of Wozzeck's death and his increasing agitation are reflected in the irregular, varied canonic forms of RH 5b beginning in m. 180 (cf. ex. 3.22, right). Although the patterns internally conflict strongly with the notated meter, they are in a five-part canon at a duration of a bar (the final statement beginning m. 184 is cut off at the downbeat of m. 185), as if the meter were trying to exert control over the RH, reflecting Wozzeck's attempts to control his fate. The meter is also supported by an underlying RH 8b spanning mm. 180–86 (the largest beat value for the RH in the scene).

On top of the conflicting canons of the altered RH 5bs, Wozzeck declares he would like a fight, to RH 3a (m. 183–84), set metrically with a beginning rest to take eight beats. The notes he sings are the Drum Major's motive (ex. 3.2d), as Wozzeck takes on the posture of the Drum Major. Margret replies with the same pitch motive (mm. 185–86), but in RH 2c in a varied form, prematurely cutting off the final two canonic RH 5bs with her chilling statement: "But what is that, there on your hand?" (*Aber, was hast du an der Hand?*).[37] The juxtaposition of the duple division 3a (m. 183) and triplet division 2c (m. 185) summarizes the opposition of these two divisions in the second section.

The final section of the scene (mm. 187ff.; only four bars are shown in ex. 3.24) consists of continuous RH 6a's in an implied $\frac{7}{2}$ meter, in conflict with the notated $\frac{2}{2}$ meter, ascending in eight statements—the number of attacks in the RH—through the whole-tone+ collection $<B\flat–C–D–E–G\flat–A\flat–A–B\flat>$ as the bass notes of interval 11 dyads (strings; woodwinds are added at m. 190). Above this bass succession, Wozzeck, Margaret, and voices from the choir enter with RHs in various canonic configurations, as Wozzeck protests his innocence while Margaret and the growing mob accuse him of murder. Berg's arrangement of the canonic entries is, characteristically, extremely varied (fig. 3.12). The fourteen (two times seven) RHs, which vary through RH 3a, 6a, 7a, and 8a, enter at twelve different time points relative to the bass RH 6a, where the time points of the RH 6a are defined as $<0–4–10–12–18–24–25–26>$ (canonic entries at RH 6a time points 25 and 26 each occur twice in fig. 3.12). The spans between canonic entries grow successively shorter as the density increases from one to four distinct voices (Wozzeck, Marie, male chorus, female chorus) above the bass ostinato.

The successively thicker texture of RHs suddenly ends at the curtain in m. 211, where three sets of canonic statements of RH 4b begin (fig. 3.13): first in four voices at a canonic interval of a quarter, quarter, and a half (mm. 211–13, time points 0, 4, 8, and 16); second, in six voices with entries at a quarter beat, dotted quarter, quarter, eighth, and eighth (mm. 213–15, time

Figure 3.12. Entries of canons in mm. 187 – 210 of *Wozzeck*, Act III, scene iii (units in eighths, W = Wozzeck entry, M = Margaret entry, W/M: = combined Wozzeck and Margaret, Ch1 = male choir entry, Ch 2 = female choir entry) in relation to time points (t pts) 0 to 26 of bass ostinato RH 6a's

						mm.				
	186	190	193	197	200	202	203	206	208	210
RH	6a	6a	6a	3a 6a	3a	6a	8a 3a	7a 3a	6a 6a	3a
	W/M	W/M	W	W M	W	Ch1	M W	Ch2 W	Ch1 W	M
	—	—	—	— —	—	—	— —	— —	— —	—
t pts	(26)	26	25	24 27	25	8	16 22	12 14	2 3	17
strings	B♭	C	D	E	G♭		A♭		A	B♭
RH 6a:	m. 187	190	194	197	201		204		208	211

Figure 3.13. Time points of canons ending *Wozzeck*, Act III, scene iii (units in sixteenths)

m.	211	212	213	214
1.	0 4	10 12 18	24 25 26	
2.	4 8	14 16 22	28 29 30	
3.	8	12 18 20	26 32 33 34	
4.		16 20	26 28 34	40 41 42

m.	(216)	(217)	(218)
m.	213	214	215

m.	213	214	215	
1.	0 4	10 12 18	24 25 26	
2.	4 8	14 16 22	28 29 30	
3.		10 14	20 22 28	34 35 36
4.		14 18 24	26 32	38 39 40
5.		16 20	26 28 34	40 41 42
6.		18 22	28 30 36	41 42 43

macrorhythm: 38 39 40 41 42

points <0−4−10−14−16−18>); and third in six voices with the same durational entries as the second (mm. 216−18). In the second and third canons, the
aligned RHs create a macrorhythm of consecutive sixteenths leading into m. 219
and the following scene. The initial entrances of the second and third canons—
at a quarter, then a dotted quarter—begin similarly to the durations of the RH
itself but do not continue. These canonic combinations contain a relatively high
number of internal attack coincidences, underscored in fig. 3.13, and thus are
relatively consonant in a rhythmic sense.

The RH of Act III, scene iii is also varied by tempo changes (fig. 3.14), which
reinforce the three-part shape of the scene (mm. 122−54, 155−86, 187−211)
but also round it off, with the tempo of the first part corresponding to that of
the third.[38] In the first section (mm. 122−54), the changes in tempo correspond
with beginnings and endings of the RH, and the tempo slows by 75% from
quarter = 160 to 120. The tempo in the second section (mm. 155−86) returns to
quarter = 160, and slows from half = 80 to 60 to 40, with triplet half at 60 in
mm. 161−68. The section ends with half = 40, slowed by 50%. The final section
(mm. 187−211) is set at half = 80, quarter = 160, and slows by 75% to half =
50−60 at m. 216, roughly corresponding to the change in the first section.

The RH 6b that straddles mm. 154−59 (cf. ex. 3.24) is affected by changes in
tempo from half = 60, to 80 (quarter = 160), and back to 60. The tempo
changes contract and stretch the RH, or, in absolute terms, alter it to an RH
approximately between 5b and 6b. Similar alterations to the RH, stretching in
mm. 158−60 by a poco ritardando to RH 2c and a rallentando to RH 3a in mm.
172−73 and 178−79, demonstrate Perle's assertion that "it seems to have
occurred to no one except Berg that the integral units of a thematic or *ostinato*
rhythmic figure may be paced at different rates of speed even with a single statement of that figure, so that in an absolute sense the given pattern is annihilated,
while in a relative sense (i.e., relative to the concurrent changes in tempo) it
remains inviolate."[39] Perle also points out that the final scene v of Act III in
Wozzeck, a moto perpetuo in $\frac{12}{8}$, contains many internal changes in tempo (particularly in mm. 387−88). Although Berg may have pioneered the constructive
use of rhythmic motives, changes in tempo within established rhythmic patterns, where the pattern retains its identity, are common in tonal music.

RHYTHMIC MOTIVES: AMETRIC

Ametric rhythmic motives in Berg's atonal music tend to be rhythmically fluid,
with periodic articulation suppressed by ties and rests and shifts from duple to
triple divisions. These types of rhythms appear in the op. 2 songs (ex. 1.14), op.
4 (no. 1, mm. 24−26; no. 3, motive 4/8, mm. 9−10, no. 5, motive 4/8, mm.
31−35), op. 5 (no. 2, ex. 3.20; no. 3, mm. 14ff.), and op. 6 (see analysis of op. 6,

Figure 3.14. Tempo Changes in *Wozzeck*, Act III, Scene iii

	bar	tactus	change	description
122–145	$\frac{2}{4} = 80$	quarter = 160		metric RH
145–148	$\frac{2}{2} = 40$	half = 80		conflict, canons
149–152	$\frac{2}{2} = 35$	half = 70		
152–154	$\frac{2}{2} = 30$	half = 60		conflict
		quarter = 120	$\times \frac{3}{4}$	
154–157	$\frac{2}{4} = 80$	quarter = 160, half = 80		metric
158–160	$\frac{2}{2} = 30$	half = 60, triplet quarter = 180		metric
		triplet half = 90		
161–168	$\frac{2}{2} = 20$	triplet half = 60, half = 40		conflict, canons
		triplet quarter = 120		
169–179	$\frac{2}{2} = 30$	half = 60, quarter = 120		metric
180–186	$\frac{2}{2} = 20$	dotted quarter = $53\frac{1}{3}$		ametric
		half = 40		
		quarter = 80	$\times \frac{1}{2}$	
		triple quarter = 120		metric
187–215	$\frac{2}{2} = 40$	half = 80, quarter = 160		canons, conflict
216	$\frac{2}{2} = 25$–30	half = 50–60	$\times \frac{3}{4}$	

no. 1 below).[40] The motivic RH2 in the op. 4 songs (ex. 3.25) appears at the end of op. 4, no. 5 as a macrorhythm in a vertical presentation of motive 4/b <G–A♭–B♭–C♯–E> (mm. 54–55: oboe and bassoon, to flute and clarinet, to piano). The rhythm has five attacks with proportions of <5–2–5–9–(6)> and a time-point line of <0–5–7–12–21> (units of triplet sixteenths) with internal repeating periodicities of 5 (5–0, 12–7) and 7 (7–0, 12–5). The periodicity is more apparent when the rhythm appears in a truncated form with four attacks, as <0–5 / 7–12>, dividing into two and two. Despite its syncopated appearance, then, in the absence of a strong meter the rhythm groups in duple with agogic accents on the first and third notes.

TEMPO AND NOTATION

In several pieces by Berg, a passage appears renotated with a new tempo that yields the same durations as the original; the reasons for the change are not always clear. In op. 4, no. 3, for instance, the opening A section (mm. 1–11) is notated in $\frac{3}{4}$ with *massige Viertel*. The middle section (mm. 11–17) has triplet divisions notated in hypermeasures of $\frac{9}{8}$ with broken internal barlines indicating $\frac{3}{8}$, in a slower tempo. When the A′ section (mm. 17–25) appears, however, it is

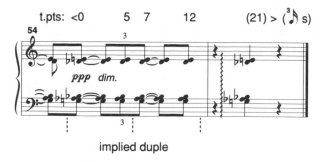

implied duple

Example 3.25. *Hauptrhythmus* (RH2) ending op. 4, no. 5, mm. 54–55. Berg 5 ORCHESTERLIEDER, OP. 4. Copyright 1953 by Universal Edition A.G., Wien. Copyright renewed. All Rights Reserved. Used by permission of European American Music Distributors Corporation, sole U.S. and Canadian agent for Universal Edition A.G., Wien.

notated in $\frac{3}{8}$ at *massiges Tempo [eighth]*; thus the A' section in $\frac{3}{8}$ is in the same tempo as the A section in $\frac{3}{4}$.[41] The middle section $\frac{3}{8}$ bars, in a slow tempo, are presumably slower than the bars in the A' section, and the continuation of $\frac{3}{8}$ in the A' section allows for a smooth transition.[42]

A similar notational change occurs in op. 3, no. 2. After the opening $\frac{3}{4}$ with *massige Viertel*, a change is made to $\frac{6}{8}$ and $\frac{9}{8}$, with internal $\frac{3}{8}$s again indicated by broken barlines (mm. 9–10). The tempo accelerates, then slows so that by m. 23 and the return of opening material the notated $\frac{3}{8}$ meter is marked *a tempo, aber breiter*, presumably now at a moderate eighth, but a bit broader than the opening. The rest of the movement is then in $\frac{3}{8}$. The reason for the change from $\frac{3}{4}$ to $\frac{3}{8}$ is obscure; it seems to contradict the indication *aber breiter*.

In op. 5, no. 4, the opening passage (mm. 1–4) is renotated in a brief restatement (mm. 11–12), which, combined with a tempo change, yields the same durations (ex. 3.16a). The opening is notated in $\frac{4}{4}$, eighth = 66, but the piano chords are each a dotted quarter in duration, as dotted quarter = 22, creating a conflicting implied meter of $\frac{3}{8}$ or $\frac{6}{8}$. Triplet divisions enter in m. 6 in a slightly slower tempo, without a change of meter. At the restatement (m. 11), Berg indicated: "the triplet eighth remains 88, so the initial dotted quarter corresponds to the present quarter + eighth triplet."[43] The opening dotted-quarter chords, at duration = 22, are rewritten as quarter plus triplet eighth in duration, also equaling 22. The same duration thus results from the combined notational changes and slower tempo. Berg's renotation in op. 5, no. 4 allows a musically smooth but visually complicated transition from the middle section (mm. 6–11) to the restatement (mm. 11–12), particularly the consistent notation of the <B–C#> motives in the piano, then the clarinet, across the sectional boundary. The rhythmic independence of the opening piano chords from the notated meter is reflected by their placement in the middle of m. 11, which creates a perceived downbeat, supplanting the notated meter. In the closing measures of the piece, the tempo slows again, with triplet eighth = quarter = 80–88 (mm. 13ff.); the renotation allows more easily readable subdivisions of the beat (into thirty-seconds) in the closing measures (ex. 3.16b).

Form and Treatment of Motives

In terms of form and motivic treatment, Berg's atonal music may be categorized simply by the presence or absence of a return of relatively sizable passages or the recurrence of motives—in the traditional sense of a pitch figure with a characteristic contour and rhythm—and formal sections. A group of pieces is characterized by through-composed forms, as in op. 2, no. 4, op. 4, nos. 1 and 4, op. 5, no. 3, and *Wozzeck*, Act I, scene iii, or by forms with only brief restatements, as in op. 5, nos. 1, 2, and 4, and op. 6, no. 3. Of these, op. 2, no. 4, op. 4, no. 4, and the op. 5 pieces contain little repetition of musical figures after their initial presentation, and hence few motives in the traditional sense. The rest of Berg's atonal music is characterized by repeated motives and formal areas in several categories: (1) thematic variation forms, in op. 4, no. 5 and *Wozzeck*, Act I, scene iv, Act II, scene ii, and Act III, scene i; (2) refrain forms, in *Wozzeck*, Act I, scenes i and v and Act II, scene v; (3) sonata forms, in op. 3, nos. 1 and 2 and *Wozzeck*, Act II, scene i; (4) ternary forms, in op. 4, no. 3 and *Wozzeck*, Act II, scenes iii and iv and the interlude in Act III; and (5) a two-part AA' form in op. 4, no. 2. The op. 6 movements are relatively experimental formally, with a retrograde return of opening material ending the first movement—a feature that returns in *Wozzeck*, Act I, scene i—the second movement a complex overlay of a rondo form with an arch-shaped introduction-waltz-development-reprise-waltz-coda, and the third movement essentially through-composed, with formal sections delineated by tempo.[44] Several scenes in *Wozzeck*—Act I, scenes ii and iii and Act II, scene iv—include relatively large internal tonal sections with corresponding popular tonal forms—songs, marches, ländler, and waltzes—with their concomitant repetition patterns.

Motivic treatments in the pieces characterized by repeated motives and formal areas consist of a blend of contrapuntal combination and developing variation of distinct motives and accompanying material, in op. 3 and *Wozzeck* (Act I, scenes i, iii–v; Act II, scenes i–v; and Act III, scene i and the interlude). Melody and accompaniment textures are found in op. 4, nos. 2 and 3, op. 6, no. 1, and the tonal songs and marches in *Wozzeck*, Act I, scenes ii and iii and Act II, scenes i and iv. In a few pieces, op. 4, nos. 1 and 5, and op. 6, nos. 2 and 3, the texture consists of a simultaneous superimposition of many motives in dense textures; in op. 4, the relatively short motives are treated contrapuntally, whereas in op. 6, nos. 2 and 3, motives are longer and are subjected to developing variation (and are consequently difficult to categorize). *Wozzeck* also includes variation forms, some described as "inventions" by Berg, based on unusual motivic or unifying elements: (1) a series of three chords in Act I, scene ii; (2) the pitch-class B in Act III, scene ii; (3) rhythmic motives in Act III, scenes iii and v; and (4) a referential "chord" or pitch-class set in Act III, scene iv. The latter recalls Schoenberg's op. 16, no. 3, "Farben," although it is stricter in its focus on a referential form of a single pitch-class set.

One consistent motivic feature of Berg's atonal music, even where movements have little or no internal motivic repetition, is the appearance of the same motives or musical figures in different movements within a work. For instance, op. 2, no. 4 ends with a passage similar to music in op. 2, nos. 1 and 2, and the second movement of op. 3 develops motives and themes from the first movement. The five songs of op. 4 form an arch by the recurring material in songs 1 and 5 and the ABA form of song 3, and, despite their lack of internal repetition, even the op. 5 pieces share a motive between movements. The op. 6 pieces are unified by many intermovement motives and include anticipations of material from *Wozzeck*, where links between scenes and acts are established by leitmotivs and "leitsektions" of music.[45]

UNUSUAL MOTIVIC TRANSFORMATIONS

Unusual motivic transformations in Berg's atonal music, some of which foreshadow later twelve-tone developments, include combined retrograde and inversional forms, contour maintenance with changing cyclic intervalic content, systematic exploration of intervalic combinations, serial order, and verticalization of segments. Retrograde transformations tend to appear almost exclusively in formal palindromic returns in Berg's music, but in the first movement of op. 3 the bridge motive is varied by a combination of inversion and retrograde (ex. 3.6b). The motive appears initially as a melodic [014] <E–F–A♭> harmonized by trichords [015], [037], and [016] (with a fourth chord [015] harmonizing the return to F); on its repeat (m. 14), these three trichords are retrograded at T−1, with an accented passing tone C♯1 added in the middle voice. The melody is, however, not the expected T−1 retrograde of <G,E,E♭>; instead it is inverted around axis F/F♯ as <G–G♭–E♭>, still yielding an [014]. The {E♭,G♭} are part of a T0 3-cycle collection overlapping from the cadence of the preceding phrase. This remarkable combination of retrograde and inversion demonstrates Berg's continual process of variation at all levels.

The use of contour to establish and maintain the identity of motives is characteristic of all of Berg's music, but intervalic content is often also an identifying feature. In op. 6, no. 2 (ex. 3.26a), however, motive 6/2 is defined exclusively by

Example 3.26a. Contour motive 6/2 <1032> in op. 6, no. 2

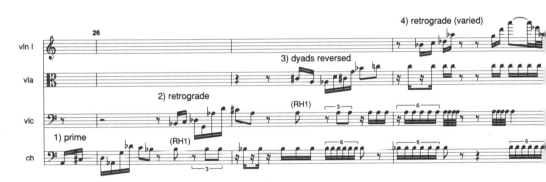

Example 3.26b. Canon on motive 4/a (with RH1), op. 4, no. 1, mm. 25–28

Example 3.26c. Systematic variation of motive 4/6, op. 4, no. 1

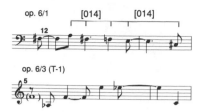

op. 6/1   [014]   [014]

op. 6/3 (T-1)

Example 3.26d. Motive 6/a from op. 6, no. 1, mm. 12–13 varied serially as motive 5 in op. 6, no. 3, mm. 5–6

its relative contour: <1032> (this notation uses numerals 0, 1, 2, . . . to indicate the relative registral position of notes; in <1032> the second note is lowest, the first note is next-lowest, the third note is highest, and the fourth note is next-highest).[46] Although, in the course of the movement, the second interval steadily increases in size, the relative contour profile remains.

In op. 4, no. 1 (ex. 3.8), the 5-cycle–based motive 4/4 is transformed successively in intervals and contour first to a whole-tone+ motive (m. 8), to motive 4/a (m. 9), and to the notes of motive 4/b {G,Ab,Bb,C♯,E} (m. 14). The gradual alterations to the contour allow a continual recognition of the motive as it is varied in cyclic content, and the transformation emphasizes the similarity in contour of motives 4/4 and 4/a and associates motive 4b with these two motives as well.

In op. 4, no. 1, motive 4/4 is set in a remarkable canon with different forms of itself related by serial order and contour (ex. 3.26b, mm. 25–28, contrabass, cello, viola, violin 1; the first two canonic statements are completed by an RH1).[47] The motive appears (1) in its original "prime" order <A–C♯–D–Ab–G–Db–C–Bb> (contrabass); (2) in retrograde order but with a prime contour (cello); (3) in prime order but with segmental dyads reversed and in inverted contour, <C♯–A–Ab–D–G–Bb–C>, except for the ascent from C♯4 to G4 (viola); and (4) in a varied, incomplete retrograde (violin 1). The third transformation, prime order with reversed dyads, foreshadows a property of the row of the *Lyric Suite*. In the latter, row IB is related to P5 by reversed segmental dyads; the structure of the row yields alternating sums from adjacent pitch-classes, and the two rows share sum 4 (fig. 3.15).[48] The intervalic structure

Figure 3.15. Shared sums in *Lyric Suite* row and motive 4/4 in op. 4, no. 1

Lyric Suite P5:	5 4 0 9 7 2 8 1 3 6 A B	IB:	B 0 4 7 9 2 8 3 1 A 6 5
dyad sums:	9 4 9 4 9 A 9 4 9 4 9	sums:	B 4 B 4 B A B 4 B 4 B
Motive 4/4:	9 1 2 8 7 1 0 A	varied:	1 9 8 2 1 7 A 0
dyad sums:	A 3 A 3 8 1 A	dyad sums:	A 5 A 3 8 5 A

Example 3.26e. Motives and vertically aligned variants in op. 3, second movement, mm. 5–6, 32–33, and op. 5, no. 1, mm. 1–2, 8–9. Berg 4 PIECES, OP. 5. Copyright 1924 by Universal Edition. Copyright renewed. All Rights Reserved. Used by permission of European American Music Distributors Corporation, sole U.S. and Canadian agent for Universal Edition A.G., Wien. Berg STRING QUARTET, OP. 3. Copyright 1925 by Universal Edition. Copyright renewed. All Rights Reserved. Used by permission of European American Music Distributors Corporation, sole U.S. and Canadian agent for Universal Edition A.G., Wien.

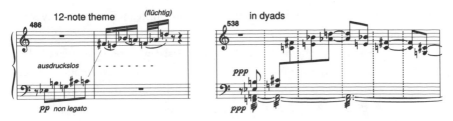

Example 3.26f. Twelve-note passacaglia theme and variation with vertical dyads, Wozzeck, Act I, mm. 486–87, 538. Berg WOZZECK, OP. 7. Full Score copyright 1926 by Universal Edition A.G., Vienna. English Translation copyright 1952 by Alfred A. Kalmus, London. Full Score copyright renewed. Pocket Score copyright 1955. Pocket Score copyright renewed. All Rights Reserved. Used by permission of European American Music Distributors Corporation, sole U.S. and Canadian agent for Universal Edition A.G., Wien.

of motive 4/4 contains a cyclic segment similar to the *Lyric Suite* row in its first five notes, consisting of alternate notes of 5 and 7 cycles, <A̱–C♯–Ḏ–A♭–G̱>, producing alternating sums 10 and 3. As with the two forms of the row, the varied version of the motive with dyads reversed retains the sum 10 dyads of the original.

Motive 4/6 in op. 4, no. 1 (ex. 3.26c, mm. 24–29) is varied systematically in a manner similar to that applied to motivic variants in Schoenberg's op. 22, as described by the composer in a radio talk on the songs.[49] The tetrachordal motive and its transformations constitute a systematic exploration of ordered intervals, 10, 3, and 1 in ascending and descending combinations (with two cases of interval 9). The contours consist of the original <3–2–1–0> and five variants, including the mirror contour <0–1–2–3>. In mm. 30–32, the motive is liquidated down to two notes before a final full inverted statement in m. 35. The motive forms are all whole-tone+ collections, [0124]s or [0236]s.

In a transformation in op. 6, a new motive is derived from an existing motive by transposition and a changed contour, with maintained rhythm. In op. 6, no. 3, motive 5 (ex. 3.26d, mm. 5–6, violin 1) derives from motive 6/a in op. 6, no. 1 (mm. 12–13, clarinet, horns) as a serial motive, transposed at T−1 and given a new contour but retaining almost the same rhythm. (The initial note F appears immediately preceding in the oboe in op. 6, no. 3).

In another transformation foreshadowing serial and twelve-tone procedures, horizontal motives appear in verticalized segments. In motivic transformations from the second movement of op. 3 and from op. 5, no. 1 (ex. 3.26e), motives are segmented and the segments superimposed vertically. In op. 3 a whole-tone+ based motive <C–A♭–D–E–F♯–G–C♯–F♯> from m. 5 (second movement) recurs segmented into verticalized <C–A♭> and <D–E–F♯> (mm. 30ff.); in op. 5, no. 1 the transformed initial clarinet figure <A♭–E♭–G–A–C–E> appears at the reprise in the piano at T−4, with the initial three notes <E−B−E♭> over the remaining <F−A♭−C> (m. 9).

In *Wozzeck*, Act I, scene iv, the twelve-note passacaglia theme is treated like a serial motive and even like a twelve-tone row in the vertical presentation of segments (ex. 3.26f).[50] The theme is grouped in (1) horizontal dyads (vars. 3, 4, and 8); (2) five vertical dyads against the other held vertical dyad (vars. 6, 7);[51] vertical trichords (var. 15); and (4) with a vertical tetrachord in the sixth to ninth notes (var. 8). In variation 7 (ex. 3.26f) the vertical dyads are set in a palindrome arch. In three variations, the theme is divided hocket-like between instruments (vars. 9 and 10 and beginning of var. 11) and combined with partial statements of the three chords from Act I, scene ii, as Wozzeck describes his previous hallucinations to the Doctor. In Act III, scene i, also a set of variations, another twelve-note motive also appears as vertical dyads and a trichord (var. 1, horns, Act III, mm. 14−16).

Finally, Berg devised a characteristic treatment of motives and figures that, like contrapuntal settings, provides variation without a loss of identity. Motives are often introduced by adding one note at a time, as in the piano coda figure of op. 5, no. 4 (mm. 17ff., ex. 3.16b), or dissolved by deleting one note at a time, in a type of liquidation, as in *Wozzeck*, Act I, scene i, mm. 80−83, flutes (ex. 3.27). This process of slow emergence, then decay, affects not only motives and figures but also larger forms, as in op. 6, no. 1, where the piece ascends from unpitched percussion through low to high registers, only to return in a retrograde motion back to the depths at its end.

Example 3.27. Motivic liquidation, *Wozzeck*, Act I, mm. 80–83. Berg WOZZECK, OP. 7. Full Score copyright 1926 by Universal Edition A.G., Vienna. English Translation copyright 1952 by Alfred A. Kalmus, London. Full Score copyright renewed. Pocket Score copyright 1955. Pocket Score copyright renewed. All Rights Reserved. Used by permission of European American Music Distributors Corporation, sole U.S. and Canadian agent for Universal Edition A.G., Wien.

FORMS WITH LEAST REPETITION

The songs op. 2, no. 4 and op. 4, no. 4 (both analyzed below) and the clarinet piece op. 5, no. 3 are Berg's most radical works with regard to form and motivic treatment. In each there is almost no internal formal or motivic repetition between sections, yet each contains links of the other movements of each work. Opus 5, no. 3 is in four distinct sections (mm. 1−4, 5−8, 9−13, and

14–18) defined by pitch material and gesture, rhythm and tempo. The only traditional motivic relationships to the surrounding movements involve the clarinet figure in mm. 5–7, a variant of a piano and clarinet motive in op. 5, no. 1 (mm. 2–5, ex. 3.15b), and the {C,E} interval 4s beginning the final section (mm. 14–15), recalling the {D,F♯} opening of op. 5, no. 2 (ex. 3.20). The other pieces in op. 5 have only brief restatements, in roughly three-part ABA' forms (fig. 3.16; the restatement in op. 5, no. 1 is somewhat more complex). Given Berg's formal tendencies, some writers have posited a four-movement organization in op. 5: a substantial opening movement, a slow movement with a pronounced rhythmic element, a soft scherzo-trio-scherzo third movement (mm. 1–8,

---

Figure 3.16. Forms in op. 5

Op. 5, no. 1	Op. 5, no. 2	Op. 5, no. 3	Op. 5, no. 4
A mm. 1–6	A mm. 1–4	mm. 1–4	A mm. 1–4
B mm. 7–9½	B mm. 5–7	5–8	B mm. 5–11
A'/Coda mm. 9½–12	A' mm. 8–9	9–13	A' mm. 11–12
		14–18	Coda mm. 13–20

9–13, 14–18), and a final weighty, slower movement of the same length (twelve bars in $\frac{4}{4}$) as the first, but with a lengthy, dramatic coda added.[52]

Opus 4, nos. 1 and 5 and op. 6, nos. 2 and 3 are characterized by the superimposition of multiple motives. Op. 4, no. 1 is a through-composed three-part form (mm. 1–19, 20–29, 29–38), with the treatment of motives defining four corresponding sections (dividing the second section into mm. 20–24 and 24–29). (The op. 4 motives are given in ex. 3.7, where motives 4/a–e occur in more than one song, motives 4/1–8 occur in one song only.) The first, third, and fourth sections in op. 4, no. 1 present, then dissolve, a group of motives; the second section contains no motives but is organized around a whole-tone wedge (ex. 3.10). The majority of motives (4/c and 4/1, 2, 3, 7, and 8) are treated contrapuntally, except for motive 4/b {G,A♭,B♭,C♯,E}, which is transposed and reordered as a pitch-class set, and the unusual transformations of motives 4/4 and 4/6 (see exx. 3.8 and 3.26c).

In the opening fifteen bars of op. 4, no. 1, motives 4/1–5, which combine initially into an aggregate, are each transposed cyclically (see fig. 3.5) and gradually liquidated, eventually coalescing on the notes of motive 4/b, {G,A♭, B♭,C♯,E} (m. 14), which then moves by interval 1 voice-leading to motive 4/c <F♯–A–B–D–F> (m. 15, ex. 3.7). In the third and fourth sections of the song the transformed motives are 4/4, 4/6, 4/7, 4/8, with motive 4/b in the voice (ex. 3.18) and motive 4/5 in the harmonium (ex. 3.19). Several motives are treated cyclically: motive 4/4 is transposed through a 3-cycle of transpositional levels P9–P0–P6–P3 (mm. 29–35, bassoon and english horn, violin 1, horn, cello, oboe, contrabassoon); the transpositional levels of motive 4/7 in mm. 25–27—P5, P6, P7, and P9 (mm. 25–27, horns)—are in the <+1, +1, +2> pattern of the end of the motive itself, and the motive is successively liquidated from 6–4–2–1 chords.

Opus 4, no. 5 is a variation form—a passacaglia with three motives 4/a, b, and c—consisting of a theme of ten bars and nine variations of five bars each.[53] Variations 6–8 restate elements of 1–3, creating a large two-part division of variations 1–5 and 6–9. The theme contains three superimposed motives, 4/a, b, and d (ex. 3.7, motive 4/a at T6 beginning on E), with motives 4/9, 4/c, and 4/e added in the variations. Of the three thematic motives, 4/a is used the least, appearing only in the theme and variations 4, 5, and 7; motive 4/d does not appear in variations 4, 8, and 9; and the most common motive, 4/b, appears in all but variation 7. Motives are mostly untransposed, except for 4/b, which appears at P7 and PA (sharing four-note 3-cycle subsets within its [01369]) and at multiple transpositional levels in variation 3; motive 4/e appears at P5 (mm. 11–12, oboe) and P4 (mm. 35–37, canon of strings, horn, and voice); and motive 4/d appears at P0 and P5 (the latter transposition of this wedge motive recalls the vocal wedge around F and the bass Fs in op. 4, no. 2, ex. 3.9). In the closing bars, motive 4c <F#–A–B–D–F> is stated in overlapping "waves" in the trombones and trumpets, truncated successively from six through two notes, with the final note of each statement "resolving" to a note from motive 4/b {G,Ab,Bb,C#,E}. The final bars present a simultaneous expansion and contraction of motive 4/b to its widest <E2–C#3–Bb3–Ab4–G5> and narrowest <G3–Ab3–Bb3–C#4–E4> (ex. 3.25) spans simultaneously.

Opus 6, nos. 2 and 3 are similarly characterized by superimposed motives; for instance, the unfolding of four motives simultaneously at the beginning of op. 6, no. 3 (ex. 3.31) recalls the opening of op. 4, no. 1. The motivic distribution in op. 6 is also similar to that in op. 4; several motives appear in different movements (motives 6/a–e, ex. 3.26d and 3.28 and fig. 3.17), whereas others appear only in one movement.[54] By comparison with op. 4, however, motives in op. 6 are longer and are fragmented, varied, and spun out in traditional ways. Motive 6/a (ex. 3.26d), based on [014]s, is varied as a serial motive in op. 6, no. 3, mm. 5–6, but returns in its original form in mm. 160–61 of the latter.[55] Motive 6/d (ex. 3.28b) has two forms: a descending 3-cycle+ melody harmonized by whole-tone+ and 3-cycle tetrachords, and the melody by itself, sometimes inverted, with an added [014] ending.[56] The op. 6 pieces also contain motives and other material that foreshadow events in *Wozzeck*, most notably the appearance in op. 6, no. 3 (mm. 79–83, low strings) of the "Hallucination" motive of Act I, scene

Example 3.28a. Motive 6/b in op. 6, no. 2, m. 37; motive 6/c in m. 38

Example 3.28b. Motive 6/d in op. 6, no. 2, mm. 5–7, inverted in op. 6, no. 3, mm. 6–8

ii (mm. 275–79) and the interval 1 ascent of a 5-cycle based chord near the end of op. 6, no. 3 (mm. 161–64) anticipating the drowning music of Act III, scene iv (mm. 285–314).[57]

Opus 6, no. 2, entitled *Reigen* ("Round Dance") and based on the waltz and the ländler, is comprised almost exclusively of motivic voices in contrapuntal combinations. The large formal groups are in a refrain binary structure AA'/ AA'/Coda, with three divisions of the A sections as a, b, and c (the latter omitted from the first A; see fig. 3.18).[58] Seven motives appear in op. 6, no. 2: motives 6/b, c, and d (ex. 3.28a–b), an extended melody beginning from the [014] of motive 6/e (ex. 3.28c), and three additional motives 6/1 (ex. 3.29), 6/2 (ex. 3.26a), and, near the end of the movement, a new motive 6/3 (mm. 98–110, 111–21). Motives are transposed, inverted, and varied intervalically but maintain relative contours; one unusual transformation is a variant of the melody of motive 6/c in retrograde in two places (mm. 59 and 67, flute), and one disguised relationship is the notes of motive 6/b <A–B♭–A–C♯–C–D– A♭–G> (ex. 3.28a) at T7 in the motive 6/e–based waltz melody in m. 20 <E–F–E–A♭–G–A/B–B♭–D♭> (ex. 3.30, bassoon and trumpet).[59] The texture is mostly in two to four parts, with the densest combination of superimposed motives in the developmental c section (mm. 83–97).

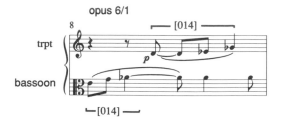

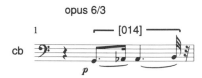

Example 3.28c. Motive 6/e in op. 6, no. 1, m. 8; op. 6, no. 2, mm. 3–5; and op. 6, no. 3, m. 1. Berg 3 ORCHESTERSTÜCKE OP. 6. Copyright 1923 by Universal Edition. Copyright renewed. All Rights Reserved. Used by permission of European American Music Distributors Corporation, sole U.S. and Canadian agent for Universal Edition.

In a passage similar to op. 4, no. 1, mm. 83–97 in op. 6, no. 2 divide into three sections (mm. 83–88, 89–93, 94–97) consisting of aligned motives 6/1, 6/2, 6/c, and 6/b and accompanying material repeated as ostinati in four or five distinct voices. Harmonically, op. 6, no. 2 is also similar to the outer sections of op. 4, no. 1, with its superimposed layers of motives, each with its own cyclic properties. The most notable harmonies are 5-cycle–based: the accompanying chords in mm. 57–58 are 5-cycle [027]s, leading to a 5-cycle sequence of [016]s (mm. 61–64, strings, initial notes <E–B–F♯–C♯–G♯> and to a twelve-note 5-cycle vertical chord, spanning F♯ to D♭ ascending (m. 66) with several following 5-cycle figures (mm. 67–68, horns, harp, and bassoons). As with other pieces by Berg, the notes D and G are focal: combined [037]s from {D,F,A}, {C♯,E,G♯}, and {E♭,G♭,B♭} (mm. 41–47, 68–70) create [013478]s—a hexachord found elsewhere in Berg's music—mm. 1–14 feature a 1-cycle bass moving from C♯2 to D3, then from D3 through <B♭2–G2–G♯2–A2–B♭2> by m. 20, to a pedal D1 in mm. 41–48, and, near the end of the movement, a prolonged bass A1–2 moves to D3 (mm. 105–10) and D2 descends to G1 via D♭2 in the closing bars (mm. 118–21).

Figure 3.17. Recurring motives between movements of op. 6

Op. 6, no. 1	Op. 6, no. 2	Op. 6, no. 3
motive 6/a		
mm. 12–13, clarinet, bass clarinet, horn		mm. 5–6, violin 1, flute
39, trombone		mm. 160–161, horn, trumpet, strings
motive 6/b		
m. 37, 39, flute, oboe, trumpet, violin	m. 6 viola	mm. 23–24, english horn, clarinet, mm. 33–34 violin
motive 6/c		
m. 38, flute, oboe, trumpet, violin	m. 7, viola	m. 93, horn, cello
motive 6/d		
mm. 44–46, celeste, violin	mm. 4–6, violin, celeste	mm. 6–8, violin
motive 6/e		
mm. 6–8, bassoon, trumpet	mm. 3–6, bassoon, trumpet	mm. 1ff., cello
chord {D,F,A,B}		
m. 42		m. 91

Figure 3.18. Form in op. 6, no. 2 (Rondo)

		a	b	c		correspondences		
A	mm.	1–13	14–19		mm.	1–19	=	42–54
						1–5	=	111–14
A'	waltz	20–23	24–31	32–41		20–23	=	94–97
						24–25	=	98–99 T1
						26–28	=	30–31 T1
						26–28	=	75–77 TA
A		42–55		56–72		58–59	=	66–67 T2
			73–82	83–97		83–88 = 89–93 = 94–97		
						88	=	120–21 T5
			dissolves					
A'	waltz	94–97	98–100	101–10				
Coda		111–21						

Example 3.29. Motives 6/c to 6/1, op. 6, no. 2, mm. 14–15. Berg 3 ORCHESTERSTÜCKE OP. 6. Copyright 1923 by Universal Edition. Copyright renewed. All Rights Reserved. Used by permission of European American Music Distributors Corporation, sole U.S. and Canadian agent for Universal Edition.

Example 3.30. Waltz theme with alternate notation for solo violin, op. 6, no. 2, mm. 20–24. Berg 3 ORCHESTERSTÜCKE OP. 6. Copyright 1923 by Universal Edition. Copyright renewed. All Rights Reserved. Used by permission of European American Music Distributors Corporation, sole U.S. and Canadian agent for Universal Edition.

Opus 6, no. 3 is in five large sections, roughly A (mm. 1–52), B (mm. 53–91), C (mm. 91–130), development (mm. 131–55), and coda/A' (mm. 155–74) (fig. 3.19). The sections correspond to Tempos I, II, and III, a mixture of the three, and Tempo I, respectively, with the closing four bars in Tempo III, although each section has, in addition, many shorter, differentiated subdivisions.[60] Within the first A section are five internal divisions: a, mm. 1–14; a', mm. 15–24; b, mm. 25–29; c, mm. 29–38; c', mm. 39–46; and a", mm. 46–52, based on varied returns of material. The first c section makes reference to the coming Tempo II in the midst of an accelerando. Within section B, a brief passage at Tempo I occurs with some fleeting references to the A material (mm. 77–83). Unlike in

Figure 3.19. Form in op. 6, no. 3

A	a mm.	1–14	maßiges Marschtempo (I)
	a	15–24	a tempo
	b	25–29	subito a tempo, aber schon etwas bewegter als Tempo I und im Tempo steigern
	c	29–38	accelerate through m. 33 Flottes Marschtempo (II) to rit.
	c'	39–46	viel langsamer, sehr zögernd
	a"	46–52	by m. 50 to Tempo I
B		53–61	Flottes Marschtempo (To II) [erroneously marked To III]
		62–66	grazioso
		66–77	a tempo
(A)		77–83	Wieder zuruckkehren zum beiläufigen Tempo I
		84–91	poco accel.
C		91–107	Allegro Energico (Tempo III)
		107–120	
		121–130	m. 126 Höhepunkt (three hammer blows)
dev.		131–135	Tempo I
		136–148	Tempo II (136–139 = 25–27)
		149–155	m. 149 Tempo III, rit. to
coda/A'		155–165	Pesante (Tempo I?) to m. 160 Sehr langsam
		166–170	slower (= 29–30, 40–44)
		171–174	Subito a tempo (III) (hammer stroke on last beat)

Berg's other pieces, the tempo recurrences in op. 6, no. 3 do not have clearly defined corresponding motivic recurrences. The texture in this movement is the densest in Berg's atonal music; almost all material is derived from the motives by developing variation and the harmonic language results almost entirely from the confluence of horizontal lines.[61] Four motives at the outset establish the military march atmosphere (ex. 3.31) with a martial dotted rhythm, trills, and triplet metric punctuations. The motive in the english horn is transposed cyclically at T_1 (P = $<5-6-7-8-9-A-B-o>$) in mm. 1–11, recalling the opening of op. 4, no. 1.

The climax in m. 126 of op. 6, no. 3 is marked by three "hammer strokes," which derive originally from motive 3 (mm. 3ff., english horn) and appear first in an extended passage with an overall crescendo (mm. 50–61) ending with a repeated statement in the entire orchestra (except violins, viola, cellos) in mm. 60–61. The three-attack rhythm returns in mm. 155–59 and the hammer stroke returns for the final attack in the movement. The three-attack rhythm climaxes in mm. 60–61 and 126, and the final hammer stroke divides the movement into three sections as a large-scale projection of the rhythm.

Example 3.31. March motives, op. 6, no. 3, mm. 1–4. Berg 3 ORCHESTERSTÜCKE OP. 6. Copyright 1923 by Universal Edition. Copyright renewed. All Rights Reserved. Used by permission of European American Music Distributors Corporation, sole U.S. and Canadian agent for Universal Edition.

Berg's op. 4, nos. 2 and 3 contain melody and accompaniment textures within clear formal repeating structures. In the AA' (mm. 1–7, 8–11) form of op. 4, no. 2 (dividing approximately at the Golden Section), the A' section is a partial retrograde of the A section in the accompanying parts in the oboe and brass against a condensed return of the opening vocal part in canon with the cellos. The contour graph (included in ex. 3.9) shows the overall shape of the piece at a glance. The ABA form of op. 4, no. 3 is defined by meter, tempo, orchestration, and tessitura (fig. 3.20). The only motive is 4/e (ex. 3.7, mm. 9–11, oboe), which is also embedded in the opening vocal line.[62] The A sections contain a dissolution and regeneration of a twelve-note chord (ex. 3.13); the B section is based on a wedge from the principal 3-cycle {G,Bb,Db,E}.

SONATA FORMS

Tonal sonata forms have the principal characteristic that themes presented in a key other than the tonic return transposed to (or closer to) the tonic; the dramatic reconciliation of the transposed material with the tonic key justifies the large formal repeat in the recapitulation.[63] In an atonal sonata form the tonal justification for a large repeat is no longer present. The choice of a sonata-form thematic framework is therefore somewhat arbitrary, but the form does provide a clear and traditional organization of the presentation and development of material, with built-in repetition. In his atonal sonata forms—movements 1 and 2 of op. 3, and Act II, scene i of *Wozzeck*—Berg adopted the traditional sonata-form thematic plan of contrasting theme groups in an exposition, a developmental section, and a varied restatement in recapitulation.[64] The distinction between sections arises from the general characteristic that, in the exposition and recapitulation, motives and themes are presented in clearly defined phrases

Figure 3.20. Form in op. 4, no. 3

A	B	A'
mm. 1–11	12–17	18–25
$\frac{3}{4}$	$\frac{3}{8}$	$\frac{3}{8}$
a tempo	slower	tempo (original quarter = 8th)
winds	winds strings percussion	strings percussion
full register	low register	high register

and sections that often group together by varied repetition, whereas formal divisions in the development are less well defined, with extended and expanded passages. Although this formal outline is generally descriptive of the presentation of themes and motives in Berg's sonata forms, however, in practice all three sections contain both expository and developmental sections.

The String Quartet op. 3 consists of two related movements.[65] The first movement is a sonata form with clear formal divisions; the second can be interpreted as a sonata form with rondo characteristics, perhaps as a sonata-rondo.[66] The second movement also has the function of a development section to the first, with motives from the latter developed, reshaped into new motives, and restated in their original forms.[67]

In the balanced formal proportions of the first movement (fig. 3.21), the exposition and recapitulation are about the same length, eighty (mm. 1–80) and eighty-three bars (mm. 105–87), respectively, with a shorter development of twenty-five bars (mm. 81–105). The two theme areas in the exposition are each forty bars in length (mm. 1–40, 41–80) and return in the recapitulation at thirty-three and forty-two bars, with a coda of eight bars. Both theme areas are ternary forms; the first area has the proportions 1:2:1 (9, 18, and 9 bars) with a four-bar transition, which returns as 2:2:1 (14, 13, and 7 bars) in the recapitulation. The first theme area contains a main theme (MT) (ex. 3.6a) and a bridge motive (BM) (ex. 3.6b), plus four subsidiary motives: a secondary main theme (SMT) derived from the MT (ex. 3.6a), a cyclic motive (CYC) from aligned ascending 5- and descending 1-cycles, a wedge motive (WGE), and a figure (BMf) derived from the upper voice [014] of the BM (ex. 3.5, m. 21 <A–E–F–Ab>). MT and SMT are both whole-tone+ collections, and MT is related to

Figure 3.21. Form in op. 3, first movement (underlining indicates alterations in the recapitulation compared with the exposition)

Exposition			No. of bars		Recapitulation		
			[80]	[83]			
1st area:			(40)	(33)			
A a MT/CYC/WGE		1–4½	9	14	105–107 MT/CYC	a	A
					108–110 CYCdev		
a' MT/WGE/SMT		4½–9			111–113 2ndth1/SMT	a'	
					114–119 CYC dev		
B b	BM/MT	10–13	18	13	119–121 BM/MT	b	B
b'	BM/BMf/MT	14–20			122–125 BM/MT	b'	
					126–131 NTH	c	
dev	BMf	20–27			132–138 BM/NTH/MT		(A')
transition: MT/BM		28–31	4				
A' a T = 7 MT/WGE		32–35½	9	7			
a'	SMT	35½–40					
2nd area:			(40)	(42)			
A	2ndth1	41–47	12	20			
a	2ndth2	48–49			149–150 2ndTH2	a	A
a'		50–52			151–152	a'	
					153–157 CYC dev/MT/SMT		
B 2ndth3/2ndth1/BM		52–57	10	7	138–148 2ndth1/2ndth3 dev		B
2ndth4/BM		58–60			158–159 2ndth4		
WGE		61			160–164 WGE		
A'	dev. 2ndth2	62–72	19	15	165–171 2ndTH2		A'
					171–176 MT/WGE/BM		
2ndth2		73–75					
2ndth1/2		75–76					
2ndth4		77–80			177–179 2ndth4		
				8	180–182 BM/MT (182 = 175–76)(A)		
					183–187 MT/CYC		Coda
Development			25				
2ndth4/BM		81–82	(58–60)				
2ndth4		83–89	(77–80)				
2ndth3/WGE/2ndth4		90–97					
2ndth1/4		98–101 (climax)					
2ndth1/ CYC/WGE		102–105 (retransition)					

BM and BMf by its internal [014]. The WGE motive comprises a number of wedge formations, which frequently spin off the ends of other motives.

Of the four distinct motives in the second area, three are closely related (ex. 3.6c−e): 2ndth2 is a subset of 2ndth1, with a change in contour of the opening two notes, and 2ndth4 is a slightly varied retrograde of 2ndth1. 2ndth2 appears in two forms, one a whole-tone+ collection, the other a 1 cycle+ collection, with a change from descending intervals 2s to descending interval 1s (ex. 3.6c). These two forms of 2ndth2 are reflected in the successive interval 1 and 2 wedge-like expansion of 2ndth3 <G−A♭−G−A−G> (ex. 3.6d). The new theme (Nth), which appears in the recapitulation, begins with an [014] in the same rhythm as BM and is similar in its end portion to the descent of 2ndth2 (ex. 3.6f).[68]

In the first movement of op. 3, motives are treated contrapuntally for the most part, retaining contour, rhythmic proportions, and intervals. For instance, the Nth (ex. 3.6f) is begun in the viola (m. 126), imitated in violin 2 (m. 127), and initiated and completed in violin 1 (m. 128), with subsequent entries in the viola and cello (mm. 130, 131). Only a few motives are varied in interval content (CYC, mm. 108−10, 114−18, 153−56, ex. 3.4; BM, mm. 52−60 and 81−82) or with added ornamental notes (BM, m. 50). Two motives receive unusual treatment: the [014] from BM is spun out as a small cell (mm. 10−27, ex. 3.5), and 2ndth2 appears in two intervalic forms, one with even interval 2s, the other with odd interval 1s (mm. 63−80, 160−61). Other motives have added wedge figures emerging from their final notes (MT, mm. 1−4; CYC, mm. 2−4; 2ndth1, mm. 102−4; and 2ndth3, mm. 148, 193). At the end of the development section, 2ndth1 appears in three-voice parallel cyclic-based trichords (mm. 98−101): 3-cycle [036], 5-cycle [027], 4-cycle [048], then motivically-related [016]s.

The second movement of op. 3 has a broad three-part ABA design that can be interpreted loosely as a sonata form, but in which the exposition and recapitulation are rondos, with short, highly fragmented subsections (fig. 3.22).[69] The large-scale divisions are again relatively balanced: a seventy-one-bar exposition (mm. 1−71), seventy-eight-bar development (mm. 72−150), and eighty-one-bar recapitulation (mm. 151−232). The second movement has seven themes, but MT, CYC, 2ndth1, 2ndth2, and the WGE figure from the first movement all reappear in the second (underlined in fig. 3.22). A remarkable cyclic transformation occurs between the main theme of the first movement and a recurring figure of the second movement that appears first in m. 25 and incorporates both whole-tone and 5-cycle aspects: if the main theme of the first movement, <F−E♭−D♭−A−C−B>, is transposed (T9) to <D−C−B♭−F♯−A−G♯> but a descending 5-cycle <F−C−G> substitutes for the descending 2-cycle <D−C−B♭> around the common middle note C, it yields the figure <F−C−G−F♯−A−G♯−(F♯−E)> (violin 1, m. 25).[70]

Figure 3. 22. Form in op. 3, no. 2 (underlines indicate material from the first movement)

Exposition			Recapitulation		
1st area		[72]	[81]		
A	Th1, Th2a	mm. 1–3	151–164	Th1 developed	A
B	Th2, WGE, pedal D	4–9	165–176	pedal D, MT/CYC	B
A'	Th1a, Th7 hint,	10–22			
B	pedal D, Th2, WGE	23–33			
2nd area					
C	Th3, Th4, Th5	34–41	177–178	Th3	C
			179–184	Th2, WGE developed	B
A"	Th2a, Th1	42–49	185–189	Th2a	A"
D	2ndth2	50–53			
			190–194	Th4 developed	C
			194–199	Th5, Th2a	A/C
E	Th6	54–60	200–208	Th6, Th5	E/C
A	Th1	61–63			
B	pedal D, WGE	64–72	209–217	Th2, WGE developed	B
			Coda		
			217–222	Th2, Th3,	B/C
			223–225	Th1, WGE	A
			226	Th3	C
			227–229	MT	B
			230–232	pedal D	B'
Development			[79]		
	pedal G–D–A, 2ndth2		72–78		
	pedal E, Th5, 2ndth2		78–88		
	Th1a, Th3		88–111		
	Th4 to 2ndth1, Th2/6 varied		111–118		
	Th7, liquidation, Th5 inverted		119–146		
	Th5 inverted, pedal E♭, ADGC				
	5 cycle		146–151		

In atonal sonata forms, the relationship between exposition and recapitulation has to be reconsidered, given that the recapitulation no longer has a tonal motivation. In the recapitulation of the first movement of op. 3, most of the first- and second-area motives return at pitch, and the only passage substantially altered in the recapitulation is the development of 2ndth3 in mm. 138–48 (fig. 3.21). The latter motive appears only briefly in the exposition (mm. 52–57) and the development (mm. 90–94), and thus the recapitulation is motivated to give it a fuller presentation. Its presentation is highlighted by the reordering of materials in the second key area: the exposition's initial mm. 41–47 are omitted from the recapitulation, with mm. 138–48 appearing instead, though these latter bars restate mm. 52–57 from the exposition.

A similar situation occurs with the CYC motive, presented briefly in the exposition (mm. 1–5) and at the end of the development (mm. 102–5), then developed at the beginning and within the recapitulation (mm. 106–10, 114–18, 153–56). The recapitulation is also differentiated by a new theme (mm. 126–36, ex. 3.6f), which substitutes for the bridge motive, and by motives crossing area boundaries in the recapitulation: 2ndth1 appears briefly in the first area (mm. 111–13), and first-area motives recur three times in the second area (mm. 153–57, 171–76, and coda, mm. 180–87, changes to recapitulation material underscored in fig. 3.21). The development section is similarly motivated by motivic factors; it is comprised mainly of 2ndth4 (mm. 81–89, 95–98), which appears only briefly in the exposition (mm. 58–60, 77–79) and the recapitulation (mm. 177–79). A measure of continuity over the formal divide between development and recapitulation is created by the gradual emergence of the latter's opening CYC motive in the end of the development (mm. 102–5, cello).

The second movement of op. 3 is similar to the first in its treatment of the development and recapitulation sections (fig. 3.22). Themes briefly stated in the exposition are expanded upon in the development and the recapitulation (Th4, presented in mm. 37–38, developed in mm. 111–18 and 190–99; Th5, presented in mm. 39–40, developed in mm. 78–88 and 194–201), and a new theme appears in the development (Th7, mm. 119–46) with only a brief antecedent in the exposition (mm. 13–15, violin 2). The second movement also contains developments of motives from the first movement (2ndth2, mm. 50–53, 72–88; 2ndth1, mm. 111–18), and, in the recapitulation, motives from the first movement substitute for second-movement motives (MT and CYC for Th2, mm. 165–76), linking the two movements.[71] The pedal D that concludes the movement recalls the emphasis on this pitch-class throughout, and, with the concluding bass note G of the first movement, continues the emphasis on these two notes that pervades Berg's entire oeuvre.

WOZZECK, ACT II, SCENE I

The sonata form in *Wozzeck*, Act II, scene i is notable for the links between the dramatic action and the form (fig. 3.23).[72] Each of the four themes—first, transition, second, and closing—is a leitmotiv in the opera: the first theme is the "Earrings" motive (whole-tone+), the transition theme the "Child Rebuffed"

Figure 3.23. Form in *Wozzeck*, Act II, scene i

Exposition		Reprise	Recapitulation
introduction	mm. 1–6		
first theme			
antecedent	7–15	60–70	128–136
consequent	16–28	71–80	137–149
transition	29–42	81–89	
second theme	43–53	90–93	150–161
closing theme	53–59	93–96	162–166
Development	mm. 97–127:	Climax mm. 115–116	

motive (3-cycle+ [0147]), the second theme Marie's "Cradle Song" motive (5-cycle based, ex. 3.2b), and the closing theme a Wozzeck motive (a purely whole-tone version of the "Anguish" motive. The return of musical material in the sonata is motivated by recurring text and action on stage, except for the recapitulation, in which the curtain descends at m. 140 and the remaining first theme consequent, second, and closing themes (the transition is omitted) recur, finishing the musical sonata form as an interlude.

The harmonies of the sonata form stem from the two cadential chords ending the previous Act I, reiterated at the beginning of Act II, scene i (ex. 3.1f). The first chord is a whole-tone+ collection <G–D–A–B–F–A–C♯> [013579] associated with Wozzeck, the second a 5-cycle–based collection <G–D–A–D♯–F♯–B> [013589] associated with Marie. The Wozzeck chord contains whole-tone+ subsets {D,F,A,C♯} [0148] and {D,B,F,A,C♯} [02458], both with subset {F,A,C♯} [048]. The Marie chord contains [0147] {D,A,D♯,F♯}, a 3-cycle+ chord that combines the Mother leitmotiv [014] (also a subset of [0148]) with an interval-class 5 and 5-cycle–based [0158] {F♯,G,B,D}. The [0147], which also appears as {A,C,D♯,E} in the introduction, is associated with the child in Act II, scene i and may be regarded as a cross between Marie's [014] mother motive and her characteristic interval-class 5 from the cradle motive (theme 2 in the sonata) and Wozzeck's even intervals. The cyclic treatment of the child's motive, with 5-cycle+ transpositional levels (mm. 29–34 <T5–T5–T1>), confirms the relationship to Marie. These tetrachords associated with the three characters group into pentachords [02458] and [01478] and Z-related hexachords [012569] and [013478] throughout—recalling the combination of cyclic and pitch-class set relationships found in Opus 5 where the same hexachords appear—and in the course of the scene all materials are transposed to contain two or three notes of the referential [048] {F,A,C♯} from the Wozzeck chord.[73]

The climax of the development section is signaled by new musical material (mm. 114–127), which musically and dramatically refers outside the scene to the overall tragedy, represented by the "Wir arme Leut" leitmotiv in one of its three pivotal statements in the opera (the others are in Act I, scene i [ex. 3.1b] and in the interlude in Act III, mm. 361–65). As Wozzeck reflects on the bleak future in store for his child, he sings the whole-tone+ "Wir arme Leut" <F–D♭–F♯–A–B> motive accompanied by a twelve-note aggregate of three 3-cycle [0369] chords (at T2 from the parallel statement at the climax of Act I, scene i [ex. 3.1b]), which builds to a climax that is followed by the sudden reduction in pitch, register, orchestration, and dynamics leading to the famous C-major triad section (mm. 116–27). This poignant, simple triad sounds as Wozzeck gives money to Marie for herself and the child. Musically the triad is a subset of both [0148] and [0147] and can be interpreted as combining an even interval 4 from Wozzeck, an interval-class 5 from Marie, and an interval 3 from the child. The added notes in Wozzeck's vocal line, an interval 1–based group {B♭,B,A, A♭,G,F♯}, combine with the C-major [037] to create [0147], [0148], and other tetrachords found throughout the scene. Dramatically, the distinctive string sound—violin 2 on the lower C and violas divided on the {E,G} all muted—creates a halo around Wozzeck as he performs his selfless task.

WOZZECK: FORMS AND LEITMOTIVS

The opera *Wozzeck* is in three acts, with five scenes per act; a formal chart is given in figure 3.24. Despite Berg's assertion in his lecture of an overall three-act ABA design, the form is not analogous to the ABA' in *Lulu*, where the third act is, to a great extent, a recapitulation of music from the first. Significant repetitions of passages of music in *Wozzeck*, Perle's "Leitsektions," show a closer connection between Acts I and II; correspondences of leitmotivs, character appearances, and shorter passages associated with characters are evenly distributed through the opera.[74] The Act III interlude is a development section of many of the leitmotivs and motivic figures in the opera, except for those associated with Marie; Marie's leitmotivs appear together at the moment of her death in Act III, scene ii, as if her life passes quickly before her eyes (mm. 103–8).

Leitmotivs in *Wozzeck* have distinct dramatic associations and harmonic identities and are identified not only by traditional maintenance of contour and relative rhythmic proportions, but even by referential pitch-class or pitch level. In general, Wozzeck's leitmotivs are whole-tone+ collections (ex. 3.1) whereas Marie's are 5-cycle–based collections (ex. 3.2); as Perle has noted, many referential levels of leitmotivs contain the fateful notes F and B, associated with Wozzeck and Marie, respectively.

Figure 3.24. Formal chart of Wozzeck

Wozzeck: Dramatic and musical structure

Drama		Music
Act I		
Exposition		*Five character pieces*
Wozzeck in relation to his environment		
Wozzeck and the Captain	scene 1	Suite
Wozzeck and Andres	scene 2	Rhapsody
Wozzeck and Marie	scene 3	Military March and Lullaby
Wozzeck and the Doctor	scene 4	Passacaglia
Marie and the Drum Major	scene 5	Andante affettuoso (quasi Rondo)
Act II		
Dramatic Development		*Symphony in Five Movements*
Marie and her child, later Wozzeck	scene 1	Sonata Movement
The Captain and the Doctor, later Wozzeck	scene 2	Fantasia and Fugue
Marie and Wozzeck	scene 3	Largo
Garden of a tavern	scene 4	Scherzo
Guard room in the barracks	scene 5	Rondo con introduzione
Act III		
Catastrophe and Epilogue		*Six Inventions*
Marie and her child	scene 1	Invention on a Theme
Marie and Wozzeck	scene 2	Invention on a Note
A low bar	scene 3	Invention on a Rhythm
Death of Wozzeck	scene 4	Invention on a Hexachord
Orchestral interlude		Invention on a key
Children playing	scene 5	Invention on a regular quaver movement

VARIATION FORMS

Act I, scene iv and Act III, scene i of *Wozzeck* are both variations on themes, and both include a twelve-note motive and numbers of bars, beats, and tempos based on sevens and threes. In Act I, scene iv, the twelve-tone passacaglia theme, <E♭ – B – G – C♯/C – F♯ – E – B♭ – A/F – A♭ – D>, features overlapping C♯/C whole-tone collections with a closing 3-cycle collection, and it is treated like a serial motive, arranged with verticalized segments (ex. 3.26f). In variation 21 the theme is set in massive chords, with a bass descending interval 1, from D to E♭, against the theme's succession from E♭ to D. The first and eighth to eleventh chords are whole-tone+ collections and the final chord is [01469], a sonority familiar in Berg's music from the op. 2 songs. In the strict cyclic manipulations of a whole-tone+ motive in the scene, <F♯–E–D–C–F>, most notably an arrangement in a horizontal overlapping T−1 sequence and vertical imitation in successive T4s to create vertical 5-cycle chords (mm. 512ff. and 620ff.), Berg may be parodying his own techniques, as the cyclic manipulation from m. 620 accompanies the Doctor's immortal cry, set to the whole-tone+ motive extended and transposed to <D♯–C♯–B–A–G–C>, "Oh meine Theorie!"

Act III, scene i is a theme with seven variations, each seven bars or beats in length, followed by a double fugue of twenty-one bars (3×7) with a first subject of seven different notes (fig. 3.25).[75] The main chord {D,F♯,A,G,B♭,E♭} [013478] of the scene is familiar from the Z-related hexachords [013478] and [012569] in Act II, scene i (and from the earlier op. 5 pieces). Characteristically, the chord is presented in the context of a G focus, segmented into triadic {D,F♯,A} and {E♭,G,B♭}; in this "tonal" appearance of V- and ♭VI-chords it recalls the tonal ländler in Act II, scene iv (mm. 421–24) and the musical collision by the drunken stage band as several members careen off into ♭VI of G at a half cadence. The four motives in Act III, scene i (initially motive 1 in mm. 3–6, motives 2–4 in mm. 7–9, motive 2 low strings, motive 4 violins, and motive 3 trumpet to clarinet) in the variations are fashioned into two fugue subjects (initially mm. 52–57 and 57–62). The theme and variations each divide into two sections, the first with only motive 1 and Marie's *Sprechstimme* reading of

Figure 3.25. Form in *Wozzeck*, Act III, scene i

	motive 1 / 2, 3, 4		
Theme:	mm. 3–6/7–9	7 bars	$\frac{4}{4}$, quarter note = 56
Var. I:	mm. 10–13/14–16	7 bars	
Var. II:	mm. 17/18	7 beats	
Var. III:	mm. 19–22/23–25	7 bars	$\frac{3}{8}$, eighth note = 112
Var. IV:	mm. 26–27/28–32	7 bars	
Var. V:	mm. 33–35/36–39	7 bars	$\frac{4}{4}$, quarter note = 56
Var. VI:	mm. 40–41/42–44	14 beats	$\frac{4}{4}$ $\frac{2}{4}$
Var. VII:	mm. 45–46/47–51	7 bars	$\frac{1}{4}$
Fugue:			
1st subject exposition	mm. 52–57	P7, P3, P7, PA, P2 = motive 1	$\frac{4}{4}$, quarter note = 56
2nd subject exposition	mm. 58–62		quarter note = 49
both	mm. 62 (last beat)–72		

the Bible, the second with combined motives 2, 3, and 4 and Marie's singing prayers.[76] The motives are subjected to contrapuntal imitation, transposition, and some variance in interval content, but they are also treated as serial motives, altered in contour and rhythm. The twelve-note motive 2 appears in mostly vertical dyads in variation 1 <A♭/B–G–B♭/C♯–C/E♭–A/E–D/F–G♭> [horns], recalling similar vertical dyads in the twelve-note passacaglia theme of Act I, scene iv [ex. 3.26f]), and all the motives are transposed over the course of the variations in mostly descending interval 1 cycles. The fugue subjects maintain their traditional contour and rhythm but are transposed and subject 1 is inverted.

The first fugue subject has a five-part exposition (mm. 52–57) beginning on the notes of the referential harmony, <G–E♭–G–B♭–D>, with notes {G, E♭, F♯, B♭} marking the initial notes of accompanying gestures. It also accompanies the exposition of subject 2. In the closing stretto, which steadily increases in density, 5-cycle and whole-tone+ harmonies are built up by parallel entrances: subject 1 in parallel whole-tone [026]s (m. 63, clarinets, trumpet, trombones), 3-cycle+ [0147]s (m. 64, oboes, clarinets), and whole-tone [0246]s (m. 66, contrabass, cello, viola, horns, trombones, tuba, bassoons, bass clarinet), and subject 2 in parallel 5-cycle–based [0158]s (m. 65, flute, clarinets, adding violins in m. 67), leading to a dissolution in all voices. In addition to their cyclic identities, the harmonies [0158] and [0147] are subsets of the main harmony [013478] {D,F♯,A,G,B♭,E♭}, recalling the similar relationship of hexachords to tetrachordal subsets in Act II, scene i and the op. 5 clarinet pieces.

RONDO FORMS

The fifth scenes of Acts I and II, which share several musical passages, were both described by Berg in his lecture as rondos. The former scene is, however, more through-composed than in rondo form; the only refrain element is the "Drum Major" motive (ex. 3.2d) appearing in mm. 666–68, 676, 694–98, and 714–15.[77] The interval 5 of this motive is the basis of the most easily recognizable passage occurring in both scenes: the canonic "Fight" music (Act I, scene v, mm. 693–98) accompanying the struggle between first the Drum Major and Marie, then the Drum Major and Wozzeck (Act II, scene v, mm. 787–95). In Act II, scene v, after the introduction (mm. 737–60), the sections of the rondo are separated by occurrences of the "Drum Major" motive as in Act I, scene v, but the scene also has a clear rondo theme (mm. 761–67, 785–88, 805–14; see ex. 3.32).

The three pentachords with which Act II, scene v begins, [01348], [01367], and whole-tone+ [02348] (ex. 3.33), are at T6 from their original levels in Act I, scene ii and return at another T6 (mm. 756–58), thus their original (T0) level.

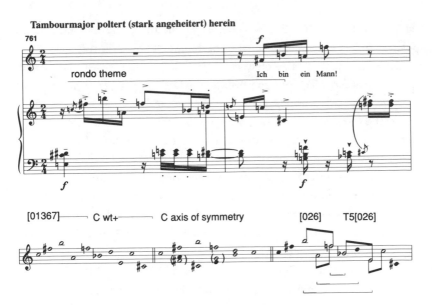

Example 3.32. Rondo theme, *Wozzeck*, Act II, scene v, mm. 761–62, with analysis showing cyclic segments and symmetries. Berg WOZZECK, OP. 7. Full Score copyright 1926 by Universal Edition A.G., Vienna. English Translation copyright 1952 by Alfred A. Kalmus, London. Full Score copyright renewed. Pocket Score copyright 1955. Pocket Score copyright renewed. All Rights Reserved. Used by permission of European American Music Distributors Corporation, sole U.S. and Canadian agent for Universal Edition A.G., Wien.

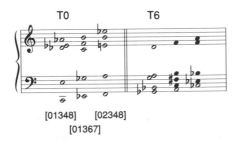

Example 3.33. Three chords at T0 and T6 (common tones indicated by filled-in noteheads), from *Wozzeck*, Act I, scene ii and Act II, scene v

Since the second and third chords at T0 contain internal {F,B,F♯/G♭,C} [0167] and {A,F,E♭,B/C♭} [0268], respectively, transposition by 6 retains four invariant notes in each. The first pentachord contains no interval 6s and thus no common tones; at T6 it yields the three notes {G,B♭,D} omitted from the T0 series. The first chord does contain, however, two internal interval-class 3s, {D♭,E} and {E♭,C}, which each complete a [0369] when transposed at T6, {G,B♭} and {A,G♭}. Finally, the bass interval 5 outlining the three chords combines with itself at T6 into [0167] <C–F–G♭–C♭>. Thus, the three chords and their T6 transposition reflect Berg's characteristic combining of the three multicyclic sets [0167], [0268], and [0369]. Also characteristic is the cyclic expansion of voice-leading intervals (in the T0 configuration on the left of ex. 3.33): from intervals 1, 2, and 3 between corresponding notes of the first and second chords, to intervals 2, 3, 4, and 6 from those of the second to the third.

The first five notes of the rondo theme of Act II, scene v (ex. 3.32) are the same pitch-classes as the second of the three chords at T6, <C–F♯–B–A–F> [01367] (ex. 3.33), and the remainder is a whole-tone+ collection <B♭–D–E–C–C♯>. The theme shows a remarkable approach to symmetry and cyclic content. The notes are roughly symmetrical around C5 (sum 0)—the only repeated note—with the exception of A4 and E4, which displace F♯4 and G4, respectively (given in filled-in noteheads in ex. 3.32). However, A4 and E4 are themselves symmetrical around G4/F♯4, and the axes of F♯5/E4 and F5/A4 are B4 and C♯5, symmetrical around C5 (and similarly the axes of F5/E4 and F♯5/A4 are B♭4/B4 and C♯5/D5, themselves symmetrical around C5.[78] From another viewpoint, if the notes above and below C5 are grouped as {F♯,B,F,D} and {A,C♯,E,B♭}, both are 3-cycle+ [0147]s, related at sum 3 with an axis of C♯5/D5 disturbed only by the octave-displaced setting of C♯4; thus, it follows that if the notes F♯4 and G4 were substituted for E4 and A4, the resulting note groups {F♯,B,F,D} and {F♯,C♯,G,B♭} would still both be [0147]s, related at sum 0 and almost entirely symmetrical around C5.

If the rondo theme is analyzed using the coordination of intervalic and durational distance set out by Lewin (ex. 3.32, bottom stave, right),[79] descending interval 6s over three-note spans occur as B–F and B♭–E, which combine into [0167], a subset of the [01367] first pentachord, and ascending interval 8s over two-note spans occur as A–F and E–C [0158]. These groupings and the retrograde T5 relationship between [026] <B–A–F> and T5 [026] <B♭–D–E> support the harmonic division [01367]/[02346] between notes <F–B♭> and reflect the origin of the second whole-tone+ collection in the final three-note [026] of the initial [01367]. It is also noteworthy that the recurring interval 8s are initiated by A and E, the notes outside the registral symmetry around C in the theme.

Tonal and Folk Settings in Wozzeck

Throughout Berg's *Wozzeck*, sections of tonal forms appear, characterized by periodic phrases and regular meters.[80] Most of the forms are repeating structures, often of the ABA variety. In his lecture on *Wozzeck* (1929), Berg commented on the tonal folksong sections: "I believe I have succeeded in composing all sections requiring the atmosphere of *Volkstümlichkeit* in a primitive manner which applies equally to the style of atonality. That particular manner favors asymmetrical arrangement of periods and sections, it utilizes harmonies in thirds and especially in fourths and a type of melody in which whole-tone scales and perfect fourths play an integral part. . . . Also the so-called polytonality may be counted among the devices of a more primitive brand of harmony. We find a popular element in them in the Military March (with its intentionally wrong basses) and in Marie's Lullably (with its harmonies in fourths)."

The harmonies in thirds, fourths, and whole-tone collections described by Berg are actually simplified versions of his own cyclic materials, and they allow, for the most part, folksongs and tonal passages to fit comfortably into the existing harmonic framework. It is the simplified harmony, tonal allusions and even tonal progressions, and the consistently metrical grouping of small-scale repeating formal structures that distinguishes the folk sections.

Act I, scene ii is characterized by contrasting material alternately representing Wozzeck then Andres: Wozzeck is accompanied by variations on three chords (To, ex. 3.33) in $\frac{3}{4}$, and his vocal line is in *Sprechstimme* (except mm. 237–39 and 240–41); Andres sings three strophes of a folksong in C major in $\frac{6}{8}$ (mm. 213–22, 249–56, and 259–69) beginning with the whole-tone+ folksong motive <D–G–A–B–A–C♯–D♯>, each strophe more elaborate but also with the regularity of meter and harmony increasingly broken down by Wozzeck's interjections, which inject the three chord harmonies into the C-major context.[81] The two characters are related by the C orientation of the three chords, but they differ in the clash between tonal chords and the intervalic qualities of the three chords, particularly the whole-tone+ third chord.[82]

Act I, scene iii contrasts tonal forms, a march accompanying the Drum Major on parade (mm. 326–63) and a folksong accompanying Marie as she sings to her child (mm. 363–427), with an irregular atonal section accompanying Wozzeck in his visit to Marie and the child (mm. 427–84). The scene is, unlike others, a concatenation of the three sections of music.[83] The military march is characteristically metrical, but the harmony is polytonal: the melody is mainly in C major/minor, but the accompaniment revolves around the bass notes C/C♯/D/E♭/E, eventually cadencing on C in m. 345. The trio (mm. 346–61), set in overlapping five-bar phrases, begins on "♭VI" (A♭) but continues in a 7-cycle, <A♭–E♭–B♭>, to lead into the transition and then back to a C/C♯ focus for the return of the march.

The lullaby in Act I, scene iii is one of three folksongs associated with Marie; the other two are the second-theme song in the sonata movement in Act I, scene i and Marie's song of repentance in Act III, scene i.[84] The lullaby, which begins with the cradle song motive (ex. 3.2b), is in two large strophes with an incomplete third instrumental strophe (fig. 3.26), each section constituting a three-part

Figure 3.26. Cradle song in *Wozzeck*, Act I, scene iii, and Act II, scene i, second theme

Strophes			a	a'	b	
I:		A	mm. 372–73	374–75	376–79	
		B	380–81	382–83	384–87	
II:		A'	388–89	390–91	392–95	
		B'	396–97	398–99	400–3	
III:		A"	403–4	405–6		instrumental
			407–9	410–11		instrumental
II/i		Folk song (second theme)				
		A	43–44	45–46	47–53	(extended)
		A'	90–92			diminution, irregular
		A"	150–61			diminution, irregular

aa'b Bar form. The cradle song melodic and harmonic material appears in Act II, scene i as the second theme of the sonata form but is now changed to reflect Marie's agitated state: the song is about the "bogeyman" to scare the child, and its successively more irregular phrasing reflects Marie's increasing vexation with the child and her dread of the coming confrontation with Wozzeck (fig. 3.26). In Act III, scene i, Marie rebukes the child (variation 3, mm. 19–25) to music recalling the transition section of the sonata form in Act II, scene I, but she relents (end of variation 4, mm. 26–32), and sings a folksong about a poor child with no father and mother—foreshadowing her own and Wozzeck's deaths and the child's fate. The song, in the final three measures of variation 4 (mm. 30–32), all of variation 5 (mm. 33–39), and the first two measures of variation 6 (mm. 40–41), is in F minor, with the harmonic rhythm regular and metrical. The concluding 5-cycle in the bass, <G–C–F>, leads back into the "atonal" context. The last suggestion of Marie's folksong material occurs in Act III, scene iii, when Wozzeck is at the inn, where his boisterous bar song is set to the "Cradle" motive (ex. 3.2b), betraying his thoughts of the dead Marie (mm. 145ff.).

Act II, scene ii is an invention or fantasia (mm. 171–285) and fugue (mm. 286–362) on three subjects associated with the Captain, the Doctor, and Wozzeck; throughout the scene, the characters' leitmotivs sound only when they speak or sing, and so the invention and fugal form reflects the drama virtually line for line.[85] In an opening scene of pure camp comedy with *commedia dell'arte* overtones,[86] the Doctor terrifies the Captain with a grotesque prognosis of the latter's fate, set ironically to a lilting waltz with following mock funeral march. In the combination of the Captain's and the Doctor's motives at the outset (ex. 3.34), the former begins with a 5-cycle–based collection <F♯–G♯–C♯–B>,

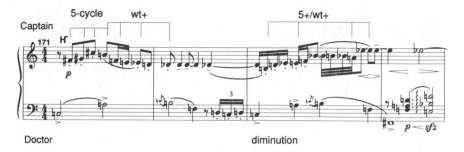

Example 3.34. "Captain" and "Doctor" leitmotivs, *Wozzeck*, Act II, scene ii, mm. 171–74. Berg WOZZECK, OP. 7. Full Score copyright 1926 by Universal Edition A.G., Vienna. English Translation copyright 1952 by Alfred A. Kalmus, London. Full Score copyright renewed. Pocket Score copyright 1955. Pocket Score copyright renewed. All Rights Reserved. Used by permission of European American Music Distributors Corporation, sole U.S. and Canadian agent for Universal Edition A.G., Wien.

then pivots on B to a whole-tone–based <B–F–E♭–D♭> descent (with 1-cycle–based passing notes). The Doctor's motive, <C–A–C–B–F–D>, is a reordered subset at T6 of the Captain's motive—the T6 relationship is reflected by the opening notes of the two motives, C and F♯—and it maintains the dyad {F,B}, expressed as a descending B–F in both. Given the evidence that this scene was the first written, it is remarkable how the fundamental elements of the opera pervade the music of these two subordinate characters.

The Waltz in Act II, scene ii originates in Act I, scene iv, where a brief waltz figure in variations 13 and 18 accompanies the Doctor's diagnosis of Wozzeck. The introduction sets the G focus and two-bar hypermeasures (mm. 202–7), but when the waltz theme enters (mm. 208–15) it has an extended internal three-bar group (mm. 210–12), breaking up the periodic regularity in the characteristic melodic pattern analogously to the added dissonances in Berg's "cycle+" pitch collections. The cadence on F minor at the end of an interlude (mm. 226–31), in the overall context of G, foreshadows the same tonal relationships in Act III, scene i.

The periodic funeral march following the waltz, with which the Captain mourns his untimely demise (ex. 3.35a), foreshadows Wozzeck's death, with its bass focus on A and whole-tone+ upper voice, <B–A–G–F–E♭–D>. The march begins a path that goes through the harmonic setting of Wozzeck's anguish motive in the invention and fugue sections (mm. 273–74, 276–77, 281–82, 313–17), which returns as the climax of the scene (mm. 341–42, ex. 3.35b), to the climax of the opera (Act III, mm. 364–68, ex. 3.35c). Harmonically, the climax of Act II, scene ii (mm. 341–44, ex. 3.35b) occurs over a D chord after a prolonged G/A dyad in the bass (mm. 334–41), with the Wozzeck

Example 3.35a. Funeral march, *Wozzeck*, Act II, scene ii, mm. 262–65

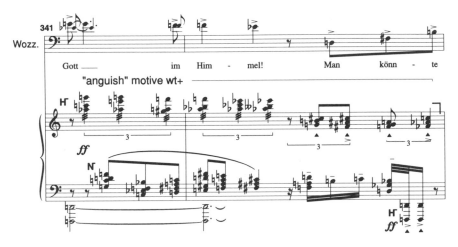

Example 3.35b. Climax setting of "Anguish" leitmotiv, *Wozzeck*, Act II, scene ii, mm. 341–42

"Anguish" motive as the upper voice <G–F–E♭–C♯–A–C>. The climax of the opera has the same motive, harmonized in tetrachords similar to the funeral march chords, but with uniform [0237]s in the context of the local implied key of D minor (Act III, m. 365, ex. 3.35c). Thus, Act II, scene ii, the first written, anticipates the climax of the entire opera.[87]

The three-part interlude in Act III, an "invention on a tonality," has outer tonal sections and an inner developmental section of motives from throughout the opera related to Wozzeck (Act III, mm. 320–45, 346–64, 365–70).[88] The tonal sections are strongly metered in two-bar hypermeasures. The key is D minor; the opening phrase (ex. 3.1e) prolongs D with tonal elements but also sets D in a whole-tone context. The passage continues with a modulation to F, and D♭ as ♭VI of F. The middle section is underlaid with directed elements: an interval 1 descent from A to C♯ (mm. 343–46), pedal notes C♯ to G (mm.

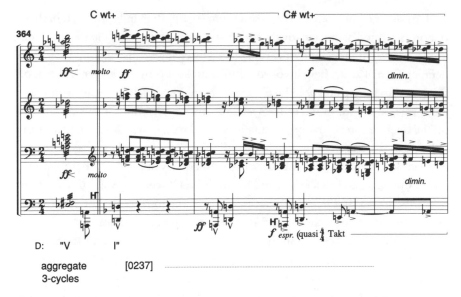

Example 3.35c. "Aggregate" dominant leading to climax setting of "Anguish" leitmotiv, *Wozzeck*, Act III interlude, mm. 364–68. Berg WOZZECK, OP. 7. Full Score copyright 1926 by Universal Edition A.G., Vienna. English Translation copyright 1952 by Alfred A. Kalmus, London. Full Score copyright renewed. Pocket Score copyright 1955. Pocket Score copyright renewed. All Rights Reserved. Used by permission of European American Music Distributors Corporation, sole U.S. and Canadian agent for Universal Edition A.G., Wien.

346–56), and finally E♭ as ♭II of D (mm. 362–64), leading to V–I in D, with the aggregate V chord made of three superimposed 3-cycles (m. 364, ex. 3.35c) for the return of D minor harmonizing the climactic "anguish" motive statement (mm. 365 ff.). In the final section, the theme is set in duple groupings against the triple meter (indicated by Berg as *quasi 4/4 Takt*, ex. 3.35c), as a continuing reflection of Wozzeck's fate. This climactic statement of the Wozzeck anguish motive, set to the chords of the funeral march from Act II, scene ii, acts as the final dramatic outburst and a conduit for the audience's response to the tragedy that has unfolded before them.

Orchestration

> "It has been my endeavor . . . to satisfy my desire for unity and integration, as well as for variety and multiplicity of form, by utilizing the possibilities of orchestration and of instrumental combination."

With this comment from his *Wozzeck* lecture (1929), Berg indicated that orchestration is treated as imaginatively and systematically as other elements of his music. Along with the traditional role played by changing instrumental forces in defining formal areas, Berg invoked "obbligato" solo ensembles reminiscent of the concerto grosso and used instrumental combinations for evocative and dramatic roles in the songs and in *Wozzeck*. Adorno devoted most of his comments on the opera to orchestration, noting its central role, in which "the entire compositional structure, from large-scale divisions to the tiniest capillaries of motivic development, become clear through color values."[89] Of Berg's atonal music, opp. 4, 6, and 7 (*Wozzeck*) are for orchestra. Overall, op. 4, influenced by Schoenberg's op. 16 Orchestral Pieces, contains the most radical orchestration, with its treatments of chords and motives in fragmented colors and textures recalling *Klangfarbenmelodie*, and instrumental effects such as glissandos to indeterminant notes (op. 4, no. 1, m. 7, strings).[90] Opus 6 is more traditional than op. 4, with fewer effects and more continuity of lines within the same instrumental colors.[91] *Wozzeck* is largely similar to op. 6 in the use of the orchestra, although with pockets of special effects recalling op. 4.

DRAMATIC, EVOCATIVE USES OF ORCHESTRATION IN *WOZZECK*

A comment from his *Wozzeck* lecture indicates the extent to which Berg integrated purely musical and dramatic elements: "[The] two initial bars [in *Wozzeck*] . . . contain . . . two short introductory string chords. In order to underline the crescendo leading from the first to the second chord, a soft, but gradually increasing, roll on the side drum bridges the two bars. This was a purely instrumental affair of musical sonorities. When I heard it for the first time, I noticed to my great surprise, that the general military atmosphere of the opera could hardly have been hinted at more poignantly and succinctly than by means of that little drum-roll." Evocative and dramatic uses of orchestration abound in *Wozzeck*. In the return of the chords of Act I, scene ii at the beginning of Act II, scene v (mm. 737–43, 759–60; ex. 3.33), for instance, the timbre is "snoring soldiers": a five-part male chorus singing with half-opened mouths. The chorus enters softly as the raucous waltz ending the previous scene suddenly stops.

In three scenes in *Wozzeck*, an added ensemble or instrument is used onstage as a supplement to the orchestra. In Act I, scene iii (mm. 326–63), the Drum Major is introduced at the head of a military band of twenty players (piccolo, two flutes, two oboes, two E♭ clarinets, two bassoons, two horns, two trumpets, three trombones, tuba, and percussion—triangle, small drum, cymbal, and large drum). The band, part of a military parade from behind the stage scene outside Marie's window, plays a whirling parody of a military march. In a stunning dramatic gesture, the band music abruptly stops (m. 363) when Marie slams the window and her poignant "Mother" motive appears in the fresh sonority of the strings (ex. 3.2a).

In Act II, scene iv, the inn scene consisting of a traditional scherzo 1 (ländler, mm. 412–47, reprised as mm. 592–634), trio 1 (mm. 447–80, reprised as mm. 605–50 and 713–23), scherzo 2 (waltz, mm. 481–559, reprised as mm. 671–96, 704–12, and 724–36), and trio 2 (mm. 560–89), reprised as mm. 637–40) (also an added section as an interlude, mm. 651–70), the external action is associated with tonal metrical music, first in the orchestra (ländler, mm. 412–441; waltz, mm. 670–736), but for the most part in an onstage band: two fiddles tuned a tone higher than normal, C clarinet, accordian, two to four guitars, and bass tuba or bombardon (ländler, mm. 442–47, 592–635; waltz, mm. 481–559, 649–85).[92] Wozzeck's inner turmoil is represented by the atonal orchestra (accompaniment to the apprentice's song, mm. 447–80, 634–36, 639–57; Wozzeck's entrance, m. 495; music underlying Wozzeck's agitation at seeing Marie and the Drum Major, mm. 517–29, 553–60; ländler, mm. 589–605), which alternates and conflicts tonally and metrically with the stage band music throughout (particularly in mm. 592–604, with notated $\frac{3}{4}$ against $\frac{5}{4}$). In a brilliant musical and dramatic stroke, in the midst of this conflict the stage band stops briefly (mm. 599–602), but the $\frac{3}{4}$ meter is maintained by the dancers on stage, who are instructed to keep dancing until the band enters again; the dancers' beat is indicated by three diamond-shaped quarter-duration noteheads in an added stave marked *Ländlertempo*. The atmosphere is enhanced by Berg's references to Mozart's *Don Giovanni* (*Wozzeck*, Act II, mm. 439–42, from the minuet in Act I, scene v, which has its own metric conflicts consisting of three orchestras playing in $\frac{2}{4}$, $\frac{3}{4}$, and $\frac{3}{8}$), the Drum Major acting as Don Giovanni, Marie as Zerlina, and Wozzeck as Masetto—and to Strauss's *Rosenkavalier* (*Wozzeck*, Act II, mm. 430–34, from Act I, mm. 249ff. in Strauss's opera). The scene also includes an a capella chorus (mm. 560–76, 581–90, 637–38) and a song with solo guitar accompaniment (mm. 577–90, 639–40), both among the drinking songs at the inn.

At the end of Act III, scene ii and Marie's murder, in another brilliant use of instrumentation for dramatic effect, the stunning crescendo on a unison note B with full orchestra is followed by a dance played on an out-of-tune upright piano in Act III, scene iii. The piano evokes the music at the inn in Act II, scene iv, accompanying the action and Margaret's song (mm. 122–45, 148–57, 168–79).[93] As in Act II, scene iv, the tonal stage instrument reflects the outer world while the orchestra represents Wozzeck's inner anguish.

The dramatic confrontation between Wozzeck and Marie in Act II, scene iii is reflected by two opposed ensembles: Marie is associated with the orchestra (strings, timpani, four trumpets, trombone, bass tuba, and large drum), Wozzeck with a chamber ensemble consisting of the fifteen instruments used in Schoenberg's Chamber Symphony op. 9, clearly marked in the score by Berg and noted in his lecture as a homage (eight woodwinds: flute/piccolo, oboe, english horn, E♭ clarinet, A clarinet, bass clarinet, bassoon, and contrabassoon; two brasses: two horns; and five solo strings (see fig. 3.27).[94] In mm. 395 ff., however, the chamber orchestra accompanies Marie as she cries "Leave me alone! Better a knife in my heart than lay a hand on me." When Wozzeck repeats Marie's words "Lieber ein Messer" to the note C♯3 and a rhythm recalling his automaton-like answer to the Captain in Act I, scene i, "Jawohl, Herr Hauptmann" (ex. 3.1b), it becomes clear that Marie will die by Wozzeck's hand. Marie's fate is thus fore-shadowed by the change from her orchestral accompaniment to Wozzeck's chamber orchestra.

Figure 3.27. Instrumental forces in *Wozzeck*, Act II, scene iii

mm. 367–87:	Wozzeck with chamber orchestra
mm. 387–94:	alternating Wozzeck with chamber orchestra, Marie with orchestra
mm. 395–97:	Marie with chamber orchestra, "ein Messer"
mm. 398–402:	Wozzeck with chamber orchestra
mm. 402–5:	alternation of chamber orchestra and orchestra

Act I, scene I is comprised of separate, self-contained dance forms, each dance characterized by an obbligato ensemble (fig. 3.28). Overall, the orches-tration begins with strings and woodwinds and gradually adds more brass—with two breaks in this progression for the solo cadenzas—until the air, which is mostly for strings. The contrast between the Captain and Wozzeck throughout is reflected instrumentally: the loud brass of the gigue (mm. 90–96) highlights the Captain's mocking laughter (using the rhythm of Wozzeck's pathetic "Jawohl, Herr Hauptmann" (ex. 3.1b—and his pious pronouncement that Wozzeck had a child, "ohne den Segen der Kirche" ("without the sanction of the church," mm. 121–22, 125–26) is set with a woodwind and brass accompaniment scored to resemble an organ. Wozzeck's poignant replies, using the same melody, "ob das Amen daruber gesagt ist eh' er gemacht wurde" ("just because nobody said Amen before he was made," mm. 130–31, clarinet) and "Laßet die Kleinen zu mir kommen" ("Suffer the little children to come to me," mm. 131–32), and his subsequent statements in the air are set with prominent strings, in a Christ-like halo (which returns in the string C-major triad in Act II, scene I, mm. 116–27, when Wozzeck gives money to Marie for the child). Underlying his climactic statement in the air, "Wir arme Leut," is the rhythm of the "Jawohl Herr Hauptmann" motive, now set powerfully in rhythmic aug-mentation in the lower strings (ex. 3.1b).

Figure 3.28. Obbligato ensembles in *Wozzeck,* Act I, scene i

Prelude	(mm. 1–29):	woodwind quintet: oboe, english horn, clarinet, bass clarinet, bassoon
Pavane	(mm. 30–50):	3 tympani, harp, small/bass drums
Cadenza	(mm. 51–64):	solo viola
Gigue	(mm. 65–108):	3 flutes, celeste
Cadenza	(mm. 109–14):	solo contrabassoon
Gavotte	(mm. 115–26):	4 trumpets
Double 1	(mm. 127–32):	4 horns
Double 2	(mm. 133–36):	4 trombones
Air	(mm. 136–153):	strings
Postlude	(mm. 153–172):	woodwind quintet: oboe, english horn, clarinet, bass clarinet, bassoon
Interlude	(mm. 173–200):	3 choirs: brass, winds, strings

KLANGFARBEN ORCHESTRATION

Opus 4 is characterized throughout by changes in color in the presentations of motives and unusual sounds such as the harmonium in the first song. The most notable treatment of the orchestra appears in op. 4, no. 3, an ABA' form with formal sections defined by orchestration and register (fig. 3.29). In the A section, a twelve-note chord sounds in twelve instrumental voices in the winds and brass, covering an expansive range (ex. 3.11). The chord repeats five times, with notes of the chord changing colors each time among the twelve instrumental voices.[95] The final A' section twelve-note chord, with the same pitch-classes and vertical order, is built up successively by ascending notes in uniform timbre: string harmonics, doubled by the celeste (with a continuous tam-tam roll) in a high tessitura, ascending from C4. The middle section (mm. 11–17) has a thin texture in the low register, with a wedge expanding and changing color from horn, low strings, bass clarinet, and bassoon to harmonium, harp, violin 1, and trombone.

Wozzeck also contains passages with varied use of *Klangfarben.* In Act III, scene ii, an invention on pitch-class B, this note is presented in all registers and orchestral colors (including vocal lines from Wozzeck and Marie), with an overall motion of low to high (m. 92), then spanning the full register (to m. 100) back to a low register (m. 106), and ending on a mid-range B3 (m. 109; see fig. 3.30).[96] The appearances of B in different octaves constantly change color. At the end of the scene, in one of the most famous moments in the opera (m. 109), the *Hauptrhythmus* of Act III, scene iii is created by the timbral rhythm in the entrances of the winds, brass, and strings on the note B3 in canon (ex. 3.21).

Figure 3.29. *Klangfarben* in A section of op. 4, no. 3 (mm. 1–7)

B	E♭ clarinet	flute	oboe	trumpet	clarinet 1
F	clarinet 1	E♭ clarinet	trumpet	oboe	flute
E	flute	oboe	E♭ clarinet	clarinet 1	trumpet
C	oboe	trumpet	flute	E♭ clarinet	english horn
A	trumpet	bassoon	clarinet 1	flute	horn
F♯	english horn	clarinet 1	bassoon	bass clarinet	E♭ clarinet
E♭	bass clarinet	english horn	trombone	horn	oboe
B♭	horn	trombone	english horn	tuba	bass clarinet
G	bassoon	tuba	bass clarinet	english horn	trombone
D	trombone	contrabassoon	contrabassoon	bassoon	tuba
A♭	tuba	bass clarinet	horn	contrabassoon	contrabassoon
C♯	contrabassoon	horn	tuba	trombone	bassoon

The orchestra crescendos, then suddenly breaks off after articulating the downbeat of m. 114 (with the chord of Act III, scene iv; ex. 3.3), leaving an *Hauptrhythmus* statement in the bass drum, after which the orchestra resumes with a deafening crescendo on three octaves (B2–B4). This crescendo is followed by a wholly unexpected new sound, the out-of-tune piano of Act III, scene iii, a stunning dramatic gesture.

In the "Invention on a Chord," Act III, scene iv, variations are created partially by timbre. The chord begins in close position (mm. 220ff., ex. 3.3) in the woodwinds and horns and reappears in close position in the strings (mm. 257–58), then in the woodwinds and brass (mm. 259–63), harp (mm. 262–66), solo strings (mm. 267–69), and full orchestra (mm. 270–83). The drowning music is invoked by rising parallel chords (mm. 284–301) constantly regenerating, like waves, in overlapping alternating choirs: strings, woodwinds, muted strings (col legno), horns and bassoons, muted strings (*am Steg gestrichen*), muted brass, muted strings (*am Griffbrett*), woodwinds, and muted horn. The music is foreshadowed in op. 6, no. 3, mm. 161–63, where parallel chords rise in pizzicato strings and staccato woodwinds. The "croaking of toads" mentioned by Berg in his lecture on *Wozzeck*, in reference to the drowning music in Act III, scene iv, indicated in the clarinets in mm. 301–14, is similar to the passage "like toad's croaking" in Mahler's First Symphony (third movement, mm. 135–37), in the woodwinds and horn.

CYCLIC USES OF ORCHESTRATION

In a few places, Berg treated orchestration somewhat analogously to the cycles in his pitch and rhythmic language. In op. 4, no. 4, the five cellos in mm. 22–29

Figure 3.30. Use of pitch-class B in *Wozzeck*, Act III, scene ii

m.			register
71	B/B1	contrabass	low
73	B1	trombone 4	
75	B/B1	contrabass	
77	B2	bassoon 1,2 (trill with C♯)	
78	B2–B1	bassoon 3 (chromatic slide)	
78	B1	bassoon/contrabassoon	
79	B	contrabass	
80	B6	violin 1 harmonic	high
80	B3	horn, span from B3 to F3	med
82	B3	clarinet B–D trill	
82	B4	horn/harp	
83	B4–3–2–1	harp/horn	med to low
83	B1	tuba A♯/C neighbors	low
84	B	contrabass, B–F–B	
85	B–B6	strings successive gliss	low to high
86	B6/B5	violins tremolo	high
91	B6–3	violin, octave jumps	high to mid
91	B4	trumpet flutter-tongue	med
92	B5	flute flutter-tongue	high
93	B2	trombone 4/timpani B–D	low
94	B2–B5	clarinet octave jumps	low to high
96	B2	vocal: "Nixe"	low
97	B–6	strings	low to high
100	B–6	strings, with harp	low to high
101	B2	timpani	low
103	B5–3	Marie death scream, with timpani	high to mid
106	B/1	harp, part of waiting motive	low
109	B3	orchestral canon on RH,	
		voices added successively	med
117	B2–3–4	full orchestra crescendo	

playing the note E4 as a harmonic are reduced by one part at a time at intervals of one bar (mm. 24–28) down to one cello. In op. 4, no. 3, the twelve-note chord dissolves one note and one instrument at a time, at successive intervals of an eighth note from the bass up in mm. 6–8 (recalling the similar dismantling of a piano chord in op. 5, no. 2, m. 7). In op. 6, no. 1, mm. 5–7, the number of unpitched percussion instruments declines successively from five to three to two to one.

In the stage band music in Act II, scene iv of *Wozzeck* (mm. 627–29), Berg arranged the three upper parts, fiddle, C clarinet, and guitar, in a series of three-part chords (ex. 3.36). The three instrumental parts shift between the registral voices in the chords, and a stave labeled *Klang* (sound) is given below the music to clarify the results of the three voices. This arrangement clearly recalls the fourth song in Schoenberg's *Pierrot Lunaire*, "Eine blaße Wäscherin," in which three instruments, flute, A clarinet, and violin, similarly play three-part chords, with each part shifting between registral voices. Schoenberg also provided a piano reduction below the instrumental parts to clarify the voice-leading underlying the three instrumental voices.

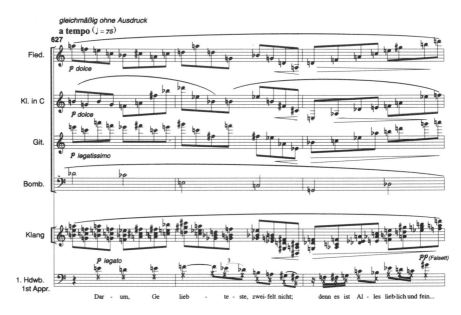

Example 3.36. Non-linear orchestration, including *Klang* stave, *Wozzeck*, Act II, scene iv, mm. 627–29. Berg WOZZECK, OP. 7. Full Score copyright 1926 by Universal Edition A.G., Vienna. English Translation copyright 1952 by Alfred A. Kalmus, London. Full Score copyright renewed. Pocket Score copyright 1955. Pocket Score copyright renewed. All Rights Reserved. Used by permission of European American Music Distributors Corporation, sole U.S. and Canadian agent for Universal Edition A.G., Wien.

OPUS 2, NO. 4

The song op. 2, no. 4, composed in 1909–10, is the last of the four songs op. 2 and Berg's first "atonal" piece. The text, from the collection of poems *Die Glühende: Glühende in einem neuen Heimat-Urgefühl* (1896) by Alfred Mombert (1872–1942) (fig. 3.31), contrasts idyllic images of nature, warm breezes, sunny meadows, and the nightingale with the tragic story of a maiden, feverish with love, whose tears are reflected in the melting show and who dies heartbroken alone in the "dark forest" and the "somber tree trunks."[97] The evocative descriptions of a menacing nature suggest an expressionist atmosphere, foreshadowing the nightmarish nature scenes in *Wozzeck* and Schoenberg's *Erwartung*.[98] The text is set entirely syllabically, except for a melisma on the word *singen* (mm. 7–8) and the *tonlos* intonation on the word *Stirb* ("die," m. 19).[99]

Although the voice and piano parts are independent, the form of the song reflects the divisions of the poem. The opening two lines comprise a self-contained section (mm. 1–6), the third line a transitional passage (mm. 7–9). The scene of the maiden's story, high on a mountain, is established by an ascent from low to high register (mm. 9–11). The story itself is set in a section of increasing register and intensity (mm. 12–16) until the maiden's cry of anguish (m. 16), at registral and dynamic extremes. The vocal G#5 in m. 16, at the point when the maiden realizes that her love has left her waiting, is the highest vocal note and marks the climax (at the Golden Section, the sixty-second quarter-note beat in a total of one hundred quarters). Her death is reflected by a descent to a low B♭1 in a "Fate" rhythm (mm. 17–19), which returns in the closing bars (ex. 3.37a). The epilogue in the final two lines of the poem is set to the descending chords

---

Figure 3.31. Text of op. 2, no. 4

mm. 1–6	Warm die Lüfte, es spreißt Gras auf sonnigen Wiesen, Horch! Horch es flötet die Nachtigall.
mm. 7–9	Ich will singen:
mm. 9–11	Droben hoch im düstern Bergforst es schmilzt und glitzert kalte Schnee,
mm. 12–15	Ein Mädchen in grauen Kleide lehnt an feuchten Eichstamm, Krank sind ihre zarten Wangen, Die grauen Augen fiebern durch Düsterriesenstämme.
mm. 15–19	"Er kommt noch nicht. Er läßt mich warten."
mm. 20–25	Stirb! Der Eine stirbt, da neben der Andre lebt; Das Macht die Welt so tiefschön.

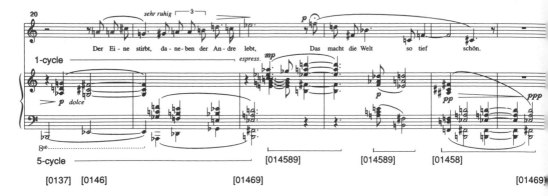

Example 3.37a. Closing cyclic pattern of chords in op. 2, no. 4, mm. 20–25

Example 3.37b. Alignment of 1- and 5-cycles yielding [0137] and (Tn) [0256] tetrachords in op. 2, no. 4 and op. 2, no. 1

in the closing section (mm. 20–25), where the harmonies refer to the first two songs of op. 2 and associate the maiden's death with the sleeping death of the previous poems.[100]

The six self-contained sections of op. 2, no. 4, mm. 1–6, 7–9, 9–11, 12–15, 15–19, and 20–25, group musically by register, gesture, and internal repetition. The elemental motives include a complete neighbor (mm. 1–2, piano; mm. 5–6, piano and voice; mm. 9–10, piano; and mm. 15–16, voice) and a rising interval (usually interval 8) followed by a stepwise descent (voice, mm. 5–6, 7–8, and 10–11). The registral connection of a bass C2 (mm. 1–6, 11, 15; ex. 3.38), leading through B♭1 at the climax (mm. 17–20) to close on B1, suggests a double-neighbor motive that encompasses the entire song. The neighbor motive stems from the vocal incomplete neighbors in op. 2, no. 3, mm. 6–8, and op. 2, no. 1, the ascending vocal motive from the primary motive of op. 2, no. 2

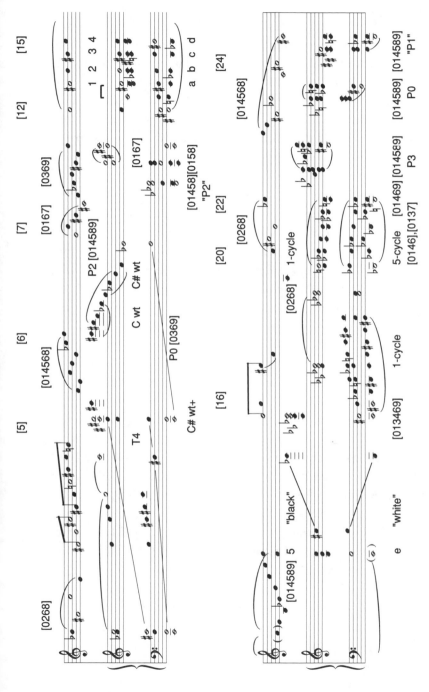

Example 3.38. Cyclic pitch structure in op. 2, no. 4 (priority notes given in open noteheads)

(opening vocal). The vocal line is a compilation of material from previous songs (ex. 3.38): the opening <B♭–F♯–C–E> [0268] recalls op. 2, no. 2, and the rising arpeggio <G♯–A–C–D♯–E> [01478] in m. 3 recalls the vocal opening in op. 2, no. 3 (ex. 1.18). In the piano, the ascending 5-cycle from B♭ in mm. 20–22 (ex. 3.37a) restates the beginning of op. 2, no. 2 (ex. 1.16a), and the chord <B–F♯–D♯–A–D> (mm. 22–25) is a pitch-transposed version of the <D–A–F♯–C–F> chord opening op. 2, no. 1 (ex. 1.15). In op. 2, no. 1, the chord's upper note F is a dissonance that resolves downward by semitone; in op. 2, no. 4, which lacks a tonal harmonic distinction between consonance and dissonance, the chord does not require resolution. Even the presence of the analogous "note of resolution," C♯4, as the final note in the voice (m. 24, ex. 3.37a) has no destabilizing effect. The transformation of this chord from unstable dissonance to relatively stable harmony reflects the transformation of the language in op. 2 from tonal to non-tonal.[101]

The primary link between the op. 2 songs is the alignments of ascending interval 5 and descending interval 1 cycles that occur throughout. As described in chapter 1, the cycles align in tonal contexts in the first three songs (ex. 1.13), but in op. 2, no. 4 the alignment (mm. 20–22, ex. 3.37) creates "atonal" chords. A parallel descending 1-cycle voice added to the [026] model (open noteheads in the upper system in ex. 3.37b) creates alternating Tn [0137] and Tn [0256] (TnI [0146], the Z-related all-interval-class tetrachords).[102] In retrospect, the same harmonies and voice-leading result in op. 2, no. 1 from neighbor chords <E♭–G–C♯–F♯> and <A–G–C♯–F♯> progressing to <D–F♯–C–F> (mm. 6–10, ex. 3.37b).[103]

In its pitch-class and intervalic language, the song is initially structured primarily around the notes {C,C♯,F♯,G} Po [0167] and their interval-classes 5, 6, and 1 (ex. 3.38), with the emergence of interval-class 4 as an organizing force toward the end of the song.[104] Relationships between interval-classes (ics) throughout are embodied in the three multi-cyclic interval 6–based tetrachords: [0167], with ics 1, 5, and 6; [0268], with ics 2, 4, and 6; and [0369], with ics 3 and 6. The analogous formations from combined [04]s are the 4-cycle–based [048] and [014589], along with the closely-related [014568].

Once established in the opening bars (mm. 1–6), notes {C,C♯,F♯,G} recur throughout in motivic figures and as boundary notes in the piano and vocal parts (given in open noteheads in ex. 3.38). The outer-voice dyads {C,G} and {F♯,C♯} in m. 5 return in the upper voice of mm. 10–11, then descend to the low register to initiate a wedge cyclic alignment which governs the middle mm. 12–15. The wedge consists of sum 7 dyads in the left hand, expanding from F♯2/C♯3 to C2/G3, joined by the right hand and an underlying ascent in the voice to create five-part whole-tone+ [01468] chords ascending by interval 1

against the descending bass. The upper voice of the wedge in the piano is articulated and rhythmically displaced by a recurring motivic <C–F♯>, and the left-
hand dyads and right-hand trichords unfold successively in characteristic patterns: the left-hand dyads, lettered a, b, c, d, and e in ex. 3.38, unfold as ab/
abc/bcde, and the right-hand trichords, numbered 1,2,3,4,5, as 12/13/14/15.
The wedge is followed by a registrally expanded wedge of upper "black" notes
against lower "white" notes; the combined "black" and "white" note glissandos,
which may be regarded in the context of surrounding emphases on interval-
class 5 as 5-cycle segments, complete their cycles to create an aggregate.[105]

The primary {C,F♯,G,C♯} note group is also fragmented and recombined; for
instance, {C,F♯} joins with {E,B♭} as an [0268] in the opening vocal gesture
<B♭–F♯–C–E> and in m. 17. Both of these sets feature adjacent interval-class
4s {Gb,B♭} and {C,E}, reflecting the role of [0268] as a mediator between the
interval-class 6 and 4–based elements in the song. When the opening vocal gesture returns as <A–C♯–G–E♭>, varied with inverted contour in the closing
section (mm. 20–21), the other interval-class 6 from {C,F♯,G,C♯}, {C♯,G}, combines into an [0268] with {A,E♭}. The interval-classes of [0268] also exert an
influence over the boundary notes of the twelve successive vocal phrases:
<B♭4–E4, F♯4–D5, F5–E♭5, G4–C♯4, F4–G4, G♯4–D5, D♭4–G4, C♯5–C♯5,
A4–F4, F5–A4, A4–E♭5, F5–C♯3>, interval-classes <64262660446>. The two
pitch-classes omitted from the vocal boundary tones are the prominent notes C
and B in the bass of the piano part (mm. 1–6, 22–25).

The whole-tone property of [0268] is reflected in the opening piano note
groups: the initial bars group into an upper C whole-tone collection with lower
boundary E4 and a lower C♯ whole-tone+ collection with upper boundary D♯4.
As becomes customary in Berg's atonal music, the added dissonant note in the
lower collection, C, is part of an interval 7 that includes the lowest note of a
chord, lending it a "tonal" stability. In the course of mm. 1–6, the piano chord
evolves into a C♯ whole-tone+ chord, with the upper neighbors {F♯,G♯} the only
vestiges of the upper C whole-tone collection, but maintaining the bass {C,G}
dyad and its concomitant stability. The opposition of whole-tone–based materials continues through the rapid descent of C whole-tone <G♯–F♯–D–B♭>
then C♯ whole-tone <G–E♭–B–F–E♭–A> collections in the piano (mm.
6–7), and the C whole-tone-based collection of the vocal part in mm. 7–8, with
the "dissonant" boundary notes {G,C♯} combining with the left-hand interval-
class 6 dyad {A,E♭} in a C♯ whole-tone–based [0268]. After this point, however,
whole-tone–based elements largely disappear, returning only in the [0268] in
m. 17.

The piano chord of m. 6 collapses inward by interval-class 3 motion from the
expansive outer voice notes {C2,F♯6} to the closed {A3,E♭4} of mm. 7–8 (the

upper E♭ is anticipated by the vocal part in m. 6); the associated {C,F♯} and {A,E♭} dyads form tetrachord [0369]. Interval 6 {A,E♭} returns prominently within the climax chord immediately preceding m. 16, which contains [0369] {A,C,E♭,G♭}, and also in the vocal [0268] of mm. 20–22 and final chord of the song. The remaining interval-class 6s, {G♯,D} and {B,F}, the complement of the vocal [0268]s {B♭,F♯,C,E} in m. 1 and {A,C♯,G♯,E♭} in mm. 20–21, appear prominently in whole and in part throughout: in the vocal part in mm. 4 and 7–11; {F,B} within the chord in mm. 5–6 (at T4 from the corresponding {G,C♯} in the first chord, {F,B} and {G,C♯} combine into [0268]) and as the final two bass notes; {F,G♯} in the upper vocal and piano lines in mm. 4–6 and at the vocal climax in mm. 15–16; <F–D> beginning the final vocal phrase (mm. 22–23); and {B,D} as the outer notes of the closing chord. Finally, the axis interval 6s are stated consecutively in two places: in the ascending 1-cycle from D♯2/A3 to G♯2/D4 in the piano (mm. 16–17), and within the descending [016] trichords of mm. 20–22, in retrograde order as D4/A♭3 to A3/E♭3.

The {C,E♭,F♯,A} [0369] of mm. 6–7 has sums of 9/3, reflected in the vocal boundary group {G,D,G♯,C♯} with the same sums in mm. 7–11. Sum-9 pairs continue in two chords in mm. 9–10: {G,D,B,G♭,B♭} has sum-9 pairs G/D and B♭/B, with the G♭ pairing with the previous E♭, and {A,E,C,F,A} has sum-9 dyads F/E and A/C. Both chords combine adjacent interval-class 5s and 4s; {A,C,E,F} [0158], with its internal interval-class 5s and 4s, is a counterpart to [0268], with its interval-class 4s and 6s. The G-based [01458] chord turns out to be a catalyst for the emergence of interval 4, particularly in the cadential chords of the song. Its upper interval 4 {G♭,B♭} appears as the first two vocal notes, the upper notes in the climax chord of m. 15 and the [0268] {C,E,G♭,B♭} of m. 17, and returns in the closing measures in the vocal part and the penultimate chord of the song. In retrospect, interval 4 is foreshadowed at the outset as an internal transpositional level in the opening chords, mapping [026] {G2,F3,C♯4} to {B3,A4,F5}.

The larger harmonic collections stemming from the G-based [01458] in mm. 9–10 are [014568] and [014589]. The former appears as <F–E–C–B–G–E♭–F–E♭> [014568] in mm. 5–6 (vocal part) and the same set, reordered, as <F–E–B–E♭–G–C–E–F> in mm. 14–15 (vocal part—a restatement that formally connects the opening vocal line with the climax, extending the upper-voice register from F5 in m. 6 to G♯5 in m. 16. In both sets, an [014589] results if G♯ replaces F; in m. 6 a G♯ is the upper neighbor note in the piano, which "replaces" the upper neighbor note F in the voice (and spawns its own P2 [014589]), and at the climax in mm. 15–16 the line <F5–G5–G♯5> leads from F to the climactic G♯, the highest note in the voice. Set [014568] returns at sum 5 in the closing vocal <F–D–F♯–B♭–C–F–C♯>.

In terms of [014589], the chord {G,D,B,G♭,B♭} in mm. 9–10 may be regarded as an embryonic interval 4–based P2 [014589]—with the missing E♭ in the previous E♭/A dyad. In fact, a P2 [014589] leads into the E♭/A dyad in a segment of the descending piano line ending in m. 6 <F♯–D–B♭–G–E♭–B>. The three chord pairs comprising the cadence of the song begin, respectively, with P3 [014589] <E–G–B–C–E♭–A♭>, P0 [014589] <A–C–E–F–A♭–D♭>, and <F–D–F–A♯–C♯–F♯> (sharing five of six notes {F,D,F♯,B♭,C♯} with the closing vocal [014568]), which may be regarded as an embryonic P1 [014589], lacking {A} (found in the surrounding cadence chords). Thus, the G-based chord in mm. 9–10 and the three penultimate cadence chords comprise the four distinct transpositional levels of [014589]: P2, P3, P0, and P1.

In another view, the three cadence chords are related in a 5-cycle, as a continuation of the bass ascending 5-cycle from m. 20, <B♭–E♭–A♭–D♭–G♭–B> to <E–A–(D)>, where E descends by interval 7 to A and the final D is displaced by a bass F (which allows for a final interval 6 F–B bass motion). The successive T5s between the [014589]s translate in a mod-4 context as successive T1s, from P3, P0, and P1–another reflection of the interaction of 1- and 5-cycles in the song.

The cyclic progression in the piano from m. 20 to m. 22 consists of [016]s in a descending 1-cycle in the right hand against an ascending 5-cycle in the left, creating alternating tetrachords Tn [0256] and [0137] (cf. ex. 3.37). The ascending interval 5 bass voice consists of five interval 5s spanning an interval-class 1, <B♭–E♭–A♭–D♭–G♭–B>, while the upper descending interval 1 voice spans an interval 5, <G–F♯–F–E–E♭–D>. At the chord beginning m. 22, the sequence is broken with a descending interval 7 from F♯ down to B, emphasizing the B chord, with an added F♯ to create [01469] <B–F♯–E♭–A–D>—a chord anticipated by the [013469] <C–D♭–A–E♭–G♭–B♭> climax chord in mm. 15–16, with which it shares a T5-related [0347] subset. Finally, the bass 5-cycle <B♭–E♭–A♭–D♭–G♭–B–E–A–(D)> ending the song is balanced by the complementary notes in a 7-cycle in the opening mm. 1–11, in the bass interval 7s of chords: <C–G–D–A–E>. The omitted note in the cycle, F, is the bass note of the altered penultimate cadence chord.

Berg's initial atonal effort shows many of the characteristic features of his emerging style: interacting 1- and 5-cycles, wedges, opposing whole-tone areas, focuses on different interval-classes within collections (such as the interval 4–based [014589]s), the [01469] sonority of the final cadence chord with its bass interval 7, and the use of bass interval 7s in many chords, particularly where a note of the interval 7 is dissonant in the harmonic context, as in the whole-tone based chords of the piano in mm. 1–6. The appearance and subtle inter-relation of the three interval-class 6–based tetrachords [0167], [0268], and

[0369] is particularly characteristic, as these multi-cyclic collections establish and mediate between areas of different cyclic or intervalic collections. In following pieces, Berg developed his cyclic materials, establishing the harmonic identity of motives with cyclic collections and contrasting motives and harmonic areas by an opposition of two primary cyclic collections, as hinted at by the opposition of interval classes 4 and 6 in op. 2, no. 4.

OPUS 4, NO. 4

Berg's orchestral songs op. 4, composed in 1912, use as texts the "Picture-Postcard Texts" (*Texte auf Ansichtskarten*), nos. 60–66 in *Das neue Altes* (1911), a collection by Peter Altenberg (1859–1919).[106] The text images—an intertwining of emotions and nature—are strikingly similar to those in the Mombert text for op. 2, no. 4. The imagery of winter, thunderstorms, and clouds as representations of emotional trauma followed by renewal appears in the first, second, and fifth songs. The fourth and fifth songs speak of a forsaken soul, with "ash-blond, silken hair around my pale face" and "immeasurable sorrow," who finds peace only by escape, but with tears reflected in the snow that "drops gently into pools of water." The third song, which begins "Beyond the bounds of the universe you glanced musingly," expresses "the Romantic yearning to transcend the finite world and the limitations of man's earthly existence."[107] In Berg's setting the finite world of tonality is transcended, and the new limit of the twelve tones in the crystalized form of a twelve-tone chord and theme emerges.

Several instances of word painting occur in the op. 4 songs. The "snow-storm" in no. 1 is reflected in the "blizzard" of motives in the opening mm. 1–15. The successively longer melismas elaborating the important motive <G–A♭–B♭–C♯–E> on *gewartet* in song 4 emphasize the reference to waiting. Also in song 4 (fig. 3.32), the fluttering blond hair is reflected in flitting lines in the oboe, clarinet, and flute (mm. 22–32). Although *Sprechstimme* is not used, several vocal effects occur. In the first song, the voice sings initially with a closed-mouth hum, then half-open, and finally fully open (mm. 20–22, notated conventionally), marked "like a breath—starting and stopping" (*Wie ein Hauch an- und abzusetzen*). In the third song, the voice tonelessly whispers the text "sud-

---

Figure 3.32. Text of op. 4, no. 4

mm. 1–8	Nichts ist gekommen, nichts wird kommen für meine Seele—
mm. 9–15	Ich habe gewartet, gewartet, oh—gerwartet!
mm. 16–21	Die Tage werden dahinschleichen,
mm. 22–32	Und umsonst wehen meine aschblonden, seidenen Haare um mein bleiches Antlitz!

---

denly, all is over" (*plötzlich ist alles aus*, mm. 16–17); although the notation, a stem with an *x* in place of the notehead, is somewhat similar to the *Sprechstimme* notation of a regular notehead with an *x* on the stem, the effect is quite different: the singer whispers in a monotone. The designation is similar to the *tonlos* setting of *Stirb* in op. 2, no. 4, which is, interestingly, on the same pitch, A3.[108]

The vocal setting in op. 4 is mostly syllabic except for melismas on *schöner* (more beautiful) in songs 1 (m. 23) and 2 (m. 5), *Gewitterregen* (thunderstorm) in song 2 (mm. 9–10), *sinnend* (musingly) in song 3 (mm. 6–7, 24–25), and *gewartet* (waited) in song 4 (m. 13). In the first four songs, the vocal part is largely independent of the accompaniment: in no. 1 the voice is only doubled briefly by the english horn (mm. 24–26) and the violin (mm. 31–32) and in no. 4 by the violin (mm. 10–13); in addition, the vocal part participates in the main motives of the work only in songs 1 (mm. 29–32) and 4 (*gewartet*, mm. 10–13), both on motive 4/b <G–A♭–B♭–C♯–E>, and in a variant of motive 4/a in no. 2 (mm. 2, 8–9, [0167] <E♭–B♭–A–E>). The fifth song marks a break with the others, however, as the voice participates in the motivic content and is doubled throughout (see discussion, p. 49).

The text of op. 4, no. 4 presents a bleak picture of waiting for solace or perhaps for love (fig. 3.32), with the highest point of emotion—corresponding to the loudest and most expansive vocal gesture (m. 13)—at the end of the second line, followed by resignation.[109] The setting of the four lines corresponds to the four sections of the song: mm. 1–8, 9–15, 16–21, and 22–32, but the vocal line groups into three phrases, mm. 1–8, 9–15, and 20–32, the latter emerging from the instrumental end of the third section. The song is through-composed, with only a hint of a return of the opening spare texture in the closing bars. The form is generated largely by register (cf. exx. 3.39 and 3.40): the primary register around F4 contrasts, first, with a separated high dyad {Bb6-B6} in a register that returns briefly in mm. 10–15 but is fully explored only at the end, where the initial {B♭6–B6} dyad returns, and second, with a low F♯3 in m. 9, which introduces the low register unfolded only in mm. 16–22, reaching its low point of A2.

Only one motive from surrounding songs appears, 3-cycle–based motive 4/b <G–A♭–B♭–C♯–E> [01369] (ex. 3.40, mm. 10–15, violin, voice, xylophone), and an altered form {F,D,B,E,A♭} (m. 16, clarinet), but several figures are close variants of motives: a whole-tone+ inverted variant of motive 4/a in the third section <A♭5–E5–D5–B♭4–F♯4–C♯4–G♯3–D3> (descending solo viola, mm. 19–21); descending <G5–D5–C♯5–C5–B4–A4–C♯5> similar to motives 4/e, 4/6, and 4/8 in the first section (english horn, mm. 6–8, ex. 3.39); and the [014]s in the opening vocal line. In addition, the opening vocal <F–E–A♭–G–F♯–D♭> together with the flute notes <B♭–B> yields [01234679], which shares six notes with the opening vocal line of op. 4, no. 2,

Example 3.39. Opus 4, no. 4, mm. 1–10. Berg 5 ORCHESTERLIEDER, OP. 4. Copyright 1953 by Universal Edition A.G., Wien. Copyright renewed. All Rights Reserved. Used by permission of European American Music Distributors Corporation, sole U.S. and Canadian agent for Universal Edition A.G., Wien.

<B♭–B–G–F♯–F–E♭–B♭–A–E> [01234689]; the latter begins with pitch-classes <B♭–B> foreshadowing the opening flute line in op. 4, no. 4.

Sections 2 and 4 of op. 4, no. 4 are characterized by chords in *Klangfarben*. The first, a whole-tone+ chord [0135] <F♯3–E♭4–C♯5–F5> (mm. 8–15; see exx. 3.39, 3.40), moves through five mixed color combinations to end in the uniform color of clarinets (fig. 3.33); the colors include fourteen of the seventeen available instruments (excluding the percussion section), reserving the viola for the solo statements in mm. 14–21. The timbres overlap and grow out of one another; soft (*pp*) entrances are masked by loud (*ff*) ends, yielding alternating crescendo, subito *pp*, crescendo, and so on. The second chord, [013468] <A2–E♭3–B3–E4–G4–F♯5> in mm. 22–26, is set in mixed colors, but only the low A changes color. The chord dissolves with staggered endings where each part fades out, in the order <G/F♯–A–E–B–E♭>; the timpani part ends with a descending glissando, and the cello parts are cyclically dissolved by deleting one cello at a time. The other sections in the song have distinctive timbres as well: the opening mm. 1–7 feature only voice with accompanying flute,

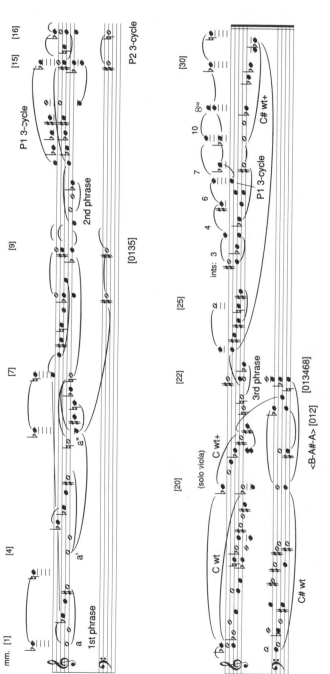

Example 3.40. Cyclic and registral pitch structure in op. 4, no. 4 (priority notes in open noteheads)

Figure 3.33. *Klangfarben* in op. 4, no. 4

first chord:

mm. 8–15

F5:	violin 2	oboe 1	cello	trumpet 1	english horn	clarinet 1
C♯5:	english horn	horn 1	flute 1	trombone 1	trumpet 2	clarinet 2
E♭4:	cello	violin 1	bassoon	tuba	horn 2	clarinet 3
F♯3:	horn 2	bass clarinet	trombone 2	contrabass	bassoon	bass clarinet

second chord:

mm. 22–26

added upper line	violin/oboe		clarinet	flute
G/F♯	celeste		—	—
E	5 celli		4 3	2 1
B	trumpet		—	—
E♭	timpani		—	—
A	bassoon	bass clarinet	trombone	horn

then english horn (ex. 3.39), and the third section (mm. 15–20) has a solo viola line against a descent passing from the clarinets to low brass.

The formal and pitch structure of op. 4, no. 4 is organized primarily around unfoldings and registral completions of pitch interval cycle 1–based [012]s in various symmetrical and neighbor configurations (ex. 3.40; cf. ex. 3.39). The opening vocal subphrase defines the primary register [012] <F4–E4–F#4>, which is embellished by motivic shapes and motions to other registers in mm. 1–8, then returns in mm. 9ff. with the second vocal phrase and again at the veiled return in the third vocal phrase, mm. 20ff. Other significant [012]-related registers are defined by (1) the incomplete dyadic [01] <Bb6–B6> in the opening mm. 1–7 and closing mm. 30–32; (2) the <F3–F#3> dyad in mm. 9–16, completed by E3 in mm. 19–21; and (3) the [012] <B2–A#2–A2> in mm. 17–28. Of these, the upper-register <Bb6–B6> remains incomplete, with attempts at completion in m. 15 by {Ab6} and in m. 29 by {C7}. Its unfulfilled state is reflective of the text.

In the three-part opening phrase (mm. 1–3, 4–5, 6–8, labeled a, a', a" in ex. 3.40), the primary notes <F#4–F4–E4> begin and end each subphrase. The motivic <F–E–Ab> [014] embellishing the underlying <F–E–F#> in the first subphrase expands up to Db5 in the second subphrase and to G5 in the third, which is completed instrumentally (english horn). With this third subphrase and its instrumental continuation, the registral space from <Db5–Ab4> opened up in the second subphrase is filled in by an interval 1 descent. Meanwhile, a lower descent from <F4–B3–F#3> (mm. 1–8) mirrors the ascent from <Ab4–Db5–G5>, reversing and inverting the intervals <+5, +6> to <−6, −5>. A somewhat similar symmetrical registral expansion occurs in the third phrase return in mm. 20ff., where the voice begins with the primary <F#4–E4–F4> register but leaps up to D5, only to descend to F#4 in [012] segments, then continuing with a C# whole-tone descent from F4 to Ab3, completing a 3-cycle–based symmetry of <Ab3–F4–D5>.

The second vocal phrase (mm. 9–15) begins similarly to the first, but the registral expansion upwards proceeds by the P1 3-cycle–based <G–Ab–Bb–C#–E–Ab> motive, anticipated by the preceding interval 3 <D4–F4>. The initial <G–Ab> is foreshadowed at the outset in the motivic <F–E–Ab–G–F#>, and the upper Ab5 held through mm. 15–19 similarly connects registrally with the G5 in m. 6.

The initial interval 3 and the 3-cycle–based continuation in the second phrase (mm. 9ff.) mark the second cyclic interval type in the song and act as a contrast to the interval 1–based [012]s. In retrospect, interval 3 is announced at the outset in <F4–Ab4> of the motivic <F–E–Ab>, and its influence returns with this motive in mm. 15–16 as <F5–Ab5> and again in mm. 20–21 as <F3–E3–A♭3>. The 3-cycle basis in the second phrase, P1 <G–A♭–B♭–C♯–E>, continues into the harmonic change in mm. 15–16, where the initial *Klangfarben* chord yields to P2 3-cycle–based <F3–D4–B4–E5–A♭5>, and returns in the closing bars, as P1 3-cycle+ <E5–D♭6–G6–B♭6–B6> (mm. 29–31, flute) in the upper register, linking up with the final [01] <B♭6–B6>. The third 3-cycle collection, P0, does not appear in complete form, although notes {F♯,E♭} and {A,E♭,F♯} are prominent in the two *Klangfarben* chords.

The third cyclic type in the song is whole-tone–based. The first *Klangfarben* chord is [0135] whole-tone+ {F♯,E♭,C♯,F}, which leads, as noted, to a 3-cycle–based chord in mm. 15–16. The latter dissolves almost immediately into whole-tone–based descents (mm. 16–21, clarinets) in offset duple and triple durations. As the descent completes, a solo viola held {A♭5} descends through C whole-tone+ <A♭5–E5–D5–B♭4–F♯4–C♯4–G♯3–D3>. The A♭5 continually changes status: dissonant in the earlier <G–A♭–B♭–C♯–E> 3-cycle+ arpeggiation (mm. 10–15), it is consonant in the harmonic <F–D–B–E–A♭> 3-cycle+ collection (m. 16), then consonant again as part of a C whole-tone collection. In the course of the solo viola descent, the added note C♯4 creates a momentary contrasting 5-cycle segment <F♯4–C♯4–G♯3>. The whole-tone cycle returns in the closing vocal line, in the descent from F4 in the C♯ whole-tone collection to end with the dissonant A♭3. This motion recalls the opening motive <F–E–A♭> as well as the held A♭ of the 3-cycle+ collection <G–A♭–B♭–C♯–E> in mm. 1off., and points up the important role of A♭ throughout the song.

With the combined return of the opening <B♭6–B6> dyad as well as 3-cycle and whole-tone collections, the final bars act as a summation for the song. The vocal line from m. 20 expands out symmetrically from F4 to D5/A♭3, with the upper span defined by interval 1 and the lower by whole-tone motion. In retrospect, the first two vocal phrases also expand out symmetrically from F4 to E5/A3 by m. 13, with the spans defined first by interval 1, then interval 3, collections. The final bars contain several other events: descending "fluttering" lines in changing instrumental and intervalic colors (mm. 23–27, oboe, clarinet, flute) and a somewhat cyclic successive increase of intervals <3–4–6–7–A> in the celeste <F♯5–A5–C♯6–G6–D7–C8> to end on the highest note in the song, C8. The final glissando in the celeste matches glissandos in the cellos and timpani as the instrumental parts fade into effects, leaving only the high flute and low voice.

The pivotal harmonic motions in mm. 15–16 and 20–22 both mark formal junctures. In the first of these, the initial *klangfarben* chord, a whole-tone+ [0135] <F♯–E♭–C♯–F> bounded by the notes F/F♯, changes to a 3-cycle+ [01369] <F–D–B–E–A♭> by way of a bass motion of <F♯3–F3> and an upper-voice return of the motivic <F−E−Ab> motion from the opening. The second chord then dissolves into the descending whole-tone lines in the following bars. The next important harmonic point occurs in mm. 20–22, where the non-cyclic second *Klangfarben* chord {013468] (which contains [0135] as a subset and shares [0136] with [01369]) emerges from the somewhat whole-tone low-register oscillations accompanying the descending viola line. The harmonic move is confirmed by the completed [012] bass motion <A#2−B2−A2>.

The meter in op. 4, no. 4 is supported only in the opening bars, by the vocal part and the first attack of the *Klangfarben* chord in m. 8. The final section is characterized by triple and duple divisions, first by the double time signature $\frac{2}{4} = \frac{6}{8}$ (m. 21), then by $\frac{3}{8} = \frac{1}{4}$ (mm. 22-23), the voice part in $\frac{1}{4}$ changing to $\frac{3}{8}$ in m. 24. This region of metric change (mm. 19−24) between the third and fourth sections is highlighted by the viola part in an implied $\frac{3}{16}$ against the notated $\frac{2}{4}$ or $\frac{6}{8}$ in mm. 19−21. The passage of the first *Klangfarben* has two aspects: the time-point attack, and the point at which the new timbre is audible as the previous one fades. The patterns of these time points in mm. 8−15 conflict with the notated meter (fig. 3.34). The initial attacks occur at durations of <7−6−4−5−4−5> eighths, and the timbral durations—the durations marking the aural beginning of each new timbre as the old one fades—occur in units of <10−5−4−7−3−3> eighths. Although no obvious pattern arises from these durations, they conflict with the barlines, contributing to the rhythmic freedom in the song.

OPUS 5, NO. 1

Berg's clarinet pieces, written in 1913 but not performed until October 17, 1919, are his most aphoristic, least characteristic pieces.[110] Several authors have compared the four movements to a symphony, with the substantial outer movements, a slow second movement, and scherzo-like third movement. Although cyclic collections appear throughout, particularly in op. 5, no. 2 (ex. 3.13), the harmonies derive largely from the opening clarinet motto in the manner of pitch-class set relationships.

Formally, op. 5, no. 1 is in three sections, dividing clearly at mm. 6−7, but the boundaries of the third formal division are complicated by the differing positions of the returning opening material in the clarinet and piano. The clarinet part groups into three sections: (1) the motto in mm. 1−2 (ex. 3.41); (2) a traditional three-fold sequential development of a figure (taken from the piano in m. 2, ex. 3.15b) leading to a high point in m. 4, then dissolution into the low register in m. 6; and (3) a brief statement—the highest and loudest point marking the climax (mm. 7−8)—ending with a three-fold varied figure derived from the opening of the motto (mm. 7−9, ex. 3.26e) that dissolves into the low register, then slowly focuses symmetrically on the final note G3 (mm. 9−12). The piano

Figure 3.34. Chord durations in op. 4, no. 4, mm. 8–15 (time point 0 = m. 8, units = eighths)

mm.	8	9	10	11	12	13	14	15	16
notated ²⁄₄ bars:	0	4	8	12	16	20	24	28	32
chord attacks:									
F5	0	7		13	17	23	27		(32)
C♯5	2	7		13	17	23	27		(32)
E♭4	3.5	7		13	17	23	27		(32)
F♯3	0	7		13	17	23	27		(32)
difference		7 /		6 /	4 /	6 /	4 /	5	
timbral durations:	0			10 /	15 /	19 /	26 /	29 /	32
difference		10 /		5 /	4 /	7 /	3 /	3	

part is also in three sections: (1) it introduces the figure taken up by the clarinet in m. 2, then accompanies the clarinet to m. 4 before ascending to its climax in m. 6, marked by three chords; (2) it introduces then accompanies the clarinet statement from m. 7, ending in m. 9 on a cadence of a D-based whole-tone+ chord with a fermata (ex. 3.26e); and (3) the third section begins with a transposed reference to the opening clarinet motto on the second beat of m. 9, followed by reiterated cadential chords in three dissolving groups.

The tempo changes support both the clarinet and piano divisions, defining two large parts each with two internal divisions: (1) the clarinet motto with quarter note = 76 (mm. 1−2) and the second clarinet and first piano sections (mm. 2−6) in a slower tempo of quarter = 58, ending with a ritardando to quarter = 40−44; and (2) the beginning of the third clarinet and second piano section (m. 7), marked by an accelerando to an *a tempo* quarter = 76, and the piano's third section (m. 9 $\frac{1}{2}$) with a slower quarter = 52. The return of quarter = 76 in mm. 7−8 emphasizes the formal and gestural parallel between the clarinet figures of mm. 1 and 7−8. These two points are also connected in the registral expansion unfolding through the piece: G2/Ab5 (mm. 1−2) to Bb1/Eb6 (mm. 7−8) and B/Ab7 (m. 12).

The initial meter of $\frac{4}{4}$ is supported by the clarinet and piano until a dissolution in mm. 5−6, in which the clarinet progresses in a cyclic diminution of rhythmic values culminating in a trill in m. 7. In mm. 7−8 the piano groups in $\frac{3}{8}$, briefly matched by the clarinet at the end of m. 7 until both parts again dissolve into the fermata of m. 9 (ex. 3.26e). The piano left hand cadences to this point with a metric cyclic pattern of diminuted note values (quarter, eighths, triplet eighths, and sixteenths, mm. 8−9) emphasized by an accelerando; the right hand has a similar but ametric cyclic pattern of diminuted note groups in an ascending line of <G#4−A4>, <Bb4−A4>, <B4−A4>, <C#5−A4>, <D5−A4> in <8−6− 6−5−4> sixteenths, the last held into the fermata. The notated meter is not supported in the final section following the fermata; the three voices are each in a relative pattern of successively larger note values, emphasized by the *Poco rit.* but with no discernible periodicity. The piano low B, articulated on the second half of the notated beat 1 in m. 12, seems to assert a final referential downbeat, but no meter or rhythmic resolution emerges.

In its pitch language, op. 5, no. 1 is structured around the components of the opening clarinet motto (ex. 3.41): (1) interval-classes 1, 4, and 5 in various combinations; (2) notes {Ab,Eb,E,A} P3 [0156] arranged as interval 1 pairs A/Ab and E/Eb at T5 or sum 0 and as interval 5 pairs Eb/Ab and E/A at T1 or sum 0; (3) boundary notes {G4,F#4,Ab5,A5} P6 [0123]; (4) the wedge motion from <Ab5−Eb5−G4> to <A5−D5−F#4> as sum-3 pairs F#/A, G/Ab, or sum-B pairs Ab/Eb, A/D; (5) the cyclic sequence of intervals, from <Ab5−Eb5−G4−

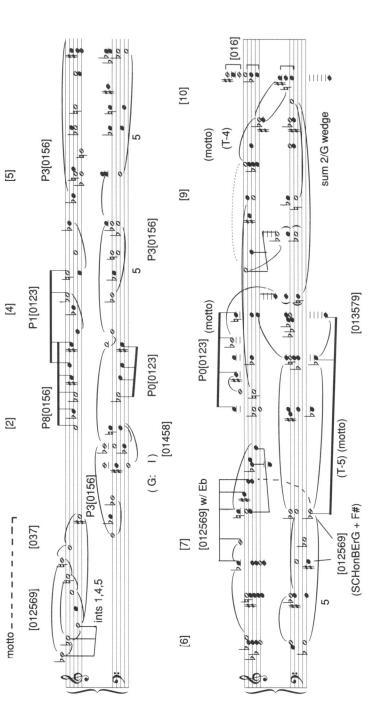

Example 3.41. Cyclic pitch structure in op. 5, no. 1 (priority notes in open noteheads)

A4–C5–E5–A5–D5–F♯4–(A3)>, pattern <−5,−8(=−1),+2,+3,+4,+5(6) −7,−8,−9 (to A3 in piano)>; (6) the emphasis on D, by the voice-leading <E♭5–E5–D5>, and D as part of a D triad {A,D,F♯} "dominant," with the lower F♯ a neighbor to the preceding "tonic" G; and (7) the set-class [012589] (TnI[012569]) of the initial six notes.[111]

The primary notes {A♭,A,E♭,E} and tetrachords [0156] and [0123] are significant throughout op. 5, no. 1 (ex. 3.41): in mm. 2–4, the piano P3 [0156] in interval 1 pairs <A/A♭–E/E♭> leads by T5 to the clarinet P8 [0156] <A4–A♭4–C♯5–D5> with common tones {A,A♭}; the latter overlaps with P1 [0123] <D5–C♯5–E♭5–E5>, restoring {E,E♭} in their original registers as <E♭5–E5>. Underneath, in mm. 3–4, the piano's P0 [0123] shares {E♭,D,C♯} with the upper P1 [0123] (due to the T1 relationship between the two), and the piano cadences in m. 4 with P3 [0156] <A–A♭–E–E♭>, wherein the two interval 5s E3/A3 to A♭3/E♭3 reverse the order to succession of E♭/A♭ to E/A in the opening clarinet figure. The notes {A,E♭,E,A♭} return in the piano (m. 5–6) in an ascent through A♭4–A4 to E♭5–E5 to A5, while the clarinet descends symmetrically through <A3–A♭3–E3> (m. 6). The clarinet's climax (mm. 8–9) features a P0 [0123] arranged symmetrically as sum-3 pairs <D–C♯–E♭–C>, at TB from the P1 [0123] in m. 4, sharing pitch-classes {C♯,D,E♭}. The lower grace note creates boundary tones {A,E♭}. The notes {E,E♭} return as the boundary notes of the restated opening trichord of the motto as <E5–B4–E♭4> in the clarinet (m. 8) and piano (m. 9) at T−4 from the opening. The G♯7 (A♭) as the upper note of the final piano chord is the culmination in the expanded register of the upper boundary notes: A♭5–A5 (m. 1) to E♭6 (m. 8) to G♯7 (mm. 10–12).

The opening three-note clarinet figure <A♭–E♭–G> [015], intervals <−5, −8>, returns in various configurations, most notably in the bass of the piano as T−5 <E♭2–(D♭2)–B♭1–D1> (mm. 7–8), and in mm. 8–9 in the clarinet, then piano, both at T−4 <E5–B4–E♭3(4)>.[112] The latter states the transposed notes of the opening of the clarinet motto, but in the rhythm of the end three notes of the latter <A–D–F♯>. The entire opening clarinet motto actually appears at T−4 in the piano (m. 9) with <F–A♭–C> in the left hand (ex. 3.26e). The final chord in the piano also contains a T−8 version of the motto initial figure as <C4–G3–B>, with the B projected down two octaves. The four statements thus begin on notes {A♭,E♭,E,C} of a 4-cycle+ collection drawn from the initial six notes of the clarinet motto.

The parallel between the opening motto and mm. 7–8 in the clarinet is emphasized by wedge formations. The opening motto has wedges of sums 3 (A♭/G to A/F♯) and B (A♭/E♭ to A/D); sum 3 returns in the <D/C♯–E♭/C> upper-register clarinet figure in m. 7. The successive three-voice figures in m.

8—varied from the first three notes of the clarinet motto—<E♭6 – C6 – D2> and {E5 – B4 – E♭3}> combine sums 3 (E♭/C to E/B), similar to the opening motto, but add sum 2 (C/D to B/E♭). The clarinet continues with sum 2 in it symmetrical focus on G3 to end the movement. Sum 2 has a larger role to play as well; the final chord, <B – G – C – F – F# – B♭ – E – A – D – G#>, is a superset of the opening clarinet motto inverted at sum 2, with the addition of notes {E,A}. (The two notes missing from the final chord, {E♭,E♭}, begin the clarinet line in op. 5, no. 2.) The final chord segments registrally into [016]s patterned as <+5,+6>—<G – C – F#>, <F – B♭ – E>, <A – D – G#>—in a variant on the combination of interval-class 5 and boundary interval-class 1 in the opening trichord [015] <A♭ – E♭ – G>.

The focus on G and D, with the latter in a hierarchical position analogous to a dominant, is established at the outset, in the lower-voice interval 1 descent <G – F#>, with F# part of {D,F#,A} in the clarinet, followed by a G-based triadic figure in the piano in m. 2 ([01458] {F#,G,B♭,B,D} is an abstract subset of [012569], sharing notes G and D with the clarinet motto). In mm. 3 – 4, D4 is established as a center of symmetry and simultaneously begins a descent through interval 5s interspersed with interval 1s, <D4 – A3/A♭3 – E♭3/D3 – A2/A♭2 – E♭2 – B♭1/(D1)>, to the downbeat of m. 8. The final low D1 is the bass of a whole-tone+ collection <D – G♭ – A♭ – B♭ – C – F> which, in its cadential position at the fermata, acts analogously to a dominant of the final clarinet G3. The low B in the final measure is part of the emphasis on that note.

In pitch-class set terms, the first six notes of the motto form set P7 [012589] (TnI [012569]) <G – A♭ – A – C – E♭ – E>; at sum 7 the pitch-class content {E♭,C, B,B♭,E,G} yields the SCHönBERG name motto. The two sets share the maximum of four notes {C,E♭,E,G} and exchange {A,A♭} and {B♭,B}. The latter set appears as the third chord of the piano climax (m. 6) + F#, <F#2 – E3 – C4 – E♭4 – G4 – B4 – B♭5>, followed by another statement in the descending line (downward stems in the score) in m. 7 <C5 – E5 – B4 – B♭4 – G3> when combined with the piano bass E♭2. The upper piano line begins with <B♭5 – A5> (the initial notes so A̲lban B̲erg), part of <B♭5 – A5 – B5 – F#5 – D5>, which with E♭ yields an [012589] sharing notes {A,B♭,E♭} with the Schönberg motto set.

Set-class [012589] ([012569]) occurs throughout op. 5, no. 1: in addition to those instances just cited, as <F4 – D4 – D♭4 – B♭3 – A3 – G#3> (clarinet, mm. 4 – 6), and <G2 – F#2 – E♭2 – D♭2 – B♭1 – D1> (piano, bass descent, mm. 6 – 8). In the final chord of op. 5, no. 1, the entire motto appears at sum 2, in a ten-note collection that excludes D♭ and E♭. The [012589] portion appears as {G,F#, F,D,B,B♭}, at the same level as the G-based "tonic" figure in m. 2 ({G, F#,B♭, G,D,B} in the left hand of the piano), reaffirming the "tonic" status of the final chord around G2.

The Orchestral Pieces op. 6 were written in 1913–15, with the first two movements premiered on June 5, 1923, but the complete premiere delayed until April 14, 1930.[113] The three pieces increase in length and complexity roughly in the proportions 1:2:3, from the *Präludium* at 56 bars, through *Reigen* at 121 bars, to the *Marsch* at 174 bars.[114] The first movement has a symmetrical three-part ABA' form defined by tempo, instrumentation, and musical material, in which the density, dynamics, and register expand until the climax in m. 36 (approximately 64 percent of the way through the movement), then decrease to the end (fig. 3.35).[115] The three internal aa'b subsections of the first A section return in reverse order, as ba'a and mm. 1–8 in the final a are restated in retrograde as mm. 49–56; Berg's tempo indications clearly point to the correspondences between mm. 9 and 42 and mm. 8 and 49. The A and A' sections do not correspond exactly, however, for the b subsection of mm. 12–15 returns embedded near the end of the B section (m. 39) in the climax and transition subsection, prior to the beginning of A' in m. 42. The middle section has two formal aspects: melodically it groups as an antecedent (mm. 15–24) and varied inverted consequent (mm. 25–36); harmonically, however, mm. 15–24 consist of a varied version of mm. 1–14, whereas mm. 25–36 have their own harmonic organization. The dual status of mm. 15–24 as a harmonic variant of mm. 1–14 and melodic antecedent to mm. 25–36 creates continuity across the three-part form of the movement.

The orchestration of the opening mm. 1–8 and closing retrograde mm. 46–55 is particularly distinctive, as the movement seemingly emerges from and returns to the depths of a primeval world. The opening bars evolve from

---

Figure 3.35. Form in op. 6, no. 1

A	a	mm. 1–8	*langsam* quarter, *Tempo I*, motive 6/e
	a'	mm. 9–12	a tempo, motive 6/e
	b	mm. 12–15	rhythmic, motive 6/a
B	a/c	mm. 15–24	*wenig bewegter Tempo II* (antecedent)
	a/c'	mm. 25–36	Tempo II, *Wenig bewegter Tempo II* (consequent)
	db	mm. 36–41	motives 6/b,c, climax, transition
	(b	m. 39	= mm. 12–15, motive 6/a)
A'	a'	mm. 42–44	Tempo I of corresponding m. 9 (mm. 9–12)
	e	mm. 45–46	motive 6/d
	a'	mm. 47–48	motive 6/e–D-based chord
	a	mm. 49–56	*sehr langsam*, corresponding to m. 8 (mm. 8–1 retrograde), motive 6/e

---

unpitched percussion to pitched percussion, with increasing rhythmic activity, instrumental density, and expanding register, moving to low brass and strings, then to a plaintive melody in the high register of the bassoon (mm. 6–8) followed by a similarly high register figure in the trombone (mm. 9–11). The opening percussion sounds group in $\frac{5}{8}$ beginning from the first attack, ending with decreasing $\frac{7}{8}$, $\frac{5}{8}$, and $\frac{4}{8}$ groups in mm. 6–7, conflicting with the notated meter created and supported by harmonic and melodic events.

In the corresponding bars ending the movement, the instrumental tension is eased dramatically by the melodic use of flute and bassoon (mm. 42–44) and violin (mm. 51–52) in their low registers, in place of the previous high-register trombone and bassoon notes. Overall, the music regresses back to the low register, with increasingly less activity through pitched and finally unpitched percussion. The implied meter is $\frac{7}{8}$ from m. 53 to m. 56 (beginning from beat $3\frac{1}{2}$ in m. 52); from this point, notes and rests are inversely related: notes with durations of <4–3–2–1> eighths and rests of <3–4–5–5> eighths. The symmetry of the A and A' sections is enhanced by the appearance of unpitched percussion at the climax of the movement, near the end of the B section, at the point of greatest registral span, instrumental density, and dynamics.

The outer sections of the movement are characterized by a recurring rhythmic motive set with $\frac{4}{4}$ meter (ex. 3.42), in mm. 9–10 (trombone), 13–14

Example 3.42. Rhythmic motive in op. 6, no. 1, mm. 9–10

(percussion, low strings, brass, and harp), 36 (horns), and 42–43 (flute, bassoon). The rhythm characteristically switches from duple to triple divisions with suppressed beats by ties, but it is metrical, spanning a measure unit in its total duration. The second half of the B section (the beginning of the consequent statement, mm. 25ff.) is marked by two related juxtaposed rhythms: the first (violins, m. 25) has time points <0–8–16–24–36–60–(96)> (units of triplet sixty-fourths) in a characteristic decelerating pattern of relative durations of <2–2–2–3–6–9>, and the second (bassoons) has syncopated time points <6–24–30–45–60> (the $\frac{4}{4}$ beats are <0–24–48–72–(96)>). The two rhythms coincide at time points 24 and 60 (beats 2 and 3.5), in units of 24 and 36 or an asymmetrical 2 + 3 + 3 pattern (in eighths) within the bar. The middle section also features a strongly metric recurring dotted rhythmic figure, dotted-eighth–sixteenth (m. 21, flute, oboe; mm. 23–24, trumpet, violin, cello, clarinet; mm. 31–34, violins 1–2, bassoon). This dotted rhythm returns to provide the initial impulse for the transition back to the A' section, combined with the opening [014]s (mm. 39–41, clarinets, trumpets, trombones).

The climax (m. 36) is marked by the recurrence of the 5-cycle+ motive <C–Bb–Eb–Ab> in five durations simultaneously: half notes (trombones), triplet halves (trombones), quarters (clarinets, trumpets, xylophone), eighths (flute), and sixteenths (glockenspiel, violins), counterpointed by the rhythmic motive from the A section (horns, ex. 3.42). The notated $\frac{4}{4}$ meter is generally supported by all of these durational groups, beginning with the unison attack on the downbeat of m. 36.

Although five of the recurring motives in op. 6 appear in the first movement, only motives 6/a (mm. 12–14, ex. 3.26d, and m. 39) and the [014]-based 6/e (m. 8, ex. 3.28c) play integral roles. The other motives appear only once, as precursors: motives 6/b and 6/c immediately after the climax (6/b, mm. 38–40, flute, oboe, trumpet, viola, then flute, clarinet, violin, viola; 6/c, m. 38, flute, oboe, trumpet, violin, viola, to horn); motive 6/d inserted as a parenthesis in the A' section (mm. 44–46, violin, cello).

The harmonic language of op. 6, no. 1 is based on several interrelated elements: (1) primary 5-cycle–based and secondary whole-tone–based collections; (2) the pervasive use of [014]s, from motives 6/a and 6/e, on the surface and in transpositional levels; (3) a sum-10 relationship between surface materials (this level, mapping F/F and B/B, returns throughout Berg's music, particularly in the *Chamber Concerto*); and (4) a tonal implication or focus on G and D, with G hierarchically superior to D. The harmonies in mm. 1–14, consisting of ten chords, are almost entirely 5-cycle–based (numbered 1–10 in ex. 3.43), either as continuous segments, with gaps in the cycle, as in the first chord, or with added notes as 5-cycle+ collections (all labeled with "5" in ex. 3.43, non-5-cycle notes are indicated with filled in note heads).[116] The close voice-leading connections throughout are exemplified in the succession of the first two chords, where the upper interval 5 notes <Eb–Ab>, the last two notes of the gapped 5-cycle of chord 1 <G–(C)–F–Bb–Eb–Ab>, are held over to become the first two notes of the 5-cycle of chord 2 <Eb–Ab–C#–F#–B>, but placed over the rest of the cycle in a reverse of the relative position of this dyad in the first chord's 5-cycle. The gap between G2 and F3 in the first chord is filled in registrally by the C#3 in chord 2; this change from the expected C3 reflects the T1 transposition of {F3,Bb3} to {F#3,B3}. In chords 2 to 3, the interval 5 F#–B is held over, but B becomes dissonant in the C whole-tone+ context of chord 3. Each of the upper-voice notes in mm. 1–14, <Ab–Bb–Eb–Db>, which together form a 5-cycle collection [0257], is initially consonant, but the Eb in chords 4–7 alternates in status from dissonant to consonant, before the final C# is consonant with chord 10.

Example 3.43. Cyclic pitch structure in op. 6, no. 1 (priority notes in open noteheads)

Example 3.43. Cyclic pitch structure in op. 6, no. 1 (priority notes in open noteheads)
(*Continued*)

Within chords 1–10, two symmetrically placed intervening chords interrupt the pattern of 5-cycle events: the whole-tone+ chord 3 and 3-cycle+ chord 8. The whole-tone+ chord is reflected in the bass line from chord 4, which unfolds first a C whole-tone segment <D–B♭–C>, then a C♯ whole-tone collection <D♭–E♭–F–B–G> (extending over the section to the repeat of chord 1 in m. 15). The whole-tone organization of the bass line returns in the second part of the middle section (mm. 25–32), where the bass is organized around the C whole-tone collection as <F2–D2–C2–A♭1–F♯1–E2–B♭2–C2–B♭2–G♯2>.

Chords 1, 2, and 3 return to begin the first part of the middle section of op. 6, no. 1 (mm. 15ff.), followed by chords 4, 5, and 6 transposed first at T3 (mm. 20–22; in the transposed chord 6, a G♭4 substitutes for G4, creating a whole-tone+ chord), then sequentially at T4 (mm. 22−24). In the closing mm. 42−55, chords 4, 5, and 6 return, followed by a simplified version of chord 4 as whole-tone+ cycle collection{D,F,A,B}, then, in retrograde, chords 3, 2, and 1. The formal return to 5-cycle harmonies is foreshadowed by the emergence of 5-cycle material towards the end of the middle section: the bass <G#2−C#3−(E3)−E♭3−B♭2> in mm. 32−34 restates the melody notes of mm. 1−14 in a different order, and the climax chord in m. 36 is a seven-note 5-cycle collection spanning D through A♭ with an added note B.

In addition to the melody notes <A♭4−B♭4−E♭5−C#4> in mm. 1−14, the upper melodic voice includes [014]s <E4−G4−A♭4> and <D4−E♭4−G♭4> (m. 8) and [03458] <F#4−A4−F4−E4−C#4> from two conjoined [014]s <F−F#−A> and <F−E−C#> (mm. 9−12). The first two [014]s each have two notes in the prevailing C whole-tone+ harmony of chord 3; the [03458] is dissonant over chords 8 and 9 until the final C# aligns consonantly with the 5-cycle chord 10. The first two [014]s return over chord 1 to begin the middle section in m. 15; the <E−G−A♭> is gradually spun out into a long continuous sequential melody in mm. 15−24. At m. 25, an inverted [014] <A♭5−F5−E5>, with two notes E and A♭ consonant and the F dissonant in the recurring C whole-tone+ harmony <G3−D4−F#4−B♭4>, is repeated; then, at m. 28, it similarly spins out a consequent melody, its contour inverted from the corresponding melody in mm. 15−24. The [03458] <F#−A−F#−F−E−C#> from mm. 9−12 returns as a chord in m. 32, with an added bass G#2 that initiates the <G#2−C3−E♭3−B♭2> restatement of the opening melody notes; then it reappears in its original motivic shape in the bass of mm. 38−40, where the final C#2 serves as a "leading tone" to the bass D2 beginning at A' restatement.

The internal interval-classes 1, 3, and 4 of [014] act as transpositional levels within and between surface materials. Within mm. 15−24, chords 4−6 return transposed, first at T3 (mm. 20−21), then at T4 (mm. 22−23). The [014]s <E−G−A♭> and <D−E♭−G♭> (m. 8) are related to the [03458] [014]s <C#−E−F> and <F−F#−A> by T−3 and T3 respectively. These first two [014]s, <E−G−A♭> and <D−E♭−G♭>, relate to each other at sum 10, symmetrically arranged around F4; the same sum-10 relationship obtains between <F−F#−A> and <F−E−C#>, from mm. 9−12, again symmetrical around F4. Chord 7, accompanying the beginning of <F#−A−F#−F−E−C#>, with the A of the [03458] included, is comprised of sum-10 symmetrical pairs D♭/A, G/E♭, C/B♭, and F/F; chord 10 also is based on sum 10 pairs B/B, E/F#, and A/C#. Sum-10 pairs also appear within and between chords: the outer voices of chords 1 and 4 are in sum-10 pairs G/E♭ and D/A♭. When <E−G−A♭> and <D−E♭−G♭> combine with chord 1 in m. 15, all notes are in sum-10 pairs: E/G♭, G/E♭, F/F, and A♭/D, and the T3-transposed chord 4 in m. 21 also has sum-10 pairs F/F, G/E♭, C/B♭. The same sum returns in the climax chord (m. 36), pairs D/A♭, G/E♭, C/B♭, F/F and B/B, followed by the return of the sum-10–based [03458] from mm. 9–12.

The harmonies in op. 6, no. 1 are also oriented around a focus of D and G, in hierarchical relationships analogous to I and IV or V and I. The opening chords 1–4 may be interpreted as I [VII]–V in G; the interpretation of chord 3 as a dominant to D relates to its whole-tone+ construction by positing the traditional function of a whole-tone chord as dominant. The D-based chord 4 is emphasized by the unique internal interval 7s in its lower notes, in place of the interval 5s of surrounding chords. In the beginning of the second part of the middle section (mm. 25ff.), a chord succession alternates 5-cycle chords with whole-tone+ cycle collections built over G. Characteristically, the "dissonant" G is nonetheless a bass note supported by upper interval 7 note D, lending it the illusion of a "tonal" stability, supported by surrounding emphases on G. A D-based chord returns at the climax in m. 36, followed by the [03458] figure from mm. 9–12 that ends with oscillating C♯–E to lead back to D and begin the A' section, recalling the bass of chords 2–4 from the opening. A simplified D chord, as triadic {D,F,A,B}, returns in m. 48, before chords 3–1 reappear to end on a bass G; because of the retrograde, the implied tonal progression of the opening does not function as a nonsensical V–VII/V–I, but the end nonetheless leaves a strong impression of a G focus.

4 The Twelve-Tone Music: Introduction

After completing *Wozzeck*, Berg took the first steps toward incorporating Schoenberg's techniques of "composition with twelve tones" into his music with the *Chamber Concerto*, a work that straddles Berg's atonal and twelve-tone periods, as the op. 2 songs link his tonal and atonal music.[1] The extraordinary "Open Letter" on the *Chamber Concerto*, dated February 9, 1925, and published by Berg in a public dedication to Schoenberg, is a veritable declaration of the compositional principles that characterize the rest of his music.[2] Berg outlined both extramusical and purely musical features in his letter. The former are the programmatic, symbolic, and autobiographical aspects, which include numerology, quotation and other musical references, and names set in musical notation. As described in the introduction, these elements continued through the rest of his compositions. The second aspect referred to is the musical language, including pitch relationships described by Berg as "tonal," "completely dissolved tonality" and "twelve-tone," systematic thematic and formal relationships, and motivic and formal uses of rhythm, meter, and tempo. Although the twelve-tone techniques are at an early stage in the *Chamber Concerto*, where "rows" are actually only themes, the language foreshadows the extensions of Berg's cyclic collections and techniques to twelve-tone procedures that characterize the rest of his music.

We may define "twelve-tone" music as music in which all pitch events in a piece can be traced, without an unreasonable amount of difficulty, to the common source of the ordered intervals of a twelve-note row, taking pieces like Schoenberg's *Variations for Orchestra* op. 31 and Webern's *Symphony* op. 21 as examples. In these and similar pieces, material derived from rows by partitions—the compositional grouping of notes non-adjacent in the row or extracted from two or more row forms—generally either (1) replicates ordered or unordered pitch-class sets or set-classes from row segments; (2) appears in the context of the ordered row; or (3) is part of a compositional process stemming from the intervalic properties of the row in which every step in the process is derived directly from the previous step. By strict application of these criteria, Berg's later music, from its tentative beginnings in the *Chamber Concerto* to the mature Violin Concerto, is not truly twelve-tone—except perhaps for the second version of the song "Schließe mir dir Augen beide"—despite the presence of rows and characteristic twelve-tone techniques. It is also not the case that Berg "fused" twelve-tone techniques with tonality (a tonal center supported by triadic tonic and dominant functions) in his later music.[3] The two systems are fundamentally incompatible. Instead, the basis of Berg's pitch language in his later music continues to be the cyclic collections of his earlier period, developed with regard to order-position relationships and aggregate completion, and still capable of tonal allusion by registral spacing and intervalic emphases, but similar enough to his atonal music that Berg's adaptation of Schoenberg's twelve-tone ideas marks a difference in degree rather than in kind.[4] The extended passages from the Violin Concerto in examples 5.74, 5.75, and 5.76, for instance, although containing many notes more or less derivable from rows as well as seemingly dissonant notes and resolutions, plus vertical spacing and linear connections strongly implying tonal progressions, are more consistently interpretable in terms of the mixture of 5-cycle+, whole-tone+, and 3-cycle+ collections characteristic of Berg's earlier music.

BERG AS THEORIST AND ANALYST

Berg left a rich legacy of sketches, drafts, and comments on his music from the *Chamber Concerto* to the Violin Concerto, along with analyses written for Willi Reich and Rudolf Kolisch and letters to Reich, Webern, and Schoenberg, among others.[5] These materials consistently demonstrate the extent to which Berg approached his music analytically, consciously working out formal possibilities and, in his twelve-tone charts, carefully relating derived material to the original row by the use of order-position numbers.[6] Berg's comments and calculations throughout indicate his fascination with ordered relationships based on numerology and cyclic or symmetrical relationships, as well as his belief in the somewhat mystical underlying unity that they represented.

Berg's twelve-tone sketches provide ample evidence of the continuing influence of interval cycles and cyclic collections on his composition. His comments on the row used in the first movement of the *Lyric Suite* include a sketch of the 5-cycle trichords in order positions 024, 135, 68A, and 79B, which he reordered to make a continuous 5/7-cycle (cf. exx. 5.11a and d). In the same movement he also extracted a four-note segment from the row and transposed it by a 3-cycle in a non-aggregate context (ex. 5.9), in a characteristic cyclic but non-row procedure. The initial row sketches (July 17, 1927) for *Lulu* contain an extraction of the two whole-tone collections (ex. 5.36i), two versions of an extracted interval-class 5 and segmentation of the remaining notes into two 5-cycle collections (exx. 5.36n–o), and partitions of combined 3-cycle [0369]s and the multicyclic [0167], which serve as basic cells in the opera (ex. 5.36p–r). Materials derived for *Lulu* at a later date, the late summer of 1929, also amply represented in sketches, consist of a cyclic treatment of order positions, as in the new rows created from the main row by extracting notes in cyclic series. For instance, the row associated with the character Alwa is created by taking every seventh note of the principal row, beginning with the first, in a 7-cycle of order positions 07294B6183A5 (ex. 5.37). In sketches for the Violin Concerto, the pitch 7-cycle on every other note—or on the 2-cycle of order positions 02468—is highlighted in the opening bars, and the whole-tone segment in the final four notes is used as a point of invariance with the chorale theme in the final movement (cf. exx. 5.64 and 5.73).

Berg's analyses of and commentary on the *Lyric Suite* document many of the characteristic features of his twelve-tone techniques: (1) the row is rotated and may be regarded as a "ring," with relationships that include the wrap-around intervals; (2) the content of segments is reordered; (3) the potential for tonal allusion within segments is encouraged; (4) segmental invariance between rows is exploited; (5) segments are extracted from the row and used in non-row contexts, and the residue (with fewer than twelve distinct pitch-classes) is used as a separate compositional unit; (6) the row is partitioned into motives that appear independently of the row context; and (7) partitioning creates motivic rhythms from order positions within the row, and these rhythms are used outside the row context. The most characteristic of these aspects is Berg's derivation of materials, both pitch and rhythmic, from a row, followed by their use independent of the row context—placing the structural role on the intervalic properties of the derived materials rather than the source row.

In his "Open Letter" on the *Chamber Concerto*, Berg described the rhythmic organization of the third movement, with three rhythmic motives set in a *rondo ritmico*, and noted the precursor to this movement in Act III, scene iii of *Wozzeck* and the last movement of Schoenberg's Wind Quintet op. 26. Motivic rhythms also appear in constructive roles in *Der Wein*, *Lulu*, and the Violin Concerto. The derivations of rhythms from order-position partitions in rows in the *Lyric Suite* and in *Lulu* demonstrate the level to which Berg integrated aspects of his earlier music with twelve-tone techniques.

FUNCTION OF ROWS

Berg's sketch materials indicate the extent to which he painstakingly related derived materials to original rows, using order-position numbers 1 – 12, but the fact that these relationships are not always made explicit on the surface of the music has led to debate on the structural role of these rows in his later music. For instance, Jarman, Perle, Reich, and Reiter differ on the role of the principal row as a unifier in the opera *Lulu*, the relevance of the derivational procedures, and whether or not Berg reveals the row relationships in an audible way in the music.[7] The controversy revolves around the cyclic order-position derivations of rows, in which notes from the main row are extracted in cyclic successions to create new rows—mentioned above in relation to the character Alwa's row—and with materials requiring several steps for their derivation, as with the collections and serial motives associated with the character of Countess Geschwitz. In his early (1936) analysis of *Lulu*, Reich referred to a letter from Berg in which the latter states: "The unity of the music is assured by the fact that the whole opera is constructed upon a single twelve-note row, the subdivision, inversion, and reforming of which made possible in turn not only the great variety but in many instances what is practically a leitmotive treatment of both melodic and harmonic elements."[8]

Many writers have commented on the "unity" provided by the source row in light of the abstract nature of the derivations of materials.[9] Although Reiter and, more recently, Hall have extended the derivations given by Reich and shown by detailed sketch study that many more of these relationships are present than previously uncovered,[10] Perle has claimed that the derivations in and of themselves are irrelevant to analysis; the only information of use is the invariances and other relationships that obtain between the materials themselves.[11] Jarman has claimed that derivational procedures have relevance only if the derivations are demonstrated clearly on the surface.[12]

My position on this question is that any relationships that Berg reveals between rows and material on the surface may have dramatic associations or even local musical structural bases, but they are not necessary for musical coherence. Since the rows are not central, their treatment or relationship to the surface need not be consistent. Thus Berg can reorder rows and even add or omit notes without disturbing the language. Although he often carefully related derived materials to the original row, the use of row-derived materials in non-row contexts, the reordering of row segments, and the free addition of non–row-derived notes suggests that the basis of the language is not the rows but the smaller derived and non-derived materials, which are mostly, as in his atonal music, cyclic-based collections. With twelve-tone rows thus regarded as one means to an end, rather than an end in and of themselves, questions concerning the extent to which Berg's later music follows Schoenberg's stated strictures on the number of rows in any one piece or as to whether the row occupies a central position and is audibly related to all events in the piece are not central to analysis. Since musical coherence does not depend on the row as the main referent, no requirement exists for a consistent treatment of rows.

My assertion that Berg's twelve-tone music is neither row-based nor tonally-based might be challenged on the basis of the sketches. Berg's twelve-tone sketches include row charts and drafts that clearly identify rows by labels and by order positions numbered 1–12; even the most esoteric derivations of material are shown in their relationships to the order of the rows. In addition to his row labels, in the sketches—particularly those for the Violin Concerto—Berg included Roman-numeral "tonal" analyses of his materials, indicating that he regarded these materials as at least alluding to such relationships.[13] Despite the row and tonal indications in Berg's sketches, however, I reject the notion that such evidence applies directly to the music as the only possible explanation. As I and others have argued elsewhere, the relationship between sketch and finished piece can never be assumed to be a one-to-one correspondence, even where the same notes appear in both. The goals and musical context of sketches are not the same as in the finished piece, which provides a context not present in the sketches. Sketches can serve as confirmations or suggestions in the context of an analysis, but they can never direct the analysis.[14] Sketches are, nonetheless, a great help in analysis, and, outside the realm of analysis, Berg's sketches have provided invaluable information about the composer, his compositional process, the chronology of his compositions, and incomplete works, and have allowed such seminal events as the discovery of the film music scenario in *Lulu*, the completion of Berg's second opera, *Lulu*, and the uncovering of the hidden song in the final movement of the *Lyric Suite*.

Although rows are not the primary basis of pitch relationships, they play an important role in Berg's later music. In addition to their thematic role, traditional row relationships, such as ordered and unordered segmental and non-segmental pitch, pitch-class, and set-class invariance abound, although systematic combinatorial row combinations are rare. The sketches show derivations of material from rows by methods ranging from those dependent on the order of pitch-classes in the row to those independent of the order, stemming only from properties of the aggregate. Compromises between order and aggregate content abound, exemplified by partially ordered rows such as that of the character Schigolch in *Lulu*, in which the three ordered [0123] tetrachords are internally ordered in different ways, in complete and incomplete forms (ex. 5.36m).[15]

The cyclic operations on order positions as a method of deriving new material, even new rows, from a source row—noted above in the row associated with the character Alwa in *Lulu*—along with Berg's frequent use of pitch 5-cycle collections, suggest an isomorphism between this treatment of pitch-classes and that of order positions.[16] Although attractive, the analogy is limited, since the two are perceived quite differently. Cycles of pitches and cyclic collections are audible as pitches and intervals, but order-position cycles are perceptible in rhythmic relationships, as durational intervals. A clear instance of Berg's structural use of rhythmic "intervals" or durations of order positions in different rows occurs in the film music of *Lulu*. Here a series of rows follow one another, representing the parade of witnesses at the trial of *Lulu* (mm. 670–80). The principal row and the Alwa row are the first to appear, both in continuous sixteenth notes, with the notes {E,A,B♭,E♭} in the referential principal row order positions 0268 punctuated to create rhythms within the rows (ex. 5.37). Because of the invariances between a 1-cycle 0123456789AB (the principal row) and a 7-cycle 07294B6183 (the Alwa row) of 02468A or a 2-cycle of order positions, the rhythm of order positions 0268 is identical, as a rhythmic manifestation of the order-position relationships.[17] Another example occurs at the death of Dr. Schön (ex. 5.51), where the notes of this character's row are embedded in an equal-duration presentation of the principal row of the opera, and the rhythmic proportions of the row notes reflect the order-position 02591468B37A derivation of the Schön row from the principal row.

TONAL ALLUSION

Although Berg took advantage of the tonal appearance of interval cycles and cyclic collections in his previous music, it is remarkable that, even as he adopted the more classical style of twelve-tone composition in his later pieces, such tonal allusions become more prominent, as in the final movement chorale variations in the Violin Concerto.[18] Berg indicated in several comments and writings that he intentionally explored the tonal possibilities of his materials: "all the more since a movement in my second quartet [*Lyric Suite*] being written now presents the attempt to write the very strictest twelve-tone music with strong *tonal* elements, which was certainly *possible*."[19] "In any case, if you could derive from them [Willi Reich's rows derived by cyclic operations on order positions], so that something tonal (or, let's say, something of the rules of the old tonality) is included in twelve-note composition, that would be a great gain for the musical side."[20]

With regard to *Lulu*, Schoenberg wrote about a conversation with Berg in which the latter noted that "as a dramatic composer he did not believe he could do without the possibility of contrasted characterisation, including an occasional recourse to major and minor."[21] In *Lulu*, the row associated with Dr. Schön has a "major triad" in its first three notes, whereas Alwa's row has a "minor triad" in the same position (see ex. 5.37); the father-son relationship is represented by the sound and associations of this "major-minor" duality, realized in many passages throughout the opera. The surroundings are not tonal, however, and in fact the structural basis is the inversional relationships between the two rows, a feature exploited particularly with regard to Dr. Schön's materials, but the triads present a familiar distinctive difference yet also a recognizable similarity in sonority.[22] In the Violin Concerto, the triadic row segments allow for an often "tonal"-sounding surface, and, in places, analogous procedures, such as the mixing of "minor" and "major" by adding additional notes outside the purview of the row (see trio 1, ex. 5.69, where the D in the first "triad" is an added note, creating a "major/minor" momentary "mixture").[23]

The use of Bach's harmonization of the chorale melody "Es ist genug" in the Violin Concerto is a well-known instance of an apparent juxtaposition of twelve-tone and tonal elements. The chorale appears without disrupting the musical coherence because its tonal progression and the rows intertwined around the voices of the chorale are both underlaid by the cyclic collections that govern the entire piece (exx. 5.74–76 show passages from the fourth-movement chorale variations interpreted cyclically). Beyond the invariance of the opening of the chorale melody and the last four notes of the row, a whole-tone tetrachord [0246] (exx. 5.64 and 5.73), both row and chorale setting are shaped by the 5-, 3-, and whole-tone-cycle–based collections that occur throughout the concerto. The chorale maintains its symbolic, extra-musical associations, which exceed the bounds of the piece, but its tonal language seamlessly emerges from and dissolves into the surrounding cyclically-based passages.

ROWS, DERIVED MATERIALS, AND CYCLES

Developments in Berg's cyclic materials in his later music include the greater use of aggregate formations and the incorporation of cyclic collections within rows as segments or as partitions, in cyclic and non-cyclic order position patterns.[24] Cycles easily form into aggregates by continuation, as in 1- or 5-cycles, or with continuation and transposition, in 2-, 3-, 4-, and 6-cycles (ex. 1.1). Aggregate completion, which occurs to a lesser extent in Berg's earlier music, is frequent in the twelve-tone music, particularly, of course, in the context of rows.

The *Chamber Concerto* marks a preliminary step in the use of cyclic collections as row segments. The "rows" in this piece are mostly twelve-note themes only, or themes that contain the twelve distinct notes within them. Cyclic collections are incorporated as segments in only a few cases. For the most part, non-cyclic–based melodic materials are set in cyclic harmonic contexts, as in the setting of a theme from the second movement in parallel five-voice 3-cycle+ [01369]s (theme 8, ex. 5.2b). In general, the melodic and harmonic domains are related less consistently here than in later works. The dichotomy between the cyclic vertical language and the horizontal ordered aggregate themes is solved in subsequent pieces by a consistent use of cyclic collections as row segments.

The preeminent role of 5-cycle–based collections in pieces after the *Chamber Concerto* is reflected in the intervalic content of row hexachords: the rows of "Schließe mir" (second setting) and the first movement of the *Lyric Suite* (the same row) and the principal row of *Lulu* have the same 5-cycle–based hexachords [024579] (ex. 5.8 [row 1] and 5.36a); the rows of *Der Wein* and of Alwa and Dr. Schön in *Lulu* have hexachords of 5-cycle+ [012479] and gapped 5-cycle [013568] (ex. 5.27 and 5.37); and the row of the character Lulu in the opera has hexachords of 5-cycle+ [023579] (ex. 5.36h). The row of the Violin Concerto has a 7-cycle succession in order positions 02468 that is partitioned out in the opening bars (ex. 5.64).

In *Lulu*, most of the derived and non-row musical materials also have 5-cycle characteristics: (1) the Acrobat's 5-cycle piano clusters of "white" notes [013568A] and "black" notes [02479]; (2) the three 5-cycle–based collections [05], [02479], and [01378] associated with the Countess Geschwitz (ex. 5.57); (3) the interval-class 5 content of the "Picture" trichords [015], [027], [025] (ex. 5.36g); and (4) the diatonic [013568A] collections of the Wedekind tune used in Act III. Two of the basic cells (BCs) of the opera also have important 5-cycle components: BC I [0167] and BC II [01378].[25]

The 5-cycle source of material in the opera allows multiple invariance possibilities. For instance, the Acrobat piano clusters and one of the Countess Geschwitz collections are both pentachord [02479], a feature exploited in the invariant collections accompanying their discussion in Act II, scene ii (mm. 722–73). Another of the Countess collections, [01378], is also BC II of the opera and a subset of the opening [013568] hexachords of the Alwa (order positions 01245) and Dr. Schön rows (order positions 01234). A dramatic instance of this invariance occurs when, at the moment of death, Dr. Schön sees the Countess emerging from the closet, to [01378] {E,A,B,C,F} acting both as a Countess collection and as 01234 of Dr. Schön's inverted row (Act II, scene i, mm. 605–6). The tendency throughout for materials to divide into "white" note

[013568A] groups and mostly "black" note [02479] groups in characteristic transpositional levels also stems from the shared 5-cycle basis.

The primary basic cells in *Lulu* are the multi-cyclic collections [0369] and [0167] and, also appearing but to a lesser extent, [0268]. As described earlier, each permits two or three cyclic interpretations: [0369] as 3- or 6-cycle collections; [0167] as 1-, 5-, or 6-cycle collections; and [0268] as 2-, 4-, or 6-cycle collections. The three BCs are related by their common interval-class 6s; together they include all six interval-classes and thus provide a maximum of variety and possibilities of interaction with the materials in the opera. These collections are highly redundant, with only three ([0369]) or six ([0167], [0268]) distinct pitch-class realizations, and so may be combined into aggregates and derived from rows in multiple ways. The collections are also prominent in *Der Wein*, where three interval-class 6s are partitioned from the row and combined in pairs as [0268] and [0167], with the residue [012678] divided into 1-cycle [012]s (cf. ex. 5.29, 5.32).

In the first movement of the *Lyric Suite*, the emphasis on the 5-cycle content of the hexachords, rather than the order, is reflected in the three versions of the row hexachords: (1) the all-interval arrangement of the main theme (ex. 5.11a), (2) an ordered 5-cycle accompaniment and in a version of the main theme in the coda (ex. 5.11d), and (3) in diatonic "scalar" forms comprised of intervals 1 and 2, as the closing theme, and in a version of the main theme (ex. 5.11c). The row properties stem from its 5-cycle basis: since complementary hexachordal 5-cycle segments are related by T6, the two hexachords are related at T6; as a result, the pivotal T6-related notes B and F never appear in the same hexachord. Instead, they stand at the boundaries of the four principal main rows used: P5, PB, I5, and IB.

The *Lyric Suite* row in its all-interval form also has a latent 3-cycle structure emerging from properties of the 5-cycle basis. Both within a single 5-cycle hexachord and between two complementary 5-cycle based hexachords, notes can be arranged in symmetrical pairs related by interval-class 3s. Thus, within the symmetrically arranged 5-cycle hexachords (ex. 5.8, row 1) with interval pattern <B89A7652341>, dyads in corresponding notes in the two hexachords are related by interval-class 3. An alignment of the two hexachords exploiting this property occurs at the beginning of the second setting of "Schließe mir die Augen beide": <F−E−C−A−G−D> with <Ab−Db−Eb−Gb−Bb−B>. As another result of this arrangement of interval-class 3−related pairs, the row is capable of trichordal combinatoriality at T = 3-cycle {0369}, {147A}, or {258B}, as occurs partially in a transition section in the first movement of the *Lyric Suite* (mm. 15−18, 18−19).[26]

As another consequence of the cyclic structure in the all-interval order of the *Lyric Suite* row, with segments of a 7-cycle on order positions 024 and 68A and an inversionally-related 5-cycle on order positions 135 and 79B (ex. 5.11b), adjacent notes in paired order positions 01 23 45 67 89 AB or 12 34 56 78 9A B0 are from inversionally-related 5/7 cycles and have the same sums (or indices).[27] In the row P5, for instance—<F – E – C – A – G – D – A♭ – D♭ – E♭ – G♭ – B♭ – B>—the sums are 9 between {F,E}, {C,A}, {G,D}, {A♭,D♭}, {E♭,G♭}, and {B♭,B} and 4 between the alternate dyads {E,C}, {A,G}, {D, A♭}, {D♭,E♭}, {G♭,B♭}, and {B,F}. Of the four main rows in the first movement of the *Lyric Suite*, P5 and PB (sums 4, 9) and IB and I5 (sums B, 4) share sum 4; thus, dyads in order positions 01 23 45 67 89 AB of P5 or PB are the same as those in 12 34 56 78 9A B(0) of IB or I5, respectively (exx. 5.11a and 5.11e show P5/IB–shared dyads). In the recapitulation of the movement, IB substitutes for P5 (m. 45) and is slurred to maintain the sum-4 dyads. Finally, the interlocking 5- and 7-cycles insure that each segmental trichord includes at least one interval-class 5 and that segmental tetrachords and pentachords include at least two interval-class 5s.

The "scalar" form of the *Lyric Suite* row anticipates a similar construction in the first hexachord of the row of *Der Wein*, lending it properties similar to those of a diatonic scale: "stepwise" interval-class 1 and 2 segments, "thirds" or interval-class 3s and 4s on every other note or on a 2-cycle of order positions, and fourths or interval-class 5s and interval-class 6s between notes separated by three, or a 3-cycle on order positions (ex. 5.27). In several places, interval 1 cycles are created by the interweaving of different rows. The row of the Violin Concerto is constructed oppositely to that of *Der Wein*: segments are interval-class 3s or interval-class 4s, and a 2-cycle on order positions yields interval-class 5s (ex. 5.64). As in the row of *Der Wein*, however, "stepwise" or even 1-cycle successions are created by interweaving two or three rows. The Violin Concerto row is derivable from that of *Der Wein* by a varied 2-cycle on order positions of the latter, 024613AB7859 (ex. 5.27); in addition, two interwoven rows from the Violin Concerto, P8 and PA (m. 145), yield pitch-classes <8AB1357>, close to the P8 row order positions 0123456 (pitch-classes <8AB1347>) of *Der Wein*.

The Violin Concerto row is based on both 5- (or 7-) cycles on non-adjacent notes and whole-tone+ collections on non-adjacent notes and segments (ex. 5.64). The interweaving of these two cycles in the row creates overlapping segmental [037] trichords that themselves are related in 5-cycles (ex. 5.66, mm. 11–15). This tonal appearance establishes the context into which the tonal choral "Es ist genug" enters without disturbing the fabric of the musical language.

As in Berg's atonal works, his later pieces usually feature two cyclic collections as primary, with a third secondary, from the whole-tone, 3-cycle, and 5-cycle collections; 1- and 6-cycles appear, as in his earlier music, in combination with one of the primary cycles. In the *Lyric Suite*, for instance, the 5-cycle first movement contrasts with the rest of the quartet, in which the row is successively altered to make a total of four rows. Rows 2, 3, and 4 are characterized by segmental whole-tone+ collection [0126]s, a set particularly prominent in its {F,A,B♭,B} form in movements 2−4 (ex. 5.8). Along with [0126], three other whole-tone+ tetrachords, [0236], [0258], and [0137], are prominent in the work, all with whole-tone subset [026], relating row and non-row material in the quartet—including the quotes from Zemlinsky's *Lyric Symphony*, based on [0236], and the opening of Wagner's *Tristan und Isolde*, based on [0126] (exx. 5.21 and 5.25). Set [0236] is also a 3-cycle+ collection, and it appears in this context in movement 2 (ex. 5.14 m. 5).

Berg's incorporation of twelve-tone rows into his cyclic language, along with the use of collections such as the multicycled [0167] in *Lulu*, raises his cyclic language to a high level of integration. His "thematicization" of highly characteristic and complex cyclic materials may be compared with Beethoven's thematic use of the highly characteristic elements of tonality, triads, thirds, and half-steps, in works like the *Pathétique* Sonata and the *Eroica* Symphony. In a similar way, but in an operatic context, Berg infused the most characteristic cyclic materials—the basic cells [0167], [0268], and [0369]—with both musical and dramatic significance in *Lulu*, a work which may be regarded as the apex of his ability to extract the maximum cyclic consequences from his material.

ROW DERIVATIONS AND ORDER-POSITION CYCLES

Many of Berg's derivations of material from rows have been described in terms of cycles of order positions. As mentioned above, Berg's consistent use of order-position cycles suggests that intervals between pitches and "rhythmic intervals" between order positions may have been regarded in analogous ways. The two interact in interesting ways; for instance, in the Violin Concerto, the extraction of every other note, a 2-cycle of order positions 02468, yields a 7-cycle of pitch-classes, with P7: <G−D−A−E−B> (ex. 5.64). Figure 4.1 contains a list of cyclic operations on order positions in rows, with corresponding collections from Berg's music. The chart includes possibilities not used by Berg in his pieces, some of which appear in his sketches. The derivations in the a and b categories in figure 4.1 are alignments of vertical and horizontal row segments, yielding non-segments in the opposite dimension, familiar from much twelve-tone music. The derivations in the c categories are more removed from the row, since they consist of concatenated cyclic patterns of order positions, without regard for row segments. These types of derivations appeared first in *Der Wein*, where a 2-cycle on order positions groups the row into tetrachords and hexachords. The emergence of the derivations of type c in *Lulu* followed the composition of *Der Wein* in the summer of 1929, after Berg had begun *Lulu*, as part of the two-stage compositional process for the opera.

A characteristic feature of almost all of Berg's music is the use of repeated motives or, in the operas, leitmotivs and even longer themes or sections. The identity of this motivic material is paramount: motives and themes are consistently characterized by traditional contour associations, rhythm, order, and even pitch or pitch-class level. They are most often treated contrapuntally rather than developed or varied; retrograde orders rarely occur, except as part of formal palindromes.

As is the case with Schoenberg's early serial music, Berg's *Chamber Concerto* themes almost all contain the twelve distinct pitch-classes, but in different numbers of total notes (exx. 5.1 and 5.2).[28] The themes are treated contrapuntally, for the most part, and inverted and retrograded within formal sections entirely based on these transformations. Except when undergoing these basic transformations, however, the twelve-note themes are not, for the most part, used as rows. In only a few places do other characteristic twelve-tone features, such as changes in contour, verticalization of segments, combinatorial arrangements of segments, reordering of segments, and partitioning, occur.

In the works after the *Chamber Concerto*, traditional contour and rhythmic characteristics are used for themes and motives, which are often varied by beginning on different notes of rows, rotating the intervalic and pitch-class content. In "Schließe mir" (second setting), Berg used only two forms of the row, P5 and I8, the latter rotated to begin with its second hexachord as 6789AB012345. Thematic statements are created by the equivalent contour and rhythm of P5 in m. 1 and the rotated I8 in m. 11 (see exx. 5.5 and 5.6).[29] In *Lulu*, a similar thematic setting of a rotated row, in the case of a rotation of an inverted Alwa row in the contour and rhythm of the rondo theme, is used by Berg in a wry commentary on the esoteric nature of such a row transformation, with the text "No one at the office knows what to write."[30] In the first movement of the *Lyric Suite*, the main thematic contour and rhythm are set originally to P5, but later these motivic features are set with a rotated P5 beginning on order position 8, (m. 7) as well as in the alternate orders of the row, the 5-cycle and scalar orders (exx. 5.11a and 5.11c−e). Thus the main theme is independent of its intervalic order.

RETROGRADES

Berg rarely used retrograde row forms except in formal sections, as in the second half of formal palindromes. In the *Chamber Concerto*, the theme-and-variations form of the first movement is organized around the presentation of themes in prime (theme, variations 1 and 5), retrograde (variation 2), inversion

Figure 4.1. Cyclic operations on order positions of rows in Berg's twelve-tone music. CC = Chamber Concerto; SM II = "Schließe mir"; LS = Lyric Suite; DW = Der Wein; L = Lulu; VC = Violin Concerto.

original: 0123456789AB

a) vertical	b) horizontal	c) concatenations of horizontal
1) 2-cycles		
01	02468A mm. 18–19, SM II	02468A13579B Acrobat's row in L (ex. 5.37)
23	13579B recap. in LS, mvmt. 1, mm.	0246 8A13 579B tetrachords in DW (ex. 5.33)
45	42–44 (ex. 5.11b)	68A024 3579B1 hexachords in DW (ex. 5.35)
67		0246 1357 opening of VC (ex. 5.64)
89		
AB		
2) 3-cycles 012 tetrachords in DW (ex. 5.33)	0369 2479 Picture trichords	0369147A258B Schoolboy row in L (ex. 5.37)
345	147A as 036A L (ex. 5.36g)	2479036A158B Lulu row in L (ex. 5.36h)
678	258B 158B	
9AB		
3) 4-cycles		
048	0123	04815926A37B
159	4567	
26A	89AB	
37B		
4) 5-cycles a) 05A3816B4927 Countess Geschwitz source row in L (ex. 5.37)		
7294B6183A50 Alwa row in L (ex. 5.37)		

Figure 4.1. Cyclic operations on order positions of rows in Berg's twelve-tone music. *CC = Chamber Concerto; SM II = "Schließe mir"; LS = Lyric Suite; DW = Der Wein; L = Lulu; VC = Violin Concerto. (Continued)*

| | original: 0123456789AB | |
a) vertical	b) horizontal	c) concatenations of horizontal
5) 6 cycles: 06 17 28 39 4A 5B	012345 Painter dyads in L (ex. 5.36b) 6789AB SM II	06172839 4A5B 0167 2389 45AB Painter tetrachords in L (ex. 5.36c)
6) gradated cycles 02591468B37A 0136A/39/269B	series 23443223443 series 12345654321	Dr. Schön row in L (ex. 5.37) Chorale row from Alwa/principal/Schön rows in L (ex. 5.37)

(variation 3), and retrograde inversion (variation 4) forms of the material.[31] In "Schließe mir" (second setting) the row has no distinct retrograde; since Pn = R(Pn+6), any "retrograde" row can be interpreted as a prime or an inversion form. Berg creates a retrograde, however, by setting P5 in palindromic segments by contour and rhythm, in a thematic use surpassing the purely intervalic properties of the row (ex. 5.7).[32]

In the *Lyric Suite* and in *Lulu*, retrograde-based relationships prompted Berg to alter his materials. Of the former (which uses the same row as the second setting of "Schließe mir"), Berg wrote to Schoenberg that "the symmetry [of the row] also has a serious disadvantage. For the *second* half is a mirror image of the *first* half transposed down a diminished 5th <[A♭−D♭−E♭−G♭−B♭−C♭> second half = R(T6) of <F−E−C−A−G−D> first half] . . . from which it follows that this row has *no* independent retrograde form. As a matter of fact the retrograde is the original row R transposed down a diminished fifth [P(n+6) = R], which with appropriate transposition is equivalent to the row [P = R(n+6)]. For that reason . . . I decided in my next efforts to alter the row."[33]

Berg subsequently exchanged notes between the two hexachords of the row to make two other rows, then derived a fourth row from the third by a rhythmic-motivic partitioning (ex. 5.8). Given Berg's avoidance of retrograde row forms, however, it was probably the lack of variety due to the identity of intervals in the two hexachords, as well as the creating of the programmatically related note group {B♭,A,F,B}, rather than the lack of a distinct retrograde per se, that prompted him to alter the row.

In *Lulu* a somewhat similar situation arose. The relationship between the derivation of Alwa's row and a row initially intended for the Countess Geschwitz is that of prime and retrograde: R(Alwa's row) = the Countess row (ex. 5.37). This situation results from the inverted order-position relationship between the derived Alwa 7-cycle 07294B6183A5 and the initial 5-cycle 05A3816B49270 derivation used in the Countess materials. Berg noted this relationship in his sketches and subsequently altered the Countess materials to avoid the direct retrograde relationship. As in the *Lyric Suite*, however, it may have been the lack of intervalic variety rather than the prime-retrograde relationship that prompted Berg's altering of the retrograde-related row.

The row of the Violin Concerto, P7 <G−B♭−D−F♯−A−C−E−G♯−B−C♯−D♯−F> has an interval pattern of <34433443222(2)>, so that a prime form is equivalent to a rotated retrograde inversion: R(IB) <C♯−D♯−F−G−B♭−D−F♯−A−C−E−G♯−B> rotated to begin on G. As Perle has noted, the "free" use of the row in the concerto, a use based more on the content of row segments rather than the ordered identity of rows, along with the rotated retrograde inversion invariance, effectively eliminates retrograde forms from analytical consideration.[34] Even the identification of prime and inversion forms is tied largely to thematic and motivic statements.

NON-CYCLIC TRANSFORMATIONS

A recurring derivation in Berg's later music is the division of rows into segmental or non-segmental four-note groups and eight-note residue rows.[35] Berg pointed out the importance of the four-note group {F,A,B♭,B} in the *Lyric Suite*, and similar four-note groups and eight-note residue rows occur in "Schließe mir" (second setting) and in the film music of *Lulu*.[36] In "Schliesse Mir (II)" one of the two rows, a rotated I8, appears in an eight-note version, with the four-note group {F,E,C,A}—the first four notes of P5—partitioned out of the row. The eight-note residue row appears, with {F,E,C,A} superimposed but displaced from their original positions in the row, in a horizontal aggregate before the final chord (ex. 5.6b). In the piano part of mm. 12–15, the same eight-note residue row is segmented into palindromic accompanimental figures (ex. 5.6a). In his description of row characteristics in the *Lyric Suite*, Berg pointed out the four-note motive used to relate row forms in the third movement. In row 2, the four-note motive [0126] is present in four places in the row, and Berg chose four forms, PA, P5, P8, I3, that have the motive at the level {F,A,B♭,B} (ex. 5.18). The four-note motives appear independently of the rows, and each of the rows appears in twelve-note and eight-note forms. Berg referred to the four-note motive [0126] as a "four-note group" that acts "somewhat like an ostinato."[37]

In *Lulu*, a division of rows into four-note and eight-note groups occurs in the film music. A succession of six rows—the principal row and the rows of Alwa, Dr. Schön, the Acrobat, the Schoolboy, and the Countess Geschwitz—is stated once whole, then repeated with the rows as eight-note residue rows with the four-note group BC I [0167] {E–A–B♭–E♭} extracted from each (mm. 670–74; cf. ex. 5.37). (The Schigolch row also appears, in an eight-note form, with one of the three [0123] tetrachords omitted.) The combination of eight-note rows and <E–A–B♭–E♭> repeats, transposed successively by T2, so that <E–A–B♭–E♭> combines with <F♯–B–C–F> and <G♯–C♯–D–G> to complete an aggregate. At each transpositional level, the eight-note rows combine into eight-note verticals—the complement of the prevailing [0167]—when each row pauses on a different note.

Form

Like his earlier music Berg's twelve-tone music is characterized by clearly defined formal sections identified by thematic material, tempo, and meter.[38] Most forms are repeating structures of the sonata-form, ABA, or rondo variety, or in two parts, often with the second a retrograde of the first. The second movement of the *Chamber Concerto* is, for instance, a large palindromic binary with internal ternary sections. In the three-part ABA' third movement of the *Lyric Suite*, the third section is an abbreviated retrograde of the first. *Der Wein* also consists of a three-part ABA form, in which the middle song has an internal palindrome (mm. 112−41, 141−172), and the third song is comprised mostly of a condensed restatement of the music of the first song, with the music of the introduction (mm. 8−14) returning as a coda (mm. 208−16). The latter suggests a parallel with *Wozzeck*, in which Berg remarked that the closing oscillating chords could link up to the beginning of the opera, so that the entire musical and dramatic flow could repeat in a circle. In *Der Wein*, the final chord, {D,F♯,G♯,C}, is an elaboration on the {D,F♯,C} chord stated at the beginning of song 1 in m. 15 at the entrance of the voice. By ending with the introduction, the implication is that the closing m. 216 could be replaced by m. 15, and the whole piece begun again, in a circular form.

Lulu features the palindromic film music interlude between Act II, scenes i and ii, which accompanies a palindromic scenario, and the palindrome in the sextet in Act i, scene iii, which reflects the circular comments surrounding Lulu after she faints and is being urged to return to her dancing on stage. In Act III of *Lulu*, Berg recapitulates much of the music in the first act in connection with dramatic parallels between characters and situations. In the prologue, the Animal Tamer, played by the Acrobat, introduces the characters to the audience as animals; when this music returns in Act III, scene i, the Acrobat is directing the ceremonies at the gaming tables in Paris, with all the same characters present, except for the dead Medical Specialist, Painter, and Dr. Schön, who return as their alter egos the Silent Professor, the Negro, and Jack the Ripper in Act III, scene ii. The "Lied der Lulu" in Act II, scene i (mm. 491−538), originally Lulu's credo stated to a threatening Dr. Schön, returns in a parallel statement of her new self-awareness to the Marquis, who is also threatening her, in Act III, scene i (mm. 125−45). The rondo music that originally accompanies Alwa's overtures to Lulu, in Act II, scenes i and ii (mm. 243−336, 1001−150) returns in Act III, scene ii when the Countess brings Lulu's portrait to the attic, and the four characters, Alwa, the Countess, Schigolch, and Lulu, recall the past (mm. 957−99). Finally, the return of Lulu's victims in the guise of her tormenters, the Medical Specialist, the Painter, and Dr. Schön, as the three clients who visit her in her final role of prostitute, the Silent Professor, the Negro, and Jack the Ripper, is reflected musically by the return of the corresponding music from Act I in Act III, scene ii.

The *Chamber Concerto* and *Lulu* contain the most complex forms in Berg's twelve-tone music. In the *Chamber Concerto*, several forms are superimposed.

The first movement is a theme and five variations, with aspects of a sonata form, a concerto, and even a five-movement symphonic form. The second movement is, as noted, a binary palindrome, with ternary ABA divisions in each half. The third movement, labeled *rondo ritmico*, superimposes the form of the first movement on that of the second and adds a rondo with sonata-form characteristics based on rhythms, in which pitch themes from the two movements are superimposed on three rhythmic motives.

In *Lulu*, individual scenes are not closed forms, as Berg claimed was the case in *Wozzeck*. Instead, forms associated with different characters are interwoven horizontally in time across different scenes, with extended or brief interruptions between the sections of the forms. The character forms are: Dr. Schön with a sonata form and a five-part strophic aria; Alwa with a rondo; the Painter with a *monoritmica*—a large formal section delineated by repeated statements and variations on the *Hauptrhythmus* of the opera—and the related Prince/Manservant/Marquis characters with sets of variations. Dr. Schön's sonata-form material accompanies him onstage: the exposition and first reprise appear in Act I, scene ii (mm. 533–990) when he confronts Lulu with his wedding plans;[39] the development and recapitulation occur later, in Act I, scene iii (mm. 1209–361), when Lulu in turn confronts him with her possible wedding to the Prince and Schön is reduced to helplessness. The interruption of the sonata form thus corresponds to the drama. In Act II, scene i, Dr. Schön sings a five-strophe aria (mm. 387–552), which is similarly interrupted between the fourth and fifth strophes, now by the "Lied der Lulu" (mm. 491–537).[40]

Alwa's rondo is divided into two parts. In Act II, scene i (mm. 243–336), he makes his feelings known to Lulu; then in Act II, scene ii (mm. 1001–150), after Lulu has escaped from prison and he is again alone with her, he declares his love in the same stage setting as the previous scene. The resumption of the form again follows the drama. In the *Symphonic Pieces* from *Lulu*, a suite that Berg arranged to publicize the opera, the rondo appears in uninterrupted form as the first movement, with the intervening music between the two large halves and the numerous interjections by the Manservant and Dr. Schön in the first half of the rondo omitted (see fig. 5.20).

The variations in Act III, scene i (mm. 83–230), associated with the Marquis but actually part of a continuing set of variations on the material associated with three related characters, the Prince, Manservant, and Marquis, in Acts I, II, and III (actually, four characters, since the Acrobat takes the place of the Manservant in Act II, scene ii), are interrupted by intermezzos consisting of the return of the English waltz of Act I, scene iii (Act III, mm. 89–98, 158–81) and by the music of the "Lied der Lulu" from Act II, scene i (Act III, mm. 125–45). In the interlude between Act III, scenes i and ii, four variations occur on the Wedekind theme. The first variation has already appeared as the "Lied des Mädchen-händlers" in the first intermezzo of the Marquis variations (Act III, mm. 103–18), and the theme and second variation return separately in Act III, scene ii.

As in Berg's earlier music, internal movements and sections of pieces are linked by recurring motivic and thematic material. In the *Chamber Concerto* and the *Lyric Suite*, themes and motives foreshadowed in one movement are developed in the next. In the *Chamber Concerto*, a motive from the second movement appears briefly in the first (first movement, mm. 87–90, described as cell 1 in figure 5.1), and the RH (one of three rhythmic motives) of the third movement appears in the second (second movement, mm. 297–301, 306–8, and 312, and mm. 413–15 and 420–27 in retrograde); the third movement combines the musical material of the first two. The solo instruments also make brief but dramatic appearances in each other's movements, the violin in the first movement (mm. 111–12), the piano in the second movement, at the center of the palindrome (mm. 358–63). In the *Lyric Suite*, each movement builds on an element, usually a row, of the previous movement. In the Violin Concerto, the trio 1 material of the first large movement (first movement, mm. 137–54) reappears in the second (second movement, mm. 44–89), and the introductory gestures of the opening (first movement, mm. 1–10, 92–103) return at the end (second movement, mm. 229–30). These two large movements divide into four smaller submovements in which the second and fourth are linked by the return of the Carinthian folk tune (first movement, mm. 214–28, and second movement, mm. 201–13).

The links between movements even extend to links between pieces, as in Mahler's music. The row of "Schließe mir" (second setting) and the *Lyric Suite* appears near the end of the *Chamber Concerto* (ex. 5.3).[41] In "Schließe mir" (second setting), the opening four notes of the main row, {F–E–C–A}, separated and used as a motive in the second half of the song, comprise the chord associated with Alwa in *Lulu*.[42] In addition, the first of the palindromic piano accompanimental figures in mm. 11–15, a 3-cycle–based [0147] rising and falling in the piano, foreshadows a motive associated with Lulu in the opera that first appears in the prologue, when Lulu is introduced, as an arch form ascending then descending [01369] (with [0147] in its upper four notes) on the piano. Finally, the tango music from *Der Wein* returns as the English waltz in *Lulu*, and the chord at the center of the palindrome (m. 141) in *Der Wein* is the precursor to the central chord in the film music of the opera.

Rhythm and Tempo

Throughout his later music, Berg continues and extends the rigorous treatment of rhythm and tempo found in his earlier music.[43] The opera *Lulu*, in particular, features rhythmic motives, meters, and tempos as integral parts of the large-scale formal and dramatic organization. Motives and themes in Berg's twelve-tone music have consistent rhythmic settings, but, as in his earlier music, rhythmic motives independent of pitch content also appear and are varied in ways analogous to pitch variations: by augmentation, diminution, metric setting, alteration of internal durations, and tempo. Berg indicates rhythmic motives as *Hauptrhythmen*, with an RH label as an adaptation of Schoenberg's H (*Hauptstimme*) marking. The RH label appears in the scores of the *Chamber Concerto*, *Lulu*, and the Violin Concerto, and in the sketches for *Der Wein* and the *Lyric Suite*.

In the third movement of the *Chamber Concerto*, pitch themes from the previous two movements appear set to three rhythmic motives (ex. 5.4). In movements 3 and 6 of the *Lyric Suite* (exx. 5.19 and 5.26), as well as in the Schigolch row derivation (ex. 5.36m), and the film music of *Lulu* (ex. 5.37), rhythmic motives derive from the order positions of pitch motives extracted from equal duration presentations of the row. These rhythms then appear independently of the row context. For instance, the Schigolch row derivation rhythm is associated with the Medical Specialist (ex. 5.36m); it and the film music motive are both in four-attack rhythms, variants of the RH of the opera.

In *Lulu*, the Countess Geschwitz is associated with a cyclic rhythmic motive, a palindromic accelerando-decelerando of successively smaller, then larger, durations (first in Act II, scene i, mm. 5–10; ex. 5.58). The Countess's "suicide" scene in Act III, scene ii (mm. 1146–187) is organized around statements of her characteristic rhythmic motive. The most cogent rhythmic feature of the opera is, however, the recurring *Hauptrhythmus* (ex. 5.38a). This RH, which appears at the end of each act, is associated with the fated death of almost all the characters. The *Monoritmica* in Act I, scene ii, at the death of the painter, is an extended version of smaller "monoritmicas" based on the RH that appear at crucial formal and dramatic points, particularly the deaths of characters, throughout: in Act I, scene i, at the death of the Medical Specialist (mm. 196–257, with the variant of the RH from the derivation of Schigolch's row, ex. 5.36m, lower voice); in Act I, scene ii, at the death of the Painter in the large-scale *monoritmica* (mm. 669–1957); as the underlying rhythm in Dr. Schön's coda theme (ex. 5.48b); at Schön's realization that he is unable to free himself from Lulu at the end of the first act (mm. 1360–61); and at his death in Act II, scene i (mm. 380, 473, 548–651, recalled in 1015). Alwa's death is foreshadowed at the end of Act II (m. 740) and occurs in Act III, scene ii (mm. 1090–1122). The corresponding music from Act I represents the three clients, with the corresponding husbands' music and RH passages, which now signify Lulu's death: the Silent Professor/Medical Specialist passage returns in Act III, scene i (mm. 772–89), the Negro/

Walter (Painter) *monoritmica* (mm. 1056–105) returns associated with Alwa's death, and Jack/Dr. Schön's coda theme with Lulu's death (mm. 1213, 1292). The RH accompanies Lulu's cry just before her death (Act III, m. 1292), and the death of the Countess Geschwitz at end of the opera is associated with the deaths of Schön and Alwa, with the three chords of these characters all set to the RH (ex. 5.61).

The cyclic qualities of rhythm and meter and of Berg's cyclic transformations of rhythm described in the previous chapter continue in the twelve-tone music. The *Hauptrhythmus* of *Lulu*, for instance, has a structure analogous to a cyclic + collection: its relative durational pattern is <3313> (when the last duration is defined), a "3-cycle + collection" of durations, where the periodic pattern of 3s is broken by an added duration (ex. 5.38a). In the *monoritmica* in Act I, scene ii, the rhythm is set in $\frac{5}{4}$ with the <3313> durations in eighths, with an alternate setting in $\frac{4}{4}$ from the proportions <3311>, with the duration of the last note shortened.

In his later music, Berg continued the practice begun in *Wozzeck*, Act III, scene iv, of organizing at least one formal section per piece rhythmically. The third movement of the *Chamber Concerto* is a sonata-rondo form based on three rhythmic subjects (see fig. 5.1). In the *Lyric Suite*, the outer sections of the third movement are based on rhythms derived from the row (see ex. 5.19), and sections of the fifth movement are based on the ordered cyclic proportions <1−2−3−4−5>. The second song scherzo of *Der Wein* is characterized by a dotted rhythm recalling the rhythm of the second movement scherzo of Beethoven's Ninth Symphony. In *Lulu*, the RH is the basis of the *monoritmica* of Act I, scene ii, the mini-*monoritmica* at the death of each character, and the coda of the Schön sonata form; the arietta "Das mein Lebensabend" has its own rhythmic ostinato patterns, and the Countess's suicide scene and her character throughout are associated with her characteristic accelerando-decelerando rhythms. The decelerando of the Countess's rhythm has its counterpart in the slowing of the tempo throughout the final scene of *Lulu* from quarter = 184 to 42.[44] Finally, the third submovement of the Violin Concerto is characterized by an RH that occurs in almost every measure (ex. 5.71).

The tempo relationships between the six movements of the *Lyric Suite* illustrate a treatment of tempo analogous to pitch cycles. The succession of diverging tempos, accelerating in movements 1, 3, and 5 and decelerating in movements 2, 4, and 6, respectively, creates a large-scale form. This form transfers to tempo both the interweaving of inversionally related interval 5/7−cycles in the row in the first movement of the quartet and the patterns of accelerating and decelerating durational values that characterize Berg's rhythmic language.

The palindromes that occur in the second movement of the *Chamber Concerto*, the third movement of the *Lyric Suite*, song 2 of *Der Wein*, and the *Lulu* film music and sextet in Act I, scene iii present two possibilities for rhythmic realization. In the retrograde half of the palindrome, either the durations between attack points of the original rhythms are stated in retrograde or the attack points are replicated in retrograde. The difference between the two is exemplified in the <3313> RH of *Lulu*, which is <3133> as a durational retrograde and <1333> as an attack-point retrograde (ex. 5.38a).[45] The few exact retrograde passages in the palindromic second half of the *Chamber Concerto* are durational retrogrades, with the original note values written in reverse order. Berg apparently first developed the attack-point retrograde in the third movement of the *Lyric Suite*.[46] In *Der Wein*, rhythms in the second half of the palindrome are mostly durational, as in the sextet in *Lulu*, where the palindrome is similarly created from durational retrogrades. In the *monoritmica* in Act I, scene ii, the RH appears in the attack-point retrograde form exclusively. In the palindromic film music of *Lulu*, most retrograde rhythms in the second half, including the retrogrades of the RH, are durational, except for the notable recurrence of the RH (from m. 680) in its prime order in the retrograde half (m. 694) and the passage in mm. 701−4 corresponding to mm. 670−74 (ex. 5.37). In this passage, the notes <E♭−B♭−A−E> are articulated in a series of retrograde rows stated in continuous sixteenths, yielding attack-point retrogrades.

In *Wozzeck*, Act II, scene iv, Berg alternated popular, tonal, metric dance music with ametric atonal music as a juxtaposition of the outside world with the internal world of Wozzeck's torment. Within the scene, for the most part the stage band plays the popular metric music and the orchestra plays the ametric music. But occasionally the two are juxtaposed, as Wozzeck's inner and outer worlds collide. A similar procedure is used in Act I, scene iii of *Lulu*, where Alwa and Lulu chat to metric dance music played by an offstage band (Act I, mm. 992−1020), Alwa sings of his inner feelings to his ametric rondo music (mm. 1021−39); then the dance music strikes up again and the conversation returns to mundane, everyday matters (mm. 1040−93). Later in the scene, when Lulu faints and returns to her dressing room, the jazz band plays a ragtime in $\frac{2}{2}$ juxtaposed with the orchestra playing in $\frac{3}{4}$ (mm. 1155−168), until the door is closed and the jazz music suddenly stops.[47] *Der Wein* also contains a section of similar popular music in its tango (song I, mm. 31−63 and 179−95), associated in the text with gambling, drinking, and prostitution.

In Act III, scene ii of *Lulu*, the Wedekind tune, with its periodicity and simple tonality preserved, represents the seedy world of the Marquis Casti-Piani as the "Lied des Mädchenhändlers" (mm. 103−18). The tune returns as the basis of the variations between scenes i and ii, which progress from a tonal, metric setting to a "polytonal," then "atonal," and finally "twelve-tone" setting, each successively freer from the notated meter. In scene ii, a simplified tonal, metric version of the tune recurs in an orchestration recalling a hurdy-gurdy, representing the outside street life of London, which contrasts with the inner life in the attic, set to the more complex language characteristic of the opera as a whole.

The Violin Concerto is somewhat different in this regard. The two metric passages, the Carinthian folk tune and the chorale, do not stand out as much rhythmically because the entire concerto is organized to a large extent metrically, at least on the level of the notated barline, even in the chaotic third section. The Carinthian folksong has a clear meter, even hypermeter, and presents a nostalgic moment of calm in the second section and a mood of remembrance in the fourth. The chorale has a similar strongly metric basis largely reflected in its setting.

This overview of Berg's compositional techniques in his later music demonstrates the close relationship with his earlier music. The oft-cited twelve-tone themes in the *Altenberg Lieder* and *Wozzeck* are emblematic of the aggregate possibilities of cyclic completion and clearly indicate Berg's path to twelve-tone composition. His early choice of cyclic materials made such a path perhaps not inevitable, but certainly predictable. The *Chamber Concerto* shows the beginning of Berg's identification of row segments with cyclic collections, a process realized in the rows of "Schließe mir" (second setting) and the *Lyric Suite*—a row that, while not created by Berg (but by his student Fritz Heinrich Klein), has its cyclic potential exploited in characteristic fashion. By the opera *Lulu*, which uses the same row source hexachords as the earlier song and quartet, Berg had fully realized the cyclic potential of his twelve-tone row materials and integrated them with the multicyclic tetrachords [0167], [0268], and [0369] that appear throughout his compositions. The later Violin Concerto indicates the extent to which he could seamlessly incorporate tonal relationships into these materials. These two final works constitute such a high and complete level of cyclic integration and tonal allusion in an aggregate context that it is difficult to imagine how Berg could have gone further in either direction had he lived to write subsequent works.

5 The Twelve-Tone Music: Detail and Analysis

Chamber Concerto

Berg's *Chamber Concerto*, completed in 1925, is a double concerto in three movements for piano, violin, and thirteen winds.[1] The first movement features the piano as soloist (mm. 1–240), with a brief appearance by the violin (mm. 111–12); the second movement spotlights the violin (mm. 241–480), with a matching momentary entry by the piano (mm. 358–63); and the third movement begins with a cadenza for violin and piano (mm. 481–534) followed by the combined solo instruments and ensemble (mm. 535–785). The complement of fifteen players (the two soloists and thirteen accompanying instruments) originates, as Berg noted in his "Open Letter," in the "holy number of this kind of instrumental combination since [Schoenberg's] Opus 9."[2] Prior to the beginning of the concerto, three musical motives, associated with the names of Schönberg (in the German spelling), Webern, and Berg, appear as a motto in three parts, the solo piano and violin and the horn, representing the ensemble (see ex. 5.1a).

As in a traditional concerto, the first movement opens with a double exposition: the opening thirty bars are an exposition of the movement's materials by the ensemble, followed by a repeated statement in the solo piano. Both piano and ensemble participate in the body of the movement, trading lead and accompaniment roles (mm. 61–180), until the recapitulation (mm. 181–240), in which piano and ensemble restate their material in canon. In the two-part second movement, the violin plays the main thematic material, for the most part, exchanging only one theme with the ensemble in the retrograde second half. The third movement opens with a virtuoso duo-cadenza for the violin and piano (mm. 481–534), after which the two instruments combine with the ensemble except for a brief duet (mm. 638–44). The material consists of superimposed themes from the previous movements, with the solo instruments playing each others' themes, exchanging leading and accompanimental roles. In the closing coda, the violin plays the final notes pizzicato over a fading held piano chord.

FORM

The most remarkable feature of the concerto is the combination of different forms in each movement (fig. 5.1). The first movement (mm. 1–240) is a theme and five variations overlaid with elements of sonata, symphony, and concerto movements. The second movement (mm. 241–480) is a palindromic binary form, with each half subdivided into a ternary ABA'. The third movement (mm. 481–785) superimposes the musical material of the first two, in order, and adds a rondo with sonata aspects, based on three rhythmic motives. (In figure 5.1, corresponding sections of movements 1 and 2 combined in movement 3 are aligned horizontally; the underlying items indicate anomalies as described below.) Internal divisions within each movement are defined largely by repeated statements of themes and other materials in prime, inversion, retrograde, and retrograde-inversion forms and orders, as well as by tempo and meter, and in the third movement also by the overlaid form defined by the rhythmic motives. Berg indicated in the formal chart from his "Open Letter" that sections within each movement occur in multiples of three. The six sections of the first movement, the themes and five variations, are of 30 (mm. 1–30), 30 (mm. 31–60), 60 (mm. 61–120), 30 (mm. 121–50), 30 (mm. 151–80), and 60 bars (mm. 181–240), for a total of 240 bars. The six internal ABA–R(ABA) sections in the palindromic second movement, three in each half, are of 42 (mm. 241–82), 48 (mm. 283–330), and 30 bars (mm. 331–60) and, in retrograde, 30 (mm. 361–90), 48 (mm. 391–438), and 42 bars (mm. 439–80), for a total again of 240 bars (mm. 241–480). In the third movement, the superimposed material from the first two is extended from 240 to 305 bars (mm. 481–785), but a large internal repeat of mm. 536–710 adds 175 bars (36 percent of the movement) to attain 480 bars, equal to the sum of the previous two movements. Including the repeat in the third movement, the entire concerto is 960 bars in length, with the movements in a 1:1:2 proportion.

The initial section of the first movement presents the three mottos (ex. 5.1a), derived from the names Schönberg, Webern, and Berg, with six themes (exx. 5.1b–f). These group into four subsections: the three mottos and theme1; themes 2–3; themes 4–5; and theme 6 (these subsections are divided by double barlines in the theme and in variation 1, except at m. 8; they are marked inconsistently in the rest of the movement). These subsections are maintained in the movement except for the canonic variation 5, where some overlap occurs between the piano and the ensemble. The subsections are also defined by tempo. The theme and variations 2 and 5 group internally into three tempos: Tempo I (dotted half = 66) with the mottos and themes 1–3, Tempo II (a slightly brisker dotted half = 72) with themes 4–5, and Tempo III (a slower dotted half = 60) with theme 6. Variations 3 and 4 each maintain one tempo throughout: in the former the tempo is between Tempo I and Tempo II (dotted half = 69), and in the latter the tempo is double that of variation 3 (dotted quarter = 138). The theme and variations 1 and 3 are written as 30 bars in $\frac{6}{4}$, variations 2 and 5 as 60 bars of $\frac{3}{4}$, and variation 4 as 30 bars of $\frac{6}{8}$. Thus, compared in terms of a dotted half note unit, variations 1, 2, and 5 are similar in length and tempo, variation 3 is a bit quicker, and variation 4 is both half as long and notably faster. The overall tempo is shaped by the slight accelerando in variation 3 leading to the quickest tempo in variation 4 before a return to the initial tempo and meter.

The variations are distinguished not only by the order but the form of themes. The theme and variations 1 and 5 present the mottos and themes in prime form and order; variation 2 presents them in retrograde form and order, variation 3 in inversion form and prime order, and variation 4 in retrograde-inversion form and retrograde order.[3] Deviations from this order and treatment of themes, underscored in figure 5.1, occur in variation 4, the retrograde-inversion variation, where R(5P) and R(3P) themes mix with their R(5I) and R(3I) counterparts (mm. 157–75) and the Schönberg motto appears prematurely, in aligned prime and inversion forms (mm. 166–69, flute, horn 1). This displaced motto has a corresponding statement in the third movement (mm. 687–90), where the spectacular setting includes a broad registral span and dense, whole-tone–based harmonies.

In the sonata-form outline of the first movement (given by Berg in a chart in his "Open Letter"), the theme and variation 1 constitute an exposition and reprise, variations 2–4 a development, and variation 5 a recapitulation.[4] In this view, the development is not the usual working-out of material with developing variation; instead, it consists of varied presentations in the twelve-tone forms of

Figure 5.1. Form in the *Chamber Concerto* (underlining indicates irregular occurrences of events)

Movement 1

Theme/exposition: prime
1–7	1P, mottos
8–15	2P, 3P
16–24	4P, 5P
25–30	6P

Var 1/reprise: prime
31–37	1P, motto
38–45	2P, 3P
46–54	4P, 5P
55–60	6P

Var 2/development: retrograde
61–72	R (6P), waltz
71–90	R (5P), R (4P), <u>cell 1</u>
91–109	R (3P), R (2P), <u>waltz</u>
110–20	R (1P), mottos
111–12	<u>violin G–D–A–E</u>

Movement 2   *Prime*

A prime
241–59	7P
260–70	8P, cell 3
271–82	<u>8P</u>, 9P, <u>10P</u>

B prime
283–93	10P, cell 1
294–302	11P, cells 1, 2, 3, <u>RH</u>
303–10	10P, cell 2, <u>RH</u>
311–13	11P, <u>RH</u>, cell 2

B inversion
| 314–21 | 10I, cells 1, 3 |

B prime
| 322–30 | 12P |

A inversion
331–49	7I, <u>7P</u>
350–360	<u>8P</u>, 8I, cell 3
	<u>piano twelve C#s</u>

Movement 3 (sonata/rondo)

RH: cadenza/introduction
481–90	
491–506	
507–23	<u>no cell 3</u>
524–34	<u>no 8P, 10P</u>

MR: exposition 1st theme/A
| 535–39 | <u>RH</u> |
| 540–49 | <u>RH</u> |

SR: 2nd theme/B
| 550–67 | <u>RH</u> (<u>MR</u> var) |
| 565–70 | <u>RH, no cell 2</u> |

MR: Reprise 1st theme/A
571–76	MR, <u>RH, no cell 3</u>
577–90	
591–601	

SR: 2nd theme/B
602–21	<u>MR</u>
622–30	<u>RH</u> on Db
628–29	violin chords

Figure 5.1. Form in the *Chamber Concerto* (underlining indicates irregular occurrences of events) (*Continued*)

Movement 1	Movement 3 (sonata/rondo)	Movement 2	Retrograde
Var 3: inversion	RH/R (RH): development/C	A R (inversion)	
121–27 1I	631–37	361–71 R (8I, 8P), cell 3	
128–35 2I, 3I	638–51	372–90 R (7I, 7P)	
		B R (prime)	
136–44 4I, 5I	652–62	391–99 R (12P)	
		B R (inversion)	
145–50 6I	663–70	400–407 R (10I), cell 3	
Var 4: retrograde inversion		B R (prime)	
151–56 R (6I)	671–76 no cell2	408–10 R (11P), cell 2, no R (RH)	
157–65 R (5I, 5P), R (4I)	677–84 R (MR), no R (RH)	411–18 R (10P), R (RH)	
166–75 R (3I, 3P), R (2I), Sch motto P/I	685–695 no cell2, SR	419–27 R (11P), R (RH), cells 1, 2, 3	
	696–706 SR	428–38 R (10P), cell 1	
176–80 R (1I), mottos	707–9a		
Var 5/recapitulation: prime	MR: Recapitulation 1st theme/A	A R (prime)	
181–94 1P, mottos	710b–25 no R (8P)	439–50 R (8P, 9P), R (10P), 8P, 9P	
	SR: 2nd theme/B		
195–210 2P, 3P, mottos	726–37 RH, no 8P, cell 3	451–61 R (8P), cell 3	
211-19 4P, 5P	738–50 no 5P		
	MR: 1st theme/A.		
220–40 5P, 6P, waltz	751–80 row of Lyric Suite, RH	462–480 R (7PB), Sch motto, cell 3	
	780–95 RH		

Example 5.1a. Opening mottos, *Chamber Concerto*

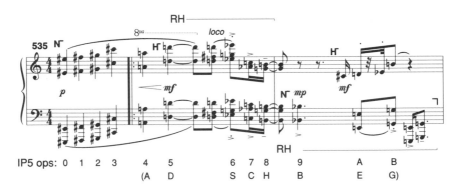

Example 5.1b. Theme 1P5 with *Hauptrhythmus* (RH), *Chamber Concerto*, third movement, mm. 535–37

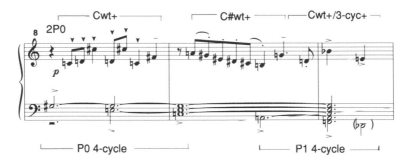

Example 5.1c. Theme 2P0, *Chamber Concerto*, first movement, mm. 8–10

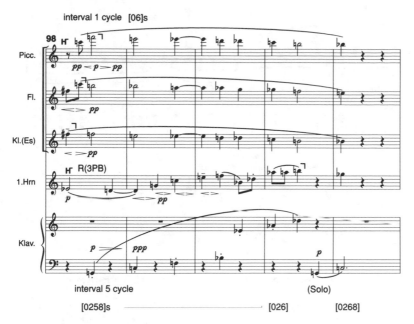

Example 5.1d. Theme R(3PB) segment in aligned 1- and 5-cycles, vertical [0258]s, [026]s, *Chamber Concerto*, first movement, mm. 98–102

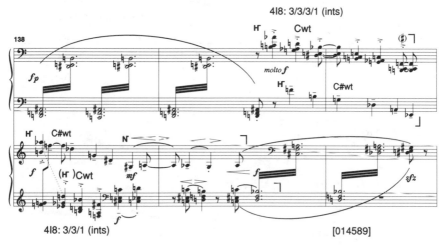

Example 5.1e. Theme 4, 3-cycle-based, in "hocket" alternation yielding horizontal whole-tone collections, *Chamber Concerto*, first movement, mm. 138–40

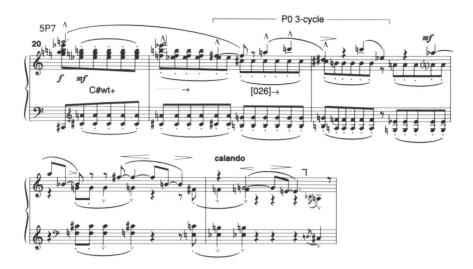

Example 5.1f. Theme 5P7 in whole-tone+ setting, *Chamber Concerto*, first movement, mm. 20–25

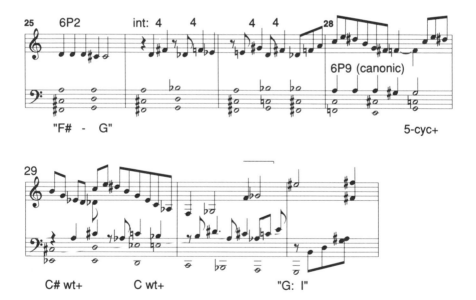

Example 5.1g. Theme 6P2 in "tonal" setting with canonic 6P9, *Chamber Concerto*, first movement, mm. 25–31. Berg KAMMERKONZERT. Copyright 1925 by Universal Edition. Copyright renewed. All Rights Reserved. Used by permission of European American Music Distributors Corporation, sole U.S. and Canadian agent for Universal Edition A.G., Wien.

retrograde, inversion, and retrograde inversion. In the sonata-form context, the displaced Schönberg motto in variation 4 (mm. 166–69) might be interpreted as a false recapitulation—a signal to mark the imminent return of the recapitulation in variation 5 (mm. 181ff). The return of the waltz accompaniment from variation 2 (mm. 61–72, 91–120, piano) in the recapitulatory variation 5 (mm. 229–40, piano) may be interpreted as material from the development reappearing in the recapitulation.

The first movement may also be viewed as a symphonic form, somewhat akin to the symphony in *Wozzeck*, Act II, with the exposition and reprise (theme and variation 1) grouping together as an opening movement, a waltz second movement (variation 2), an adagio third movement (variation 3), a scherzo fourth movement (variation 4), and a canonic return in a finale (variation 5), with a recall of the waltz from the second movement in the closing bars.[5] In addition, the first movement begins in a traditional concerto format with a double exposition, to complete the multiple formal aspects of theme and variations, sonata, symphony, and concerto.

The second movement also presents six themes and three smaller motivic fragments or cells (ex. 5.2); the latter are similar in size and usage to the first movement mottos but they do not appear in as orderly a fashion (fig. 5.1). The A sections contain themes 7–9 and cell 3, the B sections the other three themes 10–12 and cells 1, 2, and 3. Five tempo indications correspond to themes 7–8, 9, 10, 11, and 12: Tempo I (quarter = 48), Tempo II (half = 24), and Tempo V (quarter = 48) are actually the same but the beats are grouped in different meters—$\frac{2}{4}$, $\frac{2}{2}$, and $\frac{4}{4}$, respectively—whereas Tempo III (quarter = 54) and Tempo IV (quarter = 72), both in $\frac{4}{4}$, are successively faster. As in the first movement, internal sections are distinguished by the form and order of the themes and cells: a succession of prime and inversion materials in the first half is retrograded in the second half. Themes 7, 8, and 12 are, like themes 1–6, introduced separately; theme 9 is presented along with themes 8 and 10 in mm. 271–82 and 439–50 (yet alone in the corresponding mm. 524–34 of movement 3, piano), but is apparently omitted from the A inversion and retrograde inversion sections, although it may be regarded as represented by the aggregate setting of cell 3, which is similar to the first four notes of theme 9 (detailed below, mm. 350–60, 361–71). In a few other variant appearances of themes (underscored in fig. 5.1), theme 7 in prime recurs with itself in inversion in the A' section (mm. 331–49, 372–90), as does theme 8 (mm. 350–60, 361–71), and theme 9 appears with itself in prime and retrograde forms (mm. 439–50).

Many authors have noted the discrepancy between the form of the second movement and the form chart given in Berg's "Open Letter" (fig. 5.2).[6] In the revised proportions, Berg's divisions at mm. 319 and 403 are moved ahead to m.

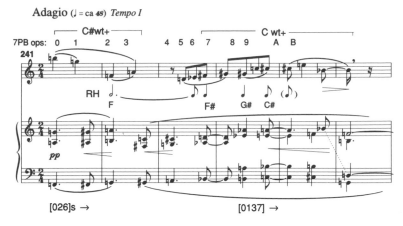

Example 5.2a. Theme 7PB, *Chamber Concerto*, second movement, mm. 241 – 45

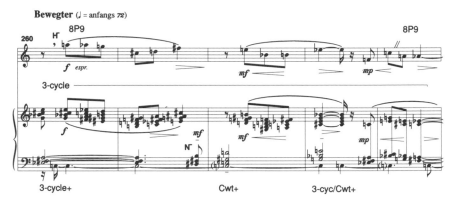

Example 5.2b. Theme 8P9 in 3-cycle+ setting, *Chamber Concerto*, second movement, mm. 260 – 64

322 and back to m. 400, respectively (a change of 3, interestingly, given the importance of this number throughout). Berg's numbers yield a symmetrical pattern of bar lengths within each half of the palindrome, which the revised proportions eliminate; the revisions are, however, strongly corroborated by musical evidence, including double barlines in the score.

Although the second half of the second movement is largely a retrograde of the first half, the palindrome is not strict throughout: the palindromic bars are mm. 356–60/361–65, 283–311/410–38, and 271–282/439–50, with some variance. In the final A section (mm. 451–80), however, the solo violin changes to arpeggiated triadic chords, implying a pitch-class focus on C, and the surrounding parts in mm. 456–70 are varied substantially from their corresponding bars in the first half mm. 246–60.[7] The corresponding tempos in the

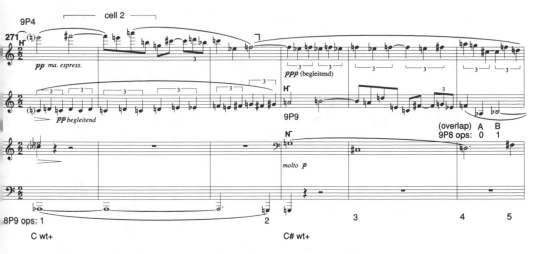

Example 5.2c. Theme 9 (with theme 8P9), *Chamber Concerto*, second movement, mm. 271–78

Example 5.2d. Theme 10P1, with cells 1 and 2, *Chamber Concerto*, second movement, mm. 283–86

two halves are the same except for mm. 372–90, with quarter = 120–44, which is about three times faster than the corresponding mm. 331–49, at quarter = 48. More significantly, in the first half, a *Höhepunkt* appears in m. 314, placed formally at approximately .61 of mm. 241–360 (the Golden Section); the elements of this highpoint are, however, largely omitted in the varied corresponding bars in the second half, mm. 405–9 (mm. 312–16). This climactic point shapes the first half of the movement, but its formal proportion makes no sense in reverse, and its omission in the second half breaks the retrograde symmetry of the movement.

The formal sections and themes, mottos, and cells of the first two move-

Example 5.2e. Theme 11 with cell 1 and RH in canon, *Chamber Concerto*, second movement, mm. 294–95.

Example 5.2f. Theme 12P7, *Chamber Concerto*, second movement, mm. 323–26.

ments are superimposed in order in the third movement (see fig. 5.1; only added or omitted elements are indicated, with underlining, in the third-movement columns; corresponding material from the first and second movements is otherwise assumed to be included: themes, 1P, 7P, and mottos in mm. 481–90, etc.), with the pitch material varied in rhythm, meter, instrumentation, and tempo.[8] The third movement adds a rondo- or sonata-like form delineated by three rhythmic motives (see ex. 5.4): a *Hauptrhythmus* (RH), main rhythm (MR), and subsidiary rhythm (SR), which are also presented in varied forms with alterations to the durational patterns.[9] The MR and SR are in separate sections, but the RH crosses over sectional boundaries, appearing throughout (occurrences

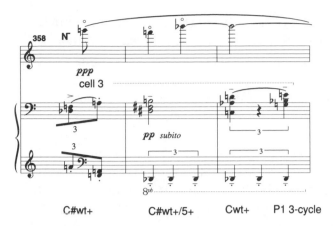

Figure 5.2. Chart of the second movement of the *Chamber Concerto*

Berg's chart

	A		B		A'	A'	B		A		
	A		B		A'	A'	B		A		
mm.	241	271	283	319	331	361	391	403	439	451	(480)
	30	12	36	12	30	30	12	36	12	30	
	30	12	39	9	30	30	9	39	12	30	
mm.	241	271	283	322	331	361	391	400	439	451	(480)
	A		B		Λ'	A'	B		A		

Revised chart

---

of RH and MR outside their own formal sections are underlined in fig. 5.1, as are appearances of RH in the second movement). The principal tempo (*Hauptzeitmass*) is quarter = 90 for the MR and SR, with the RH more variable in extremes of quarter = 60 and 120. Thus, in the third movement the tempo of themes from the first movement is slower but that of themes from the second is faster.

Although the third movement is labeled a *rondo ritmico*, a sonata-form outline is clearly implied, with the MR statements either as the rondo A section or as a sonata-form first theme, the SR as a rondo B section or a sonata-form second theme, and the RH as a rondo C section or a sonata-form's transitional or developmental element. The RH is actually a roving element that recurs throughout the movement. The sonata-form divisions of the third movement correspond to formal divisions in at least one of the other two movements, except for the "SR: 2nd theme/B" sections (mm. 550–70, 602–29, and 726–50, fig. 5.1), and the final "MR: 1st theme/A" (mm. 751–85).

The third movement has musical material of 305 bars, but an internal repeat of 175 bars (mm. 536–709) in the exposition-development of the sonata-form outline yields a total 480 bars—double the 240-bar length of the first two movements. The repeat seems anomalous, since large-scale exact repetitions are rare in Berg's music (the only other instance is the repeated exposition in the Piano Sonata op. 1), and an exact repeat merely to fit a predetermined numerical scheme seems to be contrary to statements by Berg and Schoenberg on the importance of continual variation.[10] In addition, without its repeat, the third movement is symmetrically arranged around m. 631 (mm. 481–631–785, or about 150:154 bars), which corresponds to both the palindromic middle of movement 2 (mm. 360–61) and the midpoint of movement 1, between variations 2 and 3 (mm. 120–21). The repeat is, however, asymmetrical around m. 631, as mm. 535–631–710 (a proportion of 96:80 bars, or about 19:16). With the ever-present variation in restatements in Berg's other music, as in the third act of *Lulu*, the exact repeat in the concerto is unique in Berg's later compositions.[11]

As in other pieces by Berg, the movements are linked by shared motivic material. Cell 1 from the second movement is foreshadowed in the first (variation 2, mm. 87–90, winds to piano), and the second movement contains the *Hauptrhythmus* of the third (mm. 294–313, 411–27, underscored in fig. 5.1). The third movement is, of course, comprised entirely of pitch themes from the first two, combined with the three rhythmic motives. In the closing measures of the third movement (mm. 775–80), Berg extended the principle of inter-movement motivic connections to inter-piece sharing of motivic material, by including the row of his next two works, "Schließe mir die Augen beide" (second setting) and the first movement of the *Lyric Suite* (ex. 5.3). The row is presented as P4, a level not used in the following two pieces, and, although arranged in two successive variants of the RH, its inclusion is a conceit—it is not integrated into the language of the concerto except that it is twelve-tone—pointing to the future.[12]

TREATMENT OF THEMES

The *Chamber Concerto* features six themes and three mottos in its first movement and six themes and three cells in its second; all are combined in the third movement (see exx. 5.1 and 5.2, also appendix). The themes almost all contain twelve distinct pitch-classes but different total numbers of notes; the mottos and cells

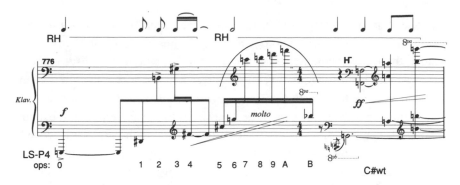

Example 5.3. *Lyric Suite* row in RH, *Chamber Concerto*, third movement, mm. 775–80. Berg
KAMMERKONZERT. Copyright 1925 by Universal Edition. Copyright renewed. All Rights
Reserved. Used by permission of European American Music Distributors Corporation, sole
U.S. and Canadian agent for Universal Edition A.G., Wien.

are related to the themes but are used separately. The pitch materials generally
maintain contour, rhythm, and order, with inversional contour and retrograde
ordering in the corresponding forms. Since motivic identification is paramount,
developing variation is rare; themes are combined contrapuntally and, in the
third movement, are varied by orchestration, tempo, and changes in rhythm.

Although the themes are, for the most part, used traditionally rather than as
rows, there are a few serial and twelve-tone transformations: changes in contour
indicating pitch-class identity, verticalization of segments, combinatorial alignments, reordering of segments, partitioning, and *Klangfarben* partitioning.[13] The
most notable twelve-tone–style relationships obtain among the three mottos
and theme 1: the eight-note Schönberg motto <A–D–Eb–C–B–Bb–E–G>
contains the Berg <A–Bb–E–G> and Webern <A–E–Bb–E> mottos as subsets, and it is preceded by its complementary 5-cycle + collection <F–F#–G#–
C#> [0237] to create the twelve-tone theme 1 (cf. exx. 5.1a and b, theme 1P5 is
given with order position numbers [ops] due to its twelve-tone treatment). A
striking vertical arrangement occurs in variation 3, where segment 01234
<F–E–D–A–C#> of theme 1I5 (the label indicated the inversion form begin-
ning on 5, or F, of theme 1) is aligned with itself vertically in two altered rotations, 23014 <F–E–D–A–C#> and 30124 <A–F–E–D–C#> with 4 (C#)
shifted to end each segment (m. 123, clarinets). In the characteristic harmonic
setting, these mostly white-note upper voice 5-cycle–based collections are set
against lower black-note 5-cycle–based collections; the two coalesce in the final
5-cycle collection {C#,Gb,Ab}.

Several cases of partitioning occur with different themes. In theme 7's initial
appearance, the notes <F–F#–G#–C#> in order positions 2679 of 7PB are

punctuated by simultaneous attacks in the accompanying brass in a rhythm close to the RH (ex. 5.2a, mm. 241−44); the same notes are <u>0123</u> of theme 1P5, relating these two themes.[14] *Klangfarben* partitioning with octave displacement occurs when Theme 6I8 (mm. 145−47) is presented in a hocket-like alternation of piano and ensemble, with a "result" (*ergebnis*) stave added to show the continuous row underlying the fragmented surface.[15] In the corresponding bars in the third movement (mm. 663−67), the entire theme is in the violin, but accompanying chords in the ensemble imitate the previous partitioned setting.

Finally, theme 4I8, a 3-cycle−based theme from cycles of 3/1 (<A♭−F−E>), 3/3/1 (<A♭−F−D−D♭>), and 3/3/3/1=(<A♭−F−D−B−B♭>), is partitioned with alternating notes in different voices (mm. 136−40, ex. 5.1e). The separate voices are whole-tone collections: in m. 138, 3/3/1-cycle <A♭−F−D−D♭−B♭−G−G♭−E♭−C> partitions into whole-tone+ collections <A♭−D−B♭−F♯−C> and <F−D♭−G−E♭>; in mm. 139−40, 3/3/3/1-cycle <A♭−F−D−B−B♭−G−E−D♭−C−A−F♯−E♭> partitions into the two complete whote-tone collections <A♭−D−B♭−E−C−F♯> and <F−B−G−D♭−A−E♭>.[16] The accompanying harmonies [012367] and [014589], although grouped into [037] and [015] trichords, result from 3/3/1- and 3/1-cycles, respectively (<0367[A]12>, <145890>).

In the first movement, Berg states almost all the themes at the same pitch level in prime as 1P5, 2P0, 3PB, 4P2, 5P7, and 6P2, and at the same relative inversional level—sum 10 (a characteristic sum for Berg that maps B−B and F−F)—as 1I5, 2IA, 3IB, 4I8, 5I3, and 6I8. Of the prime-form themes, only theme 6 appears at a different level, in a single canonic statement in the theme section, as 6P9 (mm. 28−30, horn 1; see ex. 5.1g). The 6P9 is incomplete, but, of the notes missing in its immediate continuation, <G−B−B♭−F−D−C♯−C> (corresponding to the bracketed notes on 6P2 in m. 28 of ex. 5.1g), five appear in the following variation 1 (mm. 31ff.), where the left-hand piano accompaniment is {G,B,D,A♯}, altered from the original 1P5 <u>89</u>AB {G,B,E,A♯}. Combined with the upper E♯ in the right hand (from 1P5 <u>0</u>), the altered set yields {G,B, D,A♯,E♯}. The same altered left-hand collection {G,B,D,A♯} returns to initiate variation 2 (m. 61 piano) and creates a momentary confusion; the variation begins as if it were in prime, but R(6P2) enters in the next bar (m. 62) to signal that the variation is in retrograde, although set over the waltz accompaniment.[17]

A few inversional themes appear simultaneously with their corresponding prime forms to yield sum-10 dyads F/F, F♯/E, G/E♭, A♭/D, A/D♭, B♭/C, B/B: the displaced Schönberg motto (mm. 166−69 flute and horn 1) and R(3PB)/ R(3IB) (mm. 169−70, piano, left and right hands). In dyads at sum 10, notes B and F map into themselves; however, in the latter alignment of R(3PB)/R(3IB), R(3PB) is altered to avoid a B,F doubling. A few transposed inversional rows appear: R(5I3)/R(5I9) (variation 4, mm. 157ff., canon between horn and piano) and R(2IA)/R(2I3) (variation 4, mm. 171–73, canon, piano left and right hands); in variation 3 (mm. 140–44), a version of the inverted theme 5 is given in a descending 1-cycle sequence of overlapping canonic statements: 5I3 (trombone), 5I2 (bass clarinet), 5I1 (horn), and 5I0 (bassoon).

Almost every theme in the first movement appears in canon at least once: 6P2 and 6P9 in mm. 25–30 (flute and horn 1, ex. 5.1g); R(5P7) in four-part (mm. 71–81, flute, oboe, clarinet, and piano) and three-part canons (mm. 591–604, A clarinet, oboe, and trumpet), as well as the inverted canon just described, from 5I3, 5I2, 5I1, and 5I0 in mm. 140–44; R(3PB) in three-part canon (mm. 91–97, flute; oboe; clarinet, horn, and bass; clarinet; and bassoon); R(5I3)/R(5I9) in canon (mm. 156–61, piano and horn); and R(2IA)/R(2I3) in canon (mm. 171–73, 696–97, piano, right and left hands). Variation 5 consists entirely of a canon between the piano and the ensemble, except for theme 3PB, which is divided between the horn and the ensemble. The ensemble begins the canon in m. 181, followed by the piano in m. 188, but by the end of the canon the piano has overtaken the ensemble. The piano drops out of the canon for theme 3PB in mm. 199–211, its part taken over mostly by the horn; this momentary hiatus allows the piano to overlap with the beginning and ending of the 3PB canon: first finishing 2P0 (mm. 198–202) and overlapping with the beginning of the 3PB canon (oboe, m. 200, <B–A–A♭–D♭–G♭–F–E>, etc.; horn, m. 201), then entering with a variant of 4P2 before the end of the 3PB canon (mm. 207ff.). Within the 3PB canon, mostly between horns 1 and 2 and the ensemble, the *comes* narrows the gap between itself and the *dux* from six eighth-note durations (between *dux* oboe and *comes* horn, m. 199) to 1.5 eighth durations (between *dux* E♭ clarinet and *comes* horn and bassoon, mm. 209–10). The piano enters, now with the lead advantage (m. 207), and pulls farther ahead in themes 4, 5, and 6 (mm. 207, 215, 220; ensemble, mm. 211, 220, 229), until it ends its part of the canon in m. 230; the extra mm. 230–239 constitute a return to the waltz of variation 2 in retrograde. In the setting of variation 5 in the third movement, the canonic voice of Variation 5 does not appear, but themes 5P7 and 6P2 are aligned in mm. 751–79 as they are in variation 5 (mm. 220ff.).

Of the themes in the second movement, 7PB, 8P9, and 12P7 are untransposed, but themes 9, 10, 11 occur at many levels. In theme 9, the first and last intervals form interval 2s with notes related by TB; thus, in a descending interval 1 cycle, the last two notes of one theme may overlap as the first two of the next (ex. 5.2c, m. 276), as in the sequence 9P9, 9P8, and 9P7 (mm. 274–82, trumpet, bassoon, contrabassoon). Only themes 7, 8, and 10 appear inverted, with 7IB (7PB) and 8I1 (8P9) at sum 10, as in the first movement, and sum-10 dyads are created by simultaneous statements of 8P9 and 8I1 (mm. 350–55, offset in the corresponding mm. 366–71).

Theme 8 is treated somewhat differently than the other themes in its partial recurrences in the second half of the palindrome and in the third movement.[18] As 8P9, it is set in five-part parallel 3-cycle+ [01369]s (mm. 260–70, ex. 5.2b), then as a cantus firmus against theme 9 (mm. 271–79, contrabassoon, ex. 5.2c).[19] In the corresponding bars in the second half of the palindrome, it reappears as R(8P9) with theme 9 (mm. 442–50, trombone), but then is reduced to a brief, partial statement (m. 456, trumpet); in movement 3 it appears as 8P9 alone (mm. 507–14, violin, interspersed with 4-cycle and 3-cycle collections), but then is omitted entirely (mm. 724–37). Theme 8 also appears as juxtaposed 8I9 and 8P1 (mm. 350–55, 366–71) in both halves of the palindrome of movement 2, but in the corresponding bars in movement 3 it is again reduced to a mere suggestion (as 8P8, mm. 619–21, E♭ clarinet <A–G–F♯–C–B>, and mm. 635–37). In the third movement, theme 8 appears in full only in the cadenza (spread out with intervening notes over mm. 507–14, violin, beginning on A5 in m. 507 and ending on C6 in m. 514).

Cell 1 is a four-note motive consisting of three notes at interval 1 followed by a leap of variable size. The cell, foreshadowed in variation 2 of movement 1 (mm. 87–89, ensemble, piano), is associated with the openings of themes 8 and 10 (ex. 5.2d) and is used as a prefix to theme 11 (ex. 5.2e), also, in one instance, to theme 2 in the third movement (m. 540, english horn), but it appears separately in the outer B prime sections of the second movement (mm. 291–93 and 428–30; brass, mm. 299 and 422). At the *Höhepunkt* in mm. 314ff., three simultaneous statements of the inverted theme 10 appear in different durations (10I8, piccolo, flute, A clarinet, trumpet; 10IB, oboe, english horn; and 10IB, E♭ clarinet, violin), with the corresponding cell-1s isolated and highlighted.[20]

Cell 2 is a four-note motive with contour <2130> and varied intervals; it is associated with the beginning of theme 9 and the end of theme 10 (exx. 5.2c, 5.2d), but it also appears separately (mm. 297–300 and 421–24, violin, A clarinet, flute; mm. 311 and 410, violin). Cell 3, an ascending 5-cycle collection [0257], appears harmonized in three tetrachords, creating an aggregate (ex. 5.2g). In its 5-cycle [0257] collection, cell 3 is related to the opening of theme 9 and can be heard to imply theme 9 when cell 3 occurs around the center of the palindrome in mm. 358–60/361–63, where theme 9 is omitted. Cell 3 occurs with an upper voice <A–B–D–E>, for the most part; its most notable appearance is around the middle of the palindrome (mm. 358–60/361–63) in an aggregate setting of three whole-tone+ collections with a final 3-cycle collection, including the mysterious twelve low C♯s on the piano. Its final three statements are a 3-cycle of transpositions, with each cell in retrograde: {A,B,D,E}, {C,D,F,G}, and {E♭,F,A♭,B♭} (a ten-note combination omitting C♯ and F♯, mm. 457–60, 462–64, and 464–65). Including the two transposed statements, cell 3 appears ten times in the second movement, in four palindromic pairs (mm. 260–63/457–59, 300–301/420–21, 314–17/404–7, 358–60/361–63) with two additional varied occurrences (mm. 462–64 and 464–65).

RHYTHM AND METER

For the most part, the rhythms associated with the themes in the first two movements are maintained consistently as identifying features, whether the theme is in prime or retrograde aspect, with the exception of themes 1 and 5, and the mottos—although the Schönberg motto appears in variation 4 (mm. 166–68) in its original rhythm. The formal retrogrades have rhythms written in durations (rather than attack points), reversed with few alterations of the type that appear in Berg's later palindromes. The most striking rhythmic variations befall theme 5. The 5I8 (mm. 140–44, piano) is set in a quadruple pattern to the dotted half-note duration in $\frac{6}{4}$, and unfolds by Berg's characteristic procedure of adding one additional note in each three-note cycle (012, 123, etc.) At m. 145, where a transition is made back to a triple division, Berg wrote a quadruple division in the piano part but indicated the corresponding triplet division below the staff, marked *Rhythmus-Umwandlung*. Theme 5 also varied, in canon as R(5I9) and R(5I3) (mm. 157–160, piano left hand and horn), by statements in repeated sixteenth-note values, with the rhythm evened out.

The third movement contains, as Berg describes it in his "Open Letter," three rhythmic motives: a "main rhythm" (MR), a "subsidiary rhythm" (SR), and "a rhythm that can be considered as a sort of motif" (RH) (ex. 5.4). The themes of the first two movements are set to the three rhythmic motives in the third movement, with the exception of theme 8 (fig. 5.1).[21] RH (and R(RH)) sets the pitch A and its sum-10 pair C♯ (mm. 297, 302, 306, 414, 416, 420, 481, 545, 685), theme 1 (mm. 483, 535, 631–32), theme 2 (m. 638), theme 6 (mm. 571, 675, 751), theme 7 (m. 645), theme 11 (mm. 294, 311, 409, 425, 542, 565, 673, 694), and the

Example 5.4. Three rhythmic motives, *Chamber Concerto*, third movement

Lyric Suite row and chord {F,G,A,B} ending the movement (mm. 775–80, ex. 5.3); the MR sets theme 2 (m. 540), theme 5 (mm. 591, 751), theme 6 (m. 579), theme 9 (m. 710), theme 10 (mm. 535, 563, 571, 678, 710), and theme 12 (m. 579); and the SR sets theme 1 (m. 627), theme 2 (m. 616), theme 3 (mm. 602, 692), and theme 4 (m. 550).

Both SR and MR are organized and set metrically, for the most part. RH has a built-in accelerando, with durations <6221()>, which fits easily into duple metric beats (ex. 5.4). The rhythm appears first, however, with theme 11 (mm. 294–96, violin, ex. 5.2e) with durations <62213> (in sixteenths) in a repeating pattern of seven eighths, causing it to shift in relation to the meter in a characteristically cyclic series: from beat 1, then beats 4.5, 4, and 3.5 of the $\frac{3}{4}$ bars. In the following bars, the RH sounds six times, three times on the note A (mm. 297–392 contrabassoon and trombone, trumpet and trombone), once on an A/B♭ dyad (mm. 304–5, violin) and twice on C♯—the sum-10 pair of A (mm. 306–8, bass clarinet and bassoon). The second half of the palindrome contains the corresponding R(RH)s (mm. 413–15, bass clarinet and bassoon on C♯; mm. 416–17, violin on A/B♭; mm. 420–23 on A, trumpet and trombone, trombone and contrabassoon; and mm. 425–27, R(theme 11), violin).

RH returns at the outset of movement 3 in the cadenza, in a characteristic successive cyclic diminution of note values by one-half (initial dotted-half duration (mm. 481–82) to dotted quarter (m. 483) to dotted eighth (m. 483), solo violin, mm. 481–84), with an underlying piano RH in the largest durational values (initial dotted half). This rhythm appears in various variant and retrograde forms in the third movement, including the prominent metric statements on the note A in mm. 685–89, underlying the dramatic return of the Schönberg motto. In the bars corresponding to the center of the palindrome in the second movement (mm. 360–61), the ominous piano low D♭s are adorned with RH and R(RH), changing in number of attacks from twelve to ten. Perhaps most unexpectedly, the added P4 row of the *Lyric Suite* (mm. 775–80, piano, ex. 5.3) has its first 5 notes in RH, and its sixth to twelfth notes are grouped together, along with the articulation of the final piano chord, in an augmented version of RH.

PITCH LANGUAGE

The *Chamber Concerto* occupies a transitional position in Berg's assimilation of Schoenberg's twelve-tone techniques into his cyclic language. In Berg's subsequent twelve-tone music, row segments are largely cyclic collections; in the concerto, however, not all the themes hold cyclic collections as segments. In the case of theme 8, for instance, which is harmonized as part of 3-cycle l [0369] collections, the 3-cycle+ context is imposed; it is not present in the theme itself (ex. 5.2b). Overall, 3-cycle+ and whole-tone+–based collections are primary, with 5-cycle+ collections secondary.[22] As in most of Berg's music, horizontal ascending and descending interval 1 cycles appear frequently, creating directed motion by their voice-leading associations (for instance, mm. 13−14, 166−68, 260−70, and 309−18).

The opening three mottos may be partitioned into 3-cycle+ [0136]s and [0147] (ex. 5.1a). The [0147] <B−B♭−G−E> is subsequently arranged as dyads <B−G> and <A♯−E> in m. 1; <B−G> combines with theme 1 note E♯ and <A♯−E> with F♯ in whole-tone [026]s. With the 3-cycle <E−A♯−C♯> in m. 2 (final beat), the harmonies alternate between the principal 3-cycle P1 {E−G−B♭−C♯} and whole-tone+ collections, but the first section ends with a P2 3-cycle {D,F,A♭,B} "resolving" locally to an implied "tonic" in C major. In the corresponding bars in variation 5 (mm. 188−93), the principal P1 3-cycle is more emphatically stated, and, at the return of mm. 1ff. at the opening of the third movement (mm. 481−90), theme 1P5 0123 5-cycle+ <F−F♯−G♯−C♯> and 89AB 3-cycle+ chords <B−B♭−G−E> (piano) combine with whole-tone theme 7 0123 <G−B−F−A> (piano) and the principal P1 3-cycle collection {G−B♭−C♯−E} (violin).

The whole-tone+ segments of theme 2P0 are complemented by the 4-cycle−based accompanying chord <D♭−F−A/C−E−G♯> (mm. 8−10, 38−40, ex. 5.1c) initially, and throughout by 4-cycle−based harmonies (mm. 171−75, 491−506, 540−41, 696−97). The whole-tone+ segments of theme 2 are also reflected in the setting of 2IA in vertical interval 2s in variation 3 (mm. 128ff., 638ff.). In other places, however, theme 2 is accompanied by an allusion to the waltz focus on G (mm. 102−9) and a 3-cycle context (mm. 725−29), the latter reflecting the dual status of the final tetrachord.

The 5-cycle+ segments in theme 3PB are emphasized in its initial setting by [025]s in ascending 2 cycles (mm. 10−15). Later, however, 5-cycles take over the accompaniment, in mm. 97−102, with a characteristic alignment of descending 1-cycles in parallel interval 6s and ascending 5-cycles mimicking a "circle of fifths" of "dominant seventh chords" or whole-tone+ collection [0258]s (R(3PB), ex. 5.1d), which leads to a bass G and subsequent cadential motion to G (mm. 102ff.) in the tonal allusion to the waltz. This alignment, as well as a setting of theme 8 with aligned 1- and 5-cycles yielding vertical 3-cycle+ collections (mm. 621−24) is similar to the 1- and 5-cycle alignments in Berg's earlier works. In other appearances, theme 3 is harmonized by whole-tone+ collections (mm. 42−43, 203−6, piano; mm. 643−44, where the piano in interval 2s reflects a similar setting of 2P0 in mm. 638ff.; mm. 675−76, violin, contrabassoon, and bassoon) and combined 3- and 5-cycle collections (mm. 495−506, piano).

Theme 4 is constructed in three sections of 3-cycle+ collections, with 3-cycle [03]s, [036]s, and [0369]s hooked together by interval 1s to complete the aggregate: 4P2 as <D–F–F♯–A–B♭–D♭>, <D–F–A♭–A–C–E♭–E–G–B♭>, and <D–F–A♭–B–C–E♭–G♭–A–B♭–D♭–E–G> (mm. 16–19). Theme 4 is initially accompanied by 3+, 5-cycle, and whole-tone+ collections over a descending interval 5 cycle, moving from G2 to C1 (mm. 16–20, trombone to bassoons; mm. 46–50, piano). In variation 3, theme 4 appears as 4I8 in a *Klangfarben* alternation yielding linear whole-tone collections (ex. 5.1e). The extremely cyclic nature of this theme is reflected in other materials; in variation 5, for instance, a descending 3/3/1-cycle similar to the middle section of theme 4 appears in the piano part (mm. 186–87), harmonizing the Schönberg motto. In its appearances in the third movement (mm. 595–601, 653–57, 681–84, 738–40), theme 4 is varied in its final section but maintains its 3/1-based cyclic construction.

Theme 5 is initially harmonized by whole-tone+ collections based on descending parallel [026]s (mm. 19–23, ex. 5.1f; also mm. 50–54; 140–44, piano; 157–60, and 216–19), contrasting with the internal 3-cycle collection. In other appearances, however, the 3-cycle+ segment of theme 5 is complemented by a 3-cycle+–based harmonization, as in mm. 69–80, where theme 5 appears in a four-part canon with accompanying 3-cycle–based chords, building successively from two to six notes. In variation 4, theme 5 is introduced by a wedge of descending C♯ whole-tone and ascending C whole-tone collections, creating odd-interval sum-5 dyads (m. 155). (The wedge whole-tone collections connecting R(6I8) to R(5I3) in variation 4, mm. 155–56, piano, foreshadow a similar whole-tone harmonization of combined themes 6P2 [violin] and 9P4– 9P9–9P8–9P7 [piano] in the cadenza, mm. 524–32).

Theme 6, largely from successive interval 4s, is harmonized mostly by a "tonal" implication of G created by alternating "F♯-minor" and "G-minor" triads, in larger whole-tone+ and 5-cycle+ contexts (ex. 5.1g). The G focus recurs when R(6P2) is set over the waltz pattern in variation 2 (mm. 61–68), where the waltz chords are altered "I" and "V" chords in G: [0347] {G,A♯,B,D} and [0137] {A♭,C,D,E♭}. In variation 4, the ending 4-cycle collection <A–F–D♭> of R(6I8) (m. 154, oboe, english horn) is accompanied by alignments of itself with an ascending 1-cycle, creating a series of twelve different intervals in a 7-cycle: pitch-classes <9519519519519 51> over <AB0123456789>, yielding intervals <B6183A507294>;[23] the series is followed by the exclusively odd intervals from aligned C/C♯ whole-tone scales.

Theme 7, with its internal whole-tone+ collections, is harmonized on its first appearance by whole-tone+ collections from parallel [026]s and [0137]s (mm. 241–47, ex. 5.2a) and later in canon in primarily whole-tone+–collection contexts (mm. 375–90). It also appears harmonized by 3-cycle+ collections (mm. 254–59, as 7IB, mm. 338–44). The first four notes of theme 7, the C♯ whole-tone collection {F,G,A,B}, are used as the basis of whole-tone+ collections in the cadenza (mm. 481–90) and the coda (mm. 781–85), where the piano plays {G,F,A,B} in octaves over the full register of the instrument, in the RH (ex. 5.3), holding these notes while the upper instruments noodle with other themes until the final violin gesture of <G,F,A,B>. When theme R(7IB) appears in vertical dyads <u>B975</u> over <u>A864</u> (m. 650, oboe and english horn), with horizontal voices in a 2-cycle of order positions, the same voices also have cyclic pitch content, with 5-cycle+ <C–A–D–G> and whole-tone<F#–Bb–E–Ab> collections. This manipulation in particular foreshadows later developments in *Lulu*.

Theme 8, although lacking internal 3-cycle collections, is presented in five parallel voices, creating vertical 3-cycle+ [01369] collections (mm. 260–70, ex. 5.2b). The notes of the main 8P9 row are the "added notes" to the 3-cycle chords; the other rows are 8P7, 8PA, 8P4, and 8P1—from the principal 3-cycle collection {G–Bb–C#–E}. In the third-movement cadenza, theme 8 appears with the 3-cycle+–based theme 4 (mm. 507–14). Later in the third movement, the end of theme 8 is followed by a combination of interval 1s in parallel [0369]s against a descending 7-cycle bass—in a characteristic alignment of 1- and 5-cycles—creating vertical 3-cycle+ [01369]s (mm. 622–23).

Themes 9 (with eleven distinct pitch-classes), 10, and 11 are presented in varied, less well-defined cyclic contexts. Theme 9 is almost completely symmetrical, at 9P4 <E–F#–A–B–G–C#–D–Bb–C–Eb–F> in symmetrical sum-9 pairs E/F, F#/Eb, A/C, B/Bb, and G/D, with C# lacking its partner G#.[24] In mm. 271, successive 9P4 (violin), 9P9 (trumpet), 9P8 (bassoon), and 9P7 (bassoon, contrabassoon) are presented along with 8P9 and 10P1 in a whole-tone+ context (mm. 271ff., ex. 5.2c); later, in mm. 283–86, 10P1 appears in a whole-tone+ context (ex. 5.2d). In a climactic statement (mm. 314ff.), inverted theme 10s appear in three different durations—quarters (10I8), eighths (10IB), and sixteenths (10IB/I3)—simultaneously; the event is foreshadowed in mm. 303–5 by appearances of cell 1 in successive quarters (trumpets, trombones), eighths (horns and clarinets), and sixteenths (bass clarinet and bassoon).[25] The climax in m. 314 is accompanied by mostly cyclic trichords—4 cycle [048]s, triadic [037]s, whole-tone [026]s, and 3-cycle [036]s—appearing successively in parallel ascending interval 1s (bass clarinet, bassoon, contrabassoon; similar cyclic combinations harmonize theme 10 in mm. 287–91 [clarinet, contrabassoon, trombone] and 430–34 [clarinet, horn 2, piano]), similar to the succession of whole-tone to triadic to 3-cycle collections accompanying theme 7 at the beginning of the second movement (mm. 241ff., trumpet, horn, trombone; ex. 5.2a). In movement 3, theme 10 is juxtaposed with the interval 3-cycle+–based theme 4 (mm. 550–62, violin, ensemble; mm. 677–84, piano, ensemble).

The whole-tone+–based theme 11 is set to RH and given a prefix cell 1, accompanied by 3-cycle+–based [01369] and [01367] harmonies (mm. 294–302, bassoon, trumpet, horn, trombone, ex. 5.2e; mm. 419–27, flute, oboe, english horn) and by vertical 4-cycle [048]s (mm. 312–14, horn, trombone; mm. 698–701, trumpet, horn, trombone). Theme 12, with internal whole-tone+ collections, is accompanied by its own final [016] <C–F♯–B> segment (ex. 5.2f). It repeats several times, varied intervalically but largely retaining its whole-tone+ segmental context (bass clarinet, mm. 325–27; solo violin, mm. 327–28; bassoon, mm. 328–29). In the third movement (mm. 652–57, piano, ensemble), R(12P7) appears with the [016]s expanded and combined into larger whole-tone+ and 3-cycle+ collections.

FOCAL PITCH-CLASSES

The note G is a focal pitch-class throughout the *Chamber Concerto*, emphasized cyclically as a member of the principal whole-tone+ collection {F–G–A–B–C♯–D} and the principal 3-cycle collection {G–B♭–C♯–E}, and in 5-cycle contexts with tonal allusions and with note D as a recurring "dominant." The other notes of the primary whole-tone+ and 3-cycle collections are also emphasized in various ways throughout. Most notably, the note A begins each of the mottos, and the notes E–G–B♭ end the mottos. The first movement begins with C♯ whole-tone notes {E♯,G,B} and ends with a nine-note chord that excludes {C♯, F,G} from the same collection. The second movement begins with C♯ whole-tone tetrachord {F,G,A,B} (ex. 5.2a); A and C♯ are emphasized throughout, particularly when set to RH; the chord at the center of the palindrome in the context of cell 3 is 3-cycle {C♯–E–G–B♭} (ex. 5.2g), and the movement ends with tetrachordal C♯ whole-tone+ {D,G,F,B} (not including the piano). The third movement ends with a D-based whole-tone+ chord in m. 780, leading to a held C♯ whole-tone tetrachord {F,G,A,B} in the piano and final notes in the violin. In the sum-10 pairs between most materials, F/F and B/B map into each other and the G whole-tone collection to itself (although the latter property is true of any even-sum mappings).

In other instances of the focal notes, C♯ is prominent as the highest voice beginning 2P0 and as the lowest note in the accompanying {D♭,F,A,C,E,G♯} chord (mm. 8–10); 3P11 begins with B; theme 4 spans D to G, and its accompanying 5-cycle begins on G and ends on C♯ (mm. 16–20); theme 5P7 spans G to C♯; theme 6P2 begins on D and is harmonized by F♯/G triads (mm. 25–31, 55–60, 220–40, 525–32, 751–65), and, in variation 1, C♯ is emphasized by octave repetition as part of 6P2. The waltz in variations 2 and 5 is based on a "tonic" of G (accompanies R(6P2), mm. 61–68 and mm. 229–40; 3PB, mm. 91–97; R(2P0), mm. 102–5; and 12P7 with R(5P2), mm. 577–87). A focus on E♭, with E♭ "minor triads," underlies 1I5 (mm. 121–24), then 6I8 (mm. 149–51), and, as a pedal tone under R(5I8) (mm. 161–65); acting analogously to scale; degree $\hat{6}$ in G, E♭ eventually "resolves" to D.

The only focus in the concerto not included in the G whole-tone and 3-cycle+ collections is C. A local inflection of C in m. 7 and the "resolution" of G to C in the bass in variation 4 (mm. 61–72, piano) of the first movement anticipates the tonal focus on C in the violin part at the end of the second movement. The tonal elements occur as C and G triads and 3-cycle "diminished seventh" [0369]s in the violin part of this movement (mm. 451–62), and in the transposition of the <A–B–D–E> cell 3 to <C–D–F–G> and <B♭–A♭–F–E♭>, each note part of chords that seem to imply a center of C (mm. 457–65). At m. 475, the alternate ending to the second movement begins, leading to a cadential C-based whole-tone+ chord, <C–E–B♭–A♭–D♭> (alternate ending, m. 485). The implied progression of G to C here, with its extension of the 5-cycle D–G–C, perhaps recalls the final movement of Berg's opus 5 pieces.

The language also includes quarter notes, which Berg characteristically includes integrally as the logical end of a cyclic succession of ever smaller intervals in the solo violin part: in mm. 277–80, the violin descends by interval 2s <C–B♭–A♭–F♯–E> and <[C]–B–A–G–F>, then by interval 1's <C–B–B♭–A–A♭–G>, and by quarter tones, from C down to A, indicated by Zs on the note stems.[26]

"Schließe mir die Augen beide"

For his first fully twelve-tone piece, Berg chose to reset the poem "Schließe mir die Augen beide" by Theodor Storm, a text he had previously set in 1907. He juxtaposed the two songs in a dramatic flourish for the twenty-fifth anniversary of Universal Edition, as an illustration of the extent to which music had changed during that period, from the C-major key of his first setting to the twelve-note all-interval row used in the second setting. The resetting of the song also had a private meaning for Berg; whereas the first version was dedicated to his future wife, Helene Nahowski, the second version was the first in a succession of pieces with hidden references to his infatuation with Hanna Fuchs-Robettin.[27]

Berg's second setting, hereafter referred to as "Schließe mir" without qualification, features many of the characteristics found throughout his later music. The contours and registers are expansive, and lines move in sweeping gestures, as if straining to break free of the bounds of the piece. The formal sections are balanced and clearly defined, and numbers of beats and bars are in integral ratios related to 23 and 10: the twenty bars in the song divide formally into ten plus ten, the $\frac{3}{4}$ meter organizes the corresponding sixty beats ($2 \times 3 \times 10$), and the voice reaches its apex in m. 13, at approximately .63 (the Golden Section) of the way through the song. Overall, the notes F and B are emphasized as beginning and ending notes of rows, formal sections, and registral extremes.[28] The dynamics are somewhat unusual for Berg in their constrained expression, varying only from $\textit{pp}$ to $\textit{p}$ for most of the song, except for the brief crescendo to $\textit{mf}$ near the end (mm. 18–19).

The all-interval row and the setting of the vocal line express the greatest diversity in intervalic and pitch-class content, while the small number of row forms and row-related harmonies—mostly segmental 5-cycle collections—provide a high degree of consistency in the language. In this brief piece, the close relationship between 5-cycle–based language and the row hexachords makes it virtually academic to distinguish between the two—in that sense, it is Berg's only "true" twelve-tone work, in which all events can be directly related to one row. The two row forms used, P5 and I8, both appear as vertical chords (mm. 10–11, 19–20), but the latter row appears only in a rotated form, beginning from its second hexachord, which gives it the same boundary notes F and B as P5. The row derivations on I8 are quite sophisticated: the row is not only partitioned into a four-note group and eight-note residue, but the eight-note row is rotated and segmented to derive further material.

TEXT, VOCAL LINE, AND FORM

The text of "Schließe mir" is arranged in two stanzas of four lines each, in the rhyme scheme abab cddc (fig. 5.3).[29] The number of syllables per line reflects the rhyme scheme, in the cyclic arrangement 8787 7887. Berg set the eight lines in eight vocal phrases, grouped by stanzas of four lines in each half of the song. The vocal line uses only one row form, P5 (ex. 5.5) and is entirely syllabic, with one note per syllable; thus, the sixty syllables constitute five vocal rows, with two and a half rows per stanza. With the same number of notes per phrase as syllables, the 8787 7887 cyclic arrangement yields a maximum variety of phrase boundary notes from P5: in the sixteen boundary notes, each note and order position appears at least once, with order positions $\underline{0}$, $\underline{5}$, $\underline{8}$, and $\underline{B}$ (notes <F–D–E♭–B>) appearing twice. Two of these notes, F and B, are the first and last notes, respectively, in the vocal line.

In the first half of the song, the ten bars divide in half (mm. 1–5, 6–10) by line pairs in the text, row use, and texture. Further equal subdivisions of mm. 1–2$\frac{1}{2}$, 2$\frac{1}{2}$–5, and 6–8$\frac{1}{2}$, 8$\frac{1}{2}$–10 result from the entrance of the second row in the accompaniment in m. 2$\frac{1}{2}$ and the accompanimental palindromes centered around mm. 5–6 and 8$\frac{1}{2}$. In the second half, the row use and texture divide into mm. 11–16 and 16–20, but the text setting is accelerated so that the seventh

Figure 5.3. Text and row setting in "Schließe mir"

	rhyme	syllables	P5	boundaries	
1. Schließe mir die Augen beide	a	8	<u>0</u>–7	F–D♭	mm. 1–2
2. mit den lieben Händen zu;	b	7	<u>8</u>–2	E♭–C	3–4
3. geht doch alles, was ich leide	a	8	<u>3</u>–A	A–B♭	5–7
4. unter deiner Hand zur Ruh.	b	7	<u>B</u>–5	B–D	8–10
5. Und wie leise sich der Schmerz	c	7	<u>6</u>–0	A♭–F	11–12
6. Well' um Welle schlafen leget,	d	8	<u>1</u>–8	E–E♭	13–14
7. wie der letzte Schlag sich reget,	d	8	<u>9</u>–4	G♭–G	14–17
8. füllest du mein ganzes Herz.	c	7	<u>5</u>–B	D–B	17–19

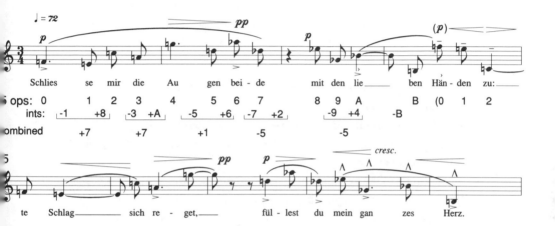

Example 5.5. First and last vocal rows, "Schließe mir," mm. 1–4, 16–20. Berg "Schließe mir die Augen beide" (1925). Copyright 1955 by Universal Edition A.G., Wien. Copyright renewed. All Rights Reserved. Used by permission of European American Music Distributors Corporation, sole U.S. and Canadian agent for Universal Edition A.G., Wien.

vocal line begins in m. 14, before the formal division at m. 16, breaking the text distribution pattern of two lines per five measures to signal the impending end of the song.

Of the five vocal rows, the first and last have the same contour (ex. 5.5) and contain all eleven intervals (within an octave); thus the closing phrase constitutes a return at the end of the song. The accompanimental I8 row beginning the second half of the song in the piano right hand (mm. 11–13, ex. 5.6a) is very similar in relative contour to the opening and closing vocal rows, emphasizing the formal halves. The overall arch-contour of the main row (the combined

Example 5.6a. Forms of row I8, "Schließe mir," mm. 11–13

I8: 8-note row

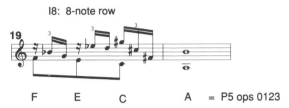

F   E   C   A   = P5 ops 0123

Example 5.6b. Final I8 row with <F–E–C–A> extracted, "Schließe mir." Berg "Schließe mir die Augen beide" (1925). Copyright 1955 by Universal Edition A.G., Wien. Copyright renewed. All Rights Reserved. Used by permission of European American Music Distributors Corporation, sole U.S. and Canadian agent for Universal Edition A.G., Wien.

intervals between paired notes reveal the large ascent, then descent, ex. 5.5) is reflected throughout the song in vocal arcs in mm. 1–4, 13–15, and 15–19, and the piano left hand in mm. 5–6, 7–8, and 12–14; even the verticalized rows ending each formal half arpeggiate to form an inverted arch—descending in m. 10 and ascending in m. 20.[30]

In contrast to the first and fifth rows, the middle three vocal rows are set with diverse contours and eight distinct pitch intervals each. In terms of relative placement of notes, each of the twelve pitch-classes in the five vocal rows appears in two octaves. The registral placements of notes in the five P5 rows may be listed as pairs of low/high numbers: F-3/2, E-3/2, C-1/4, A-4/1, G-2/3, D-1/4, Ab-3/2, Db-1/4, Eb-2/3, Gb-3/2, Bb-1/4, and B-2/3. The lack of a 5/0 or 0/5 pattern reveals that all notes are varied in octave placement at least once.

In the first vocal row, successive dyads are grouped in pairs, order positions 01 23 45 67 89 AB, by the contour pattern and by the textual stress on the upper first note of each dyad (ex. 5.5). By this grouping, patterns of every other note—or a 2-cycle on order positions—combine as 02468A and 13579B. The corresponding pitch patterns are an ascending 7-cycle in 024 <F–C–G> and a descending 7-cycle in 79A <Db–Gb–B>, and an ascending 5-cycle 135 <E–A–D> and a descending 5-cycle 68A <Ab–Eb–Gb>. The natural crescendo of the ascent is, however, contravened by the decrescendo indicated in the vocal part of mm. 1–2, from *p* to *pp*. The dyadic pairs in the first vocal row are shifted throughout by the irregular groups of seven syllables in lines 2, 4, and 5.

The vocal part begins with dyads from o͟1, then shifts at C4 *zu* (m. 4) to the 1͟2 3͟4 5͟6 7͟8 9͟A B͟o dyads, back to o͟1 dyads at D4 *Ruh* (m. 9), and again to 1͟2 dyads at F5 *Schmerz* (m. 12). As a consequence of these shifts, the final row, which marks a return to the contour of the initial vocal row, has the opposite dyad pairs grouped, 1͟2 3͟4 5͟6 7͟8 9͟A B͟ (ex. 5.5). Thus, Berg arrives at characteristic variety in the formal return.

ROW PROPERTIES AND DERIVED MATERIALS

As Berg commented in his notes to the *Lyric Suite*, which in its first movement uses the same row as "Schließe mir," the all-interval row has no independent retrograde, yielding only twenty-four distinct row forms with P(n) = R(Pn+6).[31] The hexachords are 5-cycle collections [024579], arranged with 7-cycles in o͟2͟4 and 6͟8͟A and with 5-cycles in 1͟3͟5 and 7͟9͟B (of prime form rows). This cyclic structure results in adjacent dyads at alternating sums: sum-9 dyads appear in o͟1 2͟3 4͟5 6͟7 8͟9 A͟B from pitch-classes (P5) <54 09 72 81 36 AB> and sum-4 dyads in 1͟2 3͟4 7͟8 9͟A B͟o from pitch-classes <40 97 22 88 13 6A B(5)>.[32] The change in dyadic grouping in the vocal part from o͟1 dyads to 1͟2 dyads thus alternates between sum-9 and sum-4 pairs. These sums appear in vertical dyads as well: in m. 16, even-interval sum-4 dyads <C/E–B/F> appear, and in the accompaniment in m. 18, sum-9 dyadic pairs <B♭/C♭–E♭/G3–A♭/D♭–G/D> are aligned vertically, yielding odd interval-classes 1, 3, 5, and 5.

Although the row permits hexachordal combinatoriality, vertical row alignments are generally not combinatorial, except in the opening five bars, where the two hexachords of P5 are aligned in the voice and piano: <F–E–C–A–G–D> over <A–D♭–E♭–G♭–B♭–B>. In this note-for-note alignment of the two hexachords, the dyads are all interval-class 3, as a result of the cyclic structure of the row: a 5/7-cycle divides into four trichords, related to one another by interval-classes 3 or 6; for instance, <5–o–7 / 2–9–4 / B–6–1 / 8–3–A>. The corresponding arrangement of 5/7-cycle trichords in each hexachord of the row thus yields the interval-class 3 pairing: <F–C–G> o͟2͟4 / <A♭–E♭–B♭> 6͟8͟A and <E–A–D> 1͟3͟5 / <C♯–F♯–B> 7͟9͟B.

Of the two row forms P5 and I8, the latter occurs only in rotated order, beginning with its second hexachord (ex. 5.6a). With I8 rotated, P5 and I8 hold the 3-cycle notes {F,D,A♭,B} in the same relative positions, as the first, sixth, seventh, and twelfth notes. In contrast to the straightforward presentations of P5, I8 undergoes several complex transformations. The row I8 is presented immediately prior to the final chord with the notes 6͟7͟1͟3 <F–C–A–E> [0158] displaced from their original positions and set in even eighth notes in the order of the first four notes of P5 as <F–E–C–A> (ex. 5.6b). The two rows are thus linked by this four-note group. The eight-note residue row I8 8͟9͟A͟B͟o͟2͟4͟5

<Bb–G–Eb–D–G#–C#–F#–B> constitutes the remaining notes (the 5-cycle end segment highlights the importance of this interval throughout the song). This eight-note residue row, left over from the extraction of {F,C,A,E} from I8, is the source of the left-hand accompanimental figures in mm. 12–15.[33] The residue row I8 89AB0245 <Bb–G–Eb–D–Ab–C#–F#–B> is rotated with the note B 5 omitted, leaving 2489AB0 <C#–F#–Bb–G–Eb–D–Ab>. The segments 2489 <C#–F#–A#–G> [0147] and AB0 <Eb–D–Ab> [016] are extracted and used, along with a combined {Bb} and {E,A} (from {F,E,C,A}) as {E,A,Bb} [016] (ex. 5.6a). The [0147] is an unusual harmony in the song, although it has an internal interval-class 5 and [037]; as a 3-cycle+ harmony, it reflects the invariant 3-cycle notes, {F,Ab,B,D}, between P5 and I8, and the interval-class 3 pairing of P5 012345 / 6789AB in mm. 1–2.

Other harmonic events in the song evince varied row alignments and segmentation, including rotation. The alignment of P5 in the voice and I8 in the piano at the beginning of the second half of the song pairs the two rows' order positions 6789AB, yielding sum-1 dyads in odd interval-classes <31515>: <Ab–Db–Eb–Gb–Bb> / <F–C–Bb–G–Eb>. Immediately thereafter (mm. 13–14), the rows are aligned but offset by one, P5 34567 over I8 23456, yielding alternating interval-classes <43>: <A–G–D–Ab–Db> / <C#–E–F#–B–F>.[34] The initial accompanimental rotated P5 in the piano (mm. 1–5) is arranged in vertical segmental tetrachords, of 5-cycle+–based 6789, [0257], 2345 [0257], and AB01 [0167], with non-segmental voice-leading. The harmonic motion through 5-cycle chords in different positions along the cyclic continuum by conjunct voice-leading, for instance, from <A–D–G–C> to T6 <Eb–Ab–Db–Gb> with voice-leading <A–Gb>, <C–Db>, <G–Ab>, and <D–Eb> in mm. 3–4—also found in the first movement of the *Lyric Suite* (mm. 11–12)—is analogous to the alternation of whole-tone+ collections by odd-interval voice-leading found throughout Berg's music. Corresponding vertical segmental tetrachords and trichords, now from 5-cycle–based [0158] 789A, [016] 456, and [0358] 0123, appear near the end of the song, in conjunction with the return of the opening row contour and intervals; these chords are arranged with the outer voices in a wedge pattern of complementary interval 1 cycles from {C4,E4}, outer voices <E–F–Gb–G–F–Gb> / <C–B–Bb–Ab–A–Ab> (mm. 16–19).

Finally, although the row itself, with symmetrical interval pattern <B89 A7652341>, has no distinct retrograde forms, Berg nonetheless creates the impression of a retrograde by palindromes from contour, rhythm, and pitch in the first half of the song (ex. 5.7, mm. 4–10; the implied retrograde form is shown with the corresponding prime form numbers). The midpoints of the palindromes in mm. 5–6 and 8½ serve formal functions, dividing mm. 1–10 into 1–5 and 6–10, and mm. 6–10 into 6–8½ and 8½–10. These palindromes have

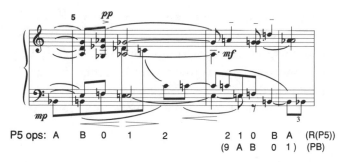

P5 ops: A B 0 1 2   2 1 0 B A (R(P5))
              (9 A B 0 1) (PB)

Example 5.7. Palindromic setting of lower-voice row, "Schließe mir," mm. 5–7. Berg "Schließe mir die Augen beide" (1925). Copyright 1955 by Universal Edition A.G., Wien. Copyright renewed. All Rights Reserved. Used by permission of European American Music Distributors Corporation, sole U.S. and Canadian agent for Universal Edition A.G., Wien.

parallels in the second-half palindromic arch figures in the left-hand piano accompaniment in mm. 12–15.

Lyric Suite

The *Lyric Suite*, Berg's second string quartet, written in 1925–26 and first performed January 8, 1927 in Vienna, is in six movements with a recently discovered song for soprano in the last movement.[35] The song is part of the secret dedication to Hanna Fuchs-Robettin, which includes numbers of bars and beats and tempo indications in multiples of 23 and 10, symbolic tempo and performance indications, and an emphasis on the "initials" note group {A,B♭,B,F}. Publicly, the quartet is dedicated to Alexander Zemlinsky and takes its name from his *Lyric Symphony*; Berg quoted a melody from the symphony in the fourth movement, and included as well a quote from the opening of Wagner's *Tristan und Isolde* in the sixth movement.[36] Berg left detailed analyses of the six movements in the quartet in letters and an analysis for Rudolf Kolisch, outlining the individual forms and the treatment of rows and motives.[37]

 The six movements in the *Lyric Suite* progress in interwoven inversionally repeated tempo cycles—analogous to the alternating 5/7-cycle construction of the row in the first movement—accelerating in movements 1, 3, and 5 and decelerating in movements 2, 4, and 6, so that successive movements become more extreme in their expression and in their contrast with the previous movement.[38] On a relative scale of 1 (fast) to 6 (slow), the tempo progresses cyclically through movements 1 to 6 as <3–4–2–5–1–6>. As the tempos increase in movements 1, 3, and 5, however, the movements also increase in length, so that movement 5 is substantially longer than 1 or 3; as the tempo slows in movements 2, 4, and 6, correspondingly, the number of bars decreases, so that the movements stay close in absolute duration.

In his notes to Schoenberg on the composition of the *Lyric Suite*, Berg observed that the initial row, labeled here as row 1, lacked a distinct retrograde, and, seeking variety, he altered the row by exchanging notes in the two hexachords. In successive alterations, Berg created four rows (ex. 5.8): row 2 from

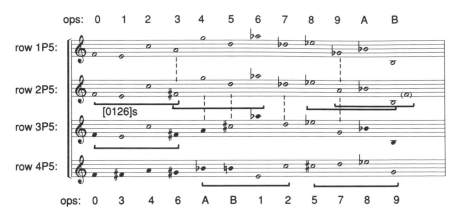

Example 5.8. The four rows in the *Lyric Suite*

row 1 by exchanging pitch-classes in order positions 3 and 9; row 3 from 2 by exchanging pitch-classes in order positions 4 and 9, and 5 and 7; and row 4 from row 3 by partitioning and concatenating notes in order positions 0346AB / 125789. The derivation of row 4, which is clearly demonstrated in the music in the fifth and sixth movements (mm. 375–85 and mm. 30–31, respectively), stems from a partitioning of row 2 in movement 3 as 03469AB / 12578, which is used to create two motivic rhythms. The two partitions differ only in the changed position of 9, a relationship unveiled by their juxtaposition in movement 6 (mm. 30–32; see example 5.26). The rows appear in movements 1 (row 1) and 6 (rows 3 and 4), the outer sections of movement 3 (row 2), and the internal sections of movement 5 (rows 3 and 4); the remainder—movements 2 and 4, the middle section of movement 3, and sections of movement 5—are in Berg's "atonal" idiom, with largely thematic appearances of the rows: rows 1 and 2 in movement 2, and rows 3 and 4 in movement 5.

The combined twelve-tone and atonal elements in the quartet both stem, however, from the common denominator of Berg's cyclic language. The first movement is, uniquely in the quartet, wholly 5-cycle–based, with 3-cycle elements secondary. The second movement is principally 3- and whole-tone-cycle–based, with 5-cycle elements in an internal section. The third movement is whole-tone+−based, stemming from the emphasis on [0126] and its seg-mental appearances in row 2. Two motives derived from row 2 by a rhythmic partition are 1-cycle collections, from the other cyclic aspect of [0126]. The set [0126] is also prominent in movements 4, 5, and 6, with its accompanying whole-tone+ context. The second and fourth movements also feature the whole-tone+ or 3-cycle+−based motive [0236], related to the quote from Zem-linksy's *Lyric Symphony*. The sixth movement contains whole-tone+ collections from aligned prime and inversion rows at even sums, and features whole-tone+ collections [0126] and [0258] in connection with the quote from the beginning of Wagner's *Tristan und Isolde*.

In the succession through the four rows, the interval patterns change from an even distribution in the all-interval row 1 <B89A7652341> (prime form) to a predominance of interval-class 1s in row 4, <13B21581114> (prime form) (ex. 5.8). Each row after the first features at least one segmental [0126], although [0236] is not segmented in any row. Row 1 has [0158]s as its end tetrachords, related by T6 or (in P5) by inversion at sum 3, {E,F,A,C} and {B♭,B,E♭,G♭}; [0167] {D♭,D,G,A♭} is the middle tetrachord, with internal sums 3/9. By exchanging the sum-3 − related notes A and F♯ in 3 and 9 to create row 2, the end tetrachords become [0126]s related at sum 3 {F,E,C,F♯} and {E♭,A,B♭,B}, with the middle tetrachord unchanged. In his letter to Schoenberg, Berg demonstrated that row 2 contained the segmental tetrachord {F,E,C,F♯} {0126] in four forms, in 0123, 3456, 89AB, and 9AB0, referring to it as a "four-note group" that acts "somewhat like an ostinato." In his later notes on the suite, and in the music, the rows used are 2P5, 2P8, 2PA, and 2I8, with segmental {B♭,A,F,B} [0126] in each case (see ex. 5.18). This note group appears once in the first movement (m. 56 viola, where A4 is added AB0 <Bb−B−F> of row 1P5 to create <A−B♭−B−F>) and six times in the second (in 2P8, mm. 24−25, 30−31, 94−95, and 98−99; also non-row, mm. 56−59 and 105−6). As {F,A,B♭,B} and, more generally, as [0126], the tetrachord dominates movements 3 to 6 and prepares for the quoted opening of *Tristan* in movement 6, which begins with [0126] <A−F−E−E♭> and is sur-rounded by the notes <A−F/B♭−B>. The notes of the Tristan chord itself {F,G♯,B,D♯} [0258] are segmental as 1234 in row 3P4 (see ex. 5.25).[39]

The quote from Zemlinsky's *Lyric Symphony* has its own related tetrachord, [0236] (see ex. 5.21).[40] Sets [0236] and [0126] share subset [026], and although both are whole-tone+−based chords, [0236] also has 3-cycle+ potential. Tetra-chord [0236] first appears in a repeated figure in the second movement (see ex. 5.14), and it returns in movement 4 immediately prior to the Zemlinksy quote (m. 31). The recurring [0126] and [0236] tetrachords unify the suite and are the most prominent of a group of tetrachordal whole-tone+ motives, supersets of [026], which include [0246], [0146], [0157], [0268], [0258], [0248], and [0137].

The importance of tetrachords throughout is foreshadowed in the first movement by the introductory 5-cycle tetrachords (see ex. 5.10), the independent cyclic treatment of [0158] 89AB before the recapitulation (mm. 41−42; see ex 5.9), and the vertical tetrachords [0158], [0167], and [0158] from P5 to end the movement. These tetrachords are among the materials that link movements: row 1 from movement 1 and row 2 from movement 3 both appear in movement 2; the upper-voice <E−F−G−B> [0137] tetrachord ending movement 1 is the same set as the opening T = −1 <E−D#−A#−F#> of the main theme of movement 2 (cf. exx. 5.10 and 5.14); the middle-section trio of movement 3 is the exposition of movement 4; movement 4 contains the main theme and the [0236] figure of movement 2, leading to the Zemlinsky quote; movement 5 introduces the two rows 3 and 4 used in movement 6 and restates the insistent short-long rhythm of movement 2 (mm. 56−59, 131−35) in reverse as an important rhythmic motive throughout (mm. 15−19, 30−35, 124−29, 133−47, 183−95, 200−211, 306−25, 329−39, 401−6, 415−20, and 446−60); and movement 6 includes a figure recalling movement 1 (first movement, mm. 5−6, 38−39, in sixth movement, mm. 10−11, 37−39).[41]

MOVEMENT I

The first movement of the *Lyric Suite* is in sonata form, with traditional formal features (fig. 5.4). The proportions of exposition to combined development-recapitulation are approximately 1:1; a thirty-six-bar exposition (mm. 1−36), seven−bar development (mm. 36−42), and twenty-eight-bar recapitulation (mm. 42−69).[42] Each formal section within the exposition has a characteristic theme or motivic figure and tempo: a main theme in ternary form on two levels (aba', and xyx' within a), a second theme in ternary form (cdc'), and a closing theme; a brief development; a condensed recapitulation; and a brief coda. As is characteristic of Berg's forms, motives cross sectional boundaries: the main theme appears in an inverted contour variant in the second theme area (mm. 25−26, violin), and the y motive from the first theme area appears with the closing theme (mm. 33−34, 59−60).

Berg's adaptation of the sonata principle in the first movement features themes and motives from the exposition both transposed and inverted in the recapitulation, at levels designed to stay within the main row family of P5, PB, I5, and IB, their hexachords Po/P6 [024579] {F,E,C,A,D,G} / {Ab,Db,Eb,Gb,Bb,B} in P5/PB and P1/P7 [024579] {F,F#,A#,C#,D#,G#} / {D,A,G,E,C,B} in I5/IB, and rows with equivalent hexachords by pitch-class content: P5/I4, PB/IA, P6/I5, and Po/IB (see the row chart in the appendix). With these rows and hexachords, transformations that stay within the main row family include: (1) transposition at T6 between P5-PB and I5-IB—the b material of the first theme and the c

Figure 5.4. Form in the *Lyric Suite*, first movement

Exposition: mm. 1–35 (35)			Recapitulation mm. 42–69 (28)	
introduction m.	1			
main theme mm. 2–22		Tempo I, ♩ = 100	mm. 42–52	main theme
	a	mm. 2–12	mm. 42–48	a
		x mm. 2–4	mm. 42–44	x
		y mm. 5–6 poco pesante		
		x' mm. 7–12 a tempo	mm. 44–48	x' sum 4
	b	mm. 13–15	mm. 49–51	b T6
bridge		mm. 15–19	mm. 51–52	bridge
	a'x	mm. 20–22		
2nd theme mm. 23–33		Tempo II poco più tranquillo	mm. 53–62	2nd theme
	c	mm. 23–28	mm. 53–58	c T6
	d	mm. 28–30	mm. 58–62	d + ay chords
	c'	mm. 31–33		
closing theme		mm. 33–35 poco accel. Tempo I	mm. 62–69	closing theme/ codetta

Development mm. 36–42 (7)   Tempo I

mm. 36–37 = mm. 21–22   a'x with scalar MT
mm. 38–39 = y in m. 38 = m. 6 at sum 4, m. 39 = m. 5, poco pesante
mm. 40–42   retransition, P5 89AB in 3-cycle sequence

material of the second theme return in the recapitulation at T6 (mm. 13–15 returning in mm. 49–51, mm 23–28 returning in mm. 53–58); (2) inversion at sum 4 between PB-I5 and IB-P5—the y material from the first theme (m. 6, ex. 5.13a) appears in the development (m. 38) at sum 4, and the main theme x', initially from P5, returns at sum 4 IB in the recapitulation (mm. 7–12 in mm. 44–48); and (3) transposition at T7 between P5-P0 and I4-IB, and between PB-P6 and IA-I5—the closing theme from (either) P5/I4 returns at T7 P0/IB in the recapitulation (m. 33, ex. 5.13b, in mm. 62ff.).

The main row family also expands into two 3-cycle–related secondary families P2,P5,P8,PB and I2,I5,I8,IB. Rows related by T3 share invariant 5-cycle segments: Pn 024, 135, 68A, 79B = Pn+3 531, 79B, 024, A86, respectively. This expanded family of rows appears in transition sections in the exposition and development: P2,P5,P8,PB at mm. 15–17, I2,I5,I8,IB at mm. 18–19, and I2, I5,

I8, PB at mm. 51–52. In the initial alignment, a trichordally combinatorial arrangement results from the rows aligned in <u>01234</u>, with vertical [0369]s (mm. 15–16, after which the alignment is broken). Row P2 also occurs in the second theme area: the second theme appears as P5-IB (mm. 23–24, violin 2) and returns in three-part canon as I5 (viola to violin 1), P2 (cello), and IB (violin 2) in mm. 31–33 (these three rows actually begin at the end of m. 26 in the accompaniment to the second theme; the second theme return in m. 31 begins with <u>7</u> of each row). Rows P2 and P8 also appear in the second theme area in the recapitulation (mm. 58–61: P2, cello; m. 62: P8, violin 2 to viola), and in the closing theme and coda P2,P5,P8, and PB occur in the scalar order of hexachords (mm. 62–69), and P2 appears in vertical tetrachords (violin 1, m. 67).[43]

In addition to their roles in the expanded row family just described, 3-cycles return in the retransition, ending the development section (mm. 41–42), where the segment <u>89AB</u> [0158] of P5, <E♭,F♯,B♭,B>, is extracted from its row context, arranged in paired voices, and sequenced at a complete 3-cycle (ex. 5.9). The succession is, however, similar to successive PB, then P5, rows—<B–B♭–G♭–E♭–D♭–(A♭)–D–(G)–A–C–E–F/F–E–C–A–G–(D)–A♭–(D♭)–E♭–G♭–B♭–B>—because the [0158]s in <u>0123</u> and <u>89AB</u> are related at T = 6. The actual series is only ten distinct notes, however, since it is impossible to construct an aggregate from three [0158]s. The passage is remarkable not only for the relationship between row and cycles but also in that, through judicious voice-leading and note doubling, a 3-cycle of [048]s (a 4-cycle harmony) may be interpreted (ex. 5.9). This multicycle setting foreshadows the complex cyclic language of *Lulu*.

The introduction to the first movement sets the harmonic context with four 5-cycle chords, three [0257] tetrachords and an [024579] hexachord, segmenting a continuous 7-cycle from P5 and IB hexachords (ex. 5.10). The boundary notes

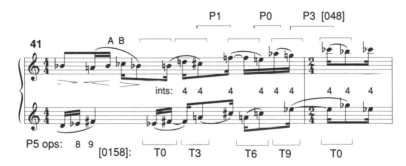

Example 5.9. 3-cycle transposition of row segment [0158], *Lyric Suite*, first movement, mm. 41–42. Berg LYRIC SUITE. Copyright 1927 by Universal Edition. Copyright renewed. All Rights Reserved. Used by permission of European American Music Distributors Corporation, sole U.S. and Canadian agent for Universal Edition A.G., Wien.

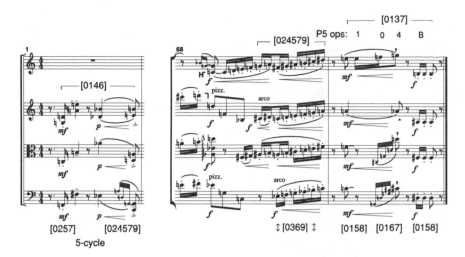

Example 5.10. Cyclic tetrachords and hexachords, opening and closing of *Lyric Suite*, first movement, mm. 1, 68–69

(lower) F and (upper) B initiate the registral and row-order position emphases on these pitch-classes that occur throughout the movement, and the combined 5-cycle chords with the upper-voice <D–E–B♭–B> all-interval class tetrachord [0146] foreshadow the row's combination of intervalic diversity with harmonic homogeneity. These tetrachords reappear in two forms at the end of the movement: first, as 5-cycle [0257] chords in an aggregate from a 4-cycle of transpositional levels, <F–B♭–E♭–A♭>, <A–D–G–C>, and <C♯–F♯–B–E> (mm. 65–66);[44] and, second, as tetrachords from P5 (m. 69, ex. 5.10). The upper voice <E–F–G–B> [0137] from P5 104B, foreshadowed by the same pitch-classes as a chord in m. 67 (violin 1, from P2 456A), is the Z-related all–interval-class tetrachord to the opening melodic [0146].

The main theme, identified by its contour and rhythm, appears in various guises, corresponding to three orders of the row hexachords: (1) the all-interval order of the row, as P5 (mm. 2–4, 20–22, ex. 5.11a); (2) in the scalar order of hexachords from PB at the beginning of the development (mm. 35–37, ex. 5.11c); and (3) in the 5/7-cycle order of the hexachords from P5, at the beginning of the codetta (mm. 64–66, ex. 5.11d). The main theme also appears as rotated rows P5 8–7 (mm. 7–10) and IB 1–A (mm. 44–48, ex. 5.11e), and partially as IB 0–7 at the end of the second theme area (mm. 32–33, 56, violin 1), and is reflected in an inverted contour variant IB 8–B as part of the second theme area (violin 1, mm. 25–28).

As described above, the all-interval row features alternating-sum dyads: at P5 <F–E–C–A–G–D–A♭–D♭–E♭–G♭–B♭–B> the sums are 4,9. The row IB <B–C–E–G–A–D–A♭–E♭–D♭–B♭–G♭> has sum dyads of 4,B, sharing

Example 5.11a. Main theme, *Lyric Suite*, first movement, mm. 2–4

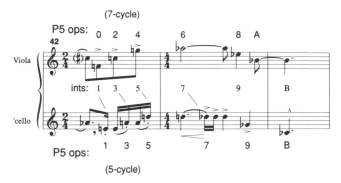

Example 5.11b. Cyclic partition at recapitulation of main theme, *Lyric Suite*, first movement, mm. 42–44

Example 5.11c. Scalar form of main theme, *Lyric Suite*, first movement, mm. 35–37

Example 5.11d. Seven-cycle form of main theme, *Lyric Suite*, first movement, mm. 64–66

sum 4 with P5. The opening P5 theme 1 (ex. 5.11a) has the sum-9 dyads slurred, but when row IB substitutes for P5 in the recapitulation (mm. 44–48, ex. 5.11e), the opposite sum-4 dyads are slurred (recalling the changed dyadic groupings in the vocal rows of "Schließe mir," ex. 5.5). At the beginning of the recapitulation, the 5/7-cyclic structure underlying the all-interval form of the

Example 5.11e. Substitute row IB for P5 in main theme, *Lyric Suite*, first movement, mm. 45–46. Berg LYRIC SUITE. Copyright 1927 by Universal Edition. Copyright renewed. All Rights Reserved. Used by permission of European American Music Distributors Corporation, sole U.S. and Canadian agent for Universal Edition A.G., Wien.

row is revealed by the row partitions 02468A (viola) and 13579B (cello) (ex. 5.11b). The vertical intervals formed by superimposing 024 over 135 and 68A over 79B are <1 − 3 − 5 − 7 − 9 − B>—increasing in a 2-cycle.[45]

The b material in the first theme area consists of vertical segmental trichords and tetrachords from P5, IB, PB, and I5 (ex. 5.12), with an upper-voice eleven-note collection (lacking B) of segmental [037]s related by T5, T6, and T1 (reflecting the P0/P6 and P1/P7 of the main row family hexachords) and [026]: <C−G−E♭>, <C−A♭−F>, <F♯−C♯−A>, <B♭−D−E>. The trichords accompany a C♯ whole-tone+−based melody (cello) based around notes B and F. In the recapitulation, the b passage is transposed by T6 to rows PB, I5, P5, and IB, which may also be regarded as retrograde rows (since PB = R(P5), etc.), yielding

Example 5.12. Partitions in first-area b material, *Lyric Suite*, first movement, mm. 13–15. Berg LYRIC SUITE. Copyright 1927 by Universal Edition. Copyright renewed. All Rights Reserved. Used by permission of European American Music Distributors Corporation, sole U.S. and Canadian agent for Universal Edition A.G., Wien.

Twelve-Tone Music: Detail and Analysis   255

the vertical tetrachords of the original in reverse order. The closing theme is the scalar version of the row, hexachords P0/P6 [024579], under the y chords from the first theme area (mm. 33–35, ex. 5.13b). At T7 in the recapitulation (mm. 62ff., violin 1), the hexachords rotate, to begin on the pivotal notes B and F (i.e., <B–C–D–E–G–A> instead of <G–A–B–C–D–E>), accompanied by a continuous 5-cycle from P8 (cello). In the coda, the [024579] scalar hexachords of the closing theme appear at 3-cycle–related T = {0,3,6,9}, from row groups P0/P3/P6/P9 and P2/P5/P8/PB (ex. 5.10). In the penultimate gesture (m. 68), the aligned P = <3–9–0–6> [024579] hexachords create six successive vertical [0369]s (two complete aggregates), leading to the vertical tetrachords of P5 and, by way of conclusion, juxtaposing the primary 3- and 5-cycle collections of the movement.

Example 5.13a. First-area y motive, *Lyric Suite*, movement 1, mm. 5–6

Example 5.13b. Combined y motive with closing theme, *Lyric Suite*, first movement, mm. 33–34. Berg LYRIC SUITE. Copyright 1927 by Universal Edition. Copyright renewed. All Rights Reserved. Used by permission of European American Music Distributors Corporation, sole U.S. and Canadian agent for Universal Edition A.G., Wien.

The twelve-note main theme of the second movement begins with [0137] <E–D♯–A♯–F♯> at T−1—a fateful interval in the quartet—from the upper line [0137] <E–F–G–B> ending the first movement (cf. exx. 5.10 and 5.14). Row 1 also appears in the second movement, where the head motive of the first movement's second theme (mm. 23–26) begins the second-movement's B theme in mm. 16–23 (at T3, violin 1, as 1P8, ex. 5.15), continuing with rows 1I2 and 2P8.

Example 5.14. Main theme and [0236] motive, *Lyric Suite*, second movement, mm. 1–6. Berg LYRIC SUITE. Copyright 1927 by Universal Edition. Copyright renewed. All Rights Reserved. Used by permission of European American Music Distributors Corporation, sole U.S. and Canadian agent for Universal Edition A.G., Wien.

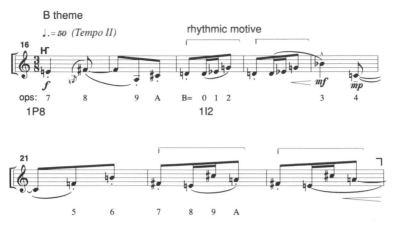

Example 5.15. Rows 1 and 2, with rhythmic motive, in B section, *Lyric Suite*, second movement, mm. 16–23. Berg LYRIC SUITE. Copyright 1927 by Universal Edition. Copyright renewed. All Rights Reserved. Used by permission of European American Music Distributors Corporation, sole U.S. and Canadian agent for Universal Edition A.G., Wien.

Tetrachordal sets [0126] and [0236] are prominent throughout the second movement: [0126] in the main theme, as {F,A,B♭,B} in row 2P8 (mm. 24–25, 30–31, 94–95, 98–99) and beginning the C sections (mm. 56–58, 105–106); [0236] in a motivic figure in the A sections (first in m. 5, ex. 5.14). The main cyclic collections throughout are whole-tone+ and 3-cycle+, with secondary 5-cycle collections in the C area theme.

Formally, the second movement is a rondo, with three distinct sections differentiated by material, meter, and tempo (see figure 5.5). Some overlapping of material occurs, however; the [0236] motive of the A sections emerges near the end of the first B section (mm. 33–40, violin 2) to foreshadow the return of A' in m. 41, where the formal division is obscured by the delay in the return of Tempo I until m. 43. The final C section (mm. 113–42) contains material and corresponding tempos from the A and B sections, in the nature of a development. At the movement's climax (mm. 131–42), in three-bar hypermeasures marked *Dreitaktig* and grouped by the augmented upper-voice [0236] motive (ex. 5.16) from the A section (violin 1), this motive is juxtaposed with a headmotive of the C theme (violin 2), which groups in $\frac{3}{8}$ against the notated meter, the repeated Cs of the B section (viola), which group in a conflicting $\frac{4}{8}$ with an internal syncopated rhythm, and the motivic shape and characteristic rhythm derived originally from row 2 in the B sections (cello; cf. exxs. 5.15 and 5.16). The combined pitch-classes of the whole-tone+ or 5-cycle+ collection [0247] {G♭,A♭,B♭,D♭} in violin 2, {C} in the viola, whole-tone {B,A,G,E♭} in the cello, and {F,E} from violin 1 create an eleven-note collection, omitting D (no D

Figure 5.5. Form in the *Lyric Suite*, second movement: rondo with developmental reprise

A mm. 1–15   Tempo I $\frac{6}{8}, \frac{3}{8}, \frac{9}{8}$ main theme, [0236]

B mm. 16–40   Tempo II $\frac{3}{8}$, B theme from rows 1 and 2, incomplete
                                        [0236] 33–40

A' mm. 41–55   Tempo I   (m. 43) $\frac{6}{8}, \frac{3}{8}, \frac{9}{8}$

C mm. 56–80   Tempo III $\frac{2}{8}$, [0126] {F,A,Bb,B}, C theme

Reprise/Development

A mm. 81–93   Tempo I $\frac{6}{8}$ main theme

B mm. 94–113   Tempo II   (m. 91) $\frac{3}{8}$, 94–100 = 24–33, 101–4 = 16–19 row 2

C mm. 113–142   with B, A material (mm. 114, 131ff.)
                                       mm. 105–8 = 56–60, 110–12 = 21–23,
                                       120–21 = 66–67

Coda/A

    mm. 143–50   Tempo I   main theme, "domestic" tetrachords

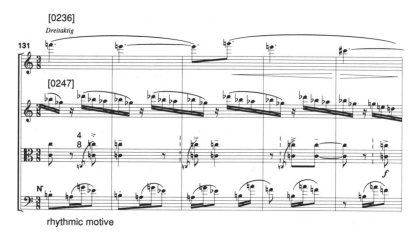

Example 5.16. Combined motives ending the reprise-development, *Lyric Suite*, second movement, mm. 131–36. Berg LYRIC SUITE. Copyright 1927 by Universal Edition. Copyright renewed. All Rights Reserved. Used by permission of European American Music Distributors Corporation, sole U.S. and Canadian agent for Universal Edition A.G., Wien.

appears from m. 128 to m. 143, and, somewhat uncharacteristically, D is not prominent in the entire quartet). The climax is foreshadowed at the juncture of the B and A' sections, where parallel [0236] motives (violins 1 and 2) combine with a motive from row 2 (viola, cello, mm. 39–40).

The main theme of the second movement consists of twelve tones divided gesturally into hexachords [013467] / [012369], with end tetrachords [0137] and [0158], from the close of the first movement and the end tetrachords of row 1, and [0126] within the second hexachord (mm. 1−2, ex. 5.14).[46] The theme begins with [016] <E−D♯−A♯>, which returns at T-2 <D−C♯−G♯> in its eighth to tenth notes; the {D6} completes the latent registral [0126] in <E6−D♯6−A♯5>, and, in a similar fashion, the C6 following <D6−C♯6−G♯5> completes an [0126] (and the underlying linear interval 2 descent E6−D6−C6). Remarkably, the main theme is constructed with 3-cycle [036]s in alternate order positions 024 (<E−A♯−G>), 135 (<D♯,F♯,A>), and 79B (<D−G♯−F>), leaving a remaining [012] in 68A (<B−C♯−C>). These underlying 3-cycles are reflected in the 3-cycle setting of the theme and in its T3 recurrences (mm. 81ff., 114−17). The cyclic construction also allies this theme with row 1 of the *Lyric Suite* and the later row of the *Violin Concerto*, where 5/7-cycles emerge from similar every-other-note partitions.

The theme appears in full at the outset as P4, with a 3-cycle counterpoint (mm. 1−2). It returns in full in the A' section, as P0 in imitation with its first hexachord at P8 (mm. 41ff.); at the beginning of the reprise-development as P7 in a four-part imitation (mm. 81ff.); and within the reprise-development as P7 (mm. 114−117). Elsewhere the theme appears with its first hexachord only: P4, in two-part varied imitation with 3-cycle counterpoint (mm. 9−10); P0, with an octave shift after the first trichord (m. 45); in the developmental section, inverted in imitation at I1, IA, IA, I6 (mm. 89−90) then liquidated further to the [016] opening trichord in imitation; and I2,I9,I7, and finally as a P8 hexachord beginning the codetta (m. 143). The primary levels of the main theme throughout, P4,P0,P7, and P8, form a 4-cycle+: P4 and P7 hold the maximum number of four notes invariant in the first hexachord; P8 holds three notes invariant with P7's first hexachord. If the main theme is viewed in the context of its 3-cycle counterpoint, the four levels P4,P0,P7,P8 represent all three 3-cycles P1,P0,P1,P2 (mod 3).

The [0236] motive, like the main theme, appears in full and partial forms. After its initial appearance in mm. 5−6 (ex. 5.14), it returns in its first half at T5, combined with the main theme P4 and a whole tone+−based figure (mm. 9−11), followed by a reordered [0236] at its original pitch-class level (m. 12). In a similar combination in mm. 45−50 at T7, [0236] returns with the PB main theme (altered in its first two notes from <B−A♯> to <C−B>) and the whole-tone+ motive; the latter is set in four-part stretto (mm. 48−50), with the first entry continued to an aggregate by an added [0268] <E♭−A−G−C♯> and the fourth entry followed by another T5 [0236] motive (violin 1). In its full form, the [0236] motive recurs at the climax, near the end of the reprise-development, again at T5 (mm. 131−39, ex. 5.16).

The B section theme, with an internal rhythmic motive, is based on rows 1 and 2 (ex. 5.15): 1P8 7-B̲, 1I2, o̲-A̲, 2P8 o̲-B̲ (the latter row not shown in ex. 5.15). The C section opens with an introduction based on [0126] at its referential {F,A,B♭,B} level (mm. 56–59); this figure returns in mm. 105–9 to interrupt the B theme 1I2 (mm. 101–4 and 110–13). The C section theme is based on 5-cycles divided by interval 3s and 4s (mm. 66–73, ex. 5.17; also mm. 72–73, violin and cello [sum-7 dyads], and mm. 120–24). The theme is truncated to a 5-cycle+–based [0247] in the section ending the reprise-development (mm. 124–42; cf. 5.16, violin 2).

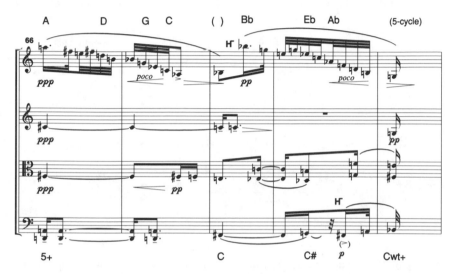

Example 5.17. Five-cycle based C theme, *Lyric Suite*, second movement, mm. 66–70. Berg LYRIC SUITE. Copyright 1927 by Universal Edition. Copyright renewed. All Rights Reserved. Used by permission of European American Music Distributors Corporation, sole U.S. and Canadian agent for Universal Edition A.G., Wien.

Harmonically, the opening of the second movement is organized in 3-cycles (mm. 1–2, ex. 5.14), leading to alternating whole-tone+ harmonies (mm. 3–6) that set the [0236} motive. The juxtaposition of 3- and whole-tone+–cycle collections reflects the two cyclic aspects of [0236] and the whole-tone+ aspect of [0126]. In the climactic combination of motives (ex. 5.16), the cello motive is whole-tone+, the second violin begins with 5+ cycle (or whole-tone+) [0247] and changes to whole-tone+ [0148] (m. 135), and the upper-voice violin 1 is the 3 cycle+ or whole-tone+ [0236]. The closing bars feature unfolded P1 and P2 3-cycles (mm. 145–46 violin 2, viola), then 5-cycle+ collections (m. 147, [01257] on beat 2½) until the closing chord, a whole-tone+ [02458]. The primary whole-tone+ collections mark cadential points throughout (m. 55, from formal section A' to C; m. 80, from sections C to A of the development; m. 86; m. 148; and the final cadence, m. 150).

MOVEMENT 3

The third movement of the *Lyric Suite* is a scherzo with trio, the outer scherzo sections twelve-tone and the inner trio "atonal," with [0126] {F,A,B♭,B} the unifying element. The reprise of the scherzo is in retrograde, with the original sixty-nine bars shortened by one-third to forty-six, omitting passages corresponding to mm. 30–39 and 46–58.[47] Of the four main rows used in the scherzo, 2P5, 2P8, 2PA, and 2I3 (ex. 5.18), each contains segmental [0126]s in 0123, 3456,

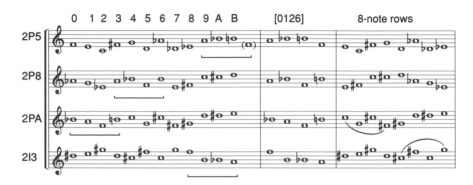

Example 5.18. Four rows, [0126]s, and eight-note rows, *Lyric Suite*, third movement

89AB, 9AB0, including one {F,A,B♭,B}, and each appears in both complete and eight-note versions, with the {F,A,B♭,B} [0126] removed.[48] Materials in the third movement are characterized by motivic rhythms, and the contrast between areas with these rhythms (mm. 6–9, cello; also mm. 10–17, 22–29, 30–37, 43–45), those with continuous sixteenths (mm. 1–9, 17–19, 26–29, 34, 37–40, 46–69), and those with chordal homorhythmic passages (mm. 19–21, 40–42) helps to delineate formal sections.[49]

Two pairs of motivic rhythms derive from the row itself. In the first, given by Berg in his analytical notes, two 1-cycle–based pitch motives are extracted from a continuous-duration presentation of the row (ex. 5.19a). The rhythm of order positions 03469AB and 12578 yields the durational series <3 – 1 – 2 – 3 – 1 – 1 – 1> and <1 – 3 – 2 – 1 – 1> (the final duration in each is variable). These two rhythms, labeled RH1 and RH2, encompass seven and five attacks, respectively. The two interval 1–based pitch-class motives appear in their characteristic rhythms throughout, except at the end of the scherzo (mm. 44–45 and 67–69, 95–93), where they are set in continuous sixteenths in a reversal of their original derivation. A secondary rhythmic pair is created as variants of RH1 and RH2, to

Example 5.19a. Derivation of RH1 and RH2 from row 2P5, *Lyric Suite*, third movement, mm. 10–12

Example 5.19b. Canonic pairs in SR1 and SR2, *Lyric Suite*, third movement, mm. 30–31. Berg LYRIC SUITE. Copyright 1927 by Universal Edition. Copyright renewed. All Rights Reserved. Used by permission of European American Music Distributors Corporation, sole U.S. and Canadian agent for Universal Edition A.G., Wien.

accomodate the division of the row into eight notes and repeated units of {F,A,B♭,B} (mm. 30–38; see ex., 5.19b). The eight-note rows (labeled 8-2PA and 8-2P5) are set in an eight-attack rhythmic pattern of <3–1–2–3–1–1–1–2>, while the repeated {F,A,B♭,B}s are set in overlapping five-attack rhythms of <1–3–2–1–3>. These two variant rhythms are labeled SR1 and SR2, respectively.[50] The rhythmic organization of the movement is based on the RH1, RH2, SR1, and SR2 rhythms and their augmentation, diminution, and variation.

If the metric weights are determined (by a process similar to that described in chap. 3) from the time points of the rhythms RH1 <0–3–4–6–9–10–11>, RH2 <0–1–4–6–7>, SR1 <0–3–4–6–9–10–11–12>, and SR2 <1–4–6–7–10>, each has the greatest weight at units of three and six, thus grouping most naturally into threes and sixes, mostly in sixteenth notes. The canonic imitation and constant interplay of these rhythms, in threes and sixes when considered separately, but notated and combined in duple groups of four, accounts in large part for the rhythmic independence from the notated ¾ barlines of the movement.

The first scherzo (mm. 1–45 [138–105]) divides into three parts, the second a varied repeat of the first, and each of the first two parts subdivides into four smaller sections (see fig. 5.6). The second scherzo, a palindrome of the first, is shortened in its part 2, where the passage corresponding to mm. 30–41 is represented only by m. 108, and its part 3, where the passage corresponding to mm. 46–57 is omitted. The first section (mm. 1–9) begins with {F,A,B♭,B} motives isolated in the orders of the different rows, with the eight-note rows subsequently added. The first violin's initial <B♭–A–F–B> from 2PA repeats then adds the eight-note residue (marked *Hauptstimme*); this sequence repeats until mm. 7–9, where only the eight-note residue row remains. The second violin and viola present similar sequences in canon, with rows 2P5 and 2P8 beginning with <A–B♭–B–F> and <A–B♭–F–B> motives (respectively), ending with only eight-note residue rows. In mm. 6ff., approximately where the three upper rows

Figure 5.6. Form of scherzo sections in *Lyric Suite*, third movement

	Scherzo I			Scherzo II		
				corresponding palindrome		
	part 1	part 2	part 3	part 3	part 2	part 1
mm.	1–9	25–29	46–69	104–93	113–109	138–129
	10–17	30–38		(58–69)		128–121
	17–21	39–41			108	121–117
	22–25	42–45			107–105	116–113

are in their eight-note versions, the cello (mm. 6–9) plays {B♭,A,F,B} successively in the orders of the three rows: <B♭–A–F–B> from 2PA, <A–B♭–B–F> from 2P5, and <A–B♭–F–B> from 2P8. The three statements are set to the twelve attacks of the RH1 and RH2 stated successively (durations of a dotted quarter, eighth, quarter, etc., then an eighth, dotted quarter, etc.; cf. the RH1 and RH2 shown in ex. 5.19a); so that the second group <A–B♭–B–F> straddles the two rhythms; thus, the RH1 and RH2 actually appear before the demonstration of their derivation (mm. 10ff.).

The opening bars contains a typically cyclic patterning of rhythms: the four-sixteenth notes motive {F,A,B♭,B} is grouped with the following sixteenth rest, creating a five-sixteenth unit within the $\frac{2}{4}$ meter. As the motive is stated successively in the violin 1, violin 2, and viola parts, the initial attack point shifts each time, yielding a total of twelve metric placements in a 5-cycle, to begin on each possible sixteenth-note subdivision of the three beats in a bar (i.e., beats 3.4, 2.1, 3.2, etc.). The pattern breaks with the entrance of <B♭–A–F–B> in mm. 5–6 (violin 1). The opening setting of the four-note motive {A,F,B♭,B} in a five-unit grouping foreshadows its later placement in the five-attack SR2 (mm. 30–38, ex. 5.19b).

The three eight-note rows from 2PA, 2P5, and 2P8 in the violins and viola are set in five different alignments in mm. 6–9. While there are no octaves or unisons in the alignments—an important criterion for counterpoint throughout the movement—only three of the alignments theoretically yield this result. With the three eight-note rows, 2PA <C–G–D♭–F♯–A♭–D–E♭–E>, 2P5 <E–C–F♯–G–D–A♭–D♭–E♭>, and 2P8 <E–F♯–C–D♭–D–A♭–G–E♭>, the five alignments Berg used are (in order 2PA/2P5/2P8): (1) superimposed notes C/E/D (m. 6), (2) C/D♭/D♭ (mm. 6–7), (3) C/D♭/D (mm. 7–8), (4) C/D♭/E (mm. 8–9), and (5) C/A♭/E (m. 9). The second alignment is arranged such that the two D♭s do not meet, and in the fifth alignment the viola has a repeated A♭ to avoid what would be a G unison. The alignments that do *not* yield octaves and unisons are the first, third, and fourth. These row alignments foreshadow the complex system of similar alignments, but of twelve-note rows, in mm. 46–67.

In the shortened repeat of the opening in part 2 of the scherzo (mm. 25–29), continuous {F,A,B♭,B} motives in the viola (mm. 26–28, ordered from 2P8, 2I3, 2PA, 2P5, 2P8, 2PA, 2PA, 2P5, and 2P8) are accompanied by eight-note versions of the other rows, set to SR1 (m. 26: 2P5, cello, 2P8, violin 2; m. 27: 2PA, violin 1). A 2P8 in the viola (m. 29) ends the section.

The section in mm. 10–17 consists of the four full rows arranged in canonic pairs of instruments set to RH1 and RH2. The first canonic pairs, 2P5 (viola and violin 1, ex. 5.19a) then 2I3 (cello and violin 1) are set with the rhythms in eight-note durations, the remaining pairs with the rhythms in sixteenth-note durations

(m. 12, P8, violin 2, viola, etc.). The durational intervals of the canons shrink successively until m. 16, anticipating the change in texture beginning in m. 17. In the corresponding section in part 2 (mm. 30−38), the four instruments pair off in canons (ex. 5.19b): violin 1 and cello are in canon at one beat, presenting eight-note rows set in the SR1; violin 2 and viola are also in canon at one beat, both with {A,B♭,B,F} in SR2; the violin 2−viola canon is broken in mm. 34−35 and 37−38 by continuous sixteenths in both voices.

In mm. 17−21, a three-part canon on 2P5 (cello and viola, violin 2, violin 1) leads to descending vertical segmental trichords of the eight-note rows 8-2P5, 8-2P8, 8-2PA. In the corresponding mm. 39−41, the four rows are stated simultaneously (in the alignment shown in ex. 5.18); to avoid the octave B♭s in $\underline{A}$ of 2I3 and 2P5, $\underline{1}$ (E) and $\underline{A}$ (B♭) are exchanged in 2I3. This note-for-note alignment of the four rows with avoided octaves recalls the eight-note row alignments in mm. 6−9 and foreshadows the alignments in mm. 46−67.

In mm. 22−24, the four instruments again pair off in canons. Violin 2 and viola, with rows 2PA and 2P5, begin their canons at two sixteenths on D♭1 of 2PA (violin 2) and E4 of 2P5 (viola), in a variant of the SR1/RH1 in sixteenth-note units. Eventually, both parts pass 2PA notes back and forth in a hocket formation (mm. 24−25). Violin 1 and cello are also in canon at two sixteenths using 2I3 (rotated to begin with <F−B−B♭−A> in the violin); both are also in a variant on SR1/RH1 (in eighth-note units). In the corresponding mm. 42−45, violin 1 has the complete 2P8 in RH1 (in eighths, with four notes of the row acting as grace notes), and violin 2−to-cello and viola line features 2P5 divided into RH1 and RH2 (RH1 rotated in violin 2 to begin with its final three notes); the lower three voices then repeat their aggregate 2P5 pitch motives—1-cycle <F♯−G−A♭> in violin 2, 1-cycle−based <E−C−D−D♭−E♭> in the viola, and <A−B♭−B−F> in the cello—in continuous sixteenths.

The third part of the first scherzo (mm. 46−69, 104−93 = 69−58; mm. 46−57 are omitted from the second scherzo section) is devoted to four-part canons on the four main rows. At each of the twelve occurrences of each row, the row is transposed by interval 1, in a 1-cycle of transpositions, and rotated by one order position, in a 1-cycle of rotations (fig. 5.7, "2P6-$\underline{1}$" indicates the row 2P6 rotated to begin on its order position $\underline{1}$ note, etc.). In reference to the canons, Berg wrote to Schoenberg on July 13, 1926: "Nobody in the world— excuse me, *only you*, dearest friend, can imagine the difficulties I encountered in working out the *possible* 4-voice canons (there are 17) in these 4 forms (RI [1PA], II [2P5], III [2P8] and U [2I3]). That's why the slow progress."[51] In his analytical notes on the *Lyric Suite,* Berg remarked: "Finally after [m.] 46 all possible (those that do not form unisons) [canons] between the four forms [of the twelve-tone row] can be used."[52]

Figure 5.7. Rows in *Lyric Suite*, third movement, mm. 46–67

mm.	46			66
violin 1:	2P5,	2P6-<u>1</u>,	2P7-<u>2</u>, . . .	2P4-<u>B</u>
violin 2:	2P8,	2P9-<u>1</u>,	2PA-<u>2</u>, . . .	2P7-<u>B</u>
viola:	2PA,	2PB-<u>1</u>,	2P0-<u>2</u>, . . .	2P9-<u>B</u>
cello:	2I3,	2I4-<u>1</u>,	2I5-<u>2</u>, . . .	2I2-<u>B</u>

The seventeen possible canons mentioned by Berg are those in which the rows 2P5, 2P8, 2PA, and 2I3 align in a four-part continuous canon without resulting octaves or unisons.[53] Since Berg's canon consists of twelve instances of the four rows, in twelve different alignments, we can assume that he worked out the seventeen possibilities and chose the twelve that he wanted to use. The initial alignments of Berg's twelve chosen canons are given in figure 5.8, with the remaining possibilities; all are displayed relative to the referential I3 set to <u>o</u>. The actual alignments with the rotated and transposed rows are given as well (the final P7 of the second violin part is completed in the viola, m. 67). The order of the voice entries in the canons is also given in figure 5.8, along with the durations in sixteenths for each row. The voices have staggered entries; after each row statement Berg added combinations of rests and row segments before the next row is stated. The total durations of the row and this after-row material make up the total number of sixteenth-note durations for each row statement. For instance, in the first canon, the order of rows is 2I3, 2PA, 2P8, 2P5, and the 2I3 row takes twenty sixteenth-note durations: twelve sixteenths for the row and eight added sixteenth-note durations in rests or repeated segments of 2I3. The other rows enter in a staggered pattern: 2PA after four sixteenths, 2P8 seven sixteenths, and 2P5 eleven sixteenths. These rows then have their own total durations: 2PA takes nineteen sixteenths, twelve for the row and seven for added rests or repeated segments, and 2P8 and 2P5 have eighteen and fifteen durations (in sixteenths), respectively. Thus, the first four rows in the canon have durations of 20, 19, 18, and 15 sixteenths, but because of the staggered entries the order of rows in the second alignment in the canon is still 2I3, 2PA, 2P8, and 2P5. By the fourth alignment, however, this order begins to change because of the total duration occupied by each row. The final rows in the upper two voices are cut off and so have durations of only five and seven sixteenths. In one place two rows overlap by two notes in double stops: m. 54, overlapping P0 <u>23</u> (G–C♯) in the viola and second violin, and P1 <u>56</u> (B♭–E) in the second violin (the four affected notes are in interval-class 6 pairs and form a 3-cycle [0369]).

Thus, Berg's intention seems to have been to create a canonic section of

Figure 5.8. Canons in *Lyric Suite*, third movement

		alignments used												other possibilities					
		1	2	3	4	5	6*	7	8	9	10	11	12	13	14	15	16	17	18
violin 1	2P5	1	6	5	6	B	3	6	B	7	1	6	5	7	B	0	7	7	B
violin 2	2P8	5	7	7	5	1	7	7	0	B	5	7	7	B	7	4	B	5	1
viola	2PA	8	9	8	B	4	8	0	5	1	7	1	0	0	8	B	4	1	7
cello	2I3	0	0	0	0	0	0	0	0	0	0	0	0	0	0	0	0	0	0

actual alignments with rotated and transposed rows:

	1	2	3	4	5	6	7	8	9	10	11	12
violin 1	2P5-1	P6-7	P7-7	P8-9	P9-3	PA-8	PB-0	P0-6	P1-3	P2-A	P3-4	P4-4
violin 2	2P8-5	P9-8	PA-9	PB-8	P0-5	P1-0	P2-1	P3-7	P4-7	P5-2	P6-5	P7-6
viola	2PA-8	PB-A	P0-A	P1-2	P2-8	P3-1	P4-6	P5-0	P6-9	P7-4	P8-B	P9-B
cello	2I3-0	I4-1	I5-2	I6-3	I7-4	I8-5*	I9-6	IA-7	IB-8	I0-9	I1-A	I2-B
mm.	45–48	48–50	49–51	51–53	53–54	54–55	56–58	58–60	59–61	61–63	63–65	65–67

		order of voices												durations in sixteenths for each row												
violin 1	2P5:	4	4	4	3	4	3	2	3	3	1	4	4	(11)	15	16	14	15	12	13	19	16	15	26	16	5
violin 2	2P8:	3	3	3	4	2	2	1	2	2	4	3	3	(7)	18	15	17	12	12	14*	19	13	27	17	15	7
viola	2PA:	2	2	2	2	1	1	3	4	4	3	1	2	(4)	19	16	12	15	12	24	21	16	15	13	16	12
cello	2I3:	1	1	1	1	3	4	4	1	1	2	2	1		20	15	15	20	16	16	12	12	21	19	15	12
canons		1	2	3	4	5	6	7	8	9	10	11	12		1	2	3	4	5	6	7	8	9	10	11	12

twelve different alignments of the four rows successively transposed and rotated, with no octaves or unisons. There are, however, three alterations to this theoretical framework. The first discrepancy is Berg's sixth alignment (mm. 54–55), which is actually not one of the seventeen theoretical possibilities. It would yield a unison or octave of PA 7 (violin 1) and I8 4 (cello), F♯–G♭ (m. 55 third sixteenths), but it does not do so because of Berg's arrangement of the entrances of the rows, which avoids aligning PA 7 with I8 4. A possible explanation lies in the similarity of alignments 6 and 14 shown in figure 5.8. These two alignments differ only in the alignment of the first violin row. If PA in the first violin were shifted, so that m. 54 had <G–D♭–G♭–A♭–D> beginning with the fifth rather than the first sixteenth note (extending the previous row by four additional notes), Berg's sixth alignment would be altered to that given as alignment 14, and the number of alignments would be corrected to seventeen, rather than the eighteen listed in figure 5.8.

The second discrepancy appears in m. 49, in alignment 2: the combination of rest and row segment following the PB row in the viola causes octave G♭s on the last sixteenth of the bar, from 2 of PB (viola) and 1 of P6 (violin 1). The alignment of rows is correct, but the added sixteenth rest in the repeated segment following the PB row (viola, third-to-last sixteenth in m. 49) creates the unison. This unison could be easily remedied by moving the sixteenth rest to the end of the repeated segment.

The third discrepancy appears in m. 62, in alignment 10, where an extra note D (m. 62, seventh sixteenth) is added between Io 2 and 3 (D♭4–F4, cello); D also appears in the repeated segment at the end of the row (m. 64, second sixteenth). These extra notes cause eight unisons or octaves: D4–D5 (cello and second violin, m. 62, seventh sixteenth), B3–B5 (cello and first violin, m. 62, ninth sixteenth), B♭3–B♭5 (cello and second violin m. 63, first sixteenth), E4–E5 (cello and second violin, m. 63, fourth sixteenth), A♭2–G♯4 (cello and first violin m. 63, sixth sixteenth), G2–G5 (cello and second violin m. 63, seventh sixteenth), D♭3–D♭5 (cello and second violin, m. 64, first sixteenth), and F♯4–F♯4 (cello and first violin, m. 64, seventh sixteenth). The same octaves and unisons occur in the retrograde half of the palindrome.

One thing is strange about this third discrepancy: Berg's following row alignment 11 (in m. 64) is correct; the addition of D to the previous alignment 10 does not alter it. The octaves and unisons are all with rows or after-row rests and segments of the tenth alignment (except for the first D between the cello and violin 2 in m. 62, third-to-last sixteenth, wherein the second violin note is from the after-row segment of the previous row). Thus, if the additional Ds were removed as copying errors, the following alignments would be wrong. The removal of the two "extra" Ds would require that two sixteenth rests or notes

be inserted after the tenth alignment row in the cello (m. 64, first and second sixteenths) to keep alignment 11 and the rest of the alignments correct.

Although the added note D is emphasized at the end of the first scherzo (m.
67)—the two pitch motives from the derivation of RH1 and RH2 from P5
return in continuous sixteenths, <F–F♯–G–G♯–A–A♯–B> symmetrical at
sum 4, and <E–C–D–D♭–E♭> is reordered to <E–C–C♯–E♭–D>, to end
on the axis note D—it is difficult, to say the least, to hear any D priority as a
reason for the change in row alignments. The discrepancies in the canonic section raise interesting questions, especially in light of the alignments of eight-
note rows in mm. 6–9, where two of the alignments also do not "work" in the
sense yielding unisons or octaves. Did Berg intend the theoretical model of
alignments without octaves and unisons to be the finished version? Or did he
then change the model in the score, even though octaves and unisons were created? Do the discrepancies appear in the early parts? Why the added Ds but following correct alignment? Was Berg ever aware of the "problem," if it is one?

The "mistakes" also raise issues with regard to the critical edition. Should a
critical edition of the *Lyric Suite* give the passage in two versions, one as in the
score, the other with the "mistakes" corrected and the "theoretical" conception
restored?[54] If so, what about mm. 6–9, where similar "mistakes" occur? If the
cello row in mm. 6–7 and viola row in m. 9 are each shifted back one sixteenth,
the alignments "work"; Berg's addition of a repeated A♭ in m. 9 indicates he was
aware of the latter problem here. It is interesting to speculate on whether he
ever found problem doublings in the later passages, or what he might have done
to remedy them.

TRIO AND MOVEMENT 4

The trio of the third movement, which doubles as the exposition of the
fourth movement, is based largely on [0126] {F,A,B♭,B}, appearing throughout
in full (mm. 69–70, violins; mm. 74–75, viola; and m. 84, violins) and in separate boundary notes of gestures (m. 75, violin 1, B♭; m. 77, violin 1, B♭; m. 78,
cello, B; m. 79, violin 1, B♭; and mm. 85–86, violin 1, B–Γ). The two main
motives in the trio are both contour-and-rhythm motives, with varied intervals
and pitch-class content (ex. 5.20, fig. 5.9), and both are initially presented in
whole-tone+–based contexts. The first motive (example 20a) is a sequential
figure (mm. 70–74) with upper-voice groups in threes, then fours <F – B♭– A♭ /
E–C–B / C♯–E♭–A–D – G–F♯–G♯–C>, in a sentence phrase structure.
The fourteen-note melody has twelve distinct notes (with G♯, C repeated at the
end) in which the two four-note groups are [0126]s; the first six notes hold
[0126] as a subset ({B♭,E,C,B}) and the first two notes {F,B♭} have accompanying {A,F} to yield [0126] {F,A,B♭,B}. The melody also has internal interval 4-

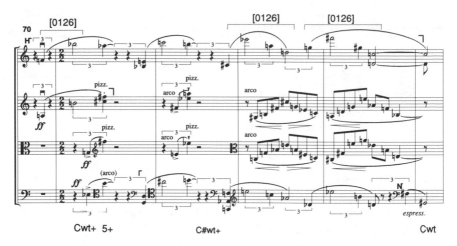

Example 5.20a. Opening and first motive, *Lyric Suite*, third movement, trio, mm. 70–74

Example 5.20b. Second motive, *Lyric Suite*, third movement, trio, mm. 74–75. Berg LYRIC SUITE. Copyright 1927 by Universal Edition. Copyright renewed. All Rights Reserved. Used by permission of European American Music Distributors Corporation, sole U.S. and Canadian agent for Universal Edition A.G., Wien.

cycle, 2-cycle, and 5-cycle trichords: <F−B♭ / A♭−E−C / B−C♯−E♭ / A−D−G / F♯−A♭−C>, or may be regarded as three overlapping whole-tone+ collections <F−B♭−A♭−E−C / B−C♯−E♭−A−D−G / F♯−A♭−C>. The accompanying melody in the cello, from the pickup to m. 72, consists of reordered incomplete segments of the first-violin melody: <F−E−C−A♭/D♭−E♭−B/D−F♯−G♯>, with internal 4-cycle and 2-cycle collections.

Figure 5.9. Form in *Lyric Suite*, trio and fourth movement

Trio

mm.			
70–73	motive 1		A
74–75	motive 2		B
76–78	transition		
79–84	development of motive 1		A'
86–86	canons on motive 2		B'
87–89	transition		
90–92	motive 1 variant		A"

Fourth Movement

mm.		
1–11:	(from trio, mm. 74–75) motive 2, wedge variant, motive 3	B/C
12–13:	(from trio, mm. 70–73) motive 1	A
14–20:	motive 3 developed	C
21–23:	(from trio, mm. 81–83) motive 1	A'
24–26:	motive 2 canon	B'
27–28:	motive 1 canon	A'
29–33:	motive 3, main motive, [0236] motive from second movement	C
32–33:	Zemlinsky quote in $\frac{6}{8}$	D
34–35:	(from trio, mm. 86–87, T4): motive 4	B"
35–44:	(from trio, mm. 88–92, T4): transition, motive 1, [0126]	A'
45–50:	Zemlinsky quote in $\frac{4}{4}$	D'
51–58:	wedge, [0126] episode	A"
59–69:	coda, [0126], Zemlinsky opening [013]	D"

The second motive (ex. 5.20b, mm. 74–75) begins with a slow oscillation <D–C♯>, leading to notes <B–B♭–F–(E)–B–A> (viola) from [0126] {F,A, B♭,B}, paired with an inverted statement at sum-4 (cello), mapping B onto F. The other two voices (violins) are similarly in sum-4 pairs (except for the second note D4 in the second violin, which "should" be an E under sum 4), arranged so that each vertical is a whole-tone+ collection. The second motive is also similar to the main theme from the second movement in its descending [016] gesture (cf. ex. 5.21); the relationship is confirmed by the appearance of the main theme of the second movement in the fourth.[55] The second motive is developed in canon (mm. 85–86), where it assumes an alternate form with [0145] <F♯– D–D♭–F>, which becomes motive 4 in the fourth movement.

In contrast with the essentially ametric scherzo, rhythmic groupings in the trio change in relation to the barline: the rhythm supports the notated bar in the opening (mm. 70–74, ex. 5.20a), shifts emphasis to the notated second (half-) beat (mm. 74–78), then is essentially free of the notated barlines (mm. 79–84) until the two voices of the canon on motive 2 (mm. 85–86) reinstate the notated meter. Measures 90–92 are characterized by a hemiola in m. 92 before the return of the scherzo. This grouping conflict, a feature of the entire trio, is reflected in the rising transitional gesture in mm. 76–77, where the four instruments ascend, each on a different subdivision of the beat, to join on the downbeat of m. 77.

The highly sectionalized fourth movement, which constitutes the climax of the quartet, consists mainly of the two motives introduced in the exposition of the preceding trio arranged in A and B sections, respectively, with motive 2 gaining a variant wedge opening, alongside two other motives, 3 (section C in fig. 5.9, m. 29, viola <E–C–E♭–D–F♯>) and 4 (m. 34, violin 1 <B♭–G♭–F–A>), as well as the Zemlinsky quote (ex. 5.21, from section D). The motives are varied

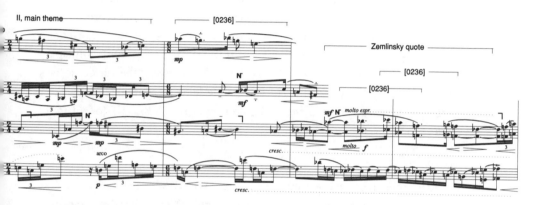

Example 5.21. Main theme and [0236] motive from second movement, preceding Zemlinsky quote, *Lyric Suite,* fourth movement, mm. 30–33. Berg LYRIC SUITE. Copyright 1927 by Universal Edition. Copyright renewed. All Rights Reserved. Used by permission of European American Music Distributors Corporation, sole U.S. and Canadian agent for Universal Edition A.G., Wien.

and alternate in successive developmental sections. Passages from the trio are reworked; for instance, the trio passage from mm. 86–92 is transposed at T4 in the fourth movement (mm. 34–39; see fig. 5.9), which yields upper-voice {F,A,B♭,B} in mm. 38–39; in its wake, [0126] {F,A,B♭,B} reemerges in its own episodic sections.

The passage from mm. 30–33 (ex. 5.21) includes the main theme of the second movement, confirming its resemblance to motive 2, as well as the [0236] motive from movement 2 and the Zemlinsky quote, which is a whole-tone+ collection, making explicit the relationships between these materials. The beginning three notes of the Zemlinksy quote, <B♭–C♭–D♭> [013], related to the fourth to sixth notes of the main theme of the second movement, also appear in various guises throughout the fourth movement, from as early as mm. 2–3 (viola), and are particularly prominent in the closing bars.

The Zemlinksy quote, marked by Berg as *Zitat aus Zemlinskys Lyrischer Symphonie* (mm. 32–33, viola, ex. 5.21; mm. 46–50, violin 2), is taken from the third movement of the *Lyric Symphony* for baritone and orchestra.[56] The quote first appears in $\frac{6}{8}$ (mm. 32–33) but returns, varied, in $\frac{2}{4}$, and marked *ganz frei recitativisch* (mm. 46–50). In its latter appearance, the quote is preceded by [0126]s including {B,F,A,B♭} (mm. 43–44), and the following passage (mm. 51–62), encompassing the climax in mm. 54–55, ends with [0126] {F,B♭,B,A}, pointing up the internal [0126] {B♭,B,A,E♭} in the quote. The second setting (mm. 45ff.) is somewhat polytonal, with the E♭/B♭–based quote over a held D-based chord, creating a familiar but distorted version of the melody. Characteristically, the note D is also immediately presented in cyclic contexts: the quote is preceded by 5-cycle–based harmonies forming an aggregate (mm. 45–46) over a horizontal 4-cycle <D–F♯–B♭–D>, in which the upper notes <B♭4–B4–D♭5> anticipate the first three notes of the Zemlinsky quote;[57] following the quote, a bass <D–F–A♭> 3-cycle ensues (mm. 51–53), underlying an aggregate "wedge" of diverging interval 1 cycles in the viola, and leads to {A,B♭,B,F} [0126] in all voices at the climax (mm. 54–58).[58]

MOVEMENT 5

The fifth movement of the *Lyric Suite* has an ABA'B'A" form with coda (fig. 5.10), in which the A sections are "atonal" with assertive forte contrapuntal themes, many of them of twelve tones, and the B sections are twelve-tone, using rows 3 and 4, in sustained vertical segmental chords changing slowly in tentative flautando pianissimo textures. Each successive section takes a greater number of bars, until the twenty-bar coda. Set [0126] appears in row contexts, often as a held vertical chord ({D,D♭,C,A♭}, mm. 85–120 or at T5 {G,G♭,F,D♭}, mm. 200–239). A notable rhythmic feature in both A and B sections is the organization of passages into fives or cyclic sequences <1–2–3–4–5> or <5–4–3–2–1> with regard to numbers of bars, durations, and beats. In several places, five-note chords are built up one note at a time: [02347] (mm. 15–19), [01469] (mm. 30–35), and whole-tone+ [02458] (mm. 125–29), Other chords are similarly built up and broken down systematically: whole-tone [0268] {E♭,F,G,A}, mm. 183–89; whole-tone [0246] {F♯,G♯,A♯,B♯} mm. 189–95; and {E,G,D♯, B,F♯,A♯,C♯,A}, mm. 330–40.

The A sections of the movement are characterized by a motive that appears in both eleven-note form, with the missing note immediately following (mm. 1–4, end note E), and twelve-note form (ex. 5.22).[59] The motive, which has inter-

Figure 5.10. Form in *Lyric Suite*, fifth movement

A	mm.	1–50	(50)	atonal
B	mm.	51–120	(70)	twelve-tone
A'	mm.	121–211	(90)	atonal
B'	mm.	212–325	(110)	twelve-tone
A"	mm.	326–440	(115)	atonal
Coda	mm.	441–60	(20)	twelve-tone

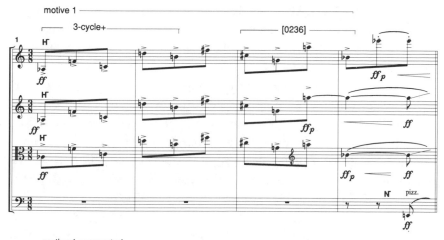

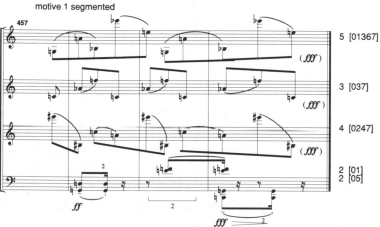

Example 5.22. Motive 1, *Lyric Suite*, fifth movement, mm. 1–4; segmented, mm. 457–60. Berg LYRIC SUITE. Copyright 1927 by Universal Edition. Copyright renewed. All Rights Reserved. Used by permission of European American Music Distributors Corporation, sole U.S. and Canadian agent for Universal Edition A.G., Wien.

locking 3-cycle+ and whole-tone+ segments and includes the three whole-tone-cycle+ [0236]—but which might be seen more programmatically to begin with "F-minor" and "B-minor" triads—begins each A section: mm. 371–74 in twelve-note form, and mm. 342–45 and 441–60. At the end of the movement, the series segments into groups of three, four, and five notes—violin 2 [037], viola [0237], and violin 1 [01267] (ex. 5.22), reflecting the cyclic <12345> rhythmic and formal relationships in the movement. The cello is arranged with lower interval 7s {C,G}, {G,D}, {D,A}, {G,D}, and {C,G} in a 7-cycle (mm. 446–60) arranged at durational intervals of <5−4−3−2−1> bars, lending the impression of a tonal resolution on C, and canonic upper-voice dyads {D♭,E♭} and {A♯,B} and, at T5, {F♯,G♯} and {E,F}, also in durational intervals of <5−4−3−2> bars (the final one-bar unit is cut off by the end of the movement).

Row 3 appears in the B sections of the movement as vertical segments (mm. 51–82, 82–120, 133–47, 211–46, 241–60; see fig. 5.11). In a later passage (mm. 261–97), row 3P3 is partitioned non-segmentally into 03469A / 12578B, which yields two [012345] 1-cycle collections (ex. 5.23a). The partitioning derives from the 03469AB / 12578 partition of the characteristic rhythms (RH) in the third movement, which also yield 1-cycle collections (ex. 5.19a). The partition is also close to the 0346AB / 125789 derivation of row 4; the actual derivation of this row occurs in mm. 281–90, where violin 1 plays 3I9 0346AB and violin 2 and viola play 125789. The row 4I4 then appears in mm. 375–85 (ex. 5.23b); in mm. 380–85 the notes of its second hexachord 6789AB (viola) double as 125789 of a simultaneous 3I4 (viola and cello), again demonstrating the derivation of row 4I4 from 3I4.

MOVEMENT 6

The sixth movement of the *Lyric Suite* includes, in an autograph study score, the text *De profundis clamavi*, no. 31 of a section of poems entitled *Spleen et Ideal* from *Les fleurs du mal* by Charles Baudelaire, in the German translation by Stefan George (fig. 5.12).[60] The text is a sonnet, divided into four stanzas of 4, 4, 3, and 3 lines, with combinations of ten and eleven syllables in patterns that follow the rhyme scheme. The vocal part, a doubling of notes present in the instruments, is almost completely syllabic except for 3P3 (9−A) <F−A♭> on *Blei* (m. 18, first violin) and 3P9 (234567) <E−B♭−C♯−F−C−F♯> on *riesengroß* (mm. 31–32); in the latter the melisma emphasizes the giganticness of chaos. The vocal line is mostly of rows 3 and 4; the only non-row phrase is the first in stanza 4, a Po 3-cycle−based line of <D♯−G♯−E−F♯−B−G−A−D−B♭−E−C>. Berg set the first three lines of stanza 2 in a palindrome (rows 3Io, 4PB, R(3Io)), with the central *Dunkel* ("darkness") on C♯4 (4PB−B) at the end of m. 23 (viola), the midpoint of the movement. The palindrome reflects the circular state of the abyss

Figure 5.11. Row settings in *Lyric Suite*, fifth movement

3I4: <E–F–A–E♭–C–A♭–D♭–G–G♭–D–B–B♭>
012/ 3456/ 789/ AB01/ 234/ 5678/ 9AB0/ 1234/ 567/ 89AB (mm. 51–82)
[015] [0237] [015] [0167] [036] [0127] [0146] [0258] [016] [0148]

3P1: <D♭–C–A♭–D–F–A–E–B♭–B–E♭–G♭–G>
0123/ 456/ 789/ AB4/ 567/ 89AB/ 0123 (mm. 82–120)
[0126] [015] [015] [012] [016] [0148] [0126]

3I4: 012/ 3456/ 789/ AB01/ 234 (mm. 133–47)
[015] [0237] [015] [0167] [036]

3P6: <G♭–F–D♭–G–B♭–D–A–E♭–E–A♭–B–C>
0123/ 456/ 789/ 4AB/ 4567/ 89AB (mm. 211–46)
[0126] [015] [015] [012] [0156] [0148]

3P3: <E♭–D–B♭–E–G–B–F♯–C–C♯–F–G♯–A>
0124/ 1345/ 4567/ 89AB (mm. 241–60)
[0158] [0358] [0156] [0148]

3P3: 03469A in canon, to 3P9, 3P4, 3P9 (mm. 261–80)
12578B

3P3: mm. 298–320

3P5: <F–E–C–F♯–A–C♯–D–D♯–G–A♯–B>, mm. 402–5

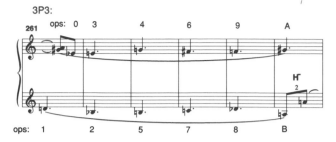

Example 5.23a. Row 3 partition, *Lyric Suite*, fifth movement, mm. 261–66

Example 5.23b. Row 4I4 with derivational context of row 3I4, *Lyric Suite*, fifth movement, mm. 375–85. Berg LYRIC SUITE. Copyright 1927 by Universal Edition. Copyright renewed. All Rights Reserved. Used by permission of European American Music Distributors Corporation, sole U.S. and Canadian agent for Universal Edition A.G., Wien.

in the protagonist's heart: six days the sun appears, but without warmth, and for six days the sun does not shine.

The form of the song follows the four stanzas of the poem, with an introduction and an epilogue consisting of the last line of stanza four (fig. 5.13). The introduction encompasses mm. 1–12, including an anticipation of the vocal line in the first violin (mm. 7–8, 4I9, ex. 5.24) and a cello melody from 3P7 (mm. 10–12). The final line of stanza 2 is set to the *Tristan* quote (ex. 5.25) from segments of three rows, and the climax occurs at m. 31, in the final line of the third stanza *und dieser Nacht! ein Chaos riesengroß!* ("And of this night, a gigantic Chaos!"). The score at this point is a flurry of arpeggiations in all four instruments, beginning with the {G,B,D} [037] of 3P9 89A and adding successively notes B012345 <F♭–A–G♯–E–B♭–C♯–F> of the same row. The fourth stanza

Figure 5.12. Setting of *De profundis clamavi* and rows in *Lyric Suite*, sixth movement

	syllables	vocal line		mm.
Zu Dir, Du einzig Teure, dringt mein Schrei;	10	4I3	0123456789	13–14
Auf tiefster Schlucht darin mein Herz gefallen.	11	4I3	AB 3I7 012345678	14–15
Dort ist die Gegend tot, die Luft wie Blei	10	3P3	0123456789A	17–18
Und in dem Finstern Fluch und Schrecken wallen.	11	4I5	001013478A	19
Sechs Monde steht die Sonne ohne Warm,	10	3I0	0125789AB	22
In sechsen lagert Dunkel auf der Erde.	11	4PB	4568AB/A8654	23–24
Sogar nicht das Polarland ist so arm.	10	R(3I0)	BA98765210	25
Nicht einmal Bach und Baum noch Feld noch Herde.	11	3PA	3012 3P4 04 3P9 03 3PA 346	26–27
Erreicht doch keine Schreckgeburt des Hirnes	11	non row		29
Das kalte Grausen dieses Eisgestirnes	11	3P5	12346AB 3P0 0346	30
Und dieser Nacht! ein Chaos reisengroß!	10	3P5	9AB 3P9 8B01234567	31–32
Ich neide des gemeinsten Tieres Los,	10	3P5	012345668A = 4IA 0	33–34
Das tauchen kann in stumpfen Schlafes Schwindel . . .	11	4IA	123456789AB	34–35
So langsam rollt sich ab der Zeiten Spindel!	11	3I1	123456789AB	40

Figure 5.13. Form in *Lyric Suite*, movement 6

introduction:	mm. 1–12	Tempo I, quarter note = 69
	mm. 1–6	3I5/3P5, 4I5/4P5
	mm. 7–8	violin 1 4I9 melody anticipates vocal opening
	mm. 9–12	cello 3P7 melody under vertical row tetrachords 3P7, 3PA, 3P1
stanza 1	mm. 13–19	Tempo II, quarter = 46
interlude 1:	mm. 20–21	
stanza 2:	mm. 22–28	*Tristan* quote mm. 26–27
stanza 3:	mm. 28–32	climax m. 31, largo, half note = 46 to Tempo I, quarter = 69,
stanza 4:	mm. 33–35	Tempo II {F,A,B♭,B}
interlude 2:	mm. 36–39	(= first movement, mm. 5–6), Tempo I
epilogue:	final line of stanza 4 m. 40, mm. 41–46 final ten rows: no {F,A,B♭,B}

Example 5.24. Sum-10 alignments of 3P5 with 3I5, and 4P5 with 4I5; anticipatory melodic 4I9. *Lyric Suite*, sixth movement mm. 6–8. Berg LYRIC SUITE. Copyright 1927 by Universal Edition. Copyright renewed. All Rights Reserved. Used by permission of European American Music Distributors Corporation, sole U.S. and Canadian agent for Universal Edition A.G., Wien.

ends with a pronounced <B♭–A–F–B> from 3PA 0123, harmonized in vertical trichords 048, 159, 26A, and 37B (mm. 34–35). The final line of stanza 4 begins the epilogue of despair, with ten rows fading into the final {F,D♭} oscillation of 4I3 AB in the viola, directed by Berg to be continued for an indeterminate amount of time, ending eventually on the F—so that the quartet begins

Example 5.25. Palindrome around middle (mm. 23–24) and *Tristan* quote (mm. 26–27), *Lyric Suite*, sixth movement (all numbers are ops.). Berg LYRIC SUITE. Copyright 1927 by Universal Edition. Copyright renewed. All Rights Reserved. Used by permission of European American Music Distributors Corporation, sole U.S. and Canadian agent for Universal Edition A.G., Wien.

and ends with this note. The middle of the song (m. 23) is marked by a palindrome in mm. 22–23/24–25 (ex. 5.25).[61]

Several features within the sixth movement recall the first. The material in mm. 10–12, 37 and 39 is from first movement, mm. 5–6 (m. 37 from m. 5 inverted at sum 8, and m. 39 from m. 5 at T_5). In mm. 28–29 of movement 6, the hexachord <F–F♯–A–C♯–D♯–A♯> (interval pattern <13427> [013589] is sequenced in a 3-cycle+, T = <0–3–6–9–(0)> (successive hexachords share three notes; the aggregate is completed by the D beginning the fourth hexachord); the collection is a variant of the hexachord of row 1 (I_5 <F–F♯–B♭–D♭–E♭–A♭> intervals 14325) retaining the unique interval-class multiplicity, and the 3-cycle sequence recalls the similar treatment of [0158] prior to the recapitulation in the first movement (mm. 40–41, ex. 5.9). Under the hexachord, [0135] is also sequenced in a 3-cycle+, T = <4–7–A–1> (violin 2: successive tetrachords share only one note; the aggregate is completed with the fourth tetrachord).

The opening bars of the sixth movement set out rows 3 and 4, all bounded by F,B, and aligned in sum-10 pairs that map F and B into themselves (ex. 5.24): the rows are added one at a time, first $3I_5$ in the cello, $4I_5$ in the viola, $4P_5$ in the first violin, then $3P_5$ in violin 2. The mostly whole-tone–based tetrachordal harmonies in m. 6 are combinations of even sum-10 dyads. The opening passage has a remarkable cyclic combination of a successive accelerando of decreasing note values (quarter to triplet quarter to eighth to triplet eighth—integral proportions 6:4:3:2) with a balancing simultaneous decelerando of successively slower tempos (slowing the half-note beat from 34.5 to 23), giving the perhaps programmatic illusion of ever greater activity that nonetheless accomplishes no more.[62]

In the midst of the central palindrome of the song (mm. 22–25, ex. 5.25), the notes {B–A♭–D–F♯} [0258] are held, anticipating the *Tristan* quote (the notes of the upper line in the opening of *Tristan* are <G♯–(A–A♯)–B–(C–C♯)–D–(D♯–E–E♯)–F♯>). The quote (mm. 26–27), which begins with [0126] <A–F–E–E♭> and is surrounded by [0126] <A–F,B♭–B>, is formed from notes of three different rows: 3PA, 3P4, and 3P9; the *Tristan* chord {F,B, D♯,G♯} is, however, a segment of $3P4$: 1234 [0258].[63] In the setting of the text "Not even brook and tree, nor field nor flock," a reference to *Bach* ("brook") is given with <B♭–A–C–B>, which holds three of four notes invariant with {F,A,B♭,B} (end of m. 25).

The derivation of row 4 from row 3 is demonstrated in m. 30, $4P_5$ from $3P_5$, with the order-position partition and rhythm 0346AB / 125789 (ex. 5.26). Immediately following, 3P0 is partitioned using the RH1 and RH2 rhythms of the third movement, 03469AB / 12578, demonstrating the close similarity between the two procedures and between the resulting motives in movement 3 and row 4 in movement 6.

Example 5.26. Row 3P5 partitioned into 4P5 segments, 3P0 partitioned into RH1 and RH2 rhythms from third movement; *Lyric Suite*, sixth movement, m. 30. Berg LYRIC SUITE. Copyright 1927 by Universal Edition. Copyright renewed. All Rights Reserved. Used by permission of European American Music Distributors Corporation, sole U.S. and Canadian agent for Universal Edition A.G., Wien.

The final section of the song is preceded by one last gasp of {B♭,A,B,F} in m. 39 (violins), after which ten final rows unfold in continuous eighths, with overlapping invariances from rows 4P 9AB = rows 3P 012. The final row, 4I3 in the viola (which was the first vocal row), ends with an oscillation between its final two notes, F and D♭, with instructions to end on the upper note F. A diminuendo to morendo is marked, so that the final movement and the *Lyric Suite* fade, as described by Berg in the annotated score, "dying away in love, yearning, and grief."

Der Wein

Der Wein is a concert aria, an orchestral song in three parts, with a text from three of the five poems comprising *"Le vin"* by Charles Baudelaire, nos. 104–8 from *Les fleurs du mal* (written in the 1840s, published in 1857), in the Stefan George translation; Berg's choice of Baudelaire is of course interesting in light of the revealed text for the sixth movement of the *Lyric Suite*.[64] The vocal part in

Der Wein was set to both the German and French versions, the latter as an "ossia" line employing repeated and added notes.[65] The three sections, hereafter "songs," are entitled "Die Seele des Weines" ("L'âme du vin" or "The Spirit of the Wine"), "Der Wein der Liebenden" ("Le vin des amants" or "The Wine of Lovers"), and "Der Wein des Einsamen" ("Le vin du solitaire" or "The Wine of the Lonely One"). Berg composed the aria on commission from singer Růžena Herlinger from late May to June 23, 1929, followed by approximately two weeks of scoring and copying; the first performance was on June 4, 1930.[66]

TEXT AND FORM

The first poem has six stanzas of four lines each, all in the pattern of $11-10-11-10$ syllables except stanza 6, where the pattern is $11-11-11-10$ (fig. 5.14).[67] The second and third texts are sonnets, with four stanzas of 4, 4, 3, and 3 lines. The syllable schemes vary from six to nine syllables in the second song and return to eleven and ten syllable lines in the third song.[68] Berg sets the text almost completely syllabically (the only melismas are a four-note group on *brust* in song 1, stanza 6, line 3 (mm. $127-28$) and a three-note group on *singen* in song 1, stanza 1, line 1 (m. 16), and repeated notes are relatively rare (two extended repeated-note passages occur in song 1, stanza 1, line 1, in mm. $15-16$, from P2, and in stanza 5, lines $1-2$, in mm. $64-65$ and $172-73$, on $<A-C-E\flat>$ and $<G-B-D-F>$; also in the *Schwebend* section of song 2, stanza 2, lines $1-2$, mm. $97-102$, on [0268] $<E-C-B\flat-F\sharp>$), so that, for the most part, as in "Schließe mir" and the song in the final movement of the *Lyric Suite*, the number of syllables in the poem lines determines the number of notes in each vocal phrase. Since in songs 1 and 3 the poetic lines are ten and eleven syllables long, the twelve-note row forms are adjusted to fit, so that no single line of text is set to one row, and in only one place—the first two lines of the first song—is a complete row stated consecutively in the vocal part. Yet, aside from IB in the first song (mm. $21-22$, $51-53$) and the opening two rows P2 and I3 (mm. $15-20$ return in mm. $73-76$), no row appears twice in the vocal part. Thus, the music of the third song, largely an instrumental recapitulation of the first, has quite different vocal lines: the only similarities are the vocal part from song 1, mm. $64-65$ in song 3, mm. $173-75$; the piano part from song 1, mm. $3-4$ in the vocal line of song 3, mm. $175-77$; the vocal line from song 1, mm. $73-74$ in mm. $196-97$; and the vocal line from song 1, mm. $33-34$ at $T-3$ in song 3, mm. $200-201$. The combination of recapitulated instrumental part with altered vocal line yields a characteristic unity with variety and sets a precedent for much of Act III of *Lulu*.

The poetic stanzas correspond to the main formal divisions in the songs (see fig. 5.15, where corresponding passages from songs 1 and 3 are aligned hori-

Figure 5.14. Text and rows in *Der Wein* (dashes indicate the presence of slurs with more than one note per syllable)

"Die Seele Des Weines"	syllables	vocal line	bars
Des Weines Geist begann im Faß zu singen:	11	P2 0001122343–4	15–16
"Mensch, teurer Ausgestoßener, dir soll	10	P2 56789ABB I3 01	17–18
Durch meinen engen Kerker durch erklingen	11	I3 234567889AB	18–20
Ein Lied von Licht und Bruderliebe voll!	10	IB 23456789AA	21–22
Ich weiß: am sengend heißen Bergeshange	11	non-row	23–24
Bei Schweiß und Mühe nur gedeih ich recht	10	non-row	25–26
Da meine Seele ich nur so empfange;	11	I0 12345679AB	27–28
Doch bin ich niemals undankbar und schlecht.	10	non-row	29–30
Und dies bereitet mir die größte Labe,	11	P3 0123456789A	32–33
Wenn eines Arbeitmatten Mund mich hält,	10	P6 0123345–69A	33–34
Sein heißer Schlund wird mir zum kühlen Grabe	11	F♯ PA A98 P0 1234569	35–36
Das mehr als kalte Keller mir gefällt.	10	P0 AB0 I8 B012345	37–38
Hörst du den Sonntagsang aus frohem Schwarme?	11	R (IA) 6565433211̲0	47–50
Nun kehrt die Hoffnung prickelnd in mich ein:	10	IB 23456789AB	51–53
Du stülpst die Ärmel, stützest beide Arme,	11	P5 01233 012344	56–58
Du wirst mich preisen und zufrieden sein.	10	PB 9AB I2 0123456	59–63
Ich mache deines Weibes Augen heiter	11	non-row A–C–E♭	64–65
Und deinem Sohne leih' ich frische Kraft;	10	non-row G–B–D–F	66–67
Ich bin für diesen zarten Lebensstreiter	11	I6 0123456788A	68–69
Das Öl, das Fechtern die Gewandtheit schafft.	10	R (P9) 54543210BB	69–71

Figure 5.14. Text and rows in *Der Wein* (dashes indicate the presence of slurs with more than one note per syllable) (*Continued*)

"Die Seele Des Weines"	syllables	vocal lines	bars
Und du erhältst von diesem Pflanzenseime,	11	A♭ – F – D♭ – G♭ P2 56789AB	73–74
Den Gott, der ewige Sämann, niedergießt,	11	I3 00123456788 (2)	75–76
Damit in deiner Brust die Dichtkunst keime,	11	P8 0123456789A	77–79
Die wie ein seltner Baum zum Himmel sprießt."	10	I1 0123456788	75–76

"Der Wein der Liebenden"	syllables	vocal line	bars
Prächtig ist heute die Weite,	8	13–P6 88012344	88–89
(Stränge und Sporen beiseite)	8	P6 456789AB	90–91
Reiten wir auf dem Wein	6	13–P9 880123	92–93
In den Feeenhimmel hinein!	8	P9 456789AB	94–96
Engel für ewige Dauer	8	E–C	97–99
Leidend im Fieberschauer;	7	F#–B♭	100–102
Durch des Morgens blauen Krystall	7	P7 23456789	104–7
Fort in das leuchtende All!	8	F–B♭ P8 123456	107–8
Wir lehnen uns weich auf den Flügel	9	non-row	114–18
Des Wirdes, der eilt ohne Zügel.	9	E I7 1234 I3 2345 B	118–22
Beide voll gleicher Lust	6	non-row	123–25
Laß Schwester uns Brust an Brust	7	P4 12345–4–569A–B	126–29
Fliehn onhe Rast und Stand	6	I6 012345	129–33
In meiner Träume Land!	6	I6 6789AB	134–40

Figure 5.14. Text and rows in *Der Wein* (dashes indicate the presence of slurs with more than one note per syllable) *(Continued)*

"Der Wein des Einsamen"	syllables	vocal rows	bars
Der sonderbare Blick der leichten Frauen,	11	A–C–E♭	173–75
Der auf uns gleitet wie das weiße Licht	10	I2 789AB01232	175–76
Des Mondes auf bewegter Wasserschicht	10	I2 345678989A	176–77
Will er im Bade seine Schönheit schauen,	11	non-row	178
Der lezte Taler auf dem Spielertisch,	10	P8 9AB IB B012345	179–81
Ein frecher Kuß der hagern Adeline,	11	I3 654B012 B 23465	183–86
Erschlaffenden Gesang der Violine,	11	P7 0 F♯ 0 G♯ 12 B 3 C♯ 45	188–90
Der wie der Menschheit fernes Qualgezisch:	10	D P5 01201254 B	191–93
Mehr als dies alles schätz ich, tiefe Flasche,	11	F P2 6789ABBB P1´ 01	196–97
Den starken Balsam, den ich aus dir nasche	11	P1 23 = I3 456789ABB0	198–99
Und der des frommen Dichters Müdheit bannt.	10	P3 60123456 C♯–C	200–201
Du gibst ihm Hoffnung, Liebe, Jugendkraft	11	PA 89AB01267 G♭ E♭	202–4
Und Stolz—dies Erbteil aller Bettlerschaft	10	F C♯ P0 012345 A♭ G♭ G	204–5
Der uns zu Helden macht und Gottverwandt.	10	I2 0123456789	206–8

Figure 5.15. Form in *Der Wein* (q = quarter-note duration, dh = dotted half note)

Introduction:	mm.	1–14	$\frac{4}{4}$,	q = 36–44 Tempo I
Song 1: exposition	mm.	15–87	$\frac{4}{4}$,	q = 46–52 Hauptzeitmass (24–30 $\frac{3}{4}$, q = 42, 36)
Song 2: scherzo	mm.	88–172	$\frac{6}{4}$,	dh = 60, q = 44–52
Song 3: recapitulation	mm.	173–208	$\frac{4}{4}$,	q = 36–44 to 46–52 Tempo I
Coda:	mm.	208–16		

Detail

Song 1

mm.			
1–14	orchestral	introduction	
15–23	1st theme	stanza 1	
24–30	transition	stanza 2	
31–38	intro to Tango	stanza 3	
39–63	2nd theme/Tango	stanza 4	
64–72	2nd theme B	stanza 5	
73–87	closing theme	stanza 6	
(73–76 = 17–20)			

Song 3

mm.		
1–5, vocals of 64–65 = 173–77		stanza 1
29–30 = 178		
31, 37–38 = 179–180		stanza 2
39–50 = 181–93		
71–72 = 194–95		
73–74 = 196–98		stanza 3
32–34 = 199–201		
202–208		stanza 4
8–14 = 208–16 Coda		

Song 2

mm.			
88–96	A		stanza 1
97–103	B		stanza 2
104–11	A'		
112–22	C	Tango allusion, beginning of palindrome	stanza 3 (overlaps to m. 125)
123–41	A'	to center of palindrome	
141–59	A'	retrograde second half of palindrome	stanza 4 (from m. 126)
160–72	C	Tango allusion, balance of palindrome, mm. 171–72 added	

zontally), except in the second song, where, at the return of A' in m. 123, the last line of the third stanza corresponds to the beginning of the musical section (text stanza 4 begins at m. 126).[69] The overall form of the three songs, ABA, is a type of da capo aria, or, alternately, a sonata form with an exposition in song 1, a scherzo instead of a development in song 2, and a recapitulation in song 3. Formal areas are delineated by tempo and meter: songs 1 and 3 are similar in this respect, whereas song 2 is in a contrasting meter and tempo. The recapitulation in song 3 is condensed: it omits mm. 15–23, 33–36, 60–71, and 75–87 from song 1 and adds its own mm. 202–8, then the concluding mm. 209–15 restate mm. 8–14 of the introduction. The sonata-form interpretation is supported by (1) the return of the transitional and second-theme material (the tango) in the recapitulation initially transposed (by T^{-4}); (2) a motivic resemblance between the first-theme material (mm. 17–20) and the closing theme (mm. 73–76; song 3, mm. 196–97); and (3) an allusion to the tango of songs 1 and 3 in song 2 (mm. 112–22, 160–70). The sonata-form interpretation is unusual, however, in that the first-theme material of the first song (mm. 15–23) does not return at the beginning of the recapitulation (the third song), a feature which occurs in all other of Berg's sonata forms. Instead, the opening of the recapitulation (mm. 173–77) combines music from the introduction (mm. 1-5), with the melody from the song-theme B (mm. 64–65).

Song 2 divides in a proportion of about 1:3: an ABA' of twenty-six bars (mm. 86–111), then a palindromic CA'/A'C of sixty bars (mm. 112–41/141–72). The palindrome begins in m. 112, at the halfway point in the aria's total of 215 bars, whereas the middle of the palindrome is about .65 of the way through the second song and the entire Aria. The vocal line from the first half of song 2 is taken by instruments in the purely instrumental retrograde half of the palindrome (vocal mm. 114–124 return in mm. 168–158 [trumpet], 125–130 in 157–152 [alto saxophone], 131–134 in 151–148 [violins], and 135–141 in 147–141 [clarinet]).

MUSICAL MATERIAL

Der Wein was composed after Berg had derived the initial materials for *Lulu*, among them a row associated with Lulu herself. [70] The row of *Der Wein* is similar to this row (ex. 5.27)—at P2 of both, the notes B♭ and B switch hexachords, and two ordered segmental note groups <D–E–F–G–A> and <D♭–G♭–A♭> and one unordered group {C,B,E♭} are invariant. The hexachords of the two rows, [023579] of the Lulu row and [013568] / [012479] of *Der Wein*, share 5-cycle subsets [02457] / [02479]. The row of *Der Wein* appears often with a unidirectional contour in the first hexachord, similar to the Lulu row settings (ex. 5.39c), and in a few cases (mm. 77 and 123, flute, and m. 127 clarinet 1) with the characteristic opening turn figure of the Lulu row.

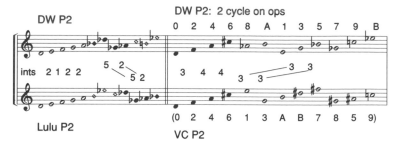

Example 5.27. Comparison of row from *Der Wein* (DW), Lulu row from *Lulu*, and row from the Violin Concerto (VC)

The scalar motion of the first hexachord of the row of *Der Wein* lends it properties similar to a diatonic scale: stepwise segments, "thirds" or interval-class 3s and 4s on every other note (or in a 2-cycle of order positions), and "fourths" or interval-class 5s between notes separated by two intervening notes (in a 3-cycle of order positions). A transformation by a 2-cycle on order positions—a transformation used in *Der Wein*, *Lulu* and the *Violin Concerto*—yields a row very similar to that of the Violin Concerto (ex. 5.27). In both pieces, interval 1 cycles are created by interweaving two rows; for instance, in *Der Wein* (mm. 188–90), the vocal <G–F♯–G–G♯–A–B♭–B–C–C♯–D–F> derives from interlaced P7 001234 <G–A–B♭–C–D> and P6 012345 6 <F♯–G♯–A–B–C♯–D–F> (see mm. 56–58, piano, for an ascending figure in interval 1s and 2s from four rows PB, P8, P2, and P3). As in other of Berg's twelve-tone pieces, the row of *Der Wein* appears mostly in prime and inversional forms, except within the large formal palindrome in the second song.[71]

The principal cyclic collections in *Der Wein* are whole-tone+ and 5-cycle+, with 3-cycle collections secondary. The row hexachords [013568] / [012479] are both 5-cycle+ collections, and a recurring derived motive, collection [0268], is whole-tone. The opening mm. 1–7 present five subphrases, with two types of motivic material distinguished by cyclic collections and instrumentation (ex. 5.28). In the first four subphrases, the initial gestures are both extended cyclically: horizontal motive a [013] <D♭–C–E♭> (mm 1–2) in the woodwinds is extended to motive a' [0136], 3-cycle+ <D♭–C–E♭–F♯>; horizontal motive b [015] <C–C♯–G♯> (mm. 2) in the strings, with the inverse contour of a, is extended to b', 5-cycle+ overlapping <F♯–B–E–D♯> (mm. 3–4)—in its second to fourth notes also a retrograde of b <C–C♯–G♯> at T3—in a continuing phrase ending in a liquidation back to the essential interval 5, <F♯–C♯> (mm. 5–6). In the first a to b succession (mm. 1–2), the two gestures are related by the linking <E♭4–C5> of a P0 3-cycle, and in a' to b' the gestures are related by the overlapping F♯4, part of a P0 3-cycle <C4–E♭4–F♯4>. The final E5 of the b' motive

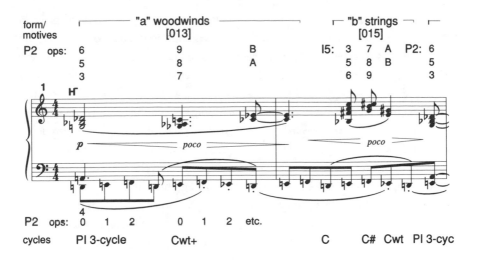

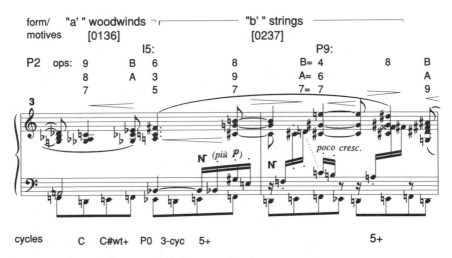

Example 5.28. Rows and cyclic harmonies in *Der Wein*, mm. 1–4 (rows labeled with order-position numbers). Berg DER WEIN. Copyright 1966 by Universal Edition A.G., Wien. Copyright renewed. All Rights Reserved. Used by permission of European American Music Distributors Corporation, sole U.S. and Canadian agent for Universal Edition A.G., Wien.

(m. 4) is consonant in the horizontal 5-cycle <F♯4–B4–E5> but resolves as a dissonance to D♯5 in the vertical 5-cycle+ collection <C♯–F♯–G♯–D♯>.

The initial note D♭4 is consonant in a PI 3-cycle+ collection that includes the bass note E rather than D, motivating the oscillation in the bass; at the end of m. 2 the <G–B♭–D♭> upper trichord is set over E but retains the dissonant note A2. Characteristically, this A also hovers over the bass D as a supporting interval 7, lending D the air of a "tonic" or focus. In a', the extension to F♯, <C4–E♭4–

F♯4>, is harmonized by E♭, completing the P0 3-cycle, but with an added B♭ again at interval 7 above the bass E♭—lending the neighboring E♭ an air of stability (the two instances foreshadow the important roles of bass notes D and neighboring E♭ throughout the work). In the bass line, interval 3 <D–F> is continually unfolded as <D–E–F> and <F–E♭–D> [013]s, with the wandering notes both consonant and dissonant in the cyclic harmonic collections of the upper voices, propelling the motion forward. The latent P2 3-cycle of <D–F> is completed only at the end of the passage (m. 7) by an added bass <G♯–B>. This complete P2 3-cycle complements the unfolded horizontal P0 3-cycles and later P1 3-cycles in the upper voices. When this opening instrumental material returns at the beginning of the third song (mm. 173–77), the vocal part of mm. 64–66 is superimposed as a P0 3-cycle segment <A–C–E♭>, supporting the upper 3-cycle voices. The passage (mm. 64–66) presents a combination of P0, P1, and P2 3-cycle–based and 5-cycle–based harmonies similar to the opening.

When the voice enters to begin the first song of *Der Wein*, a characteristically complex combination of cycle collections, tonal allusion, formal function, and significant row derivations ensues (mm. 15–18, ex. 5.29). The voice has the referential row P2, related symmetrically at sum 4 to the bass I2. The inner voices are derived from I9, with three [06]s (A2, 79, 63) and two [012]s (B01, 458), derived non-segmentally from the row (described as derivation 2 below). The combined harmonies in mm. 15–16 are mostly whole-tone+ based, with horizontal interval 1 voice-leading, but these harmonies also allude to a tonal "circle of fifths" progression, a combination of a bass 5-cycle <D–G–C> and upper-voice descending 1 cycles in parallel interval 6s <C/F♯–B/F–B♭/E> of the type found throughout Berg's music. By m. 17, however, the tonal allusion fades, and the remainder of the passage (mm. 17–18) moves to 5-cycle+ collections resulting from rows IB and I2 in vertical arrangements (derivations 5 and 1, described below) with motives 1 [013] <B–D♭–D> and 2 [037] <G♯–F–C♯>. Similar combinations of whole-tone+ and 5-cycle elements appear at the end of song 1, the beginning of song 2, and the end of song 3.

The middle chord of the palindrome in the second song (m. 141, ex. 5.30) reflects the tonal and cyclic implications of the Aria in its several possible interpretations. The C♯ in the bass may be seen in a "tonal" role as the "leading tone" of the referential D in the piece, under two "triads" with F and B as roots.[72] Cyclically, the C♯ alters each "triad" to a whole-tone+ collection, {F,A,C,C♯} and {B,C♯,D♯,F♯}, or, in the latter set, to a 5-cycle+ collection. Perhaps most relevant, however, is the observation that the three [06]s, {B,F}, {D♯,A}, and {F♯,C}, combine into [013679]. This hexachord stems from the [06]s derived from the row in mm. 15ff. and other places (ex. 5.29; see derivation 2 below), which form [012678]; along with the purely whole-tone [02468A], these three set-classes are

Example 5.29. Entrance of voice in *Der Wein*, song 1, mm. 15–18. Berg DER WEIN.
Copyright 1966 by Universal Edition A.G., Wien. Copyright renewed. All Rights Reserved.
Used by permission of European American Music Distributors Corporation, sole U.S. and
Canadian agent for Universal Edition A.G., Wien.

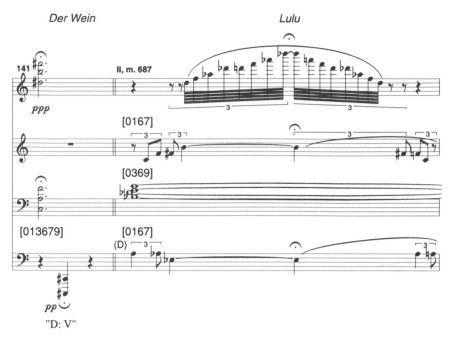

Example 5.30. Central palindrome chords in *Der Wein*, m. 141, and *Lulu*, Act II, m. 687

the only ones available by combining [06]s, as extensions of the multi-cyclic tetra-chords [0167], [0268], and [0369] common in Berg's music. The set-class [013679] returns as part of an important motive in *Lulu* (see ex. 5.40a), and the chord in *Der Wein* is a subset, at T2, of the corresponding central chord in the palindromic film music of *Lulu* (ex. 5.30, including <D–F–A♭–D♭> in the latter).

ROW DERIVATIONS

Prior to composing *Der Wein*, Berg had experimented with the main row of *Lulu*, subjecting it to a number of complex manipulations, clearly sketched out in row charts, to derive musical material (see ex. 5.36), in a pattern he would follow for his final three pieces. In *Der Wein*, he added more sophisticated row manipulations, which lead eventually to the expanded materials for *Lulu* as described below (ex. 5.37). In *Der Wein*, material generated from rows results from segmental and partitioned collections, grouped here into seven derivations, most with distinct cyclic aspects: 5-cycle (derivation 1a), 3-cycle (derivations 3 and 7), combined 5- and 3-cycle (derivation 1), whole-tone–based (derivations 4 and 5, and 13-note row), and 1-cycle (derivation 4).[73]

Derivation 1 is based on a 3-cycle order-position alignment 012/345/678/9AB with vertical 5-cycle–based tetrachords 0369 [0127], 147A [0257], and

<u>2</u>58B [0257] (mm. 11–14 and 212–15, winds; mm. 18 and 74, strings, see ex. 5.31). Successive rows are related at T−3: I4, I1, IA, then I8, I5, I2, allowing overlap between rows by the invariances In <u>2</u>, <u>5</u> = I(n+9) <u>0</u>, <u>3</u>. The upper line created from successive overlapping <u>012</u>s is a descending 1/2 (= 3) cycle, which resembles a row statement; for instance, the upper line <E–D–C#–B–Bb–Ab> in m. 11 is close to I4 <E–D–C#–B–A–Ab>. A related derivation 1a consists of vertical dyadic [05]s from aligned <u>0126B/34578</u>—pairing order positions related by 3—with horizontal 1-cycle collections (mm. 42ff.; see ex. 5.35). The rows P8 and I1 (piano, bassoon, mm. 42–46, 186–87), are related at sum 9, yielding invariant dyads {C#,G#}, {C,A} and {D,G}.

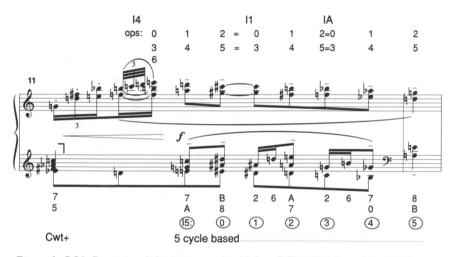

Example 5.31. Derivation 1, *Der Wein*, mm. 11–12. Berg DER WEIN. Copyright 1966 by Universal Edition A.G., Wien. Copyright renewed. All Rights Reserved. Used by permission of European American Music Distributors Corporation, sole U.S. and Canadian agent for Universal Edition A.G., Wien.

Derivation 2 stems from row properties shown in a sketch given by Berg to Reich for program notes to the first performance (ex. 5.32). In IB, row segments are identified as "5-tone major" in <u>01234</u> [02357], "3-tone minor" in <u>567</u> [037], and "4-tone major/minor" in <u>89AB</u> [0347].[74] In realizations, the segments align to create vertical [037]s, with <u>13</u> as grace notes to <u>024</u> (mm. 90–91, horns), or they are concatenated in a partially ordered row, <{<u>01234</u>},{<u>567</u>},{<u>89AB</u>}> (mm. 100–103, low strings). The vertical chords appear in song 2, often set to a characteristic rhythm of dotted quarter, eighth, quarter (described below as RH3: in mm. 88–90, horns, strings, and clarinet, P3 and I4; and in mm. 90–96, strings, I4, R(I1), and R(I5), winds, PB and R(P3)). The partially ordered row is an arpeggiated accompaniment figure in song 2 (mm. 97–105, strings, I2,

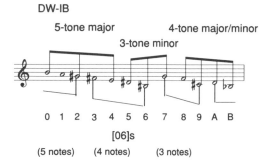

Example 5.32. Derivation 2, from Berg's sketch of row IB, *Der Wein*

R(P3), PB, and R(I0)). These "triadic" derivations from the row combine into the overall 5-cycle orientation of the second song.

Derivation 3, a segmental 3/4/3/2 division of 0̲1̲2̲/3̲4̲5̲6̲/7̲8̲9̲/A̲B̲, characterizes the introduction (mm. 1–7 [see ex. 5.28], also the return in mm. 173–77). In the opening P2, 0̲1̲2̲ [013] sounds horizontally against vertical whole-tone+/3-cycle+ tetrachords 3̲4̲5̲6̲ [0236], whole-tone trichord 7̲8̲9̲ [026], and dyad A̲B̲ [04]. The successive rows are P2, I5, P2, I5, P9 (varied 3/3/3/3 row segments), IA, and R(P0) (3/3/3/3 row segments from 1̲). An ostinato [013] in the bass, invariant in multiple row forms, <D–E–F> (P2 0̲1̲2̲, P9 3̲4̲5̲) and <F–E♭–D> (I5 0̲1̲2̲, IA 3̲4̲5̲, R(P0) 3̲2̲1̲), underlies the melody, participating in the cyclic collections discussed above.

Derivation 4 consists of the extraction of non-segmental [06s] in 3̲6̲, 7̲9̲, and A̲2̲ [06]s and 1-cycle [012]s in B̲0̲1̲ and 4̲5̲8̲, partitioning the row into two [012678]s. The three partitioned [06]s derive from groups of three, (7̲9̲), four (3̲6̲), and five (A̲2̲) notes, counterpointing the segmental 5–4–3 grouping found in Berg's sketch (ex. 5.32). In. mm. 15–16, the three vertical [06]s are voiced in horizontal [012]s (<C–B–B♭>, <F♯–F–E>), and the remaining [012]s are related by [06]s (<G♯–A–G> and <D–C♯–E♭>, ex. 5.29). The remarkable combination of tonal, row-derivational, formal, and cyclic aspects of this passage has already been discussed. Dyadic [06]s appear in non-row contexts throughout *Der Wein*, particularly in [0268] combinations in mm. 24–30 and the closing measures 214–15, with 1- and 5-cycles in mm. 51–53 and at the center of the palindrome as [013679] in song 2, m. 141 (ex. 5.30).

The rows in song 2 are altered by the addition of a note from order position 8̲ at the beginning, yielding [06] between 8̲ and 0̲, as in 13-P6 <C–F♯–G♯–A♯–B–C♯–D–F–B♭–C–E–E♭–G> (with A♯ instead of A) in mm. 88–89. The resulting thirteen-note rows (labeled by the corresponding twelve-note row) appear in m. 88 (13-P6), m. 92 (13-P9), m. 104 (13-P7), m. 107 (13–P8), and m. 124 (13-P4). The added first note creates not only an additional [06] but whole-tone [026] with <u>801</u>, and even whole-tone [0246] with <u>012</u> in the altered 13-P6 in m. 88, where <u>2</u> is A♯ instead of A. The additional note—often within the characteristic RH3 rhythm described below—also notably alters the distinctive unidirectional contour of the first hexachord of the row to <−6, +2, +2, +1, +2>.

Three derivations stem from a 2-cycle on order positions, <u>02468A</u> <u>13579B</u>, created by extracting every other note (ex. 5.27). The 2-cycle order-position (2-cycle-op) row, which contains mostly successive interval 3s and 4s, is implied in mm. 10−11 (strings), 19−20 (clarinet and viola P7 <u>024613A</u> <G−B♭−D−F♯−A−C−E>), and 64−67 and 172−77 (voice and surrounding parts, <A−C−E♭−G−B−D−F>). Derivations 5 and 6 partition the 2-cycle-op row into further order-position 4 and 3 cycles.

Derivation 5 consists of vertical tetrachords from the 2-cycle-op row <u>0246</u> <u>8A13</u> <u>579B</u>, as whole-tone+−based collections [0148] [0347] [0258] (ex. 5.33, from rows IB and I5). These tetrachords appear in mm. 10−11 (woodwinds, I3, I4) and 13−14, and 214 (winds, IB, I5). In mm. 13−14, the upper-voice <u>017</u> [024]s of T6: related IB and I5 yield a descending 2-cycle <B−A−F−G−E♭−C♯>; this melody line and the vertical whole-tone+ collections of derivation 5 contrast with the surrounding 3-cycle−based melodies and 5-cycle vertical collections of derivation 1 (from I2 and I3, ex. 5.33).

Derivation 6 consists of vertical trichords from the 2-cycle-op row: <u>024</u>

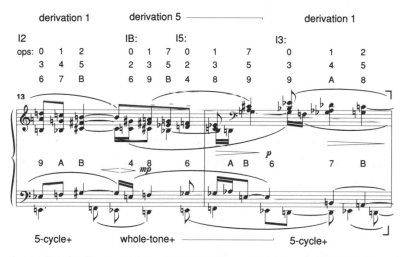

Example 5.33. Derivations 1 and 5, *Der Wein*, mm. 13−14. Berg DER WEIN. Copyright 1966 by Universal Edition A.G., Wien. Copyright renewed. All Rights Reserved. Used by permission of European American Music Distributors Corporation, sole U.S. and Canadian agent for Universal Edition A.G., Wien.

[037], 68A [025], 135 [036], and 79B [036] (ex. 5.34). The trichords appear in mm. 8–10 (clarinets, I7, I3), where they combine with the bass P2 to create mostly 5-cycle–based [0258], [0358], and [0158] chords. Derivation 7 stems from rotated 2-cycle-op row hexachords in the tango (ex. 5.35). In m. 40, hexachord 02468A appears as a 3-cycle+ chord <F–G–A–C♯–E> over a held bass B♭, and complementary hexachord 13579B is rotated to 531B97 <G♯–B–D–E♭–F♯–(C)>, with two 3-cycle segments, as a trumpet melody. The trumpet figure is repeated (not shown), varied from the 02468A hexachord of R(I1) to appear, again, as a 3-cycle+ collection <D–E–G–B♭–D♭> (mm. 45–46).

Example 5.34. Derivations 5 and 6, *Der Wein*, mm. 8–10. Berg DER WEIN. Copyright 1966 by Universal Edition A.G., Wien. Copyright renewed. All Rights Reserved. Used by permission of European American Music Distributors Corporation, sole U.S. and Canadian agent for Universal Edition A.G., Wien.

In addition to the row derivations, *Der Wein* includes three pitch motives and three rhythmic motives. Motive 1 [013] appears throughout in many guises, as at the opening <D♭4–C4–E♭4> (ex. 5.28) and in combinations of 1/2 (=3) cycles (ex. 5.33, mm. 11–14). Motive 2 [037], a row segment, appears with a <+9, −4> contour in m. 17 (violin 1, ex. 5.29) as <G♯–F–C♯> <8ΛB> of I2, and at the climactic vocal entrances in mm. 73 and 196. Following their double statement in m. 17 (ex. 5.29), a brief development consisting of figures that combine the contour of motive 2 and the [013] of motive 1 occurs in mm. 18ff. harmonized by the derivation 1 setting. Such motivic transformations are common in *Der Wein*.

Motive 3 [0268], often appearing as {D,F♯,G♯,C}, with D in the lowest voice, is associated with the [06]s of derivation 2. It appears in mm. 24–30 (and m. 178), at the end of the first song, as the *Schwebend* melody in the second song (mm. 97–102, transposed to {E,C,F♯,B♭}), and as the final chord in m. 216. Two

Example 5.35. Beginning of tango, rhythmic motives I (RHI) and 2 (RH2), derivation 1a, *Der Wein*, mm. 38–43. Berg DER WEIN. Copyright 1966 by Universal Edition A.G., Wien. Copyright renewed. All Rights Reserved. Used by permission of European American Music Distributors Corporation, sole U.S. and Canadian agent for Universal Edition A.G., Wien.

aspects of motive 3, its referential {D,F♯,G♯,C} level and its internal [o6]s, are significant throughout *Der Wein*. In fact, the referential {D,F♯,G♯,C} of motive 3 explains a transposition in song 3. The song is, for the most part, a recapitulation of material from song 1 at the same pitch level, as is characteristic of restatements in Berg's music. At the beginning of the restated tango, however, mm. 181–83 are transposed down by interval 4 from the corresponding mm. 39–41 (ex. 5.35).[75] At m. 184, the original transpositional level is attained by wholesale repetition of m. 183 at T4. By the interval 4 transposition, the solo piano right-hand {C,F♯} in m. 39 is restated as {A♭,D} in m. 181, associating the two [o6]s to complete a large-scale motivic {D,F♯,A♭,C} [o268].

The emphasis given to pitch-class D as the lowest voice of motive 3 {D,F♯,G♯,C} reflects the emphasis on this pitch-class throughout *Der Wein*, where, as in many of Berg's works, D has a referential status and E♭ a secondary, neighboring, status; unlike in Berg's earlier works, however, the note G is not included along with D in a privileged place. The most prominent row P2, which begins <D−E−F−G−A−B♭−C♯> and ends with E♭, appears as the first and last horizontal rows (mm. 8−12, ex. 5.34; mm. 209−13), and as the first vocal row (ex. 5.29, mm. 15–18).[76] The note D is emphasized registrally and timbrally in the bass ostinatos <D–E–F> and <F–E♭–D> in the opening bars (ex. 5.28), in the piano (mm. 7–8) as a lowest-register D1 led to locally from C♯1, and on a larger scale from C♯1/C♯2 in the piano at the center of the palindrome in m. 141 (ex. 5.30) to the concluding piano D1/D2 in mm. 215–16, supporting a {D,F♯,G♯,C} [0268] final chord. This chord is partially stated at the beginning of song 1 both vertically—in m. 15, at the entrance of the voice, the chord is <D–C–F♯>—and horizontally, in a <D–C–F♯> melodic outline in the bass in mm. 15–17 (ex. 5.29). A similar juxtaposition of vertical and horizontal statements of <D–C–F♯> and {D,F♯,G♯,C} occurs near the center of the palindrome (mm. 128–31 and 150–54, bass and piano). Finally, in a particularly cogent example using formal position to emphasize the hierarchical status between the notes D and E♭, to conclude song 1, a "tonic" {D,F♯,G♯,C} [0268] in m. 86 is followed by a "dominant" {E♭,G,A,D♭} [0268].

The other component of motive 3, the [0268] interval structure, is most prominent in mm. 24–30, where vertical pairs of [06]s diverge by inversionally-related 1 cycles, in a wedge. The resulting vertical chords are groups of [0268] and [06].[77] In the passage, [06] {C,F♯} appears repeatedly, arpeggiated through extreme registers, and is omitted from the surrounding rows, I9 (piccolo), I0 (clarinet 1, voice), and P0 (bass clarinet); the procedure foreshadows a passage in *Lulu* (Act 1, scene 1, mm. 170–76), where, in the canon between Lulu and the Painter, [06]s {E/B♭}, {B/F}, and {F♯/C} are similarly arpeggiated and omitted from surrounding rows.

RHYTHM AND METER

Although there are no *Hauptrhythmus* markings in the score of *Der Wein*, three structural rhythms occur, helping to delineate material and formal areas.[78] The first motive, RH1, is the three-attack upbeat gesture associated with vocal and instrumental entrances, as in the first vocal entrance (m. 15, ex. 5.29; also m. 16, horn; m. 17, violin 1, motive 1, ex. 5.29; and mm. 39–40, ex. 5.35, and 181–82, tango, vocal line, mm. 64, 66, 68, 70, 179, 183, 202, and 206). The third rhythmic motive, RH3, from a dotted quarter, eighth, and quarter in the proportions <3-1-2>, acts as the scherzo rhythm to the second song, particularly associated with the thirteen-note rows (mm. 88–107, 123–141; in retrograde in mm. 142–72). The second motive, RH2, is associated with the tango rhythm, with proportions <1–2–1–2–1–1> grouping into a syncopated <3–3–2> within a defined metric group of 8 (ex. 5.35; also mm. 31–32, horns, and mm. 179–80 brass; mm. 38–39, piano, and m. 181, woodwinds; motive 2, mm. 43–46, and mm. 186–88, alto saxophone and clarinet). From m. 39 to m. 40, RH2 is diminuted from eighths to sixteenths (ex. 5.35). In the piano setting in m. 39, the rhythm is accompanied by its own retrograde pattern of <2–3–3>, with a macro-rhythm of continuous sixteenths.[79] RH2 is characterized melodically by pairs of descending intervals, as in m. 39; in another form, the intervals are descending interval 9s (mm. 43–48 and 186–92, alto saxophone and solo violin; m. 47, voice, R(IA), 65, B–D; mm. 114–20 and 162–68, the allusion to the tango in song 2, flute and violin).

Although the tango begins strongly metric, with syncopation, durational canons consisting of variations on the tango proportions of <3–3–2> undermine the notated meter with conflicting meters and syncopations that imitate the popular jazz style. In mm. 41ff., the piano right and left hand have units of five sixteenths set in canon at a duration of three sixteenths. With the odd length and interval of imitation, the two parts constantly change beats (similar to the opening of the third movement of the *Lyric Suite*): the right hand (from m. 41) begins on beats 1.1, 2.2, 1.3, 2.4, 2.1, 1.2, 2.3, 1.4, while the left hand begins on 1.4, 1.1, 2.2, 1.3, 2.4, 2.1, 1.2, 2.3, 1.4. The canon continues, at two sixteenths, between the violin, cello and contrabass, and clarinets (mm. 47–51). Beginning in mm. 43ff., the bassoon and the violin and viola have gestures in units of three eighths (six sixteenths) set in canon at two eighths. Both canons conflict with the $\frac{2}{4}$ meter. Later (mm. 54–58), the glockenspiel, then the bass clarinet and trombones and the flutes and violin play figures in three–eighth-note units, against a piano pattern in three–sixteenth-note units (mm. 56–58). These syncopations and conflicts against the struggling "jazz" regular meter ultimately overwhelm any regularity, as the tango music dissolves into the following section (mm. 60–63).

Lulu

Lulu is Berg's second opera, written from about 1927 to 1935.[80] On November 30, 1934, a suite of pieces from the opera was performed, containing a rondo compiled from music associated with the character Alwa; an Ostinato of music intended to accompany a film between Act II, scenes i and ii; Lulu's aria, the "Lied der Lulu"; the variations Interlude of Act III; and an Adagio consisting of the Countess's contemplation of suicide and her *Liebestod* to Lulu at the end of the opera.[81] The opera itself was, however, apparently left incomplete, and from its premiere in Zurich on June 2, 1937 until 1979 was performed in a two-act version, with two excerpts from the third act—the variations and Adagio movements from the *Lulu Suite*—played as an epilogue. As it turned out, Berg had completed most of the third act in sketches and drafts, and, despite obstacles, the opera was completed from Berg's notes by the Austrian composer Friedrich Cerha. Following the death of Helene Berg, the three-act *Lulu* was premiered in Paris on February 24, 1979.[82] Cerha's edition is considered to be true to Berg's intentions, and has come to be regarded as definitive.[83] All references here are to Cerha's completed version of *Lulu*.

For the text of the opera, Berg condensed two plays by Frank Wedekind, *Erdgeist* and *Die Büchse der Pandora* (1892–1903), dividing the action into three acts of three, two, and two scenes each.[84] This three-part division may be labeled ABA' in terms of the return of musical material from Act I in Act III, but a case can be made for ABA'B' due to the inclusion of material associated with the Countess Geschwitz and the Acrobat–Animal Tamer, the "Lied der Lulu," and Alwa's rondo music from Act II in Act III. However defined, the three-part division counterpoints dramatically and musically a two-part division that is reflected in many details, but most notably by Lulu's two-part ascent and descent in fortune, which pivots around the palindromic film music interlude between Act II, scenes i and ii.[85]

The music within scenes is shaped into successive defined small song forms, with labels such as *Aria Arietta*, *Arioso*, *Canzonetta*, *Duet*, *Interludium*, *Kavatine*, *Lied*, and *Recitativ*, whereas larger forms across scene boundaries—mostly interrupted and divided internally by intervening music—are identified as absolute and more generic musical forms and associated with specific characters: a *Kammermusik* associated with Schigolch in Act I, scene ii (mm. 463–530, a wind nonet of piccolo, flute, oboe, english horn, clarinet, bass clarinet, bassoon, contrabassoon, with some string, piano, and vibraphone interjections); a *Sonate* associated with Dr. Schön in Act I, scenes ii and iii—Schön is also associated with the *Arietta* "Das mein Lebensabend" in Act II, scene i and the *Fünfstrophige Arie* in Act II, scene ii—a *Rondo* associated with Alwa in Act II, scenes i and ii (foreshadowed in Act I, scene iii), and a set of *Variationenen* associated with the related characters of the Prince-Manservant-Marquis across the three acts, with related variations on a melody from a lute song by Wedekind in Act III.[86] The Painter is associated with a *Canon* in Act I, scene i and a *Monoritmica* in Act I, scene ii, the latter comprising a large formal area characterized by repeated statements of a rhythmic motive, the *Hauptrhythmus* or RH.

COMPOSITION AND MUSICAL MATERIALS

The composition of *Lulu* proceeded in two stages.[87] Act I, scene i and the opening part of scene ii, mm. 86–529—a total of 444 bars—is based on materials derived directly from one row, found in sketches dated July 17, 1927. The amount of music was substantially more than Berg had written using one row to this point. In a letter to Schoenberg of September 1, 1928, Berg described his first stage musical materials for *Lulu*, and added that "if this should not be sufficient, I would construct a new series, similar to the manner in my *Lyric Suite* in which the series underwent some minor modifications (through transposition [exchanging of order positions] of a few notes) which was then, at any rate, very stimulating for my work."[88] In time, the materials did turn out to be insufficient. In the summer of 1929, Berg composed *Der Wein* and experimented with some new types of derivations, extracting notes in cyclical combinations (see exx. 5.27, 5.33, and 5.34). Following *Der Wein*, influenced by conversations with Willi Reich, Berg greatly increased his compositional resources for *Lulu* by creating several new derived rows, which then served as sources for the types of derivations originally used on the main row. These second-stage rows and derived materials combine with those of the first stage in the rest of the opera, including the *prolog*, which was composed last.[89]

First Stage   In a letter to Schoenberg of September 1, 1928, Berg indicated that he had completed three hundred measures of *Lulu* (out of the projected three thousand)—approximately mm. 86–386; in fact, mm. 86–529 are based solely on the material of the sketches dated July 17, 1927.[90] These sketches consist of row charts containing the principal row in all twelve transpositions of prime and inversion rows, with the derived materials in each row written out and identified by order-position numbers 1–12 (ex. 5.36).[91]

The first-stage derivations fall into three categories. The first is based on the order of the main row: a division into two 5-cycle–based hexachords [024579] related by T6 (ex. 5.36a); an alignment of the two hexachords yielding six dyads of even interval-classes <646444>, known as the "Painter" dyads for their association with this character (ex. 5.36b); these dyads combined into whole-tone+ [0248], [0268], and 3-cycle+ [0147] tetrachords, known as the "Painter" tetrachords although they appear in various contexts (ex. 5.36c); verticalized segmental trichords, sets [015] [027] [025], sharing interval-class 5, associated with Lulu's portrait and known as the "Picture" trichords (ex. 5.36g); a row derived from the horizontal voices of the trichords, 2479036A158B, with 5-cycle–based hexachords [023579], associated with the character Lulu, particularly in her role as a dancer (ex. 5.36h); verticalized segmental dyads with partitioned 2B or 4A, associated with the Medical Specialist (ex. 5.36j); and the row with intertwined second tetrachord 6475 (example 5.36l). The three 1-cycle [0123] tetrachords associated with the character Schigolch stem from a rhythmic partitioning of this intertwined row (example 5.36m).

The second category of derivation from the main row of *Lulu* is based on properties of the 5-cycle [024579] hexachords: a division of hexachords into [037]s in T6 pairs (ex. 5.36d); and the extraction of an isolated non-segmental interval-class 5, from 29 or 18, leaving two 5-cycle collections (exx. 5.36n–o). The third category is derived by non-systematic row partitions stemming not

Example 5.36. First-stage sketches for the principal row of *Lulu* (upper numbers in each stave are intervals or set-classes, lower numbers are order positions)

from the order of the row but from the content of the aggregate: a partitioning of trichords [036], [048], and [037] (ex. 5.36e); of [037]s and [048]s (ex. 5.36f); of the two whole-tone collections (ex. 5.36i); an alignment of two whole-tone collections in interval 5 dyads (ex. 5.36k); and the multicyclic [0167]s and [0369]s, which occur throughout the opera as basic cells (exx. 5.36p–r).

The materials described above include those associated with the four main characters in Act I, scene i and the first part of scene ii: Lulu, with her row and Picture trichords (exx. 5.36g–h); the Painter's dyads and tetrachords (exx. 5.36b–c); the Medical Specialist's dyads (ex. 5.36j); and Schigolch's "row," used as three partially-ordered [0123] collections (ex. 5.36m). The rhythm of the lower part in example 5.36m is associated with the Medical Specialist (initially in Act I, mm. 112–14) and is an early form of the *Hauptrhythmus* of the opera; it is also part of the derivation of Schigolch's materials (Act, mm 458–63). Uncharacteristically, the musical connection does not reflect a corresponding dramatic connection between the two characters.

All of Berg's first stage materials either embody or are related to cyclic collections. In particular, the three multicyclic tetrachords [0167], [0369], and [0268] are all present, with the first two particularly prominent throughout the opera in many musical and dramatic connections. In the sketches, however, Berg also added several "tonal" interpretations of material. The "triads" in examples 5.36d, e, and f are identified by letters (for example, *gis* for a G♯-minor triad, or *dur* and *moll* for major and minor triads, as in the sketch for the row of *Der Wein*); the row associated with Lulu has an extra note at the beginning added in parentheses, recalling the thirteen-note rows in *Der Wein*, with segments <E♭–F–G–A♭–B♭–C–D–G♭–E♭> and <E–A–B–C♯> identified as tritone-related "E♭ major" and "A-major" collections; and the Medical Specialist dyads are grouped in threes and similarly labeled with tritone-related "C-major" and "F♯-major" segments (ex. 5.36j). These labels clearly indicate that Berg was aware of the possible tonal allusions or relationships inhering in his materials, which may have motivated his choice and combinations of these derived materials.

Second Stage For his second-stage materials, Berg developed rows and related materials for the characters Dr. Schön (Schn), Alwa, the Countess (CG), the Schoolboy (Schy), the Acrobat (Acbt), and the chorale (Ch) row associated with the related Prince-Manservant-Marquis, which are themselves sources of further derived materials, like those discussed above. The rows are created by cyclic operations on order positions of the main or principal row (PR), a process that can be defined as extracting notes from the principal row in cyclic series and can be represented by using the order-position numbers of this row as referential (ex. 5.37).[92] The Alwa row is derived by a 7-cycle on order positions, or, taking

Example 5.37. Second-stage derivations of rows from the principal row of *Lulu*

every seventh note, beginning with the first: <u>07294B6183A5</u>. The Countess's row is originally a 5-cycle row <u>05A3816B49270</u> (shown to the right in ex. 5.37 as CG-5), but it is then inverted and rotated, and an adjacent note pair exchanged (<B♭4−E♭5>) to yield her row. This row is, however, rarely used; the Countess is represented for the most part by ten-note rows and further derived 5-cycle collections [05], [024579], and [01378] (described below)—similar to the first-stage derivations in which [02479]s and [05]s are partitioned from the principal row (exx. 5.36n−o). The Acrobat's and the Schoolboy's rows are created by a slightly modified cyclic extraction procedure: the Acrobat's row is created from a 2-cycle on order positions, but with a place marker added to the cycle to avoid repetition and arrive at all twelve notes: <u>02468A</u> (+1) <u>13579B</u>; the Schoolboy's row is similarly created from a 3-cycle on order positions, with two added places to yield all twelve notes 0369 (+1) 147A (+1) 258B (the Schoolboy row directly related to the principal row beginning on E is shown at the right in ex. 5.37; in the music it is transposed at $T-2$).[93] The Acrobat is also associated with 5-cycle piano "white-" and "black-note" collections, which can be derived from this character's row at P4, rotated, with segmental hexachords [013568] / [012479] (the same hexachords as appear in Schön's and Alwa's rows) represented in 9AB012 / 345678 as $<C-D-F-E-A-B /B\flat-E\flat-G-A\flat-G\flat-D\flat>$, with G transferred to the first hexachord.[94] Dr. Schön's row results from a gradated series $<2-3-4-4-3-2-2-3-4-4-3>$ of order positions 02591468B37A, and the chorale row is similarly created by a gradated series $<2-3-4-5-6-5-4-3-2>$ on, successively, Alwa's row, the principal row, and Dr. Schön's row. Specifically, the chorale row at P(n) is derived from Alwa P(n) 0259, the principal row P(n + A) 28, and Schn P(n + ·3) 158AB. This chorale row is an eleven-note row, the missing note often appearing with the row in the music (similar to the eleven-note version of the main theme in the fifth movement of the *Lyric Suite*; see ex. 5.22).

Relationships between rows derived by order-position cycles stem from invariances within the cycles themselves, and these invariances can be realized in rhythms. In a passage from the film music interlude between Act II, scenes i and ii, for instance, the principal row and five character rows are presented consecutively in equal-duration presentations (mm. 670–74).[95] In each, the ordered collection $<E-A-B\flat-E\flat>$ [0167] is punctuated, creating rhythms from the order positions of this collection in each row (ex. 5.37). The largely cyclic relationships between the rhythms add a layer of musical and dramatic structure to the passage. In the order-position 7-cycle derivation of Alwa's row from the principal row, notes in 02468A are held invariant, so that the rhythms of $<E-A-B\flat-E\flat>$ 0268 in the main row and Alwa's row are identical (proportions 2:4:2:4, in sixteenth-note units), reflecting Alwa's central role in the drama.[96] The order-position 2-cycle creating the Acrobat row yields a 0268 rhythm, which is a cyclic diminution by one-half of the rhythms in the principal and Alwa rows and an apt representation of the character of the Acrobat. The rhythm of the $<E-A-B\flat-E\flat>$ note group in the Schön row, proportionally 1:5:1:5 is an exaggerated form of the Alwa–principal row rhythmic proportion 2:4:2:4, symmetrically transformed at $<+1, -1, +1, -1>$, and is similar to the Countess Geschwitz row proportion 1:6:1:4 (an analogous exaggeration of $<1:5:1:5>$, but at $<0,-1,0,+1>$; the rhythmic relationships reflect the triangle of Lulu's three principal lovers. Finally, the Schoolboy row is transposed to begin on D, producing ordered $<E-A-B\flat-E\flat>$ to yield a rhythm that is almost a durational retrograde of the Schön row rhythm.

Dr. Schön and Alwa also share family ties in the opera as father and son, and this relationship is reflected by invariances between their rows. In Alwa's row <07294B6183A5>, adjacent order-positions differ by 7, and in pairs by 14 = 2 (mod 12); in the Schön row <02591468B37A>, successive order positions differ either by 2 or by combinations of 3s and 4s in 7s. As a result, identical gradations are no more than two notes away in the two rows, and two of three pitch-classes in each trichord of the rows are identical. Moreover, in the sum-1 inversion between Schn P4 and I9, pitch-class dyad pairs C/C♯, B/D, B♭/E♭, A/E, A♭/F, and G/F♯ map into one another. Thus, the rows Alwa P4 and Schn I9 have the same trichordal and hexachordal pitch-class content (ex. 5.37); the shared trichords and hexachords are [037], [036], [027], [016] and [013568] / [012479].

Berg's second-stage derived materials hold invariances with one another and with the first-stage materials by their shared cyclic content.[97] The 5-cycle–based materials are the principal row hexachords [024579], the Picture trichords and Lulu row hexachords [023579], the Alwa and Dr. Schön row hexachords [013568] / [012479], the Countess Geschwitz collections [05], [01378], and [02479], the Acrobat piano clusters [02479] and [013568]. In addition, the Countess collection [01378] is prominent throughout the opera as basic cell II, appearing as 01234 and 56789 in Dr. Schön's row and as 01245 in the first hexachord of Alwa's row. The Schoolboy row tetrachords [0248], [0156], and [0248] and the Painter tetrachords [0268], [0147], and [0248] consist of outer wholetone collections—a cyclic collection largely associated with Lulu throughout.

The Schigolch tetrachordal [0123]s are just one of a number of interval 1–based tetrachords and trichords derived throughout: Dr. Schön's row is partitioned into [0123], [01234], and [012] in order positions 089B, 1456A, and 237, when the character arrives at the house at the end of Lulu and Schigolch's conversation (Act I, scene ii, mm. 530–32); the Acrobat row is partitioned into [012]s 04B, 123, 567, and 89A (Act II, m. 139, 750–73); Alwa's row is partitioned into a two-voice counterpoint, with lower voice [0123] 2467 (see ex. 5.54), and the [0123] appears independent of the row context in accompanying voices throughout the Alwa rondo;[98] and, in the verticalized tetrachordal presentation of the rows of Dr. Schön–Jack the Ripper, the Schoolboy, Alwa, the Acrobat, and Schigolch in Act III (mm. 752–70), as Schigolch and Alwa wait for Lulu and her first customer to arrive, the upper voices of a series of tetrachords are all [0123]s: from Schön's row in order positions 237A, Schoolboy 147B, Alwa 138B, Acrobat 8923, and Schigolch 89AB, and, later in the scene, again with Schigolch and Alwa waiting (m. 842), upper-voice [0123]s emerge from Alwa I9 order positions 146B.[99]

Of the dyadic derivations, the Painter dyads, interval-classes <646444>, are similar to the alignment of the Countess Geschwitz collections ([02479] /

[01378]) yielding vertical interval-classes <65464> (Act III, scene ii, m. 1320; also ex. 5.58) and to the Medical Specialist dyads, interval-classes <445335> and <443333> with alternate Countess Geschwitz collections alignments yielding interval-classes <32332> and <54464> (Act III, scene ii, mm. 1321–22).

The second-stage materials also include a characteristic rhythm, the *Hauptrhythmus* (RH) of the opera (ex. 5.38a). This rhythm is a varied form of the

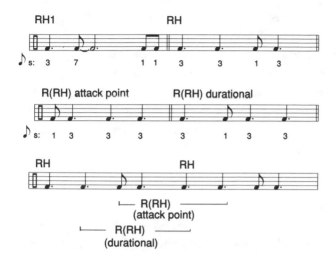

Example 5.38a. Forms of the *Hauptrhythmus* (RH) in *Lulu*

Example 5.38b. Counterpoint of the *Hauptrhythmus* (RH) and five gun shots, *Lulu*, Act II, scene i, mm. 533–55

rhythm associated with the Medical Specialist in the first-stage materials, RH1, with the second proportion reduced from 7 to 3 (cf. ex. 5.36m). RH has a structure somewhat analogous to the cyclic+ pitch-class collections: the proportions of the RH are <3 – 3 – 1 – 3>, a 3-cycle+ of durations (when the final duration is defined by a following attack). The 1 duration is "dissonant" in the overall context, as it breaks the pattern of equal durations. RH appears in many guises, even governing subtle details, such as the hammer blows when Alwa hangs Lulu's portrait on a nail in the attic setting of Act III, scene ii (m. 956). RH also appears in two forms as a retrograde: as an attack-point retrograde with relative durations $<1-3-3-3>$, and as a durational retrograde with relative durations $<3-1-3-3>$; both retrograde forms are contained with repeated statements of RH.

The moments in the opera associated with fate or death are brought into clear relief by a harmonic focus on the 1-, 5-, and 6-cycle combinations of Basic Cell I(BCI) [0167] (with either interval-class 5 or 6 emphasized) and the 3-cycles of BC III [0369], usually in aggregate formations, and by a rhythmic focus on RH. Like leitmotivs, these collections and rhythm not only accompany disastrous events as they occur but foreshadow events by underscoring earlier moments that draw characters to their fates.[100] The most obvious instances of RH occur at the end of each act, accompanying the chords associated with Lulu's three principal lovers: Dr. Schön (end of Act I), Alwa (end of Act II), and the latter two plus a third associated with the Countess Geschwitz (end of Act III; see ex. 5.61), but the death of each character is accompanied by sections based on RH, which may be labeled, following Berg, as monoritmicas.

LULU

The central character Lulu, although onstage for almost the entire opera (absent only in the *monoritmica* of Act I, scene ii, mm. 669–754; Act II, scene ii, mm. 40–58, when Dr. Schön sings "Das mein Lebensabend"; Act II, scene ii, mm. 722–952, when she is in the prison hospital; and Act III, scene ii, where she is on the street or in the adjacent room), is somewhat of an enigma. Her *Erdgeist* nature is manifest in her mysterious origins, her relationship to Schigolch, her child-like innocence, her power over men, and her ability to recover from cholera. She is, however, largely passive, defined by those around her, as represented by the portrait that follows her throughout, symbolizing the images that others have of her.[101] Her name varies depending on who is addressing her: Nelly to the Medical Specialist, Eva to the Painter, and Mignon to Alwa and Dr. Schön; she refers to herself as a "beast" (*Tier*, Act I, scene ii, mm. 512–16), and only Schigolch calls her Lulu. In the "Lied der Lulu," she comments on her role as a mirror for other's desires, telling Dr. Schön, "I've never in the world wanted to seem anything other than what I've been taken for, and no one has ever taken me for anything other than what I am."[102]

In the first half of the opera, Lulu's fortunes are continually on the rise, but her life is controlled mostly by Dr. Schön; even when she asserts her will over him and forces him to confront her at last in marriage, it is merely the next step in the life that he has—perhaps unintentionally—created for her. The moment of truth for Lulu comes at the moment she shoots Dr. Schön and takes charge of her own life. Ironically, as she gains self-awareness in the second half of the opera, her fortunes decline. The music of the "Lied der Lulu" returns when

Lulu rejects the Marquis Casti-Piani's blackmail proposal to send her to an Egyptian bordello, telling him that in the prison hospital she achieved self-realization and her eyes were opened to her destiny. Initially, known as the murderess of Dr. Schön, she is now referred to as Lulu not only by Schigolch but by Alwa, who identifies "Lulu's portrait" (Act III, scene ii, mm. 911–13), and in the *Leibestod* the Countess calls her "Lulu" (Act III, scene ii, mm. 1315–26). Despite her new awareness and identity, however, her situation deteriorates. Her portrait returns to haunt her in the attic in London (Act III, scene ii) as a stark contrast between the past and present; although, for a moment, Alwa, Schigolch, Lulu, and the Countess are transformed by the portrait, and the music of the rondo returns (Act III, mm. 919–1023), the dismal present soon intrudes and Lulu heads back to the street (Act III, mm. 1020–23). She has chosen to prostitute herself, despite the protests of Alwa and the Countess, a decision that leads to her death at the hands of Jack the Ripper.

Unlike other characters in the opera, Lulu is associated with no large musical form; her only solo material is the relatively brief "Lied der Lulu." Instead, she interacts with other characters and their musical forms or passages: with the Painter in the canon and duet in Act I, scene i (mm. 132–95, 305–28), Schigolch in the *Kammermusik* of Act I, scene ii (mm. 462–530), Dr. Schön in the sonata of Act I (scene ii, mm. 532–668; scene iii, mm. 1209–361) and the five-strophe aria of Act II, scene i (mm. 380–551), Alwa in the ragtime of Act I, scene iii (mm. 992–1020, 1040–93) and the rondo of Act II (foreshadowed in Act I, scene iii, mm. 1020–40; Act II, scene i, mm. 243–337, and Act II, scene ii, mm. 1004–150), Schigolch, the Acrobat, and the Schoolboy in the music based on Lulu's freedom-entrance motive in Act II, scene i (mm. 145–223), and the Marquis Casti-Piani in the chorale variations of Act III (mm. 83–230). In the final scene, she plays her part in the return of the Medical Specialist's music with the Silent Professor (Act III, mm. 769–823, 850–865), Alwa's rondo when the Countess returns with Lulu's portrait (Act III, mm. 957–99), the painter's *monoritmica* with the Negro Prince (Act III, mm. 1058–1100), and the Schön sonata and aria "Das mein Lebensabend" when Jack arrives to kill her (Act III, mm. 1188–278, 1304–14).

Musical Materials   Lulu is associated with several musical figures or leitmotivs which are generally characterized by whole-tone+ collections. Her portrait is depicted musically by the Picture trichords, four vertical trichordal segments in the principal row (PR), 012 [015], 345 [027], 678 [025], and 9AB [025], with a consistent contour and horizontal voicing: 2479, 036B, and 158A (ex. 5.36g). These Picture chords, however, which occur whenever Lulu's portrait appears or is referred to, feature prominent interval-class 5s, which represent musically surrounding characters' reflections on Lulu, as the portrait does dramatically. Characteristic cyclic settings of the Picture trichords include a 4-cycle creating an aggregate from the upper-voice [0235]s (ex. 5.39a, from rows PR-P1, P5 and P9, in Act I, mm. 93–97), horizontal T6-related pairs, yielding an upper-voice interval 2/1 cycle (ex. 5.39b, upper rows PR-P6 and P0, in the introduction to the canon between Lulu and the Painter, Act I, mm. 132–133, 143–44, and 149–50), and in vertical pairings at T5 and T7 (ex. 5.39b, from rows PR-P1/P6 and P5/P0, Act I, mm. 132–33), with resulting 5-cycle verticals. Throughout the duet between Lulu and the Painter (Act I, mm. 300–21), the 5-cycle–based Picture trichords contrast with the mostly whole-tone Painter tetrachords (ex. 3.36c), in a harmonic setting characteristic of Lulu throughout the opera. The Picture chords are also prominent in the ragtime music in Act I, scene iii (mm. 994–1004, 1005–13, 1014–20), and they appear in Act II, scene i as Dr. Schön is dying and gazes once more at Lulu's picture (mm. 590–92, horns), at the center of the film music (Act II, mm. 685–86), in Act III, scene ii, when the Countess returns with the portrait (mm. 913–18), and, perhaps most movingly, to accompany the Countess as she prays for mercy under Lulu's portrait (Act III, mm. 1180–85).

Lulu's row, associated with her dancing and seductiveness, derives from the 2479036A158B horizontal voices of the Picture trichords and has 5-cycle hexachords [023579] and a whole-tone+ segment in its 2345678 (ex. 5.36h). The row appears first as two whole-tone collections (ex. 5.36i) in Act I, scene i, when

PR: P1   P5   P9

Example 5.39a. Picture trichords in 4-cycle, *Lulu*, Act I, mm. 93–97

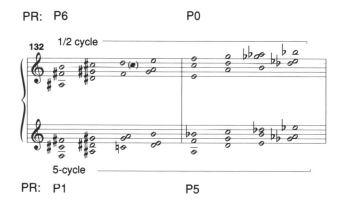

Example 5.39b. Picture trichords at T6 in 5-cycle alignment, *Lulu*, Act I, mm. 132–33

Picture trichords from PR-P0

Example 5.39c. Lulu P5 row with Picture trichord harmonization, *Lulu*, Act I, mm. 116–18. Berg LULU Acts 1 & 2. Copyright 1964 by Universal Edition A.G., Wien. Copyright renewed. Revision © Copyright 1985 by Universal Edition A.G., Wien. All Rights Reserved. Used by permission of European American Music Distributors Corporation, sole U.S. and Canadian agent for Universal Edition A.G., Wien.

Lulu mentions her dancing for Alwa's new stage music (mm. 99–102), then in its true form as Lulu P5 (mm. 115–18, ex. 5.39c, where it is harmonized with three groups of Picture trichords) in its characteristic contour and rhythm with an opening turn figure. The Lulu row is the melodic basis of the canon between the Painter and Lulu in Act I, scene i (mm. 156–85), in a canon with ever shorter intervals between *dux* and *comes*, reflecting the chase. Lulu also sings a figure derived from the Medical Specialist dyads (ex. 5.36j), initially the cazonetta "Auf einmal springt er auf" at the death of the Medical Specialist (Act I, scene i, mm. 258–62); the same music returns at the deaths of the Painter (mm. 868–71) and Dr. Schön (Act II, scene i, mm. 610–12).

The most memorable motive associated with Lulu, by its sheer beauty as well as its dramatic affiliation, is the "Freedom" motive, named for its appearance when Lulu cries "O Freedom" (*O Freiheit*) after escaping from prison (Act II, mm. 1000–1004).[103] The motive (ex. 5.40a) does not appear to have a convincing direct derivation analogous to Lulu's other materials but is related to basic cell II [01378]. The motive features registrally separated trichordal [026]s and [037]s combining into 5-cycle–based hexachords, [013578], [023579], and the characteristic [0167] / [0369] superset [013679] in an aggregate combination (open noteheads in ex. 5.40a).[104] The opening holds basic cell II [01378] {E, A,B,C,F} as a subset, a chord arpeggiated in the middle voices, along with its T1 transformation {F,B♭,C♭,D♭,G♭}. The motive appears in Act II, scene i (m. 145) and returns at T1 (m. 163), following basic cell II's transposition, ending with the

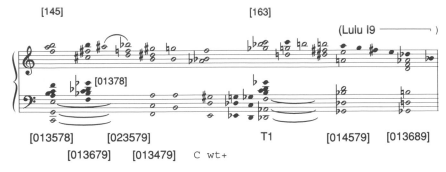

Example 5.40a. Freedom motive, *Lulu*, Act I, mm. 145–69

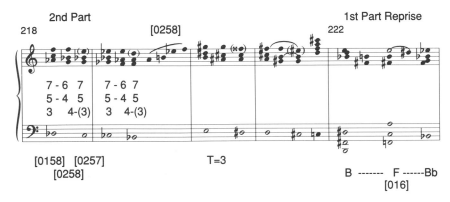

Example 5.40b. Freedom motive, second part, with varied return of first part at m. 222, *Lulu*, Act I, mm. 218–22

Example 5.40c. Freedom motive in film music interlude, *Lulu*, Act II, mm. 683–84, 690–91

Lulu I9 row and a final upper-voice sonority of 3-cycle–based [0147] <D–F–A♭–D♭>, a chord that recurs throughout the opera in a cadential role (most notably at the central chord of the film-music palindrome, Act II, m. 687, ex. 5.30). In another form, the motive has a T6-related (Tn) [047] added at the beginning, displacing the bottom voices of the first chord (ex. 5.40b, m. 222); the bass progression of [016] <B–F–B♭> is a subset of basic cell I [0167].

The second component of the passage is a succession of chords that feature stepwise resolutions of 5-cycle–related [0158]s, [0258]s, and [0257]s, mimicking tonal progressions with "half-diminished" and "dominant-seventh chords" and the tonal voice-leading of resolving seventh-chords (ex. 5.40b).[105] The upper notes do not resolve in each case (as "4–3" suspensions)—to what would be the dominant chord at the end of each bar (the unstated notes of resolution are given in parentheses in ex. 5.40b)—leaving "dissonant" [0257]s. The chord succession spans interval 3 (mm. 218–19) and sequences at the same interval (mm. 220–21), to complete a 3-cycle in its boundary tones. When it precedes the freedom motive's initial part, as it does here leading into m. 222, the succession strengthens the allusion to a V-I cadence, or, with the added first chord, a ♭II–V–I progression in the tonal allusion of the Freedom motive.

The Freedom motive and associated chord succession appear first in the prologue (mm. 44–62), at the same level as shown in examples 5.40a and b, when Lulu is introduced to the audience by the Animal Tamer and described as *Die Urgestalt des Weibes* ("the true nature of woman").[106] It appears for the first time within the drama in Act II, scene i when, after Dr. Schön has left, Lulu enters, at the height of her powers, to her coterie of lovers: Schigolch, the Schoolboy, the Acrobat, and, hidden behind stage, the Countess Geschwitz (mm. 145–223). The text for this ravishing statement of the motive is paradoxically bizarre and somewhat banal: to the glorious climax, Lulu sings "if only you're [the Acrobat's] ears weren't so big" (*Wenn Sie nur nicht so lange Ohren hätten*, mm. 218–23). The contrast between music and text is striking and comical, reflecting the pathetic group of males and their arguments about who will end up with Lulu.

The Freedom motive returns in the film music palindrome between Act II, scenes i and ii, close to the center. Unlike all other materials of the palindrome, however, the motive is in retrograde order in the first half (mm. 683–84), then is restored to prime order in the second half (mm. 690–91), so that the second half of the palindrome is motivated to "correct" the motive's aspect (ex. 5.40c). It is the only motive so treated in the interlude. The setting reflects the state of Lulu's freedom: in the first half of the film music and palindrome, she is incarcerated, and so her Freedom motive appears in retrograde. In the second half, she is on her way to escaping, and her Freedom motive now sounds in its prime order, to reflect her new-found liberation. After she has escaped, Lulu sings of her new freedom to the Freedom motive (Act II, scene ii, mm. 1001–3), at the level of bass notes <G♭–C–F>, then, at the characteristic intensifying sequence at T1 a few bars later (mm. 1010–15), at the level of bass notes <D♭–G♭>, when she sees her portrait and is reminded of the past. The motive also appears twice in the second part of Alwa's rondo (Act II, scene ii): in a sequence at T6, from bass <C♭–E> to <F–B♭> outlining [0167] (mm. 1030–37), and near the end (mm. 1080–86), at the same level as in the prologue and Act II, scene i, to Alwa's memorable line: "If it weren't for your two childlike eyes, I should say you were the most designing of whores and bitches who ever inveigled a man to his doom," and Lulu's equally stunning reply, "I wish to God I were."[107]

Finally, the entire Freedom motive passage from Act II, scene ii (mm. 145–72) returns in Act III, scene ii at T8, when Lulu begs Jack to accompany her into her bedroom. At this moment, as Lulu is trapped and facing her imminent death, the ironic appearance of her Freedom motive creates one of the most powerful and poignant scenes in the opera (mm. 1267–75).

"Lied der Lulu"   The music of the "Lied der Lulu," which encompasses all of the material associated with Lulu except for the Freedom motive, appears in two places in the opera: first in Act II, scene i, in the midst of Dr. Schön's five-strophe aria (mm. 491–538), and second in Act III, scene i, as an intermezzo within the Marquis Casti-Piani's chorale variations (mm. 125–45). The later appearance of the "Lied" is foreshadowed by the inclusion of the chords eventually associated with the Marquis in the first appearance of the "Lied" (mm. 516–521), where the chorale accompanies the text "If you sacrifice to me the evening of your life," reflecting Lulu's later dealings with the Marquis, who wants Lulu to sacrifice the evening of her life to his employers.[108] The first "Lied" is also a movement in the *Lulu Suite* and was dedicated to Anton von Webern on the latter's fiftieth birthday in December 1933.[109]

In the preceding five-strophe aria in Act II, scene i, Dr. Schön is jealous, paranoid, and enraged; he gives Lulu a gun and orders her to shoot herself. Instead, she draws away and sings the "Lied," telling Schön that he knew who and what she was when he married her. The text of the "Lied" is arranged in five sentences, each with internal paired dialectical clauses (fig. 5.16).[110] The dialectic in the text is reflected by the parallel musical dialectic of prime and inversion, in which the clauses are set in musical phrases of successive prime and inversion pairs (fig. 5.17).[111] The accompaniment varies from figures in prime-inversion pairs at the same index number or axis of symmetry as in the vocal line, to those with different indices and axes and to others not in prime-inversion pairs. Each of the five sentences is delineated by double barlines in the score, and each phrase is set off by double barlines in the vocal part only, except for the first sentence (which receives slightly different treatment).[112] Each sentence, and in some cases each internal phrase, has its characteristic ensemble, with the highest instrumental density in the second phrase of sentence 5.

The principal components of the harmonic language in the "Lied" are whole-tone+ collections stemming from the Painter tetrachords [0268], [0147],

Figure 5.16. Text of the "Lied der Lulu"

1. Wenn sich die Menschen um meinetwillen umgebracht haben, so setzt das meinem Wert nicht herab.

2. Du hast so gut gewußt, weswegen Du mich zur Frau nahmst, wie ich gewußt habe, weswegen ich dich zum Mann nahm.

3. Du hattest deine besten Freunde mit mir betrogen, Du konntest nich gut auch noch Dich selber mit mir betrügen.

4. Wenn Du mir Deine Lebensabend zum Opfer bringst, so hast Du meine ganze Jugend dafür gehabt.

5. Ich habe nie in der Welt etwas anderes scheinen wollen als wofür man mich genommen hat.

Und man hat mich nie in der Welt für etwas anderes genommen als was ich bin.

Figure 5.17. Paired prime and inversion phrases in sentences of the "Lied der Lulu"

		prime	/	inversion
Sentence 1	mm. 491–497:	491–494		495–497
Sentence 2	mm. 498–507:	498–502		503–507
Sentence 3	mm. 508–515:	508–511		512–515
Sentence 4	mm. 516–521:	516–518		519–521
Sentence 5	mm. 522–539:	522–528		529–539

---

and [0248] (ex. 5.36c), particularly in sentence 5, and from the chorale chords in sentence 4 (see ex. 5.62). The middle sentence 3 is set in the contrasting 5-cycle–based Picture trichords [015], [027], [025], and [025]. The vocal lines consist of the principal row, the Lulu row, a derived "Lied" row, and 1/2–cycles from the upper line of juxtaposed T6-related Picture trichords (ex. 5.39b). Basic cell I [0167], itself inversionally symmetrical, appears in the accompaniment to the second phrase in sentence 1 (mm. 495–97 <D–G–A♭–D♭>) and in sentence 5 in the vocal part (mm. 527–28 <A–D–E♭–A♭> and mm. 534–39 <A–E–E♭–B♭>).

The vocal phrases in the first sentence (mm. 491–94, 495–97, ex. 5.41) are not arranged in P/I pairs. Instead, the vocal PR-Po in the first phrase is counterpointed by an inverted canonic PR-I7 (cello); the stretto acts as a transition from the simultaneous prime and inversion statements in the preceding aria to their successive statements in the remainder of the "Lied." The second vocal phrase, a rotated PR-IA, overlaps by <C♯–D♯> with PR-Po (Po <u>AB</u> = IA <u>45</u>). [113] The rotation causes the second vocal phrase (m. 495) to begin with the same hexachordal pitch-classes as in PR-Po {E,D,C,G,A}, but with an exchange of B

Example 5.41. Opening two phrases, "Lied der Lulu," *Lulu*, Act II, mm. 491–97. Berg LULU Acts 1 & 2. Copyright 1964 by Universal Edition A.G., Wien. Copyright renewed. Revision © Copyright 1985 by Universal Edition A.G., Wien. All Rights Reserved. Used by permission of European American Music Distributors Corporation, sole U.S. and Canadian agent for Universal Edition A.G., Wien.

and F (recalling this hexachordal relationship in the row of the first movement of the *Lyric Suite*). The harmonic basis of the first sentence is whole-tone+ collections in characteristic interval 1–based wedge voice-leading (especially evident in the middle stave, mm. 491–93, of ex. 5.41), thus alternating between the two distinct collections, but it ends with 5-cycle–based collections, a change marked by the added [0167]s in mm. 495–96. The vocal phrases are punctuated by inversionally-related Painter tetrachords (from PR-I7 and P1, mm. 491, 495), which are whole-tone+ in their outer chords; they are arranged with outer voice [037]s and [015]s, however, foreshadowing the Picture trichords.

The vocal sentence of the second section is set to an ordered aggregate (ex. 5.42), labeled "Lied P6," derived initially from row segment <F#–D–C#> of the principal row I6 012. This "row" has whole-tone+ hexachords, reflected in the whole-tone+ harmonies. The second phrase is set almost completely in inversional pairs at sum 0 to the first (fig. 5.18). The third statement (mm. 508–11, 512–15) is dominated melodically and harmonically by the 5-cycle–based Pic-

Example 5.42. First phrase of second sentence; "Lied der Lulu," *Lulu*, Act II, mm. 498–502. Berg LULU Acts 1 & 2. Copyright 1964 by Universal Edition A.G., Wien. Copyright renewed. Revision © Copyright 1985 by Universal Edition A.G., Wien. All Rights Reserved. Used by permission of European American Music Distributors Corporation, sole U.S. and Canadian agent for Universal Edition A.G., Wien.

ture trichords. In the first half, the trichords ascend from T6-related principal rows PR-Po, P6, and Po, then descend via PR-I11 and I7 (oboes to strings), yielding the characteristic 1/2–cycle upper voice. The vocal line follows the upper voice of the chords and adds coloratura interval 1 and whole-tone figures. The corresponding trichords in the second half are from retrograde rows PR-R(PA), R(P4), R(PA), R(I3), and R(I9) (related at sum A, mapping F/F and B/B), rather than inversions PR-I11, I7, I1, Po, and P6. The substitute retrograde rows yield Picture trichords that are very similar to those of inversional rows (specifically, R(Pn) and I(n+3) rows yield two invariant notes per trichord; see ex. 5.43). The use of retrograde rows instead of inversional rows in the second

Figure 5.18. Second-sentence prime-inversion pairs in the "Lied der Lulu"

mm.		mm.	
498–502	vocal Lied P6	503–7	vocal Lied I6
498–500	Lulu P5 (alto sax)	503–4	Lulu I7 (alto sax)
500–2	violin 1 line	505–6	Contrabass line (altered)
498–99	PR I6 (horn)	503–5	PR P6 (horn)
499–501	cello line	504–6	violin line (altered)
501	Painter tetrachords from PR–P6 (strings)	506	Painter tetrachords from PR-I6 (strings)
500–1	violins, viola	505–6	violin II/Contrabass
502–3	wedge viola and cello bridges two phrases		

Example 5.43. Picture trichord invariances at PR-I1/R(PA) (open noteheads)

phrase of sentence 3 creates the impression of a palindromic center at this midpoint of the five sentences of the "Lied."

In the fourth sentence (mm. 516–21), the first vocal phrase row Lulu I5 is answered by Lulu P7 in the second phrase; Lulu I5 is left incomplete, and its final note A begins the second phrase as order position 1 of P7, which precedes order position 0 because of the characteristic opening turn figure of this row. The accompaniment consists not of P/I pairs but of chorale wholetone–based chords in the first phrase (see ex. 5.62) and whole-tone [026] trichords in the second.

The final, longest sentence of the "Lied" (mm. 522–28, 529–38) begins with three dyads on stopped horns from the Painter tetrachords (from R(PA)), which recall a similar gesture at the beginning of the "Lied" (ex. 5.41) and formally delineate the final phrase. The vocal rows in the first phrase, PR-P4, and I5 (overlapping by one pc) leading to BCI [0167] <Eb–Ab–A–D> and culminating on D6, are answered by inversional pairs at PR-IA (overlapping), P9 (at sum 2), and BC I [0167] <A–E–Eb–Bb>. The paired prime-inversion vocal phrases are reflected in the surrounding parts. Whereas the harmonies from the

Painter tetrachords are predominantly whole-tone+, the outer voices of the successive Painter tetrachords are predominantly [037] and [015] (see outer voices of Painter tetrachords in ex. 5.41), contrasting the two primary harmonic collections of the "Lied."

In the final bars (ex. 5.44), the vocal line [0167] <A–E–E♭–B♭> descends in a whole-tone+ context to end with a reference to Alwa, Lulu's next lover and victim. Over an {E♭,B♭} pedal bass, row Alwa PA appears in the two-voice counterpoint setting found in the rondo. The language changes from whole-tone based to 5-cycle when the Alwa motive appears, to lead back into the fifth strophe of Dr. Schön's five-strophe aria.

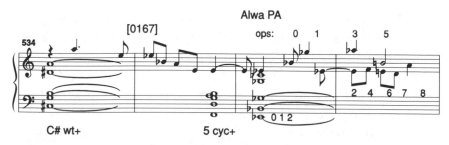

Example 5.44. Closing bars with Alwa reference, "Lied der Lulu," *Lulu*, Act II, mm. 534–37. Berg LULU Acts 1 & 2. Copyright 1964 by Universal Edition A.G., Wien. Copyright renewed. Revision © Copyright 1985 by Universal Edition A.G., Wien. All Rights Reserved. Used by permission of European American Music Distributors Corporation, sole U.S. and Canadian agent for Universal Edition A.G., Wien.

Lulu's Death   Lulu's blood-curdling death-cry chord in Act III, scene i (*Todesschrei*) is preceded by a 5-cycle+ collection that emerges from the end of the Countess's vows to start a new life (mm. 1290ff., ex. 5.45). This collection thins into an [0258] "Tristan" chord, <G♯–D–F♯–B> (the same chord that is held prior to the *Tristan* quote in the *Lyric Suite*, sixth movement; see ex. 5.25), which is sustained below Lulu's cries of "Nein, nein" set to [0167] <C–F–F♯–B> in the *Hauptrhythmus*. The two chords, which share dyad {B,F♯}, combine into [013679]—ironically, the characteristic chord of the Freedom motive. The death-cry chord itself is an aggregate from three segmental [0167]s. The interval [0167]s ascend in order, beginning with the lower {A,E,E♭,B♭}, climbing upward in successively smaller durations, as vertical interval 7 dyads, and culminating with {A,E} repeated in the upper register (mm. 1296ff.). The [0167] {C♯,G♯/G,D} similarly ascends to culminate in a repeated {C♯,G♯} dyad (mm.

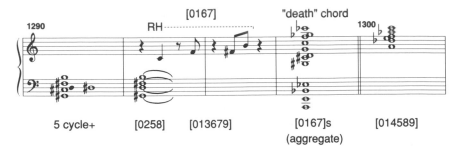

Example 5.45. Events surrounding Lulu's death, *Lulu*, Act III, mm. 1290ff.

1298ff.), and [0167] {F,C/B,F#} climbs to a repeated {F,C} (mm. 1299ff.). The hexachordal [014589] from these interval-class 5 dyads, one from each [0167], {A,E,F,C,C#,G#}, exploits the interval-class 5 component of [0167], but recombined in a 4-cycle of transpositions.

The hexachord continues over material from Dr. Schön's–Jack's row, arpeggiated and accompanied by its complementary [014589] hexachord in oscillating {D,B} and {B♭,E♭} dyads—{D,B,B♭,E♭} [0145] in the middle-voice—and trichord {F,F#,G} [012] in the lower voices (mm. 1301ff.). The music dissolves into material related to Dr. Schön–Jack, as Jack kills the Countess and takes his leave (mm. 1303–14). In the few bars preceding the Countess's *Liebestod* (mm. 1313–14), [0167]s at T1 combine into [012678] <E–A–B♭–E♭>, <D–A–A♭–E♭>, reasserting the original [01567]-based relationships of the death cry chord after the contrasting combination of T4-related [05]s in [014589]. The parallels between this passage—composed at the height of Berg's mature output—and procedures related to contrasts between the cyclic guises of interval-classes 6 and 4 in his first atonal work op. 2, no. 4 are striking.

DR. SCHÖN

The dual nature of Dr. Schön, the strong public man, a newspaper magnate, and the weak private man, slave to his passion for Lulu, is manifested in each of his three primary musical passages in the opera: the sonata in Act I, scenes ii and iii, the *Arietta* "Das mein Lebensabend" and the following *Kavatina* in Act II, scene i, and the five-strophe aria in Act II, scene i. In the course of the sonata, Dr. Schön descends from a position of strength and control over Lulu in the exposition and reprise to weakness and submission in the development and recapitulation. In the sonata, arietta, and aria, Schön's dual nature is reflected in the opposition of prime/strength and inversion/weakness forms of his rows and related materials. Dr. Schön regains his former position of dominance when his alter ego Jack the Ripper appears in Act III, along with the coda of the sonata music, to humiliate and murder Lulu. The three passages associated with Dr. Schön are interrelated primarily by the underlying basis of his row, but also by textual connections and recurring themes and motives.

Sonata The most notable formal feature of the sonata associated with Dr. Schön is its divided presentation, a feature it shares with many of the musical forms in the opera (fig. 5.19, in which corresponding passages are aligned horizontally). The exposition and a shortened reprise appear consecutively in Act I, scene ii (mm. 533–624, 625–68), but the coda of the reprise is cut short by the intrusion of the Painter (mm. 669–957) and does not resume until its extended statement as the interlude between Act I, scene ii and iii (mm. 958–92). The development and recapitulation of the sonata do not appear until the middle of Act I, scene iii (mm. 1208–88, 1289–1361). In the recapitulation, the coda music is again restated only briefly; it returns in its full form in Act III, scene ii, to accompany Jack's appearance (mm. 1235–65).

The musical divisions of the sonata are, as might be expected from Berg's earlier sonata form in Act II, scene i of *Wozzeck*, motivated by topics in the text: the condensed reprise of the exposition accompanies a shortened repeat of the textual topics associated with the main theme, transition, second theme, and closing-coda themes. Even subtle details in the ordering of topics are reflected in the musical setting; for instance, in the reprise, the first theme area is interrupted by the transition music (mm. 633–40), reflecting the intrusion of the dramatic topic associated with the transition.[114]

Most of the sonata's musical material is derived from the row associated with Dr. Schön (ex. 5.46), which has 5-cycle–based hexachords [013568]

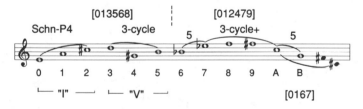

Example 5.46. Row of Dr. Schön at P4, intervallic properties

[012479], with interval-class 5s in 01, 67, AB.[115] The same interval-classes in 01 and AB allow for successive Schön rows to overlap by two notes (Pn with P(n+3) and I(n+8)), as occurs in the prologue when the "tiger" (Dr. Schön) is introduced, accompanied by rows Schn-P4 and I3, then Schn-P4 and I0 overlapping by two notes {C,G} (mm. 20–24). The interval-class 5 in AB and [016] in 9AB allow for overlap between Schön rows and BCI [0167}, as in the exten-

Figure 5.19. Form of Dr. Schön's sonata in Act I of *Lulu* (rows are the Schön rows)

	Exposition: mm. 533–624	First reprise: mm. 625–68	Second reprise: mm. 1289–1361
Main Theme:	mm. 533–53	mm. 625–32, 641–(53)	mm. 1289–98
A:	533–43 P8, P1/I8, P4, P5	625–32 P6, PB/I6, P4, P5	1289–95 overlapping P8, P6, I4, PB, IB
B:	544–46 IA, I5	641–46 IA, I5	1296 Lulu IA
A':	547–53 P2, P7/I2, P0, P6	647–(53) P2, P7	1297–98 P6
Trans.	554–86	633–40	1299–1303
A:	544–62 P9, P0, Lulu P6	P9, P0, Lulu P6	P9, P0, Lulu P6
	562 Theme2 foreshadowed		
B:	563–78 P8, PB		
A':	579–86 P9, P0, Lulu P6		
Theme2:	587–614	650–65	1304–55 expanded, "letter canon"
Gavotte	587–94 P3, P3, I8	648–55 P3, P3, I8	1304–25 RH
Musette	595–600 P7, I2	656–61 P7, main theme P8 canon	1326–35 [0167], RH
Gavotte	601–5 P3	662–66 P3	1336–50 Lulu row, Picture trichords
Musette	606–10 P4 main theme P8 two-part canon		1351–55 + Lulu row, [0164], RH, Picture trichords
Gavotte	611–14 P3		
Coda	615–24 P8, PR–P4	666–68 shortened	1356–61 + cadence chords
		958–92 extended	Act III, scene ii, mm. 1235–65
Development:	mm. 1209–36		
	mm. 1236–88		

sion of Schn-PA by [0167] <F#–C#–C–G> in the development of the sonata (mm. 1216–19).

The Schön row also has 3-cycle + segments in 345 and 789A, and these segments are reflected in the setting of the first theme of the sonata (ex. 5.47, mm. 533–34, 1289–91), Schn-P8, which has a P0 3-cycle segment {G♭,C,E♭} in 345 harmonized with the P1 3-cycle+ collection {F,G,B♭,C#,E} (including the first two notes <D♭,F> of the sonata main theme).[116] The setting balances interval-class 3s against 5s: the interval-classes between the theme and its counterpointing accompaniment are initially <5–1–1–5> over the 3-cycle collection, then in m. 534 they change to interval-class 3s as the accompaniment changes to a 5-cycle+ basis, with voice-leading also by interval-class 3 from <G♭3–A2> to <B♭3–G3>. In the continuation of the theme (m. 537), Schn-P4 then P5 are set in three-voice parallel 3-cycle [036]s (mm. 537–40, 628–32), which, with added notes from the melodic bass line, yield 3-cycle+ collections. Immediately following the initial main theme, simultaneous paired rows Schn-P1 and I8, at index 9, yield vertical odd intervals (mm. 535–36, ex. 5.47); added notes create a mostly 5-cycle context. The simultaneous prime and inversion forms (and their sum-9 relationship) foreshadow the texture for much of the later five-strophe aria.

In traditional sonata forms, the second theme material returns transposed. In the Schön sonata, however, transpositions occur within the first area. The first theme area is in a three-section ABA' (fig. 5.19): (1) main theme (MT) Schn-P8, P1/I8, P4, P5 (mm. 533–43); (2) inversional MTs from Schn-IA, I5 (mm. 544–46); and (3) MT transposed by T6 as Schn-P2 (altered, beginning with D5-B4, to imitate briefly the opening contour of inversional forms of the theme; cf. m. 544) and paired P7/I2 (mm. 547–53), followed by P0, P6. At T6, P2 and P8 are maximally dissimilar by hexachords, with only two common tones in corresponding hexachords, but the same sum-9 dyads obtain between P1/P8 and (T6)P7/I2. In the first reprise (mm. 625–32), MT returns transposed by T−2 at Schn-P6, a level at which three notes per hexachord are invariant, with paired PB/I6 at sum 5. In the development (m. 1228), the PB/I6 aligned rows appear at T6 P5/I0, yielding maximally dissimilar hexachords but maintaining sum 5. In the recapitulation, the P8 and P6 row levels of MT both appear (mm. 1289–98), but the subsequent prime and inversion forms are in canon rather than aligned: P6–PB against I4–IB at sum 10. The "B" section rows are omitted in the recapitulation, replaced by row Lulu IA, when she refers to the Prince (m. 1296). The final section is reduced to one MT statement at Schn-P6 (mm. 1297–98).

The coda theme features the Schön row, the principal row, and RH, all intertwined.[117] Dr. Schön initially enters to a brief but dramatic foreshadowing of the coda theme rising out of the dwindling ascending interval 1 cycles accompanying Schigolch's exit (mm. 530–31, example 5.48a); the theme is from Schn-

Example 5.47. Schön sonata, main theme, rows and cyclic structures, *Lulu*, Act I, mm. 533–37. Berg LULU Acts I & 2. Copyright 1964 by Universal Edition A.G., Wien. Copyright renewed. Revision © Copyright 1985 by Universal Edition A.G., Wien. All Rights Reserved. Used by permission of European American Music Distributors Corporation, sole U.S. and Canadian agent for Universal Edition A.G., Wien.

P4 divided into trichords 012, 345, 679, ABo, [037]s and [036], with a bass line 3-cycle+ collection <A–Ab–Eb–C> [0147]. In the coda theme of the exposition (mm. 615–24, ex. 5.48b) the Schön and principal rows are unfolded simultaneously; the initial Schön and principal row pairs, Schn-P8/PR-P1 and Schn-P4/PR-P4, share the maximum number of five invariant notes in corresponding hexachords. Within the Schön row, the tonal I–V allusion in the [037] in 012 and the 3-cycle [036] in 345 lends a stability, based on a referential Db, to the passage. This "tonal" interpretation is encouraged by the stepwise voice-leading throughout, implying resolutions of dissonances around the implied "key" of Db.[118]

Example 5.48a. Schön sonata, coda theme foreshadowed, *Lulu*, Act I, mm. 530–31

Example 5.48b. Schön sonata, coda theme, Schn and PR rows intertwined, *Hauptrhythmus* setting, *Lulu*, Act I, mm. 615–21. Berg LULU Acts 1 & 2. Copyright 1964 by Universal Edition A.G., Wien. Copyright renewed. Revision © Copyright 1985 by Universal Edition A.G., Wien. All Rights Reserved. Used by permission of European American Music Distributors Corporation, sole U.S. and Canadian agent for Universal Edition A.G., Wien.

The melody of the coda theme groups into five varied motivic figures, each with a gesture of a slow ascent and a dramatic descent, which group across the four-attack RHs that underlie the melody. The melodic figures have different intervals and order positions at each turn: Schn-P8 ()23560 whole-tone+ <E–F–G♭–E♭–D–G♯> (mm. 615–16), P4 0123 5-cycle + <E–A–C♯–D> (mm. 617–18), 4567 5-cycle+ <G♯–B–B♭–E♭> (mm. 619–20), 70345 <E♭–E–D–A♭–B> (mm. 622–23), and 789 <E♭–F–G♭> (m. 624). The first three figures gradually descend from high points of E♭5 to C♯5 and to B4, before the final two figures return to the higher registers at A♭5 and F♯6. The return of the first-figure gesture in the fourth creates a two-part form in mm. 615–21 and 622–25.

Harmonically, almost every chord in the coda theme is a form of [0258], a collection that can be either whole-tone+ or 3 cycle+ but also has a strongly "tonal" sound. The [0258] harmonies and stepwise voice-leading create the impression of consonant and dissonant notes, respectively, by tonal criteria. The initial chord, a [01469] <D♭-A♭-F-B-E>, recalls the op. 2 songs, except that the upper note E "resolves" up to F, the "third" of the chord—whereas the earlier motion was the opposite (cf. ex. 1.15, 3.37b, and 5.48b). Somewhat tonal as well is the congruence between the large and the small levels: the large-scale move from the D♭ to the concluding E (m. 625) is reflected in the opening vertical interval 3 <D♭-F♭> and the D♭ to E triads in the first two bars (mm. 615–16, ex. 5.48b). In cyclic terms, the bass 3-cycle+ <D♭–C–G–E–()–B♭> and overlapping C whole-tone+ cycle <B♭–F♯–F–E–D–C> reflect the two possible interpretations of the vertical [0258]s.

The expanded coda music in the interlude between Act I/scenes ii and iii (mm. 958–990) is in a large three-part form: A, mm. 958–67; B, mm. 968–78; and A' mm. 979–92. The A sections are the same as in the previous coda theme. The B section consists of fifteen melodic statements of the Schön row. In the lower voices, three simultaneous prime statements (Schn-P4, PB, and P8) in parallel Tn [047]s, characteristically at intervals <+7, +9>, are followed by three simultaneous inversional statements (Schn I5, I0, and I8) in parallel [037]s, intervals <+7, +8>, as a horizontal succession of the prime and inversion row forms that characterize the music associated with Dr. Schön. In the upper voice rows, the sonata main theme occurs in canonic inversionally related pairs Schn-P6 and I8 (mm. 968–69), T6, P0 and I2 (maximally dissimilar hexachords, but same sum 2) (mm. 970–71), and P6 combined with P0 (mm. 972–75). The end bars of the B section (mm. 976–78) lead from [0167] <A–D–E♭–A♭> over a <D–A> bass through A♭ to D♭. Prior to the statement of A' and the return of D♭, a transposed T7 statement of the first bar of the coda theme on a bass A♭ acts as a "dominant" to the following D♭-based theme (m. 978), strongly supporting the tonal allusion.

"Das mein Lebensabend" and the Five-Strophe Aria   In "Das mein Lebensabend" and
the following *Kavatine*, inversional forms reflect Schön's desperation and para-
noia; as he becomes violent, however, the prime forms of his material return.
The text of "Das mein Lebensabend" refers to the "circle" of Schön's family; the
main row, Schn-19, shares its trichordal pitch-class content with his son's row,
Alwa P4 (ex. 5.37). The arietta divides in two sections (Act II, mm. 40–50, ex.
5.49, and mm. 51–60) with the return of the opening setting at the parallel text

Example 5.49. Schön arietta "Das mein Lebensabend" with ostinato rhythm, *Lulu*, Act II,
mm. 40–41. Berg LULU Acts 1 & 2. Copyright 1964 by Universal Edition A.G., Wien.
Copyright renewed. Revision © Copyright 1985 by Universal Edition A.G., Wien. All Rights
Reserved. Used by permission of European American Music Distributors Corporation, sole
U.S. and Canadian agent for Universal Edition A.G., Wien.

Das mein Familienkreis, but also into three parts through the two durational series
underlying the bass ostinato, which group into aba' sections: first series, mm.
40–45; second series, mm. 46–53; first series return, mm. 54–60. The gapped
5-cycle ostinato bass <D–Eb–Bb–Ab–G–C#–F#> (Schn-19 56789AB) is a
seven-note series set isorhythmically to two repeating durational series, the first
of six durations, the second of eight. The first durational series is in units of
<2–3–1–1–1–4>, totaling twelve rhythmic units (in sixteenth notes; three
quarter-note beats); this durational series repeats eight times over seven repetitions of the pitch series (mm. 40–45). The second durational series is
<1–1–3–1–1–1–3–4>, totaling fifteen rhythmic units (in sixteenths; three
and three-quarters quarter-note beats); it repeats nine times (mm. 46–53), again
set isorhythmically over the pitch series, which recurs about ten times, but the
ninth instance of the rhythm series is altered to <1–1–3–1–1–1–4> (m. 53)
as a transition back to the first series <2–3–1–1–1–4>. The second durational
series also has a section in three-part canon at durational intervals of four six-

teenths (mm. 50–53; a fourth voice varies the bass pitch and durational ostinatos). The canonic intervals of four and eight sixteenths yield the minimum
number of simultaneous attacks possible between statements of the second
rhythmic pattern, with a macrorhythm of continuous sixteenths. The restated
first series theme repeats seven times, but this time the pitch series breaks down
(m. 57). The arietta returns briefly in Act III, scene ii, after Jack has stabbed the
Countess and is looking for a towel to wipe off the blood (mm. 1305–6), where
the ostinato <D–E♭–B♭–A♭–G–C♯–F♯> occurs in changing rhythms of proportions <1–1–1–1–1–3>, again <1–1–1–1–1–3>, and <1–3–1–1–1–1>,
under the complement collection <A–E–C–B–F> in the voice.

Dr. Schön's five-strophe aria features an extended passage of paired prime
and inversional material reflecting the two sides of his character.[119] The aria is
characterized throughout by 5-cycle collections, principally by combinations of
the 5-cycle elements of Schön's row, the BC I [0167], and, in the third strophe,
by the materials of the Countess Geschwitz, and by the simultaneous presentation of prime and inversion forms of materials, principally at sums 9 and 7 (ex.
5.50). The beginning of the first strophe pairs Schön rows P2 and I7, with
[0167] {G,G♯,C♯,D}, in a pattern that proceeds cyclically throughout. With the
return of [01378] {E,A,B,C,F} on the downbeat of mm. 553, the aria ends,
immediately followed by the *tumultuoso* as Lulu fires five shots into Dr. Schön.

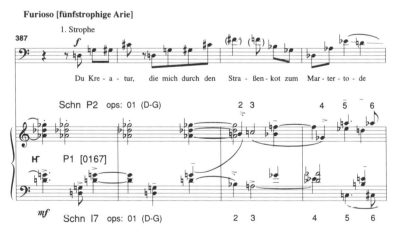

Example 5.50. First strophe opening of Schön's five-strophe aria, *Lulu*, Act II, mm. 387–90.
Berg LULU Acts 1 & 2. Copyright 1964 by Universal Edition A.G., Wien. Copyright renewed.
Revision © Copyright 1985 by Universal Edition A.G., Wien. All Rights Reserved. Used by
permission of European American Music Distributors Corporation, sole U.S. and Canadian
agent for Universal Edition A.G., Wien.

Schön's Death The *tumultuoso* passage following the aria restates the sum-9 {E, A,B,C,F} with {B♭} combination of the *tumultuoso* preceding the aria. As Lulu fires at Dr. Schön, the five revolver shots are set in five sixteenth-note units, against the four-sixteenths–based meter and in counterpoint with continuous RHs (ex. 5.38b, mm. 553–55). The RHs then continue in various canonic relationships, in a mini-monritmica. In the course of Schön's death scene, his row and the principal row occur in greater frequency, until Schön's P4 row is absorbed back into the principal row P4 (mm. 587–604, ex. 5.51). At the point of Schön's death, the Countess suddenly emerges, and the {E–A–B–C–F} [01378] motive that ultimately unites the three characters, Alwa, Dr. Schön, and the Countess, reappears (mm. 605–8).

Example 5.51. Row Schn-P4 absorbed into PR P4 at Dr. Schön's death, *Lulu*, Act II, mm. 591–602 (rhythmic proportions of Schn P4 order positions given above stave, units = quarter notes)

Dramatically, the absorption of Schön's row back into the principal material of the opera graphically depicts his demise; musically, the absorption reverses the original derivation of his row. Dr. Schön's row is derived from the principal row by a numerical series of order-position extractions PR 02591468B37A, which corresponds to the numerical series <2–3–4–4–3–2–2–3–4–4–3>. Schön's death is illustrated by, first, his own P4 (Act II, mm. 587–90), then Schn-P4 and PR-P4 intertwined, with the latter in quarter notes, so that the duration of the notes of Schn-P4 reflect the order-position relationships between the two rows (Act II, mm. 591–602, ex. 5.51), and finally only PR-P4

(Act II, mm. 603–4), with the Schön row completely subsumed as he dies. This remarkable illustration of a dramatic death by a musical means integral to the entire opera (row derivations by order-position operations) indicates the level to which Berg had integrated his language with the text in *Lulu*.

Jack the Ripper   In Act III, scene ii, when Jack appears, most of the music associated with Dr. Schön returns: the sonata first theme (mm. 1188–92, 1313–15), the coda theme (mm. 1193–99) and coda music (mm. 1235–61), the *Kavatine* (mm. 1200-29), and music from the arietta "Das mein Lebensabend" (mm. 1305–6). The second hexachord of Schn-P4 is used prominently as a chord, ordered <C–F–F♯–G–B♭–E♭>, underlying the first hexachord of the row (Act III, mm. 1310–14). Whereas in Acts I and II Schön's music signaled his progressive descent into death, in Act III the same music marks Schön's re-emergence as Jack the Ripper and the death of Lulu. The evocative coda music, rewritten in $\frac{3}{4}$, is particularly effective in accompanying the reversal of the two roles. The reason for the renotation from $\frac{4}{4}$ to $\frac{3}{4}$ is not clear, however, since the effect is the same; the change recalls similar apparently inexplicable renotations in Berg's atonal music.

ALWA

Alwa is a central figure in the opera; along with Lulu he is the only character to appear in every scene. Although he is Dr. Schön's son, he becomes one of Lulu's suitors even while his father is alive. After Schön's death, Alwa conspires to help Lulu escape from prison, but, as with the other characters, his association with her brings disaster. In Paris he loses the fortune he gained from selling his father's newspaper empire, and in London, reduced to living off Lulu's prostitution, he is killed by her second client, the Negro. In the *Lulu* plays, Alwa is a writer, but Berg changed his occupation to a composer and identified himself with the character.[120] In the prologue, the Animal Tamer (played by the Acrobat) invites the audience into the show but uses Alwa's row in his vocal line (mm. 9–12, Alwa-P9; mm. 73–75, Alwa-P4 with english horn and alto saxophone in the contour of the third rondo theme), indicating that the invitation stems from Alwa/Alban Berg.[121] The first words in the opera itself are Alwa's "May I enter?" (m. 86, *Darf ich eintreten?*) as he enters the room where the Painter and Dr. Schön are eying Lulu; his question also allows the audience to "enter" the opera. In Act I, scene iii, Berg's association with Alwa is marked dramatically when Alwa muses that Lulu's life would make an interesting, if improbable, opera, to the strains of the opening chords of *Wozzeck* (Act I, scene iii, mm. 1095–109), followed by brief restatements of the music associated with Lulu's first two husbands, the Medical Specialist and the Painter, then the coda theme from Dr. Schön's sonata, as Alwa describes the plot of such an opera (mm. 1100–1112). In Act II, scene ii (m. 826), Berg provides critical commentary to his own opera when the Acrobat tells Alwa: "You've composed an opera of horrors in which my fiancée's [Lulu's] two legs have the principal roles and which no decent theatre will put on."[122] Berg's identification with Alwa is also evident in Alwa's *Hymne* to Lulu (Act II, scene ii), when he compares her body to music; Berg changed the musical terms used by Wedekind to include references to the movements of the *Lyric Suite*.[123]

Musical Materials   Alwa is represented musically by his own row, derived by a 7-cycle of order positions from the principal row (ex. 5.37) and derived material. His row has the same 5-cycle–based hexachords [013568]/[012479] and trichords [037] [036] [027] [016] as Dr. Schön's row. In the opening of Act I, scene i, Alwa's 5-cycle row segments are intertwined with those of the principal row, revealing the high level of invariance between the two rows. Alwa's first line (Act I, m. 86), "May I enter?" (*Darf ich entreten*), to <F–D–G> 234 of PR-P0, is also Alwa P9 123; the first hexachords of the two rows share [02479] {C,E,F,D,A}. The [037] partitions of the principal row in this passage, 235 <G–Bb–Eb> and 014 <A–C–E> (cf. ex. 5.36d) foreshadow the opening "major" and "minor" trichords of the Schön and Alwa rows. Alwa's row appears only a few times before his rondo music: as P7 in Act I, scene i (mm. 98–99), again in combinations close to the diatonic hexachords of the principal row, and in Act I, scene ii, after the death of the Painter, where Berg indulges in a little twelve-tone parody, setting Alwa's words "No one at the office knows what to write" (concerning a "revolution in Paris") to uncharacteristic rotated retrograde inversion forms of the Alwa row (mm. 789–93, 928–30, and 945–46).[124]

Rondo   Alwa's principal music appears in the rondo of Act II, scenes i and ii, which surrounds the middle of the opera symmetrically, and the partial return of this music in Act III (figs. 5.20, 5.21). The rondo accompanies the dialogue between Alwa and Lulu in Act II, scenes i and ii; like the Schön sonata, the rondo is interrupted by musical-dramatic interjections, is separated into two scenes, and is partially restated in Act III, scene ii.[125] Alwa's rising passion in the Act II, scene i section of the rondo is illustrated in his vocal line, which progresses successively from speaking (mm. 243ff.) to *Sprechstimme* (mm. 268ff.) to a brief outburst in half- and full singing (m. 273), before retreating to *parlando gesungen* (mm. 275ff.), then proceeding to *poco cantabile* (mm. 281ff), half singing (mm. 285–86), and finally to full voice *molto cantabile* with the third rondo theme (mm. 320ff). The successive stages in Alwa's vocal expression recall the begin-

Figure 5.20. Form of Alwa's Rondo in *Lulu* (h = half note, dh = dotted half note, q = quarter note, dq = dotted quarter note)

Rondo		Tempo	Sonata
foreshadowing:			
R ritornello	Act I, scene iii mm. 1020–1040		introduction
	Act II, scene i mm. 145–72	$\frac{3}{4}$ dh = 56	
	interlude: canon mm. 173–94	$\frac{6}{4}$	
transition	mm. 195–208	$\frac{2}{2}$ h = 56, $\frac{6}{4}$, $\frac{3}{4}$	bridge
R ritornello	mm. 209–23	$\frac{2}{2}$ h = 84	transition theme
	interlude mm. 224–42	$\frac{6}{4}$ dh = 69	
I			Exposition
A rondo theme I	mm. 243–49	$\frac{4}{4}$, Tempo I q = 69	main theme
	interlude: Manservant mm. 250–61 subito recit.		
B episode	mm. 262–73	a tempo (I) 262–68 268–73	transition theme
	interlude: Dr. Schön m. 274		
A rondo theme II	mm. 275–80	a tempo (I)	transition theme
	mm. 281–86	Tempo I	theme 2
	interlude: Manservant mm. 287–93		
	interlude: Dr. Schön m. 294		
	interlude: Manservant mm. 295–97		
C episode	mm. 298–306	Tempo I	theme 2
	mm. 306–9	$\frac{4}{4} - \frac{2}{4}$, Tempo II q = 54	transition
	interlude: Acrobat mm. 310–13		
	interlude: Dr. Schön mm. 313–17		
C episode	mm. 318–19	$\frac{4}{4} - \frac{2}{4}$, Tempo II q = 54	transition
A rondo theme III	mm. 320–24	$\frac{3}{4} - \frac{2}{4}$, Tempo II	closing theme
codetta	mm. 325–36	$\frac{2}{4}, \frac{3}{4}, \frac{4}{4}$, Tempo II	codetta

Figure 5.20. Form of Alwa's Rondo in *Lulu* (h = half note, dh = dotted half note q = quarter note, dq = dotted quarter note) (*Continued*)

Rondo			Sonata
II			Development
Act II/scene ii			
R ritornello	mm. 1001–4		introduction
B (mm. 275–80)	mm. 1004–9	animato	transition theme
R ritornello	mm. 1010–15	a tempo	introduction
transition	mm. 1016–29	$\frac{4}{4} - \frac{3}{2}$ Tempo II	transition
R ritornello	mm. 1030–37	$\frac{3}{2}$, quasi Tempo I	introduction
A rondo theme III	mm. 1038–47	Tempo II	closing theme
D Lulu row	mm. 1048–54	Tempo I	new material
transition/codetta	mm. 1055–59	accel.–allarg.	transition
III			Recapitulation
A (mm. 243–49)	mm. 1059–65	$\frac{4}{4}$, a Tempo I	main theme
B (mm. 265–67)	mm. 1066–69	animato	bridge
A (mm. 281–86)	mm. 1069–74	a tempo	theme 2 (at T1)
C (mm. 318–19)	mm. 1075–76	$\frac{4}{4} - \frac{2}{4}$, Tempo II	transition
A (mm. 320–22)	mm. 1077–79	$\frac{3}{2}$, Tempo II	closing theme
R ritornello	mm. 1080–86	$\frac{2}{4}$, Tempo II	introduction
transition/musette:	mm. 1087–96	$\frac{4}{4}$, grazioso	
coda/hymn:	mm. 1097–1150	$\frac{12}{8}$ sostenuto dq = 44–54 quasi Tempo II	
introduction	mm. 1097–1101		
D:	mm. 1102–11		
E:	mm. 1112–30		
F:	mm. 1131–36		
musette (rondo):	mm. 1137–44		
Coda:	mm. 1145–50		

Figure 5.21. Rondo music from *Lulu*, Act II, scene i, in Act III, scene ii

II/i,	mm. 265–7	B	III/ii,	mm. 957–58	T = −2
	mm. 1059–65	A		mm. 959–73	2:1 augmentation
	mm. 1102–11	hymn		mm. 974–90	varied 2:1 augmentation
	mm. 1131–35	hymn		mm. 991–97	varied 2:1 augmentation
	m. 1139	hymn		mm. 998–99	varied repetition

nings of op. 4, no. 1 and of Act I, scene ii of *Wozzeck*, but in the context of *Lulu* they associate Alwa with the Animal Tamer, who has a similar series of successive changes in voice quality in the prologue.

The rondo, in three large sections followed by the hymn, is characterized by a ritornello based on Lulu's Freedom motive and related rondo themes, each derived from Alwa's row. Characteristically, the form may be described in terms of a rondo or a sonata form (fig. 5.20). The main requirement of a sonata form, a transposed recapitulation of the second theme, occurs when the second rondo theme (rondo theme II), first heard in Act II, mm. 281–86, 298–306, returns transposed at T1 in the recapitulation (mm. 1069–74). The rondo has two tempos, Tempo I with quarter note = 69 (recalling the *Lyric Suite*) and Tempo II with quarter = 54; the latter differentiating the C episode, rondo theme II, and the codetta. The rondo music is introduced in Act I, scene iii (mm. 1020–40), when Alwa is alone with Lulu in her dressing room at the theatre; part 1 appears in Act II, scene i, after an introductory section featuring the ritornello freedom motive (mm. 145–242). The middle section is developmental, with some added material, and part 3 is recapitulatory, omitting only a secondary theme from part 1 (from mm. 275–80), which also appears in the development section (mm. 1004–19). The hymn acts as a developmental coda, with some new material added.

The three Rondo themes are based on the Alwa row, in a consistent opening contour, initially <+8, −3, +5>, more generally as relative contour <0213> and in a characteristic pattern of unfolding by repetition with one added note each time. The distinctive contour also migrates to other rows and material in the episodes, acting as a unifying device. The harmonies vary from whole-tone+ collections to 5-cycle collections with strong triadic or tonal implications, from the [037] and [036] trichords in the Alwa row 012 and 345, and also from the 5-cycle–based Picture trichords, which recur throughout the rondo music in connection with Lulu.

Rondo theme I consists of a slightly altered Alwa P2 (omitting 6 and 8) to a rotated P4 (omitting 6, ordered 79AB, sequential at T2 with the previous P2 579AB) (ex. 5.52a). The initial melodic C♯–D changes the harmony from a 5-

Example 5.52a. Rondo theme 1, *Lulu*, Act II, mm. 243–49. Berg LULU Acts 1 & 2. Copyright 1964 by Universal Edition A.G., Wien. Copyright renewed. Revision © Copyright 1985 by Universal Edition A.G., Wien. All Rights Reserved. Used by permission of European American Music Distributors Corporation, sole U.S. and Canadian agent for Universal Edition A.G., Wien.

Example 5.52b. Sketch of row Alwa P2, with derived [0123]s from 059A, 138B, 2467

cycle {C♯,B,E,F♯} to a C whole-tone+ collection {D,E,F♯,B}, and the theme is set in mostly whole-tone+ collections, based on [026]s in descending interval 1-based accompaniment, until the closing 5-cycle harmonies from the Picture trichords (mm. 248ff.) appear. The [026] harmonies create an impression of a series of dominant chords moving by "chromatic" (1-cycle) voice-leading, lending a directed motion to the passage strongly reminiscent of late-nineteenth-century tonal music. The theme is set with similar whole-tone+ harmonies, from Alwa P4/P6 in Act I, scene iii (mm. 1020–33) and later in Act II, scene i (mm. 1059–65) and Act III, scene ii (mm. 960–73), where the rows have canonic voices at T5: Alwa P2/P7, P4/P9 (with the maximum number of four invariant notes in corresponding hexachords).

An important motive, 1-cycle [0123], initially from Alwa P2 579A <E♭–G♭–E–F> (m. 245), recurs throughout the inner voices in the theme and is especially prominent in the following B section as <+2, −1, −2>, from the end of m. 249 (ex. 5.52a). In the brief rondo passage in Act I, scene iii (mm. 1020–40), Alwa's vocal line consists almost exclusively of concatenated [0123]s except for row Alwa-P4 towards the end (mm. 1036–38). A sketch from Berg's materials for *Lulu* shows a derivation of three [0123]s from the Alwa row in 138B, 2467, and 159A (ex. 5.52b).

The second rondo theme, in two interrupted statements (mm. 281–86, 298–306), consists of Alwa P4 unfolded in four successively longer statements of two, three, six, and finally twelve notes (from <E–C–A–D–B–F–B♭–A♭–E♭–F–G♭–G>), in a mostly whole-tone+ context, with virtually continuous [0123]s in the inner voices. The theme's first half dissolves, as Alwa breaks off his thoughts (mm. 285–86), into a repeated group of P4 row segments ([013] <B–C–D>, [06] <G–C♯>, [05] <A–E>, and [0257] <F–B♭–G♯–D♯>; the missing note, F♯, begins the following Manservant interruption (m. 287). At the corresponding point in the theme's second half (m. 302), the row segments recur, down by TA (mm. 302–3), then sequenced at T1 (mm. 304–305); the three transposition levels T0–TA–T1 outline the intervals of the upper voice [013]. In part 3 of the overall form, rondo theme II returns in a single statement, but, unusually for the rondo, transposed up a half step (mm. 1069–74). The transposition corresponds to the second-theme transposition in the recapitulation of the sonata; the T1 level creates the minimal presence of two invariant notes in corresponding hexachords of the Alwa row, but also heightens the passion in Alwa's tone at the prospect of "ein Kuß!" Surrounding sections are, however, not transposed from their previous levels.

The three statements of the rondo theme III, the only theme to appear in all three parts of the rondo, are linked by textual allusions to Lulu's eyes: "A spirit arriving in Paradise and rubbing the sleep out of its eyes" (Act II, mm. 320–24), "your eyes shimmer like the surface of a deep well into which a stone has been thrown" (mm. 1038–47) and "Were it not for your large child-like eyes" (1077–79).[126] Rondo theme III (mm. 320–24) consists of Alwa P1 in a single statement and appears in an extended form in part 2 followed by Alwa P8 (mm. 1038–43, ex. 5.53). The harmonization is 5-cycle based, with a strongly implied tonal context of an F♯–C♯ chord motion, extended to G♯ (m. 1044), which "realizes" the implied I–VII in the trichords {C♯,A,F♯} 012 and {B,G♯,D} 345 of Alwa P1—recalling the tonal implications of the coda theme of the Schön sonata.

Example 5.53. Rondo theme III, *Lulu*, Act II, mm. 1037–41. Berg LULU Acts 1 & 2. Copyright 1964 by Universal Edition A.G., Wien. Copyright renewed. Revision © Copyright 1985 by Universal Edition A.G., Wien. All Rights Reserved. Used by permission of European American Music Distributors Corporation, sole U.S. and Canadian agent for Universal Edition A.G., Wien.

As Alwa unreservedly expresses his passion for Lulu, an exquisitely romantic passage ensues (mm. 306–9), interrupted, as is characteristic of Alwa's music throughout the opera: as Alwa sighs over Lulu, the Acrobat sticks his head up but is motioned away by Lulu and seen by an onlooking Dr. Schön, in a scenario characteristic of a slapstick comedy (mm. 311–17). The material accompanying Alwa's ardor is a partitioned two-part counterpoint from his row (ex. 5.54) in

Example 5.54. Alwa's two-part counterpoint from P5 and P9, *Lulu*, Act II, mm. 306–9. Berg LULU Acts 1 & 2. Copyright 1964 by Universal Edition A.G., Wien. Copyright renewed. Revision © Copyright 1985 by Universal Edition A.G., Wien. All Rights Reserved. Used by permission of European American Music Distributors Corporation, sole U.S. and Canadian agent for Universal Edition A.G., Wien.

which two non-segmental motives are created, from 0135 whole tone+ [0135] <+8,+2,−9>, relative contour <1230>, and the familiar 1-cycle [0123] from 2467. The gesture is also generated from inverted rows, and the sketches show many derivations of the two-part counterpoint, with altered intervals, from Alwa and principal rows. The two-part counterpoint creates step-wise voice-leading in parallel tenths, which, from an initial quasi-tonal succession, dissolves into 5-cycle collections. The counterpoint appears initially from Alwa rows P5, P9, and P2, in successive "triadic" levels of T = 4,5 (mm. 306–19); returns in the codetta after rondo theme III, in three statements from Alwa P8, P3, and P4, T = 7,1 (the levels forming a [015] subset of the melodic [0135], mm. 323–28) in conjunction with the Picture trichords; after rondo theme III in part 2, once, from Alwa P3 (mm. 1044–45); and in part 3, once, from Alwa P2 (mm. 1075–76 correspond with mm. 318–19); it is associated each time with Alwa's passion.

The two motives from the two-part counterpoint are also used independently of their derivation and, as happens elsewhere with regard to other materials in the opera, actually appear before their derived statements. Set [0123] appears throughout the rondo; the [0135] upper-voice motive appears near the end of the B section (m.279) in string and piano chords, and later as the upper voice of segmental and non-segmental Alwa row tetrachords, especially in the hymn, with the same contour but altered intervals.

The concluding hymn is Alwa's erotic song of praise to Lulu, in which he compares parts of her body to musical forms (fig. 5.20). It opens with a distinctive texture of pizzicato strings doubled by the piano and harp, setting trichords of the Alwa row—[037], [036], [027], and [016]—in the familiar <021> opening contour of the rondo theme (ex. 5.55). The melody is from the principal row at P7, but <C–A–D> is also a segment of Alwa P4 <u>123</u> (recalling a similar doubling of notes between these two rows in Alwa's initial statement in Act I, scene i), in

Example 5.55. Opening of Alwa's hymn, *Lulu*, Act II, mm. 1097–1101. Berg LULU Acts 1 & 2. Copyright 1964 by Universal Edition A.G., Wien. Copyright renewed. Revision © Copyright 1985 by Universal Edition A.G., Wien. All Rights Reserved. Used by permission of European American Music Distributors Corporation, sole U.S. and Canadian agent for Universal Edition A.G., Wien.

an uncharacteristically strongly metric setting of hemiola duple rhythms against the triple divisions of the $\frac{12}{8}$. This opening section dissolves in a cascading descent of [0167]s (m. 1101), a gesture which recurs as a cadential element in the first part of the hymn, dividing it into mm. 1097–101, 1102–6, 1107–11, and 1112ff.

In the course of the hymn, the Alwa trichords are stated vertically, Alwa-PB <B–E–G>, <C–F#–A>, <F–Bb–Eb>, and <D–Ab–Db>, with the upper-voice whole-tone [0268] <G–A–Eb–Db> extracted, transposed, and combined with other materials, such as the Picture trichords. The Alwa row tetrachords (mm. 1131–36) appear with the [0123] motive as the upper-voice <u>26A7</u>, over cyclic tetrachords: whole-tone+ [0148] <G♭–B♭–D–F>, 3-cycle+ [0147] <A–C–D♯–E> and whole-tone+ [0146] <G♯–B–C♯–G>, with G "resolving" to F♯ over 5-cycle [0257] <G♯–B–C♯–F♯>. The upper-voice motive of the Alwa two-part counterpoint also dominates the texture, increasing in density successively by parallel [04]s, [037]s, and finally [0158] chords (mm. 1135–36). At a climactic moment, the harmony becomes exclusively whole-tone, the cycle associated with Lulu, on a pause at the "Andante" of desire in m. 1110 on [0268] {D,F♯,G♯,C}.[127] The final cadence of the hymn and of Act II (mm. 1147–50, ex. 5.56) builds from the low register, combining 3-cycle [0369]s and [0167]s and

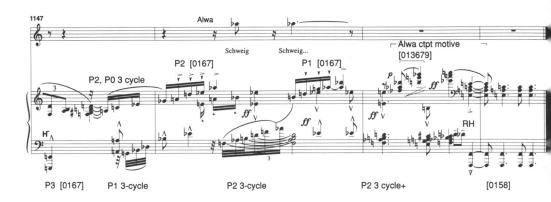

Example 5.56. End of Act II, *Lulu*, mm. 1147–50. Berg LULU Acts 1 & 2. Copyright 1964 by Universal Edition A.G., Wien. Copyright renewed. Revision © Copyright 1985 by Universal Edition A.G., Wien. All Rights Reserved. Used by permission of European American Music Distributors Corporation, sole U.S. and Canadian agent for Universal Edition A.G., Wien.

adding the upper motive of the Alwa two-part counterpoint <D♭6 – B♭6 – C7 – E4> (m. 1149), harmonized by T6-related [037]s {F♭,A♭,D♭} and {D,G,B♭} combining into [013679] (from Lulu's Freedom motive). Alwa's cadential chord {F,E,A,C}, [0158] from Alwa P4 012 <E–C–A> with the bass note F representing Lulu, concludes the act, set in the RH. The voice-leading in the succession of 3-cycle [0369]s to the final chord suggests resolution: the middle voice <F–A♭–B–D> moves by oblique and stepwise motion to <F–E–A–C>.

Alwa's Death In Act III the Countess Geschwitz brings Lulu's portrait to the attic in London and, in a quartet, she, Schigolch, Alwa, and Lulu remember the past, in a recapitulation of some of the rondo music (fig. 5.21). Rondo theme III sounds for a final time after Alwa's death in Act III (mm. 1120–22) as a grim reminder of the love for Lulu that lead to his demise. The theme appears as Alwa P8, over a drone A – E/C♯ – G♯ [0158], holding A – E with the primary transpositional level of Alwa's cadence chords <F−A−C−E>. Alwa dies at the hands of Lulu's second client, the Negro, vainly trying to protect her; the return of the Painter's RH-based *monoritimica* with this second client thus reflects Alwa's death. The funeral music following Alwa's death, described below, is from the variations on the Wedekind song.

COUNTESS GESCHWITZ

The Countess Geschwitz enters in Act II, scene i and appears in each subsequent scene. Alone among Lulu's lovers she is selfless: she sacrifices her liberty and health to get Lulu out of prison (Act II, scene ii), her body to save Lulu from the Acrobat's blackmail (Act III, scene i), and finally her life as she tries to rescue Lulu from prostitution and Jack the Ripper (Act III, scene ii). Because of her devotion to Lulu with little reward, her death is perhaps the most tragic in the opera.[128] Unlike Lulu's other principal lovers, Dr. Schön and Alwa, however, the Countess has no associated large form. Aside from the few moments in Act I, scene iii when Alwa is alone on stage in Lulu's dressing room (mm. 1095−112), however, the Countess has only completely solo passages: in Act III, scene ii her contemplation of suicide (mm. 1146−87), her determination to leave Lulu and get on with her life (mm. 1279−91), and her "Liebestod" (mm. 1315−26), which ends the opera.

Musical Materials The materials associated with the Countess Geschwitz have their origins in a derivation from the principal row by extracting every fifth note, or a 5-cycle on order positions. The result (CG-5), a rotated retrograde of the 7-cycle order position creating Alwa's row, was further altered (ex. 5.57).[129] The partitioning of this derived row to yield the three collections associated with the Countess has its source in the derivations from the principal row. In the early sketches, three collections, [05] and two [02479]s, are partitioned from the row in two ways: [05] 2,9, [02479]s 01345 and 678AB; and [05] 2,7, [02479]s 01345 and 689AB (cf. exx. 5.36n−o). In the initial 5-cycle Countess row (CG-5), an [05] and residue [02479] and [01378] are similarly extracted and used as collections (CG-C). The prime and inversion forms that share the same [05] differ in only one note in their respective [02479]s and (Tn-class) [01378]/[01578]s: CG-CP1 {C♯,G♯} {D,C,E,G,A} {F,E♭,G♭,B♭,B}, and CG-CI8 {C♯,G♯} {A,G,C,D,F} and {B,G♭,E,E♭,B♭}. The collections are labeled by the lower note of the interval 7 realization of the [05] in prime, and by the upper note in inversion.[130] In many cases, the two five-note collections are aligned, yielding dyads of mostly even intervals (ex. 5.58); these are grouped with the similar Medical Specialist and Painter dyads in Act III, scene i (cf. exx. 5.36b and j).

The residue notes left over from an extracted [05] in 1,5 of the Countess's 5-cycle row are also used as a ten-note row, but inverted and ordered from order

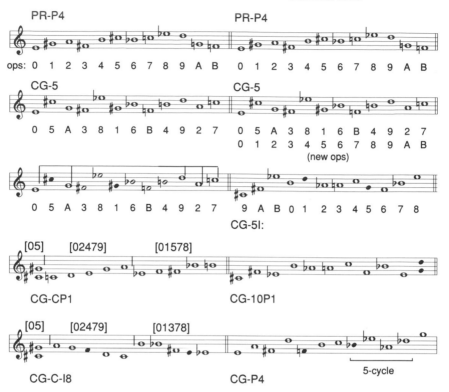

Example 5.57. Materials associated with the Countess Geschwitz

Example 5.58. Rhythmic palindromes with Countess materials CG-CP1 and I8, *Lulu*, Act II, mm. 89–91. Berg LULU Acts 1 & 2. Copyright 1964 by Universal Edition A.G., Wien. Copyright renewed. Revision © Copyright 1985 by Universal Edition A.G., Wien. All Rights Reserved. Used by permission of European American Music Distributors Corporation, sole U.S. and Canadian agent for Universal Edition A.G., Wien.

position 9, with the [05] as an accompanying harmony (CG-10). A twelve-note version, with the [05] restored, appears only in the film music interlude, with pitch-classes in order positions 7 and 8 exchanged—E♭ and B♭ in row CG-P4; the exchange creates a four-note 5-cycle <B♭–E♭–A♭–D♭> in the row). If the twelve-note CG-P4, Alwa-P4, and Schön-P4 rows are compared, as they appear successively in the film music, a high degree of similarity is revealed; two of the three notes per trichord are invariant in all three rows (except for the final trichord of Schön-P4/CG-P4 with one note invariant) (ex. 5.37), reflecting their status as Lulu's three principal lovers.

The other characteristic feature of the Countess is the setting of her material into series of palindromic accelerating and decelerating rhythms (ex. 5.58). These paired opposite rhythms, ultimately circular, suggest the dual nature of the Countess, as Lulu observes in Act III, scene i: "You are no human thing . . . not like others. Not enough for a man's anatomy. And you've too much brain in your skull to be a woman" (mm. 276–83). Lulu's remarks, although crude and cruel, point out the problems facing the Countess in society at that time.[131] The symmetrical cyclic rhythms are familiar from Berg's atonal music.

The Countess appears at the outset of Act II, scene i, marked musically by her 5-cycle–based collections and ten-note row; after leaving the house, she sneaks back inside (mm. 88–93), accompanied by her collections in a palindromic rhythm (ex. 5.58) in vertical dyads. In the Countess's appearances in Schön's five-strophe aria, her 5-cycle materials are part of the overall 5-cycle orientation. She returns in Act II, scene ii, as Lulu's savior, exchanging places with her in the hospital after purposely contracting cholera, then follows her to Paris in Act III, scene i, where Lulu uses her to entice the Acrobat into a situation where Schigolch can kill him. In Act III, scene ii, the Countess again returns, ever faithful, bringing Lulu's portrait, but Lulu again spurns her and retreats to the street.

Suicide Scene   Alone and in despair in the attic in the final scene, the Countess contemplates suicide (Act III, scene ii, mm. 1146–87), in a passage governed by 5-cycle harmonies and 3-cycle transpositional levels. The passage divides into two parts, mm. 1146–74 and 1174–87. Part 1 subdivides into five sections, corresponding to the methods of suicide she contemplates: a revolver for ten bars (mm. 1146–55), drowning for eight bars (mm. 1156–63), a knife for six bars (mm. 1164–69), a hanging for three bars (mm. 1170–72), then just "quickly" for two bars (mm. 1172–73) (fig. 5.22). The alternating accelerando and decelerando rhythms, along with the ascending and descending prime and inversion forms of material that accompany her actions, reflect her indecision as to how and whether to kill herself.

Figure 5.22. The Countess's suicide scene, part I, *Lulu*, Act III, scene ii

first section			second section			
mm. 1146–51	CG-C	P1/P8	1152–55	CG-10	P4, IB	6 / 4 = 10 bars
mm. 1156–59	CG-C	P4/PB	1160–63	CG-10	P7, I2	4 / 4 = 8 bars
mm. 1164–66	CG-C	P7/P2	1167–69	CG-10	PA, I5	3 / 3 = 6 bars
mm. 1170–72	CG-C	PA/P5				3 bars
mm. 1172–74	CG-C	P1/P8				2 bars

The successively shorter sections within part I—10,8,6,3, and 2 bars—form a large-scale accelerando that reflects the rhythmic accelerandos characteristic of the Countess's materials. In the first subsection of each, the CG-collections are doubled at interval 7 and the [02479] collections ascend while the [01378] collections descend in a pattern of accelerating and decelerating rhythms (ex. 5.59). The first paired collections, from CG-C P1 and P8, have their respective [05] collections {D♭,A♭} and {A♭,E♭} represented by only the common tone {A♭}. In each successive A section, the CG collections are transposed up by T3, in a complete cycle, and the rhythms are shortened by the first and last durations, so that the first durations of the sections shrink from 8, 6, 4, 3, to 2 sixteenths (fig. 5.23). Although the palindromic rhythms are not strictly maintained in each case, the overall pattern is distinct.

In the second subsections of the phrases in part I, two inversionally related CG-10 rows that share the same [05] are segmented into dyads 01 [05], 23 [04], 56 [03], and 89 [06], with a horizontal trichord [014] 479 (ex. 5.59). The dyads occur in inversionally related contours in the two rows. The first pairs of rows, CG-10 P4/IB, share [05] F,B♭—the final [05] of the first subsection, which is held over to be the first [05] in the next section—and both rows hold the notes

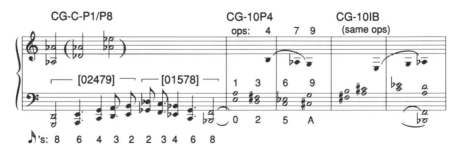

Example 5.59. Countess's suicide scene, part I, *Lulu*, Act III, mm. 1146–55. Berg LULU, Act 3. © Copyright 1977, 1978 by Universal Edition A.G., Wien. All Rights Reserved. Used by permission of European American Music Distributors Corporation, sole U.S. and Canadian agent for Universal Edition A.G., Wien.

Figure 5.23. Pattern of rhythms and collections in A sections of the Countess's suicide scene, part I, *Lulu*, Act III, scene ii

```
                [02479]                    [01378]
sixteenths:  8   6   4   3   2   /   1   2   3   4   6   8
bass notes:  G   A   C   D   E   /   Gb  F   Gb  F   Eb  Cb  Bb   1. CG–C–P1/P8    mm. 1146–51
             Bb  C   Eb  F   G   /   A   Ab  Gb  D   Db           2. CG–C–P4/PB    mm. 1156–59
             Db  Eb  Gb  Ab  Bb  /   C   B   A   F   E            3. CG–C–P7/P2    mm. 1164–66
                 E   F#  A   B   C# / D#D C   G#                  4. CG–C–PA/P5    mm. 1170–72
             3   2   1   2   3   /   2   1   2   3
                 2   2   1   1   /   2   1   1   1
                 G   A   C   DE  /   F#  F   Eb  BBb              5. GC–C–P1/P8    mm. 1172–74

                                                                 (1–5; 3-cycle)
```

in 56 and 79 invariant. The same relationships hold in the subsequent rows, each successively transposed by T3. The bass [05]s thus move through a complete 3-cycle {G,D}, {Bb,F}, {Db,Ab}, {E,B}, and back to {G,D}.

Part 2 of the passage begins with the Picture trichords overlapping the end of part 1 in mm. 1173–74, when the Countess Geschwitz kneels before Lulu's portrait. The "Liebestod" theme, so-called because it returns in the Countess's closing song, emerges from successive interval 6–related CG-10 P3 and CG-10 P9 rows (ex. 5.60); the theme groups the internal [037]s in 234 (<F–Db–Bb>) and 567 (<Cb–D–G>) of the row, recalling the opening trichords of the Alwa

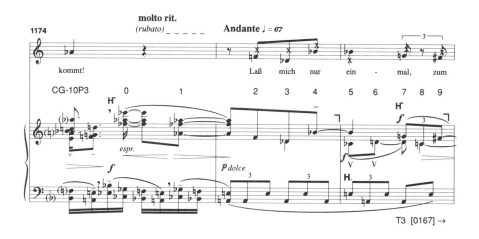

[0258]

Example 5.60. Countess's "Liebestod" theme, *Lulu*, Act III, mm. 1174–77. Berg LULU, Act 3.
© Copyright 1977, 1978 by Universal Edition A.G., Wien. All Rights Reserved. Used by permission of European American Music Distributors Corporation, sole U.S. and Canadian agent for Universal Edition A.G., Wien.

and Schön rows. The bass {A,E} (mm. 1175–76) and {E♭,B♭} (mm. 1177–79) combine to form basic cell I [0167] {A,E,B♭,E♭}, as do the prominent opening descending interval 7 dyads of both rows, {E♭,A♭} and {D,A}. The final order positions 89 interval-class 6 {C,F♯} of CG-10 P3 (invariant in CG-10 P9) are held to combine with the [05] {B♭,E♭} of CG-10 P9 to form [0258] {E♭,B♭,C,G♭}.

Part 2 ends with the 5-cycle–based Picture trichords in contrary-motion inversional pairs in accelerating rhythms (mm. 1180–87). In the upper voices, T6-related pairs of trichords from PR-I3/I9, I5/IB, and I7/I1 form three 1/2–cycles, grouped into a larger T2 cycle, over the lower-voice trichords from PR-P8/P2, P6/P0, and P4/(PA) pairs in the same relationships (cf. ex. 5.39b). The rhythmic patterns in the upper voice are similar to those in the first sections of part 1 of the passage, in successively foreshortened patterns, forming a larger accelerando. The cadence chord, [012479] {C,F,F♯,G,B♭,E♭}, the same set as the second hexachords of the Schön and Alwa rows, prepares for the arrival of Schön-Jack.

The Countess witnesses the confrontation between Jack and Lulu (mm. 1188–278), and when they go into the back room she sings of her intention to leave and return to school (mm. 1279–91), using material based on a 3-cycle of the "Liebestod" theme over a [0167] bass line: from CG-10 P3 over bass A/E, P0 over bass F♯/C♯, P9 over E♭/B♭, and P6 over bass C/G, with a final T5 descent to CG-10 P1 over bass G/D. The section coalesces on [0258] {G♯,B,D,F}, held over into Lulu's [0167] <C–F–F♯–B> protests and her death cry (mm. 1292–93, ex. 5.45). As Jack emerges from the other room, he stabs the Countess and leaves (mm. 1294–1314).

"Liebestod" The final section of the opera, marked *Grave*, is the Countess's "Liebestod," in which she cries that she will be near Lulu in eternity. The song begins with a varied restatement of part 2 of the Countess's suicide passage (mm. 1174–79) in mm. 1315–18, with the CG-10 P3 and CG-10 P9 rows and interval 7 bass A–collections {A,E} to {E♭,B♭} (cf. ex. 5.59). The bass moves to T = 7/1–related D/A and A♭/E♭: D/A accompanies CG-10 P9, and A♭/E♭ accompanies the CG-collections from I3, <A–G–E–D–C> over <C♯–B–A♭–F♯–F>. The bass interval 7 dyad then sequences down through {E,B}, {C,G}, {A,E}, and octave {F,F}, outlining [0158] {F,A,C,E}, the cadential chord of Alwa and Act II and the second-to-last chord at the end of the opera (ex. 5.61). Above the {E/B} and {C/G} dyads, the CG-collections IB and P0 align in different intervals (in m. 1322, the [02479] collection is {B♭,A♭,F♯,E♭,C♯} rather than {B,A♭,F♯,E♭,C♯}). Over bass {A/E} a descending <A♭–G♭–E♭–D♭–C♭> [02479] is set in 5-cycle tetrachords, overlapping with whole-tone+ segment <E♭–D♭–C♭–G–F–E♭–C♯–(C)–B> harmonized with whole-tone+ [0148], then 5-cycle

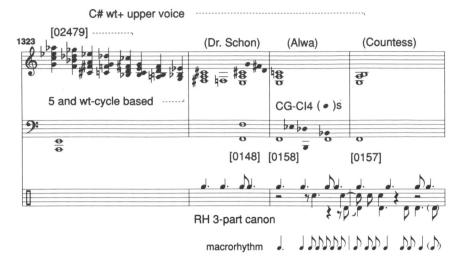

Example 5.61. *Lulu*, end of Act III, mm. 1323–26

[0258], tetrachords. In the closing bars, the CG-C I4, {A,E}, {G,F♯,D,C,B} and {A♭,E♭,D♭,B♭,F} are arranged among the three final cadence chords.[132]

The final three chords consist of the cadential chord of Act I, {F,A,C♯,E}, whole-tone+ [0148], representing Dr. Schön, with the first trichord of Schn P4, {E,C♯,A} [047] as a subset (m. 1324); the cadential chords of Act II, {F,A,C,E} 5-cycle–based [0158], representing Alwa, with the first trichord of Alwa P4, {E,C,A} [037] as a subset (m. 1325); and the final cadential chord, {F,A,E,B}, whole-tone+ [0157], representing the Countess Geschwitz, with the first dyad of the CG-P4 row {E,A} as a subset, and also as a subset of 5-cycle+ {A,E,B,C,F}, BC II [01378], and the C-collection of CG-C P7—the principal level of the CG-Collections. The bass F is the initial pitch-class of the Lulu P5 row, representing Lulu; an alternate reading of the last chord is as representing Lulu herself, bounded by F/B. The upper-voice B of the third chord is anticipated by a bass F–B in the penultimate m. 1325.[133] The upper-voice descending 1-cycle [012] <C♯–C–B> can be interpreted as part of an unfolded Lulu IA <(B♭–A♭)–G–F–E♭–D♭–A–C–B–(F♯–E–D)> in the closing bars as well. The trichord is also a transposition at T7 of the oscillating <F–F♯–G> in the chord <C–B♭–E♭–F–F♯–G> associated with Jack in the scene, from the second hexachord of Schn-P4. The <A–E> invariant dyad of all three chords sounds in the strings as a vertical interval 7 over a three-octave range.[134] The chords, interval 7 <A–E>, and bass F occur in the *Hauptrhythmus* in a three-part canon to close the opera, at a duration of five and three eighths. The canon is quite "dissonant": the canon at five eighths yields no simultaneous attacks, whereas the third entrance at four eighths yield only one simultaneous attack with the second voice (m. 1326, beat 2) and one with the first voice (mm. 1326, beat 4). With this "dissonance" a maximum of attacks appears in the macro-rhythm from the canonic RHs to close the opera.

VARIATIONS

The third large form in *Lulu*, after the sonata and rondo, is a set of variations throughout Act I, scene iii, Act II, scenes i and ii, and Act III, scene i, symmetrically placed about the middle of the palindromic film music interlude in Act II and associated with the character of the Prince in Act I, scene iii (solo cello), the Manservant in Act II, scene i, and the Acrobat masquerading as the Manservant in Act II, scene ii (solo viola), and the Marquis Casti-Piani in Act III, scene i (solo violin) (fig. 5.24).[135] The variations are based on a thirty-six note chorale melody and an eleven-note chorale row (Ch) derived cyclically from the chorale, harmonized with cyclic tetrachords (ex. 5.62). The chorale melody and row are derived in Act I, scene iii (mm. 1113–22, strings) in connection with the Prince. The rows Alwa P5, PR P3, and Schn P8 are stated in a palindromic rhythmic pattern of $<1-2-3-4-5-6-5-4-3-2-1>$ numbers of notes (fig. 5.25; cf. ex. 5.37). The concluding notes in each group, set in the longer durations of three eighth notes, are emphasized, creating the eleven-note chorale row from Alwa 0259, PR 28, and Schn 158AB (ex. 5.62; the twelfth note, C, is often added to both the beginning and end of the row). The row (ch-P5) contains opening and closing interval 5s $<F-B\flat>$ and $<A-E>$, with intervening 1-cycle [012]s $<F\sharp-G-A\flat>$ and $<D-C\sharp-E\flat>$ and an internal [0167] $<G-A\flat-C\sharp-D>$. The tetrachords harmonizing the chorale are mostly cyclic, of whole-tone, 3-, and 5-cycle+ origin; the bass voice unfolds first a P1 3-cycle+ $<G-E-B\flat-E-B-A\sharp>$, then a P2 3-cycle+ $<G\sharp-B-F-B\flat-A\flat>$. The chorale acts as a cantus firmus in the following *Konzertante Choralbearbeitung* (mm. 1123–48).

In Act III, scene i, the Marquis Casti-Piani, a pimp who infects Lulu with venereal disease and tries to blackmail her into an Egyptian brothel, has an extended dialogue with Lulu set to the *Konzertante Chorale-Variationen* (mm. 83–230, fig. 5.24). The set of twelve variations is interrupted by two intermezzos and the *English Waltz* from Act I, scene iii, linking the Marquis with the Prince from that scene. Another interruption in the variations is the return of the "*Lied der Lulu*" music (Act III, mm. 125–45).

The variations divide into four sections: variations 1–4, 5–7, 8–10, and 11–12, based on the return of variation I material in variations 5 (at T7) and 11, and the 7-cycle in the transposition of the material in variations 8, 9, and 10. The predominant variation technique is to treat the chorale row as a cantus firmus, and the predominant cyclic procedure is 5/7 – cycle transpositions. The chorale row chords (ex. 5.62), with their whole-tone+, 5 cycle+, and 3 cycle+–based

Figure 5.24. Chorale variations in *Lulu*

Prince:

Act I, scene iii: Chorale with chords mm. 1113–22

Chorale row, vocal mm. 1115–18

Chorale as cantus firmus mm. 1123–48, horns, tuba, harp

Chorale motive from Alwa 12345, solo cello, mm. 1123–24, 1148–49

Chorale mm. 1123–29, varied, solo cello

Manservant:

Act II, scene i: Chorale motive, m. 231, solo viola

Chorale, mm. 250–61, woodwinds

Chorale row, mm. 252–56 vocal (beginning with C)

Chorale row mm. 251–52, 258–59, solo viola

Chorale, notes 2–10, solo viola mm. 260–61

Chorale at T1, mm. 287–97, solo viola

Acrobat (Manservant):

Act II, scene ii: Chorale row, mm. 878–81, 887–88 solo viola

Marquis: *Konzertante Choral-Variationen*

Section 1:

Variation 1 (mm. 83–88): $\frac{3}{4}$, bassoon Ch–P5, Ch–P5, P9 solo violin, wt+ chords, characteristic rhythm

English Waltz (mm. 89–98): $\frac{3}{8}$, from Act I, scene iii, mm. 1040–94

Variation 2 (mm. 99–102): $\frac{3}{2}$, Ch–P5 chords, solo violin Ch–P5

First Intermezzo (mm. 103–18): "Lied des Mädchenhändlers," varied Wedekind tune solo violin

Second Intermezzo (mm. 119–45): "Lied der Lulu" in mm. 125–45

Variation 3 (mm. 146–49): Ch–P9 chords (T4)

Quasi Recit. (mm. 150–53): solo violin 3-cycle+ [01369], [0147]

Variation 4 (mm. 154–57): Ch–P0 chords (T7), solo violin on 12th note (G)

English Waltz (mm. 158–81): from Act I, scene iii, mm. 1040–94, rondo theme

Section 2:

Variation 5 (mm. 182–87): T7 variant of Variation 1, Ch–P0, solo violin Ch–P0, P4

Variation 6 (mm. 188–91): (Var. 2) Ch–P5 chorale chords, solo violin arpeggiations

Variation 7 (mm. 192–97): four-part canon of 5-cycle Ch–P0 (CH1, tuba), P5 (CH2, trombone), PA (CH3, horn), and P3 (CH4, trumpet); four-part canon of Ch P7 (solo cello), Ch P9 (solo viola), Ch P7 (solo violin), Ch P8 (solo viola)

Section 3:

Variation 8 (mm. 200–7): Ch–P2 as bass chorale, Painter tetrachords, [01369]

Variation 9 (mm. 208–15): T7 of Var. VIII, Ch–P9 as bass cantus firmus, [01369], [0167]s

Variation 10 (mm. 216–23): T7 of Var. IX, Ch P0 as bass cantus firmus, [0369]/[0167]

Figure 5.24. Chorale variations in *Lulu (Continued)*

Section 4:

Variation 11 (mm. 224–27): (Var. I), Ch–P5 chords, solo violin Ch–P5, P6, PB

Variation 12 (mm. 228–30): "stretta" with Ch–P4 Chorale chords, Alwa–P2 voice

Variations on the Wedekind Song

Variation 1, "Lied des Mädchenhändlers" (mm. 103–18): I–VI in C major

Variation 1, Grandioso (mm. 693–707): I–VI in C major (C–A), $\frac{3}{4}$ a tempo
(quarter = 92)

Variation 2, Grazioso (mm. 708–19): I–VI (C–A) / I–VI in G♭ (G♭–E♭), $\frac{4}{4}$ a tempo

Variation 3, Funèbre (mm. 720–29): I–VI in A major (A–F♯), $\frac{5}{4}$ (3+2) a tempo

Variation 4, Affettuoso (mm. 730–36): I–VI in F♯ (F♯–D♯), $\frac{7}{4}$ (3+4, 4+3), $\frac{10}{4}$
(4+3+3)

Thema, mm. 737–52: E♭ major /A major (mm. 737–44), C minor (mm. 744–52),
$\frac{3}{4}$, a tempo

Thema, mm. 828–42: E♭ major (mm. 828–34) and C minor (mm. 835–42)

Variation 2, mm. 1024–47 from mm. 708–19, polytonal canon in C major/G♭
major and A minor/E♭ minor

Variation 3, mm. 1110–19 from mm. 720–29, but in reverse order, first in F♯,
then in A, Funèbre, at the death of Alwa.

Example 5.62. Chorale row (Ch P5), with harmonizing cyclic tetrachords

content, are hinted at in variation 1, set to a characteristic rhythm that fore-shadows the rhythm of Alwa's funeral march from the variations interlude (ex. 5.63a); they appear complete in variation 2.

THE WEDEKIND SONG

Wedekind incorporates a real-life figure, Jack the Ripper, into the *Lulu* plays in the role of Lulu's executioner. Similarly, Berg brings in an outside musical "character" to enhance the mood of the final scene—a lute song by Wedekind himself.[136] This tune is associated first with the Marquis, then varied in the variations between Act III, scenes i and ii; parts of these variations recur

Figure 5.25. Proportions in derivation of chorale melody and row in *Lulu*

rows:	Alwa (ops)			PR (ops)			Schn (ops)				B: chorale melody
order positions:	0	12	345	6789	AB012	345678	9AB01	2345	678	9A	B
notes:	1	2	3	4	5	6	5	4	3	2	1
eighths:	3	13	113	1113	11113	111113	11113	1113	113	13	3
total units:	3	4	5	6	7	8	7	6	5	4	3: chorale row

1. Variation

funeral rhythmic motive

CH.-P5

Example 5.63a. Rhythmic motive foreshadowing Alwa's funeral march, beginning of chorale variations, *Lulu*, Act III, m. 83

III. Variation Funèbre

Wedekind melody in A major

Example 5.63b. Alwa's funeral march in variation 3, *Lulu*, Act III, mm. 720–24. Berg LULU, Act 3. © Copyright 1977, 1978 by Universal Edition A.G., Wien. All Rights Reserved. Used by permission of European American Music Distributors Corporation, sole U.S. and Canadian agent for Universal Edition A.G., Wien.

throughout Act III, scene ii, notably at the death of Alwa, with a funeral march. Within the *Konzertante Variationen* on the chorale material, the first intermezzo is the "Lied des Mädchenhändlers" (mm. 103–18), in which the Marquis describes to Lulu how he takes young women and sells them (fig. 5.24). The solo violin part is marked *zu einem Wedekind'schen 'Lied zur Laute' in der Sologeige*. This setting of the tune returns as the first in the set of variations that forms the interlude between Act III, scenes i and ii. The melody moves from C major to A minor, with regular phrases and meter and a diatonic collection similar to the hexachords of the principal row P0, noted by Berg in order-position numbers inserted into a sketch of the song.[137]

The organization of the interlude in Act III—the variations on the Wedekind melody—comprises several layers simultaneously (fig. 5.24).[138] On one level, the transposition of the melody, indicated in the music by key signatures, moves through a descending 3-cycle, from tonics with mediant relative minor keys that become major tonics in the following variation: C−a/A−f♯/F♯−d♯/D♯ (MAJOR-minor). The melodies in variation 2 and in the *thema* combine T6-related keys, G♭/C and E♭/A. On a second level of organization in the variations, the tonality of the melody is functional only in variations 1 and 2, and in the *thema*. The language proceeds systematically through the four variations, from tonal in C major, to "polytonal" in C/G♭ major, to contextual or "atonal," with Berg's characteristic cyclic harmonies along with a funeral march rhythm (ex. 5.63b) foreshadowing Alwa's death, to twelve-tone, where fragments of the Wedekind song are grouped into row segments. The rhythmic notation begins in $\frac{3}{4}$, supporting the Wedekind melody, but changes to $\frac{4}{4}, \frac{5}{4}, \frac{7}{4}$ and even $\frac{10}{4}$ in the increasingly ametric setting, before a return to $\frac{3}{4}$ with the ending *thema* section. The variations thus chart a tonal and metric course similar to the musical events in Vienna of 1900−1935, including, of course, Berg's own music. The variations end with the theme in E♭, in a simple setting orchestrated to sound like a street hurdy-gurdy; the theme and material from the variations then recur throughout Act III, scene ii.

CONCLUSION

This discussion of Berg's longest and most complex work has demonstrated that *Lulu* constitutes the high point of Berg's techniques of generating a consistently rich set of cyclic, intervallic, and serial relationships from his basic pitch, rhythmic, and formal materials, allowing multiple tonal allusions, in parallel with a complex dramatic situation, giving each character and situation clearly identifying and characteristic motives and musical passages. Although serial operations and relationships on and between the principal and secondary rows are extensive, the unifying features of the work spring most decisively from the pervasive use of the three multicyclic tetrachords [0167], [0268], and [0369] in pitch realm, and the 3-cycle+ *Hauptrhythmus* in the rhythmic realm, in relation to surrounding cyclic-based pitch and rhythmic events. As such, *Lulu* is a summation of the processes developed in Berg's music, beginning from the op. 2 songs, with both direct references backward and forward-looking innovations. For instance, in one passage in the film music, the quasi development section palindromic interlude between Act II, scenes i and ii, meant to accompany a film depicting Lulu's incarceration and liberation, a series of cyclic canons on the principal row occur, similar to those in the third movement of the *Lyric Suite* (mm. 663–69). Perhaps the most significant and forward-looking musical moment occurs when, in the same music, basic cell I [0167] <E–A–B♭–E♭> is partitioned non-segmentally from six consecutive rows (mm. 670–80): PR–P4 (clarinet, Schn-P4 (bassoon), Alwa-P4 (saxophone), Schoolboy-P2 (oboe), CG-P4 (flute), and Acrobat-P4 (contrabassoon) (ex. 5.37). The punctuation of <E–A–B♭–E♭> demonstrates rhythmically the ordered relationships between rows and the extent to which Berg had absorbed and refined Schoenberg's twelve-tone language. The direction he took in his final work, the Violin Concerto, is away from the multicyclic collections as a connecting thread and toward more tonal allusion—within the row itself—even to the point of seamlessly incorporating a complete, self-contained tonal piece within the last movement.

Violin Concerto

The Violin Concerto, Berg's last completed composition, was composed on a commission from violinist Louis Krasner in the summer of 1935, but was not performed until after Berg's death, on April 19, 1936, in Barcelona.[139] The concerto combines a tonal chorale, "Es ist Genug, in a harmonization by J. S. Bach, a Carinthian folk song, a focus on pitch-classes B♭ and G, a *Hauptrhythmus*, and the regularity and meter of tonal phrasing and rhythm with a row that has triads as overlapping segments arranged in a 7-cycle (ex. 5.64).[140] As in his previous works, but even more notably, the apparent intertwining of tonal and twelve-tone elements stems from the common source of Berg's cyclic language.[141]

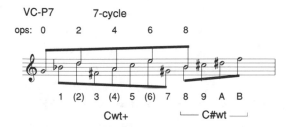

Example 5.64. Cyclic properties of row, Violin Concerto

FORM

The concerto is in two parts of roughly equal length (257 and 230 bars), each of which is divided into two smaller movements: Andante (I, mm. 1–103, 103 bars), Allegretto (I, mm. 104–255, 152 bars), Allegro (II, mm. 1–135, 135 bars), and Adagio (II, mm. 136–230, 95 bars). Although there is no palindrome, as in two-part forms in Berg's earlier music, the internal forms within each of the first three movements are symmetrical, as are the pairing, relative length, and divergence in the relative tempos of the movements, Andante-Allegretto and Allegro-Adagio. As is customary in Berg's twelve-tone music, besides the row itself the movements share distinctive thematic material; most obviously, the arch figures that open and close the first movement return at the end (I, mm. 1–10 and 94–103; II, mm. 229–30). Also, the second and third movements share the trio 2 material (I, mm. 155–66, and II, mm. 44–53 and 78–89), and the second and fourth movements both feature the Carinthian folk song (I, mm. 214–28, and II, mm. 201–13).

Despite the shared materials, the first two movements are distinct in mood and form compared with the last two: the initial movements are in large- and small-scale symmetrical arch structures, whereas the third movement is based on a recurring *Hauptrhythmus* and the fourth movement is comprised of variations on the chorale. On the level of phrases, many passages in the first, second, and fourth movements fall into balanced presentations of repeated or antecedent-consequent phrases, with the consequent an inversional form. The Carinthian folk tune has repeated one- and two-bar motives within periodic phrases and periods, and the Bar-form chorale is in alternating repeated phrases of successively shorter length.

MUSICAL LANGUAGE

The language of the Violin Concerto is embodied in the row's 5/7- and whole-tone cycles and cyclic collections (5- and 7-cycles are equivalent in a cyclic analysis but are distinctive in terms of tonal allusion and are thereby noted differently in the Violin Concerto discussion), and in the first two notes of P7, G and B♭, which are referential throughout (ex. 5.64). The opening ten bars establish the opposition between these cycles by presenting rows in segments derived from a 2-cycle on order positions (ex. 5.65), yielding 7-cycle pitch collections in 0246 and 2468 and whole-tone–based collections in 1357 and 89AB. The two collectional types alternate in two-bar groups: a 7-cycle in m. 1 and combination in m.2, then whole-tone based in mm. 3–4 and 7–8 and 5/7–cycle based in mm. 5–6 and 9–10. The whole-tone mm. 3–4 and 7–8 alternate whole-tone collections, as is customary in Berg's use of whole-tone–based materials, and both the whole-tone and 5/7–cycle based collections have dissonant elements completing added-note collections. The rows used in the opening ten bars— PA, P7, I2, and IB—have high degrees of invariance resulting from the fact that I2 is a rotated retrograde inversion of PA (where P(n) $012 \ldots$ = R(I(n+4)) $876 \ldots$) and IB is similarly related to P7; thus, in P7/IB and PA/I2, $02468 = 86420$, $1357 = 7531$, and $89AB = 0BA9$, respectively.[142]

Example 5.65. Row order positions and cycles, Violin Concerto, I, mm. 1–10. Berg VIOLINKONZERT. Copyright 1936 by Universal Edition. Copyright renewed. All Rights Reserved. Used by permission of European American Music Distributors Corporation, sole U.S. and Canadian agent for Universal Edition A.G., Wien.

The solo violin opening with arpeggiations on its open strings, <G–D–A–E>, from P7 0246, creates a simple yet striking correspondence between the instrument, 5/7–cycles, and the row, integrating these three significant features of the concerto.[143] Many derivations throughout are based on the 02468 5/7–cycle partition of the row: (1) the 012, 234, 456, 678 derivation of trichords in the opening statement of the first movement (I, mm. 11–37; see ex. 5.66) (2) a gapped 5-cycle collection is created by partitions 234789 [013568] (<Ab–C–Eb–D–F–G>, I, mm. 40–42); (3) the accompanying bass 024 to the scherzo theme (I, mm. 104–9, ex. 5.68a; also in mm. 132–36, 173–75); (4) a figure based on the alignment 02468 / 1357A from the b section of the scherzo (I, mm. 110–11, ex. 5.68b; also mm. 126–30, 180–86); (5) the trio 1 first motive (designated motive 2), with partitions 012 678 and 345 9AB (I, mm. 137–38, ex. 5.69; also mm. 141–44 [varied], 151–54 [varied], 167–68 [violin and orchestra parts exchanged]); (6) a figure with upper voice 02469-8 from trio 1 (the completed 5-cycle <C#–F#–B–E–A> is delayed by the interpolated G–Bb, I, mm. 140–41, 147–50, 240–49); and (7) in the cadenza of III, the organization of the solo violin figures around the violin open strings (II, mm. 5–22, 35–42, 65–74). A good example of the tonal potential of 5-cycle materials occurs with the accompanying chords in I, mm. 40–41: through emphasized 5-cycle bass notes <C#–F#–B>, with the triadic formations on C# and F#, they seemingly imply a tonal function, but here as elsewhere in the concerto the "resolution" to a whole-tone chord built on B (m. 41) negates the apparent tonality. Similar examples of cadential expectations unfulfilled by whole-tone ends occur with the chord progressions "in G minor" in mm. 11–17 (ex. 5.66) and "in Bb" in mm. 216–17 (ex. 5.76).

Whole-tone–based materials are also found throughout in the concerto. In addition to the opening bars (ex. 5.65), they appear: in the partition 123567 in I, m. 41 (<Fb–Ab–C–Gb–Bb–D>); from intertwined rows, related at T = 2, in the whole-tone 123 or 567 segments, or as extensions of the segment in 89AB0 in the whole-tone and whole-tone+ scalar segments in the solo violin part in the first movement (I, mm. 72–74) and in the cadenza in the third (II, mm. 21–22); in the scherzo theme as whole-tone+ 1356 and 789AB (I, mm. 104–9, ex. 5.68a; also mm. 132–33, 173–75, 208–9); and as the cadence chord at the end of the first part, whole-tone+ 0123 P7 {G,Bb,D,F#} [0148] (I, m. 257). Possibly the most dramatic use of whole-tone+ collections occurs at the climax of the third movement (II, m. 125–35, ex. 5.72): here a succession of nine chord pairs slowly descends in register, decreases in number of notes, durations and number of attacks in the *Hauptrhythmus* setting, and evolves toward pure whole-tone collections by chord pair 6 (even-numbered whole-tone notes shown as open noteheads, odd as filled-in noteheads in ex. 5.72). The accompanying solo violin part divides into trichordal whole-tone [024]s alternating source whole-tone collections in a descending 5-cycle, and a single note B♭ building into whole-tone [0246] (which foreshadows the opening of the chorale) alternating whole-tone areas in a 1-cycle+ series <B♭–D♭–D–E♭>.

As is characteristic of Berg's earlier music, the two primary cycles, whole-tone and 5-cycles, are accompanied by a secondary cycle, here 3-cycle collections; two of the few instances of 3-cycle collections articulate formal divisions in the first movement (I, mm. 60–62) and the third (II, m. 60, the beginning of the cadenza). Transformations by 3-cycles are, however, significant. The T3 relationship between G and B♭ is central to the relationships of rows: in the opening bars (ex. 5.65), the opening T3-related 7-cycle tetrachords beginning on B♭ overlap on G and create a seven-note segment <B♭–F–C–G / G–D–A–E> outlining T6 B♭–E. Underlying these 7-cycle tetrachords is an ascending line (bass clarinet) that places G and B♭ in a T1 3-cycle context, spanning <B♭2–D♭3– (D3–E♭3)–E3–(F3–F♯3)–G3–(A3)–Bb3> in mm. 1–10. The varied repeat of the opening (mm. 1–4 in mm. 5–8) at T7 combines T3-related 7-cycles <F–C– G–D / D–A–E–B> (the first F is displaced by E♭, which participates in the ascending interval 1 bass line), with outer span T6 F–B. The total span of the two 7-cycle collections is thus T1, B♭ to B. On the third repetition, back at the initial pitch-class level (mm. 9–10, harp), 7-cycle <B♭–F–C–G> leads to T9 <G–D–A–(E)>, which then backtracks down through C to a low G to begin the movement proper (m. 11). This backtracking anticipates the end of the concerto (II, mm. 229–30) where the 7-cycle figures return as <G–D–A–E / E–A–D–G–C–F–B♭>, spanning G to B♭ in a reverse of the initial move of B♭ to G. The alternating string and harp 7-cycle–based figures also return at the end of the first movement (I, mm. 92–103), where they are transformed by a 4-cycle through rows P4, P0, and P8 (as [0257]s, completing the aggregate), then by a 6-cycle P8 to P2—the latter beginning on D, at T7 from the initial emphasis on G, to lead into the scherzo second movement.

Interval 3 also has two large-scale transformational roles in the concerto, in restatements of material from part I in part II: the trio 2 melody returns at T−3 (I, mm. 155–62, in II, mm. 44–53) and the Carinthian folk tune at T3 from the parallel keys of C and G♭ (I, mm. 214–28) to E♭ and A (II, mm. 201–13), completing a 3-cycle.

Relationships at T6 are similarly less evident on the surface than in transpositions between materials. The row segment 89AB spans interval 6, matching the first tetrachord of the chorale, and throughout the variations in the fourth movement, the chorale is transposed in whole and in part by interval 6, mostly at levels PA and P4. In the scherzo, the opening [04] dyads of the theme are T6-related D♭–F and G–B (ex. 5.68a), and varied statements in mm. 108–9 are related at T6, from rows P2 and P8, with F and B major triads supporting in the bass, proceeding "tonally" to the C-based m. 110. The polytonal settings of the Carinthian folk song, with a melody and tritone-related harmony, are foreshadowed in the juxtaposed C/G♭ and F/B triads that follow the reprised scherzo theme ending the first scherzo A section in the second movement (cello and solo violin, mm. 135–36).

The folksong is simplicity in itself: a sectional period, with phrasing and hypermeasures in one-, two-, four- and eight-bar units and a clear I–V–V–I harmonic outline. It appears first in G♭, but harmonized with a progression in C (I, mm. 214–21, 222–28) and, when it returns in the fourth movement at T3, in E♭ harmonized with A (II, mm. 200–207, 208–13; the final two bars are cut short by the return of the chorale, m. 214).[144] Despite the enharmonic chordal relationships between the keys, D♭ as ♭II of C = V of G♭, and G / (A♭♭ as ♭II of G♭ = V of C, the apparent tonal juxtaposition is a contradiction: two simultaneous tritone-related tonics cannot exist.[145] The tonal impossibility of the setting reflects the "impossible" situation of the young girl, Manon Gropius (to whom the concerto is dedicated) corresponding to the folksong melody with its implied simple harmonies, and her death, corresponding to the disjunction between the tritone-related chords.

In a pitch-class set context, the central sonority of the folksong setting is two T6 [037]s combined in an [013679], a collection familiar in Berg's later music as the central palindrome chord in *Der Wein*, related to the extracted [06]s from the row (ex. 5.30), and in *Lulu* in the Freedom motive (ex. 5.40), and the polytonal setting of the Wedekind tune (variation 2 in the variations interlude), both related to the central [0167] basic cell I of the opera. In the Violin Concerto, however, the lack of motivic T6 or [0167] relationships in cyclic context leaves the [013679]s isolated. The harmonization of the Carinthian folk tune, in sharp contrast to its metric and tonal simplicity, is not reconciled with the language of the rest of the concerto: it cannot be interpreted tonally, it is outside the row, and its central [013679] collection is outside the cyclic collections used throughout.[146] The musical contradiction reflects the programmatic setting of the life and premature death of Manon Gropius.

The chorale, in its tonal setting by Bach, in contrast to the folk tune setting, is reconciled with the twelve-tone rows by the related 5-cycle and whole-tone+−based vertical elements and whole-tone and interval 1–based horizontal elements in both. The 5-cycle elements of tonality are incorporated into the row, as well as the opening whole-tone segment of the chorale (in 89AB), and they mediate the coexistence of row and chorale. The reconciliation expresses the peace found in the acceptance of death. In a symbolic gesture near the end of the concerto, the closing folk tune statement, the symbol of conflict and incompatibility, is cut off by the entrance of the final statement of the chorale (m. 214), the agent of peace and harmony.

FIRST MOVEMENT

The first movement is a symmetrical form in which the introduction returns as the coda, the A material returns in reverse order of presentation, and the B material repeats immediately (fig. 5.26).[147] Within the A sections is a smaller aba', with the b material defined by motive 1 (ex. 5.67) and the a' subsection omitted from the A' return. Across this sectional scheme, the violin gradually becomes more agitated, moving cyclically from row statements in large note values and soft dynamics to non-row figures in shorter durations at louder dynamics, climaxing in m. 74 before a sudden quieting leading into the restated A' section.

In the introduction, the bars group in pairs, alternating 5/7-cycle and whole-tone+ collections (ex. 5.65) with an internal division into mm. 1–4, 5–8, and 9–10 by parallel gestures, but with continuity from an overall rising bass line, crescendo, and arch-shaped ascent and descent. The introduction material returns as a coda (mm. 92–103), introduced by a V^7–I cadence gesture emphasizing C (mm. 91–92), after which the 7-cycle figures continue to

---

Figure 5.26. Symmetrical form in Violin Concerto, movement I

introduction mm. 1–10: 1–4, 5–8, 9–10

A	a	mm. 11–37:	mm. 11–20/21–27	antecedent/consequent
	b		mm. 28–29/30–31	motive 1
	a'		mm. 32–37 = 11–20/21–27	at T–1, superimposed
B		mm. 38–53	mm. 38–41/42–46	antecedent/consequent
			mm. 47–48/49–50	antecedent/consequent
			51–53	
B'		mm. 54–76 = expanded 38–53		
			mm. 54–58/59–62	(38–46) antecedent/ consequent
			63–66/67–70	(47–50) antecedent/ consequent
			71–76	(51–53) augmented
A'		mm. 77–91 (in reverse order of presentation)		
	b		mm. 77–80	(mm. 28–31) motive 1
			81–84	7 cycle F–C–G
	a		84–91	(mm. 11–19)
coda		mm. 92–103		(introduction, mm. 1–10)

Example 5.66. Three occurrences of "a" section trichordal row segments, Violin Concerto, I, mm. 11–15, 21–25, 32–34. Berg VIOLINKONZERT. Copyright 1936 by Universal Edition. Copyright renewed. All Rights Reserved. Used by permission of European American Music Distributors Corporation, sole U.S. and Canadian agent for Universal Edition A.G., Wien.

a bass D, at interval 7 from the opening emphasis on G, to begin the scherzo second movement.

In the initial a subsection, the memorable gesture is derived from overlapping trichords P7 <u>012</u> <u>234</u> <u>456</u> <u>678</u> <u>89AB</u> followed by a horizontal statement of P7 (mm. 11–20, ex. 5.66), then a corresponding inversional consequent statement of trichords and melodic row from I7 (mm. 21–27). The trichordal arrangements, with stepwise voice-leading, strongly suggest a tonal progression, as, for instance, in G minor: ascending fifths i, V, ii, and V of ii, followed by a hint of an augmented sixth chord in G, but any tonal function is local; most of the "tonal" successions are 5/7–cycle based collections with a tonal appearance only.[148] The I7 inverted consequent, if exact, would have presented a descending-fifths progression of (MAJOR/minor triads) C, f, Bb, and eb, but, significantly, it is altered to yield a bass line of <C–Db–Bb–B> (I7 <u>296A</u>), a 1-cycle [0123] and inverted form of the "BACH" motive (ex. 5.66). The third a figure combines both the previous prime (P6, solo violin, woodwinds) and inversion (I6, contrabass, horns) statements simultaneously at T−1 (mm. 32–38), beginning with juxtaposed B and F♯ triads. The a gesture returns at the end of the movement in a 7-cycle of rows: P7, P2, P9 (mm. 84–91). The violin plays the bass line of the a figure trichords, then evolves into the arpeggiated figure of the introduction to begin the coda (mm. 92–103).

The b passage within the first section is based on motive 1 (ex. 5.67). This motive, not apparently derived from the row, is foreshadowed (mm. 17–18, solo violin; m. 20, bass clarinet; mm. 26–27, alto saxophone, solo violin) before its definitive first appearance as an [0134] articulated as two [013]s (<C–D–Eb>

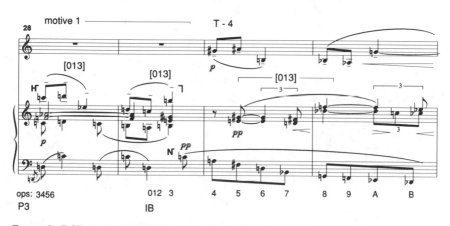

Example 5.67. Motive 1, Violin Concerto, I, mm. 28–31. Berg VIOLINKONZERT. Copyright 1936 by Universal Edition. Copyright renewed. All Rights Reserved. Used by permission of European American Music Distributors Corporation, sole U.S. and Canadian agent for Universal Edition A.G., Wien.

and <D–C–B>) horizontally and rhythmically, but also by register (<C6–D6–B5> and <E♭5–D5–C5>), in both mm. 28–29 and 30–31 at T−4 (one common tone, B). Motive 1 recurs in the restatement of the opening section (I, mm. 77–80, inverted at sum 0 and varied in m. 80). The shape and rhythm of motive 1 are developed beginning in m. 37, where it is expanded into the four-note motive that is the basis of mm. 37–50 and 54–63.

SECOND MOVEMENT

The second movement continues the symmetrical, sectional formal divisions of the first, as scherzo-trio 1-trio 2-trio 1-scherzo-coda, and a smaller symmetrical form within the scherzo of abcb'a' (fig. 5.27). The scherzo theme (ex. 5.68a), in a lilting 9/8 meter, combines a 7-cycle bass accompaniment <D–A–E>, largely "diatonic" melody with added G♭ (<F–G–G♭–C–B♭–C–A>, and an accompanying voice creating vertical whole-tone+ harmonies, and is presented, as is

---

Figure 5.27. Symmetrical form in Violin Concerto, movement 2

Scherzo A a		mm. 104–9	104–5/106–7, 108/109 paired transposed statements
	b	mm. 110–17	<u>01234</u> and T = <u>45678</u> in overlapping I7, I5, I3
	c	mm. 118–21/122–25	(from first movement, mm. 47–50) antecedent/consequent
	b'	mm. 126–31	
	a'	mm. 132–36	
Trio 1 B a		mm. 137–39	theme
	b	139–41	motive 2
	a'	141–44	
	c	145–47	
	b	148–50	(grows from motive 2, mm. 140–141)
	a	151–54	(141–44)
Trio 2 C a		mm. 155–62	theme
	a'	163–66	
Trio 1 B a		mm. 167–68 =	137–38
	b"	169–72	transition
Scherzo	a	mm. 173–75 =	104–5
	b	176–87	ländler variation = 110–12
	c	188–207	200–3/204–7 antecedent/ consequent =112–25
	a'	208–13 =	132–36
Coda:		mm. 214–28	folk tune 214–17/218–21 222–25/226–28
		mm. 228–57	mm. 240–49 from Trio 1 b (140–41, 147–51)

---

most of the material in the second movement, in sequential repetitions: the T−1 relationship of P2/I9 in mm. 104−5 to P1/I8 in mm. 106−7 recurs with I2 to I1 in mm. 110−11 and 111−12, where a countertheme appears with the 5-cycle–based 0246 / 1357 row partition (ex. 5.68b). In mm. 114−115, the redundancy of row intervals <3443> and the T2 relationship of 01234, 45678 are used to overlap rows I7, I5, and I3.

Trio 1, more aggressive in tone than the scherzo, features a theme and a motive (motive 2), both presented in sequential repetitions.[149] The theme (first in I, mm. 137−38, ex. 5.69), with row partitions 012 678 and 345 9AB, groups two rows together to yield [037]s in T3 consecutive pairs from the "roots," and

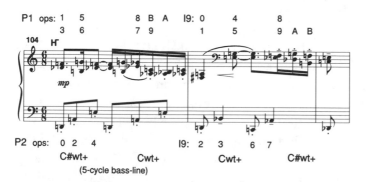

Example 5.68a. Scherzo theme, Violin Concerto, I, mm. 104−6

Example 5.68b. Scherzo countertheme, Violin Concerto, I, mm. 110−12. Berg VIOLINKONZERT. Copyright 1936 by Universal Edition. Copyright renewed. All Rights Reserved. Used by permission of European American Music Distributors Corporation, sole U.S. and Canadian agent for Universal Edition A.G., Wien.

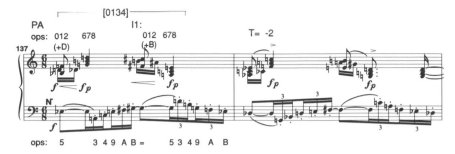

Example 5.69. Theme of trio I, Violin Concerto, I, mm. 137–38. Berg VIOLINKONZERT. Copyright 1936 by Universal Edition. Copyright renewed. All Rights Reserved. Used by permission of European American Music Distributors Corporation, sole U.S. and Canadian agent for Universal Edition A.G., Wien.

in $T-1$ symmetrical pairs from PA ("minor," "MAJOR") "b♭" to "G" triads; to I1 "F♯", to "a" triads in m. 137, all sequenced at $T-2$ in P8/IB in m. 138. The added D in the first triad creates a mixture "B♭-major," then "B♭-minor" triad as an example of the non-row quasi-tonal processes in the piece. The T3 relationship between the first two triads (b♭ to G) recalls the B♭- and G-based harp and violin figures in the introduction. The upper notes of the theme <F–D–C♯–E>, form a [0134], recalling motive 1 in the opening movement (ex. 5.67). The trichordal segments characteristic of this theme are also used in an accompanimental role (mm. 139–41), where P9 vertical trichords 012, 345, 678, 9AB harmonize a melodic P1, yielding 5- and whole-tone-cycle–based tetrachords [0347] [0258] [0247] [0257] [0258] and [0358].

The trio 1 motive, "motive 2," based on the 012 / 234 / 456 / 678 / 9AB 5-cycle division of the row and [037] chords in a characteristic dotted rhythm and contour <3625041> (I, mm. 140–41, 146–54), returns in the coda to the second movement (mm. 240–49), first in its dotted rhythm, then in variants in a continuous, undifferentiated rhythm. In the latter bars (mm. 245–49), the upper-voice ostinato 5-cycle+ <C♯–F♯–B–E–G> is harmonized by [037] triads stemming from overlapping row segments yielding "triads" (MAJOR, minor) I1 F♯ b E a followed by [024], but the settings vary through non-row "mixture" and "third-related chords" to f♯ b E A [024] (mm. 245–46, aggregate), f♯ B E a [024] (mm. 246–47, aggregate), A B E c♯/[024] (mm. 247–48), and D♭ eb G a [024] (mm. 249–50, aggregate). Passages like this one—and the "mixture" note D added in m. 137 (ex. 5.69), invite comparison with tonality, but the triads are non-functional—whether row segments or not—and are structional only within the cyclic harmonic context.

The trio 2 theme (I, mm. 155–58, 163–66, ex. 5.70) presents a fourteen-note melody, containing the aggregate, fashioned from partitioned trichords of suc-

Example 5.70. Theme of trio 2, Violin Concerto, I, mm. 155–58. Berg VIOLINKONZERT. Copyright 1936 by Universal Edition. Copyright renewed. All Rights Reserved. Used by permission of European American Music Distributors Corporation, sole U.S. and Canadian agent for Universal Edition A.G., Wien.

cessive rows, with a tag of descending 1-cycle+ (the first trichord, <C–C♯–B> is anticipated by the solo violin in the previous m. 154). The initial three successive trichords expands the first interval, <+1,−2> [012] to <+4,−1> [014] and to <+6,−1> [016], and the initial notes of the four divisions, <C–D–E–A♭>, form a whole-tone collection. The harmonies alternate 5/7–cycle and whole-tone+–cycle collections. The trio 2 melody returns twice in the third movement: first, at T−3 (II, mm. 44–53), with the harmonies arpeggiated in the solo violin part in an expanded six-beat variant of the *Hauptrhythmus* of the movement; and varied (with the interval between the seventh and eighth notes changed to interval 5, yielding only eleven distinct notes), as a tour-de-force four-voice successive T−7 canon, beginning on the notes <F–B♭–E♭–A♭> in the solo violin cadenza (II, mm. 78–90).

The coda to the second movement begins with the Carinthian folk tune (mm. 214–28), shortened in its last two measures by the abrupt resumption of the scherzo material: the G♭ triad in the last measures is taken over by I6 012 (m. 228), cutting off the last two-bar unit of the tune and breaking the regularity. The second movement ends with whole-tone+ collection P7 0123, with G in the bass.

The third movement is largely an accompanied violin cadenza, with A sections punctuated by a rising arpeggiated row figure (II, mm. 1–3, 14–15, 19–20, 96–97, 121–25), B sections characterized by a *Hauptrhythmus* (RH), and a C section based on the trio 2 material from movement 2, all in a loosely symmetrical form of ABC, cadenza B' A A'/B (fig. 5.28). The introduction (mm. 1–6) begins with the complement of P7 0123 from the end of the second movement, 456789AB of P7, with 0123, reiterated by the violin, reordered as 0213 <G–D–Bb–F♯> in the unidirectional contour of the opening arpeggiated 7-cycle figure of movement 1 (ex. 5.65). The cadenza figures are based around the 7-cycle open strings of the violin and thus are an elaboration of the introduction to the first movement; this relationship is confirmed by the <G–D–A–E/E–A–D–G> open-string arpeggio in the transition from the C section to the cadenza in m. 90. As well, the succession of rows P7–I9–P9 (mm. 7–14) outlines the consecutive 7-cycle open string notes of P7 0246 <G–D–A–E>. Throughout the A section, rows are segmented in various proportions and exchanged between the orchestra and violin (mm. 15–20, P7, IA, I3, P2; mm. 20–22, P0, P2, PA).

The B section is dominated by the syncopated RH (ex. 5.71). The five-attack RH has relative proportions <3–1–2–3–3>; with time points <0–3–4–6–

Figure 5.28. Form in Violin Concerto, movement 3

Cadenza:			
introduction		mm. 1–6	
A	a	mm. 7–14	
	a'	mm. 14–20	
	a"	mm. 20–22	
B	b	mm. 23–26,	27–34 RH
	b'	mm. 35–43	(= m. 27–34)
C		mm. 44–53	melody from trio 2 = T9 (I/mm. 155–60)
		mm. 54–60	
		mm. (58)–77	cadenza
		mm. 78–90	four-part canon on trio 2 melody
		mm. 91–95	transition
Cadenza		mm. 96–103	
B'	b'	mm. 104–8	(= 35–43, RH)
	b	mm. 109–20	(= 23–26, RH)
A		mm. 121–24	
A'/B		mm. 125–35	climax

Example 5.71. *Hauptrhythmus* (RH) settings, Violin Concerto, II, mm. 23–26, 27, 31, 32. Berg VIOLINKONZERT. Copyright 1936 by Universal Edition. Copyright renewed. All Rights Reserved. Used by permission of European American Music Distributors Corporation, sole U.S. and Canadian agent for Universal Edition A.G., Wien.

9–(12)> the rhythm groups most metrically into threes as in $^{12}_{8}$. In Berg's metric setting in $^{3}_{4}$, however, the rhythm is strongly syncopated. RH underlines several different row segmentations: whole-tone+ collections 0123/4567/89AB (II, mm. 23–26), [037] 012/ 3 cycle+ collection 3456/ whole-tone+ collection 789AB (mm. 27–42), whole-tone+ collection 0123 / [037] 456 / whole-tone+ 789AB (m. 31), and imbricated segments 012, 123, 234, 345, 4567, 89AB (mm. 32, 34). In mm. 23–26, the T4 row sequence of <I8–I0–P1–I8> has P1 substituting for I4; the substitution maintains the sequential frame, by P1 01 = I4 01 {C♯,E}, but varies the whole-tone collection harmonies. The succession of rows in mm. 27–31 pairs inversionally-related rows by invariances in their opening trichords, again changing from "minor" to "major" triads: P7 {G,B♭,D}/ I2 {D,B,G} (mm. 27–28) / I4 {E,C♯,A}/P9 {A,C,E} (mm. 29–30), continuing in a varied form of either P1 or I3, based on the invariances between these two rows (P1 0123, 789AB = I3 1234, 789AB) (m. 31). In the accompanying parts in mm. 27–34 and 35–42, the violin, then the orchestra, plays sequential figures highlighting cyclic successively larger intervals <3–4–5–6–7–A–B>.

The C section, using the trio 2 material from the second movement at T–3 (II, mm. 44–53), is underlined by the violin accompaniment in a modified *Hauptrhythmus* followed by intertwined rows P8 and P9 (mm. 54–57). A rhapsodic cadenza based on row segments and open strings (mm. 58–74) leads to the four-part solo canon on the trio 2 melody, at T-levels of <F–B♭–E♭–A♭>, arranged in a descending 7-cycle, and at a durational interval of three quarter-note beats, maintaining the metric grouping in the original (mm. 78–89). The harmonies are 5- and whole-tone+–cycle based.

The *Höhepunkt* of the movement, and the concerto, occurs in mm. 125–35 (ex. 5.72), in a monumental combination of pitch and rhythmic cycles. Nine successive chord pairs, set to RH, appear: the pairs are successively reduced in total number of attacks (<5–5–5–4–3–2–2–2>, by truncation of RH from the front), durations (in sixteenths, <20–20–19–17–12–10–16–16–6>), and intervals between their upper notes (<–B,–9,–8,–8,–6,–4,–3,–3,–1>), and they descend in register. The upper notes of the chord pairs, eighteen in number (<C♯7–B6/E6–G5/G♯–C5/E♭5–G4/A♭4–D4/B♭3–G♭3/D3–B2/E2–D♭2/ G1–F♯1>), contain eleven distinct pitch-classes; the twelfth, F, is held as a bass note throughout, as a long-range interval 5 ("dominant") to the B♭ "tonic" of the following chorale. The chord pairs become successively more whole-tone in content, moving to the C whole-tone collection (open noteheads in ex. 5.72). Of the nine chord pairs, the sixth is pure whole-tone and the shortest duration; the last three pairs are longer (the final dyad <G–F♯> is cut off by the chorale) and mixed in pitch and interval content, leading to the chorale.

Example 5.72. Climax with *Hauptrhythmus* (RH) liquidation, orchestral chords, solo violin [024]s, and [0246]s (open noteheads from C whole-tone collection, filled-in noteheads from C♯ whole-tone collection). Berg VIOLINKONZERT. Copyright 1936 by Universal Edition. Copyright renewed. All Rights Reserved. Used by permission of European American Music Distributors Corporation, sole U.S. and Canadian agent for Universal Edition A.G., Wien.

The first six chord pairs are each followed by a [024] violin figure, which alternates whole-tone collections and descends in an interval 5 cycle, and a low register violin build-up to the initial whole-tone tetrachord of the chorale: <B♭>, <D♭–E♭>, <D–E–F♯>, and <E♭–F–G–A>—the latter, after several repetitions, is doubled at the lower octave in the viola as a canonic voice to the chorale which begins at T7 <B♭–C–D–E> (mm. 132–36). This four-note whole-tone segment actually appears previously in the movement, in mm. 43 and 68 (solo violin), spanning complementary <F–E♭–D♭–B> and <B–C♯–D♯–F>. The combination of chords, violin [024], tetrachord fragments, and bass note F within each chord pair creates an aggregate until chord 6.

FOURTH MOVEMENT

The chorale variations constitute the fourth movement of the concerto (fig. 5.29). The chorale tune, originally set by Bach in A major, consists of three large phrases in AA'B (Bar) form (ex. 5.73).[150] The setting is twenty bars in length; the first two phrases (mm. 1–6, 6–11) are each five-and-one-half bars long, with the second phrase beginning shifted to beat 3 of m. 6. The third phrase has an internal aab Bar form (mm. 12–14, 15–17, 18–20) with each of the a subsections a contrasting three bars in length; the b subsection contains a repeated cadential motive that begins first on beat 2, then is shifted to beat 4, similar to the shifting of the phrase beginning in the A' section. This cadential motive rounds out the chorale by presenting a tonal inversion of the opening motive: <B♭–C–D–E> becomes <F–D–C–B♭>.

In Berg's setting, the metric shifts in the A' phrase and the last b subsection of B are removed (fig. 5.30). The second A' phrase is shifted to begin on the downbeat (II, mm. 142, 165, 184), like the first A phrase, and the second cadential motive in the b subphrase of B is shifted to beat 2 in variations 1 and 2 (mm. 175–77, 194–96), but, in the final chorale statement, these two cadential motives are stated as upbeats (mm. 222–24) and as an upbeat in an augmented setting (doubled note values, mm. 225–26). By these rhythmic changes, Berg's settings of the chorale would occupy 6 + 6 + 9 = 21 bars, an odd number; but overlaps (mm. 147, 152, 169, 192, 194) and three-bar codettas (mm. 155–57,

Figure 5.29. Form in Violin Concerto, movement 4		
Chorale	mm. 136–57	aab Bar form
Variation 1	158–77	
Variation 2 inverted	178–200	
Folk tune	201–13	
Coda: Chorale Variation 3	214–30	

Example 5.73. Melody of chorale with inversion, "Es ist genug; so nimm, Herr, meinen Geist," from Bach, Cantata 60, *O Ewigkeit, du Donnerwort*

197–99) maintain two-bar metric units throughout. In two places, canons at an interval of one bar (variation 1, mm. 159–64, and variation 2, mm. 185–90) group one-bar units against the prevailing two-bar hypermeter.

The chorale melody and Bach's harmonization clearly resonated with Berg. The opening tritone motive <B♭–C–D–E> (in Berg's transposition at T1 from A to B♭ major) fits with 89AB of the row. Bach's harmonization, particularly of the opening and the Ba' subphrase, is particularly chromatic; the [0258] and [026] harmonies and the descending interval 1-cycle are all similar to Berg's language (see Bach's harmony in ex. 5.76b, mm. 219–22, lower stave). Even the "incidental" harmonies from combinations of chord tones and non-chord tones—for instance, in Bach's harmonization, the third melody tone is set over a first-inversion major triad with an accented neighbor tone, creating a local whole-tone+ [0148]—are points of intersection between Berg's and Bach's languages.[151]

In Berg's initial setting of the chorale, a statement of phrase A in its twelve-tone guise (mm. 136–41) is followed by Bach's harmonization of mm. 1–4

Figure 5.30. Setting of chorale in Violin Concerto, movement 4

	A phrase bars	A' phrase bars	B phrase a bars	a'	b	codetta	total bars
Theme:	6 mm. PA 136–41	6 mm. 142–47	8 mm. 147–49	150–52 /	152–54	mm. 155–57	= 22
Var. 1:	6 mm. P4/PA 158–63 canon PB 159–64	6 mm. 164–69	9 mm. 169–71	172–74 /	175–77		= 20
Var. 2:	6 mm. IA 178–83	6 mm. 184–89 canon I9 185–90	6 mm. 190–92	192–94 /	194–96	mm. 197–99	= 18
Var. 3:	6 mm. PA 214–219		8 mm. 220–22	223–24 / (offset metrically)	225–27	augmented	= 14

from A and 10–11 of A' (mm. 142–47). The Ba phrase then appears, in a twelve-tone guise (mm. 147–49), with the following Ba' phrase in Bach's harmonization (mm. 150–52). The subsequent closing Bb subphrase has a twelve-tone setting, then repeats in Bach's initial setting (Bach, mm. 18–19), with its deceptive cadence motion (mm. 152–54), and the chorale closes with the final subphrase of the Bb section extended and segmented by alternating violin and ensemble parts (mm. 155–57).

In the first phrase, containing the chorale melody transposed to begin on B♭ (mm. 136ff.), the melody is derived from rows: P6 89AB <B♭–C–D–E>, PA 2458 <F–C–E♭–D>, P6 9AB3 <C–D–E–F>, and I4 03 <E–F>. A canonic voice at T−7 (mm. 134ff., viola) precedes it in an inner-voice <E♭–F–G–A>, which continues as <A–B♭–F–F–A♭–G>, harmonizing the beginning of the melody and implying a "B♭ major" harmonic context (m. 138). Surrounding voices and notes are drawn from rows. The first phrase is thus in a twelve-tone context, but with a strong implication of B♭ major, leading to the Bach harmonization in B♭ major of the second melodic phrase, but using the harmonization of (Bach's) mm. 1-4 in the first phrase and 10-11 of the second phrase. Within this tonal setting, violin interjections of the melody's opening [0246] realize the latent whole-tone+ aspects of Bach's harmonies (m. 143, <B♭–C–D–E>; mm. 145–47, <G♯–F♯–E–D>) and point to the intersection of Berg's cyclic language and tonality.

The two a subphrases beginning the third phrase are similarly arranged first in Berg's twelve-tone context (mm. 147–49, I0 0B <C–D>, P3 036 <E♭–D–C>), then in Bach's tonal harmonization (mm. 150–52), as are the two parts of the final subphrase: mm. 152–53, I6 789A <F–D–C–B♭>, and mm. 153–54. The second, tonally harmonized part (mm. 153–54), ends with a deceptive cadence (which actually appears with the first of the final subphrases in the Bach version) to motivate a repeat of the final measures (mm. 154–57), in which orchestra and soloist extend the cadence by repeating dyads in alternation, contrasting the tonal and twelve-tone settings, the latter with the row in vertical tetrachords, whole-tone+ 0123, 4567, and 89AB (I2, mm. 154–57, solo violin).

The first variation arranges the chorale in alternating phrases, using chorale levels PA, T = 6–related P4, and PB in canon with P4. The T6-related PA and P4 begin by filling in interval 6 {B♭,E} with the two whole-tone complementary tetrachords <B♭–C–D–E> and <E–F♯–G♯–B♭>. Since the chorale melody includes only six notes, {B♭,C,E,E♭,D,F} [012346], interval-class vector <443 211>, at T6 between PA and P4 there are only two common tones (yielding a ten-note set when the two are combined), and at T5 between P4 and PB the minimum one common tone (yielding an eleven-note set when the two are combined). The first A phrase, P4, is followed in canon by PB (mm. 158–64); the second A' phrase is transformed at T6 to PA beginning on B♭2 (mm. 164–69, ex. 5.74a, marked CH in m. 164); the B phrase appears again from P4 a (mm. 169–71, ex. 5.74a, beginning on F♯3, marked CH), then back to PA a (mm. 172–75, ex. 5.74a, beginning on C4, marked CH), ending with both P4 and PA b cadence figures (<B–G♯–F♯–E>, <F–D–C–B♭>, mm. 175–77). The violin melody (the *Klagegesang*) that begins with the second phrase (mm. 164–75) is created from intertwined P1/P3 (or R(15)) and P0/P2 (or R(14)) rows, dividing into mm. 164–72, then mm. 173–76 at TB (ex. 5.74a). The horizontal alignment of the rows creates multiple intervalic variants on the contour figure <0132>, as in m. 165 <C♯4–D♯4–F♯4–E4>.[152] The solo violin melody is doubled in successively larger instrumental forces: adding first and second violins (mm. 170–78), then violas (mm. 179–93).

In variation 2 (mm. 179–200, ex. 5.75a) the inverted form of the chorale theme removes the tonal implications of the prime form, since the inversion destroys the tonal organization (see ex. 5.73). The inverted forms are all sum 8,

Example 5.74a. Intertwined rows over chorale melody (CH) in variation 1, Violin Concerto, II, mm. 164–73. Berg VIOLINKONZERT. Copyright 1936 by Universal Edition. Copyright renewed. All Rights Reserved. Used by permission of European American Music Distributors Corporation, sole U.S. and Canadian agent for Universal Edition A.G., Wien.

Example 5.74b. Cyclic pitch structure, Violin Concerto, II, mm. 164–73

the sum at which E and B♭ map into themselves: chorale P4, PA, and PB appear in inversion as 14, 1A, and 19. The chorale melody is, as in variation 1, stated partially in canon, partially in single voices alternating T6 levels. The melody is stated first at IA (mm. 178–83, horns, beginning <B♭–A♭–G♭–F♭>, then continuing from F♭3 at the start of ex. 5.75a). The second phrase, at the climax (mm. 184ff.), is stated at T6 in I4 (horn 1, trumpet 1, <E–D–C–B♭, . . .>), with I7 in parallel interval 9s (horn 2, trumpet 2, <G–F–E♭–D♭, . . .>), and a canon at one-bar from T5-related I9 (mm. 184–90, harp, contrabass, <A–G–F–E♭, . . . >; the T5 canon is the inverse of the T7 canon in the first variation). The third B phrase a is stated at T6-related IA (mm. 190–92, trombone 1), the repeated a returns to I4 (mm. 192–94, trombone 2), then follow the final cadential b motives from I4 (mm. 195–96, trombone 2), and at T6 from IA (mm. 196–97, cello), and the two repeat (mm. 197–99, trombone 1, cello).

The violin melody over variation 2 is created from three alternating rows, P0, PB, and P1, yielding successive [012]s <−1,+2> at T = successive prime row interval pattern <3–4–4–3–3–4–4–3>, until the alternation is relaxed (mm. 180, starting at order position 8, ex. 5.75a). At the climax of the movement (mm.

Twelve-Tone Music: Detail and Analysis   379

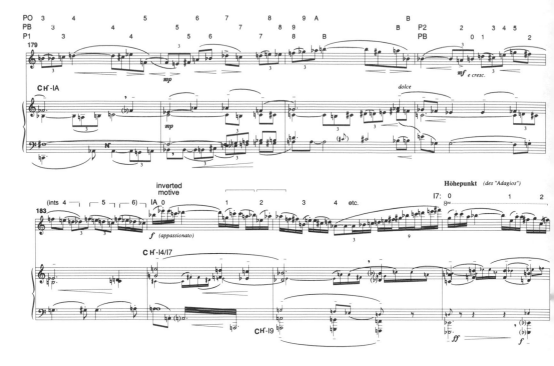

Example 5.75a. Intertwined rows over inverted chorale melody (CH) in variation I, inverted motive, Violin Concerto, II, mm. 179–86. Berg VIOLINKONZERT. Copyright 1936 by Universal Edition. Copyright renewed. All Rights Reserved. Used by permission of European American Music Distributors Corporation, sole U.S. and Canadian agent for Universal Edition A.G., Wien.

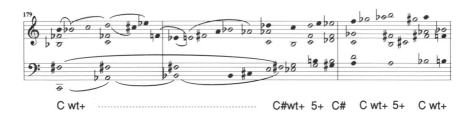

Example 5.75b. Cyclic pitch structure, Violin Concerto, II, mm. 179 – 84.

184ff.), the violin melody consists of a motive from m. 3 of the inverted chorale, initially <B♭−E♭6−C5−D♭6>, sequenced at the T-levels of IA 01234 <B♭−G−E♭−B−A♭> (mm. 184−85), I7 01234 <G−E−C−A♭−F> (mm. 186−87), and I0 2345 <F−D♭−B♭−G> (mm. 187−89). Thus, the violin begins on B♭ 0 of IA (m. 184), then G 0 of I7 (m. 186) at the climax.

The complex harmony throughout variations 1 and 2 is based on a combination of whole-tone+ and 5-cycle+, and a small number of 3-cycle+, collections (exx. 5.74b, 5.75b). Dissonant tones (labeled with filled-in noteheads) in the cyclic contexts compel the music forward in search of resolution or symmetry (which never arrives); held notes change quality from dissonance to consonance, or become consonant in a new cyclic context. The violin melody, in particular, constantly changes status as it weaves its way upward, with its contour <0132> figures in varied consonant and dissonant relationships.

In detail, in mm. 164ff. (ex. 5.74b) the initial P1 3-cycle chord has a dissonant F♯3 that resolves up to G3; the chorale dissonant passing tone C3 is paralleled with A3 and leads to a 5-cycle chord, in which the upper C♯4 is now dissonant. The first chord in m. 166 is, however, another P1 3-cycle chord in which the C♯4 is consonant, but the bass C2, initially consonant in a 5-cycle context as the end of a descending 7-cycle <A3−D3−G2−C2>, becomes dissonant in the 3-cycle chord. This chord is prolonged for the entire bar, with the violin D♯4/F♯4 acting as double neighbors to the consonant E4. The bass C2 becomes consonant again in the following 5-cycle context (m. 166), moving by interval 5 to F2 (5-cycle <C−F−B♭−E♭−A♭>); the F2 moves up to a consonant F♯2 in a P0 3-cycle {F♯,A,C,E♭}, but with a dissonant A♭3, which is held over the bar line and the change of chord to become consonant with E♭5 in an emerging 5-cycle context that completes itself on the second half of m. 167, as the A♭3 passes to a consonant B♭3. The bass note F♯2, dissonant locally, moves by a consonant interval 5 to the C♯2 beginning m. 168.

In mm. 168−69, the bass outlines a P1 3-cycle horizontally, while the individual notes are also part of vertical 3-cycle+ and whole-tone+ collections: C♯2 and B♭2 are dissonant in a P2 3-cycle {D,F,G♯,B} context, but then G2, E2, and B♭1 become consonant in vertical whole-tone contexts in m. 169. The passage then slowly reverts to 5-cycle+ collections (mm. 170−73), with an interval 1−based bass line strongly implying directed tonal motion.

Similar harmonic and melodic motions occur in the second variation (ex. 5.75b), with a greater occurrence of whole-tone+ harmonies, until the 3-cycle basis at the climax. The opening whole-tone context (mm. 179−80) has dissonance provided by notes from the opposite collection. In mm. 181−83, 5- and 3-cycle contexts intervene, leading to the climax. The initial chord in m. 184, has the P1 3-cycle {C♯,E,G,B♭} over bass A; as elsewhere in Berg's music, this impor-

CODA

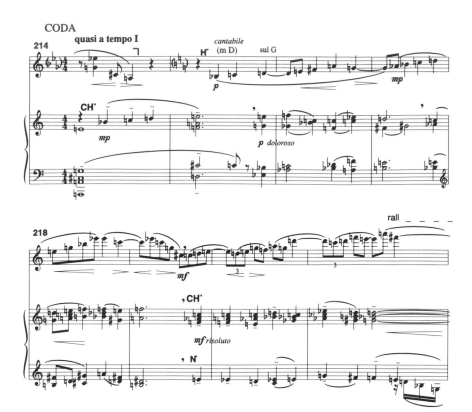

Example 5.76a. Final chorale setting, Violin Concerto, II, mm. 214–21. Berg VIOLINKONZERT. Copyright 1936 by Universal Edition. Copyright renewed. All Rights Reserved. Used by permission of European American Music Distributors Corporation, sole U.S. and Canadian agent for Universal Edition A.G., Wien.

Example 5.76b. Cyclic pitch structure, Bach harmonization in mm. 219–22 compared, Violin Concerto, II, mm. 214–22

tant formal moment has a strong tonal allusion due to this added note's acting comparably to a root. The same note hangs on into the next bar, similarly dissonant in the same cyclic context, but now with its tritone pair added, creating an embryonic contrasting Po 3-cycle, but also with strong 5-cycle tendencies that are realized in the following two bars. The passage ends with [01469]—a recurring harmony in Berg's music, from the op. 2 songs onward, and, finally, a 5-cycle on D (m. 190), a focal note at interval 7 from G.

Variation 2 leads into the final statement of the Carinthian folk song (mm. 200–13), by a successive transformation of the final <E♭–G♭–A♭–B♭> tetrachord of the inverted chorale melody, changing the upper final note through the notes <B♭4,A4,B4,C5> in a reference to Bach (mm. 198–201, cello). This folksong statement is cut off by a final chordal variation of the chorale theme. In this third variation (mm. 214–30, ex. 5.76a and b), the repeat of the A' section and the second a subphrase of the B section are omitted (fig. 5.30). The PA chorale melody is harmonized in tetrachords with an added violin commentary, in characteristic 5-cycle and whole-tone+ collections. The first phrase begins over an apparent V–I in D, which proceeds to a V–I at T6 in A♭ (forming bass [0167] <D–A–E♭–A♭> and then to an apparent similar progression in B♭ minor. The "cadence" arrival in m. 217 on a C whole-tone chord over a dissonant bass B3, however, dissolves the momentary implied tonal function.

Berg's setting of the first B section subphrase is somewhat similar to Bach's harmonization (mm. 219–22): in ex. 5.76b, Berg's harmonization is given in the upper stave, with Bach's harmonization in the lower stave.[153] Bach uses a descending interval 1 cycle, <B♭–A–G♯–G–F♯–F–E> (given here transposed to B♭); Berg's descending interval 1 cycle begins at T6, however, substituting E for B♭ (the boundary notes of the chorale opening tetrachord) in a reflection of the important T6 relationships throughout the chorale variations. Berg's harmonies are mostly whole-tone+, of the [0258] variety, as are Bach's chords, save for the pure triads. This parallel setting is a graphic illustration of Berg's cyclic settings with tonal allusions and of how they relate to chromatic tonal practice.

The following b subphrase cadential figure <F–D–C–B♭> repeats through three octaves (beginning on F6, solo violin, F5, trumpet, and F4, horn), with a final whole-tone descent <C♯–B–A–G> (horn, mm. 228–230), to end on G. Underlying the cadential figure are the successive rows P2, P1, Po, P5, and PA, in the interval 1 and 5 cycles found throughout the concerto. The piece ends with a return of the introduction's 7-cycle arpeggios, which end on B♭ under the chord <B♭–D–F–G>; this harmony with a focus on B♭, contains interval-class 5s {B♭,F}, {D,G} and interval-class 3s {B♭,G}, {F,D}. The concerto thus ends with a summary of the structural relationships developed throughout, maintaining the tonal allusion of the 5/7–cycle material to the end.

Conclusion

Berg has traditionally been described as the member of the Second
Viennese School who retained the gestural, rhetorical, and, to varying extents, harmonic language and voice-leading characteristic of
late-nineteenth-century tonal music. In the seeming alliance between
tonal and atonal or twelve-tone pitch and rhythmic organization in his music, he
is often regarded as the heir to Mahler, who somewhat analogously combined
and contrasted simple folk-like melodies, harmonies, and phrases with complex,
highly chromatic passages. Although the juxtaposition of styles is an important
component of the emotional and spiritual affect in the music of both composers, Mahler stayed within one system, operating at both extremes of the
tonal language, whereas it is usually asserted that Berg, under the influence of
Schoenberg, took the process a step further by adopting aspects of atonal and
twelve-tone techniques and balancing these with tonal features even within the
same piece.

I have attempted to demonstrate that Berg's surface juxtaposition of compositional styles, although significant in many respects, is underlaid by a unified
language. As is the case with many composers, but to a greater extent, Berg
adapted the disruptive elements in nineteenth-century tonal music—symmetry,

transpositionally and inversionally invariant pitch-class collections, and interval cycles and cycle-based collections—for his own use. These elements became the basis of an integrated cyclic language that not only is the common organizational denominator for his "tonal," "atonal" and "twelve-tone" methods of organization, taking on new guises of complementation and serial order, but that also acts as a mirror, reflecting its tonal origins. Ultimately, however, no matter how clear the image in this mirror, the language operates according to its own internal intervalic logic.

In addition to the continuity and complexity of his cyclic pitch organization, Berg's music is characterized by his extension of systematic cyclic relationships to rhythm, meter, dynamics, serial order positions, tempo and even orchestration. The treatment of these other elements reflects and complements the pitch language, lending the music a great depth of isomorphic relationships and developing variation in all its aspects. Berg's striving for a total cyclic integration, alongside his stylistic retention of the surface features and rhetoric of nineteenth-century music, can be seen, in retrospect, as a precursor to many musical developments up to the present day.

In *The Listening Composer* and the chapters added in the second edition of *Twelve-Tone Tonality*, George Perle extends his analytical views from Berg to the music of Varése, Scriabin, Schoenberg, Webern, and Bartók. Complementing Perle's writings on symmetry and cycles are Bruce Archibald's and David Lewin's studies on the role of inversion in Schoenberg's and Webern's music, Philip Lambert's studies of cyclic organization in Ive's music, Ernö Lendvai, Jonathan Bernard, and Elliot Antokoletz on symmetry and cycles in Bartók's oeuvre, Ann McNamee on interval cycles in Szymanowski's works, and Steven Stucky on the cycles of vertical chords in Lutoslawski's music. Given the increasing evidence, including the present analysis, it seems clear that, under the general rubric of "atonal," we may add symmetry-based organization to the existing theory of pitch-class set relationships in a list of two definite and defined classes of atonal structures. The two are not, of course, mutually exclusive, but they have many interrelationships, and many pieces fall, in varying degrees, in both categories. Nonetheless, they are distinctive enough to constitute two comprehensive "theories" for music of the twentieth century.

What remains for the theory of symmetry is a systematic formalization of objects and transformations, consonance and dissonance, and controlling and controlled structures, comparable to that of set theory and Schenkerian theory. In this volume I have attempted to explain one composer's body of work in terms of the symmetry of cyclic collections. I have asserted that cyclic structures are not prolonged in the tonal sense, but they certainly establish a hierarchy with which to parse the surface, and they allow for short- and long-range connections—if only associative—between motives, passages, and sections, even in large-scale contextual contrasts and reconciliations. Thus, for instance, Berg's op. 4 songs are governed by 3-cycle and 5-cycle collections, with whole-tone–based collections secondary, with those collections containing the note G referential and acting as a basis from which other collections are measured. The hierarchical possibilities are indicated in the graph of op. 4, no. 2 given in example 3.9, which illustrates the unfolding of 3-cycle collections based contextually on a hierarchically superior P_2 3-cycle {F,G#,B,D}, with a contrasting P_0 3-cycle {F#,A,C,E♭} in the chord in m. 7, and an accompanying P_1 3-cycle {C#,E,G,B♭}. This local referential status of {F,G#,B,C} is nested within an overall referential status for P_1 3-cycle {G,B♭,C#,E} in op. 4 as a whole. In the final song, op. 4, no. 5, the emphasis on the note G in this cycle characteristically assumes the form of a tonal allusion, particularly in variation 8 and at the ending. This allusion is not part of the symmetrical system, however, but is Berg's particular stylistic adaptation.

For the rest of op. 4, no. 2 (again in ex. 3.9), the contrasting 5-cycle–based collections—including the multicyclic [0167]—act in a secondary role. Thus, the 5-cycle–based motive 4/a collection appears at the outset in the guise of motivic [014]s and [0167]s, only later (in the cello lead-in to m. 7) in its interval 5 setting. The [014] motive, found in many of Berg's atonal pieces, is a stylistic adaptation by itself remaining undefined in cyclic terms. Other surface symmetries support the overall symmetrical basis—as in the wedge from F as another interpretation of the role of this locally important pitch-class, aside from its membership in 3-cycle {F,G#,B,D}.

In *Wozzeck*, Act III, scene iii, the various metric tendencies of the *Haupt-rhythmus* act somewhat analogously, as cyclic guises for this rhythm. Berg's basic contrast between duple and triple organization in the scene is a simple reflection of the possibilities for these different cyclic tendencies, and the varying settings in different meters and tempos throughout are a working-out of the metric potential. In other pieces, as in the first of the op. 4 songs, the rhythmic cycles are not metric. The constant play between the rhythmic layers in yet another work, op. 5, no. 2, illustrates the extent to which Berg varied rhythm within the smallest confines. Meter can be regarded analogously to tonality in this context; it is a stylistic guise for rhythmic cycles, as tonality is a stylistic stance for pitch cyclic collections.

The isomorphisms with rhythmic and other musical elements are an attractive aspect of the theory of symmetry; many features can be described in cyclic terms, so long as perceptual factors—such as the differences between pitch intervals, time intervals, and order-position intervals—are taken sufficiently into account. Berg clearly draws an effective parallel between the three in the film music of *Lulu* (mm. 670–74), where the successive rows display serial invariance based on cyclic patterns of order positions evidenced in rhythms, with the multicyclic [0167] as the pitch component. This instance is only the most obvious of a number of examples, many of which I have drawn attention in the preceding pages.

The easiest criticism of my presentation of a cyclic basis for Berg's music is that the notes omitted to yield the cyclic+ collections are part of more complex pitch groupings, explainable only in pitch-class–set or some other terms, and that I have merely found in my interpretations what I was looking for in a highly chromatic texture that could yield multiple readings based on any intervalic criteria, merely by choosing different notes. I have not as yet solved the essential problem of the theory of symmetry—a systematic explanation for all notes in a passage not part of a proposed symmetrical collection—but I hope at least to have provided enough evidence for a plausible basis for such an investigation. I regard the creation of a true theory of symmetry, with defined limits as to repertoire and composers, and transformations between "consonant" and "dissonant" states, as a vital step in the evolution of our view on the music of this century.

Berg's generation is unique in music for encompassing the change from tonality to a post-tonal world, in which tonality gained an entirely new and different meaning through its novel status as one organizational method among many. The situation is perhaps comparable only to that of composers like Monteverdi, who witnessed the change from an established language, Renaissance counterpoint, to the new Baroque harmony, lending the former an unprecedented emotional and stylistic quality determined by its contrast with the latter, to be exploited compositionally. Thus, later composers could invoke Renaissance counterpoint in compositions like masses to great effect, as a novel expression invoking an ever-more distant past. In the historicist atmosphere of the early twentieth century, where a new choice had to be made—one unknown to previous generations—Berg actively invoked the changed emotional power of tonal gestures and relationships, but he was concerned enough about unity and internal coherence—properties learned from the classical masters by way of lessons with Schoenberg—to create a language that subsumed tonal harmonies, progressions, and voice-leading as one option among many within a larger cyclic universe. Nonetheless, the symbols he found in tonality—nostalgia, vulgarity, folk images, deconstructed waltzes and marches, peace and tranquility—retain their potency, regardless of the level of integration. This balanced retention of tonal elements—both musical and "extra-musical"—to which I have alluded several times, defines an essence difficult to explain in words but unmistakable to the ear and heart when listening to Berg's music.

Finally, it is remarkable that, as Berg moved further along his compositional path, his increasing sophistication in language was accompanied by ever greater numbers and complexity of related private and public programmatic references. He continually and obsessively stamped the music as his own with autobiographical elements, lending it a virtual identity with the course of his own life. In this he followed a tendency found in many arts in the nineteenth century. In his paradoxical yet somewhat circular path, Berg's refusal to objectify his music by separating himself and his life from his art links him securely with the Romantic past, but his simultaneously highly individualized treatment and development of all musical elements in analogous transformations mark him as a modernist, innovative figure of the twentieth century. In our time we have come to separate clearly these two inclinations, imbuing them with ideological, institutional, and political, as well as artistic, meaning. Yet, in an earlier time, they were connected—even within one artist. Ultimately, perhaps, it is the enigma of these two apparently contradictory tendencies coexisting that feeds our continued fascination with this remarkable musician, Alban Berg, and with his life, his culture, and his music.

Appendix: Theme and Row Charts for Chapter 5

Chamber Concerto Motives

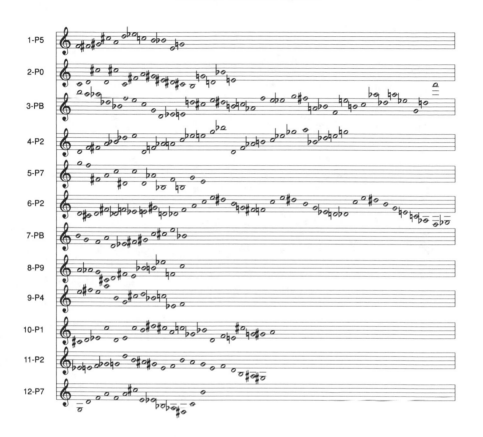

Lyric Suite Row 1

Lyric Suite row 2

Lyric Suite row 3

Lyric Suite row 4

Der Wein

Lulu Principal Row

Dr. Schön row

Alwa row

Violin Concerto

Notes

1 "Vorher möchte ich aber an Sie, meine Damen und Herren, eine Bitte richten! Und zwar die Bitte: Alles das, was ich Ihnen hier Theoretisches und Musikästhetisches zu erklären versucht habe, alles das zu vergessen, wenn Sie nunmehr am Dienstag oder später der Aufführung der Oper "Wozzeck" auf den Brettern dieses Theaters beiwohnen werden!" Alban Berg, *Wozzeck Vortrag*, translation from Jarman 1989b (pp. 169–70).

"Um wieviel mehr also sind wir berechtigt, ja—wollen wir uns ein Urteil über die Musik bilden—gezwungen, uns hievon auch in musiktheoretischer Hinsicht Rechenschaft zu geben und das in möglichst präziser, lückenloser Weise." Alban Berg, "Die musikalische Impotenz der 'neuen Ästhetik' Hans Pfitzners," translated by Cornelius Cardew in Reich 1965 (p. 214).

2 Adorno 1991 (p. 14).

3 Jarman 1991b (p. 18).

4 For instance, David Schroeder (1988, 1990) compares Berg's *Chamber Concerto* to Franz Werfel's *Spiegelmensch*, pointing out autobiographical elements in other writers well known to Berg: Strindberg, Balzac, and Baudelaire. Redlich 1957 (p. 113) noted that Berg's "mania for allusive quotations from other composers has parallels in modern literature," citing Ezra Pound's *Cantos* and T. S. Eliot.

5 For Op. 6, No. 3, see Brand, Hailey, and Harris 1987 (p. 208); Berg's asthma returns in the character of Schigolch in *Lulu*. Berg 1971 (p. 224) contains comments on Wozzeck. See also Perle 1980 (pp. 56, 129) and Jarman 1979 (p. 227). Berg described aspects of the *Chamber Concerto* in an open letter which appears in Brand, Hailey, and Harris 1987 (pp. 334–37), and was originally published in the journal *Pult und Taktstock*, vol. 2 (February–March 1925), pp. 23–28.

6 See Dalen 1989. Dalen (1989, p.157) shows a sketch of the *Chamber Concerto* where the letters AHDE (from mAtHilDE, Schoenberg's first wife) are extracted from the musical note equivalents <A,D,E♭,C,B,B♭,E,G> (ArnolD SCHönBErG) by an almost uniform cyclic extraction of letters: A (+4) H [B] (+5) D (+5) E. Interestingly, a similar extraction process on order positions of twelve-tone rows characterizes Berg's derivations of material from rows in *Der Wein*, *Lulu*, and the Violin Concerto, as described in chap. 4.

7 Perle 1977b, 1985. Berg scholars have long suspected the existence of a programmatic element in the *Lyric Suite*. Berg described the changes in the row throughout the quartet as "submitting to fate" (Reich 1965, p. 149). Erwin Stein 1927 described the suite as "lyric dramatic, a climax of atmosphere and expression [*eine lyrisch-dramatische, eine Steigerung der Stimmung- und Ausdrucksintensität*]" (also referred to by Leibowitz 1949, p. 156). Redlich 1957 called the suite "a psychological experience of great intensity" (pp. 138–39). Reginald Smith Brindle 1957 found ref-

erences to the number 23 and to Zemlinsky's name. Rognoni 1977 described the quartet as "highly dramatic in form, an amplified inner drama with no connection to a literary theme" (p. 112); he related Berg's "submission to fate [*Schicksal erleidend*]" to the appearance of this phrase "in German poetry from Hölderlin up to the late romantics, and which reflects the Nietzschian concept of *Amor fati*" (p. 114). Schweizer 1970 (pp. 88–89, 96–98) identified formal proportions in terms of Berg's self-appointed number 23 in the first movement, m. 23 being the centre of a brief palindrome in the last movement, and the placement of the second note of the *Tristan* quote (F_4) on the one hundred thirty-eighth quarter beat, or 6 × 23. Mosco Carner (1975, 110; 1983, p. 122) expressed his belief in an "inner drama too intimate, too personal to be divulged in words." Jarman 1979 cited a letter from Rudolf Kolisch stating that "the *Lyric Suite* had a programme based upon an event in Berg's life"; Jarman (1979, p. 228), had already suspected that such a program existed and had previously discovered the lines of text in sketches for the final movement which were also separately discovered and eventually deciphered by Douglass Green in 1976 (see Green 1977b).

That Adorno knew about the secret dedication is indicated in many of his comments, such as the description of the second movement as an "interior domestic scene" (1991, p. 108), his recall of Berg's comment in a rehearsal about the repeated octave Cs to reflect "the way one threatens children" (1991, p. 109), and his references to "strophes" in the sixth movement (1991, pp. 112–13). He described the suite as a "latent opera" and posited a "musical protoganist" who "cannot master the alien world through love" (1991, p. 104). Adorno wrote a letter to Helene Berg on April 16, 1936, confessing he knew about Berg's affair with Hanna Fuchs-Robettin, and cited the evidence in an essay on the *Lyric Suite* (in Brosche and Hilmar 1985, pp. 173–75). He wrote about Berg's affair in 1955, stipulating that his account not be published until after the death of all concerned; see the letter in Metzger and Riehn 1979 (pp. 8–10).

8 Green 1977b and personal communication.

9 Albine, born Dec. 4, 1902, was Berg's daughter to a servant girl named Marie Scheuchl working at the Berg family's Berghof summer home. See Jarman 1982a, Jarman 1989b (pp. 66–67), and Erich Alban Berg 1979, 1980. See also Knaus 1976, Perle 1985 (pp. 255–57), and Pople 1991 (pp. 60–64). Green 1991 (pp. 311–13) has, however, argued for caution in attributing a secret program to the concerto, in view of the lack of documentation.

10 For numerology in Berg's music see Carner 1983 (p. 148), Jarman 1982, Neuwirth 1981, Pernye 1967, and Stadler 1981. For encoded names see Floros 1971 (p. 75), Perle 1985 (pp. 18–19), Redlich 1957 (p. 113), Stadler 1981 (pp. 173–74), and Watkins 1988 (pp. 374–75).

11 See Perle 1977b and 1985 (pp. 24–25). Redlich 1960 and 1957 (p. 131) has compared the relationship between the song setting and the following *Lyric Suite* (1925–26) to Wagner's *Wesendonck-Lieder* "Im Treibhaus" (1858) and "Träume" (1857) and his opera *Tristan und Isolde* (1857–59). The parallel is made explicit by

the quote from the opening of *Tristan* in the final movement of the *Lyric Suite* (VI, mm. 26–27).

12 For programmatic elements in *Lulu* and *Der Wein*, see Perle 1977b and 1985 (pp. 17–29, 139); also Hall 1989, 1991; MacDonald 1988; Watkins 1988; and Headlam 1990.

13 See Jarman 1979 (p. 18n. 1) and Archibald 1989 (p. 111). The key or the focus on D is also prominent in music by Schoenberg and Webern: Schoenberg: 1897 String Quartet, *Verklärte Nacht, Pelleas und Melisande*, the String Quartet Op. 7, the choral song *Friede auf Erden* Op. 13, the *George-Lieder* Op. 15, the *Klavierstück* Op. 11, No. 2, and "Vorgefühle" from Op. 16; Webern: Passacaglia Op. 1 and song Op. 3, No. 1. See Schroeder 1988 on Strindberg, who used D-based musical pieces as parts of his texts: Bach's Violin Partita No. 2 in *Charles VII*; Beethoven's Piano Sonata Op. 31, No. 2 and Piano Trio Op. 70 in *A Ghost Sonata* and *Crimes and Crimes*. Berg's later reference to Beethoven's Ninth Symphony in *Der Wein* suggests this work may have been influential in the symbolic significance of D. See also MacDonald 1988, Watkins 1988 (pp. 13–14), and Headlam 1990.

14 See Berg's notes in Rauchhaupt 1971. The alterations to the row, deemed necessary for the musical reason of its redundant retrograde invariance, successively add interval-class 1s to the interval succession, as if the chromatic scale or interval 1 cycle represented fate. This reading supports Perle's assertion that the character Schigolch in *Lulu* represents fate, with a row that is close to an interval 1 cycle, as the ultimate source of the drama and musical material of the opera; see Perle 1985 (pp. 102–3).

15 Redlich 1957 (p. 113) notes a "suspension of the present and . . . a magic reversal of time"; see also Dalen 1989 (pp. 146–53); Jarman 1979 (pp. 240–41), 1989b (chap. 7); Morgan 1991; and Perle 1985 (pp. 6, 102–6).

16 Jarman 1970b.

17 See, for instance, Burkholder 1991.

18 The title *Reigen* of Berg's Op. 6, No. 2 calls to mind the novelette of the same name by Arthur Schnitzler (1862–1931). The ten dialogues of "Reigen" (1896–97) concern conversations between two people immediately before and after lovemaking. In each successive dialogue, one character continues into the next dalliance, until the end wraps around to the beginning: (1) prostitute (Leocadia) and soldier (Franz); (2) soldier (Franz) and chambermaid (Marie); (3) chambermaid (Marie) and young gentleman (Mr. Alfred); to (9) actress and count; and finally (10) count and prostitute (Leocadia). In dialogue 7, the "sweet girl" (süße Mädel) character calls the poet a doctor in an autobiographical reference to Schnitzler himself, who was both a doctor and writer. A connection between Berg and Schnitzler is suggested by the circular nature of the novelette, and the characters Franz and Marie suggest a relationship to *Wozzeck*. A reference to a friend of the count's named Lulu in dialogues 9 and 10 and the deception in the successively linked sexual partners and hypocrisy across different social classes foreshadow the world of *Lulu*. I am indebted to John Covach for suggesting the cir-

cular form of Schnitzler's *Reigen* and its possible relation to Berg's music. Watkins 1988 (p. 377) draws a parallel between Marie Scheuchl—the mother of Berg's child Albine—and the "süße Mädel" of German literature. Schnitzler printed two hundred copies of *Reigen* in 1900; the work was published in 1903, but sale in Germany was forbidden in 1904. The first performance of the play in Vienna took place in 1921. Berg referred to Schnitzler in letters to Schoenberg of March 1, 1913, and April 20, 1915 (Brand, Hailey, and Harris 1987, pp. 159, 236.). See Eislin 1989 for comments on Schnitzler.

19 Adorno 1991 (p. 74).

20 Perle 1980 (p. 18). See also Adorno 1991 (p. 82) on the catastrophic climax in "Marsch" that foreshadows impending war. Selz 1957 (p. 267) describes similar premonitions in an abstract Kandinsky work of the same time, *Improvisation No. 30* (1913), whose abstract surface is broken by two cannons in the right-hand corner, which seem to fire into the painting.

21 Jarman 1991a (pp. 94–101) discusses *Lulu* in the context of contemporary operatic trends as "epic theatre." See Adorno 1991 (pp. 115–17) on Berg's adaptation of jazz, and Redlich's (1957, pp. 178–79) comments on the influence of Schoenberg's opera *Von Heute auf Morgen* (1928-29, first performed 1930).

22 Redlich 1957 (p. 156), compares *Der Wein* in its relation to *Lulu* with the second "Schliesse mir die Augen beide" setting in its relation to the *Lyric Suite*. He points out the similarity between the tango in *Der Wein* (mm. 40ff.) and the English waltz in *Lulu* (Act I, scene iii). Berg's use of jazz reflects his time. In Germany, the 1920s saw the emergence of dance- and popular-music operas, such as *Jonny spielt auf* by Ernst Krenek (1927), a "Zeitoper" or "topical opera." Schoenberg's "Zeitoper," *Von Heute auf Morgen*, was partly a polemical statement against the younger generation of Weill, Krenek, and Hindemith. See Cook 1988.

23 The text and music of Wedekind's song are in Wedekind 1920, translated in Jarman 1979, appendix 2 (pp. 245–48).

24 Adorno 1968, trans. in John 1990 (p. 37).

25 See Jarman 1989b (chap. 7) and Perle 1980 (chap. 2) for overviews of text-music relationships in *Wozzeck*. The rediscovery of Büchner's *Woyzeck* and the problems of creating a definitive version are given in Franzos 1901, as well as in the Jarman and Perle passages cited.

26 See Jarman 1991a (pp. 98–99) for a discussion of *Lulu* in the context of Berg's operatic heritage.

27 Redlich 1957 (p. 113).

28 Green 1981; Stadler 1981 places Berg's numerology in a historical revivalist context.

29 Eliot 1932 (p. 10).

30 Straus 1990 (p. 1).

31 Straus 1990 pp. 9–15.

32 Straus 1984, 1990.

33 Berg's comment is in his notes on the *Lyric Suite*; see Reich 1965 (p. 151).

34 Even if we accept Richard Taruskin's criticisms of Straus's interpretation of this

term, we could hardly say that, in Berg's case, repression and misreading were involuntary, caused by anxiety. See Taruskin 1993 (p. 127).

35 References are given in the relevant discussions in the introductory section of chap. 1 and in chaps. 2 and 4.

CHAPTER 1: TONALITY, CYCLES, AND BERG'S OPUS 1 AND OPUS 2

1 R. Hilmar 1980 (pp. 43–45) lists eighty-two songs, counting op. 2, no. 4; see also Reich 1965 (pp. 109–13), Redlich 1957 (pp. 35–40, 287–89), and Chadwick 1971. Of the early songs, forty-six have been published in Alban Berg, *Jugendlieder*, ed. Christopher Hailey, 2 vols. (Vienna: Universal Edition, 1986–7).

2 For analysis and description of Berg's early songs, including the "Seven Early Songs" and their later orchestration from 1928, see Adorno 1991 (pp. 49–53), Adorno 1959, Carner 1983 (pp. 94–98), Chadwick 1971, DeVoto 1991 (pp. 63–66), DeVoto 1989 (pp. 35–43), Leibowitz 1949 (p. 139), Morgan 1991 (pp. 140–44), Perle 1980 (pp. 1–4), and Redlich 1957 (pp. 37–40).

3 For pitch and other musical spaces see Morris 1987.

4 Schoenberg 1969 (p. 20).

5 Lewin (1987, p. 21 and p. 22n. 1) notes many such charts in writings of German music theorists since the eighteenth century; see also Bernstein 1993.

6 Schoenberg 1983, chaps. 20–21.

7 Such uses of cyclic collections are commonly referred to as factors in the eventual dissolution of tonality in the early twentieth century. For discussions of cycles in nineteenth-century music, see Perle 1962, 1977a, 1990; Bernstein 1993; Cinnamon 1984; Morgan 1976; and Proctor 1978.

8 Cinnamon 1984, chap. 5.

9 Chadwick 1971 (pp. 133–34).

10 DeVoto 1991 (p. 63).

11 Chadwick, 1971 (pp. 136–37).

12 DeVoto 1991 (pp. 64–66); Jarman 1979 (pp. 19–20); Leibowitz 1949 (p. 138); and Morgan 1991 (pp. 140–41).

13 Perle 1980 (pp. 2–3) questions the dates of the Piano Sonata, pointing out the superiority of op. 1 to the Piano Variations from, reportedly, about the same time. R. Hilmar 1980, item 262 (p. 75), reports that composition was begun in 1907; the manuscript is missing. Adorno 1991 (pp. 40–41) relates the sonata to Schoenberg's op. 9; Redlich 1957 (pp. 47–48) notes that Berg had originally planned second and third movements. For the reception history of the sonata, see Scherliess 1981.

14 Archibald 1989 (pp. 91–92) notes the influence of Schoenberg's *Chamber Symphony* op. 9 with regard to quartal and whole-tone harmonies in the sonata.

15 The use of such a graph can be justified on the basis of Berg's analysis of the opening of Schoenberg's D-Minor String Quartet, which includes a chordal reduction of a contrapuntal texture with some normalization and rhythmic realignment. See Berg 1924b, in Reich 1965 (p. 197). Example 1.9 may be compared with Schmalfeldt's graphs of the sonata, especially her exx. 2 and 12

(Schmalfeldt 1991). Schmalfeldt shows how certain sonorities arise in tonal contexts, then free themselves from those contexts to become referential, at which point they are treated as pitch-class sets. She cites the piano chord {C♯,G,B,F♯} [0157] as well as other whole-tone–based chords such as [0148] and the half-diminished seventh [0258]. While I agree that cyclic referential sonorities indeed abound in the sonata, ultimately the piece is tonal throughout; Berg's path to atonality begins with his op. 2 songs.

16 See Schweizer 1970 (pp. 49–56) on sonata characteristics in Berg's op. 1.

17 "Open" beginnings occur in several of the *Seven Early Songs*: "Nacht," "Traumgekrönt," "Im Zimmer," "Liebesode," and "Sommertage"; see Schmalfeldt 1991 (p. 91n. 24).

18 A model for Berg's beginning open phrase and formal overlap occurs in the first movement of Beethoven's Piano Sonata Op. 31, no. 3, which, like the Berg Sonata, commences with an open phrase, and features an exposition that ends in V (m. 86), and a cadential extension moving to E♭, locally IV of B♭, which then leads back to the opening bars on the repeat, so that the tonic arrives only at the cadence ending the first phrase. The development ends with a prolongation of II⁶ (mm. 128ff.), leading into the beginning of the recapitulation on II⁶₅ (m. 137), and a tonic that arrives only at the end of the first phrase. See Schmalfeldt 1991 (p. 90).

19 Schoenberg 1983 (p. 330) notes a similar [013679] from combined B♭⁷ and E⁷ chords in the last movement of Mahler's Sixth Symphony, m. 387.

20 The cycles of vertical intervals result from the difference between the aligned horizontal intervals: descending interval 4 − descending interval 1 = interval 3 (−4 − (−1) = −3), and ascending interval 1 − descending interval 4 = interval 5 (1 − (−4) = 5).

21 Most authors trace the motivic content from the opening phrase: see Adorno 1991 (pp. 42–46); Jarman 1979 (pp. 31–32); Leibowitz 1949 (pp. 143–44); Redlich 1957 (pp. 48–49); and Scherliess 1975 (p. 29). Schmalfeldt 1991 (pp. 79–90) invokes the notions of developing variation and *Grundgestalt*. Leibowitz 1949 (p. 141) notes resemblances between Schoenberg's op. 9 second theme and the main theme of Berg's sonata and between the transition theme of the former and second theme of the latter.

22 For the compositional history of the op. 2 songs, see DeVoto 1989 (p. 43) and Kett 1989 (pp. 69–71). On the sketch evidence, Kett ascertains that Berg began with the second and third songs in the summer of 1908, then proceeded to the first, and was sketching the fourth as late as the spring of 1910. Kett (pp. 69–70) refers to a painting, *Die Schlafenden* by Josef Engelhart, a Viennese Secessionist painter with whom Berg may have been acquainted, or at least have known the work. The painting reflects a 3 + 1 grouping, with "three sleeping women in the left foreground, watched by a menacing and half-hidden faun-like creature in the right background." The painting and its possible influence on op. 2 were first "suggested by Rosemary Hilmar in the catalogue of the Berg Exhibition held in Vienna 1985." The grouping, and the "faun-like creature" are very

suggestive of the combination of the three tonal and one atonal songs in op. 2. Many authors have noted the similarity between the op. 2 songs and Ravel's *Gaspard de la nuit*; see DeVoto 1989 (p. 44). Watkins 1988 (pp. 46–52) notes the influence of Ravel and mentions the *Jugendstil* lettering on the title page of Berg's op. 2 and his piano sonata as evidence of an awareness of "contemporary French musical values" (p. 51).

23 Kett 1989 (p. 68) identifies the three poems as nos. 56, 57, and 70 of eighty-seven; a Mombert collection published in 1942, however, has corresponding poems 58, 59, and 72 from a total of eighty poems.

24 Redlich 1957 (pp. 40–41).

25 Kett 1989 (p. 79) reports that a sketch of op. 2, no. 2 exists written a major third higher, with a key signature of three flats, and speculates that E♭ major and minor were integral to the overall tonal plan. A+ a major third higher, however, the song would be in G minor, at T_5 from the D key of op. 2, no. 1, and $T-1$ from the A♭ key of op. 2, no. 3.

26 In the three-voice model and its four-voice realizations in op. 2, nos. 1–3, the [06] component has the property that $P = 1,7$ (or $P = 11,5$; both $T = 6$) is invariant. Thus, transposition of the [06] by a descending interval 1 is the same as a transposition by ascending interval 5, and the [06] retains its relative intervalic relationship with the ascending interval-5 voice. As a consequence, the successive chords are in the same set-class.

27 See Redlich 1957 (pp. 41–44) and Wennerstrom 1977; Kett 1989 labels these chords "A" and "B" and emphasizes their importance in op. 2.

28 See Kett 1989 (p. 79) and Jarman 1979 (p. 148). The rhythms are remarkably similar to those in Ravel's *Histoires naturelles*, no. 2, mm. 16–17; see n. 22 above.

29 "To sleep, to sleep, nothing but to sleep / No awaking, no dreaming! / Of those sorrows that afflicted me, / Hardly the faintest memory, / So that I, when life's abundance / Echoes down into my rest, / Shall enshroud myself all the more, / And close my eyes even tighter." Translation reprinted by permission of Deutsche Grammophon, Hamburg.

30 This palindromic return is the first instance of this characteristic of Berg's music. See Kett 1989 (p. 74) and Morgan 1991 (pp. 134–35); DeVoto 1989 (p. 43) refers to a *Bogenform*.

31 The coda is similar to the end of the Piano Sonata (ex. 1.11c); the latter's repeated C–B corresponds to the neighbor motion F♯–F—the pivotal notes in the tonic chord's roles as tonic D or dominant of G in op. 2, no. 1.

32 These two chords foreshadow the cadential chords in *Wozzeck*; cf. ex. 3.1f.

33 The chord on the last eighth note of m. 15 should have a C♭4 instead of a C4. This change, found in the corrected second edition of 1920, did not make it into the 1928 edition. Personal communication from Steven Kett.

34 "Sleeping I am carried / To my homeland. / From afar I come / Over mountain and ravine / Over a dark ocean / To my homeland." Translation reprinted by permission of Deutsche Grammophon, Hamburg.

35 See Ayrey 1982 and Perle 1977b.

36 "I overcame the strongest of giants / And from the darkest land / Found my way home / Guided by a fair hand from a fairytale— // The bells boom ponderously / And I totter through the streets / In the throes of sleep." Translation reprinted by permission of Deutsche Grammophon, Hamburg.

37 The impossible situation of a direct tritone relationship, as here of a D key area in an A♭ tonic piece, is discussed in Headlam and Brown 1990.

CHAPTER 2: THE ATONAL MUSIC: INTRODUCTION

1 "Über die Grenzen des All blicktest du sinnend hinaus" from "Texte auf Ansichtskarten" in Altenberg 1911, set by Berg in the *Altenberg Lieder*, op. 4, no. 3.

2 Berg 1929. This lecture, originally written to precede a performance of *Wozzeck* in Oldenburg in March 1929, appears in Redlich 1957 (pp. 311–27) and is translated in Redlich 1957 (pp. 261–85) and Jarman 1989b (pp. 154–70). All quotations are from the Redlich translation unless otherwise noted.

3 See Adorno 1991 (pp. 53–54) on op. 3. Berg also began and abandoned a symphony between op. 5 and op. 6. The *Sinfonie-Fragment*, from the summer of 1913, consists of a short score (*Particell*) with instrumental indications of forty-one bars, and a passacaglia of one hundred one bars. Jarman 1979 (p. 3) notes that the symphony was to be linked programmatically with Balzac's *Seriphita*. Schoenberg was also contemplating a work based on *Seriphita* in 1912; see Stuckenschmidt 1978 (p. 235). For a chronology of Berg's atonal works, see Jarman 1979 (pp. 1–8).

4 Adorno 1991 (pp. 3–4) describes this phenomenon as the "Kapuziner" principle after a game played by children in which the word *Kapuziner* becomes *Apuziner*, *Puziner*, and so on to *R*, then back symmetrically through *Er*, *Ner*, to *Kapuziner*.

5 Adorno 1991 (p. 64). Adorno refers to Berg as the "master of the smallest link" (*der Meister des kleinsten Übergangs*), where form and content in Berg's music exist in a dialectic that encompasses two seemingly contradictory characteristics: motivic elements are in a constant state of becoming rather than being where individual identity is subsumed by continual variation ending in dissolution, yet every note, motive, gesture, phrase, and section has a clear function in highly structured, unambigous forms. See Headlam (1993).

6 See discussions of the palindromes and circles in Berg's music in Adorno 1991 (p. 14); Jarman 1979 (pp. 230, 237–41), and 1989b (chap. 7); and Morgan 1991. In Berg's twelve-tone music, almost every piece has circular or retrograde-based sections.

7 Redlich 1957 (p. 264); see also Jarman 1989b (chap. 7).

8 In this characteristic Berg follows nineteenth- and early twentieth-century practice, in which unity across a multimovement work comes, in part, from repeated motives. Such pieces are often said to be cyclic when the same motive recurs in different movements. Because of my use of the word "cyclic" in a pitch context, however, I will not use the term in reference to formal motivic recurrence.

9 Perle 1980 (p. 94) comments that, as opposed to Wagner's consistent identification

of dramatic elements with leitmotivs, in *Wozzeck* some verbal leitmotivs and visual correspondences, such as the red moon, have different musical settings.

10 Schoenberg 1984 (p. 78): "A Self-Analysis" (1948).

11 Schoenberg 1984 (p. 88): "My Evolution" (1949). Parallels can be drawn between Schoenberg's athematic forms and Wassily Kandinsky's paintings of the same period: "Kandinsky abandoned perspective along with every other illusionist method, and reduced the objects in his pictures even further, 'abridged' them, until they only reveal themselves to the most attentive observer as abbreviations or hieroglyphs" (Hahl-Koch 1984, p. 141). Schoenberg corresponded with Kandinsky from 1911, and relationships between their art and philosophies are often noted, particularly the concurrent abandoning of the represented object in painting and of tonality in music. See also Selz 1957 (pt. 5).

12 Reich 1953 (p. 50), translated in Perle 1980 (p. 20).

13 Schoenberg 1984 (pp. 141–45): "The Relationship to the Text" (1912).

14 Ibid, pp. 144–45.

15 This new vocal setting, along with the more familiar harmony, probably accounts for Berg's classification of this song as "easiest" for the vocalist. In a letter to Schoenberg of March 9, 1913 (Brand, Hailey, and Harris 1987, pp. 140–41) Berg notes: "the Vth song (the Passacaglia) . . . is . . . more difficult for the orchestra . . . but easier for the voice, since there's almost always an instrument accompanying the voice—and since the harmony is still almost tonal. If I were to advise you, Herr Schoenberg, I would suggest—considering above all the musical simplicity of the vocal line (i.e., the pitches are easy to "hit")—the Vth song (a passacaglia). Nor would it be difficult to rehearse with the orchestra (though it is the longest of the songs, it can still be considered short, 55 measures). Naturally the song can be performed alone." Adorno 1991 (p. 64) notes the lineage of op. 4, no. 5 in the Passacaglia song "Nacht" of Schoenberg's *Pierrot Lunaire*, and relates the stylistic difference of op. 4, no. 5 from the previous songs, to how Webern's op. 3, no. 5 differs from the preceding songs in that opus. For a study of Berg's op. 4, see DeVoto 1967.

16 The exchange between Schoenberg and Berg is given in Brand, Hailey, and Harris 1987. Berg referred to Schoenberg's criticism and his suggestion to write an orchestral suite of character pieces in a letter of May 15, 1913 (p. 178). In a letter of July 9, 1913 (p. 102), Berg described his ambition to write a symphony (the *Sinfonie-Fragment*) rather than the orchestral suite. However, he mentions composing the suite (which became the op. 6 pieces) in letters of March 26 (p. 208), April 10 (p. 208), and August 2 (p. 212), all from 1914. In letters of July 20, 1914 (p. 211) and late November 1915 (p. 257), Berg referred to his insecurity in writing the op. 6 pieces after Schoenberg's censure: "After all I continually have to ask myself whether what I'm expressing, measures over which I often brood for days on end—is any better than my most recent things [op. 4 and 5]. But how am I to judge? I hate *those* things so much that I came close to destroying them completely, but *this* I can't judge yet at all, because I'm in the middle of it" (p. 211). Perle 1980

(pp. 12–13, 17) points to the influence of Mahler's Ninth Symphony and describes the op. 6 pieces as "in a sense, retrogressive . . . nevertheless, essential preparation for the composition of *Wozzeck*" (p. 13). It is thus ironic that the first full performance of the op. 6 pieces had to wait until April 14, 1930, long after the premiere of *Wozzeck* in December 1925; see Reich 1965 (p. 77).

17 Brand, Hailey, and Harris 1987 (p. 257).

18 Schoenberg 1984 (p. 276): "Problems of Harmony" (1934).

19 See Jarman, 1979 (chap. 5) and Perle 1980 (chap. 1). Perle quotes Adorno, from Reich 1937 (p. 36), who stated that in Berg's use of old forms "he did not obediently pour new wine into old bottles; he did not merely cover the unaltered schemata of the sonata, the variation, and the rondo with chromatics and enharmonics in a modernistic manner. On the contrary, right from the start he shows himself determined to develop them with severity and originality from the motivic and thematic structural principles worked out by Schoenberg and adapted by Berg in the Piano Sonata [op. 1]."

20 Büchner's play was left in twenty-six fragments at his death; an edition was prepared by Emil Franzos in 1875, the first of many that preceded Berg's adaptation in his opera. See Watkins 1988 (chap. 10 and pp. 357–72). On *Woyzeck* the play and Berg's adaptation in *Wozzeck*, see Berber 1914, Carner 1983; DeVoto 1990; Franzos 1901; Jarman 1989b (chap. 2); E. Hilmar 1975; F. H. Klein 1923; Perle 1980 (chaps. 2 and 3); Petersen 1985; Redlich 1957 (pp. 74–83, 109–11); Segar 1990; and E. Stein 1922. For the work's reception history see Berg 1924a and 1927; Brosche and Hilmar 1985, items 290–381; DeVoto 1990; Forneburg 1963; E. Hilmar 1975; Jarman 1989b (chap. 8); Kolleritsch 1978b; Pass 1978 (pp. 92–124); Perle 1980 (chap. 6); Petschnig 1924; Treitler 1989; Viebig 1923; Vogelgesang 1977; and John 1990 (pp. 41–52). See Watkins 1988 (p. 357) on the naturalist elements in *Wozzeck*, Puffet 1989 (p. 203) on expressionist opera, and Mauser 1981 for a comparison of *Wozzeck* and *Erwartung*. The expressionism in *Wozzeck* has parallels in other arts; for instance, Wozzeck's drowning (Act III, scene iv, mm. 283–319) recalls the Edvard Munch woodcut *The Cry* of 1893: the writhing figure surrounded by shock waves may be associated with Wozzeck and the swirling water around him, against the two bystanders—who may be interpreted as the Captain and the Doctor. See also Selz 1957 (p. 52).

21 Berg's lecture on *Wozzeck* in Redlich 1957 (pp. 270–71).

22 Watkins 1988 (pp. 359ff.).

23 A series of articles on the subject is collected in Jarman 1989b: E. Stein 1922, F. H. Klein 1923, Viebig 1923, Petschnig 1924, Berg 1924a, and Berg 1927. See also Jarman 1979 (chap. 5) and Perle 1980 (chap. 3). Perle (p. 3) relates *Wozzeck* to Schoenberg's *Guerrelieder*, referring to "the integration within a large-scale design of self-contained individual numbers that remain clearly differentiated in spite of thematic and harmonic interrelations."

24 The formal chart of *Wozzeck* was prepared by Berg's student Fritz Mahler. See Jarman 1989b (p. 41), also Perle 1980 (p. 194).

25 F. H. Klein 1923 in Jarman 1989b (p. 135).

26 With regard to the interludes, Berg wrote, in a letter to Webern of August 19, 1918: "The combining of 4–5 scenes into *one* act through orchestral interludes tempts me also, of course. (Do you find anything similar in the *Pelleas* of Maeterlinck-Debussy?)." See Reich 1953 (p. 50); mentioned in Perle 1980 (p. 20).

27 Berg 1927. Derrick Puffet 1989 (p. 200) points out, referring to Dahlhaus, *Esthetics of Music*, trans. William Austin (Cambridge: Cambridge University Press, 1982) p. 64, that Berg takes the role of music serving drama as a given, noting particularly the leitmotiv appearances at Marie's death in Act III, scene ii.

28 Redlich 1957; see also Jarman 1979 (pp. 191–98).

29 Emil Petschnig pointed out that absolute music forms in opera are not new, mentioning canons in *Fidelio* and *Eugene Onegin* and fugue and fugato in *Die Meistersinger* and *Carmen*, to which might be added the chorale prelude in *The Magic Flute* (Petschnig 1924, in Jarman 1989b, p. 143. Jarman 1979 (p. 194) adds "Ah, taci inguisto core" in *Don Giovanni*, Act II, and the sextet in Act III of *Figaro*. With regard to *Wozzeck*, however, Petschnig found that "[Berg] deceives himself and others when he claims with this work to have done anything more than simply raise the question [of form in opera] yet again. At the very best one can only speak of feeble attempts at recreating opera through certain formal devices, but these attempts drown hopelessly in a jumble of chords and voices" (Petschnig 1924 in Jarman 1989b (pp. 146–47). Petschnig particularly objected to the forms of the five scenes in Act I (the Suite, Rhapsody, Military March, Passacaglia, and Andante Affetuoso), forms that he believed existed in name only. See Berg 1927 and 1929 for the composer's reply. Douglass Green (1982) has called the closed "absolute forms" outlined by Berg into question, describing them as "movements" rather than scenes, since they do not always coordinate with the stage curtain.

30 Adorno 1968, translated in John 1990 (p. 39). Adorno's comment, suggesting that the forms are part of an underlying structure, is particularly interesting in light of Berg's fascination with secret symbols and programs.

31 Berg 1927, in Jarman 1989b (p. 153). See also Perle 1980 (pp. 88–89).

32 F. H. Klein 1923, in Jarman 1989b (p. 137).

33 Schoenberg 1983 (p. 421).

34 Brand, Hailey, and Harris 1987 (p. 283). The letter first appeared in Perle 1977a.

35 Perle 1977a.

36 Schoenberg 1983 (pp. 418–19), ex. 340–42).

37 The principal writings on this topic are Perle 1977a, 1977c, 1980, 1989, and 1990. Perle's own compositional method, his solution to the problem of an organizing system for music based on the symmetry in the twelve-tone collection, is called "twelve-tone tonality." See also Jarman 1979 (pp. 19–22) and 1987, and Archibald 1965, 1968, 1989.

38 Perle 1990 (lecture 3).

39 Antokoletz 1984 based his work on Bartók's music on Perle's approach to symmetry, interval cycles, and inversional complementation. In Antokoletz's view,

Bartók's pitch combinations are either symmetrically based or are non-symmetrical—such as folk melodies—but subject to symmetrical transformations. The contrast and reconciliation of symmetrical material (such as octatonic collections) with non-symmetrical material, particularly tonal diatonic elements—definable in cyclic terms as 5/7−cycles—is central to Bartók's music and is strongly related to Stravinsky's harmonic language as defined in Berger 1963 and van den Toorn 1983.

40 In his analysis of Varèse's *Density 21.5*, Perle 1990 (pp. 70−83) interprets the piece as based on a 3-cycle, which changes to a 2-cycle in the closing measures, mediated by the common interval 6.

41 Perle 1955 shows how [0123] is transposed successively with invariances of three, then two, notes in analogy with tonal modulation in Bartók's Fourth String Quartet.

42 Perle's example is from Schoenberg's op. 11, no. 1, where the cyclic properties of [048] affect the role of hexachordal superset [014568]. See Perle 1990 (pp. 9−11, 19−21, 59−70).

43 Perle's "sums of complementation" are also known as index numbers. See Babbitt 1962.

44 Perle 1977a.

45 Cf. Lewin 1990 and Perle 1993.

46 Morris 1987.

47 See Marvin 1988 and 1991; Friedmann 1987; and Marvin and Laprade 1987. Schoenberg 1967 (pp. 113−15) used "contour" graphs of phrases in music by Bach, Haydn, Mozart, and Beethoven, and often stated that color, texture, and register were the most significant elements in some of his atonal music.

48 Forte 1973, 1985, 1991 and Schmalfeldt 1983, 1991.

49 The cello E as the last note is a misprint for E♯, the note that appears in an autograph copy given by Berg to Schoenberg. The manuscript is in the collection of Robert Owen Lehman.

50 Travis 1959, 1966; Salzer 1952; and Straus 1987.

51 For an analysis proposing just such a large-scale cycle, see Porter 1989−90 on Berg's String Quartet op. 3.

52 Lewis 1982−83.

53 See Jarman 1979 (chap. 4) for an extended discussion of Berg's use of rhythm.

54 Lewin 1981.

CHAPTER 3: THE ATONAL MUSIC: DETAIL AND ANALYSIS

1 Whole-tone collections as TnI-classes become more distinctive as the cardinality increases: 3 of 12 trichords (.25), 3 of 29 tetrachords (.1), 1 of 35 pentachords (.03) and 1 of 50 hexachords (.02). All whole-tone Tn-classes but [026]/[046] are inversionally invariant; [048], [0268], and [02468A] have fewer than twelve distinct forms by invariance under transposition.

2 Whole-tone+ collections (hereafter abbreviated as "wt+ collections") gain in distinctiveness as the cardinality increases: 10 of 29 tetrachords (.34), 10 of 35 pen-

tachords (.29), 4 of 50 hexachords (.8), and 1 of 35 septachords (.03). With wt and wt+ collections combined, the proportions are 13 of 29 tetrachords (.45), 11 of 35 pentachords (.32), and 5 of 50 hexachords (.1). The interval-class (ic) vectors of wt+ tetrachords contain 3 even/3 odd ics (/="and"), versus 2 even/4 odd for the rest (except for the purely wt sets); the most distinctive is [0148] with 3 ic4s. The comparison in pentachords is 6/4 for wt+ versus 4/6 for the rest, and with hexachords 10/5 versus 7/8 or 6/9.

3 Leitmotiv names are from Perle 1980; I have included characteristic repeated motives even if they only appear in one scene. My "anguish" motive is labelled *fatalistische* in a sketch; see Petersen 1985 (p. 86). Redlich 1957 (pp. 103–6), Perle 1980, Jarman 1979, and Schmalfeldt 1983 refer to wt+ collections in *Wozzeck*; Forte 1973 notes the wt+ structure of *Wozzeck* collections and of Scriabin's mystic chord. From Forte 1973 (pp. 119–123), Schmalfeldt 1983 demonstrates the wt+ sets relating to Wozzeck, positing the primary set as 4-19 [0148]. Petersen 1985 (pp. 89–100) cites {D,F,A,C#} [0148] as the source chord for Wozzeck.

4 Perle 1980 (pp. 133–34, 157–58) and Jarman 1979 (pp. 47–60) and 1989b (pp. 46–49) both identify the C# wt collection and this cadence chord as primary and show subset relationships with *Wozzeck* materials throughout. Redlich 1957 (p. 99) refers to the C# wt collection plus D as a *Grundgestalt*.

5 The waltz passage recalls one given by Schoenberg in "Problems of Harmony" (1934) (Schoenberg 1984, p. 282), wherein he shows a succession of "atonal" pentachords ending with a D-minor triad, and comments: "Strange to say, the ear accepts the final chord here just as it does a tonic and it might almost seem as if the preceding dissonances were really standing in legitimate relation to this tonic." He refers to this phenomenon as "the last prevails."

6 Perle 1980 (pp. 135–41) describes the significance of the dyad {F,B} in *Wozzeck*.

7 The chord pair recalls the two chords built on G and A♭ in op. 2, no. 1, mm. 16–17 (ex. 1.15). Jarman 1979 (pp. 60–67) discusses the second cadential chord and its relationship to Marie's material, adding a B♭ (from Act I, scene iii, mm. 317, 481). Schmalfeldt 1983 posits 4-18 [0147] as Marie's referential collection. Redlich 1957 (pp. 135–36) notes the role of interval 5 in Marie's material. Petersen 1985 (p. 149) cites {F,A,B,E} [0157] as the source chord for Marie.

8 Perle 1977a and 1990 discusses this alignment of cycles as well as others in Berg's op. 2 and 3; see also Archibald 1989 (pp. 96–105), Porter 1989–90, and DeVoto 1991 on pervasive interval 1 and interval 2 motion in Berg's music. The alignment intervals in the figure shown in ex. 3.4a differ by four ($3 + 4 = 7, 7 + 4 = B$), equal to the difference between the two generating cycles: $(-1) - 7 = 4$. Differing alignments produce permutations of 4-cycles: 0 4 8, 1 5 9, 2 6 A, and 3 7 B.

9 See Perle 1977a and 1980 (pp. 124–125); Perle cites the text ("a sin") as a motivation for the compositional procedure here, where the violin breaks the symmetry.

10 See Perle 1977a. Jarman 1979 (pp. 32–34) defines the harmonic language in op. 3 in terms of five small cells: wt-based collections, [014], [012], [027], and wedge formations.

11 The wedge could also be defined around the dyad C/B, where the upper E♭ would still arrive an octave higher in m. 7 with the lower A♭ pair omitted.

12 See Archibald 1989 (ex. 10) for wedge patterns around D in the second movement of op. 3, mm. 1–4.

13 Jarman 1979 (pp. 25, 34–37) describes cells [014] and [0167] as the basis of the melodic and harmonic structure of op. 4. My chart of motives (fig. 3.3) and some analysis are after DeVoto 1967.

14 This 5-cycle construction foreshadows the row of Berg's Violin Concerto, where a 7-cycle appears on every second note, based on the open strings of the violin: G b♭ D f♯ A c E g♯ B c♯ d♯ f.

15 The combination of [014] with horizontal and parallel interval 3 and 4 cycles in op. 4, no. 2 (1913) recalls the treatment of the same materials in *Pierrot Lunaire* no. 8, "Nacht" (1912). For op. 4, no. 2, see DeVoto 1967 (pp. 66–71) and Jarman 1979 (pp. 25–27).

16 The contour graph in ex. 3.9 was created by Alexander Brinkman and Martha Mesiti; see their "Graphic Modelling of Musical Structure," *Computers in Music Research* 3 (1991): 1–42.

17 The aggregate chord heard immediately after Lulu's death in Berg's second opera *Lulu*, Act III, scene ii is shown alongside the chord of op. 4, no. 3 in ex. 3.11. In this chord, six of the twelve notes in the op. 4 chord appear in the same registral configuration but transposed down by interval 4 (filled-in noteheads in the example).

18 See the discussion of bars 39–54 in DeVoto 1989 (pp. 60–63).

19 Compare Archibald 1989 (ex. 15), where the two wt collections in op. 5, no. 2 are differentiated throughout. The interval 3 and 4 based structure of op. 5, no. 2 is similar to that of Schoenberg's op. 19, no. 2; note especially, in the latter, the chords in m. 6 from two [036]s at T1 and in m. 9 from two [048]s at T1, and the combined ic3,4 in the motivic collection <G–B–C–E♭>. Carner 1983 (pp. 120–21) also asserts a similarity between op. 5, no. 3 and Schoenberg's op. 19, no. 2 and the silent depressing of a tetrachord in the piano at the end of op. 5, no. 4 as being foreshadowed by a similar gesture in Schoenberg's op. 11, no. 1. Defotis 1979 compares the opening thirds of op. 5, no. 2 with the opening of Strauss's *Death and Transfiguration*.

20 Jarman 1979 (pp. 23–25) notes that many intervalic "cells" derive from the opening clarinet motto in op. 5. He asserts (p. 27) that the referential opening of op. 5 foreshadows the referential cadential chords in *Wozzeck*.

21 I am indebted to David Lefkowitz for some of the set analysis of op. 5.

22 See Lewis 1981, on op. 5, no. 3, who notes the focus on D, the 4-cycle [048]s in the opening bars, the importance of sets [0258] and [0148] (wt+ collections), and the similarity between the opening clarinet line and mm. 10–12. Lewis concludes that the piece contains a duality of pitch organization, tonal focus, and pitch-class set relationships. Berry 1989 (chap. 2) approaches op. 5, no. 3 from a performance standpoint but also notes the structural use of [048]s and [036]s and [012] motives,

as well as "tonal" emphases on the notes C and D in this movement and on C, D, and G throughout Opus 5.

23 In a sketch of the opening bars of op. 5, no. 2, shown in E. A. Berg 1976 (p. 148), the parts are notated at T4 from the final published version. The initial note group is thus clarinet {E,F,G,B,C,A♭} and piano {F♯,A♯}—the notes of the final chord of op. 5, no. 4, with F the third-to-last note in the clarinet part and F♯/G♭ the penultimate clarinet note, although without a corresponding A♯.

24 See Stroh 1968, Jarman 1979, and Perle 1980. Jarman 1979 defines a "constructive rhythm" as a "recurrent rhythmic pattern which operates independently of harmonic or melodic material" (p. 147). Berg defined a *Hauptrhythmus* as "a rhythm that can be considered as a sort of motive" ("Open Letter on the *Chamber Concerto*"), but the term is applicable to his earlier music.

25 The term is from Cone 1968 (p. 25).

26 This definition is derived from Yeston 1974 (chap. 3).

27 Hypermeasure is a term coined by Cone 1968 (p. 75).

28 Lewin 1981.

29 DeVoto 1967 assigns a value of eight sixteenths to motive 4/3 and consequently arrives at 157½ bars for a realignment.

30 Jarman 1979 (p. 149) discusses the variants of this rhythm.

31 See DeVoto 1967 (ex. 25).

32 A notational discrepancy occurs in the orchestral score in the voice and violin parts in mm. 31 and 33: in m. 31, triplet quarters indicate three in the time of two; in m. 33, triplet quarters indicate three in the time of four. The latter notation should be triplet halves, as in the piano-vocal score and the celeste part in the orchestral score.

33 For a different view of the rhythmic grouping in op. 5, no. 2, see Defotis 1979, who posits a "reduced" version of the piece (p. 134), omitting extensions and delays.

34 Perle 1980 (pp. 174–83) and Jarman 1979 (pp. 163–64) discuss the RH in this scene.

35 This rhythmic gesture has been foreshadowed by the solo timpani rhythm in op. 6, no. 3 (mm. 142–43), a rhythm that is modeled in turn after similar gestures in Mahler's symphonies.

36 I am indebted to Keith Waters for this observation.

37 This setting of the previously established Drum Major pitch motive with the independent RH is what Stroh 1968 defines as a "counterpoint."

38 My chart is based on Perle 1980 (pp. 178–80).

39 Perle 1980 (pp. 181–82).

40 Discussion of these rhythmic motives appears in Jarman 1979 (pp. 148–49).

41 In a handcopied piano reduction of op. 4, nos. 3 and 4, given by Berg to Schoenberg, the direction at the A' section is augmented with *Anfangstempo [eighth]* = *[quarter] vom Anfang*, confirming the tempo relationship. This score is in the collection of Robert Owen Lehman.

42 DeVoto 1967 (p. 74) speculates that the meter change also reflects the text change from past *blicktest* to present *blickst* in the first and last lines of the text.

43 *der Triole* [eighth] *beiläufig 88, so daß das anfängliche* [dotted quarter] *dem jetzigen* [quarter + triplet eighth] *entspricht.*

44 Reich 1965 (p. 115) refers to analytical notes by Berg from April 2, 1930, in which the op. 6 pieces are described in terms of a symphony: Movement I: *Prelude*, the Scherzo movement II and slow movement III within *Reigen* (mm. 1–100 and 101–121), and a final *March* (mm. 53–129) with a development or coda (mm. 130–74).

45 Perle 1980 (p. 95) distinguishes leitmotiv from *Leitsektion*, the recurrence of a "total musical complex rather than . . . a motive."

46 This relative contour designation is taken from Morris 1987 and Marvin 1988.

47 See DeVoto 1967 (ex. 29).

48 The row of the *Lyric Suite* is, in Perle's terms, a "cyclic set," and P5 and IB are "cognate sets" due to their shared sum 4.

49 See Schoenberg 1932 and DeVoto 1967 (ex. 26).

50 See Redlich 1957 (pp. 100–101); Perle 1980 (pp. 164–65), and Jarman 1979 (p. 72) on the passacaglia theme.

51 This setting foreshadows a similar arrangement of the main row in *Lulu*. See ex. 5.36j—the Medical Specialist dyads.

52 Redlich 1957 (p. 57). Defotis 1979 (p. 136) observes that op. 5, no. 4 "adumbrates" a piece for string orchestra, with melody and accompaniment figures, including an "upbeat" designation in m. 4, more appropriate to strings.

53 Adorno 1991 likens op. 4, no. 5 to "Nacht" from Schoenberg's *Pierrot Lunaire* and its stylistic divergence from the rest of the cycle to Webern's op. 3, no. 5.

54 Jarman 1979 (pp. 37–46) points out recurrences of [014] (his cell "x"), here related to motive 6/e, and [0137] (cell "y"), here motive 6/c. See also DeVoto 1981, 1983–84 for exhaustive studies of op. 6, no. 3.

55 See Jarman 1979 (pp. 37–41) and Perle 1980 (p. 15) on [014] as a central motive in op. 6.

56 The [014] turn figure in motive 6/d, breaking the 3-cycle, is virtually a Berg signature; it recalls similar turns in the wt+ motives in *Wozzeck* (ex. 3.1a) and op. 3 (ex. 3.6a).

57 Perle 1980 (p. 19).

58 The grand pause in m. 82 is approximately at the Golden Section proportion. See Perle 1980 (p. 16). Jarman 1989b (p. 20) asserts a "rondo-like waltz" in op. 6, no. 2; Carner 1983 (p. 144) shows an introduction (mm. 1–20), waltz in tripartite form (mm. 20–100), and closing slow section (mm. 101–21); and Archibald 1989 (p. 117) posits a sonata form: introduction, mm. 1–20; exposition, mm. 20–44; development, mm. 45–94; recapitulation, mm. 94–100; and coda, mm. 110–21.

59 Perle 1980 (p. 18).

60 Jarman 1979 (p. 177), refers to a "sonata-form" for op. 6, no. 3, but, with perhaps the exception of the brief, varied return in mm. 155ff., the movement does not appear to conform to any recognizable sonata-form outline, although Carner 1983

(p. 146) defines an introduction mm. 1–32, main section mm. 33–52 and 53–90, development mm. 91–126, reprise mm. 127–54, and coda mm. 155–74. Reich 1965 (p. 115) refers to analytical notes by Berg for the premiere of the op. 6 pieces, outlining divisions of the *Marsch* as: mm. 1–53, "march-like" group; mm. 53–129, march; and mm. 130–79, developmental coda. DeVoto 1981 (p. 103) shows the varied return of the harmonies from mm. 25–27 in mm. 136–39.

61 Upon first view of the score, Adorno commented that the *Marsch* "must sound like playing Schoenberg's Orchestral Pieces and Mahler's Ninth Symphony, all at the same time." Adorno 1991 (p. 22).

62 DeVoto 1967 (p. 73).

63 Cone 1968 (pp. 76–77) defines this procedure as the "sonata principle."

64 See Jarman 1979 (pp. 176–79) and Schweizer 1970 for discussions of Berg's use of sonata forum.

65 For the history of op. 3, see Jarman 1979 (p. 5), Archibald 1989 (pp. 105–6) and Redlich 1957 (pp. 49–50).

66 See Schweizer 1970 (pp. 74–85) on the first-movement sonata form.

67 Redlich 1957 (p. 50) notes that the second movement of op. 3 is developmental and suggests Webern's Five Movements for String Quartet op. 5 and Mahler's later symphonies as models for the interdependence of the movements in Berg's op. 3. Adorno 1991 (p. 55) notes the "permanent transition" in the second movement. Jarman 1979 (pp. 32–34) shows relationships between motives in op. 3, no. 2 in terms of small cells.

68 The new theme is from the fifth in a set of incomplete piano sonatas, mm. 3off. See Krämer 1992 (pp. 73–77).

69 Adorno 1991 (p. 60) outlines the movement as: first complex, mm. 1–47; first rondo reprise, mm. 48–53; second theme and transition, mm. 54–71; development with multiple rondo entrances, mm. 72–150; reprise, mm. 151–232. Schweizer 1970 defines the movement as a rondo form, with rondo theme 1 at mm. 1, 47, 61, 151, and 203, and rondo theme 2 at m. 88, 102, and 214. Carner 1983 defines a rondo with episodes in mm. 34–46, 50–60, 72–85, and 119–50, with a free recapitulation at m. 151 and a coda at m. 217.

70 This transformation springs from Adorno's observation (1991, pp. 60–61) that the figure in m. 25 of the second movement is set in the rhythm of the main theme from the first movement.

71 See Schweizer 1970 (pp. 75–77) for other underlying relationships between the opening motives of the two movements.

72 See Schweizer 1970 (pp. 105–50), Perle 1980 (pp. 145–55), and Schmalfeldt 1983 (pp. 111–15, 185–92).

73 Schmalfeldt 1983 posits hexachords [012569]/[013478] or Forte 6-Z19/Z-44 as the nexus sets for whole opera. Perle 1980 describes the tetrachords as "basic cells," characterized by interval structures of various types or "modes" and transpositional levels of "keys." The tetrachords combine in larger sets as "characteristic harmonic details and focal elements *within* a given complex of pitch compo-

nents" (pp. 145–55). Schmalfeldt incorporates Perle's cells but uses pitch-class set relationships to show the primacy of [0147], a set she associates with Marie (pp. 177–92).

74 See Jarman 1979 (pp. 194–97) for a chart of musical correspondences.

75 Krämer 1992 (pp. 67–73) details the connections between the thematic material of this scene and an early *Klavierstück* (F 21 Berg 5 in R. Hilmar 1980) in F minor. See Forte 1985 on the tonal aspects of the scene.

76 I am indebted to Mary Linklater for her observations on the binary form of each variation; see also Petersen 1985 (p. 159) and his discussion of the speaking and singing indications throughout *Wozzeck* (pp. 251–55).

77 Perle 1980 (p. 58) calls Act 1, scene 5 "rhapsodic, a polyphonic web of melodies whose rhythm and contour are constantly transformed"; he also compares the scene to op. 6, no. 1.

78 I am indebted to Adam Ricci for some aspects of this discussion of the rondo theme.

79 GIS3 in Lewin 1987 (pp. 37–45).

80 Watkins 1988 (pp. 358–59); see also Perle 1980 (p. 99). Büchner's play *Woyzeck* contains thirteen folksong sections in rhymed verse.

81 For comparisons of the melodies of each strophe, see Forneburg 1963 (p. 31).

82 Perle 1980 (p. 138) gives "priority" to C as lowest note of the first of the three chords.

83 Perle 1980 (pp. 51–52) describes the scene as a march, cradle song, and "through-composed episode."

84 See a comparison of these melodies in Forneburg 1963 (p. 32).

85 See Chittum 1967 and Petersen 1985 (pp. 218–20) for a list of motives and their occurrences and contrapuntal details in Act II, scene ii.

86 Carner 1983 (p. 168) cites the stock *commedia dell'arte* figures of the Spanish Captain and the Bolognese Doctor.

87 Leibowitz 1949 (pp. 153–54).

88 Jarman 1979 (p. 196) and Petersen 1985 (pp. 273–77) detail the motivic occurrences in the interlude. See also Forte 1991 for a detailed analysis. Krämer 1992 (pp. 62–67) shows the connections between the interlude and Berg's incomplete Fourth Piano Sonata.

89 Adorno 1968, translated in John 1990 (p. 38).

90 Berg's effects and unusual performance directions drew the ire of Schoenberg, who questioned whether Berg used them musically or just for effect, to be "modern." See DeVoto 1989 (p. 58). Schroeder 1993 (p. 290) compares Berg's orchestration to the painter Klimt's "color and decorative design."

91 In op. 6, no. 1, the opening bassoon melody, on A♭ above middle C (mm. 6–8), changing to trombone on the E♭ a fifth above (mm. 9–11) at the top of the register, is remarkably reminiscent of the opening of Stravinsky's *Rite of Spring*.

92 The violin tuning is the same as in Mahler's Fourth Symphony, second movement.

93 Berg indicated in the score that the piano may be used to give the singers their pitches or may play with them quietly, beginning in m. 202; this may not, however, be advisable on an out-of-tune piano!

94 Berg commented in his lecture (1929): "Incidentally, I intended thereby to pay homage to my teacher and master at this pivotal point of the opera."

95 DeVoto 1967 (p. 72). The color changes in this chord are similar to those in Schoenberg's op. 16, no. 3 (Redlich 1957, p. 62).

96. See Lederer 1978 (pp. 57–67) for a discussion of the scene, with emphasis on the symbolism of the note B.

97 "In the warm breezes, grass sprouts from sunny meadows / Listen! Listen, the nightingale pipes away. / I wish to sing: / High in the dark mountain forest, cold snow melts and glitters, / A maiden clad in grey leans against the damp trunk of an oak tree. / Sick are her tender cheeks, / Her grey eyes feverish through the somber giant tree trunks. / 'He still does not come! He leaves me waiting.' / Die! The one dies, the other lives; / From such stems the world's profound splendor." Mombert, "Warm die Lufte." Translation, Glenn Watkins. Reprinted with permission of Schirmer Books, an imprint of Simon and Schuster Macmillan, from *Soundings: Music in the Twentieth Century*, by Glenn Watkins. Copyright © 1988 Schirmer Books. Opus 2, no. 4 was published in 1909 in the *Blaue Reiter Almanac*, ed. Franz Marc and Wassily Kandinsky.

98 Adorno 1991 (p. 49).

99 In a draft of the song in the Vienna Stadtsbibliothek, the marking is *ohne Stimme*.

100 The harmony suggests a reference to the second movement of Ravel's *Gaspard de la nuit*, where death is associated with the image of "le gibet," the hangman. See Watkins 1988 (pp. 49–50). The relentless octave B♭s in the Ravel work are reflected in the syncopated "Death" rhythm on B♭ in the Berg song.

101 The chord, referred to in Schoenberg's *Harmonielehre*, is a favorite of Berg's: it is transposed down a half-step, but with an upper resolution of the upper note in the Act III interlude of *Wozzeck* (m. 327), functioning as ♭VI of F. The chord, with the same resolution, begins the coda theme to Dr. Schön's sonata in *Lulu*.

102 The alternating chords result because, in any [0137], [026] at P(n) pairs with a single note ([0]) at P(n+B), and in any [0256], [026] at P(n) pairs with a single note at P(n+5). Since the +5 and −1 cycles change T levels by a total of 6, the chords alternate (these relationships are explored in Headlam 1988):

5 cycle				1 cycle			
[026]	[0]			[026]	[0]		
P (n)	P (n+B)	=	P	(n)	P	(n+B)	=	[0137]
P (n+5)	P ((n+B)−1)	=	P	(n)	P	(n+5)	=	[0256]
P (n+10)	P ((n+B)−2)	=	P	(n)	P	(n+B)	=	[0137]
P (n+3)	P ((n+B)−3)	=	P	(n)	P	(n+5)	=	[0256]

103 See Kett 1989 on the op. 2 songs, who labels these chords "A" and "B." See also Wennerstrom 1977.

104 For a different view of the song based on [0157] in adjacent and non-adjacent note connections, see Forte 1988.

105 Similar "black" and "white" 5-cycle segments appear in the hunting chorus, trio 2, in *Wozzeck*, Act II, scene iv (mm. 560–589, 637–39), where the choir

contrasts white- and black-note collections, and are significant in the *Lyric Suite* and *Lulu*.

106 For the compositional history of op. 4, see Redlich 1957 (pp. 58–60); DeVoto 1967, 1989; Perle 1980 (p. 11); Simpson 1987 (p. xiii); Eislin 1989; and Schroeder 1993. DeVoto 1967 (pp. 96ff.) points out influences on op. 4 of Schoenberg's *Pierrot Lunaire, Gurrelieder,* String Quartet op. 10, op. 16, no. 2, and the unpublished Little Pieces for Small Orchestra. According to DeVoto, op. 4, no. 4 was the first song written. On Peter Altenberg, see Simpson 1987 (pp. 125, 288, 298–304, 357), DeVoto 1967, Watkins 1988 (pp. 54–55), Hahl-Koch 1984 (p. 178n. 149), and Carner 1983 (pp. 39–40). Altenberg frequented Viennese coffeehouses as "an arch-bohemian" with a strong "commitment to social questions"; he was a foremost practitioner of "extract" theory, which exalted economy and brevity, particularly in the prose-poem form used in the *Texte auf Ansichtskarten,* and in his *Wiener Skizze,* popular 'feuilletons' in the Viennese newspapers (Simpson 1987, pp. 287–303). Altenberg's brief literary forms are reflected in and may have influenced Berg's aphoristic settings.

107 Simpson 1987 (p. 249). "Uber die Grenzen des All blicksten du sinnend hinaus." "The textual parallel to the Stefan George text in the fourth movement of Schoenberg's first atonal work, the String Quartet No. 2 op. 10, is striking: "I feel the air of another planet" ("Ich fühle Luft von anderem Planeten"), from George's "Entrückung." Schroeder 1993 (pp. 283–84) notes that the arch-symmetry in the text of the third song reflects an overall poetic symmetry.

108 In a manuscript containing op. 4, nos. 3 and 4 in a piano reduction, given by Berg to Schoenberg, the passage is marked *tonlos* with diamond-shaped noteheads beginning on a notated B and ending on A. This manuscript is in the collection of Robert Owen Lehman.

109 "Nothing is come, nothing will, to still my soul's longing. / So long have I waited, have waited so long, ah, so long! / The days will slip steathily, / And in vain flutters my ashen blond silken hair round my pallid countenance." Translation by A. Kitchin. Carner 1983 (p. 105) interprets the text as "the sadness and despair of a woman who has waited in vain for the longing of her soul to be stilled, and in this expectation has grown old." Perle 1980 (p. 10) notes that the opening word *Nichts* is set to the vanishing flute interval 1 B♭6–B6, contrasting with the end of op. 4, no. 3, where the word "all" is set to a twelve-tone chord.

110 For history and discussion of op. 5, see Redlich 1957 (pp. 55–56), Archibald 1989 (pp. 106–7), Jarman 1979 (pp. 6–7), Adorno 1991 (pp. 67–68). However, the question of why these pieces were written for clarinet has not, to my knowledge, been addressed. The pieces are usually compared with Schoenberg's op. 19 piano pieces—of which the second piece has remarkable similarities to Berg's op. 5, no. 2—and Webern's violin and cello pieces op. 7 and 11. Berg wrote to Schoenberg on April 24, 1913, that he originally planned four to six short pieces (Brand, Hailey, and Harris 1987, pp. 174, 284). Both the clarinet pieces and the op. 4 songs drew the wrath of Schoenberg, however, who criticized Berg for

their insubstantial nature (despite his own brief efforts of the time) and caused Berg to head back in the direction of larger works, in the op. 6 pieces and eventually *Wozzeck* (Brand, Hailey, and Harris 1987, pp. 256–57).

111 Jarman 1979 (pp. 23–25) describes the opening clarinet figure as the source of op. 5 musical material, dividing the figure into six and three notes, and deriving five trichordal cells, segmentally and non-segmentally ([012], [015], [014], [016], and [037]), which are used throughout. Adorno 1991 (p. 69) similarly subdivides the clarinet motive into cells.

112 The treatment of this motive recalls the large-scale unfolding of the <A5–F♯5–B4> initial chord in Schoenberg's op. 19, no. 6 as notes <E6–B5–D5>. See Lewin 1982–83.

113 For the history of op. 6, see Reich 1965 (pp. 42, 56–57, 114), Redlich 1957 (pp. 64–71), Adorno 1991 (pp. 73–74), Jarman 1979 (pp. 7–8), Archibald 1989 (pp. 110–13), Taylor 1989 (pp. 123–24), and Perle 1980 (pp. 11–14, 17–18). Most authors compare the op. 6 pieces to Mahler's music. See DeVoto 1981 for a comprehensive discussion of formal and thematic relationships in the op. 6 pieces.

114 Reich 1965 (p. 115) notes that Berg sent analytical remarks on the op. 6 pieces for the premiere dated April 2, 1930. Berg commented that the three movements approximate a four-movement symphony, with the *Präludium* a first movement, *Reigen* divided into a scherzo and a slow movement (at m. 101), and the *Marsch* the last movement.

115 Taylor 1989 (p. 134) defines the form as introduction, mm. 1–15; prime section, mm. 16–41; conclusion, mm. 42–56.

116 Jarman 1979 (pp. 41–42) labels the first chord in op. 6, no. 1 as his cell z and notes the pervasive use of "fourth" chords. Taylor 1989 considers the chord progression in op. 6, no. 1, focusing on mm. 1–15, but in terms different from those used in the present discussion, although he notes the recurring interval of a fourth.

CHAPTER 4: THE TWELVE-TONE MUSIC: INTRODUCTION

1 See Adorno's comment (1991, p. 89), "Nowhere is that phrase about a transitional work more concretely applicable than in the *Chamber Concerto*."

2 Berg's letter appeared in *Pult und Taktstock*, vol. 2 (February-March 1925), pp. 23–28; see Reich 1965 (pp. 143–48) and Brand, Hailey, and Harris 1987 (pp. 334–37). Translations are from Reich.

3 Jarman 1979 (pp. 131–33) discusses the difficulties of reconciling these two contradictory systems, but affirms that Berg accomplished this feat.

4 See Perle 1985 (pp. 86, 198ff.) on the non-row aspects of the language of *Lulu*, in which Perle reiterates his categories of "normative" and "reflexive" elements in Berg's twelve-tone music. Cyclic elements also figure in invariance relationships between rows in the music of Schoenberg and Webern. In Schoenberg's Variations op. 31, for instances, three families of rows are created from the 3-cycle collections in order positions 0178, and families of "BACH" motive rows, 1 cycle

[0123] in order positions 05AB and 1234, are formed. These cycles remain firmly in the row context, however. For discussion of the cyclic properties of the twelve-tone operators, see Morris 1987 and Morris and Starr 1977–78.

5 Reich 1936 outlines derivations of material in *Lulu* from Berg's notes; for Berg's twelve-tone sketches, see also Hall 1985, 1989, and 1991; Headlam 1995; Jarman 1978 and 1979; Green 1991b; Perle 1985; Pople 1991; and Scherliess 1977.

6 Berg, like Schoenberg, labelled rows "OI" for the referential level, then "OII" for the row a semitone below, and so forth. "UI" stood for the inversion row at the referential level, "K" for the retrograde, and "UK" for the retrograde inversion, and numbers 1–12 for order positions. See Green 1991b (p. 208). Hall 1989 (p. 236) has noted that Berg was meticulous about labeling rows in his sketches in his earlier twelve-tone pieces, but this practice was somewhat relaxed in his later pieces. See also Jarman 1978.

7 See Carner 1983, Jarman 1979 (pp. 112–25), Keller 1953, Perle 1959, 1965a, 1985 (pp. 157–58), Reich 1936, and Reiter 1973, also Headlam 1985a, 1990.

8 Reich 1936 (pp. 89, 161–62); see also Redlich 1957 (p. 178).

9 See Perle 1985 (pp. 157ff.); Carner 1983 (p. 250); Reiter 1973 (pp. 57–60); Jarman 1979 (pp. 112–25); and Hall 1985, 1989.

10 Reiter 1973; Hall 1985, 1989, 1991.

11 Perle 1985 (pp. 157–61).

12 Jarman 1979 (pp. 118–25).

13 Pople 1991, chap. 5.

14 Headlam 1995. I agree with Hall 1989 on the usefulness of sketches, but the finished piece must be the referent, not the sketches.

15 Perle 1962, 1985 describes such internally unordered collections as tropes.

16 See Lewin 1966, Rothgeb 1967, Solomon 1973, Stanfield 1984–85, Headlam 1985a, and Mead 1988–89 on row orderings.

17 The mapping of a 1-cycle onto a 7-cycle is often described as a Multiplicative or M operation; the invariances of "M7" on order positions are analogous to the pitch-class operation M7, mapping (0) (2) (4) (6) (8) (A) and (17) (39) (5B), where, for instance, pcset {0268} remains invariant.

18 Pople 1991, chap. 5.

19 "umsomehr als ein Satz meines im Entstehen begriffenen 2. Quartetts den Versuch darstellt, in der aller strengsten 12 Ton-Musik mit stark *tonalem* Einschlag zu schreiben; was jedenfalls *möglich* war." Berg, letter to Schoenberg of June 27, 1926, in Rauchhaupt 1971 (p. 92); see also Reich 1959 (pp. 45–54).

20 "Jedenfalls, wenn Sie aus ihnen ableiten könnten, daß auch in der Zwölftonkomposition Tonales (oder sagen wir: etwas von den Regeln der alten Tonalität) enthalten ist, wäre das ein großer Gewinn fürs Musikalische." Berg, letter to Reich of September 4, 1929. See Reich 1965 (p. 79) and Hall 1985.

21 Reich 1971 (p. 248).

22 See Jarman 1979 (pp. 93–100) and Adorno 1991 (pp. 127–28) on tonal implications in *Lulu*.

23 See Burkholder 1991 (pp. 45–46, 50–51) on the tonal characteristics of the Violin Concerto.

24 Perle 1989 and 1990 reaffirms the "normative" structures in Berg's twelve-tone music, comparing the use of [0167] in *Lulu* with pieces by Bartók and the sum and difference relationships with his own twelve-tone tonality.

25 Perle 1985 (pp. 88–90) and Jarman 1979 (p. 86) have defined certain collections as basic cells in *Lulu*; these recurring collections are analogous to both leitmotivs and pitch-class sets in their treatment.

26 The row is 210 012 210 012 in mod 3, with trichords [015] [027], [027] [015].

27 Perle 1977c describes this organization as cyclic sets; rows P_5 and IB, which share one sum, are cognate sets.

28 Earlier twelve-note themes appear in op. 4 and in the passacaglia theme of *Wozzeck*, in which segments are verticalized; see ex. 3.7, motive 4/d, and ex. 3.26f.

29 Equivalent contours are identified here as those with the same relative spatial orderings between elements. Morris 1987 and Marvin and Laprade 1987 have established complex criteria for contour equivalence based on the twelve-tone operators.

30 Perle 1985 (p. 98).

31 Perle 1985 (p. 2) compared this formal use of inversion and retrograde to the first movement of Schoenberg's Serenade op. 24, where the "section comprising mm. 1–8 is literally inverted at bars 17–24, and is . . . repeated . . . against new material in bars 9–16, that section being in turn inverted as a totality at bars 25–32, repeated at bars 33–40, and again inverted at bars 41–48." Redlich 1957 (p. 118) also mentions the Serenade in connection with the *Chamber Concerto*.

32 A similar palindrome from a retrograde-invariant row appears in the development section of the first movement in Webern's Symphony op. 21.

33 "Diese symmetrie hat aber auch einen schweren Nachteil. Die *zweite* Hälfte ist nämlich das um 1 verminderte Quint tiefer liegende Spiegelbild der *vorderen* Hälfte,. . . woraus sich ergibt, daß diese Reihe *keine* selbständige Krebsform hat. Tatsächlich lautet der krebs der um eine verminedte Quint tiefer gesetzten Originalreihe R[,] was bei entsprechender Tonversetzung gleich ist der Reihe: Aus diesem Grund . . . entschloß ich mich bei meinem nächsten Arbeiten zu folgender Veränderung der Reihe. Translation from Brand, Hailey, and Harris 1987 (pp. 349–50).

34 Perle 1985 (pp. 250–57).

35 Similar groups appear in Schoenberg's Variations for Orchestra op. 31, where a four-note motive {Bb,A,C,B} (BACH) is extracted from different row forms by isolating 05AB.

36 See Berg's notes on the *Lyric Suite* in Rauchhaupt 1971 (pp. 91–117).

37 "4-Ton Gruppe," "quasi als Ostinato." Translated from Brand, Hailey, and Harris 1987 (p. 350).

38 See Jarman 1979, chap. 5.

39 Berg indicates "Sonate" and "Reprise der Sonate" in the score (Act II, mm. 535, 625). Douglass Green however, notes that the term "double exposition" would be

more appropriate, as Berg, like Mahler, thought of sonata form as exposition, reprise 1, development, reprise 2 (private communication).

40 Schweizer 1970 (p. 223), in his study of Berg's use of sonata forms, offers an intriguing parallel between the music within the total span of the Schön sonata form and the second-act symphony of *Wozzeck*. In this view, the Schön sonata exposition and reprise, and the later development and final reprise (Act I, mm. 533–666, 1209–361) correspond to the sonata form in *Wozzeck*, Act II, scene i; the *monoritmica* (Act I, mm. 669–958) to the Act II, scene ii invention and fugue; the coda of the Schön sonata form between scenes ii and iii of Act I (mm. 958–92) to the confrontation scene in *Wozzeck*, Act II, scene iii; the jazz ragtime and English waltz and the Prince's chorale variations in the first part of Act I, scene iii with the inn scene in Act II, scene iv; and the section of Alwa's rondo in Act I, scene iii (and his rondo music in Act II, scenes i and ii) with the *rondo marziale* in *Wozzeck*, Act II, scene v.

41 See Congdon 1985 (p. 269) on the *Lyric Suite* row in the *Chamber Concerto*.

42 Carner 1983 (p. 72) shows a sketch from Berg's projected setting of Gerhart Hauptmann's *Und Pippa tanzt* with the same note group, {E,A,C,F}, in a rhythmic setting of eighth, quarter, eighth, eighth recalling the RH of *Lulu*.

43 For a discussion and analysis on Berg's treatment of rhythm and tempo in his later music see Perle 1985 (pp. 207–33) and Jarman 1979 (chap. 4).

44 Perle 1985 (pp. 228–29); Cerha 1979 (pp. 30ff.).

45 The attack-point retrograde of <1–3–3–3> is Berg's adaptation. A strict attack-point retrograde would be <1–3–3–1>.

46 The rhythms in this movement and the distinction between durational and retrograde rhythms are explained in Green 1977a. Green notes that Berg used the symbols RH for the longer rhythm, RN for the shorter in the sketches.

47 The sudden cut-off of the stage band music recalls the abrupt ending of the military band music in *Wozzeck*, Act I, scene iii, when Marie slams the window shut.

CHAPTER 5: THE TWELVE-TONE MUSIC: DETAIL AND ANALYSIS

1 The *Chamber Concerto* was begun in 1923 and completed February 9, 1925—in full score July 23, 1925—and premiered in March 1927 in Berlin; see Redlich 1957 (pp. 115–17); Jarman 1979 (pp. 8–9); and Brand, Hailey, and Harris 1987 (p. 334). Berg arranged the middle movement for piano, clarinet, and violin in February 1935; see Congdon 1981.

2 Berg, "Open Letter," in Reich 1965 (pp. 143–48) and Brand, Hailey, and Harris 1987 (pp. 334–37). Translations from Reich. The ensemble includes nine woodwinds—two flutes, the second doubling piccolo; oboe, english horn, E♭ clarinet, A clarinet, B♭ bass clarinet, bassoon, and contrabassoon—and four brass: trumpet, two horns, and trombone. For the history of the orchestration, see Berg 1971 (pp. 306–7, 315) and Brand, Hailey, and Harris 1987 (pp. 326–30).

3 Perle 1985 (p. 2) suggests a source for Berg's formal use of the twelve-tone operations in Schoenberg's Serenade op. 24, first movement.

4 See Schweizer 1970 (pp. 57–73) on the sonata form in this movement, and Neuwirth 1981 on formal and temporal proportions.

5 See Adorno 1991 (p. 99), who describes the "Ländler-like" second variation, "chordal" third, and the "scherzo-like" fourth variation.

6 Jarman 1979 (p. 186n. 1), notes that, with respect to the discrepancy, he was unable to check Berg's original; see also Perle 1985 (pp. 2–3) and Dalen 1989 (p. 144). Dalen comments that the discrepancy may have been a printer's error, but "evidence in the first draft of the survey suggests that Berg himself intentionally juggled the numbers, possibly to convey the impression of uniform proportional relations among the three movements, or to create the illusion of perfect symmetry within each half of the palindrome" (p. 176n. 24). It seems more likely, however, that Berg changed his mind several times and that the final version was not coordinated with his formal chart.

7 See Congdon 1981.

8 See Schweizer 1970 (pp. 71–72) for examples of combined themes from the two movements.

9 Redlich 1957 (p. 116) refers to a letter from Berg to Webern of September 1, 1923, describing the third movement as a "sonata." My formal chart of the third movement and its rhythmic designations are after Jarman 1979 (pp. 154). Jarman's labels for the rhythms are RT, RS, and RH; variants of the RH are shown in Jarman's example 189 (p. 155).

10 Pierre Boulez, in his introduction to the *Chamber Concerto*, gives his opinion that the repeat has a perceptible numerical necessity, but not a structural one, as it goes against the "principle of constant variation" in the rest of the piece (Vienna: Universal Edition, n.d.).

11 Congdon 1985 (pp. 254ff.) presents an intriguing if somewhat improbable rationale for the repeat, based on the overall formal use of retrograde in the concerto and on listeners' reactions to the repetition in terms of the embedded first and second movements in the third. In Congdon's view, the repeat adds two other symmetries. Given A ¦BA' R(A'B) ¦R(A') from movement 2 in movement 3, on the repeat the palindromic second-movement material can itself be considered a large palindrome, because BA' = R(R(BA'), and vice versa. Given theme vars. 1–2–3–4 5 from movement 1 in movement 3, on the repeat, variation 1 (prime) is heard as the substitute for variation 5; then a retrograde palindrome is created, with R(5,4,3,2) (R(P,RI,I,R)) heard instead of variations 2–5 (R,I,RI,P). The crucial substitution of R(5) for 2 is facilitated by the return of the waltz from the beginning of variation 2 at the end of variation 5. Thus, in Congdon's explanation, the repeat adds two non-coinciding palindromes in the third movement, one corresponding to the first movement material, the other to the second movement material. For my own case, while I am intrigued by the non-returning *Höhepunkt* in m. 314 of the second movement and the added statement of the Schönberg motto in m. 166 of the first movement, I have been unable to go any further towards explaining the repeat along these lines.

12 The row, created by Berg's pupil Fritz Heinrich Klein (Klein 1925), was identified in the concerto by Congdon 1985.

13 Lambert 1993 shows segmental and partitioned derivations linking some of the themes, foreshadowing Berg's later derivations of material.

14 Congdon 1981 (p. 151).

15 This added stave is similar to the *Klang* staves in *Wozzeck*, Act II, scene 4.

16 In m. 140, upper stave of ex. 5.1e, the F2 in the final chord is given a sharp to indicate that an F♯ is required to complete the cycle, while the score shows F♮.

17 See Congdon 1985 (p. 243).

18 The special treatment afforded theme 8 may be connected with its programmatic role as the "Melisande" theme. See Dalen 1989.

19 Green 1981 (pp. 58–59) and Jarman 1979 (p. 73).

20 This climactic presentation of cell 1 in different simultaneous rhythmic settings recalls the climax of op. 6, no. 1 (mm. 136ff.).

21 This type of resetting is foreshadowed in *Wozzeck*, where Marie's waiting motive (Act III, scene iii, mm. 152–53) and the Drum Major's motive (mm. 183–86) are set to the RH of the opera. Carner 1983 (p. 154) notes that in Schoenberg's Serenade op. 24, themes and motives of the finale are set to the *Marsch* rhythm, linking the outer movements.

22 Jarman 1979 (pp. 76–79) describes four "interval fields" in the concerto, based on superimposed major thirds, minor thirds, perfect fourths, and whole tones.

23 The series of intervals increases by 7 each time, thus creating an aggregate of intervals from the difference between the two generating cycles: $(-4) - 1 = -5$ or 7.

24 Lambert 1993 (p. 337). This symmetrical arrangement of theme 9, with dyads at sum 9 and Pn = R(In+1), invites comparison with the *Lyric Suite* row, with its adjacent sum-9 dyads and Pn = R(Pn+6) construction.

25 Adorno 1991 (pp. 197–98).

26 Redlich 1957 refers to the Czech composer Haba and microtones (p. 127), as does Carner 1983 (p. 152). Berg mentioned Haba and his "quarter-tone choruses and a sixth-tone quartet," and their performance in Frankfurt, in a letter to Schoenberg of March 25, 1924 (Brand, Hailey, and Harris 1987, p. 332).

27 Berg gave the date 1900 for the first setting of "Schließe mir" in his dedicatory preface, as part of the "twenty-five year" separation between his two settings of the text, but the later date 1907 is accepted as definitive; see Reich 1937 (pp. 14ff.) and 1965 (p. 109) and Redlich 1957 (p. 37). The songs first appeared in Reich 1930. Universal published the two songs in revised versions in 1960 as *Zwei Lieder (Theodor Storm)*, with Berg's dedicatory preface and an analytical essay by Hans Redlich. See Smith 1978 for a study of some sketches for the song.

28 The numbers 23 and 10 reflect Berg and Fuchs-Robettin by Berg's assignation (see Perle 1977b), and, representing her initials, F and B appear together at beats 10 (m. 4) and 23 (m. 8). The vocal register spans Berg's initials, A5 (m. 13) to B♭3 (m. 12), and Berg's musical moto {A,B♭,E,G} appears contiguously in mm. 13–14 (piano, left hand) and 15–16 (piano and voice).

29 "Close, o close my eyes at parting / with those hands I've loved so much, / that my anguish and my suff'ring / may find peace in thy sweet touch. // As my pain flows like the sea, / wave by wave to rest at evening, / when at last it ceases beating / all my heart is filled by thee." Alban Berg "Schließe mir die Augen Beide. English translation by Eric Smith. Copyright 1955 by Universal Edition A.G., Wien. Copyright renewed. All Rights Reserved. Used by permission of European American Music Distributors Corporation, sole U.S. and Canadian agent for Universal Edition A.G., Wien.

30 The formal contour arches foreshadow similar arches in *Der Wein* (especially m. 141) and *Lulu* (Act II, m. 687).

31 Berg's notes are in Rauchhaupt 1971 (pp. 91–117); see also Redlich 1960 and Jelinek 1952 (pp. 14ff.). For the row created by F. H. Klein, see Klein 1925 and Headlam 1992.

32 The row is thus a "cyclic set" in Perle's terminology (1977c).

33 Perle 1985 (p. 9) posits a PA row (beginning on B♭) as the source for these materials; with the pervading use of P5/I8 however, it seems unlikely that PA would make only one heavily disguised appearance.

34 The two alignments correspond to the sum and difference alignments of Perle's cyclic sets (1977c).

35 For the compositional history, see Jarman 1979 (pp. 9–10), Green 1977b, and Redlich 1957 (pp. 137–41).

36 Green 1977b (pp. 20–22) points out a larger context for Wagner's *Tristan und Isolde* in the final movement. For the program of the *Lyric Suite*, see Green 1977b and Perle 1977b.

37 Rauchhaupt 1971 (pp. 93–117); Reich 1959, 1965 (pp. 149–52); and Brand, Hailey, and Harris 1987 (pp. 348–51).

38 Perle 1985 (p. 13); Jarman 1979 (p. 180); Schweizer 1970 (pp. 86–88).

39 See Green 1977b, 1984, and Straus 1984.

40 Green 1977b (pp. 15–16).

41 Stein 1927 (p. 3); see also Schweizer 1970 (pp. 91–92).

42 An alternate reading of the movement is as a sonatina form, with recapitulation beginning at m. 36. I prefer the sonata-form reading due mainly to the material in mm. 40–41, which is analogous rhetorically to a dominant pedal building to the climactic return of the opening theme in mm. 42ff. See Berg's analysis in Rauchhaupt 1971 (p. 106), Stein 1927, also Adorno 1991 (p. 108) and Schweizer 1970 (pp. 85–99); Budday 1979 (p. 28) defines mm. 13–22 (49–52) as a transition.

43 The first tetrachord in m. 67 <C♯–D–A♯–F♯> should be <C♯–D–A–F♯> P2 0123, if the row is considered the criterion for note choice. See Budday 1979 (p. 34, n. 40).

44 Budday 1979 (p. 31).

45 The vertical 2-cycle of intervals results from the alignment of 7-cycles in 024 and 5-cycles in 135: 7 − 5 = 2.

46 The second movement's main theme may stem from row I16. If I16 has notes F♯

and A—the same notes that are changed in the referential forms between row 1 and row 2—and the first two tetrachords reversed, the result is the tetrachords of the main theme of the second movement:

1I6 <F#–G–B–D   A–E–Eb–Bb Ab–F–C#–C> [0158] / [0167] / [0158]

    <<u>A</u>–G–B–D   <u>F#</u>–E–Eb–Bb Ab–F–C#–C> [0247] / [0137] / [0158]

    <F#–E–Eb–Bb   A–G–B–D Ab–F–C#–C> [0137] / [0247] / [0158]

MT <E–D#–A#–F# G–A–B–D C#–G#–C–F> [0137] / [0247] / [0158]

Jarman 1979 (p. 29) posits a similar relationship between the main theme of movement 2 and row 1I1 of the first movement, in which <u>0123456789AB</u> of 1I1 is reordered as <u>645</u> <u>AB789</u> <u>0214</u>.

47 See Levin 1979 for a list of changes in the corresponding bars of the two scherzo sections.

48 Two alternate orders appear: in 2PA, <u>4567</u> <C–G–C#–F#> as <u>4765</u> <C–F#–C#–G> (mm. 30–37, cello)—anticipating the derivation of row 3 from row 2— and in 2I3, <u>4567</u> <C#–F#–C–G> as <u>5467</u> <F#–C#–C–G> (mm. 11–12, cello and viola; mm. 33–34, cello). The same note group, {C,C#,F#,G}, results from the sum-1 relationship between 2I3 and 2PA.

49 Green 1977a discusses the rhythms and retrogrades in the third movement of the *Lyric Suite*, using sketches, and the alterations and variants to row order and the rhythms. He groups ten "events" in the outer sections of the movement; these are similar to the formal divisions given in figure 5.6. See also Jarman 1979 (pp. 156–58).

50 The second SR2 in m. 31 (violin 2) is altered by delaying the second note B by a sixteenth, possibly to avoid an octave with the viola.

51 "Von den Schwierigkeiten, die es mir aber bereitete, von diesen 4 Formen (R I, II, III u U) die *möglichen* 4stimmigen Canons (es sind 17) zu finden, kann sich niemand auf der Welt, pardon, kannst *nur Du* Dir, liebster Freund, einen Begriff machen. Daher auch das langsame Vorwärts kommen." In Rauchhaupt 1971 (p. 95). Translation from Brand, Hailey, and Harris 1987 (pp. 348–51).

52 "Schließlich ab 46 *sämtliche* zwischen den 4 Formen [12er Reihe] *möglichen* [möglichen: das heißt ohne Einklänge zu bilden] Engführungen." In Rauchhaupt 1971 (p. 112). My translation.

53 Maegaard 1975.

54 Budday 1979 (p. 65) shows a "corrected" version of mm. 62–64 with the added D omitted.

55 Jarman 1979 (p. 30).

56 The suppressed text from the *Lyric Symphony* is "Du bist mein Eigen, mein Eigen" ("You are my own, my own") related to the program of the *Lyric Suite*.

57 Budday 1979 (p. 74). These arpeggiated chords (mm. 45–46) return in movement 5, mm. 356–70, at T2 and in augmentation. Perle 1985 (p. 13) describes the return of the arpeggiated harmonies as "an hallucinatory recollection."

58 The viola's diverging interval 1 wedge is an M7 transformation of the diverging interval 7s in row 1 from the first movement. See Perle 1985 (pp. 11–12).

59 Beginning with row 1P1, <C♯–C–A♭–F–E♭–B♭–E–A–B–D–F♯–G>, if C♯ and D are exchanged, the tetrachords of the first theme in movement 5 result: <D–C–A♭–F–E♭–B♭–E–A–B–C♯–F♯–G> to <A♭–F–C–D–B–F♯–C♯– G–A–B♭–E♭–E>. The rearrangement in the theme of movement 5 yields opening F- and B-"minor triads," followed two notes later by A and B♭ ("Alban Berg"), in a programmatic context. See Jarman 1979 (p. 29).

60 The song text was deciphered in Green 1977b. The vocal melody is given in Perle 1977b (pp. 10–11) and Perle 1985 (pp. 20–23). "To you, you sole dear one, my cry rises / Out of the deepest abyss in which my heart has fallen. / There the landscape is dead, the air like lead / And in the dark, curse and terror well up. // Six months without warmth stands the sun. / During [the other] six darkness lies over the earth. / Even the polar land is not so barren- / Not even brook and tree, nor field nor flock. // But no terror born of brain approaches / The cold horror of this icy star / And of this night, a gigantic Chaos! // I envy the lot of the most common animal / Which can plunge into the dizziness of a senseless sleep . . . / So slowly does the spindle of time unwind!" trans. from Green 1977b. Used by permission of Douglass M. Green. The German has George's idiosyncratic non-capitalization of nouns, but Green notes that Berg copied the poem using normal German practice; see Green 1977b (p. 22n. 5).

61 Budday 1979 (p. 80) extends this symmetrical arch to encompass the entire song.

62 The relationship of tempo and duration is discussed in Perle 1985 (p. 16).

63 The row derivation of the Tristan quote is described in Straus 1984 and Green 1984.

64 See Baudelaire 1922. For discussion of Baudelaire see Redlich 1957 (pp. 156–58), who notes that the poems of *Der Wein* date from soon after Büchner's *Woyzeck*, and Carner 1983 (pp. 108–10), who suggests Mahler's "Der Trunkene im Frühling" from *Das Lied von der Erde* as an influence on *Der Wein*. See also Adorno 1991 (pp. 117–20) and Watkins 1988 (p. 193), who note Berg's affinity for French texts and music.

65 Brand, Hailey, and Harris 1987 (p. 424).

66 Jarman 1979 (p. 11); Scherliess 1976 (p. 109); and Redlich 1957 (pp. 155–56).

67 "*The Spirit of the Wine*":
One evening, the spirit of the wine sang out in bottles:
"O Man, I cry to you, beloved deprived soul,
From within my glass prison and my vermillion seals,
A song full of light and brotherhood!

I know how much is needed, on the fiery hillsides,
In pain, in sweat and in broiling sun
To create my existence and give me life;
But I shall not be ungrateful or evil-minded.

For I generate an infinite joy when I tumble
Down the throat of a man worn out by his labors,

And his warm chest is a sweet grave
Which pleases me much more than my cold cellars.

Do you hear the echo of the songs of Sundays
And the hope which bubbles in my quivering breast?
With elbows on the table and your sleeves rolled up,
You will worship me and be content;

I will light up the eyes of your entranced wife;
I will restore to your son his strength and coloring
And will be for the weak sportsman of life
The oil which revives the muscles of those who struggle.

In you I will fall, ambrosial fruit,
Precious drops cast by the eternal Sower,
That our love should bring forth the poetry
Which will blossom toward God like a rare flower!"

"*The Wine of Lovers*":

Today the world is wonderful!
Without bit, without spurs, without reins,
Let us ride with the wine
Toward a fantastic and sublime heaven!

As two angels who are tortured
By an unending tropical fever,
In the crystal blue of morning
Let us follow the distant mirage!

Lightly balanced on the wing
Of the understanding whirlwind.
Both in an equal delirium,

My sister, swimming side by side,
We will fly, without rest or respite,
Towards the paradise of my dreams!

"*The Wine of the Single Man*":

The odd look of an elegant lady
Which sidles towards us like the white beam
That the caressing moon directs to the trembling lake
When she wishes to bathe her serene beauty therein;

That last bag of chips in the hand of a gambler;
A tender kiss from the slender Adeline;

The sounds of exciting and inviting music,
Like the faraway cry of human sorrow,

All that is not equal, O profound bottle,
To the penetrating balms that your fertile depths
Keep for the converted heart of the devout poet;

You pour out for him hope, youth and life,
—And pride, the redeemer of all poverty,
Which makes us triumphant and equal to the Gods!

Translation by Kevin Roberts. The German text is taken from the published score. In George's translation a reference to a violin in the third poem, stanza 2, line 3, "erschlaffenden Gesang der Violine" is not in the French version, but Berg reflects the change with prominent violin entries in the tangos of songs 1 and 3 (mm. 46–49, 189–93). See Redlich 1957 (p. 158n.2).

68 In the original French of the first poem, the six stanzas are arranged symmetrically, pairing stanzas 1 and 6, 2 and 5, and 3 and 4 by the number of syllables and their divisions within each line. The third song is in alexandrines in the original French; all lines have twelve syllables, divided internally into six plus six.

69 Figure 5.15 is after Jarman 1979 (p. 186).

70 See Hall 1985 and Headlam 1990. Redlich 1957 (p. 156) compared *Der Wein*'s relationship with *Lulu* to that of "Schließe mir" with the *Lyric Suite*, pointing out the similarity between the tango in *Der Wein* (mm. 40ff.) and the English Waltz in *Lulu* (Act I, scene iii).

71 Two retrograde rows appear in the voice, both only partial statements: R(IA) at mm. 47–50 and R(P9) at mm. 70–71. Twelve retrograde forms appear elsewhere: R(PO) in mm. 6–7 (strings and harp); R(Io) in m. 10 (violins); R(I7) in m. 20 (viola); R(Io) in m. 21 (5–0, violin 1); R(I4)/R(Io) in mm. 40–41 and 182–83; R(I2) in mm. 73 and 196 (2–7, strings); R(I1), R(I5), and R(P3), and R(Io) in mm. 92–105 (strings); and R(P4) in m. 120 (5–A, violin 1). The relative lack of retrograde rows may also reflect the ordered invariance between P/RI and I/R rows:

$$P2: \quad 2 \quad 4 \quad 5 \quad 7 \quad 9 \quad A \quad 1 \quad 6 \quad 8 \quad 0 \quad B \quad 3$$
$$R(Io): \quad 0 \quad B \quad 3 \quad 2 \quad 6 \quad 8 \quad 1 \quad 4 \quad 5 \quad 7 \quad 9 \quad A$$

The general ordered invariance between Pn and a rotated R(In+10) in *Der Wein* foreshadows the complete invariance between Pn and a rotated R(In+4) in the row of the Violin Concerto.

72 The chord can also be seen as comprising B- and F-major triads, associated with Hanna Fuchs-Robettin. See Perle 1985 (pp. 139–40).

73 Some of these derivations are described in Jarman 1979 (pp. 101–9 and 133–36) and 1971–72. See also Redlich 1966 and Headlam 1990.

74 See Reich 1965 (p. 154); Berg noted "5 Töne Dur," "3 moll," and "4 Moll-Dur."

75 A series of successively altered events leads to the transposition; see Headlam 1990 (p. 283).

76 In the sketches for *Der Wein* the row forms here labeled as prime are labeled "U" or *Umkehrung* (inversion). Following Jarman 1979, I have exchanged Berg's prime (O) and inversion (U) to inversion and prime. This reversed analytic labelling reflects the predominance of the here-defined prime form in horizontal statements and the corresponding emphasis and association of pitch-class D with P2. Berg's "prime" label is reflected in the almost exclusive use of his "prime" row forms (here defined as inversions) for the derivations given above in *Der Wein*. (Only derivations 2 and 3 have some of Berg's "inversion" (my prime) row sources). The predominant horizontal use of Berg's "inversion" forms, here prime forms, apparently emerged in the course of composition. See also Jarman 1979, Knaus 1981.

In the sketch in Reich 1965 (p. 154), labeled "3 Beispiele" by Berg, the upper row, labeled *Reihe*, is P2 from mm. 8–10, but it is scribbled out; instead, the rows given are I3 (mm. 18ff.), 13-P9 (mm. 92–96), with the opening note in parentheses, then IB with the analytical markings mentioned above in relation to derivation 2 (ex. 5.32). The three rows are numbered 2, 3, and 1. Why Berg scribbled out the top P2 is not clear, but it may have something to do with the changing referential status in his own mind of the prime and inversion forms of the row.

77 This arrangement of [06]s with resulting vertical [06]s and [0268]s is identical in procedure to a passage in Richard Strauss's *Elektra* (1908) (rehearsal nos. 72–74). I am indebted to Janet Schmalfeldt for suggesting Strauss's opera in this connection.

78 The third rhythmic motive recalls the scherzo of Beethoven's Ninth Symphony. The RH symbol does not appear in the score of *Der Wein* (or the *Lyric Suite* or "Schließe mir"), but at least one *Hauptrhythmus* appears in the sketches, on the last beat of m. 102, with a B♭4 indicated, tied over. This B♭4 does not appear in the score (although in the score the voice has a B♭4 that ends on beat 4 of m. 102), and although there are many of what I label as RH 3 in the vicinity, none begins on the last beat of m. 102. The *Hauptrhythmus* in the sketches is thereby suggestive with respect to RH 3, but inconclusive.

79 Adorno 1991 (pp. 116–17).

80 For the compositional history, see Jarman 1979 (pp. 10–14), Jarman 1991a (chaps. 1 and 4), and Perle 1985 (chaps. 2 and 6).

81 For the *Lulu Suite*, see Headlam 1985b, also Adorno 1960, Jarman 1979 (pp. 12–13), Jarman 1982b, Perle 1985 (pp. 241–42), and Redlich 1957 (pp. 198–200).

82 The completion of *Lulu* is documented in: Adorno 1991 (pp. 132–35); E. A. Berg 1980; Csampai and Holland 1985 (pp. 225–64); Carner 1983 (pp. 269–76); Cerha 1979, 1981; Jarman 1991a (chap. 4); Perle 1985 (chaps. 5 and 6); Redlich 1957 (pp. 200–203); and Szmolyan 1977.

83 See, for instance, Perle 1979a.

84 Berg had read *Erdgeist* as early as 1904 and attended a private production of *Pandora's Box* in Vienna on May 29, 1905. See the discussion of Wedekind and con-

temporary reactions to his plays, the *Lulu* plays, German theatre, Karl Kraus's influential talk given at the Vienna performance, and Berg's adaptation and progress in his opera, in Adorno 1991 (pp. 128–29); Carner 1983 (pp. 215–26); Csampai and Holland 1985; Dahlhaus 1981; Jarman 1991a (113–17); Perle 1985 (chap. 2); Redlich 1957 (pp. 163–76); and the text of Kraus's speech in Reich 1965 (pp. 156–59) and Jarman 1991a (pp. 102–11).

85 For the large-scale musical and dramatic form, see Hall 1991; Jarman 1979 (pp. 199–200, 209–11); Perle 1985 (pp. 60–65, 147); Redlich 1957 (p. 276); Reich 1965 (pp. 157–58); and Simms 1994.

86 For smaller forms in *Lulu*, see Perle 1985 (chap. 3), Jarman 1979 (pp. 198–222) and Jarman 1991 (chaps. 3 and 5).

87 See Hall 1985, 1989, 1991; Green 1991b; Jarman 1991a (chaps. 1–4); and Scherliess 1976 for the compositional history.

88 "Wobei ich mir noch immer vorbehalte—sollte ich dennoch nicht auskommen, eine neue Reihe zu bilden, etwa in der Art wie in meiner lyr. Suite, wo die Reihe Satz-Paar-Weise kleine Änderungen erfuhr (durch Umstellungen von ein paar Tonen) was wenigstens damals sehr anregend für die Arbeit war." See Scherliess 1976 (p. 109); translation from Carner 1983 (p. 227).

89 Scherliess 1976 (p. 110).

90 Brand, Hailey, and Harris 1987 (p. 373). The two exceptions, second-stage character rows associated with Alwa (Alwa-P7, mm. 98–99) and Dr. Schön (Schön-P6, mm. 119–22), were added later in revisions. See Hall 1985.

91 For the sketches, see Cerha 1979; Hall 1985, 1989; Reich 1960; Scherliess 1975, 1977. The names given to the motivic materials are from Perle 1985.

92 The derivation of rows has been described in Carner 1983; Hall 1985; Jarman 1979; Keller 1953; Perle 1959, 1965a, 1985; Reich 1936, 1960; Reiter 1973; and Headlam 1985. Berg used order-position numbers 1–12 as a shorthand for the rows derived by every fifth and seventh notes. Hall 1985 has described letters from Reich to Berg of September 21 and 25, 1929; these letters respond to Berg's initial presentation of rows derived from extracting every fifth and every seventh note of the main row, but counting *from* the first note, rather than beginning with the first note and counting from the second:

principal row ops.:	0	1	2	3	4	5	6	7	8	9	A	B
every fifth note:	4	9	2	7	0	5	A	3	8	1	6	B
every seventh note:	6	1	8	3	A	5	0	7	2	9	4	B

Jarman 1979 (pp. 124–25) describes other arrangements similar to the Dr. Schön row derivation.

93 This type of ordering is described in Lewin 1966; see also Rothgeb 1967.

94 Jarman 1979 (p. 89).

95 See Jarman 1979 (pp. 158–59) and Headlam 1985a.

96 The invariances are analogous to those of M7 in the pitch-class realm.

97 See Perle 1985 (pp. 161–89, 198–200); Jarman 1979 (pp. 88–92) and Jarman 1991a (chap. 6) show related invariances among musical materials.

98 A sketch of the Alwa row shows three [0123]s derived from <u>059A</u>, <u>138B</u>, and <u>2467</u>; see ex. 5.52b.

99 See Jarman 1981, 1979 (p. 93); also Perle 1985 (p. 121). Jarman 1981 has noted the connection of this "parade" of rows with the text: "The rain is drumming up a parade." See also Reich 1965 (p. 174), who refers to the A-major triad (Schön P4 <u>012</u>) that "drums up the parade."

100 See Perle 1985 (pp. 209–15, 220) and Jarman 1979 (pp. 212–15).

101 Lulu's mythic universal quality relates her to other female characters of the time: Bizet's Carmen, Zola's Nana, Manet's Olympia, Klimt's Judith and Salome, and Lola from *Der blaue Engel.* See Adorno 1991 (pp. 130–31); Carner 1983 (pp. 217–18); Csampai and Holland 1985 (pp. 170–92); Estrine 1988; Jarman 1991a (pp. 99–100); Mitchell 1954; Neumann 1974; Perle 1964a and 1985 (pp. 57ff.).; Reich 1965 (pp. 159–60); Stenzl 1981; and Treitler 1991.

102 "Ich habe nie in der Welt etwas anderes scheinen wollen, als wofür man mich genommen hat; und man hat mich nie in der Welt für etwas anderes genommen, als was ich bin." Translation by George Perle; see n. 110.

103 See Perle 1985 (p. 138), who uses the name "Entrance" motive. I use "Freedom" motive for the strong association with Lulu's cry of *Freiheit* in Act II, scene ii. The choice of m. 1000 (10 × 10 × 10) is probably not coincidental but may be a reference to Hanna Fuchs-Robettin.

104 Reiter 1973 has shown how the components of the freedom motive can be derived from the Countess Geschwitz collections at their referential level: {G,D}, {C,E,F,A,B}, {D♭,G♭,B♭,A♭,E♭} grouped into {B,A,F}, {D♭,G♭,B♭}, {C,E,G}, and {G,D}. This improbable relationship seems unlikely, however, for the use of the Freedom motive in connection with Lulu is not directly associated with the Countess. The only other such relationship is the derivation of Schigolch's row from the Medical Specialist rhythm.

105 Perle 1985 (pp. 138–39) shows that these "tonal" bars may stem from the opening "I–V" trichords of the Alwa and Schön rows.

106 Perle 1985 (p. 138 (or 23× 2 × 3)) has noted that this text is set to B–F in the bass (m. 222), in a likely reference to Hanna Fuchs-Robettin.

107 "Wenn deine beiden großen Kinderaugen nicht wären, müßte ich dich für die abgefeimteste Dirne halten, die je einen Mann ins Verderben gestürzt." "Wollte Gott, ich wäre das!"

108 The music of the Marquis is associated with the characters of the Prince in Act I, scene iii, the Manservant in Act II, scene i (and, symmetrically around the palindrome between Act II, scenes i and ii, the Acrobat, when he impersonates the servant in Act II, scene ii), and the Marquis in Act III. See Hall 1991. Thus, the reference in the first "Lied" could also be to the Prince who wanted to take Lulu to Africa.

109 See Moldenhauer and Moldenhauer 1979 (p. 404) and Peryne 1967. The dedication appears in the score of the suite as well as in the piano-vocal and orchestral scores of the opera (Act II, scene i, m. 491). Although the "Lied" of the opera

encompasses forty-eight bars (mm. 491–538), the "Lied" of the suite has an extra measure added at the beginning, unnumbered, an altered last measure, and an extra end measure added to total fifty measures. The total is somewhat confusing in the suite because of the unnumbered first bar, and the measures are numbered 1–49 from m. 2. Hall (1989, p. 247) notes that Berg apparently tried to make the "Lied" forty-six bars in length originally, likely in some programmatic 23 connection, and presumably before the dedication to Webern prompted the change, at least in the suite, to fifty bars.

110 "1. If men have killed themselves for my sake, / that doesn't lower my worth. / 2. You knew as well why you took me for your wife, / as I knew why I took you as my husband. / 3. You had betrayed your best friends with me, / you couldn't very well betray yourself with me. / 4. If you sacrifice the evening of your life to me, / you've had the whole of my youth in exchange. / 5. I've never in the world wanted to seem anything other than what I've been taken for, / and no one has ever taken me for anything other than what I am." Translation by George Perle, *The Operas of Alban Berg, Volume Two: Lulu* (Berkeley: University of California Press, 1985), p. 48. Used by permission.

111 See Krenek 1958 (p. 248); Perle 1985 (pp. 175–77); and Stenzl 1981 (pp. 31–39).

112 In the piano-vocal score, the vocal double barline is missing at m. 511, between the clauses of the third line, but it appears in the orchestral score and in the suite.

113 The overlap is an unusual procedure for Berg but one that may have been suggested by the dedication to Webern.

114 Hall 1989 (p. 239, fig. 3.4) shows Berg's textual plan for the sonata and the associations of each theme: the main theme marks Schön's dominating personality; the transition theme Lulu's other husbands; the second theme, Schön's fiancé; and the coda theme Lulu's "possession" of Schön. See also Jarman 1979 (pp. 203, 207–9), who notes that Berg changed the order of passages from the Wedekind plays to fit his musical scheme; see also Jarman 1991a (pp. 59–63) and Schweizer 1970 (pp. 165–225).

The tempo markings are detailed and important in defining the form of the sonata. Perle 1985 (pp. 224–28) has an extensive discussion of tempo relationships in the sonata; see also Jarman 1979 (pp. 168–71), who documents the tempo relationships from Act I, m. 533 (beginning of the sonata), to m. 1356.

115 See Schweizer 1970 (p. 194) and Reiter 1973 (pp. 44–47, 104).

116 Schweizer 1970 (p. 193) and Reiter 1973 (p. 44) demonstrate how the combined notes in the vocal and accompaniment parts of mm. 533–34 outline both PR-P8 and Schn P8, anticipating the later intertwining of these two rows.

117 See Hall 1989 (p. 253, ex. 5).

118 Perle 1985 (pp. 131–34), and Jarman 1979 (pp. 94ff.).

119 See Perle 1985 (pp. 167ff.) and especially Jarman 1970b and 1979 (pp. 95–100).

120 Perle 1985 (p. 59). Berg makes the connection explicit by referring to a line from Alwa in the dedication to Schoenberg. It is also interesting to speculate on correspondences between Alwa/Alban and Dr. Schön/Schoenberg.

121 Perle 1985 (p. 62) speculates that Alwa is represented in the prologue by the Animal Tamer because Alwa opens the opera itself.

122 "Sie haben eine Schauderoper geschrieben, in der die Waden meiner Braut die beiden Hauptfiguren sind, und das kein Hoftheater zur Aufführung bringt."

123 Perle 1985 (p. 84). Wedekind's text refers to Lulu's "cantabile" ankles, "capriccio" knees, and "andante" of voluptuousness; Berg's text describes "grazioso" ankles, "cantabile" round calves, "misterioso" knees (from the third movement Allegro misterioso of the *Lyric Suite*) and "andante" voluptuousness (from the second movement Andante amoroso of the *Lyric Suite*).

124 Perle 1985 (pp. 97–98).

125 The rondo appears without interruption in the rondo first movement of the *Lulu Suite*. The designation "Rondo" does not appear in the score of *Lulu*; however Jarman 1982b (pp. 14–16) discovered that the rondo of the suite was inserted into the full score of *Lulu*, but the rondo designation did not get transferred. The designation for the closing hymn, however, does appear in the opera score.

126 See Jarman 1979 (pp. 99–100) and Redlich 1957 (p. 178). "Eine Seele, die sich im Jenseits den Schlaf aus den Augen reibt," "In Deinen Augen schimmert es wie der Wasserspiegel in einem tiefen Brunnen," "Wenn Deine beiden grossen Kinderaugen nicht wären."

127 The possible reference here, linking Alwa-Lulu with Alban-Hanna, is to the last chord of *Der Wein*, and the measure 1110 refers to the number 10 of Hanna Fuchs-Robettin.

128 Berg 1971 (pp. 106–11). In the foreword to the second volume of the *Lulu* plays, Wedekind wrote that the Countess, burdened by her lesbianism, is the tragic central figure, and the vulgar Acrobat is her foil. Her submission to him for Lulu's sake is a particularly poignant aspect of her story. Wedekind's foreword and the verse prologue about the Countess from the second volume, *Die Büchse der Pandora* (reprinted in Jarman 1991, pp. 115–17), highlight this tragic character as an answer to his critics. Berg may have had an insight into the character of the Countess by way of his sister, Smargada, a lesbian, for whom Berg had great sympathy. In a letter to Helene's father of July 1910 explaining his suitability for marriage, the fourth section, titled "The 'Immorality' of Members of My Family," Berg displays understanding for his sister in terms that recall Wedekind's comments. See Berg 1971 (pp. 106–11), also Perle 1985 (pp. 39–40).

129 The retrograde relationship of the initial Countess row to the Alwa row, and the subsequent change in the former, recalls the row of the first movement of the *Lyric Suite*, in which the row's lack of an independent retrograde was a catalyst for further alteration. Although Berg uses the retrograde of the Alwa row, sparingly he apparently felt that the rotated retrograde in the initial Countess row was close enough to the original to warrant alteration before use. The forms of the material relating to the Countess Geschwitz are described in Jarman 1981, Perle 1985 (pp. 99–102), and Reich 1960 (p. 39).

130 See Perle 1985 (pp. 181–89).

131 "Du bist kein Menschenkind wie die andern. Für einen Mann war der Stoff nicht-ausreichen. Und zum Weib hast Du zu viel Hirn in Deinen Schädel bekommen."

132 Perle 1985 (pp. 190–92).

133 F/B may, of course, refer to Hanna Fuchs-Robettin, and the A in the chord plus the last note B♭ of the three-note motives to Berg's initials.

134 The chords in the vertical 7 {A,E} dyad recall the death of Marie and the vertical 7 dyads {G,D} at the end of *Wozzeck*. As Reich 1965 (p. 176) notes, the final chord {F,E,A,B} of *Lulu* has the same notes as the second chord in Marie's "waiting" motive.

135 Hall 1991 (p. 245) discovered the symmetrical correspondence of the Acrobat and Manservant and associates the three characters as representing the "slavery" of "marriage, the household, or the brothel." She also notes a reference to the wedding march of *Lohengrin* in the music of the Prince and the Marquis. For an overview of the chorale variations in each act, see Green 1981. See also Treitler 1991 (pp. 268–69).

136 Wedekind was a popular star of the German literary cabaret in Munich known as Die Elf Scharfrichter (The Eleven Executioners) from 1901 to 1903. He sang his ballads to his own melodies, accompanying himself on the lute. See Appignanesi 1975. The tune is "Konfession," no. 10 of a collection, *Lautenlieder*. The text and music are found in Wedekind 1920, translated in Jarman 1979 (appendix 2).

137 The settings of the Wedekind melody recall Berg's commentaries on popular song in *Wozzeck*. The melody has regular, symmetrical periods and sections and is harmonized in tertian harmonies, and in fourths—which also predominate in the jazz sections of Lulu, particularly the *English Waltz*—and in a polytonal setting. The most clearly tonal passages in Lulu, the Wedekind melody and the jazz music, are associated with seedy, low-class characters and activities.

138 See Jarman 1979 (pp. 144–46) on the pitch language, particularly the absorption of the Wedekind tune into the twelve-tone context, which foreshadows the similar treatment of the chorale tune in the variations of the Violin Concerto.

139 For the history of the Violin Concerto, see Perle 1985 (pp. 254–55); Pople 1991 (chap. 3); and Redlich 1957 (pp. 203–5). For the reception of its performances, see Pople 1991 (chap. 6) and Krasner 1981 and 1982. For "errors" in the published score, see Lorkovic 1989 (pp. 268–71) and Pople 1991 (p. 107n. 52).

140 Berg described the row in a letter to Schoenberg of August 28, 1935, noting the similarity of the beginning of the chorale and the end of the row. Brand, Hailey, and Harris 1987 (p. 466).

141 Pople 1991 (chap. 5) combines tonal and serial readings. He concludes that the "work . . . simultaneously . . . celebrates both reconciliation and confrontation which might be said at the same time to have reconciled—and yet not reconciled—those two inseparable and eternal opposites" (p. 102). See Perle 1985 (pp. 248–50) and Jarman 1979 (pp. 136–140, 143–44) on the ambiguous serial reading of the score of the Violin Concerto and on the apparently tonal criteria for note choices. Berg noted, with regard to the row that its intervalic properties

were "advantageous," adding "since D major and similar 'violin concerto' keys were of course out of the question" (in Brand, Hailey, and Harris 1987, p. 466).

142 See Morris 1983–84, Perle 1985 (p. 251), and Redlich 1957 (p. 272).

143 See Burkholder 1991 for an inspired reading of these opening bars.

144 Green 1981 (p. 63) points out the similarity of the C/G♭ and E♭/A keys of the Carinthian folk tune in the Violin Concerto to the 3-cycle setting C–A–F♯–E♭ of the Wedekind tune in the variations in *Lulu*.

145 Headlam and Brown 1990.

146 Krämer 1992 (pp. 56–62), has shown, however, that the Violin Concerto rows I1 <D♭–B♭–G♭–D–B–G♯ / E–C–A–G–F–E♭> and I7 <G–E–C–A♭–F–D / B♭–G♭–E♭–D♭–B–A> contain the T6-related triads {G♭,B♭,D♭} and {C,E,G} in their respective hexachords, and derives notes of the Carinthian tune from these two row forms I (mm. 214–17) under the notes <F–E♭–D♭–B> in the solo violin. He points out the triadic C/G♭ juxtaposition in mm. 134–36, with a similar <F–E♭–D♭–B> violin descent, and a hint of a similar juxtaposition in m. 175, symmetrically placed within the larger arch form of the movement.

147 Perle 1985 (p. 244) suggests a sonata-form outline: introduction, mm. 1–10; principal subject, mm. 11–37; subordinate subject, mm. 38–53; reprise of subordinate subject, mm. 54–76; concluding subject, mm. 77–83; and codetta, mm. 84–103.

148 The sketches for the Violin Concerto contain roman numerals, indicating that Berg was aware of the tonal connotations. For instance, the "minor" form of the progression in m. 11 is labelled "VI–ii–V–I." On the efficacy of applying sketch evidence directly to analysis, see Headlam 1995. For a study of the sketches, see Pople 1991 (chaps. 3–5).

149 The trio 1 theme in ex. 5.69, recalls the piano figure derived from the upper voice of Alwa's two-part counterpoint (*Lulu*, Act II, mm. 278, 1006–7); cf. exx. 5.54 and 5.56 [m. 1149].

150 In the Violin Concerto sketches, the chorale variations are partly in draft in the original A-major key, down a half-step from the final version; see Pople 1991 (p. 36). The two keys A and B♭ of course represent Berg's initials.

151 In Berg's version of Bach's arrangement, however, the alto voice of m. 1 is altered in rhythm from half-quarter-eighth-eighth to half-eighth-eighth-quarter, eliminating the distinctive beat 4 [0148] of the original. The only other change made by Berg is in the initial chords of the B♭ subsection: Bach, <G♯3–B3–E4–E5> to <A3–A3–E4–C♯4> or, in B♭, <A–C–F–F> to <B♭–B♭–F–D>; and Berg, <F3–F4–C5–F5> to <B♭3–B♭4–F4–D4>.

152 Green 1981 (p. 65) refers to these "double neighbor" figures in traditional terms, invoking the tonal implications.

153 Redlich 1957 (pp. 208–9) comments on similarities between Bach's and Berg's settings of the chorale tune.

Bibliography

ABBREVIATIONS

CI	*Critical Inquiry*
IABSN	*International Alban Berg Society Newsletter*
ITO	*In Theory Only*
ITR	*Indiana Theory Review*
JAMS	*Journal of the American Musicological Society*
JASI	*Journal of the Arnold Schoenberg Institute*
JMR	*Journal of Musicological Research*
JMT	*Journal of Music Theory*
ÖMZ	*Österreichische Musikzeitschrift*
MA	*Music Analysis*
MQ	*Musical Quarterly*
MR	*Music Review*
MT	*The Musical Times*
MTS	*Music Theory Spectrum*
PNM	*Perspectives of New Music*
SM	*Studia musicologica*
SMZ	*Schweizerische Musikzeitung*
TAP	*Theory and Practice*

WORKS CITED

Adorno, Theodor W. 1959. "Die Instrumentation von Bergs frühen Liedern." In *Klangfiguren*. (Frankfurt Suhrkamp, 1959), pp. 138–56.

———. 1960. "Berg's Lulu-Symphonie." *Melos* 27: 43–45.

———. 1968. "On the Characteristics of 'Wozzeck.'" Trans. in John 1990, pp. 37–40. Originally in *Alban Berg: Der Meister des kleinsten Übergangs* (Vienna: Elisabeth Lafite, 1968), pp. 92–96.

———. 1991. *Alban Berg: Master of the Smallest Link*. Trans. Juliane Brand and Christopher Hailey. Cambridge: Cambridge University Press. Translation of *Alban Berg: Der Meister des kleinsten Übergangs* (Vienna: Elizabeth Lafite, 1968).

Altenberg, Peter. 1911. *Neues Altes*. Berlin.

Antokoletz, Elliott. 1984. *The Music of Béla Bartók*. Berkeley: University of California Press.

———. 1986. "Interval Cycles in Stravinsky's Early Ballets." *JAMS* 34: 578–614.

Appignanesi, Lisa. 1975. *The Cabaret*. London: Studio Vista.

Archibald, Bruce. 1965. "Harmony in the Early Works of Alban Berg." Ph.D. diss. Harvard University.

————. 1968. "The Harmony of Berg's *Reigen*." *PNM* 6/2 (Spring–Summer): 73–91.

————. 1989. "Berg's Development as an Instrumental Composer." In Jarman 1989a (pp. 91–122).

Ayrey, Craig. 1982. "Berg's 'Scheideweg': Analytical Issues in Opus 2/ii." *MA* 189–202.

Babbitt, Milton. 1962. "Twelve-tone Rhythmic Structure and the Electronic Medium." *PNM* 1: 49–79.

Baudelaire, Charles. 1922. *Die Blumen des Bosen*. Trans. Stefan George. Berlin: Georg Bondi.

Beiber, Hugo. 1914. "Wozzeck and Woyzeck." *Literarisches Echo* 16: 1188ff. Repr. in Jarman 1989b (pp. 111–29).

Berg, Alban. 1913a. *Arnold Schönberg: "Gurrelieder": Führer*. Leipzig and Vienna: Universal Edition.

————. 1913b. *Arnold Schönberg: "Kammersymphonie" Op. 9: Thematische Analyse*. Vienna and Leipzig: Universal Edition.

Berg, Alban. 1913c. *Arnold Schönberg: "Pelleas und Melisande" (nach dem Drama von Maurice Maeterlinck), Symphonische Dichtung für Orchester op. 5: Kurze thematische Analyse*. Vienna and Leipzig: Universal Edition.

————. 1920. "Die musikalische Impotenz der 'neuen Äesthetik' Hans Pfitzners." *Musikblätter des Anbruch*. 2/11–12 (June); Trans. in Reich 1965 (pp. 205–18).

————. 1924a. "Die musikalische Formen in meiner Oper 'Wozzeck.'" *Die Musik* 16: 587–89. Reich 1937 (pp. 178–80). Trans. in Jarman 1989b (pp. 149–51).

————. 1924b. "Warum ist Schönbergs Musik so schwer verständlich?" *Musikblätter des Anbruch* 6 (August–September): 329–41. Trans. in Reich 1965 (pp. 189–204).

————. 1925. "'Kammerkonzert für Klavier und Geige mit Begleitung von dreizehn Bläsern' (Offener Brief an Arnold Schönberg)." *Pult und Taktstock* 2 (February–March): 23–8. Trans. in Reich 1965 (pp. 143–48) and in Brand, Hailey, and Harris 1987 (pp. 334–37).

————. 1926a. "Neun Blätter zur 'Lyrischen Suite für Streichquartet.'" (1926). In Reich 1959 and Rauchhaupt 1971 (pp. 105–17).

————. 1927. "A Word About '*Wozzeck*.'" *Modern Music* 5/1 (November–December): 22–24.

————. 1929. "Wozzeck-Vortrag" (1929). In Redlich 1957 (pp. 311–27). Trans. in Redlich 1957 (pp. 261–86). Also trans. in Jarman 1989b (pp. 154–70).

————. 1930a. "Praktische Anweisungen zur Einstudierung des 'Wozzeck'" (1930). In Reich 1937 (pp. 166–72). Trans. in Perle 1980 (pp. 203–6).

————. 1930b. "Was ist atonal?" Radio talk (April 23, 1930). *23: Eine Wiener Musikzeitschrift* 26/27 (June 8, 1936): 1–11. Trans. in Nicholas Slonimsky, *Music Since 1900*. 5th ed. (New York: Schirmer, 1994), pp. 1027–29.

————. 1971. *Letters to His Wife*. Edited, translated, and annotated by Bernard Grun. New York: St. Martin's Press.

————. 1981. *Glaube, Hoffnung und Liebe: Schriften zur Musik.* Edited by Frank Schneider. Leipzig: Reclam.

Berg, Erich Alban. 1976. *Alban Berg: Leben und Werk in Daten und Bildern.* Frankfurt: Insel.

————. 1979. "Eine naturliche Tochter: Zur Biographie Alban Berg." *Frankfurter Allgemeine Zeitung,* May 21.

————. 1980. "Bergiana." *SMZ* 3: 147–49.

————. 1985. *Der unverbesserlich Romantiker: Alban Berg 1885–1935.* Vienna: Österreichischer Bundesverlag.

Berger, Arthur. 1963. "Problems of Pitch Organization in Stravinsky." *PNM* 2/1 (Fall–Winter): 11–42.

Bernstein, W. David. 1993. "Symmetry and Symmetrical Inversion in Turn-of-the-Century Theory and Practice." In *Music Theory and the Exploration of the Past,* ed. Christopher Hatch and David W. Bernstein (Chicago: University of Chicago Press), pp. 377–408.

Berry, Wallace. 1989. *Musical Structure and Performance.* New Haven: Yale University Press.

Boa, Elizabeth. 1987. "Berg's *Lulu* and the Operatic Tradition." In *The Sexual Circus* (London: Blackwell), pp. 122–29.

Brand, Juliane, Christopher Haley and Donald Harris. ed. and trans. 1987. *The Berg-Schoenberg Correspondence.* New York: Norton.

Brosche, Günter, and Rosemary Hilmar. 1985. *Alban Berg: Ausstellung der Österreichischen Nationalbibliothek: Prunksaal.* Vienna: Österreichischen Nationalbibliothek.

Budday, Wolfgang. 1979. *Alban Bergs Lyrische Suite: Satztechnische Analyse ihrer zwölftonigen Partien.* Tübinger Beiträge zur Musikwissenschaft, 8. Neuhausen-Stuttgart: Hänssler.

Burkholder, J. Peter. 1991. "Berg and the Possibility of Popularity." In Gable and Morgan 1991 (pp. 25–56).

Carner, Mosco. 1977. "Pfitzner v. Berg or Inspiration v. Analysis." *MT* 118: 379–80.

————. 1983. *Alban Berg: The Man and the Work.* 2d ed. New York: Holmes and Meier.

Cerha, Friedrich. 1979. *Arbeitsbericht zur Herstellung des 3. Akts der Oper Lulu von Alban Berg.* Vienna: Universal Edition.

————. 1981. "Zum III. Akt der Oper 'LuLu.'" *ÖMZ* 36: 541–50.

————. 1989. "Some Further Notes On My Realization of Act III of *Lulu*." In Jarman 1989a (pp. 261–68).

Chadwick, Nicolas. 1968. "Thematic Integration in Berg's Altenberg Songs." *MR* 29: 300–304.

————. 1971. "Berg's Unpublished Songs in the Österreichische Nationalbibliothek." *Music and Letters* 52: 123–40.

————. 1974. "Franz Schreker's Orchestral Style and Its Influence on Alban Berg." *MR* 35:29–46.

Chittum, Donald. 1967. "The Triple Fugue in Berg's *Wozzeck.*" *MR* 28: 52–62.

Cinnamon, Howard. 1984. "Third-Relations as Structural Elements in Book II of Liszt's *Années de Pèlerinage* and Three Later Works." Ph.D. diss. University of Michigan.

Cone, Edward. 1968. *Musical Form and Musical Performance.* New York: Norton.

Congdon, David. 1981. "*Kammerkonzert*: Evolution of the Adagio and the Trio Transcription." In R. Klein 1981 (pp. 145–60).

———. 1985. "Composition in Berg's *Kammerkonzert.*" *PNM* 24: 234–69.

Cook, Susan. 1988. Opera for a New Republic: The Zeitopern of Krenek, Weill, and Hindemith. Studies in Musicology, 96. Ann Arbor: UMI.

Crutchfield, Will. 1989. "'Wozzeck' Speaks to Us by Mixing Musical Modes." *New York Times* (December 17).

Csampai, Attila, and Dietmar Holland, eds. 1985. *Alban Berg: Lulu: Texte, Materialien, Kommentaire.* Munich: Ricordi.

Dahlhaus, Carl. 1981. "Berg und Wedekind: Zur Dramaturgie der *Lulu.*" In R. Klein 1981 (pp. 12–19).

Dalen, Brenda. 1989. "'Freundschaft, Liebe, und Welt': The Secret Programme of the Chamber Concerto." In Jarman 1989a (pp. 141–80).

Defotis, William. 1979. "Berg's Op. 5: Rehearsal Instructions." *PNM* 17: 131–37.

DeVoto, Mark. 1967. "Alban Berg's Picture Postcard Songs." Ph.D. diss. Princeton University. Excerpts in "Some Notes on the Unknown *Altenberg Lieder*," *PNM* 5/1 (Fall–Winter, 1966): 37–74.

———. 1968. "The Harmony of Berg's *Reigen.*" *PNM* 6: 73–91.

———. 1981. "Alban Bergs *Drei Orchesterstücke* op. 6: Struktur, Thematik, und ihr Verhältnis zu *Wozzeck.*" In R. Klein 1981 (pp. 97–106).

———. 1983–84. "Alban Berg's 'Marche Macabre.'" *PNM* 22: 386–447.

———. 1989. "Berg the Composer of Songs." In Jarman 1989a (pp. 35–66).

———. 1990. "*Wozzeck* in Context." In John 1990 (pp. 7–14).

———. 1991. "Alban Berg and Creeping Chromaticism." In Gable and Morgan 1991 (pp. 57–78).

Eislin, Martin. 1989. "Berg's Vienna." In Jarman 1989a (pp. 1–12).

Eliot, T. S. 1951. "Tradition and the Individual Talent." In *Selected Essays* (New York: Harcourt, Brace, 1932), pp. 3–11.

Ertelt, Thomas F. 1986. "Hereinspaziert . . . Ein früher Entwurf des Prologs zu Alban Bergs *Lulu.*" *ÖMZ* 41: 15–25.

———. 1993. *Alban Berg's "Lulu": Quellenstudien und Beiträge zur Analyse.* Alban Berg Studien, 3. Vienna: Universal.

Estrine, Robert. 1988. "Lulu's American Relations." Unpublished paper given at the joint meeting of the American Musicological Society and Society for Music Theory, Baltimore, Md.

Floros, Constantin. 1978. "Das esoterische Programm der *Lyrischen Suite* von Alban Berg." In Metzger and Riehn 1978 (pp. 5–48).

———. 1979. "Das Kammerkonzert von Alban Berg: Hommage à Schönberg und Webern." In Metzger and Riehn 1979 (pp. 63–90).

———. 1981. "Die Skizzen zum Violinkonzert von Alban Berg." In R. Klein 1981 (pp. 118–35).

———. 1992. *Alban Berg: Musik als Autobiographie*. Wiesbaden: Breitkopf und Härtel.

Forneberg, Erich. 1963. *Wozzeck von Alban Berg*. Berlin: Robert Lienau.

Forte, Allen. 1973. *The Structure of Atonal Music*. New Haven: Yale University Press.

———. 1985. "Tonality, Symbol, and Structural Levels in Berg's *Wozzeck*." *MQ* 71: 474–519.

———. 1988. "New Approaches to the Linear Analysis of Music." *JAMS* 41: 315–88.

———. 1991. "The Mask of Tonality: Alban Berg's Symphonic Epilogue to *Wozzeck*." In Gable and Morgan 1991 (pp. 151–202).

Franzos, Karl Emile. 1901. "Georg Büchner." *Deutsche Dichtung* 29: 195ff., 289ff. Trans. George Perle in Jarman 1989b (pp. 111–29).

Friedmann, Michael. 1985. "A Methodology for the Discussion of Contour: Its Application to Schoenberg's Music." *JMT* 29: 223–48.

———. 1987. "A Response: My Contour, Their Contour." *JMT* 31: 268–74.

Fuhrmann, Roderich. 1974. "Alban Berg: Violinkonzert." In *Perspektiven neuer Musik: Material und didaktische Information*, ed. Dieter Zimmercheid (Mainz: Schott), pp. 73–109.

Gable, David, and Robert Morgan, eds. 1991. *Alban Berg: Historical and Analytical Perspectives*. Oxford: Oxford University Press.

Gerlach, Reinhard. 1985. *Musik und Jugenstil: Der Wiener Schule 1900–1908*. Laaber: Laaber-Verlag.

Gratzer, Wolfgang. 1993. *Zur "Wunderlichen Mystik" Alban Bergs: Eine Studie*. Vienna: Böhlau.

Green, Douglass M. 1977a. "The Allegro Misterioso of Berg's *Lyric Suite*: Iso- and Retro-rhythms. *JAMS* 30: 507–16.

———. 1977b. "Berg's De Profundis: The Finale of the *Lyric Suite*. *IABSN* 5:13–23.

———. 1981. "Cantus Firmus Techniques in the Concertos and Operas of Alban Berg." In R. Klein 1981 (pp. 56–68).

———. 1982. Review of George Perle, *The Operas of Alban Berg* vol. 1. *JMT* 26: 145–55.

———. 1984. "Letter (*Lyric Suite*)." *ITO* 8: pp. 4–5.

———. 1991a. Review of *The Berg Companion*, ed. Douglas Jarman. *JASI* 14: 307–19.

———. 1991b. "A False Start for *Lulu*: An Early Version of the Prologue." In Gable and Morgan 1991 (pp. 203–14).

Green, Douglass M., and Stefan Kostka. 1985. Review of Janet Schmalfeldt, *Berg's Wozzeck: Harmonic Language and Dramatic Design*. *JMT* 29: 177–86.

Hahl-Koch, Jalena, ed. 1984. *Arnold Schoenberg, Wassily Kandinsky: Letters, Pictures and Documents*. Trans. John C. Crawford. London: Faber and Faber.

Hailey, Christopher. 1989. "Between Instinct and Reflection: Berg and the Viennese Dichotomy." In Jarman 1989a (pp. 221–34).

Hailey, Christopher, and Juliane Brand. 1988. "Catalogue of the Correspondence Between Alban Berg and Arnold Schoenberg." *JASI* 11: 70–97.

———. 1989. "The Twelve Lost Letters." *JASI* 12:129–74.

Haimo, Ethan. 1990. *Schoenberg's Serial Odyssey*. Oxford: Oxford University Press.

Hall, Patricia. 1985. "Berg's Tone Rows for Lulu: The Progress of a Method." *MQ* 71: 500–519.

Hall, Patricia. 1987. Review of George Perle, *The Operas of Alban Berg: Volume II: Lulu*. *JMT* 31: 140–46.

———. 1989. "The Sketches for *Lulu*." in Jarman 1989a (pp. 235–60).

———. 1991. "Role and Form in Berg's Sketches for *Lulu*." In Gable and Morgan 1991 (pp. 235–60).

Harris, Donald. 1979. "Ravel Visits the Verein." *JASI* 3: 75–82.

Harris, Donald, and Mark DeVoto. 1971. "Berg's Notes for the *Lyric Suite*." *IABSN* 2: 5–7.

Headlam, Dave. 1985a. "The Derivation of Rows in *Lulu*." *PNM* 24: 198–233.

———. 1985b. "The Musical Language of the Symphonic Pieces from *Lulu*." Ph.D. diss. University of Michigan.

———. 1985c. Review of Janet Schmalfeldt, *Berg's Wozzeck: Harmonic Language and Dramatic Design*. *ITO* 8: 57–76.

———. 1987. Review of George Perle, *The Operas of Alban Berg: Volume II: Lulu*." *ITO* 9: 57–76.

———. 1988. "Cyclic Transformations of Pitch Sets." Unpublished paper given at the 1988 Conference of The Society for Music Theory.

———. 1990. "Row Derivation and Contour Association in Berg's *Der Wein*." *PNM* 28: 256–93.

———. 1991. Review of *The Berg Companion*, ed. Douglas Jarman, and Douglas Jarman, *Wozzeck*. *Music Library Association Notes* 47: 1139–42.

———. 1992. "Fritz Heinrich Klein's 'Die Grenzen der Halbtonwelt' and 'Die Maschine.'" *Theoria* 6: 55–96.

———. 1993. Review of *Alban Berg: Historical and Analytical Perspectives*, ed. David Gable and Robert P. Morgan, and Theodor Adorno, *Alban Berg: Master of the Smallest Link*. trans. Juliane Brand and Christopher Hailey. *MTS* 15: 273–85.

———. 1995. "Sketch Study and Analysis: Berg's Twelve-Tone Music." *College Music Symposium* 33–34: forthcoming.

Headlam, Dave, and Matthew Brown. 1990. "♯IV and the Limits of Tonality." Unpublished paper given at the 1990 Conference of the Society for Music Theory.

Hilmar, Ernst. 1975. *Wozzeck von Alban Berg*. Vienna: Universal Edition.

———. 1978. "Die verschiedenen Entwicklungsstadien in den Kompositionsskizzen." In Kolleritsch 1978a (pp. 22–26).

Hilmar, Rosemary. 1978. *Alban Berg: Leben und Wirken in Wien bis zu seinen ersten Erfolgen als Komponist*. Wiener Musikwissenschaftlische Beiträge, 10. Vienna: Hermann Böhlaus.

———. 1980. *Katalog der Musikhandschriften, Schriften und Studien Alban Bergs im Fond Alban Berg und der weiteren handschriftlichen Quellen im Besitz der Österreichischen Nationalbibliothek*. Alban Berg Studien, 1. Vienna: Universal Edition.

———. 1984. "Alban Berg's Studies with Schoenberg." *JASI* 8: 7–29.

Holloway, Robin. 1979. "The Complete *Lulu*." *Tempo* 129 (June): 36–39.

Jameux, Dominique. 1981. "Form und Erzahlung in Alban Berg's Oper LULU." in R. Klein 1981 (pp. 40–45).

Jarman, Douglas. 1970a. "Berg's Surrealist Opera." *MR* 31: 232–40.

———. 1970b. "Dr. Schön's Five-Strophe Aria: Some Notes on Tonality and Pitch Association in Berg's *Lulu*." *PNM* 8/2 (Spring–Summer): 23–48.

———. 1970c. "Some Rhythmic and Metric Techniques in Alban Berg's *Lulu*." *MQ* 56: 349–66.

———. 1971–72. "Some Row Techniques in Berg's *Der Wein*." *Soundings* 2: 46–56.

———. 1978. "*Lulu*: The Sketches." *IABSN* 6: 4–8.

———. 1979. *The Music of Alban Berg*. Berkeley: University of California Press.

———. 1981a. "Countess Geschwitz's Series: A Controversy Resolved?" *Proceedings of the Royal Musical Association* 107: 111–18.

———. 1981b. "Some Observations on Rhythm, Meter and Tempo in *Lulu*." In R. Klein, 1981 (pp. 20–30).

———. 1982a. "Alban Berg, Wilhelm Fliess and the Secret Programme of the Violin Concerto." *IABSN* 12: 5–11. Repr. in Jarman 1989a (pp. 181–96).

———. 1982b. "The 'Lost' Score of the 'Symphonic Pieces From *Lulu*.'" *IABSN* 12: 14–16.

———. 1987. "Alban Berg: Origins of a Method." *MA* 6: 273–88.

———, ed. 1989a. *The Berg Companion*. Boston: Northeastern University Press.

———. 1989b. *Wozzeck*. Cambridge Opera Handbooks. Cambridge: Cambridge University Press.

———. 1991a. *Lulu*. Cambridge Opera Handbooks. Cambridge: Cambridge University Press.

———. 1991b. "'Man hat auch nur Fleisch und Blut': Towards a Berg Biography." In Gable and Morgan 1991 (pp. 11–24).

Jelinek, Hanns. 1952. *Anleitung zur Zwölftonkomposition*. Vienna: Universal Edition.

John, Nicholas, ed. 1990. *Wozzeck*. English National Opera Guides, 42. London: John Calder.

Keller, Hans. 1953. "*Lulu* at the Holland Festival." *MR* 14: 302–3.

Kett, Steven. 1989. "A Conservative Revolution: The Music of the Four Songs Op. 2." In Jarman 1989a (pp. 67–90).

Klein, Fritz Heinrich. 1923. "Alban Berg's 'Wozzeck.'" *Musikblätter des Anbruch* 15: 216–19. Repr. in Jarman 1989b (pp. 135–38).

———. 1924. "Büchner's 'Wozzeck' als Oper." *Deutsche Kunstschau* 1: 160–61.

————. 1925. "Die Grenze der Halbtonwelt." *Die Musik* 17: 281–91.

Klein, Rudolf. 1978. "Zur Frage der Tonalität in Alban Bergs Oper *Wozzeck*." In Kolleritsch 1978a (pp. 32–45).

————, ed. 1981. *Alban Berg Symposion Vienna 1980: Tagungsbericht.* Alban Berg Studien, 2. Vienna: Universal Edition.

Knaus, Herwig. 1975. "Alban Berg's Violinkonzert." In *De ratione in musica: Festschrift Erich Schenk*, ed. Theophil Antonicek, Rudolf Flotzinger, and Othmar Wessely. (Basel: Bärenreiter, 1975), pp. 255–74.

————. 1976. "Berg's Carinthian Folk Tune." Trans. Mosco Carner. *MT* 117: 487.

————. 1981. "Kompositionstechnik und Semantik in Alban Bergs Konzertaire *Der Wein*." In R. Klein 1981 (pp. 136–44).

Kolleritsch, Otto, ed. 1978a. *50 Jahre Wozzeck von Alban Berg: Vorgeschichte und Auswirkungen in der Opernästhetik.* Studien zur Wertungsforschung, 10. Graz: Universal Edition.

————. 1978b. "*Wozzeck* und die Steiermark." In Kolleritsch 1978a (pp. 125–43).

König, Werner. 1974. *Tonalitätsstrukturen in Alban Bergs Oper "Wozzeck."* Tutzing: Hans Schnieder.

Krämer, Ulrich. 1992. "Quotation and Self-Borrowing in the Music of Alban Berg." *JMR* 12: 53–82.

Krasner, Louis. 1981. "The Origins of the Alban Berg *Violin Concerto*." In R. Klein 1981 (pp. 107–17).

————. 1982. "The Violin Concerto in Vienna." *IASBN* 12: 3–4.

Krenek, Ernst. 1937. *Über neue Musik.* Vienna: Ringbuchhandlung. Repr., Darmstadt: Wissenschaftliche Buchgesellschaft, 1977.

————. 1958. "Alban Bergs *Lulu*." In *Zur Sprache gebracht: Essays über Musik* (Munich), pp. 241–50. Trans. Margaret Shenfield and Geofrrey Skelton as *Exploring Music* (New York: October House, 1966), pp. 113–22.

Lambert, Philip. 1987. "Compositional Procedures in Experimental Works of Charles E. Ives." Ph.D. diss. University of Rochester.

————. 1990. "Interval Cycles as Compositional Resources in the Music of Charles Ives." *MTS* 12: 43–87.

————. 1993. "Berg's Path to Twelve-Note Composition: Aggregate Construction and Association in the *Chamber Concerto*." *MA* 12: 321–42.

Lederer, Josef-Horst. 1978. "Zu Alban Bergs Invention über den Ton H." In Kolleritsch 1978a (pp. 57–67).

Leibowitz, Rene. 1948. "Alban Berg's Five Orchestral Songs." *MQ* 34: 487–511.

————. 1949. *Schoenberg and His School.* Trans. Dika Newlin. New York: Philosophical Library. Repr., New York: Da Capo Press, 1975.

Lendvai, Ernö. 1983. *The Workshop of Bartok and Kodaly.* Budapest: Editio Musica.

Levin, Walter. 1979. "Textprobleme im dritten Satz der 'Lyrischen Suite.'" In Metzger and Riehn 1979 (pp. 11–28).

Lewin, David. 1962. "A Theory of Segmental Association in Twelve-Tone Music." *PNM* 1: 89–104.

———. 1966. "On Certain Techniques of Re-ordering in Serial Music." *JMT* 10: 276–82.

———. 1968. "Inversional Balance As an Organizing Force in Schoenberg's Music and Thought." *PNM* 6/2 (Spring–Summer): 1–21.

———. 1981. "Some Investigations Into Foreground Rhythm and Metric Patterning." In *Music Theory Special Topics*, ed. Richmond Browne (New York: Academic Press, 1981), pp. 101–37.

———. 1982–83. "Transformational Techniques in Atonal and Other Music Theories." *PNM* 21: 312–71.

———. 1987. *Generalized Musical Intervals and Transformations*. New Haven: Yale University Press.

———. 1990. "Klumpenhouwer Networks and Some Isographies That Involve Them." *MTS* 12: 83–120.

Lewis, Christopher. 1981. "Tonal Focus in Atonal Music: Berg's Op. 5/3." *MTS* 3: 84–97.

Liebermann, Rolf. 1979. *Lulu: Tome II*. Paris: Jean-Claudes Lattès.

Lorkovic, Radovan. 1989. "Berg's Violin Concerto: Discrepancies in the Published Score." *MT* 130: 268–71.

McCredie, Andrew D. 1977. "Alban Berg's *Wozzeck*: Its Antecedents and Influence on German Expressionist Theatre." *Miscellanea musicologica* 9: 156–205.

MacDonald, Andrew. 1988. "Hidden Symbolism in *Der Wein*." Unpublished paper.

McNamee, Ann. 1985. "Bitonality, Mode, and Interval in the Music of Karol Szymanowski." *JMT* 29: 61–84.

Maegaard, Jan. 1975. "Berg's Seventeen Four-Part Canons: The Mystery Solved." Trans. Joan Allen Smith and Mark DeVoto. *IABSN* 3: 4–7. Orig. as "Ein Beispiel des atonalen Kontrapunkts im Frühstadium," *Zeitschrift für Musiktheorie* 3 (1972): 29–34.

Marvin, Elizabeth West. 1988. "A Generalized Theory of Musical Contour: Its Application to Melodic and Rhythmic Analysis of Non-Tonal Music and Its Perceptual and Pedagogical Implications. Ph.D. diss. University of Rochester.

———. 1991. "The Perception of Rhythm in Non-tonal Music: Rhythmic Contours in the Music of Edgard Varèse. *MTS* 13: 61–78.

Marvin, Elizabeth West, and Paul A. Laprade. 1987. "Relating Musical Contours: Extensions of a Theory for Contour." *JMT* 31: 225–67.

Mauser, Siegfried. 1981. "Arnold Schönbergs *Erwartung* und Alban Bergs *Wozzeck*: Studie zur Entwicklungsgeschichte des expressionistischen Musiktheaters." In R. Klein 1981 (pp. 91–96).

Mead, Andrew. 1985. "Large-Scale Strategy in Arnold Schoenberg's Twelve-Tone Music." *PNM* 24: 120–57.

———. 1988–89. "Some Implications of the Pitch Class/Order Number Isomorphism Inherent in the Twelve-Tone System." *PNM* 26/2 (Summer): 96–163 and 27/1 (Winter): 180–233.

Messiaen, Olivier. 1956. *The Technique of My Musical Language*. Trans. John Satterfield. Paris: Leduc.

Metz, Paul W. 1991. "Set Theory, Clock Diagrams, and Berg's Op. 2, No. 2" *ITO* 12: 1–17.

Metzger, Heinz-Klaus, and Rainer Riehn, eds. 1978. *Alban Berg: Kammermusik I*. Musik-Konzepte, 4. (Repr. 1981).

———, eds. 1979a. *Alban Berg: Kammermusik II*. Musik-Konzepte, 9.

———. 1979b. "Statt eine Nachworts zur Kontroverse." In Metzger and Reihn 1979 (pp. 8–10).

Micznik, Vera. 1986. "Gesture as Sign: A Semiotic Interpretation of Berg's Op. 6, No. 1." *ITO* 9: 19–35.

Mitchell, Donald. 1954. "The Character of Lulu." *MR* 15: 268–74.

Moldenhauer, Hans, and Rosaleen Moldenhauer. 1979. *Anton von Webern: A Chronicle of His Life and Work*. New York: Alfred A. Knopf.

Morgan Robert. P. 1976. "Dissonant Prolongation: Theoretical and Compositional Precedents." *JMT* 20: 47–91.

———. 1991. "The Eternal Return: Retrograde and Circular Form in Berg." In Gable and Morgan 1991 (pp. 111–50).

Morris, Robert. 1983–84. "Set-Type Saturation Among Twelve-Tone Rows." *PNM* 22: 187–217.

———. 1987. *Composition with Pitch Classes*. New Haven: Yale University Press.

Morris, Robert, and Daniel Starr. 1977–78. "Combinatoriality and the Aggregate (Part I)." *PNM* 16/1 (Fall–Winter): 3–35 and 16/2 (Spring–Summer): 50–84.

Nelson. Robert U. 1970. "Form and Fancy in the Variations of Berg." *MR* 31: 54–69.

Neumann, Karl. 1974. "Wedekind and Berg's *Lulu*." *MR* 35: 47–57.

Neuwirth, Gösta. 1978. "*Wozzeck* I/1: Formdisposition und musikalisches Material." In Kolleritsch 1978a (pp. 46–56).

———. 1981. "Themen- und Zeitstrukturen in Alban Bergs *Kammerkonzert*." In R. Klein 1981 (pp. 161–70).

Offergeld, Robert. 1964. "Some Questions about *Lulu*." *Hi-Fi Stereo Review* 8: 58–76.

Pass, Walter. 1978. "Für und Wider im Streit um die Wiener Erstaufführung des *Wozzeck*." In Kolleritsch 1978a (pp. 92–124).

Perle, George. 1955. "Symmetrical Formations in the String Quartets of Béla Bartók." *MR* 16: 300–312.

———. 1959. "The Music of *Lulu*: A New Analysis." *JAMS* 22: 182–200.

———. 1962. *Serial Composition and Atonality*. Berkeley: University of California Press. 6th ed., 1991.

———. 1964a. "The Character of Lulu: A Sequel." *MR* 25: 311–19.

———. 1964b. "Lulu: The Formal Design." *JAMS* 17: 179–92.

———. 1964c. "A Note on Act III of *Lulu*." *PNM* 2/2 (Spring–Summer): 8–13.

———. 1965a. "Lulu: Thematic Material and Pitch Organization." *MR* 26: 269–302.

———. 1965b. "The Score of *Lulu*." *PNM* 3/2 (Spring–Summer): 127–32.

———. 1967a. "Current Chronicle: Edinburgh." *MQ* 53:100–108.

———. 1967b. "Erwiderung auf Willi Reichs Aufsatz 'Drei Notizblatter zu Alban Bergs *Lulu*." *SMZ* 107: 163–5.

———. 1967c. "The Musical Language of *Wozzeck*." In *Music Forum*, vol. 1 (New York: Columbia University Press, 1967), pp. 204–59.

———. 1967d. "Die Reihe als Symbol in Bergs *Lulu*." *ÖMZ* 22: 589–93.

———. 1967e. "Woyzeck and Wozzeck." *MQ* 53: 206–19.

———. 1971. "Representation and Symbol in the Music of *Wozzeck*." *MR* 32: 291–308.

———. 1975. "Die Personen in Bergs *Lulu*." *Archiv für Musikwissenschaft* 24: 283–94.

———. 1977a. "Berg's Master Array of the Interval Cycles." *MQ* 63: 1–30.

———. 1977b. "The Secret Program of the *Lyric Suite*." *IABSN* 5: 4–12.

——— 1977c. *Twelve-Tone Tonality*. Berkeley: University of California Press.

——— 1979a. "The Cerha Edition." *IABSN* 8: 5–7.

———. 1979b. "The Complete 'Lulu.'" *MT* 120: 115–20.

———. 1980. *The Operas of Alban Berg: Volume One: Wozzeck*. Berkeley: University of California Press.

———. 1981. "Der Tod der Geschwitz." *ÖMZ* 36: 19–28.

———. 1982a. "The Film Interlude of *Lulu*." *IABSN* 11: 3–8.

———. 1982b. "The 'Sketched-In' Vocal Quartet of *Lulu*, Act III." *IABSN* 12: 12–13.

———. 1985. *The Operas of Alban Berg: Volume Two: Lulu*. Berkeley: University of California Press.

———. 1989. "The First Four Notes of *Lulu*." In Jarman 1989a (pp. 269–90).

———. 1990. *The Listening Composer*. Berkeley: University of California Press.

———. 1993. "Communication." *MTS* 15: 300–303.

Pernye, A. 1967. "Alban Berg und die Zahlen." *SM* 9: 141–61.

Petersen, Peter. 1985. *Alban Berg: Wozzeck*. in Metzger, Heinz-Klaus and Riehn, Rainer, eds., *Musik Konzepte: Sonderband* (November).

Petschnig, Emil. 1924. "Atonales Opernschaffen." *Die Musik* 16: 340–45. Trans. in Jarman 1989b (pp. 143–48).

Ploesch, Gerd. 1968. *Alban Bergs Wozzeck*. Sammlung musikwissenschaftlicher Abhandlungen, 48. Strasbourg: Heitz.

Pople, Anthony. 1991. *Berg's Violin Concerto*. Cambridge Music Handbooks. Cambridge: Cambridge University Press.

Porter, Charles. 1989–90. "Interval Cycles in Alban Berg's String Quartet Opus 3." *TAP* 14–15: 139–78.

Proctor, Gregory. 1978. "Technical Bases of Nineteenth-Century Chromatic Tonality: A Study in Chromaticism." Ph.D. diss. Princeton University.

Puffet, Derek. 1989. "Berg and German Opera." In Jarman 1989a (pp. 197–220).

Rauchhaupt, Ursula von, ed. 1971. *Die Streichquartette der Wiener Schule: Eine Dokumentation*. Munich: Heinrich Ellermann, and Hamburg: Deutsche Grammophon.

Redlich, Hans F. 1957. *Alban Berg: Versuch einer Würdigung*. Vienna: Universal Edition. Trans. as *Alban Berg: The Man and the Music* (London: John Calder, 1957).

———. 1960. "Appendix." In *Alban Berg: Zwei Lieder*. Vienna: Universal Edition.

——— 1966. "Bergs Konzertarie 'Der Wein.'" *ÖMZ* 21: 284–91.

———. 1970. "Alban Berg's Altenberg Songs Opus 4: Editorial Problems and No End." *MR* 31: 43–53.

Reich, Willi. 1930. "Alban Berg." *Die Musik* 22: 347–53.

———. 1936. "Alban Berg's *Lulu*." *MQ* 22: 383–401.

———. 1937. *Alban Berg*. Vienna: Herbert Reichner.

———. 1953. "Aus unbekannten Briefen von Alban Berg an Anton Webern." *SMZ* 93: 49–52.

———. 1959. *Alban Berg: Bildnis im Wort, Selbstzeugnisse and Aussagen der Freunde*. Zurich: Die Arche.

———. 1960. "An der Seite von Alban Berg." *Melos* 27: 36–42.

———. 1965. *Alban Berg*. Trans. Cornelius Cardew. London: Thames and Hudson.

———. 1966. "Drei Notizblätter zu Alban Bergs Oper *Lulu*." *SMZ* 106: 336–39.

———. 1968. *Schönberg: Der konservative Revolutionär*. Vienna: Fritz Molden. Trans. Leo Black as *Schoenberg: A Critical Biography* (London: Longman, 1971).

Reiter, Manfred. 1973. *Die Zwölftontechnik in Alban Bergs Oper Lulu*. Kölner Beiträge zur Musikforschung, 71. Regensburg: Gustav Bosse.

Rognoni, Luigi. 1977. *The Second Vienna School: Expressionism and Dodecaphony*. Trans. Robert W. Mann. London: John Calder. Orig. as *La scuola musicale di Vienna* (Turin: Guilio Einaudi, 1966).

Rothgeb, John. 1967. "Some Ordering Relationships in the Twelve-note System." *JMT* 11: 176–97.

Salzer, Felix. 1952. *Structural Hearing: Tonal Coherence in Music*. New York: Charles Boni. Repr., New York: Dover, 1982.

Scherliess, Volker. 1975. *Alban Berg in Selbstzeugnissen und Bilddokumenten*. Hamburg: Rowohlt Taschenbuch Verlag.

———. 1976. "Brief Alban Bergs aus der Entstehungzeit der 'Lulu.'" *Melos* 2: 108–14.

———. 1977. "Alban Bergs analytische Tafeln zur Lulu-Reihe." *Musikforschung* 30: 452–64.

———. 1981. "Zur Rezeption der *Klaviersonate* op. 1." In R. Klein 1981 (pp. 232–44).

Schiefler, Gustav. 1923. *Edvard Munchs graphische Kunst*. Dresden.

Schmalfeldt, Janet. 1983. *Berg's Wozzeck: Harmonic Language and Dramatic Design*. New Haven: Yale University Press.

———. 1991. "Berg's Path to Atonality: The Piano Sonata Op. 1." In Gable and Morgan 1991 (pp. 79–110).

Schnitzler, Arthur. 1953. *Reigen*. Introduction by Ilsa Barea. London: Weidenfeld and Nicolson.

———. 1982. *La ronde*. Trans. Frank and Jacqueline Marcus. Introduction by Frank Marcus. London: Methuen.

Schoenberg, Arnold. 1932. Translated and annotated by Claudio Spiess as "Analysis of the Four Orchestral Songs Opus 22" in *Perspectives on Schoenberg and Stravinsky*, ed. Benjamin Boretz and Edward Cone (New York: Norton, 1972), pp. 25–45.

———. 1936. "The Teacher's Testimonial." Trans. in Reich 1965 (pp. 28–30).

Schoenberg, Arnold. 1967. "Fundamentals of Musical Composition." Ed. Gerald Strang and Leonard Stein. London: Faber and Faber.

———. 1969. *Structural Functions of Harmony*. New York: Norton.

———. 1983. *Theory of Harmony*. Trans. Roy E. Carter. Berkeley: University of California Press.

———. 1984. *Style and Idea*. Ed. Leonard Stein. Trans. Leo Black. Berkeley: University of California Press.

Schoenberg, Arnold, and Wassily Kandinsky. 1984. *Letters, Pictures and Documents*. Ed. Jelena Hahl-Koch. Trans. John C. Crawford. London: Faber and Faber.

Schoenberg, E. Randol. 1986. "Alban Berg–Arnold Schoenberg Exhibit at the Arnold Schoenberg Institute in Honor of the Alban Berg Centennial." Trans. Gertrud S. Zeisl. *JASI* 9: 236–59.

Schroeder, David. 1988. "Berg's *Wozzeck* and Strindberg's Musical Models." *Opera Journal* 21: 2–12.

———. 1990. "Berg, Strindberg, and D Minor." *College Music Symposium* 30/2 (Fall): 74–89.

———. 1993. "Alban Berg and Peter Altenberg. *JAMS* 46: 261–94.

Schweizer, Klaus. 1970. *Die Sonatensatzform im Schaffen Alban Bergs*. Stuttgart: Musikwissenschaftlicher Verlag.

Seehaus, Gunter. 1964. *Frank Wedekind und das Theater*. Munich.

Segar, Kenneth. 1990. "Georg Büchner's 'Woyzeck': an Interpretation." In John 1990 (pp. 15–22).

Selz, Peter. 1957. *German Expressionist Painting*. Berkeley: University of California Press.

Simms, Bryan. 1994. "Berg's *Lulu* and the Theatre of the 1920s." *Cambridge Opera Journal* 6: 147–58.

Simpson, Mary. 1987. *Peter Altenberg*. New York: Peter Lang.

Smith, Joan Allen. 1978. "Some Sources for Berg's "Schließe mir die Augen beide." *IABSN* 6: 9–13.

Smith Brindle, Reginald. 1957. "The Symbolism in Berg's 'Lyric Suite.'" *Score* 21: 60–63.

Solomon, Larry. 1973. "New Symmetric Transformations." *PNM* 11: 257–64.

Stadler, Peter. 1981. "Berg's Cryptography." In R. Klein 1981 (pp. 171–80).

Stanfield, Michael. 1984–85. "Some Exchange Operations in Twelve-Tone Theory." *PNM* 23 (1984): 258–77 and 24 (1985): 72–95.

Starr, Daniel. 1978. "Sets, Invariance, and Partitions." *JMT* 22: 1–42.

Stein, Erwin. 1922. "Alban Berg and Anton von Webern." *The Chesterian* 26 (October): 33–36. Repr. in Jarman 1989b (pp. 132–35).

———. 1927. Preface to *Alban Berg: Lyrische Suite*. Vienna: Universal Edition.

Stein, Jack. 1972. "From 'Woyzeck' to 'Wozzeck': Alban Berg's Adaptation of Büchner." *Germanic Review* 47: 168–80.

———. 1974. "*Lulu*: Alban Berg's Adaptation of Wedekind." *Comparative Literature* 26/(Spring): 220–41.

Stenzl, Jürg. 1978. "Franz Schreker und Alban Berg: Bemerkungen zu den Altenberg-Liedern op. 4." In *Franz Schreker: Am Beginn der neuen Musik*, Studien zur Wertungsforschung, 2, ed. Otto Kolleritsch (Graz: Universal Edition), pp. 44–58.

———. 1981. "Lulus 'Welt.'" In R. Klein 1981 (pp. 31–39).

Straus, Joseph N. 1984. "Tristan and Berg's Lyric Suite." *ITO* 8: 33–41.

———. 1987. "The Problem of Prolongation in Post-Tonal Music." *JMT* 31: 1–21.

———. 1990. *Remaking the Past: Musical Modernism and the Influence of the Tonal Tradition*. Cambridge, Mass.: Harvard University Press.

Strindberg, August. 1912. *Plays*. Trans. Edwin Bjoerkman. New York: Scribner.

Stroh, Wolfgang. 1968. "Alban Berg's Constructive Rhythm." *PNM* 7: 18–31.

Stuckenschmidt, Hans Heinz. 1965. "Debussy or Berg? The Mystery of a Chord Progression." *MQ* 51: 453–59.

———. 1978. *Schoenberg: His Life, World and Work*. Trans. Humphrey Searle. New York: Schirmer Books.

Stucky, Steven. 1981. *Lutoslawski and His Music*. Cambridge: Cambridge University Press.

Szmolyan, Walter. 1977. "Zum III. Akt von Alban Bergs 'Lulu.'" *ÖMZ* 32: 396–401.

Taruskin, Richard. 1993. Review of Strauss 1990. *JAMS* 46: 114–38.

Taylor, Michael. 1989. "Musical Progression in the 'Präludium' of the Three Orchestral Pieces Op. 6." In Jarman 1989a (pp. 123–40).

Travis, Roy. 1959. "Toward a New Concept of Tonality?" *JMT* 3: 257–84.

———. 1966. "Directed Motion in Two Brief Pieces by Schoenberg and Webern." *PNM* 4: 85–89.

Treitler, Leo. 1989. "Wozzeck and the Apocalypse." In Leo Treitler, *Music and the Historical Imagination*. Cambridge, Mass.: Harvard University Press, 1989), pp. 242–63.

———. 1991. "The Lulu Character and the Character of Lulu." In Gable and Morgan 1991 (pp. 261–86). Also in Treitler 1989 (pp. 264–305).

van den Toorn, Pieter C. 1983. *The Music of Igor Stravinsky*. New Haven: Yale University Press.

Viebig, Ernst. 1923. "Alban Bergs 'Wozzeck.'" *Die Musik* 15: 506–10. Trans. in Jarman 1989b (pp. 139–43).

Vogelsang, Konrad. 1959. *Alban Berg: Leben und Werk*. Berlin: Max Hess.

———. 1977. *Dokumentation zur Oper "Wozzeck" von Alban Berg*. Regensburg: Laaber-Verlag.

Wake, Sandra. 1971. *Classic Film Scripts*. New York: Simon and Schuster.

Watkins, Glenn. 1988. *Soundings: Music in the Twentieth Century*. New York: Schirmer Books.

Wedekind, Frank. 1920. *Lautenlieder: 53 Lieder mit eigenen und frenden Melodien*. Berlin: Dreimaskenverlag.

Wennerstrom, Mary. 1977. "Pitch Relationships in Berg's Songs Opus 2." *ITR* 1:12–22.

Whitford, Frank. 1986. *Oskar Kokoschka: A Life*. New York: Atheneum.

Yeston, Maury. 1974. *The Stratification of Music Rhythm*. New Haven: Yale University Press.

Index

Schoenberg, Arnold: (*continued*)
with Kandinsky, 409n11; Piano Piece
op. 19, no. 2, 414n19, 420n110; Serenade op. 24, 423n31, 424n3; Variations for Orchestra op. 31, 421n4,
423n35
Schweizer, Klaus: view of *Wozzeck* and
of Schön sonata in *Lulu,* 424n40

Sprechstimme, 49
Straus, Joseph N., 8–10
Symmetry: general, 10–11; inversional
complementation, 57–58; a theory
of, 366–68

Webern, Anton: Symphony op. 21,
423n32